MW01005551

The Invention of Athens

The Invention of Athens
The Funeral Oration in the Classical City

Nicole Loraux

Translated by Alan Sheridan

ZONE BOOKS · NEW YORK

2006

Printed in the United States of America.
Distributed by The MIT Press,
Cambridge, Massachusetts, and London, England

Originally published in 1981 by Editions de l'Ecole des Hautes Etudes en Sciences
Sociales, Mouton Editeur, as *L'Invention d'Athènes: Histoire de l'oraison funèbre
dans la "cité classique."* This translation is reprinted by arrangement with Harvard
University Press. The Preface to the Second Edition © 1993 Payot & Rivages.

Library of Congress Cataloging-in-Publication Data

Loraux, Nicole
  [Invention d'Athènes. English]
  The invention of Athens: the funeral oration in the classical city /
Nicole Loraux; translated by Alan Sheridan.
      p. cm.
  Includes bibliographical references and index.
  ISBN 1-890951-59-5
    1. Speeches, addresses, etc., Greek – History and criticism. 2. Funeral rites
and ceremonies, Ancient – Greece – Athens. 3. Funeral orations – History
and criticism.   4. Athens (Greece) – Intellectual life. 5. City and town life in
literature. 6. Athens (Greece) – In literature. 7. Oratory, Ancient. I. Title.
PA3264.L6713 2005
885'.01093548–dc22

                                                        2005041731

Contents

Abbreviations

AA	*Archäologischer Anzeiger*
AC	*L'Antiquité classique*
AD	Ἀρχαιολογικὸν Δελτίον
AE	Ἀρχαιολογικὴ Ἐφημερίς
AJA	*American Journal of Archaeology*
AJPh	*American Journal of Philology*
Annales ESC	*Annales: Economies, sociétés, civilisations*
A & R	*Atene e Roma*
Ath. Mitt.	*Mitteilungen des Deutschen Archäologischen Instituts, Athenische Abteilung*
ATL	Benjamin Dean Meritt, H.T. Wade-Gery, and Malcolm Francis McGregor, eds., *The Athenian Tribute Lists*, 4 vols. (Cambridge, MA: Harvard University Press, 1938–53)
BAB	*Bulletin de l'Association Guillaume Budé*
BCH	*Bulletin de correspondance hellénique*
BICS	*Bulletin of the Institute of Classical Studies*
BSA	*Annual of the British School at Athens*
BSL	*Bulletin de la Société de Linguistique de Paris*
Classen-Steup	*Thukydides*, comm. Johannes Classen, rev. Julius Steup, 8 vols. (Berlin, 1912)
C&M	*Classica et mediaevalia*
CPhil.	*Classical Philology*
CQ	*Classical Quarterly*

CR *Classical Review*
CUF Collection des Universités de France
DA Dissertation Abstracts
DK Hermann Diels and Walther Kranz, eds., *Die Fragmente der Vorsokratiker*, 3 vols. (Berlin: Weidmann, 1964)
F.Gr.Hist. Felix Jacoby, ed., *Die Fragmente der griechischen Historiker*, 15 vols. (Berlin: Weidmann, 1923–)
GG Werner Peek, *Griechische Grabgedichte* (Berlin: Akademie, 1960)
Gomme, A.W Gomme, *A Historical Commentary on*
Commentary *Thucydides*, 2 vols. (Oxford: Clarendon, 1969–71)
G & R *Greece and Rome*
GRBS *Greek, Roman, and Byzantine Studies*
GT Ulrich von Wilamowitz-Moellendorff, *Griechische Tragoedien* (Berlin: Weidmann, 1922), vol. 1
GV Werner Peek, ed., *Griechische Vers-Inschriften* (Berlin: Akademie, 1955), vol. 1
Harv. Theol. Rev. *Harvard Theological Review*
HSCP *Harvard Studies in Classical Philology*
H&T *History and Theory*
IG *Inscriptiones Graecae*, I² and II/III² (Berlin, 1893–)
JDI *Jahrbuch des Deutschen Archäologischen Instituts*
JHS *Journal of Hellenic Studies*
Meiggs-Lewis Russell Meiggs and David Lewis, eds., *A Selection of Greek Historical Inscriptions to the End of the Fifth Century* (Oxford: Clarendon, 1969)
MGO Edouard Will, *Le Monde grec et l'orient* (Paris: PUF, 1972), vol. 1
MH *Museum Helveticum*
MP Jean-Pierre Vernant, *Mythe et pensée chez les Grecs: Etudes de psychologie historique* (Paris: Maspero, 1971)

MT	Jean-Pierre Vernant and Pierre Vidal-Naquet, *Mythe et tragédie en Grèce ancienne* (Paris: Maspero, 1972)
PP	*La Parola del passato*
P & P	*Past and Present*
RA	*Revue archéologique*
REA	*Revue des études anciennes*
REG	*Revue des études grecques*
Rev. Phil.	*Revue de philologie*
RFIC	*Rivista di filologia e di istruzione classica*
RH	*Revue historique*
RhM	*Rheinisches Museum*
RHR	*Revue de l'histoire des religions*
RIDA	*Revue internationale des droits de l'antiquité*
RMM	*Revue de métaphysique et de morale*
RUB	*Revue de l'Université de Bruxelles*
SBAW	*Sitzungsberichte der Bayerischen Akademie der Wissenschaften, Philosophie-Historie Klasse* (Munich)
SHAW	*Sitzungsberichte der Heidelberger Akademie der Wissenschaften*
SPAW	*Sitzungsberichte der Preussischen Akademie der Wissenschaften* (Berlin)
Sylloge	Wilhelm Dittenberger, ed., *Sylloge inscriptionum graecarum*, rev. Friedrich Hiller von Gaertringen (Leipzig: Hirzel, 1915–24)
TAPA	*Transactions of the American Philological Association*
TAPS	*Transactions of the American Philosophical Society*
Tod	Marcus Niebuhr Tod, ed., *A Selection of Greek Historical Inscriptions from 403 to 323 B.C.* (Oxford: Clarendon, 1968)
YCS	*Yale Classical Studies*

I have adopted a double system of reference. Citations of the Greek corpus appear as footnotes. Critical notes, indicated by superscript numbers, are at the back of the book.

Preface to the First Edition

This book is the fruit of research carried out between 1970 and 1976. Thus it was begun before the topic of death had come into its own, and completed before the notion of the "imaginary" conquered, on the intellectual stage where the great watchwords follow one another, the ground left vacant by the collapse of ideology.

In an earlier form, the work was presented under the title "Athènes imaginaire: Histoire de l'oraison funèbre dans la 'cité classique'" for the degree of *doctorat d'Etat* at the University of Paris I. The jury consisted of Hélène Ahrweiler, Philippe Gauthier, Henri van Effenterre, Jean-Pierre Vernant, and Pierre Vidal-Naquet. This book incorporates various changes made largely in response to suggestions from members of the jury, and most of the Greek has been transliterated or translated. There are few references to publications since October 1976, when the original work had already been rewritten several times.

The history of this book is freighted with debts. Undoubtedly the principal one is to my colleagues at the Centre de Recherches Comparées sur les Sociétés Anciennes, which, led by Vernant, Marcel Detienne, and Vidal-Naquet, is striving to free Antiquity from modern preconceptions. By working at the center and also by studying such books as *Les Origines de la pensée grecque*, *Les Maîtres de vérité*, and *Clisthène l'Athénien*, I have learned a method, come to realize that the reading of a text is nourished by a constant interaction between its contents and its context, between the closure of the text upon itself and its openness to some mythical totality that we call "Greek culture": only then can both differences and similarities be respected. Apart from this collective debt, I must also acknowledge the immense value of many long discussions with Vidal-Naquet and Vernant: this debt will be all too evident throughout the following pages.

At the University of Paris I, my gratitude must extend first to van Effenterre, who supervised my research in a critical but always benevolent way, and to Ahrweiler, who gave this book the support of the university.

I also wish to thank Pierre Lévêque, professor at the University of Besançon, who helped to defend my research.

François Furet, Chairman of the Ecole des Hautes Etudes en Sciences Sociales, accepted *L'Invention d'Athènes* for publication by the Ecole. Without his efforts, my thesis might never have been published.

It is now up to the book to live its own history.

Preface to the Second Edition

The Invention of Athens: The Funeral Oration in the Classical City is a study of a discursive genre that was also a privileged site for the Athenian democracy's development of a model of the city — or rather, of *the* model of the city, that generic city which we are fond of calling "classical." This development takes place against the background of the public funeral, for the ideological operations most durably established in the long history of the tradition are grounded, at the moment of their production, in a collectivity's relation, if not with death, at least with the death of those they consider their own.

I finally gave in to certain friendly entreaties and decided to publish an abridged version of *The Invention of Athens*,[1] after having refused to do so for a long time, because I still have enough faith in the book's hypotheses to hope it might appeal to readers beyond those interested in a *thèse d'état* thesis abundantly supplied with quotations in Greek.[2] The original edition published in 1981, with its many notes, maps, and images and with its thoroughly argued discussions, will no doubt continue to fulfill its original purpose as a working tool for researchers. But I like to imagine that in a more abbreviated form, this reflection on Athenian democracy as it was seen within Athens might contribute to current debates on democracy and politics.[3]

A shorter version, then, but not a rewritten version. This will perhaps be regretted, and if I had to write this book again, I would

probably give it a very different form. But as it was first conceived, its framework was too narrow to allow for anything other
than a series of isolated deletions, of greater or lesser extent, in
my effort to shorten the exposition and reduce the number and
length of the notes. Thus, on principle, I did not make any
changes that would alter the content or the bibliographic grounding: in preparing this abridged version, I have made many cuts,
but I have not modified or added to the text, even when I had the
desire to do so.[4] A shorter *Invention*, then, but one that has remained the same — that, at least, is my hope.

When closely reviewing a work that is already becoming old, one
is able to measure, retrospectively the gap between what one
expected (or believed one expected) during the long period of
writing — when thought carries on a monologue with itself — and
how the work was actually received. This experience is a reality
test, to be sure, sometimes melancholic, sometimes exciting,
always fruitful. When writing a book, one tends to deceive oneself concerning one's potential audience and what they will read
into it, caught up as one is in the prolonged experience of excessive familiarity. Before *The Invention*'s publication, I had foreseen
neither the points of contention, nor the discussions — whether
actual or avoided — nor the encounters that this work would
occasion.

  For example, when I methodically developed the notion of an
Athenian ideal of the political as an "imaginary without image,"[5] I
could never have imagined that this notion would be so incom-
prehensible to the French anthropologists studying ancient Greece.
But the fact is that, in the early 1980s, in their enthusiasm for figurative representations (which they baptized precisely with the
name "images"), these scholars judged it necessary — however
strange this formulation might seem — to *choose* sight over hearing. In the name of this conversion to "imagery" (implicitly conceived as a language more authentic and less culturally overdetermined than the productions of *logos*[6]), they wanted to affirm
the necessity of seeing Athens essentially as a "city of images" and

16

of seeing images as the privileged site of "the social imaginary of classical Athens."[7] The notion of an imaginary without images had to find other readers, then, such as philosophers or political theorists, who in fact (and this is certainly not a complaint) diverted the book's reception in France away from the history and anthropology of ancient Greece.

Conversely, without any suggestive bibliographic support, I believed — naively no doubt, but perhaps necessarily for the research to proceed — that I was alone in my efforts to constitute an operative notion of "genre." I did not know then that at the very same time a serious reflection on genre was occuring in the United States, among certain classicists thinking through the question of modernity. As such, *The Invention of Athens* became a "classic" in literary criticism, so much so that it threatened, to become part of the dominant orthodoxy.[8] Nor had I realized, in my attempt to understand the nature of an institution of speech, the extent to which other disciplines that lay outside my most immediate preoccupations (such as law) were finding it necessary, according to their own logic, to elaborate — or rather to endlessly reelaborate — the very notion of "institution."[9] This involved a very close and detailed reflection that, in its specific demands, appears to the historian working on the discursive forms of ancient Greece as a call to ever greater conceptual rigor.

In short, the initial reception of *The Invention of Athens* was so full of surprises and unexpected debates that I became convinced that a book never belongs to its author alone; for this very reason, I refused to include any heavy-handed intervention in these pages. But from this experience, I also gained a clearer perspective on the ideas that continue to concern me. The reason is quite simple: if given the chance, I would again pose the same problems in quite similar terms — since these terms are precisely those the Greeks themselves used (in order to think the "fine death," for example). Further, when I did decide to pursue an idea that was only sketched here — namely, on the subject of autochthony — I may have clarified or shifted the emphasis of certain formulations, but I never abandoned them completely.

17

One such formulation is that of the "fine death." This very faithful translation of the phrase *kalos thanatos* makes the "beautiful," the "fine," resonate in *kalos*, not just the "noble," as was customary. It was meant to suggest that the classical city had a notion of the beautiful that was not only ethical and political but also aesthetic. It therefore becomes important not to separate *kalos* from its reference to the beautiful, but only on the condition of conceiving *a* beautiful whose aesthetic dimension is thought on the level of abstraction.

This implied, first, the effacement of all sensory vision, correlative to that of the materiality of bodies, always already transmuted into ashes.[10] Thus, to maintain the paradigmatic status of the "fine death,"[11] we must preserve its civic grounding in fifth- and fourth-century Athens.[12] Every conception of a heroic death centered on the beauty of the dead body must therefore be distinguished from the fine death, whatever the complex relation of affinity in difference that such a death apparently maintains with the Athenian model — a relation that still needs to be thought through methodically. Referring to the Spartans of Thermopylae who combed their hair to be beautiful in death, I once emphasized the many similarities between their behavior and that of the epic fighters; but while it was the poet Tyrtaeus who first formulated the ideal of *kalos thanein* for the Spartans — within a civic and hoplitic milieu, then it is nonetheless important to distinguish the "fine Spartan death" from the one conceived by the Athenian city for all eternity, linked as it is, in part, with the elision of seeing.[13]

It is evident, then, that there is not, and could not be, any kalos thanatos in epic. Despite the eloquent pages by Jean-Pierre Vernant, who places the beauty of the Homeric dead under the sign of fine death,[14] when Patroclus and Sarpedon are killed in the *Iliad*, it is a question not of a *fine death*,[15] but of *fine dead men* (*beaux morts*). Their immobile bodies, magnified by the final shimmering of the ultimate exploit, are rigorously opposed to the outraged cadaver mutilated by men and devoured by dogs.

Among the questions raised in *The Invention of Athens* that I
would only later develop in greater detail and in reference to the
variety of material in which these questions are inscribed, the
example I gave a moment ago was autochthony. This is not the
place to give the full history of that research. Let it suffice for me
to say that if in *The Children of Athena* I tried to diversify and
deepen the examination of this mythico-imaginary configuration,
particularly in relation to Athenian thinking on the division of the
sexes,[16] and if I later returned to certain aspects of this question in
the Athenian discourse on Athens,[17] the ground for that later
work was laid in this book on the funeral oration. I recognize that
this approach was only one of the paths leading to the autochthonous myth and that there are many others, beginning with other
autochthonies in other cities — particularly in Thebes, where the
mythic aristocracy of the Sown (the Spartans) based its legitimacy
on having been born from the civic earth.[18] But I find it remarkable that for some ten years now, there has been an increasing
amount of research into the implications of the *Athenian* ideology
of citizenship in relation to the myth of origins;[19] and this research
continues to grow, particularly in the United States,[20] where the
reflection on multiculturalism, insofar as it projects itself onto
the terrain of Antiquity, necessarily finds a counter-model and a
source of "Eurocentrism" in the Athenian opposition between the
true citizens of Athens and the others, who are by definition
immigrants even in their own city.[21] If I may say so, *The Invention
of Athens*, however limited its aims may have been, contributed in
advance, and in its own way, to this very modern use of Antiquity.

It was also in *The Invention of Athens* that I began to lay the
groundwork for the research I have undertaken on the question of
stasis.[22] My primary points of departure are already discernible in
these pages, especially in the sections examining how a model
of the unified and indivisible city is constituted; in the sections
on the avoidance of conflict in the Athenian representation of
democracy (although it would no doubt be better to state it more
generally by saying: in Greek thinking about the political, largely
dominated by the reference to Athens); and, finally, in the passages

examining the obvious embarrassment of the restored democracy, beginning in 403 BCE and extending throughout the fourth century, in evoking the oligarchic episode of the Thirty, and their efforts to conceal the fact that in the time of the city these "events" or "misfortunes," identified with a bygone past that the citizens make an oath not to recall, introduced a profound rupture.

If the *The Invention of Athens* published in France in 1981 nourished and still nourishes my work on Athenian thinking about citizenship, memory in conflict, and the political, one chapter more immediately important to me than the others (no doubt because writing this chapter led me to work on the funeral oration); these pages, on the Athenian democracy's self-representation, remain more essental to me than any other part of this book. Certainly, these pages did not create a consensus around their analyses; and (to mention only the essential) the idea that Athenian democracy, caught within an excessive conformity to the values of *aretē*, did not develop a properly democratic theory of itself provoked many reactions, ranging from categorical and unexamined rejection[23]to reasoned and argued discussion.[24] I noted the rejection, I read and meditated on the discussions, but I must confess that neither of these substantially modified my view of the Athenian question of democracy. To clarify something that (in Chapter Four of *The Invention of Athens*) was only one intuition among others under the rubric of the "implicit agon,"[25] I would like to add today that we must seek the most "democratic" presentation of democracy not among the Athenian democrats, in the end, but in the criticisms directed against democracy by its adversaries, who, the better to attack it in their writings, pushed it beyond what it was, both in the form they gave it and in the goals they ascribed to it.[26]

This brings me back to the question of writing in relation to Greek political theory. Once again, I found little to change in the chapter on democracy. More recently, several studies have specifically addressed problems of writing in ancient Greece;[27] However, concerning the thesis that the democrats did not appropriate theoretical-political writing — which is one way of saying that in the life of the Athenian city, writing remained purely *instrumental* — I continue to maintain the position I developed in my book on the funeral oration.[28]

I can thus gladly say that one will find in *The Invention of Athens* the essential part of what I consider myself able to understand and to think on the subject of democracy, at least for the present moment. This does not mean that no other possible Athens exists, or other thinkable democracies — several alternative models developed over a number of years for the perspicacious reader in search of comparisons.[29]

But even if the idea of Athenian democracy is for each person a matter of choice, we can at least attempt to reach an understanding on what is historically designated by the term "Athenian democracy." Assuming that such a thing is possible: indeed, as if democracy could not be grasped over the long duration, as if two centuries far exceeded what constitutes a unity in the history of Greece, every historian, in order to identify "Athenian democracy," has a tendency to choose, consciously or not, between the *politeia* of Ephialtes and Pericles and the regime that, in the *Constitution of Athens*, is for Aristotle both "the present constitution" and the *telos* of the Athenian constitution understood very generally[30] — that is, the democracy of the fourth century, restored in 403 BCE and functioning until 322 BCE without vicissitude. This amounts to determining a moment for democracy in Athens. It is certainly permissible to doubt the legitimacy of such a gesture, and to observe the extent to which everyone has agreed to avoid speaking of it. But the debates would unquestionably gain from a lucid recognition of this practice of selection, which determines the essential elements of the discussions. For my part, I continue to uphold the choice I made in this book,[31] which is to situate the *akmē* of the regime in the fifth century. Despite all those who claim that the fourth century is the age of authentic Athenian democracy,[32] I continue to believe that while the name *dēmokratia* is celebrated after 403 BCE, the reality of the regime was embellished, and we must see this situation as an effect of the violent rupture introduced into the temporality, practices, and civic mentalities by the experience — disavowed but traumatic — of the period of the Thirty.[33]

In analyzing the reality of Athenian democracy, does the final word fall, then, to a conflict of interpretations? It may be that we are dealing here with an irreducible element or a fatality of political history. But this should not prevent us from seeking to delineate other questions and approaches, less global, more specific, and thus newer one that allows us to enrich the political history of Antiquity — which tends to be restricted to the study of institutions — with interrogations borrowed from other disciplines, particularly from the study of discursive formations located outside the political field properly speaking.

If I now had to offer a new analysis of what Pericles said in his *epitaphios* on democracy as a name and as a reality, in order to illuminate this paradigmatic text, which as such would have received only a hasty and superficial reading, I would thus gladly suggest that we draw inspiration from recent research on what archaic Greek poetics calls the *ainos*. A coded discourse whose explicit message serves as a cipher for another message — more secret and often addressed to a different public — the ainos aims at an audience that is more restricted or better informed than the one to which it is officially addressed. The poet expects this audience of the *happy few*[34] to be capable of understanding without having everything spelled out[35] — a faculty that the majority of citizens listening are supposed, as it were by definition, to lack.[36] If we admit that Pericles's *epainos* (praise) of democracy maintains a troubling affinity with the ainos, then the analysis of the "implicit agon" might be supported and developed in this perspective. If the official orator is in fact positioned as an heir to those poets who possessed the ainos, the necessary hypothesis is that at the heart of the Athenian *dēmos*, and in the very moment when it is heard, praise of democracy distinguished between two audiences: those who hear in it only the praise of the word demokratia and those who, beyond the praise of the word, are able to understand that the reality of the regime must be based on arete. This interpretation amounts to distinguishing not between those who were

22

democrats and those who were not, but between two ways of envisioning democracy, as a pure practice without discursivity or as an ideal that can only be thought by borrowing aristocratic modes of value. This does not contradict the analyses previously presented, but it does firmly place them within a longer period of time.

I will now bring this brief review to a close by adding only two more remarks, touching on two of the book's orientations that I have not yet mentioned here: its "historiographic" dimension and its use of the concept of ideology.

With regard to the numerous effects that the genre of the funeral oration, and especially Pericles's epitaphios, had on Western culture, briefly evoked in the introduction to *The Invention of Athens*, today I would include much longer analyses of their history — or their national histories — in terms of the modern uses of Antiquity. But in its magnitude as well as its diversity, such a project presupposes many individual studies that could never be completed by a single researcher, nor within a single national tradition. But we can already observe certain partial contributions, such as the recent study on the influence of the Athenian funeral oration on the rhetoric of Abraham Lincoln who, during the Gettysburg Address, saluted the American soldiers who died for the nation on both sides.[37] And we can always imagine that other such studies will follow.

As for the notion of ideology, its use in *The Invention of Athens* has given rise to a number of questions among the book's readers. Some prefered to use this term in the general and — I must say — rather vague sense of a "system of representations." Others still prefer to speak of an "imaginary"; and still others asked me whether, now that Marxism (without distinguishing practice and theory) seems decidedly out of fashion, I would still use a term that has become so cumbersome. The answer to this last objection is not very difficult, for it involves a basic fidelity to oneself: when an idea seems to have become outdated, we need not rush to repudiate it. But alongside fidelity, there exist many other theoretical reasons, I will therefore answer all my interlocutors by saying that I still do not see a more pertinent term for designating the politico-intellectual configuration that proposes "the city" — that is, the idea of a unified city, indivisible and at peace with itself[38] — as the historically embodied model of democratic Athens, for the use of Athenians and moderns alike. One could no doubt retain the notion of an imaginary, which is infinitely less compromising, and it is true that before I submitted this book to a publisher, it was called *Athènes imaginaire*. But although I later turned, for a while, to the notion of an imaginary, the vagueness of this category finally convinced me to renounce it, even if doing so meant having to search for another term yet to be invented. Does this mean that in speaking of ideology, I am designating a phenomenon of "false consciousness"?[39] I can only hope that a (re)reading of the book will convince readers that the word is here used in a somewhat more complicated sense, as was the case in the texts by Marx to which I refer — but not, I think, without maintaining a certain distance.

Is that all? Certainly not. But I believe that I have at least explained why this book remains important to me. Or, in other words, why there is now a new and different edition of a book whose life began in 1981.

May–June 1993
Translated by Jeff Fort

A Very Athenian Invention

In the catalog of Athenian inventions, the funeral oration may not be in the forefront, but it has an honorable place: after the enumeration of the canonical benefits of the democratic city, but in the first rank of Athenian idiomatic forms. Outdistanced by the great inventions of civilization, which were of mythical origin and of universal import and which testify that, in the race for the prize of *philanthrōpia*, the Athenians came first, the *epitaphios logos* comes into its own on the glorious field of arete, where it has no rival. To prove that "among the Greeks only the Athenians know how to honor valor,* one has only to declare, with Demosthenes, that "they alone in the world deliver funeral orations for citizens who have died for their country."[†]

So the funeral oration is Athenian and only Athenian.

There is no reason not to regard this declaration as authentic evidence of the uniqueness of the Athenian funeral oration, provided we reduce "the world" to Greece — but Demosthenes had no reason to concern himself with the Roman *laudatio funebris*, an examination of which would, in any case, have merely confirmed his convictions.[1] So the existence of an epitaphios logos in Athens is in itself sufficient justification for a study of the genre.

But if we were to keep within the bounds of this realistic reading,

---

* Lycurgus, *Against Leocrates* 51.

† Demosthenes, *Against Leptines* 141 (text of manuscript 5, corrected by Gottfried Heinrich Schaefer). Cf. Aelius Aristides, *Panathenaicus*, ed. Oliver, 253.

we would fail to recognize the strange play of mirrors whereby Athenians are praised for inventing a form of oration that, at Athens, praises Athenians. Declaring that Athenians are unique in practicing the funeral oration, Demosthenes uses precisely the formula by which the authors of the *epitaphioi* proclaim the unique character of the city: *monoi tōn anthrōpōn*, the Athenians are "unique among men" in all their exploits.* Their uniqueness extends even and especially to their origin: their autochthonous birth isolates them from the motley descendants of Pelops, Cadmus, Aegyptus, Danaus, and so on.† As a specifically Athenian institution, then, the funeral oration is self-referential, and an Athenian finds it difficult to evoke the epitaphios logos, even in the context of a political speech, without borrowing its language. Conversely, the city that honors its dead with an oration rediscovers itself in the oration as the originator of the *nomos*‡ and ultimate cause of its citizens' death.§ It is therefore no accident that Demosthenes, to awaken the sense of honor in his Athenian audience, praised Athens for inventing the funeral oration; but this reader of Thucydides, this admirer of Pericles, was well aware that "where the rewards offered to merit are greatest, there, too, the city gathers its bravest men."** If all celebration is merely a discreet form of self-celebration, if, in honoring greatness, one is aggrandizing oneself,[2] it is quite likely that Athens appropriated for itself part of the praise that it lavished on its dead and on the epitaphios logos.

To praise *any* Athenians in Athens amounts, then, to praising *the* Athenians,†† all Athenians, dead and alive, and above all "we who are still living,"‡‡ the "we" who coincide with the city's pres-

---

* Thucydides 2.40.2 and 5; 41.3. Lysias 18, 20, 24. Plato, *Menexenus* 245c5. Demosthenes 4.10.

† *Menexenus* 245d2–4.

‡ For example: Demosthenes 2.

§ Thucydides 2.41.5 and 2.43.2.

** *Ibid.* 2.46.1.

†† *Menexenus* 235d3–7.

‡‡ *Ibid.* 235a5–6.

ent: such is the scarcely veiled purpose of the funeral oration exposed by Plato in the *Menexenus*. Of course the Athenian *dēmos*, as is well known, was not averse to having praise showered upon it, and we know that Pindar, after crowning the city with violets, was given an extremely warm reception by the citizens.* But it is not my purpose here to recall once more that Athens, as Aristophanes puts it, is the city of the *kechēnaioi*,† of "citizen flycatchers."[3]‡ The study of the epitaphios logos, an official oration composed in accordance with a nomos[4]§ and spoken by a politician carefully chosen for this purpose by his fellow citizens,** is a quite different matter: in the democratic city, the funeral oration was an *institution* — an institution of speech in which the symbolic constantly encroached on the functional, since in each oration the codified praise of the dead spilled over into generalized praise of Athens.[5]

A very old tradition of praise tried to exorcise death by speaking of glorious deeds[6], and it is probably not irrelevant that the Athenian citizenry gathered together in the Kerameikos to ward off death by means of a speech. But what death exactly? There is scarcely any mention of death as the universal *telos* of the human condition; or at least the orators devote themselves to declaring that on every field of battle and in each of the citizen-soldiers that fell in combat, death was vanquished by glory. Thus the account of Athenian exploits does without the verb *apothanein* (to die) — a fact that the time-honored formula *andres agathoi genomenoi* is intended to conceal[7] — and death is already fading away into the past. By the same token, the dead themselves, thus consigned by the orator to eternal remembrance, are overshadowed by the city, the ultimate authority of all Memory: the ever-living city. Of course the official speech scarcely mentioned the future, but each

---

* Pindar, *Dithyrambs* 5, parodied by Aristophanes, *Acharnians* 636–40 and *Knights* 1329; cf. Isocrates, *Antidosis* 166 and Pausanias 1.8.4.

† *Knights* 1263.

‡ *Acharnians* 635: *chaunopolitai.*

§ Thucydides 2.35.3; *Menexenus* 236d7–e1.

** Thucydides 2.34.6; *Menexenus* 234b4–10.

epitaphios was concerned to ward off the inexorable law by which "all that lives must die;"* and this formula, borrowed *in extremis* from Pericles by Thucydides, throws light retrospectively on the same orator's epitaphios (and probably on the funeral oration in general) — in a way that could not be said openly but had to be hinted at. In fact, by declaring that in Athens "there is only nobility,"[8] perhaps all the speeches were intended to place Athens *en représentation*, beyond the reach of time, in a great victory that the Athenians of the present could enjoy in advance.[9]

It was an imaginary victory, of course. But who would dare to deny reality to the imaginary — not only in fifth- and fourth-century Athenian society, but also in our relationship with that same Athens? The problem is encapsulated in that question.

An illusory mastery of time? But indeed it might even be that the Athenians, celebrating a city that conformed with their wishes, systematically elaborated for their own use and posterity's† the figure of themselves that informed and still informs, more or less implicitly, the whole history of Athens.

To begin with, the prestige of the funeral oration may not be unconnected with the fact that it was not until the second half of the fourth century that an Athenian, Cleidemus, writing an *Atthis*, produced a carefully dated chronological account of the city from its remotest origins to the present. The first of the Atthidographers, Hellanicus, was not a citizen of Athens, but this fact causes little surprise. It may well be that from the end of the fifth century right up to Cleidemus, the Athenians were officially content with the "Athenian history of Athens" repeated in every funeral oration, in which the series of warlike deeds performed by the *polis* were interchangeable and symbolic of the perennial nature of civic arete. In this form, there was no place for any thought of development; this oral history had to serve as archive and document. Furthermore, because they tended to see democracy as rooted in the city's

* Thucydides 2.64.3.
† *Ibid.* 2.41.4; Hyperides 18.

autochthonous origins, the orators paid little attention to the forms of government that had preceded it, either in the mythical tradition or in more recent times. Felix Jacoby is no doubt right that the revival of political struggles in Athens in 350 encouraged the birth of a new national history.[10] One might add that since the prestige of the written word had been established for half a century, the writers were now free to compete with, and even to ignore, the official orators.[11] Finally, the models were inevitably subjected to overuse, and one of the most used was the catalog of exploits. Of course, none of these hypotheses is absolutely verifiable; but the fact remains that if the national historiography of Athens is an invention of the fourth century, the Athenians had already, for more than a century, been recounting to one another, on the occasion of public funerals, a history in which their city was preeminent.

It may well be thought that by the end of the fourth century, the funeral oration had finally died out, since no trace of it is found after 322, whether the genre was permanently extinguished or whether it survived to the Hellenistic period. Between the Athenians and themselves and then between the moderns and Athens, other models had interposed themselves since the fifth century, and Plutarch's "famous men" had long since supplanted the glorious, anonymous Athenians of the epitaphioi, before being themselves superseded. Perhaps, but things are not so simple. Of course, one no longer learns the history of Athens or studies the military policy of the democratic city in the epitaphioi, and there is no need to appeal to the "fine death" when studying the military policy of the democratic city. However, it would be naive to assert that the funeral oration no longer provides any access to Athens. The epitaphios logos is closely bound up with the "classical Greek city," that model forged in the image of Athens in the Germany of August Boeckh and G.W.F. Hegel, whose grip has been only partially shaken by contemporary historical research. Like the corpus of the epitaphioi, the "classical period" opens with Pericles and closes with Hyperides, and the funeral oration offers a ready-made support for the "paradigmatic polarization" of Greek studies between Sparta and Athens.[12] To complicate matters still more, one might add that since he is unable to escape the suggestions of his own cultural field, the historian of Antiquity confronts the study of the "classical Greek city" in terms of the intellectual, political, and national interests of his own time. Thus, to give weight to his attack on the "mere paperworld" into which the Convention of 1792–95 had sunk, Hegel exalted the democratic reign of the logos.[13] Conversely, however, in the work of, for example, Eric A. Havelock, the democratic logos becomes a weapon against any Hegelian conception of the state: careful to reconstruct a Greek liberal thought — that of Democritus or Protagoras — that he believed Platonic philosophy had ruthlessly suppressed, Havelock began by denouncing the pernicious influence of "German idealism" on the modern history of Greek political thought.[14]

Considered one of the authorized mouthpieces of classical Athens, the funeral oration does not escape from the play of these partisan and partial readings, in which two imaginary cities — that of the ancients and that of the moderns — reinforce each other.

Recent Greek history has taken up the interpretation of the epitaphioi logoi on several occasions. Thus in 1825, in a work "sold for the benefit of the Greeks," *Eloges funèbres des Athéniens morts pour la patrie*, F. Roget distinguished between two ancient forms — "servile" and "national" — of the funeral oration and declared his faith in the living continuity of Greek civilization and liberty, from Salamis to the war of independence.[15] Over a century later, the dictator Metaxas implicitly confirmed this interpretation by forbidding the study of Pericles's epitaphios in educational institutions.[16]

But it was left above all to German scholarship to read into the funeral oration the "Greek patriotism" with which German patriotism believed it could identify.[17] Attesting to this identification are Ulrich von Wilamowitz's interest in the genre of the epitaphios logos, which he considered the true source of all Athenian eloquence;[18] the publication of contending scholarly editions of the *Menexenus* in Germany and France after 1870;[19] and the innumerable conflicting interpretations of Pericles's epitaphios during and after the two world wars of the twentieth century.[20]

Given this minefield of overdetermination, in which false

corpus; to the epitaphioi of Thucydides (or Pericles) and Plato (or Socrates or Aspasia!) must be added those of Gorgias, Hyperides, and — whether apocryphal or authentic — Lysias or Demosthenes.[*] Some scholars would add to this list a speech by Archinus, of which only a mention has survived; but this is probably a bad reading of the preamble of the *Menexenus*.[44†]

Pericles, Thucydides, Gorgias, Lysias, Plato, Demosthenes, Hyperides: a reassuring list, but one in which serious anomalies are apparent. Indeed in this list, only Pericles, Demosthenes, and Hyperides correspond to Thucydides's portrait of the official orator: "a man chosen by the city" (it goes without saying that he is a citizen: who else in such solemn circumstances would be given the task of delivering the oration?), "who is considered not to be lacking in intellectual distinction, and who enjoys considerable esteem"[‡] (certainly his prestige has placed him in the forefront of the political scene).[§] Gorgias the Sophist and Lysias the metic were by definition excluded from the tribune of the Kerameikos, and this consideration alone has done much to cast doubt on the authenticity of Lysias's epitaphios: it was enough to transfer the irregularity of the orator's status onto the oration, and with a word — the magic word "inauthenticity" — the problem was considered resolved. The epitaphios of the *Menexenus* is even more disturbing: Plato is wicked enough to attribute it to an extremely odd author and speaker — Aspasia, a woman and a foreigner, and Socrates, who, as everyone knows, was not a politician. Consequently, many scholars attempted to sweep away the irritating question of the meaning of the dialogue, and those who refuse to read it as a very accurate pastiche have concluded that the text is inauthentic.

There is even doubt about some orations of the canonical orators listed above. Of Pericles's two epitaphioi, that of Samos is

---

[*] *Ibid.* 2.35–46; Plato, *Menexenus* 236d4–249c8; Gorgias, DK, 82, B 5 a, 5 b, 6; Hyperides 6; Lysias 2; Demosthenes 60.

[†] *Menexenus* 234b9–10: "I think the choice will fall on Archinus or Dio."

[‡] Thucydides 2.34.6.

[§] Compare 2.34.6 with 2.65.8 (Pericles's eulogy).

lost except for a few fragments; and the other, more famous one, reconstituted, if not actually recomposed, by Thucydides, is situated in a highly wrought work of history of which it is an integral part. Demosthenes certainly delivered the epitaphios for the dead of Chaironeia* but the oration to which his name is attached does not satisfy everybody, and because the orator makes a few errors in mythology,† or because a few of the arguments are reminiscent of Pericles's epitaphios or closely resemble certain periods in the *Menexenus*, it, too, is under suspicion and has even been declared apocryphal. Finally, no one doubts that Hyperides's oration was written and spoken by the politician and that its author wished to publish it as it was;[45] but until the discovery in 1858 of a papyrus containing an almost complete text of the epitaphios, commentators had to be content, in the case of this authentic example of the funeral oration, with a quotation from it by Stobaeus.‡

From this perspective, the funeral oration begins to look like an ever-absent model, a ghost-oration that, with one exception, we will know only through more or less accurate copies: a historian and a philosopher were pleased to compose an exemplary epitaphios, a way of proposing a theory of the funeral oration; a Sophist and a rhetor used the official oration in order to write a fictitious logos; within the corpus, then, the "false" follows hard upon the "true," and one begins to regret that authentic epitaphioi should have remained unknown because national eloquence resisted for so long the seductions of writing. Confronted with such a discouraging first assessment, scholars have, not surprisingly, shied away from studying the genre, preferring to isolate each work in its particular relationship with its author, real or supposed.

Pericles's epitaphios once again dominates this area of research. Whether it is regarded as a purple passage that may be detached from its context, or whether it is the occasion for yet another reexamination of the status of the speeches in Thucydides's work,

---

* See Demosthenes, *De corona* 285–88.

† Demosthenes 29: Akamas, son (not grandson) of Aethra.

‡ Stobaeus, *Florilegium* 124.36.

resemblances and authentic projections are intertwined, in which the funeral oration is regarded as the authorized voice of classical Athens, which in turn is seen as an archetype for modern states, it is hardly surprising that in a new reductive equivalence, historians have generally substituted for the study of the genre an examination of some of its examples: the epitaphios of the *Menexenus* (Platonic noblesse oblige!) and above all that of Pericles — or of Thucydides — who combined the prestige of the statesman with that of the historian. Let us briefly examine this exemplary case.

A list of the editions, translations, or commentaries of this famous text would be very long indeed, because quite simply "it warms the heart,"[21] because it is seen as the finest definition of the "classical ideal,"[22] or because one has read into it, at least since Hegel, the "most profound description" of Athenian democracy,[23] if not of Greek democracy in general or even of the city-state,[24] for this play of equivalences and generalizations sets up a series of ever more abstract paradigms. And yet, in very concrete terms, it is through faithful projections of their national present that historians and sometimes politicians read Pericles's epitaphios.[25] Politicians imitate the Athenian oration by adapting it to the needs of a given historical situation: thus the funeral oration to the glory of General Nanni Strozzi, written in 1428 by Leonardo Bruni, chancellor of the Florentine Republic and a great representative of the civic humanism of the Quattrocento, is entirely devoted to exalting Florence, the new Athens. It is a biased reading, of course, but one that may still prove illuminating about the epitaphios: had he not been aware of the contradiction in the reliance of an independent city like Florence on an army of mercenaries, would Bruni have perceived the extent to which the epitaphios is an oration in time of war?[26] Conversely, in attempting to situate Pericles's speech in its own time, historians are quite willing to abandon the ideal of disinterested knowledge and, in a more or less conscious way, find in the text an echo of their own preoccupations. This tendency becomes clear from a brief examination of three readings in which three Athenses emerge: the French, the German, and the English.

In the French Athens, found in *La Cité grecque*, Gustave Glotz unhesitatingly adds fraternity to the democratic values of liberty and equality. It is a short step from this to seeing the epitaphios as the ancestor of the Declaration of the Rights of Man. And, against "the all too widespread prejudice in favor of the omnipotence of the city," Glotz declares that in reality, as in the orations, the Athenians knew how to maintain "a correct balance between the legal power of the state and the natural right of the individual."[27]

To Hegel in post-Napoleonic Germany, Pericles's epitaphios speaks of a "fine democracy," a democracy reduced to its spirit and exclusively concerned with a love of the beautiful: a strange example of political life in which the political life is absent. Hegel's summary of the speech disregards everything Pericles says about the constitution in order to concentrate exclusively on "the character of Athens."[28]* Though not entirely excluded, the military significance of the funeral oration is distorted no less profoundly: breaking with the order of the Periclean speech, Hegel subordinates the warrior spirit to the desire for beauty,"† and Athenian courage, mentioned almost reluctantly, is treated in the end as no more than incidental.[29] At the cost of this suppression is erected "the political work of art," the symbol of that Greece in which German nineteenth-century thought sought its youth,[30] and in which generations of Hellenists believed they had discovered a golden age of total harmony, miraculously preserved from the contradictions of history.

After the German universities comes London; after the lovers of the forms, George Grote's empiricism.[31] From the perspective of English liberalism, Pericles' epitaphios, inserted into a chronology in which it is at first one fact among others, assumes a certain historical solidity, and in interpreting the speech, Grote ignores neither the ordering of the nomos of the funeral, nor the eminently political act that determines the appointment of the speaker by the demos, nor the strict requirements of the genre.[32] But Grote, too, makes his choices concerning the epitaphios. The

* Cf. Thucydides 2.36.4: *epitēdeusis, politeia, tropoi.*
† Cf. *ibid.* 2.39 (*ta polemika*) and 2.40 (*philokaloumen*).

praise of *politeia* and the passage on Athens's warrior *phusis*,[*] described as an "untenable assertion,"[33] have little interest for him; all his attention is focused on the paragraph that Pericles devotes to Athenian liberty.[34][†] For Grote, the epitaphios is a hymn to individual, positive, action-oriented liberty and to classical Athens — an expanding, imperialist Athens, busy like the British Commonwealth,[35] comfortable like liberal societies.[36] Indeed, Grote considers "civil society" an Athenian invention and protests against those who draw a distinction between the total subordination of the individual to the ancient polis and the individual liberty of modern societies.[37] This reading, too, has omissions and distortions, especially the overvaluation of the Greek city as the lost paradise of "generous tolerance."[38]

It may be thought that in the final analysis, these partial readings complement one another and that, in combination, they are neutralized. Thus, adding the democratic "virtue" dear to Hegel and Glotz[39] to the *eleutheria* of the liberals,[40] one would reconstruct an epitaphios previously fragmented by divergent interpretations. But German philosophy and English empiricism cannot be reconciled easily, since they are opposed in every way, even when they are dealing with the same passage;[41] at most, they share the same reluctance to decipher in the oration a certain war ethic — not only that of the Athens at war in 430, but also that of the funeral oration as a genre.

To isolate an epitaphios from the democracy that it is supposed to describe and, even more, from the genre that it illustrates runs the risk of distortion. When concentrated into a single speech, the funeral oration dissolves and provides transparent access to a transparent political model. To restore to the genre its specificity, we must first exorcise the despotic dominance of Pericles's famous speech and the more discreet but still effective dominance of its authorized commentaries. Perhaps this is possible; let us at least wager the bet.

---

[*] *Ibid.* 2.39.2–3.
[†] *Ibid.* 2.37.2.

I lay no claim to any absolutely "better" understanding; but when confronted with democracy, with the word as well as the thing, and when confronted with Antiquity, too, I feel that I am in a strange world, and thus entitled to attempt a new reading.[42] Because the notion of a political model is so problematic today, and because the inflation of the word "democracy" contributes much to obscuring the thing, I am unwilling to accept as given that Athens was the place where democracy once existed in its pure state, in a perfect coincidence of a system and its discourse. The efforts of contemporary historians to restore to each civilization its strangeness may help me to deepen the gap that separates Athens from us without entertaining too many illusions. Finally, historians' attention in recent decades to the problems of war in ancient Greece will help me to see the epitaphioi in the context of a civic time and place that was both military and political: at the frontiers of the *astu*, between the season of battles and the "reserved season" when the internal life of the polis was given more attention than the external. In the funeral oration, praise of warlike deeds and exaltation of the political system go hand in hand, and this persistent duality, when taken seriously, militates against a choice of just one of these dimensions in a particular epitaphios, however dominant it may appear, as in the case of Pericles's.

Thus to gain access to the genre, we must circumvent the particular example to which a celebrated tradition has been pleased to reduce it;[43] but, conversely, if we are to read afresh an epitaphios that has been too often commented on, we must root it from the outset in the study of the genre as a whole.

Does this mean that if we proceed in this way, we will open up a new access to the funeral oration? To believe this would be to forget that when one moves from the particular to the general, the implications of what one is doing are seldom self-evident. A reconstruction of the genre must overcome two awesome obstacles: the loss of the large majority of epitaphioi, and the encumbering fame of those orators whose speeches have survived. There are many great names (some might say too many) for this scanty corpus; to the epitaphioi of Thucydides (or Pericles) and Plato (or Socrates or Aspasia!) must be added those of Gorgias, Hyperides, and — whether apocryphal or authentic — Lysias or Demosthenes.* Some scholars would add to this list a speech by Archinus, of which only a mention has survived; but this is probably a bad reading of the preamble of the *Menexenus*.[44]†

Pericles, Thucydides, Gorgias, Lysias, Plato, Demosthenes, Hyperides: a reassuring list, but one in which serious anomalies are apparent. Indeed in this list, only Pericles, Demosthenes, and Hyperides correspond to Thucydides's portrait of the official orator: "a man chosen by the city" (it goes without saying that he is a citizen: who else in such solemn circumstances would be given the task of delivering the oration?), "who is considered not to be lacking in intellectual distinction, and who enjoys considerable esteem"‡ (certainly his prestige has placed him in the forefront of the political scene).§ Gorgias the Sophist and Lysias the metic were by definition excluded from the tribune of the Kerameikos, and this consideration alone has done much to cast doubt on the authenticity of Lysias's epitaphios: it was enough to transfer the irregularity of the orator's status onto the oration, and with a word — the magic word "inauthenticity" — the problem was considered resolved. The epitaphios of the *Menexenus* is even more disturbing: Plato is wicked enough to attribute it to an extremely odd author and speaker — Aspasia, a woman and a foreigner, and Socrates, who, as everyone knows, was not a politician. Consequently, many scholars attempted to sweep away the irritating question of the meaning of the dialogue, and those who refuse to read it as a very accurate pastiche have concluded that the text is inauthentic.

There is even doubt about some orations of the canonical orators listed above. Of Pericles's two epitaphioi, that of Samos is

* *Ibid.* 2.35–46; Plato, *Menexenus* 236d4–249c8; Gorgias, DK, 82, B 5 a, 5 b, 6; Hyperides 6; Lysias 2; Demosthenes 60.
† *Menexenus* 234b9–10: "I think the choice will fall on Archinus or Dio."
‡ Thucydides 2.34.6.
§ Compare 2.34.6 with 2.65.8 (Pericles's eulogy).

lost except for a few fragments; and the other, more famous one, reconstituted, if not actually recomposed, by Thucydides, is situated in a highly wrought work of history of which it is an integral part. Demosthenes certainly delivered the epitaphios for the dead of Chaironeia* but the oration to which his name is attached does not satisfy everybody, and because the orator makes a few errors in mythology,† or because a few of the arguments are reminiscent of Pericles's epitaphios or closely resemble certain periods in the *Menexenus*, it, too, is under suspicion and has even been declared apocryphal. Finally, no one doubts that Hyperides's oration was written and spoken by the politician and that its author wished to publish it as it was;[45] but until the discovery in 1858 of a papyrus containing an almost complete text of the epitaphios, commentators had to be content, in the case of this authentic example of the funeral oration, with a quotation from it by Stobaeus.‡

From this perspective, the funeral oration begins to look like an ever-absent model, a ghost-oration that, with one exception, we will know only through more or less accurate copies: a historian and a philosopher were pleased to compose an exemplary epitaphios, a way of proposing a theory of the funeral oration; a Sophist and a rhetor used the official oration in order to write a fictitious logos; within the corpus, then, the "false" follows hard upon the "true," and one begins to regret that authentic epitaphioi should have remained unknown because national eloquence resisted for so long the seductions of writing. Confronted with such a discouraging first assessment, scholars have, not surprisingly, shied away from studying the genre, preferring to isolate each work in its particular relationship with its author, real or supposed.

Pericles's epitaphios once again dominates this area of research. Whether it is regarded as a purple passage that may be detached from its context, or whether it is the occasion for yet another reexamination of the status of the speeches in Thucydides's work,

* See Demosthenes, *De corona* 285–88.

† Demosthenes 29: Akamas, son (not grandson) of Aethra.

‡ Stobaeus, *Florilegium* 124.36.

it is rarely compared with other epitaphioi. When they are mentioned at all, they usually serve as a foil, and the presumed originality of the text conceals the influence of the funeral oration as a
genre on Thucydides's historical writing. Even the historian's
unconditional advocates, however, dare not conceive that a traditional form, which they somewhat hastily regard as an empty
one, could have interested a writer whose scientific reputation is
unchallenged.[46] Thus authority stands in the way of research: the
authority not only of Thucydides himself but also of Plato, for in
this respect the *Menexenus* is no better off than Pericles's epitaphios. Because the philosopher wanted to dissipate the mirage
of the funeral oration by turning the speech against itself, the dialogue has often been pronounced inauthentic; and now that its
authenticity is accepted, the reading of the Platonic epitaphios
and the understanding of the genre as a whole are threatened by
the opposite temptation, namely to take the work too seriously.
The effect of declaring that the orations of Lysias and Demosthenes are apocryphal is to preserve the prestige of the great
names: because they forget that a certain style is incumbent on
the official orator, because they despise the constraints of a solemn genre,[47] scholars are surprised at not finding Lysias's usual
elegance or Demosthenes's biting wit and avoid any further examination of the funeral oration.

Rejecting all these readings because they fall to attend to the
very special status of a form of national eloquence, I shall instead
consider the funeral orations as a model of spoken language. The
objection will be made that it is a largely lost model; but such an
objection ignores the laws that govern all oral tradition and, as it
happens, all civic *paideia*, laws according to which each orator,
real or fictitious, composes his speech in imitation of all previous
such speeches, which may be lost to us but were engraved in the
collective memory of the Athenians and in the individual memory
of each listener. The model was sufficiently powerful that it was
extremely difficult to distinguish between counterfeit epitaphioi
and the generality of speeches delivered in the Kerameikos, even
supposing that in an institutional, codified genre the question

37

of authenticity is still meaningful: to assimilate beforehand any deviation is no doubt in the character of an institution, and however diverse the restrictions may be on our own preconceptions, those preconceptions inevitably influence our interpretation.[48] Whatever reasons led Thucydides, Plato, or Gorgias to write an epitaphios, it certainly was epitaphioi that they wrote, and in each case the model surpasses the historian's abrupt rigor, the philosopher's parodic intentions, or the Sophist's display of virtuosity. So if we are to study the genre, we must agree, for a time at least, to play the game according to its own rules: provided we suspend for a time any judgment on the uniqueness of each speech, provided we admit that in an epitaphios the personality of the orator has to yield to the impersonality of the genre, the unity of the funeral oration will appear even through the incomplete corpus at our disposal.

This hypothesis and approach seem to me to be the only ones sufficiently armed against the innumerable temptations to fragment the corpus into a dust of stylistic exercises. But there is nothing arbitrary about this approach, for throughout my consideration of the corpus I shall also note traces of the funeral oration in the whole of Athenian literature in the classical period. Noting these occurrences, explicit or probable — echoes of the catalog of exploits to be found in the works of the orators and historians,[49] the Euripidean version of the praise given to the dead and to the city, the jokes of the comic writers about autochthony, grandiloquent heroism, or Marathonomania — affirms both the generative power and the unity of the epitaphios logos. Furthermore, a comparison of the official speeches with contemporary literary forms reveals the specificity of the genre. It is not irrelevant that in treating the same mythical scene, such as the aid given to Adrastus by the Athenians, the epitaphioi always adopt the bellicose version of the affair, whereas the tragedies feel free to choose between the military expedition and the peaceful solution. Nor is it mere chance that the authors of the epitaphioi prefer an aristocratic democracy to the democratic kings of Aeschylus and Euripides. These phenomena confirm the politico-military character of the funeral oration.

To study this genre, then, is to acknowledge its at once double and indissolubly single dimension, as an institution and as a literary form. The trap of formalism awaits those who, ignoring the context in which the logos is inscribed, merge the funeral oration into the epideictic genre or turn it into a form of set speech for a public occasion.[50] To treat the epitaphioi simply as epideictic speeches is to forget that the political orator must have the ascendant over the logographer: we cannot be content to list *topoi* or to decide the arrangement of the speech without interrogating the significance of those topoi and of that arrangement. For lovers of figures and periods, Gorgias's fragment of an epitaphios serves as an archetype. Some even amuse themselves by moving forward the date of birth of the funeral oration to a period late enough for rhetoric to have already been developed in Athens, as if all eloquence could be reduced to formal exercises and every institution of the spoken language to an *epideixis*, as if there had never been any interaction between the laws governing public speeches and the demands of political life. Historians have rightly likened such speculations to the comparative study of the various Athenian scenes of national celebrations, in which the arrangement and the "parts" of the speech are shown to have acquired their meaning long before the Sophists set themselves up as teachers of eloquence.

To constitute the funeral oration as a unity and to root this unity in an Athenian space in which the Kerameikos is close to the Agora, in a civic time in which orator follows orator, as magistrate follows magistrate, in a political and military practice of democracy: these two operations are interdependent and reinforce each other against all the traps pointed out so far. This does not mean, however, that all obstacles have finally been overcome.

Of course the interaction between the oration and the social practices that animate it is a necessary one. But there is a wide gap between this theoretical requirement and its realization, and in the funeral oration the distinction between inside and outside is often blurred: it is as if, to study this official genre, we must position ourselves neither too much inside nor too much outside the represen-

tations proper to it. How, then, are we to get Athens to throw light
on its oration, and vice versa? Because almost all the questions that
we can pose about the epitaphioi are already to be found in the epitaphioi themselves, we run the risk, in taking this well-trodden
path, of simply repeating the topoi of the celebration of Athens.
Thus, when the orators declare that the funeral oration is the
supreme honor accorded by the city, in its benevolence, to its
finest sons, it is very difficult for us to verify whether for those who
heard the speech it actually did fulfill the role of an ideological
stimulant. A more serious problem is our inability to achieve contact with the "reality" of the democratic city — it is not easy to
"come down from heaven to earth"[51] — and if we had no other
sources at our disposal than the epitaphioi to understand the political and military functioning of the Athenian democracy, we would
know nothing of so fundamental an institution as *misthophoria* or
even of the exact makeup of that citizen army that the orators exalt
so tirelessly. But if, on the other hand, we try to stand back and
abandon any attempt to keep prudently to the frontier zone of
Athenian texts still dominated by the influence of official oratory,
the return to the epitaphioi proves problematic: how, in a decree of
the *ekklēsia* expressing the day-to-day functioning of the democracy, can we find the "material basis" or the lineaments of the
praise of the primal equality that binds the autochthones together?
If, forgetting that at the Pnyx the topoi of the praise of Athens must
have affected the decision more than once, we reduce Athenian
politics to its positive manifestations (assembly decrees or council
deliberations), we run the risk of regarding the funeral oration as
little more than empty boastings, of negligible importance when
compared with the frank, calm relativism that guided the Athenians in their assessment of reality.[52] By the same token, we are unable to see that at the Kerameikos, the decisions of the ekklesia
found their ultimate sanction in the praise of the city and its dead.

In short, how are we to read the epitaphioi without being
totally enclosed within them but also without approaching them
from too great a distance? This question is inevitable even if one
confines oneself to the classic, perennially controversial problems

about the origin of the genre. Either one keeps within the Periclean definition of the oration as *patrios nomos* (ancestral custom) and tries endlessly to explicate this vague reference to an immemorial past,* or, following the information provided by Diodorus Siculus,† one dates the oration to the years following the Persian Wars. But there is still no guarantee that we have seen the last of the influence, direct or indirect, of the epitaphioi: repeated officially in wartime,‡ the catalog of exploits proper to the funeral oration continued to serve as a model for the rhetorical history of Ephorus, and therefore of Diodorus, who made it his principal source. So a suspicion begins to emerge: did the Persian Wars, a purple passage in the catalog, see the birth of the funeral oration? It is possible, but almost too neat. Or, finally, some scholars have tried to date the funeral oration by comparing it with other forms (oral, written, or plastic) of national celebration. But such a comparison also has its limits, for all ideological systems do not develop at the same pace, and there is no certainty that the official inauguration of the Athenian oration took place simultaneously at the Agora and the Kerameikos, at the Stoa Poikile and the *dēmosion sēma*.[53]

So in the end, we are thrown back to the genre, or rather to a comparison of texts one with another in the context of a perpetual interaction between the particular circumstances of the funeral and the concrete data of the historical juncture. In the ceaseless movement from the text, deprived of the immediacy of the logos, to its political and military context, in which it is only imperfectly inserted, we inevitably lose many illusions, including that of the oration's perfect transparency. But if, renouncing all the mirages of immediacy, we agree not to seek in the epitaphioi a pure reflection of the political life of Athens, we are better equipped to go back to the text and to see in the funeral oration the inextricable intermingling of actual Athenian history and another temporality,

---

* Thucydides 2.35.3: "since our ancestors [*tois palai*] have set the seal of their approval upon the practice"; cf. Isocrates, *Panegyricus* 74: *palai*.

† Diodorus Siculus 11.33.3.

‡ Isocrates, *Panegyricus* 74: *pollakis*.

that of celebration, which strives to turn the now into an always: bearing the marks both of the speaker's present and of a tradition's timeless orthodoxy, each of the epitaphioi attests both to the implantation of the genre in the history of the city and to the resistance offered by official discourse to any transformation of society.[54]

The following chapters operate within the framework of this dual determination. In them, I shall use the terms "funeral oration" for the genre and "epitaphios" for each example, so as to distinguish more clearly between tradition and individual speeches, between the speech model and the examples of eloquence that have survived. I shall use the epitaphioi to reconstruct the funeral oration, and I shall also refer from the funeral oration to the epitaphioi, for a model, even if hidden or lost, never ceases to exert its influence. In the quest for the funeral oration, I shall try to ascertain not only what links the *dēmosion sēma* to the asty but also how the patrios nomos of the funeral illuminates the ordinary, everyday life of the citizens. Anchoring the funeral oration in the politico-military practice of the city, in which innovation does not exclude the repetitive celebration of glory, raises the issue of the destination of such a speech: is it addressed to the dead, to the living, or to posterity? Because this triple destination is inscribed in it simultaneously, the funeral oration is much more: it is a way of conceiving of Athenian history between the fragmented time of battle and the paradigmatic timelessness of the citizens' valor. It is a discourse on "democracy," the geometric locus of arete, forever protected from conflicts and tensions, for in its origins, equality accompanies nobility. In short, it is a political genre in which, governed by civic laws, the logos becomes in turn a civic norm for speaking of Athens. From epitaphios to epitaphios, a certain idea that the city wishes to have of itself emerges, beyond the needs of the present: within the orthodoxy of an official speech, there is a certain gap between Athens and Athens.

We shall examine this gap as it appears in the funeral oration. At least such a risk seems justifiable, since we no longer believe naively that we are the posterity whom the orators exhorted to remember Athens.

Chapter One

The Funeral Oration in
the Democratic City

In their attempts to anchor the political, social, and religious practice of the democratic polis in its most concrete reality, historians of Athenian society have treated the funeral oration in an often unserious or condescending, and always parsimonious, way. It is as if, caught between the decipherment of material documents, which afforded presumably direct access to the real life of the city, and the critique of positive information provided by the Athenians about their institutions and history, they had nothing to learn from an official speech that they were glad to leave to literary historians.

So even when he devotes a long study to the Athenian nomos for national funerals, Jacoby shows little interest in the funeral oration; he sees it as an obligatory but ultimately not very meaningful item in the program of the ceremonies.[1] As a result, he no longer needs to concern himself with the possible function of the oration within the nomos, and still less with the role that it might have played in the city. There are, of course, reasons for such indifference, possibly including a firm determination to separate himself from historians of too philosophical a bent. The latter, falling into the opposite excess, overestimate the importance of the speech; Wilamowitz, for example, made the funeral oration the original matrix of all eloquence, a sort of Form of the logos.[2]

Must we choose between, on the one hand, an attempt to merge the oration into a social practice and, on the other, a belief in the total autonomy of the logos? Let there be no mistake: Jacoby and Wilamowitz are both guilty of inattention to the specific function of the funeral oration, of a refusal *to consider the oration as a practice*, and as a practice endowed with meaning. In short, the historian of the nomos and the advocate of the logos both confirm, each in his own way, the dichotomy between logos and *ergon* that for the Greeks of the classical period structured the whole of human experience and, as it happens, the Athenian custom of the public funeral.* From the time when, in the world of the cities, speech won its autonomy in opposition to action, or more generally to the real,[3] the oration, sometimes overvalued and sometimes depreciated, ceased to be an ergon; when they reflected on the funeral oration, the Athenians saw it as a logos that was different from the rest of the ceremonial and irremediably divorced from the acts that it had to celebrate.[4] Although Pericles ends the first part of his epitaphios by considering the delivery of the funeral oration as a nomos,† he has first turned it into a sort of patch, introduced after the event into an already-complete traditional ceremonial.‡ Pericles was not trying to give a detailed history of Athenian practice; he simply wanted to initiate the critique to which he was subjecting the oration. But for ancient tradition,§ as well as for most modern historians, the case is closed: the funeral oration is an adjunct that one may try endlessly to date, but whose heterogeneity distracts from its character as nomos, that is, as institution.

But what is speech making, if not an act? It might be said that in Athens, the city of speech par excellence, silence was more remarkable than logos,[5] but this would be to forget that for ancient tradition the funeral oration was one of the peculiarities

---

* See Plato, *Menexenus* 236d4: *ergoi … logoi* (cf. Thucydides 2.46: *logoi … ergoi*).

† Thucydides 2.35.3.

‡ *Ibid.* 2.35.1, and Lysias 81.

§ Dionysius of Halicarnassus, *Roman Antiquities* 5.17.3 ("indeed the Athenians later added [*prosethesan*] the funeral oration to the custom") plagiarizes Thucydides, from who he borrows the term *prostithenai*.

by which Athens distinguished herself from other cities.* Indeed an epitaphios is an odd form of speech; closer to the speech-memory of aristocratic societies than to democratic speech-debate, this oration is nevertheless a political speech, marked with the seal of democracy. Apart from the choice of prose, the "lay" mode of discourse, its political nature is proved by the facts that the speech is an act of collective praise and that the speaker is officially appointed by the city.

To study the oration for the dead from a historical viewpoint is, therefore, to reject the contingent heading of "ceremonial." But to regard the funeral oration as an institution in no way requires that the speech be removed from the context to which it belongs: although they have their own function, the epitaphioi belong nevertheless to a larger whole — to the nomos of the funeral, of course, but also and above all to the political life of Athenian democracy. To assign the oration *its* place in this "reality" is to determine what it owes and what it brings to that "reality."

Only thus is it possible to avoid, perhaps, the constraints of the opposition between logos and ergon.

A Ceremony, an Oration: The Public Funeral

For elucidating the oration by its context, there is no better guide than Thucydides, who, by way of introduction to Pericles's epitaphios, describes the Athenian practice of the funeral:

> During the same winter, the funeral of those who first fell in this war was celebrated by the Athenians at public expense. The ceremony is as follows. Three days before the celebration they erect a tent in which the bones of the dead are laid out, and everyone brings to his own dead any offering he wishes. At the time of the funeral, the bones are placed in chests of cypress wood, which are conveyed in hearses; there is one chest for each tribe. They also carry a single empty litter decked with a pall for all whose bodies have not been

* Apart from Demosthenes, *Against Leptines* 141, one might cite Aelius Aristides 253. See also Polybius 6.53–54; Cicero, *Laws* 2.26 and *Brutus* 16.61.

found and recovered. The procession is accompanied by anyone who chooses, whether citizen or foreigner; and the female relatives of the deceased are present at the funeral and make their lamentation. The public cemetery is situated in the most beautiful suburb of the city; there they always bury those who fall in war; only after the battle of Marathon, in recognition of their preeminent valor, the dead were interred on the field. When the remains have been laid in the earth, a man, chosen by the city for his reputed sagacity of judgment and moral standing, delivers the appropriate eulogy over them; after which the people depart. This is the manner of interment, and the ceremony was repeated whenever there was need for it throughout the war. Over the first who were buried, Pericles was chosen to speak. At the fitting moment he advanced from the cemetery to a lofty stage, which had been erected so that he might be heard as far away as possible by the crowd, and spoke as follows.*

I have quoted at such length from this famous passage in order to read afresh a piece of evidence that, in its detail and rigor, is the equal of modern anthropological investigations. Of course, Thucydides does not say everything: the information given by later tradition (and above all by Pausanias, who, without mentioning the ceremony, describes the public cemetery at length)† and the epigraphic and archaeological discoveries of the excavations at the Agora and Kerameikos will bring important modifications to Thucydides's account, revealing its lacunae and its partial character. But the silences of the historian are no less instructive than the information he provides, and this presentation of the nomos, which is also its first mention in a history, immediately draws attention to what is most important for us: the relationship between the oration and the practice of the funeral.

If we had nothing but this text to go on, we would know nothing of the monuments of the demosion sema, nor of that signal honor accorded men when their names were inscribed on a list of

* Thucydides 2.34.1–8.
† Pausanias 1.29.4–15.

the dead, nor of the aid provided by the city to the relatives of the fallen.[6] More important, we would be unaware of the religious dimension of the ceremony, which was in fact inseparable from its political significance but which Thucydides deliberately conceals. Finally, because the historian's account has such authority, generations of researchers have even doubted the existence of an *agōn epitaphios* simply because Thucydides makes no mention of it. In fact, the historian is not interested in the funeral as such and cares nothing about what followed it: he emphasizes the *prothesis* and the *ekphora* and mentions the demosion sema, but for him the ergon comes to an end "as soon as the earth has covered the dead," and is followed by the oration. The whole of his account is directed toward the funeral oration, and if, ignoring certain essential aspects of the nomos, Thucydides mentions the tribune of the Kerameikos, it is because Pericles is going to speak there.[7] Conversely, it is hardly surprising that once the funeral oration is over, the historian loses interest in the ceremony and, ignoring the ritual lamentations that follow the oration,* hastens to conclude: "after which one withdraws."

But by concentrating on the silences of the text, we run the risk of misunderstanding its fundamental purpose, which, before the epitaphios exalted Athens, was to present the principal features of a peculiarly Athenian ceremony. Of course Athens was not alone in according special honors to citizens who had fallen in battle; in many Greek cities in the classical period, the glory of the dead and the obligations of the state to its war victims were an important dimension of civic life;[8] thus the Spartans wrote the name of the dead man on his tomb only if he had been killed in battle.† By repatriating the ashes of the dead, Athens broke with the Greek practice of burial on the field of battle.[9] It was a break that was to last throughout the classical period; from then on, of all Athenian customs, the practice of returning ashes remained

---

* See Thucydides 2.46.2; Lysias 81; Demosthenes 37.

† Plutarch, *Lycurgus* 27.3: only women who had died in childbirth received the same honor.

47

inviolable. Even if the condemnation of the *stratēgoi* of Arginusae may be explained by the extent of the losses there, the force of the custom is no doubt largely to be found in the version that says they were executed because they failed to gather up the bodies of their fellow citizens.* At least this is how Plato interprets it in the *Menexenus*, when he expresses sympathy for the victims of that naval battle for being deprived of their place in the Kerameikos.† So the Athenians made an ancestral custom (patrios nomos) of a custom that had become second nature to them, and in Thucydides's account the Soros of Marathon, following Hellenic custom, is quite naturally presented as an exception to the Athenian rule.

So it is hardly surprising that before using the funeral oration to glorify Athens as the model city, the historian emphasizes everything that makes the official funeral the symbolic manifestation of the democratic polis. Mentioning the ten coffins that contained the remains of the dead was enough to evoke the Cleisthenean framework of the ten tribes that governed not only the order of the Athenian army on the battlefield[10] but also the organization of the funeral and the listing of the dead on the stela of the *poluandrion*. When he tells us that "citizens and strangers freely joined" in the cortege, the use of the democratic formula *ho boulomenos* (the first comer) enables him to suggest the Athenian openness that Pericles was to exalt;[11] the presence of the *xenoi*, a crowd of strangers in which allies were probably the most numerous, acquired its full significance in the imperialist city, which invited its allies to take part as colonial peoples in the Panathenaea.[12] And the fact that the description of the funeral ends with the eminently political procedure of the city's selection of the orator must not be seen as mere chance: by this choice, an act of homage to a man's merit, the city honored the most valorous of its members, the quality of the orator matching the heroism of the dead.[13]

* Diodorus 13.97–101, esp. 101.1.
† *Menexenus* 243c6–8.

In short, the Athenian city knew how to honor valor.* From exordium to epilogue,† the funeral oration repeats this theme tirelessly, and it is certainly the central idea in Thucydides's account, from the Kerameikos, "the finest suburb of the city,"[14] to the orator, "enjoying eminent esteem," via the "exceptional merit" of the men of Marathon. The same may be said of the most apparently neutral information. When Thucydides tells us that the bodies were exposed for two days, he is not unaware that for the private prothesis Solonian law granted only one day.‡ Now, although a rationalistic explanation can always be given of this discrepancy, it is quite possible to see it as a measure destined to honor the combatants, since the prothesis acquired its full meaning only in noble funerals.[15] Finally, in describing the cortege, the historian is not simply obeying a wish to be exhaustive, if even in the most harmless details; indeed the coffins of cypress wood suggest the eternity of memory,[16] and the chariots recall the aristocratic pomp of the funeral processions of earlier years. The citizens killed before the enemy were carefully distinguished from the common run of mortals by many cities;[17] but where honors were concerned, the democratic city was determined to do things particularly well.

Thus all the elements of this description help to present the official funeral as a signal distinction. But the community turned the honor paid to its most valorous men to its own account, since in doing so it expressed its cohesion and greatness, solemnly attested in the face of the universe.§ Homage to the dead and celebration of "the entire nation"** went hand in hand, and the civic spirit found its own reflection on every side: that of the dead was matched by that of the living, who come to the demosion sema to learn a lesson in patriotism while listening to the orator.

* See Demosthenes, *Against Leptines* 141.
† Exordium: Demosthenes 1–2. Epilogue: Thucydides 2.46. 1; Lysias 80.
‡ Demosthenes, *Against Makartatos* 62.
§ Demosthenes, *Epitaphios* 33.
** *Ibid.*: *pasa patris.*

Evidence on the Kerameikos, whether more complete or less developed than Thucydides's text, gives the ceremony a more concrete content but broadly confirms this eminently civic interpretation of the nomos.

Before entering this cemetery, which Wilamowitz compared to the French Pantheon, and whose link with the life of the city at war has been more scientifically demonstrated by Henri Jeanmaire, we shall consider the route taken by the cortege from the ekphora.[18] Although none of our sources informs us of the precise location of the prothesis, it is very likely that the remains of the dead were exposed in the Agora, perhaps in front of the monument of the Eponyms, since even in death citizens were grouped together in tribes. In this instance, the "cortege of citizens and strangers," in which the Athenian army in full array no doubt occupied the place of honor, moved toward the Dipylon, thus taking in, wholly or partly, the Dromos, in the opposite direction to that of the Panathenaic procession; this is only a hypothesis, of course, but the Panathenaea, about which we have much more definite information, closely links the Kerameikos and the Agora;[19] it is not impossible that two of the most important national celebrations forged, within the civic space, complementary links between these two high points of Athenian political life. Conscious of their unity, postclassical tradition referred to both as the Kerameikos — outside and inside.

After passing through the Dipylon, the cortege entered the Kerameikos on the road to the Academy, bordered on both sides by row upon row of public tombs. The principle — or chance — that governed the ordering of these tombs may well never be determined: between the classical sources, which are particularly laconic, and the repetitive rubrics of later lexicographers, the loss of antiquarian or geographic works of which only the titles survive is cruelly apparent. But the indefatigable Pausanias has conscientiously followed this route, and, despite a few obscure or patently erroneous points,[20] his description of the cemetery is extremely valuable insofar as it suggests in broad outline the appearance of this official district — Thucydides's *dēmosion sēma*.

Of course, many questions remain unanswered, all the excavations notwithstanding. To attempt to reconstruct the broad outlines of the structure of lost buildings is not an impossible task, however, provided one avoids the unrealistic wish to find at all costs the most famous.[21] Because the work of Donald W. Bradeen obeys this requirement, I am prepared to accept his very likely hypothesis, based on the obituary lists or fragments of them that have survived or been recently discovered.[22] Of course the monuments generally comprised a relief representing a battle scene and a base on which was engraved an epigram to the glory of the dead of the year, but basically they consisted of stelae on which the Athenian polis inscribed, tribe by tribe, the names of the fallen citizens. Sometimes one stela was enough to record the losses of ten tribes, but more often five or even ten stelae were erected side by side to make up a monument. All the Athenians who had fallen in the same year of war were thus gathered together in the same tomb. In this egalitarianism can be discerned the democratic wish not to make distinctions among citizens buried in the demosion sema, whom the epitaphioi designate only as *hoi enthade keimenoi* (those who rest here).* And to an even greater degree than the monument as a whole, the official list proclaims the equality of all Athenian citizens beyond death.

So everything leads to an examination of these lists of the dead, a civic honor whose crucial importance has been stressed by Jacoby, but which Thucydides does not even mention, perhaps because he preferred the anonymity of the funeral oration to the enumeration of individual names.[23]

At once homage paid to citizens and a military document recording the losses of one year of war, the list of the dead ratifies the extent of the effort bestowed by the community and at the same time exalts the courage of the polis, which was not afraid to range before the enemy the very men who constituted its power.

* Lysias 1, 20, 54, 60, 64, 66, 67, 71, 74, 76, 81; Thucydides 2.43.2; *Menexenus* 237cl, 242d6, 243e6–7, 234c7–8, 246a5–6; Demosthenes 1.

On these lists, fallen citizens had no status other than that of Athenians, twice proclaimed: under the heading *Athēnaiōn hoide apethanon* and in its political dimension by reference to the ten Cleisthenean tribes. The listing of the dead by *phulai* may not have been a specifically Athenian feature, but the democratic city was particularly careful to stress the closeness of the bond between the citizen and his tribe.[24] Thus, while preserving the balance among the *phula*, the economy of the monuments as a whole leaves to each of them its share of autonomy.[25] True, it is a very limited autonomy: between the individual and the community, membership in a tribe was merely a link, intended to remind the citizen that he owed everything to the polis — beginning with his very existence. Freed from everyday attachments to social life, the dead man was now simply an Athenian. Thus the lists of the dead mention neither patronymic[26] nor demotic:[27] freed forever from the bonds to father or family, the warrior was in effect entrusted with an official mission,[28] and the deme, in which were recorded all the ordinary stages of his career as a citizen, was ceded to the polis, the ultimate authority and sole criterion of incommensurable devotion.

In burying its dead, then, the Athenian community appropriated them forever, and at the demosion sema all distinctions, individual or familial, economic or social, that might divide Athenians even in their graves were abolished. The city promised its valorous citizens a fine tomb* and a verse epigram, once the privilege of the aristocracy, now the reward for courage, and, for much of the fifth century, only for courage, as the prohibition on all luxurious appointments in private burial places suggests. Furthermore, it is highly likely that the polis itself paid for the funeral ceremony and the erection of the public monument.[29] Conversely, the organization of the agon epitaphios, in which personal ambition once again was dominant, no doubt appealed to private wealth, probably in the form of a liturgy.† But that is another story, the business of the living.

Thus the margin left for familial initiative was a particularly

---

* Xenophon, *Hellenica* 2.4.17.
† Cf. Lysias 80 and Demosthenes 13.

narrow one, and the monuments of the Kerameikos, symbols of
the civic and military unity of the Athenian polis, are evidence of
that mistrust, not to say exclusion. For further evidence, one need
only compare the democratic demosion sema with the burial
places of the archaic period, in which all members of the same aristocratic family were buried side by side in the same necropolis. At
Eretria, for instance, the Heroon of the West Gate, in which warriors and their wives were buried together, included even ephebes,
whereas ordinary folk were consigned to the necropolis of the sea:
this geographic difference in levels made tangible the abyss between the two classes.[30] Disregarding differences of status, sex, or
age, the all-powerful aristocracy declared its group solidarity and
the strength of hierarchy. At the demosion sema, on the other
hand, a functional opposition, even within the same group of Athenians, isolated the *andres*, adults and soldier-citizens, forever separated from their parents, their children, and even their wives. The
Athenian city, which democratized military activity, opening it to
every citizen, was, perhaps more than any other polis, a "men's
club," and even the Spartan parallel between war and reproduc-
tion (dead *en polemōi*/dead *lekhō*) would be unthinkable. War was
men's business, as were civic funerals.

So the role and the place of women were strictly limited in
the funeral ceremonies. To the male assembly that met to honor
its dead, only women who were closely related to the dead
were admitted; moreover, their presence was tolerated only at the
graveside, not in the cortege,* and their role was reduced to the
customary laments.[31] So Pericles was not contravening the spirit
of the ceremony when, after deploying the rhetorical weapons of
consolation and exhortation to address the fathers and sons of the
dead, who were more closely associated with the honors because
they had a share in the male arete, he was content, in the case of
the widows, to give no more than a word of warning, just enough
to remind them to behave with due decorum and reserve.[32]†

* Thucydides 2.34.4.
† *Ibid.* 2.45.2.

53

The exclusion of women seems to be simply a particular case of the general phenomenon whereby families were pushed into the background. However, the family's lot must be distinguished from women's, for with regard to relatives the Athenian democracy was a good deal more flexible than it might seem at first, at least in the periods before and after the funerals. Private individuals were permitted to honor their dead in perfect freedom at the prothesis, and the funeral banquet, though strictly regulated, took place in private houses, at the home of the dead man's closest relatives.[33]* So, without going as far as some modern historians and declaring that the role of the family in these funerals was an essential one,[34] we should speak perhaps of a compromise between city and family. But in this compromise or handing out of roles, civic values were uppermost: they unquestionably dominated the most solemn moments of the funeral, the cortege and the burial in the demosion sema. The same goes, of course, for the funeral oration, and this predominance of the city determined the very structure of the speech, in which the consolation offered to the grieving relations usually culminates in an exaltation of civic honors and of the benevolence of the polis. Similarly, after recalling the dual significance, civic and familial, of the funeral ceremonies,† the orator in the *Menexenus* reminds his listeners that the city alone assumes every role, that of father and that of son, that of heir and that of guardian,‡ without ever losing its authority: it is benevolent but all-powerful. Whether it takes the place of a family or assigns it a very limited sphere of action, therefore, the community keeps the relatives of the dead at a distance, and in the funerals of the classical period there is no place either for the "decree of consolation" by which the Hellenistic cities honored the families[35] or for the exaltation of happy family life, which the Solonian anecdote about Tellus of Athens linked with the civic happiness of dying for one's country.§

---

* Cf. Demosthenes, *De corona* 288.

† *Menexenus* 236d6–7.

‡ *Ibid.* 249b7–c3.

§ Herodotus 1.30.

This strictly civic point of view explains the "solicitude" of the city toward the families of the dead,* which finds concrete expression in measures that have often been regarded as acts of charity or public assistance.

On the evidence of the epitaphioi alone, this aid seems to have been limited to the immediate families of the dead, parents and children, who were protected by laws against injustice and destitution;† so it is tempting to stress the limited scope of those laws, in contrast to the various measures by which the Hellenistic cities tried to win the obedience and devotion of their mercenaries (public funerals, but also medical assistance for the wounded, rewards of an honorary or financial kind, promotion for the bravest soldiers, support for the families of the dead).[36] No epitaphios mentions medical care or pensions given to the war wounded,‡ and we have very little information on this aspect of civic benevolence.[37] But this silence is in itself significant: for the Athenians, the obligations of the polis to surviving soldiers were not a matter of patrios nomos, which was devoted entirely to honoring the dead, since the gulf between life and a "fine death" was unbridgeable and irrevocably separated the assistance due to those who simply served the city and the honors merited by those who, in dying, covered it in glory.§ So, we shall first see the steps taken to assist families as *honors*; this interpretation seems to be borne out by the epilogue of Demosthenes's epitaphios, which is devoted entirely to the theme of glory,** and by a comparison of the Athenian nomos with the funerary law of Thasos, where "the ancestors and descendants of soldiers who fell in battle are included among the privileged citizens, the *timochoi*, those who possess a *timē* ... the dignitaries."[38]

* *Menexenus* 248e7 and 249c3, Hyperides 42.
† *Menexenus* 248e7–9.
‡ Plutarch, *Solon* 31.3.
§ This is the *eukleïsan patrida* theme, frequent in the collective epigrams: for instance *IG*, I², 943.
** Demosthenes 36–37. See also Hyperides 27.

Material assistance was not ignored — on the contrary, it always formed an important part of these honors; but to see it as simply a social measure would be to distort its significance and to follow those who, from the fourth century on and for all too obvious ideological reasons, sought its origin in the political practice of a demagogic tyrant* or a legislator of the archaic period,† or in the deplorable waste of public funds that marked the financial administration of the imperialist democracy.‡ Of course, state subsidization of the families was part of an overall extension of the *misthoi*, whereby war orphans and the pensioners of the prytaneum received treatment similar to that accorded prison warders.§ However, in both Athens and Thasos the compensation paid to the *orphanoi* related them more to dignitaries than to wage earners.[39]

The case of these war orphans, for whom the city acted as father,** is exemplary in this respect: in the fifth century as in the fourth, the sons of the dead[40] were placed under the authority of the polis,[41] which raised them and guaranteed them their *trophē*.†† This term has been variously interpreted, sometimes as something like a complete upbringing, sometimes — much more probably — as a mere subsistence grant.[42] The link, now well attested, between the orphans and the prytaneum‡‡ suggests that the community undertook at least to provide their food in the city's common dining hall. This may be no more than a hypothesis, but, before challenging it with the silence of the texts, we should

* Duris of Samos, *EGr.Hist.*, 76, no. 63 (Polycrates); Plutarch, *Solon* 31.3.

† Solon was the first to establish a pension for a soldier wounded in battle (Plutarch, *Solon* 31.4) or to raise at state expense the sons of soldiers killed in battle (Diogenes Laertius, *Lives of the Philosophers* 1.7.55). See also Aristotle, *Politics* 2.8.1268a8–11.

‡ Aristotle, *Constitution of Athens* 24.3 (the war orphans in the number of Athenians supported by the city); cf. Isocrates, *Peace* 82.

§ Aristotle, *Constitution of Athens* 24.3.

** *Menexenus* 249a4–5; Lysias 75.

†† Thucydides 2.46.1; *Menexenus* 249a3; Aristotle, *Politics* 2.8.1268a9.

‡‡ Decree of Theozotides, ll. 10–12.

observe that there was nothing to stop the sons of citizens constantly associated with the Tyrannicides* from enjoying, like the
descendants of Harmodius and Aristogiton, the *sitēsis en Pry-
taneiōi*. Even more significant were the honors accorded the
orphans by the polis at the precise moment of their civic majority,
when the city's guardianship came to an end and they became
men.[43] Unlike other eighteen-year-old Athenians, they were then
definitively emancipated, and, without explicitly stating that they
were excused from the *ephēbia*, our sources stress that they were
separated from the ephebes: not only did the polis endow them
with a complete set of armor‡ a year before handing a few symbolic weapons to their companions of the same age,§ but, by inviting them "to go for the first time to the parental home there to
exercise authority combined with strength, with the armor that
they have put on,"** it advanced by two years the day when the
ephebes would be "henceforth on equal terms with the other
citizens."†† It was as if the war orphans, hoplites from the start,
inheriting both the weapons and the *andreia* of their fathers,‡‡
passed without transition from childhood to full citizenship.
What they underwent was certainly a "second birth," to borrow
Plato's term.§§ But at this moment of their majority, they were
more than ever declared to be the sons of their fathers,*** since
they owed these signal honors to their fathers' fine deaths.[44]

---

* Aristotle, *Constitution of Athens*, 58.1 (same sacrifices); Pausanias 1.29.15
(monument to Harmodius and Aristogiton in the Kerameikos); cf. Hyperides 39.

† Thucydides 2.46.1; Cratinus, frag. 171 Kock; Lysias, *Against Theozotides* 2;
Aeschines, *Against Ctesiphon* 154. See also *Menexenus* 249a5–6.

‡ *Menexenus* 249a7; Aeschines, *Against Ctesiphon* 154.

§ Aristotle, 42.4.

** *Menexenus* 249a4–6 and 249b1–2.

†† Aristotle, *Constitution of Athens*, 42.5.

‡‡ *Menexenus* 249a8–bl.

§§ Plato, *Laws* 11.926d8–9.

*** Lysias, *Against Theozotides* 2: the herald calls the orphans *patrothen*, by their
fathers' names.

Because citizens "exchanged their own future for that of the city,"[45] civic death illuminated the entire community with the brightness of its glory, and all the sequences of this funeral ceremony combined to proclaim the eternal nature of the polis. So far, then, everything is clear, with the political clarity that belongs to the epitaphioi and that also characterized Thucydides's excursus.

But when we abandon this well-trodden path and pose questions about the Athenian nomos that the historian and the orators scarcely took the trouble to raise, we are again confronted with the irreducible opacity of social experience. Without forgetting that the reassuring certainties of the official celebration possessed their own truth, we shall now try to penetrate some of those shadowy areas that give the national funeral its complexity.

The irritating and unresolved question of the origin of the nomos immediately presents itself. Once again Thucydides is responsible for the terms in which it is posed; but he is so despite himself, for, in referring to the practice of the national funeral as a patrios nomos, he was no doubt emphasizing its irreducibly Athenian character. But tradition decided otherwise, and despite his efforts to escape definitively from this "historico-philological sea serpent,"[46] even Jacoby cannot prevent Thucydides's readers from forever regarding this term as historical information concerning the distant origin of the Athenian custom. Of course, there are few scholars today who, trusting the vague suggestion by Diogenes Laertius,* try to relate this practice to Solon's regulations for mourning, and there are fewer still who, giving some credence to the assertions of Anaximenes the rhetor,† make Solon the inventor of the funeral oration. While restoring to the post-411 Athenians the odd habit of attributing to Solon whatever is patrios,[47] other historians try, again in the name of fidelity to Thucydides, to associate the nomos with Cleisthenes. There are

* Diogenes Laertius 1.7.55.

† Cf. Plutarch, Publicola 9.11, which may be compared with the scholion to Thucydides 2.35.1: "the legislator: quite obviously Solon."

more serious arguments in favor of this attribution: the importance given the funeral in the Cleisthenean context, the role of
the polemarch in the celebration of the rites,[48] and perhaps, too,
the fact that from the last years of the sixth century to the last
quarter of the fifth, public funerary monuments were exempt
from the constraints imposed by the general rule of austerity. But
our ancient sources are silent on the subject of Cleisthenes.

To those who wish to reject Thucydides's authority without
abandoning entirely the controversial patrios nomos, Diodorus provides an alternative solution worth consideration. He sees the practice as originating at the time of the Persian Wars and places on the
same level the consecration of the golden tripod of Delphi, the epigrams of Thermopylae, and the institution of the nomos at Athens.*

Of course caution is needed for interpreting an account that is
so obviously animated by a desire to derive the Athenian custom
from the heroic period of the Persian Wars while giving the lion's
share to Athens.[49] Diodorus's readers could not be unaware that
the Athenians who died at Plataea were buried on the spot like
the other Greeks.† So the institution of the nomos was adjusted by
a few years in order to link it with the foundation of the Attic-
Delian League, or, rather, with the ceremonies at Athens sur-
rounding the return of Theseus's ashes:‡ founded or reorganized
in 475, the national funeral was to bear thereafter the mark of
Cimonian policy. Because it reconciled those who upheld the
antiquity of the nomos with the advocates of a more recent origin, the latter hypothesis enjoyed great favor for a very long time.
But it was based on extremely shaky arguments: there can be little
doubt that the traditional dating of the return of the ashes must
be seriously reconsidered and the link between the national funeral and the Theseia, the linchpin of this reconstruction, is still
unproved as far as the classical period is concerned.

Against all these speculations, Jacoby believed that he could

* Diodorus 11.33.3.
† Herodotus 9.85.
‡ Plutarch, *Theseus* 35–36; *Cimon* 8.

date the origin of the nomos definitively to the year 464. Without forgetting such essential stages as the official funeral for the dead of Euripus, the first to be celebrated by the Cleisthenean democracy, or the cult of the heroes of Marathon, he thought that such a ceremony could have been established only at that turning point in the history of Athens when the demos began to bring its full weight to bear in politics.[50] Once again, however, there is no solid foundation of fact on which to base this attractive hypothesis, for by accepting Pausanias's dating, according to which the demosion sema functioned for the first time in 464, at the funeral for the dead of Drabescus,* Jacoby certainly overestimates the historical value of Pausanias's "evidence."[51] But in reconstructing the progress of the funeral toward institutionalization from 506 on, Jacoby has done much to clarify the debate. Indeed, the regular institution of the public funeral should undoubtedly be seen as the culmination of a process in which the foundation of the great heroic cults to the dead of the Persian Wars played the decisive role of a precedent. I would agree with Jacoby that a decisive stage was passed after Marathon, a purely Athenian victory in which the protagonists were given honors very similar to those that Athens gave its dead in the mid-fifth century.[52] If, as Pierre Amandry has suggested, all the religious ceremonies presided over by the polemarch† were closely bound up with the heroic cult of the dead of Marathon,[53] the honors given to the dead of 490 no longer seem as exceptional as Thucydides made out,‡ but begin to look much more like a celebration that, once established at the gates of the asty and accompanied by a speech, was to be erected into a nomos.

The archaeological evidence does not seem to support Jacoby's statements; the oldest obituary identified so far (*IG*, I², 944) dates from 464. Recently, it is true, the question has been raised once again by the discovery of a *lebēs* (cauldron), a reward offered around 480 to the winner of a competition celebrated by the

---

* Pausanias 1.29.4.

† Aristotle, *Constitution of Athens* 58.1.

‡ Thucydides 2.34.5.

Athenians in honor of the war dead: it was a good opportunity to declare that henceforth the funeral ceremony existed in its entirety, including the funeral competition.[54] In fact, we probably still lack the decisive proof that has been sought for so long, for an analysis of the dedicatory formula suggests that this lebes is linked to the Eleutheria of Plataea or to the Herakleia of Marathon rather than to the agon epitaphios.[55]

On this uncertainty we shall close an investigation in which ancient and modern representations of Athenian democracy and its history have all too often taken the place of proof. Although I believe that the public funeral cannot be dated earlier than Cleisthenes and probably belongs to the years following the Persian Wars, there is no way to settle this debate, in which, for each party, the nomos provides an opportunity of choosing *its* Athenian democracy — Cleisthenean, *prōmachos* (highest-ranking combatant) of the Persian Wars, Cimonian, or progressive. At least this survey has shown that it is possible to throw historical light on the nomos from many different directions as we await some providential discovery of an inscription prior to 464 to bring, perhaps, a new element into the debate. But it would probably require more than a single discovery to give the nomos a definitive date of birth, for it is by no means certain that the funeral ceremony, despite its fine appearance of unity, was born one fine day out of civic rationality. Despite a conclusion on this note of doubt, this long examination of a classic question has at least enabled us to reintroduce some solid historical reality into a perennial practice by which Athens proclaimed its timelessness.

Behind the permanence of the nomos can be discerned, at the very heart of the ceremony, a trace of the changes and tensions marking the history of the city.

Certain phenomena are only to be guessed at. It is probably no coincidence, for example, that, from being a strategos in the fifth century, the official orator was chosen, in the next century, from among professional politicians, like Demosthenes and Hyperides, and this development may well be seen as a reflection of changes

in Athenian civic life.[56] More unexpectedly, the "crisis of the
fourth century," which restored an imbalance between the public
domain and private values, is fairly easy to detect at the very boundaries of the demosion sema. At the Kerameikos, of course, private edifices were never entirely replaced by official monuments;
but in the fourth century, family concessions developed with a
degree of luxury that, until the Peloponnesian War, the city had
reserved only for individuals or groups that it wished to honor.
Stranger still is the fact that families could celebrate individually
the memory of a citizen-soldier who had died for Athens by erecting a monument to him, which was sometimes isolated but usually formed part of those private complexes. Although the tomb of
Melanopus and Macartatus, which Pausanias mentions in his description of the demosion sema,* was probably erected at the city's
expense, the same cannot be said of the monuments to Dexileus,
Demokleides, or other Athenians who fell in battle and were celebrated out of family piety.[57] These were no doubt cenotaphs, and
there is no reason to suppose that in the fourth century the Athenians gave up burying their dead in the poluandria of the Kerameikos.[58] In their decorative themes, these tombs imitate the
public monuments. But although the collective monument remained the norm, individuals gained a good deal from this new
practice, which "duplicated" civic glory with a truly personal
glory. Thus Dexileus's name ran no risk of being forgotten: twice
exalted officially — in the inscription to the glory of the Hippeis
(Horsemen) killed in 394 and on the list of that year's poluandrion
— the young horseman was again celebrated in an epitaph† and a
relief that isolated him forever from his companions in combat.[59]

Of course the community tried hard to channel this eruption
of individuality to its own advantage, and to individuals honored
with a monument in the public cemetery, the Athenian polis
offered an even more splendid tomb. But it is by no means certain
that civic values necessarily gained by this, for the shift was already

* Pausanias 1.29.6.
† Inscription for the Hippeis: Tod, II, 104; epitaph of Dexileus: *ibid.*, 105.

under way from the collective list to the crown rewarding an indi-vidual's acts of heroism.[60]

In order to ascertain the tensions beneath the fine ordering of the nomos, we need not embark on a long history of the relations between the public and the private; we need only return to the demosion sema and examine those lists of the dead that, on first reading, seemed to embody the rigid Cleisthenean civic framework. The corpus of these lists, despite many lacunae, has an obvious unity.

Behind the apparent rigidity, there are variations from year to year, and sometimes in the same year, in the manner of recording losses and in the placement of officers' names and combat sites. There are also later additions by various hands at the bottom of the stela, on the sides, and even vertically between the columns. Of course, material circumstances and inevitable errors of trans-mission (including initial omissions of names) may account for some of these differences. But more than these factors are in-volved: variations and additions suggest that in order to place a combatant on the Athenian list of the dead, the community obeyed criteria that were strict yet always subject to redefinition: on the one hand, a real openness; on the other, an implicit hierarchy among the various battles fought in the same year, and also among the various categories of combatants.

The lists are valuable but perplexing documents. They resist any attempts at systematic classification, and it is no easy matter to determine the criteria that govern inclusion on the list. "Ste-lae ... engraved by Athenians ... displayed at Athens, for Atheni-ans,"[61] they provide scant information about the rank of the combatants, especially when they were Athenians. This very paucity of information prevents us from imposing on the hosts an arrangement corresponding to the overall organization of the Athenian army. Certain terms may therefore well remain enig-matic. The xenoi (foreigners), mentioned in several lists,* may, as Philippe Gauthier believes, be allies, but the absence of the ethnic is troubling, and it is quite possible that they were simply

* *IG*, I², 944, 949, 950, to which one might add *Agora* vol. 1, no. 3842b.

mercenaries, if not metics. Given the additional possibility that in the fifth century, hardly a period marked by conformity to convention, the manner of designating a particular category of combatants may well have varied from one list to another, matters become still more complicated.

However, a number of things are evident. To begin with, *non-Athenians are included in these Athenian lists.* The *toxotai barbaroi,* mentioned in four lists,* hardly present a problem: these "barbarians," who, if their names are anything to go by, were extremely Hellenized, constituted the troops of archers that Athens, and many other cities, employed to fight on the extreme borders of the Greek world, against barbarians who were themselves lightly armed and carried bows.[62] The presence of slaves in the poluandria of the Kerameikos, attested by Pausanias,† has been confirmed by a recent discovery.‡ Of course, the mention of *one* slave has so far remained unique in the lists of the dead, but this posthumous promotion of the *therapon* Hylas is in itself an oddity: war was a matter for a free man, and we know how seldom the Greeks departed from this principle, and then only in extreme circumstances.[63] Free "foreigners" could also appear on the same list as citizens. However, this probably occurred less frequently than Wilamowitz maintains, arguing from the celebrated "generosity" of the Athenians.[64] Of course, names that are hardly Athenian have been found on some of the lists, but that does not necessarily mean that foreign auxiliaries were systematically associated with citizens in death. When foreigners were not buried apart, in a collective monument erected especially for them at the edge of the demosion sema,§ their names were added in spaces left vacant or in an additional list, sometimes preceded by the heading *xenoi.*

* *IG*, I², 950; *Agora*, vol. 17, nos. 14, 17, 22.
† Pausanias 1.29.7.
‡ *Agora* vol. 17, no. 1, ll. 139–40.
§ Monument to the Argives who died at Tanagra: *Agora*, vol. 17, no. 4 (Meiggs-Lewis 35); one might add *Agora*, vol. 17, nos. 7 and 9 (Ionic letters: Aeolian or Ionian allies).

So no clearly stated policy seems to have governed the city's relationship with non-Athenian combatants: "once the main thing had been carried out; that is, once the Athenian citizens had been laid out, praised, and buried, they added, on occasion ... the names and corps" of these auxiliaries.[65] The degree of openness of the imperialist city no doubt underwent many fluctuations, and often only the circumstances of the moment decided the attitude to be adopted toward these second-class casualties. Nevertheless, when they buried non-Athenians in the Kerameikos, the Athenians paid them tribute by inscribing their names, if only by way of an after-thought, under the general heading *Athēnaiōn hoide apethanon* (among the Athenians, the following died). In this case, of course, *Athēnaioi* must be interpreted in the broad sense of "Athenian army" and a distinction made between the two senses of this term that are implicitly contrasted inside the stela: the Athenian warrior group is composed of Athenians, in the strict sense, and "others."

A curious logic governs the equation *Athēnaioi* = *Athēnaioi* + *x*, since in it the whole is designated by the name of the part that, though inferior in quantity, is eminently superior in quality. But only this strange equation accounts for the ordering of the lists or the very special arithmetic that, in the writings of the historians, governs the count of Athenian casualties. Thus, calculating the casualties at Delium, Thucydides observes: "There died in battle ... on the Athenian side, just under a thousand, including the strate-gos Hippocrates, not counting a large number of light troops [*psi-loi*] and servants [*skeuophoroi*]."[66*] There are, however, still more difficulties, for in both Thucydides and the lists the group of "true Athenians" does not include all citizens: there were Athenian citi-zens among the light troops at Delium, just as the stelae listed citizens outside the ten tribes, at the bottom under the heading *tox-otai*.[†] So it is as if, in matters concerning war, the word *Athēnaioi* referred either to a wider group or to a smaller group than that of the soldier-citizens. Thus the eminently ideological distinction

---

* Thucydides 4.101.2.

† *IG*, I², 929 and 949.

between "Athenians" grouped according to tribe and archers grouped according to their *technē* seems to be more serious than that between Athenians and others. Could it be that someone was less of an Athenian if he specialized in non-hoplitic warfare? Some Athenians thought so,[67] and, without really taking back with one hand what it was giving with the other, the community was concerned to make the distinction.

But over and above hierarchical refinements, the main point is that the city buried the archers in the demosion sema. No doubt it did as much for the other theses enrolled in the army, psiloi and oarsmen.[68*] Those historians who have tried to exclude the latter from the Kerameikos because their names did not appear on the hoplite registry have misunderstood the complexity of Athenian military politics[69] and confused ideological preference with democratic principle: if in their arrangement the hosts followed the model of the hoplitic catalog, could the democracy have "forgotten" citizens entirely while honoring barbarians and foreigners with the same burial as "Athenians"? There can only be one answer: if no list mentions an oarsman or a peltast as such, it is because the *thētes* were included among the Athenaioi listed under the ten tribes.[70]

Finally, these Athenaioi also include the metics enrolled as hoplites. Because Thucydides does not mention them in his description of the funeral and because the lists contain no heading referring specifically to their status, it has sometimes been thought they were not buried in the demosion sema.[71] But Thucydides clearly includes the metics among the *astoi*;[72] and if any non-Athenians were to be honored with an official funeral, it must certainly have been the metics, whom Aristophanes calls the "bran" of the city, inseparable from the pure wheat of the citizens.[73†]

It should be added that for both astoi and foreigners, the rules of inscription probably varied in the course of Athenian history:

---

* Their burial in the demosion sema is postulated in *Menexenus* 243c5–8: the bodies of the combatants of Arginusae are not in the sema, but their memory remains.

† Aristophanes, *Acharnians* 507–508.

the fifth-century lists show the democratic polis swinging between exclusiveness and openness, between a broad and a narrow
conception of the status of Athenian. As far as the gaps in the corpus allow, it should be possible to outline a history of these swings.

This history begins at Marathon, where, in death, a quite clear
line separates citizens and noncitizens: only the Athenian hoplites, whose tomb the ephebes still honored in 123–22, were declared heroes.* The slaves, however, were buried with the Plataeans,†
a fact that in no sense represented posthumous promotion: freed
before the battle so as not to detract from the dignity of the hoplite ranks,‡ they were quite naturally put with the free auxiliaries
but separated forever from the citizens.[74]§ At the end of the fifth
century, the demosion sema seems to have been wide open to foreigners, at least to those who fought in the ranks of the democrats
in 403 and whose "valor took the place of country";** the city did
not shrink from giving this composite group, comprising metics,
mercenaries, and allies, an official funeral and burial in the Kerameikos. It is true that Lysias seems to regard as exceptional those
honors that, for eternity, treat foreigners as citizens. But these
honors were exceptional, not so much in relation to earlier funerals as in comparison with the exclusiveness that, during the democratic restoration, governed reorganization of the city. It is not
so much, then, the unique character of this burial in the demosion
sema that interests the orator as the truly democratic greatness of
this measure, which is tacitly opposed to the narrow conformity
of the victorious demos, which had retreated to its privileged
position and was more inclined to follow Archinus or Theozotides
than Thrasybulus; we know that Lysias was directly concerned by

* *IG*, II/III², 1006. Pausanias (10.20.2) recalls that on their tomb was erected a
stela bearing the names of the victims tribe by tribe.
† Pausanias 10.20.2.
‡ *Ibid.* 7.15.7.
§ One might compare this with the burial of Spartans and helots in two differ-
ent tombs at Plataea (Herodotus 9.85).
** Lysias 66.

Thrasybulus's decree, which was aimed at integrating the liberated metics into the civic community. Indeed, though generous to the dead, the Athenians were less so to the living, since they rejected the proposition of the democratic leader and deprived of the "benevolence" of the city the illegitimate sons of Athenians who had died for the democracy.[75] Between the burial of the xenoi side by side with Athenians and the decree of Theozotides, with its attempt to separate citizens from noncitizens, there is all the difference between the heading *Athēnaiōn hoide apethanon* and the specification *hoposoi Athēnaiōn apethanon biaioti thanatoi* (exact number of Athenians dead from violent death).* Patronymic and demotic, absent from the lists of the dead, which draw no distinction between citizens and metics, are, on the contrary, carefully included when it is a matter of isolating the legitimate orphans of Athenian fathers. In 403, the law of 451–50 on citizenship which had fallen into disuse during the Peloponnesian War, was reactivated. This might make the burial of metics and foreigners in the demosion sema look like an exceptional decision, which it probably was not.

Unfortunately, it is not possible to follow step-by-step the fluctuations of Athenian politics between 490 and 403. However, one list of the dead — that of 464 — is remarkable for its openness and eclecticism: it mentions not only a slave but also contingents of allies; and apart from the dead of Drabescus, named at the top of the list, the dead are recorded battlefield by battlefield, in a somewhat uncanonical order that mixes citizens, slaves, and allies.† This openness may be explained by the scope of the joint effort of Athenians and their allies to found Ennea Hodoi;[76] but Jacoby no doubt saw, in what he regarded as the first list of the dead, much more: the innovatory audacity of beginnings. It was, of course, a precarious openness, one bound up with very special circumstances. Furthermore, it may well have been eroded by the Periclean law on citizenship. Conversely, after being brilliantly

---

* Decree of Theozotides, ll. 4–5.

† *Agora*, vol. 17, no. 1 (*IG*, I², 928 + *Agora*, vol. 1, no. 7009): ll. 37–38ff.

affirmed in 451–50, the shadowy solidarity of the group of Athenians was to be violated on several occasions during the Peloponnesian War; as proof, we need cite only the inscription of the "barbarian archers" on four lists of the dead, three of which certainly date from after 430.* In fact, only the slave "porters" seem to have gained nothing from this generosity of the democracy: between *astos* and slave, the gap was obviously too great.

Most of those buried in the Kerameikos were certainly Athenians, but without wishing to challenge this obvious fact, we have tried to bring out the complex reality beneath the unity given by a name. The funeral oration has been no help in deciphering the lists, for, obstinately deaf to whatever does not promote the unity of the polis, it knows no dead other than citizens, no other object than "the Athenians," that homogeneous body of warriors whose morality is implicitly hoplitic but whose group is structured by no hierarchy. Between the ergon of the funeral and the logos epitaphios, there is all too evident a gap.

The same gap is discernible between what we can glimpse of the religious dimension of the public funeral and the scarcity of information provided on this subject by the epitaphioi. It is, of course, quite natural that the Olympian cult should be absent from a speech included in a funerary ceremony, but what is more surprising is the discretion with which the speakers evoke the devotion paid to the dead whose memory they are celebrating.† Apart from a few very brief allusions, the funeral oration generally prefers to develop at length what, after all, is a political theme, namely, the immortality of civic glory.

The frequency of the ceremony is therefore not easily determined. According to Thucydides, the Athenians arranged funerals

---

* *Agora*, vol. 17, nos. 14 (c. 430) and 22 (war of Decelea); *IG, I²*, 950 (naval battle at the end of the fifth century).

† On the prohibition against mentioning the Olympian gods, see *Menexenus* 238b2–3 and Demosthenes 30–31. For allusion to the gods of the underworld, see *Menexenus* 244a5–6 and Demosthenes 34.

only "when the occasion arose," and from this it has been deduced that no such ceremony took place in years of peace.* Declaring that the decision to organize a funeral was taken on the spur of the moment by the *boulē*, Plato seems to be confirming the evidence of Thucydides, unless Plato is deliberately misstating the facts in order to strengthen beforehand his criticism of the topos of improvisation.[77][†] Furthermore, everything seems to suggest that the funeral was not always celebrated on the same date. Thucydides's statement that the first casualties from the Peloponnesian War were buried in the winter has been somewhat hastily taken to suggest a general rule.[‡] The funeral was probably celebrated, when there was a lull in the fighting; but this is no more than a probability. Moreover, Felix Jacoby tried to make this vague reference precise by proposing a date — that of the Genesia (the fifth day of Boedromion) and that of the Epitaphia, which he argues replaced Genesia on the same day.[78] But apart from the fact that these two dates are very close to the end of the hostilities and present considerable practical problems (including that of the removal of the remains), the fact that in 322 Hyperides no doubt delivered his epitaphios in early spring should make us wary of any hasty systematization.

And yet certain pieces of evidence suggest quite unambiguously that the dead were honored at a fixed date in an annual ceremony. Thus the orator of the *Menexenus* declares that the city "never fails to honor the dead; for each year it performs publicly all the ceremonies that it is customary to celebrate for each individual; furthermore, it organizes competitions of athletes, horse races, and all manner of musical competitions."[§] Did the celebration of the dead, which at the beginning of the dialogue is a circumstantial ceremony, become annual simply at the whim of the philosopher? In fact, these two pieces of information are contradictory only if

---

* Thucydides 2.34–37.

† *Menexenus* 234b–c6–7 and 235c9.

‡ Thucydides 2.34.1.

§ *Menexenus* 249b3–6.

we refuse to dissociate the funeral in the strict sense from the peri-odic celebration of the dead. In Aristotle's time, sacrifices in honor of citizens who had died in battle were among the regular respon-sibilities of the polemarch* as was the funerary competition, and from the beginning of the fourth century Lysias both distinguishes between and links together funerals and competitions.† Similarly, the funerary law of Thasos in no way implies the simultaneity of the ekphora and the sacrifices and competitions in honor of *aga-thoi*.[79] So everything seems to suggest that the dead were given a double *timē:* honored once and for all by a public funeral and an epitaphios, they were also celebrated every year by a cult. The cer-emony of the funeral ensured them eternal remembrance, but sac-rifices and competitions periodically reactivated the initial honor.‡

Light is also thrown on the status of the ceremony: officially sanctioning the death of citizens, it is a culmination, and from this point of view an orator like Pericles could be content to celebrate the victims of the past year;§ but because it links the dead of a year of war with an immemorial and glorious cohort of Athenian heroes,** it is also related to the frequency of the cult, as the epi-taphios of the *Menexenus* suggests. Because, with Pericles, Thucy-dides chose to turn it into a culmination, he treated the funeral as an autonomous ceremony, devoid of all its religious implications: so he did not mention the periodic celebrations. His too-perfect silence on the matter cannot therefore be interpreted as proof of the nonexistence in the fifth century of an agon and of sacrifices; it now seems that his silence was more in the nature of a screen, intended to mask the cult.

Between the funeral and the cult there is, then, both a tight link and a gap. So it is hardly surprising that the question of the status conferred on the dead by the official ceremony has been the object

---

* Aristotle, *Constitution of Athens* 58.

† Lysias 80.

‡ Demosthenes 36.

§ See Thucydides 2.42.1.

** *Menexenus* 246a5–6.

of endless dispute: when dealing with the complex relationship that is set up, in the funeral, between religious and political elements, historians have often hesitated to treat the national funeral of the Athenians as a true "ceremony of heroization."[80] Some have gone further and, although no text of the classical period says as much, declared with Jacoby that the official cult could be addressed only to heroes.[81] This hypothesis flies in the face of the convictions of all who believe that Athens, the most "political" of all the Greek *poleis*, was in fact the only city in the classical period not to create new heroes;[82] when these scholars do not pass over the question in silence, they speak of "special honors" by which the dead are treated *"like* heroes" without being so "in the strict sense."[83]

There are reasons for such reluctance: the category of hero, a disparate if not fluctuating one, is not easily defined, and in the cult itself the overlapping between heroic or chthonian sacrifices and Olympian sacrifices, which was greater than was long believed, confuses matters further. Moreover, the death of citizens in battle and the eternal renown promised them complicate the problem still further: how can we provide against the ambiguity of the term "hero," which, originally associated with war, very soon took on a metaphorical meaning? How are we to resist the temptation to confuse heroization and immortal glory?[84]

Nevertheless, those Athenians who fell in battle were distinguished forever from the anonymous crowd of the other dead;[85] they were the object of a *timē*, which, in many respects, defines them unambiguously as heroes.* In transferring to Athens the remains of native citizens in order to return them to mother earth,† the Athenian city seems, like the Spartan city repatriating the remains of its kings,‡ to have been obeying some need — an imperative for every polis — to ensure the protection of its national

---

* *Timē:* Thucydides 2.35.1 and 44.4, which might be compared with 3.58.4 (the Panhellenic cult of Plataea); Lysias 66, 76, 79; *Menexenus* 249b3; Demosthenes 36.

† *Menexenus* 327c1–3: "She bore them and nourished them and received them, and in her bosom they now repose."

‡ Plutarch, *Agesilaus* 40.

heroes. Buried at the city gates — like the agathoi of Thasos — the valiant citizens of Athens were perhaps also invited to mount "before the ramparts a vigilant guard":[86] at least this is how we might interpret a famous fragment of the epitaphios of Samos, in which Pericles, breaking the silence that the official orators usually observed on the heroic character of the dead, described the Athenians of the demosion sema in terms of the honors that they receive and *the benefits that they bring to the city.** Among the honors paid to heroes was the importance accorded the name of the dead,[87] as well as the sacrifices and funeral competition dedicated to them.[88] Finally, Hyperides's inclusion of the Tyrannicides at the end of the list of great men of the past, whom he has summoned to welcome Leosthenes and his companions to the underworld, should not be seen as a mere oratorical flourish. Their propinquity in Hades,† like their propinquity in the Kerameikos,‡ is the projection of a deeper kinship that officially unites citizens who died for their country with Harmodius and Aristogeiton; indeed, common sacrifices were made to them both, presided over by the polemarch, in the late fourth century, but also as early as the time of Herodotus, if the appeal to the Tyrannicides in Miltiades's speech to Callimachus of Aphidna§ is not to be regarded simply as a rhetorical topos. It would be tempting to conclude that Athens certainly granted its dead heroization. We still have to explain why such a conclusion has encountered so much resistance, ancient and modern.

In fact, when they cast doubt on the heroization of the Athenian combatants — or that of the Spartans of Thermopylae, whose tomb was nevertheless celebrated by Simonides "as an altar,"** or, again, that of Harmodius and Aristogeiton — the moderns merely

---

* Plutarch, *Pericles* 8.9. The use of the present tense seems to indicate a lasting and continuing action.

† Hyperides 39.

‡ Pausanias 1.29.15.

§ Herodotus 6.109.3.

** Simonides 5D.3.

reproduce the profound "uncertainty" of the Greek cities "concerning the status of warriors who died in battle"[89] and of the great patriotic figures in general.

This hesitation has often been explained by a wish not to impugn a status verging on the superhuman, essentially bound up with the most distant past, that of the epic. From this point of view, the formula *thyein hōs hērōi* (to sacrifice *as* to a hero) would mean that by granting mere mortals the honors reserved to the warriors of epic, the cities were concerned to mark the distance that separated the present from heroic times.[90] Thus, in a manner highly reminiscent of Callinus,[91]* Isocrates declares that only those who died in the Persian Wars deserved "the same honors as the demigods" of the Trojan epic.[†] But still more is to be read into such reluctance. Because heroization always depended on a decision by the community, the Greeks of the classical period, who were only too ready to celebrate the polis in all its manifestations, were quite happy to conceal the religious beneath the political.[92] Thus Thucydides, who says nothing about the Athenian agon epitaphios, would not have stressed the heroic character of the honors given to Brasidas by the Amphipolitans had he not been absolutely forced to do so by the requirements of his narrative.[‡]

The funeral oration carries this reserve to extremes, and, not content with never referring to the category of hero, the orators surround themselves with innumerable precautions when they officially grant happiness and immortality to those they celebrate. Thus Pericles hides behind a comparison with the cult of the gods when he declares that those citizens who died at Samos have "become immortal" like them, and, to exalt the *eudaimonia* of the dead of Chaironeia, Demosthenes feels, at several points, a need to resort to "correct reasoning."[§] So no positive argument in favor

* Callinus 1D.19.
† Isocrates, *Panegyricus* 84.
‡ Thucydides 5.11.1: the substitution of Brasidas for the former colonizer Hagnon is an indication of the break between Amphipolis and Athens.
§ Plutarch, *Pericles* 8.9; Demosthenes 32–34.

of the heroization of the dead is to be looked for in the epitaphioi. Indeed the term *eudaimon** is no more evidence of the heroization of citizens who died in battle than the reference to the Islands of the Blessed;† this adjective, a "floating signifier," tends to designate the happiness of an individual whom death has delivered from the cares of life;[93] it can hardly be seen as an official title, since the orators do not hesitate to substitute *to eutuches* for *eudaimonia*: the "happiness" of the dead is then replaced by "good fortune," a vague term that may be applied as well to a life as to a death.‡

The only tangible notion in the funeral oration, then, is that of "the posthumous glory and memory of the name" of the dead,[94] except that the epitaphioi, dominated by the rule of anonymity, give the citizens no other name than that of Athenians, no other glory but a collective one: between the list of the dead and the oration, the gap is quite obvious, as is that between the hymn and the eulogy,§ between the funeral** or heroic lament[95] and the logos. In the national funeral, these two dimensions coexist, and if we are to understand the funeral oration, it must be seen in its indissolubly religious and political context. But, again, the epitaphioi select from the complexity of the ceremony, choosing the political against the religious, after choosing the timeless against the ephemeral and unity against diversity.

Thus the logos elucidates the ergon only partially; but, conversely, the gaps so often observed between the speech and the practice lead us to move away from the context of the funeral and to compare it with other speeches and other practices in order to grasp the coherence proper to the funeral oration.

* For instance: Lysias 79; Demosthenes 32; Hyperides 42. Compare with Isocrates, *Panegyricus* 84.
† Demosthenes 34.
‡ Thucydides 2.44.1. For *eutuches*, see also Hyperides 24 and 28.
§ Lysias 3.80; *Menexenus* 239b7–8.
** Thucydides 2.46.2 and *Menexenus* 249c8; Lysias 81; Demosthenes 37.

The Glory of the Dead: From Aristocratic Celebration to Collective Eulogy

The collective funeral oration is Greek. This proposition does not try to deny the primarily Athenian character of the address to the dead, but rather to stress from the outset its profound link with the mental world of the "classical" Greek city, in which the primacy of public values was both a reality and an ideal. This fact becomes clear if we compare the epitaphios logos and the Roman laudatio funebris, funeral orations that have little in common except their name and whose dissimilarity marks yet again the irreducible gap that separates *polis* from *civitas.*

The eulogy for soldiers who had died in battle was not a Roman custom. At the time of Cicero,[96] it was at most a literary fashion, and when Cicero includes in the *Fourteenth Philippic* a funeral oration to the glory of the combatants of the legion of Mars,* it is quite evident that this piece is a pastiche or occasional borrowing, faithful to the Greek model in form, but in form only, for the context is quite different: instead of the vast auditorium of the Kerameikos, we have the Senate, and instead of symbolic celebration, a highly pragmatic project, since the eulogy was intended to orchestrate the proposal of a *senatus consultum.* Thus the glory of the dead, ratified by honors that Cicero sees as a favor unique in kind,† gives precedence to the exaltation of the survivors, whose cooperation is indispensable to the success of Cicero's policy. Finally, instead of the egalitarian anonymity of the Greek oration, we have an exhaustive listing of the leader's merits; which brings us back to the laudatio funebris.

Indeed, as Polybius presents it, the Roman funeral oration is devoted to the celebration of a man or a family; delivered in the Forum — to which the dead man has been brought — by his son or closest relation, in the presence of the assembled people, it recalls the virtues and glorious deeds of the illustrious dead man.‡ By

* Cicero, *Fourteenth Philippic* 25–35.

† *Ibid.* 30–31 and 34–35.

‡ Polybius 6.52–54. See also Dionysius of Halicarnassus, *Roman Antiquities* 5.17.2ff. (funeral of Brutus) and Livy 2.47.

installing the mortal remains opposite the rostra, by celebrating the dead man's exploits and those of his most remote ancestors, the great families were certainly trying to involve the whole community in their mourning and to give Roman youth an example of valor. But such funerals were the preserve of an elite and were not so much public as a form of publicity: an exhibition of the omnipotence of the *gentes*, not a civic celebration. True, the people seemed to be involved, but this appearance* did not hide the aristocratic reality of this ceremony, by which the noble families, speaking through the tribune, reminded the people that they were the vital kernel of the city. So at most the laudatio could arouse personal devotion, arouse in a young Roman seeking renown and valor a wish for personal glory similar to that of the dead man. A benefactor of his country,† the citizen offered his services to the state, a private act very different from the collective devotion of the Athenians,‡ as were the *erga* offered by the city to the individual acts of prowess of a Horatio, a Manlius Torquatus, or a Horatius Cocles, cited by Polybius in support of the educational value of such a custom.§

This brief comparison with the Roman funeral oration illuminates the egalitarian spirit of the epitaphios and the need to situate it in relation to that "double movement of democratization and disclosure" governing the development of every Greek city.[97] But the fact that the political logos breaks with the aristocratic mode of speech makes its advent no more "miraculous" than that of the polis, and the break cannot conceal underlying continuities; so even those who regard the funeral oration as a form existing before the full development of rhetoric are forced, by that very fact, to look for models or "antecedents" for it, which they usually find in lyric poetry.[98] My own inclination is rather to assign the funeral oration its original place between the two poles of the lament and the eulogy, which in aristocratic society

---

* Polybius 6.53: *phainesthai*.

† *Ibid.* 6.54.

‡ Thucydides 2.43.2.

§ Polybius 6.54.

expressed the relationship between the living and the dead. Thus
in declaring that from one epitaphios to another, the same formula proclaims the same prohibition against bemoaning the combatants, the same obligation to devote oneself entirely to their
praise,* we will not be content to see it as the sign of a reluctantly
accepted affiliation; even if the funeral oration derives from the
lyric *thrēnos*, there is much more in this refusal to lament, since it
involves the relationship between a community and its dead and,
through these dead, with its present and its past.

Less strict than the Thasian legislation, which absolutely forbade the mourning of the agathoi,† the Athenian ceremonial allowed ritual laments while restricting them to a minimum;
but by means of the funeral oration, the city recalled that those
who had died in battle deserved something better than laments.
In fact, beyond Athens and Thasos we must see, in this prohibition against bewailing the dead, a strictly civic prescription that
was universal throughout the Greek poleis. Thus, although certain
commentators have tried to challenge the relevance of the term
used by Diodorus, Simonides's poem to the glory of those who
died at Thermopylae was certainly an *egkōmion*‡ and not a threnos.
These verses, which substitute praise§ for lament, spring from the
same source of civic thought as the funeral oration.

To grasp the significance of this rejection of the threnos, we must
first decide, from among the many senses of this word, the meaning given it by the official orators. We know that initially *thrēnos*
referred to the poet's composed lament.[99]** Thus, in the Homeric
epic, the threnos sung by the bard over the hero's body†† is

---

* Thucydides 2.44.1; Lysias 77 and 80. Cf. also Demosthenes 32–37; Plato,
Menexenus 248c5, 247c7, 248b6, and Hyperides 42.
† Funerary law of Thasos, l. 4.
‡ Diodorus 11.11.6.
§ Simonides 5D.3.
** Solon's legislation forbade threnodies in verse (Plutarch, *Solon* 21.6).
†† *Iliad* 24.720–76; cf. Pindar, *Isthmians* 8.57ff.

contrasted in a sort of dialogue with the moans and sobs of the family and crowd. The lyric poets made a gnomic form of it in which consolation of the living was accompanied by a whole philosophy of life and death. But the classical city soon abandoned these two forms, which were too obviously bound up with an aristocratic conception of mourning and, while sometimes giving *thrēnos* its original sense of a versified lament, preferred to regard this word as simply a synonym of *goos*, the general term for any kind of lamentation.

This equivalence of *thrēnos* and *goos* illuminates in many different ways the funeral oration and its exclusion of lamentation. This exclusion may be seen as a desire to suppress displays of excessive mourning, because mourning was traditionally the prerogative of the family,[100] but also because it allowed individuals who were "full of complaints"* to lament their own lot† under cover of paying the dead the homage that was their due.‡ In short, the lament gave vent to uncontrollable, because essentially feminine, emotion: although the heroes of epic did not regard tears as incompatible with their virility as warriors, weeping was, in the classical period, women's lot.§ The Athenian city was well aware of this and, after leaving room for women's lamentation in the public funeral,** chose a man to deliver the praise of the *andres* that it was burying.†† As an indissolubly military and political speech, the funeral oration recognized as its own only male values: it therefore rejected the threnos and the appeals for pity so frequent in the aristocratic epitaphs celebrating a warrior.[101]‡‡

* *Iliad* 23.137.

† *Ibid.* 19.302, 314, 331, 339 and 24.725, 748, 773.

‡ *Ibid.* 23.9 (*geras thanontōn*).

§ Pollux was to summarize this idea thus (6.202): the female is plaintive and given to threnody.

** Thucydides 2.34.4.

†† *Ibid.* 2.34.6.

‡‡ Epitaph of Tettichos (*IG*, I², 976; *GV*, 1226), 1.2. Epitaph of Kroisos (*GV*, 1224).

But the rejection of the threnos cannot be reduced to some male "stiff-upper-lip" mentality — far from it. Even when they reduce the threnody to a lament, the epitaphioi proclaim an even more fundamental rejection of the heroic cults that in an aristocratic past merged the eulogy in ritual lamentation. Whether an *elegos* or a threnos, this "lamentation of praise" for Amphidamas of Euboea, Harmodius and Aristogeiton, or the Platonic *euthynoi*[102] sees the glorification of the dead as part of mourning. More or less the same spirit is to be found in the classical period in the funerals of the kings of Sparta. As a heterogeneous society, the Spartan polis forbade any unseemly lamentation over citizens who had fallen in battle,* reserving its heroic funerals for its kings.[†] Though strictly regulated in the case of the Peers, the ritual lament came into its own with those royal funerals, in which a distant past can be glimpsed,[‡] and which for Herodotus were reminiscent more of the customs of the "barbarians of Asia" than of those of the Greek cities of his time.[§] So by way of stressing still further the gap between the heroic threnos and the civic funeral oration, we shall, with the help of Herodotus's text, briefly compare this ceremony with the Athenian public funeral.

In both cases, funerals bring the community together, but Athenian openness has its counterpart in the Spartan law of constraint, the only effective unifying factor in the social body. In Sparta, everything was codified, everything was obligatory, from the presence of the helots forced to moan over their masters' bodies** to the compulsory externalization of suffering through striking one's head and moaning.[103] Whereas the Athenian funeral left lamentation to the women, at Sparta everyone was involved in the act of mourning: helots and freemen, men and women. In

---

* Xenophon, *Hellenica* 6.4.16 (the announcement of the disaster at Leuctra did not interrupt the celebration of the Gymnopaedia).

† Xenophon, *Lacedaimonian Constitution* 15.9.

‡ Tyrtaeus (5D) had already testified to this.

§ Herodotus 6.58.

** Tyrtaeus 5D.

fact, the ceremony *was* from beginning to end mourning* and lamentation; whereas at Athens a speech, scrupulously distinguished from the ritual laments, followed the burial, at Sparta praise of the dead man was incorporated in the ritualized mourning of which it seemed to be no more than a secondary manifestation.[104] Whereas at Athens a single orator delivered a speech that was at once like its predecessors and necessarily new, at Sparta the crowd produced a formula that was always the same. Thus the Spartan community came together to proclaim in a threnos the absolute superiority of the dead king, and for ten days the city, its political life suspended, gave itself over entirely to lamentation, as if to ward off a death that endangered the very principle of its continuity. Nothing of the kind was seen at Thasos, where the duration of mourning was limited strictly to five days,† or at Athens, where the activity of the city seemed to be interrupted only long enough to bury the dead and where the political speech had its place at the very heart of the ceremony.

A threnos was for the king, a charismatic figure whose death created a profound sense of disequilibrium;[105] for Athens's citizen-soldiers, on the other hand, there were civic honors that culminated in a prose eulogy. In refusing to lament over soldiers who had sacrificed their lives for it, the city declared that it represented all reality and the principle of all life: the *pothos* of the dead, that painful ecstasy of sobbing,‡ the all-powerful presence of the absent man, unfulfilled desire, must be replaced by the ever-renewed memory of the valor of those who had fallen.[106]

Of course, the shift from the threnos to the eulogy was not a sudden one: it had its own history, its delays (such as the hoplitic reform, which gradually integrated the warrior into the political group,[107] and, well into the classical period, its reverses. Because they were still to the *laos* what the Homeric *prōmachoi* were to the army of the Achaeans, Callinus's "poliad hero" and Tyrtaeus's *anēr*

* Called *to kedos* (Herodotus 6.58).
† Funerary law of Thasos, ll. 3–4.
‡ Cf. *Iliad* 17.439 and 23.14 and 97–98; Aeschylus, *Persians* 133–39 and 541–45.

agathos created by their deaths a gap that nothing but lamentation could fill.* Democratic Athens, where the city and its army were one, was able to accept the death of its men with greater serenity. However, the epic inspiration of an official poet or the pain of an orator was enough to cause the pothos to govern once again the community's relationship with its dead: this was the case in 432, in the epigrams of Potidaea,† and above all in 338, in Demosthenes's epitaphios.‡ But these delays and regrets are hardly surprising; they are the twists and turns inevitable in any historical process. The main thing is that the logos allowed the city to ward off mourning and to leave the last word to glory.§ The properly civic way of the funeral oration steered a middle course between demoralizing laments and the prohibition against honoring the living,[108] and consummated the break with the past once and for all.

In its concern to dramatize the confrontation between the civic present and the heroic past, Athenian tragedy did not miss the opportunity to represent this substitution of the eulogy for the lament, which Nietzsche saw as the very essence of the Greek sensibility and whose political dimension I am trying to stress.[109] When, in *The Suppliant Women*, Euripides borrows from the Athenian national tradition the story, dear to the authors of the epitaphioi, of the funeral of the warriors who fell before Thebes, he turns this "tragic epitaphios" into a dramatized reflection on the funeral oration.[110] We shall now briefly examine the principal stages, from mourning to civic speech, enacted in this play.

When Theseus, victorious after his punitive expedition against Thebes, brings back to Athens the bodies of the seven Argive chiefs, the first reaction of Adrastus and of the mothers who make up the chorus is entirely one of mourning and lamentation; tears are shed over the dead, of course, but above all they are weeping

---

* *Iliad* 24.776; Callinus 1.18–19; Tyrtaeus 9D.27–28.

† *GV*, 20 (*IG*, I², 945), 1.9: "The city regrets [*pothei*] these men, as do the people [of Erechtheus]."

‡ Demosthenes 33 (pothos of relations and fellow citizens).

§ *GV*, 20,1. 12 (*patrid' eukleisan*); Demosthenes 37 (*eudoxia*).

over themselves. The long moan of the chorus threatens the serenity of the Athenian cosmos in that it leads to the wish for self-annihilation.* The intervention of Theseus, the democratic, rationalist king, is intended, then, to shift this emotion from mourning to admiration: reduced at first to silence by the sobbing of the women,† he invites Adrastus to deliver the speech that will put an end to the morbid relish of maternal grief by giving the death of the combatants its full significance as civic devotion. To deliver Adrastus of the honeyed words from the epic and to direct him to his vocation as orator, Theseus has to pull him out of the female world of the lament; so he appeals to his man's intellect and to his reputation for eloquence.‡ Once again it is necessary to cross the frontier from choral lyricism to prose diction; what Adrastus delivers is not a threnody as in Pindar,§ but "the true, just praise" of the warriors who have fallen before Thebes.**

Thus the hero whose misfortunes were celebrated at Sicyon by tragic choruses becomes, in a tragedy, the civic orator.†† By means of his speech, death is the culmination of an intelligible, motivated act. "Where do these brave men find their shining courage?"‡‡ There is no other answer to this question than the exaltation of the city and its paideia.§§ As a didactic speech, the funeral oration does not so much console as explain and exalt. And its effect is to be felt even within the play: from threnos to logos and from logos to monody, the scene follows more or less the pattern of the Athenian public funeral, and, as at the Kerameikos, the speech purifies *pathos*, which it distances.||| Indeed, the chorus, appeased by the funeral eulogy, finally abandons the cry for a

---

* Euripides, *Suppliant Women* 828–31.

† *Ibid.* 838–39.

‡ *Ibid.* 842–43: *sophōteros, epistēmōn.*

§ Pindar, *Olympians* 6.15–17 (pothos of Amphiaraus).

** *Suppliant Women* 858–59.

†† Herodotus 5.67.

‡‡ *Suppliant Women* 841–42.

§§ *Ibid.* 905–15. See also 842–43 and 917.

more modulated lament, and at the very moment when the mothers are moved away from the funeral pyre, they are integrated for the first time into the civic universe. Referring to their sons as *kleinotatous en Argeiois* (the most illustrious of the Argives), they recognize at last the rights of the city over the children whom they had wanted entirely for themselves.*

So from now on we shall study the funeral oration as an *epainos*; it is certainly as such that the Athenians understood it. Demosthenes turns it into a celebration of valorous deeds; Thucydides, in his excursus on the funeral, describes the speech as an epainos; and Plato sees the epitaphioi as praise both of Athens and of the Athenians.† By defining the speech as a eulogy, I mean not to minimize the element of exhortation and consolation in the funeral oration but, on the contrary, to show the profound interdependence, within the epitaphioi, of *egkōmion* (praise), *parainesis* (exhortation), and *paraymthia* (consolation). Indeed, in praising the dead, the orators have a double aim: to instruct the young and to console the adults. Of course there is a thin line between lament and consolation, and when circumstances permit, Pericles or Hyperides lends himself more to praise than to exhortation; thus Hyperides's praise of Leosthenes and his companions, which is excessively stressed throughout the epitaphios, plays the role of an exhortation,‡ for the orator decided quite consciously to replace the laments on the *pathein* with praise of the *poiein*.§

Every epitaphios tries, therefore, to present itself as pure celebration, irrevocably detached from the threnos, and this theme is so fundamental to this type of speech that the individual eulogy of the fourth century, which was based on the model of the funeral

* *Ibid.* 965. The attitude of the mothers is henceforth much more civic; they condemn the gratuitous sacrifice of Evadne (1072–79) and become for Theseus guardians of the memory of Athens (1165ff.).
† Demosthenes, *Against Leptines* 141; Thucydides 2.34.4; Plato, *Menexenus* 234c4–6, 235a3, 6–7.
‡ Hyperides 10–40.
§ *Ibid.* 42.

oration, does the same: thus, praising Agesilaus after his death, Xenophon is very careful to show that he is writing a eulogy and not a funeral lament.* The threnos, it is true, was to regain pre-eminence in the Hellenistic period, and the very term *epitaphios logos* was so emptied of meaning that it came to denote a poetic lament.[112] Reading Menander the rhetor, who tries to reduce every eulogy to a lament† and repeats the prohibition against moaning only as an empty, stereotyped formula,‡ evokes reflections on the civic character of a prescription that is losing its meaning in a world in which the polis is no longer the vital center of all life.

As long as Athens was making history, the only laments that might be mentioned in an epitaphios were those of a defeated enemy bemoaning its ill fate, laments complacently referred to, for they were taken up as part of a hymn to the greatness of the city and of her citizen-soldiers. Well before Lysias expressed this idea,§ Aeschylus had made a tragedy out of those Persian tears that were the finest praise of Athens, and in the second half of the fifth century a collective epitaph in the demosion sema admirably evokes the moans of the enemy.** This hymn, made up of laments, was to be seen, then, as a mere topos of the praise of warriors, because it was universally believed that the funeral oration tended toward the epainos.[113]†† That, at least, was the ideal of the oration. In more difficult periods, laments again became established in the city, an ever-renewed temptation for the funeral oration; then the orators, without in any way abandoning the eulogy, cut short the exhortation and, dwelling on consolation, returned to the path of

* Xenophon, *Agesilaus* 10.

† Menander the rhetor, *Peri epideiktikon,* ed. Spengel, pp. 418–21 and above all p. 419, ll. 9 and 26–27.

‡ *Ibid.*, p. 421, l. 16.

§ Lysias 2: "In all places and among all people those who weep over their own misfortunes sing a hymn to the valor of our dead." See Aeschylus, *Persians,* esp. 285: "Ah! How I moan when I remember Athens."

** *IG,* I², 943.3.

†† See also Thucydides 2.43.2–3 and Isocrates, *Evagoras* 62.

the threnos. The same is true of Lysias's epitaphios, in which, in a moving passage, the orator remembers the weeping survivors bemoaning their own fate.* But, again, the song of triumph is added to the song of mourning, and eternal memory wipes away the tears.[114]† Out of this decisive confrontation between the city and death, the eulogy must emerge the victor, for the greater glory of the dead and of the city.

But the fact that the city is implicated in the eulogy in no way means that the funeral oration consisted of an epainos from the outset, that it emerged, without a model, without a past, simply from the political speech. In fact, in the same period when it rejected the threnos, civic speech took over very ancient forms of glorification and, as one might expect from a polemical form of appropriation, distorted them, transformed them, and neutralized them to its own advantage.

A comparison of Pindar's or Bacchylides's epitaphioi and *epinikia* (songs of victory) is instructive in this respect. Like the poet's words,‡ the orator's speech saves men's valor from annihilation; like the poetic eulogy, the prose speech promises the warriors remembrance by generations to come.[115]§ The resemblance between the *kleos aphthiton* (imperishable glory) of the aristocrats[116] and the *athanatos mnēmē* (immortal memory) of the city** is too evident to be fortuitous. Because in death the *agathoi andres* are victorious — over nature, over fate, over themselves[117] — their departure deserves to be celebrated by the logos, just as much as the athletic prowess of the *esthlos anēr*. But at this point, things become more complicated, for beyond all the stylistic figures

* Lysias, 71.

† *Ibid.* 80–81.

‡ For example, Pindar, *Pythians* 4.186 and *Nemeans* 7.32.

§ One might compare *Iliad* 22.305; *IG,* 1², 945.3 4; and Thucydides 2.41.4.

** For example, Thucydides 2.43.2 and 3; Lysias 6 (*athanatos mnēmē/symphora anonymos*), 28, 79, 81; *Menexenus* 249d5–6; Demosthenes 28, 32, 36; Hyperides 25, 42.

there is, between a real victory and a metaphorical victory, the gap that separates life from death — and individual renown from collective glory. Pindar celebrates survivors whom he protects in advance from the annihilation of oblivion,[118] and even when he devotes himself to the praise of a warrior, death in battle does not seem to him *a priori* more worthy of praise than a fine life.* The funeral oration, on the other hand, by definition celebrates the dead or, more precisely, exalts in them a certain type of death. In fact, this first difference conceals a number of others.

Whereas both the epitaphioi and the collective epitaphs of the demosion sema praise the Athenians for bringing glory to their country by their deaths,† Pindar prefers to glorify the winning athlete, who "makes his country share in the honors that he wins."‡ In the case of the poet, the city benefits as if by reflected glory from the renown won by one of its sons; in the oration, it grants its soldiers the homage of a memory that is merely a reflection of its own glory. But, conversely, to earn the eulogy, one has only to die in its service. This "benefit," which, like Tyrtaeus's common good (*xynon esthlon*),§ concerns all the citizens, wipes away evil** — not only the evil acts that an individual may have committed in his private life but also the evil of poverty, an insurmountable taint for an aristocrat, a mere handicap in a democracy — and both Pericles, with all his seriousness, and Plato, with his lack of it, agree that "even in the case of a man who is mediocre in other respects, bravery in war, in the service of country, deserves to hide the rest";†† or that "there seem to be many advantages in dying in battle; one is given a magnificent burial, even if one ends one's days in poverty, and a eulogy, even if one has no worth."‡‡

* Pindar, *Isthmians* 7.26–30.
† Thucydides 2.42.2; *IG,* I², 943 and 945.
‡ Pindar, *Isthmians* 6.69.
§ Tyrtaeus 9D 15.
** Thucydides 2.42.3.
†† *Ibid.*
‡‡ *Menexenus* 234c1–4.

87

Thus, offering to all what the poet reserved for an elite,* the democratic city did not distinguish among its members, and the collective character of this honor explains the need, which has already been referred to several times, for anonymity. Whereas the noble was celebrated by his name, the official orators made it a duty to grant no one man, even the *stratēgos*, the honor of a special mention,[119] and only an unhoped-for success in the wake of a number of reverses allows Hyperides to transform the eulogy of the dead into praise of Leosthenes.

This anonymity was to become a commonplace among the fourth-century orators, perhaps precisely because it was no longer observed with quite so much rigor. Recalling that the Athenians did not deprive themselves of the glory of Marathon and attribute it to Miltiades,† Demosthenes is perfectly well aware that the time has gone when the only real honor lay in not proving to be unworthy of Athens.‡ But at the time when the funeral oration was coming into being, the transformation of the notion of glory into a political concept[120] was a recent enough fact not yet to have become a topos — if, that is, Karl Jost is correct in dating it from the Persian Wars.[121] Whereas in the case of Pindar, a poet with archaic tendencies, the eulogy of the city is grafted onto that of the individual, each epitaphios can easily be reduced to an encomium of Athens, in relation to which the praise of the dead becomes secondary.[122] Of course, such a process is not perfectly coherent, and two orators such as Pericles and Hyperides may agree in devoting to the dead a particularly moving eulogy and still differ at every point in the share they give to the exaltation of the city: sacrificed to the dead in 322, the polis was still predominant in 430,§ although Pericles was obviously trying to maintain a balance between the two objects

* Pindar, *Pythians* 3.114–15.
† Demosthenes, *On Organization* 21.
‡ Demosthenes, *Against Aristocrates* 197.
§ Eulogy of the city: Thucydides 2.37–41; Hyperides 4–5. Eulogy of the dead: Thucydides 2.42–43; Hyperides 6–40.

of praise, which he wanted to be interdependent and not in competition.* Although Pericles's epitaphios does not really grant the city the central role that the Egyptian funerary inscriptions reserve to the king in the biography of the dead man,[123] the glory of the dead is nevertheless seen as being that of Athens; and that is where, for the moment, the fifth-century funeral oration remains.

The city, then, has come between the glory of the aristocrats and that of the citizen-soldiers, and it is the city that, calling upon the orator to speak, separates him irremediably from the poet. As the sole dispenser of praise and blame in an aristocratic society,† the poet alone had the power to immortalize a man's renown; the orator, on the other hand, lends his voice to the community.[124] Poetic praise was doubly marked by individuality, that of the subject of the poem, but above all that of the "master of praise." The funeral oration, on the other hand, delivered at the instigation of the polis and celebrating the anonymous group of Athenian dead before a civic audience, bears the imprint of the community even in its very form, as shown by the choice of prose, the truly "common" language, in preference to poetic meter, whose prestige is synonymous with distance‡ or fascination.[125]§ The Athenians "had no need of a Homer to glorify them":** by this haughty rejection of poetry, Pericles implicitly condemns the deceptive charms of an art of illusion. Even more, however, it represents a definitive break with a form of inspired language that derived its effectiveness from its relation to the divine.

In a triple transition from aristocratic courtyards to the public cemetery of the democracy, from the poet to the orator, and from meter to prose, the language of glory became secularized, and further proof can be found in the oration's resistance to

---

* Thucydides 2.42–43.

† See, for example, Pindar, *Pythians* 3.112–15 and *Nemeans* 7.61–63.

‡ See Aristotle, *Rhetoric* 3.2.1404b8–15.

§ Thucydides 2.41.4.

** *Ibid.*

mythical or religious representations. Myth, which was central in
Pindar's work, becomes in the funeral oration a mere annex of
history; in this discourse of a community in combat, there is no
room for the gods and heroes of epic. The Homeric poems and
the aristocratic epitaphs often attribute the outcome of a battle
to divine intervention.* In the funeral oration, however, the
supernatural had no place: the innumerable battles in which citizens had covered themselves with glory knew no other epiphany than that of Athenian valor,† and the victory of Salamis,
which Aeschylus saw as a demonstration of divine anger,‡ was
no longer anything but the sign of a wrong-redressing people's
right to hegemony.§ In the funeral oration, the Athenians even
take credit for such mythical exploits as the expeditions against
Thebes and Argos, which the tragedies, more faithful to the
spirit of myth, restore to the personal initiative of Theseus and
Demophon.** Finally, whereas the poets, lyric or tragic, praise
the Athenians through their kings by referring to them as Erech-
theidai†† or as offspring of the gods,‡‡ the orators' version is,
one might say, more strictly Athenian: born of the earth, Athenians by nature from their origins, the citizens were quite willing
to accept that the gods should quarrel among themselves as
to which of them should reign over Attica;§§ but in the spirit of

* *Iliad* 16.847ff.; *GV* 1224.2 (epitaph of Croesus, "whom once in battle's front
rank raging Ares destroyed"); Herodotus 6.117, 8.38 and 84.

† A single exception: Lysias 58 (and the epigram of Coronea: *GV* 17).

‡ Aeschylus, *Persians* 827: *Zeus kolastes.*

§ Lysias 47. In the epitaphioi, it is the Athenians who punish *hubris.* See Gorgias,
DK, B 6 (*kolastai ton adikos eutuchounton*); *Menexenus* 240d4 (*kolasamenoi*);
Hyperides 5 (*tous kakous kolazousa*).

** See Euripides's *Suppliant Women* and *Heraclidae.*

†† Pindar, *Pythians* 7.10; Sophocles, *Ajax* 202, *Antigone* 982; Euripides, *Medea*
824, *Suppliant Women* 387, 681, 702, and so on.

‡‡ Aeschylus, *Eumenides* 13 (the Athenians, sons of Hephaestus); Euripides,
Medea 825 (sons of the blessed gods).

§§ *Menexenus* 237c9–d1.

autochthony, they declared that they derived from no one but themselves.*

So those elements in the funeral oration that still testify to the poetic past are precisely those that the city is anxious to mark with its own imprint: rejection of the threnos, opposition between the lyric or tragic poiein and the civic *legein*, and a wish for anonymity are, in their negative and polemical way, so many indexes to the fact that the oration was not born out of nothing. But the quest for earlier forms must nevertheless be content with intuiting the bond at the very heart of the break, for in this confrontation between the funeral oration and earlier eulogistic literary forms, it is the break that ultimately triumphs.

Comparison of the epitaphioi and Athenian collective epitaphs provides the ultimate proof of this. Between these two forms of civic speech, one spoken at the demosion sema, the other written on the poluandria, both of which are closely bound up with the official funeral, there is an obvious interdependence; yet the funeral oration provides clearer evidence of a break between the democratic city's past and its present.

Of course, the resemblances are initially more apparent. Like the epitaphioi, the epitaphs are, for "the burying community," a way of "speaking of its dead, with pride or regret, but always in a eulogistic tone";[126] and the collective epitaphs are certainly, like Tyrtaeus's elegies, which inspired them, and like the funeral oration, eulogies of the dead and exhortations to courage much more than laments.[127] Distinguishing, in the last honors paid to the combatants, between the element of mourning or pothos and that of glory or memory (that is, of the tomb),† Tyrtaeus was already stressing the civic importance of the funerary monument.[128] And in fact, by giving an epitaph, the community was also affirming its own glory. But this aim is particularly apparent in the Kerameikos: between the two essential forms adopted in

* Demosthenes 4.
† Tyrtaeus 9D.27–28 (mourning); 29–34 (glory).

the fifth century by the collective epitaph (the *prosopopoeia* of the dead indicating the spot on which they died and the meaning of their sacrifice* or the homage solemnly paid by the city to some of its sons†), the Athenian community soon made its choice, renouncing the first, of which there is evidence at the end of the sixth century,‡ and adopting the second, in which the dead, referred to as *hoide* (these men), are at once honored and kept at a distance to the advantage of polis and *patris*, the ultimate source of all existence.[129] Dedicated to "the combatants who rest here" (*hoi enthade keimenoi andres*),§ the funeral oration is animated by the same purpose and is organized quite naturally around the same themes as the epitaphs: the same exaltation of the eternal memory of valor;** the same contrast between perishable life and immortal courage;†† the same refusal to accept the possibility that Athenians could ever be defeated;‡‡ the same importance of the theme of ancestors; the same representation of time, in which myth is fulfilled in "history";[130] last, and above all, the same democratic desire for anonymity that excludes any special mention of the strategoi,§§ even in a collective form like the epigram of Eion.***

Finally, between the logos and its versified double there is the gap, so often observed, between prose and poetic speech. Dedicated to combatants, the collective epitaph remained under the sway of epic. This, one might say, was a purely formal matter,

---

* For example, the epitaphs of Thermopylae (Herodotus 7.228.2 = *GV* 4) or the epitaph of the Corinthians at Salamis (*IG*, I², 927 = *GV* 7).

† For example, *IG*, I², 943 (= *GV* 18).

‡ Epitaph of the dead of Euripus (*Anthologia Palatina* 16.26 = *GV* 1).

§ For example, *Lysias* 1.

** *IG*, I², 943; *IG*, I², 945.

†† *IG*, I², 945, ll. 11–12.

‡‡ *GV* 17.

§§ *Ibid.* 19 (= *IG*, I², 935) is too mutilated a document to be taken into consideration.

*** Aeschines, *Against Ctesiphon* 184 (no. 2, l. 1); see Plutarch, *Cimon* 7.2–8.2.

one that may be reduced to a few linguistic suggestions.* But this would be to forget that there is no innocent influence: deaf to the political language of prose that, from the sixth century, was renewing the diction of the funerary epigram,[131] the epitaphs of the demosion sema, yielding to the prestige of epic language, sometimes seem to hark back, even in their thinking, to an aristocratic past in which the glory of the warrior who had fallen in the flower of his youth took precedence over the glory of the city,[132]† in which praise gave way to lament.‡ Subordinating men strictly to the polis, the funeral oration did not grant so much to the dead,[133] and in its rejection of archaic modes of celebration it proved itself to be resolutely democratic.

Thus, when we compare the funeral oration with related forms, everything tends to situate the oration at a time of break for the Athenian city between the present and the past and, more specifically, in the break that the democratic regime brought about in the system of moral and political values, to the detriment of individuals and to the greater glory of the community.

Does this mean that we can now date the funeral oration? If we construe the question in its broadest sense, we can reply in the affirmative: everything seems to suggest that the logos epitaphios originated after 508 in the democratic regime. But in linking the oration with this crucial period of Athenian history, we are still not giving it its date of birth, for from 508 through the first half of the fifth century, Athens was undergoing increasingly rapid change as a result of external war and internal political transformation. Established at the end of the sixth century, democracy was to "democratize" itself still further;[134] between Cleisthenes and Themistocles there was Miltiades, just as there was Cimon

---

* *Marnamenoi: GV* 13 (= *Anthologia Palatina* 7.258), 14 (*IG*, I², 946), 18 (*IG*, I², 943). *Kouroi Athenaion: GV* 14 (= *Anthologia Palatina* 7. 254). *Kydos:* ibid.

† *GV* 18, ll. 1–2: "On the Hellespont, those men lost their brilliant youth [*aglaos hebe*] in fighting, but they brought renown to their country."

‡ *Ibid.* 17, ll. 1–2: the epitaph begins *Tlemones* (unfortunates).

between Themistocles and Ephialtes, and for the moment there is no evidence to link the oration with one of these stages rather than with another. So, without harboring too many illusions about the feasibility of such an undertaking, we shall now try to locate the funeral oration more specifically in the history of the democratic polis.

The Time of the Epitaphios Logos

The funeral oration is a specifically Athenian form of speech; it expresses distinctively an awareness of the originality of Athens and the choice of a political system that separates Athenian interests from those of Sparta. This postulate, either tacitly or explicitly expressed, has led most historians to link the funeral oration with the immediate aftermath of the Persian Wars. Adopted by adherents of the unity of the nomos and also by those who see the oration as a more or less autonomous institution,[135] this dating also has the support, it is true, of ancient authors, in particular Diodorus and Dionysius of Halicarnassus. Diodorus, it will be remembered, dated the first epitaphios and the first funerary competition in the year 479, and I shall not return to this "evidence," mentioned above. Dionysius of Halicarnassus tries to prove that the laudatio funebris, delivered in 506 at the funeral of Brutus but perhaps dating from the period of the kings, is prior to the epitaphios logos. Of course, the rhetor declares, the Greeks have celebrated funerary competitions from the earliest times but "it was only later that the Athenians added the funeral oration to the practices then in force, and established it in honor of those who fought at Artemisium, Salamis, and Plataea and died for their country, or to the glory of their exploits at Marathon; in any case, the Marathon affair took place sixteen years after . . . the funeral of Brutus."* Quite obviously the precise date of the Athenian institution is of little importance to Dionysius, provided it is not too early. But confining himself to the illustrious decade that began with Marathon and ended with Plataea, the rhetor nevertheless

---

* Dionysius of Halicarnassus, *Roman Antiquities* 5.17.2–4.

94

assigns the funeral oration to a very precise moment, since he apparently does not consider proposing a later date that would just as easily suit the purposes of his demonstration; no doubt the obligatory link between the oration and the Persian Wars was already a commonplace.

Of course scholars no longer believe that the oration saw the light of day in the year 479—a date linked with too many "false" ones[136]— but, pushing back the "invention" of the funeral oration by a year or two, they have turned it into an expression of nascent Athenian imperialism, confronted by the dual necessity of honoring the soldiers who were dying in foreign expeditions and of justifying itself to the Greeks.[137] Thus, examining the catalog of mythical exploits in the epitaphioi, Wilhelm Kierdorf believes he can detect a double reference to contemporary events in the year 478–77: an allusion to Panhellenic combat (the struggle against the Amazons and Eumolpus's Thracians, symbolizing the one that Athens had waged and was still waging against the Persians) and an orchestration of the hegemonic theme (the help given to the Heraclidae against Eurystheus and to Adrastus against Creon, evoking that which, according to all the Athenian writers, the Greeks were to demand from their city against the injustices of Pausanias).[138*]

To interpret the myths of the catalog in such a way, one must postulate that from the foundation of the Attic-Delian League, Athens had at its disposal a systematically organized hegemonic ideology. The rapidity of the phenomenon may be surprising; ideological formations seldom crystallize at the same pace as events. But as it happens, the city certainly seems to have worked out the justification for its hegemony very quickly; we know at least that from the end of the Persian Wars, Athenian propaganda fully exploited recent victories. Celebrating the combatants of Salamis, who had saved the whole of Greece from slavery,[†] the first "Marathon epigram," probably engraved shortly after 479,[139]

* Thucydides 1.95.3 (*adikia*); cf. Herodotus 8.3 (*hubris*).
† Meiggs-Lewis 26.4.

proclaims Athens's Panhellenic vocation.[140] From this point of view, it hardly matters that in the second epigram, engraved later at the instigation of Cimon, Marathon is substituted for Salamis; confined within the city, the political rivalries that prompted this substitution did nothing to undermine the unity of hegemonic propaganda.[141] The important thing was that from the first years of the Pentecontaetia, the Athenians declared themselves the saviors of Greece. This is attested again by a fragment of Simonides, in which, in what Aristotle was to call an obvious enthymeme,* the poet concluded from a single exploit of the Athenian demos that Athens's claims were legitimate.† Marathon and Salamis: these were the lineaments of Athenian propaganda — prior perhaps to the Panhellenic use of myths.

Still, one must guard against overestimating the importance of the Persian Wars and the shadow they cast over the oration: the praise of democracy is as essential to the funeral oration as the account of the war against the Amazons, and to explain the mythical aid given the Heraclidae, one must do more than identify Pausanias with Eurystheus. Those who try to date the beginnings of the oration to the immediate aftermath of the victory may be a good decade too early, and in their totalizing interpretations they distort the texts.

To begin with, it will be noticed that in its egalitarian form, the funeral oration ill accords with the aristocratic reaction that probably characterized the Cimonian period. Although the ceremonial of which the epitaphioi form part is certainly, as far as the Athenian democracy was concerned, the result of a long growth in awareness of the duties of the community to its combatants, there is no reason to stop this process around 478, when in 475 — and perhaps even in 469 — the city still accorded the strategoi of Eion the honor of a special mention. Between the ethic of the prizes for bravery, for which there is abundant evidence in all the Greek

---

* Aristotle, *Topica* (= *De sophisticis elenchis*) 9.164a.
† Simonides 62D.

cities at the time of the Persian Wars,[142] and the anonymity of the official oration, the collective praise of the strategoi, magistrates elected by the community, may represent a transition. However, we must not exaggerate its importance: in the Athens of Cimon, the distribution of praise still obeyed the law of what was later to be called geometric equality, and it seems that the polis could not give the same share of glory to the ordinary soldiers as to their leaders. Furthermore, this unequal distribution is to be found in many cities in the early fifth century, and Simonides, the official bard of the dead of 480, respects this in his celebration of the Spartans of Thermopylae as well as in his eulogy of Salamis. The poet summons up Leonidas to witness the bravery of the homoioi* and carefully distinguishes between the merits of the anonymous combatants, which consist of courage and determination, and those of Themistocles, which are based on judgment and skill.† The same hierarchy can be discerned in both his versions, the Spartan and the Athenian.

And yet the process leading from a geometric distribution to the egalitarianism of the collective eulogy was irreversible. No doubt it began in the late sixth century, but rapid changes seem to have taken place within twenty years. With the Athenian soldiers who, after fighting throughout the Persian Wars, fell in the battles of the Pentecontaetia, a whole period dies; it was a period of transition that found a place for individuals' merit within collective glory. The case of Sophanes is exemplary in this respect. A citizen of Athens, he left behind him a quite personal renown: as the best Athenian combatant at Plataea;‡ as the warrior who, following a challenge during the siege of Aegina, killed the Argive pentathlon champion Eurybates,§ a "brilliant exploit"[143]** comparable to the

---

* Diodorus 11.11.6, v. 7.

† Plutarch, *Themistocles* 15.4 (for all the combatants [*koinei*]: *andreia kai prothumia;* for Themistocles: *gnōmē kai deinotēs*).

‡ Herodotus 9.73; he formed part of the *onomastotatoi* of Plataea (72).

§ *Ibid.* 9.75; cf. Pausanias 1.29.5.

** *Ibid.* 9.75: *lampron ergon.*

feats of arms of the Homeric promachoi; and, finally, more leg-endary than historical, as the hoplite who "dropped anchor," the better to keep his rank.* But his end was entirely civic: a general of the Athenians at Drabescus, he died bravely (*anēr genomenos agathos*) at the hands of the Edonians† and was probably buried in the demosion sema with his fellow combatants, who fell in large numbers.‡ Of course, the mutilated fragments of the obituary of Drabescus,§ the first of our series, do not allow us to verify this assertion, but Herodotus has nothing to say either about his death or about the honors he received, and in this silence may be a clue of the extent to which he and others respected the civic norm.[144] Henceforth the spirit of egalitarianism, already perceptible in 464, was to dominate the funeral oration. No infraction of the nomos occurs in Thucydides, who never mentions the names of the most valiant combatants; the time had gone when combat provided individuals with an opportunity of distinguishing them-selves, for battles were now fought by whole communities.

There is another clue to suggest that the custom of the col-lective eulogy dates from the decade 470–60. The almost com-plete absence of any Athenian public epitaph to the dead of the Persian Wars has often been remarked on. This anomaly is all the more surprising in that other Greek states, less glorious and less cultivated than Athens, did not fail to honor their combatants with a few lines of verse.[145] This silence on the Athenians' part is probably no accident, and it would be irresponsible to impute it to a general decline in the literary tradition, when this same tra-dition scrupulously preserved the innumerable official, semi-official, and private dedications celebrating Greek victory. In fact, the inscription of a public epitaph on the tombs of citizen-soldiers is regularly attested in Athens only after the victory of Eurymedon, and this may be a significant fact. At least during the

* *Ibid.* 9.74.

† *Ibid.* 9.75 (cf. Pausanias 1.29.5).

‡ Thucydides 1.100 and 4.102.

§ *IG,* I², 928 (464 B.C.).

Pentecontaetia, Athens seems to have paid its dead more and more attention.

These convergent pieces of evidence are, of course, extremely tenuous and are not enough to date the funeral oration; but an examination of the "parts" of the oration broadly corroborates these first impressions of a climate that would have been very favorable to the blossoming of the epitaphios logos.

To begin with, the catalog of exploits, in both structure and theme, points to the funeral oration as an undertaking of far greater scope than the isolated eulogy of famous combatants, whether they fell at Marathon or at Salamis. Indeed, by linking the dead of the day with all those of earlier wars, mythical and historical, this catalog deploys the whole of Athenian history, following a tradition that was already solidly established in the time of Pericles, since, when delivering the epitaphios, the statesman felt the need to distinguish between what he was doing and that history.* The breadth of such a point of view, which makes mythical Athenians the mere predecessors of those of the Pentecontaetia, presupposes that the city regards itself as mastering time;† and in order to master time, it must first have strengthened its grip on Greece. Of course, this unitary view of civic temporality was not arrived at overnight; but already, in the epigram of Eion, the polis joins the two ends of its history, linking the mythical Menestheus with present-day Athenians. It is true that the idea is still seeking its best form of expression and takes refuge behind the authority of Homeric poetry. Thus the present is abolished in the past,[146] and "today" is transformed into "once" by means of a pote: "Unshakable were the hearts of those men who once, near Eion . . . were the first to keep the enemy at bay."‡ However, the

---

* Thucydides 2.36.4.

† Preparing to relate all their fine actions *en tōi panti chronōi,* the Athenians at Plataea had to speak a language that was in fact that of the epitaphioi, which Herodotus used as his model (9.27.5).

‡ Aeschines, *Against Ctesiphon* 184.

stimulus is given that, on the walls of the Poikile,[147*] was to link the quite recent combat of Oinoe with the war of the Amazons and with Marathon[148] or, on the shield of the Parthenos, was to uncoil the chain of the Athenian generations.[149]

It would be pointless to deny that the Persian Wars occupied an essential place in this long succession of exploits; the structure of the catalog makes this strikingly clear, since the orators pass without transition from the actions of epic to the battle of Marathon,[†] from mythical prehistory to the recent history of the city.[150] Perhaps this may be seen as a sort of suppression of the period of the Peisistratids; but this enormous omission serves merely to bring out the exploits performed by the Athenians in 490 and 480. It does not, however, provide us with any suggestion as to the date of birth of the funeral oration. On the contrary, those who seek in the funeral oration the omnipresent mark of the Persian Wars are clearly allowing themselves to be influenced by the version of Athenian history given by the epitaphioi. Even Ephorus, Diodorus's principal source, had already fallen under the charms of this traditional history, which he accepted without the slightest mistrust.[151] Thus, through Ephorus, influenced — as were all Isocrates's disciples — by the mirage of the Persian Wars,[152] a chronology proper to the funeral oration has in turn acted on the dating of the oration, henceforth linked with the historical event to which it gave primacy; such, no doubt, is the weight of any official history. Only a comparison of the catalog of the epitaphioi with other representations of Athenian history allows us to put Marathon and Salamis in their true context: as part of a vast temporal chain whose development throughout the first half of the fifth century, in the epigram of Eion or on the walls of the Stoa Poikile, must be regarded as a crucial event.

Many transformations occurred in the mental world of the Athenian city between the Persian Wars and the middle of the fifth century, and it is highly likely that the "democratization" of the city

* Pausanias 1.15.1.

† Herodotus 9.27; *Menexenus* 239b–dff.; Demosthenes 8–10.

at the time of Ephialtes's reforms contributed appreciably to accelerating the process. In fact, if we wanted to read into the oration the mark of a particular period, we would probably have to abandon once and for all the immediate aftermath of the Persian Wars and link the funeral oration with a period stretching from the fall of Naxos, "the first allied city to be enslaved contrary to traditional practice,"* to Cimon's disgrace — that is, to the moment when Athens embarked irreversibly on the path of democratic reforms and, by breaking with Sparta, on the "first Peloponnesian war."

In the fourth century, Plato and Isocrates are inclined to link the funeral oration with those years when hegemony was transformed into "tyranny" over allies. But in the *Menexenus*, Plato claims that the dead of Oenophyta were the first Athenians to be buried in the demosion sema. This statement is not confirmed by any of our sources. It may well be an intentional mistake; but this explanation proves inadequate for anyone who reads the text carefully, for this date of 457 also marks for Plato the beginning of a new era, that of the wars between Greeks: "They were the first, after the Persian Wars, to defend Greek freedom against Greeks."† We know the extent to which the author of the *Menexenus* and the *Republic* condemned these fratricidal confrontations, to which he refused to give the name *polemos*.‡ So everything seems to lead to the conclusion that by this calculated error Plato, through the public funeral, was attacking the funeral oration, on the grounds that it bore the mark of too many struggles in which Greeks had fought Greeks. Isocrates does not argue any differently when he contrasts the blessed period that followed the formation of the League with the misfortunes brought by the wars waged by the maritime, imperialistic democracy;§ and he, too, links the practice of the collective funeral with the period of the wars between Greeks.**

* Thucydides 1.98.4.
† *Menexenus* 242b6–c2.
‡ Plato, *Republic* 4.470c–471e.
§ Isocrates, *Peace* 76 and 86.
** *Ibid.* 87–88.

The value of such testimonies must not be overestimated. But animated by a single aim — criticism of the maritime democracy — they tell us more about the ideology of fourth-century intellectuals than about the historical context of the funeral oration. Therefore, rather than comment further on them, I prefer to decipher, in the oration itself, the double trace left by the strengthening of the democracy and by a hardening in Athenian relations with other Greeks.

In those decisive years in which Athens adopted a new policy, the city's literature and art echoed these changes. Thus, in Aeschylus's *Suppliants*, tragedy details for the first time the constituents of the word *dēmokratia** by exalting the law of the popular ballot in which the majority prevails.[153] Similarly, by depicting the Athenian troops confronting the army of the Lacedaemonians on the walls of the Poikile, the fresco of Oinoe proclaims the victory of Athenian democracy over the Spartan hoplites and becomes something of a symbol: the demos, which has just repudiated the policies of Cimon, delights in proclaiming its power in that citadel of Cimonian propaganda. As an official speech, the funeral oration is quite naturally marked by this period, whether it owes its birth and themes to this climate or whether, as an already-constituted mode, it received from it the new form that was henceforth to be its own.

The obligatory eulogy of democracy presupposes that the demos had actually assumed power, and only the democracy of Ephialtes gives full significance to this eulogy, which must be seen as the heart of the speech and not as some audacious innovation by Pericles.[154] Indeed, praise of the regime goes well beyond the development attributed to it, and the ancient Athens that the orators praise at the beginning of the catalog certainly looks like the democratic city. Athens welcoming the suppliants accords perfectly well with Athens armed to defend the freedom of the Greeks. On

* Aeschylus, *Suppliants* 603–604 (*dēmou kratousa cheir*); for the idea, see also 601.

the whole, the funeral oration is organized so closely around the passage on democracy that it is difficult to see it as an addition or importation of some new "locus" in an already-constituted series.

An examination of the mythical part of the catalog broadly confirms this hypothesis. A democratic version of a national tradition is certainly being applied here.

Before we proceed to this examination, one ambiguity should be eliminated. Any study of the funeral oration is hindered by the almost-total absence of any mention of an epitaphios before that of the Samian war. Even this one remains largely an enigma; a few dispersed fragments are not enough to constitute a speech. More important, the first known epitaphios presenting a catalog of exploits is that of Lysias, composed in the early fourth century. So the historian is forced to reconstruct the first orations with the help of much later epitaphioi, a highly uncomfortable archaeological exercise. However, short of pushing back the institution of the funeral oration to the year 440,[155] we must simply put up with this inconvenience. Indeed, the reconstruction is not as dangerous as might at first appear: far from being innovative, the fourth-century epitaphioi are often content simply to repeat and no doubt faithfully reproduce whole sections that had existed for a very long time and that were presumably only too familiar to Pericles's audience.* Moreover, a comparative study of the fourth-century epitaphioi and the tragedies of the century before confirms that from 465 on,[156] the mythical themes of the catalog played an important part on the official stage of Athens, and therefore in national tradition. Last, and most important, the oration that, according to Herodotus, the Athenians delivered at Plataea leaves no doubt as to the ancient character of the catalog of exploits: listing a collection of mythical examples quite similar to that found in the fourth-century epitaphioi, this speech, in which the influence of the funeral oration has often been noted, is very similar to one of those celebrated lost early orations.† So we can go back to the

* Thucydides 2.36.4.
† Herodotus 9.27.

mythical exempla of the catalog with a relatively quiet conscience.

The spirit of these passages might be summed up in the phrase "myth without heroes." Whereas a Euripides sees the war of Eleusis as the tragic culmination of Erechtheus's gesture,* the orators exalt the heroic behavior of the Athenians before Eumolpus's Thracians but are very careful not to mention the name of the former king of Athens.[157] It was not Demophon but the Athenians who, in the epitaphioi, gave the Heraclidae decisive help;† it was Athens and not Theseus that won glory in the war of the Amazons or recovered before Thebes the bodies of the seven chiefs.‡ Of course, this silence may be interpreted as a feature of secularization, but there seems to me to be more in it than that. Let us examine the meaning of such an omission in the case of Theseus, a typically Athenian hero "created" at the end of the sixth century[158] to whom three of the actions referred to might legitimately be attributed.[159]

Demosthenes's epitaphios is the only one to mention Theseus; but in it, he is cited as a democratic hero and eponymous son,§ not as a war leader, and the orator, who names him in a purple passage, is careful, when referring to the mythical wars, not to break a silence that his predecessors respected so scrupulously.** It might be surprising that so important a hero for the tragic writers should be absent from the epitaphioi. Isocrates perhaps provides the key to this anomaly when, recounting the episode of the Theban war in the *Panathenaicus*, he substitutes the sovereign demos

* Euripides, *Erechtheus*, frag. 351–61 Nauck.

† Demophon: Euripides, *Heraclidae*. Diodorus (4.57.6) attributes this exploit to Theseus.

‡ Theseus against the Amazons: Plutarch, *Theseus* 26ff.; Diodorus Siculus 4.28; Pausanias 1.2.1. Theseus and Adrastus: Euripides, *Suppliant Women;* Plutarch, *Theseus* 29.4–5.

§ Demosthenes 28.

** *Ibid.* 8; Demosthenes, on the contrary, mentions the names of the enemy chiefs (Eumolpus, Eurystheus, Creon). Similarly, in Herodotus (9.27), Eurystheus and Polynices are named as opposing the collective "we" of the Athenians.

for the Athenians of the catalog.* Thus, while bending to the custom of the epitaphioi, the logographer refers specifically to the custom and explains it: to attribute to the demos what rightfully belonged to Theseus was undoubtedly a democratic reinterpretation of the myth.[160]

To this hypothesis it may be objected that the silence of the funeral oration, understandable where heroes of the aristocratic past are concerned, hardly explains the case of Theseus, the founder of synoecism and the symbol of Athenian democracy. But all the evidence available indicates that this representation of Theseus was imposed at a later date. Although in the fourth century he was the obligatory companion of Demos and Demokratia,[161] the king of Athens probably did not become a democratic hero before the second half of the fifth century (perhaps not before Euripides's *Suppliant Women*);[162] some historians even believe that he took on those features only in the writings of the Atthidographers of the next century.[163] In any case, neither in Herodotus nor in Thucydides does Theseus appear as a democrat, and even in Euripides he is not unambiguously so.[164]

The democracy of Ephialtes and Pericles, then, had no reason to make special mention of Theseus; on the contrary, it had every interest in attributing the legendary actions of the hero to the demos. Furthermore, in 460 this silence assumes the character of a manifesto, proclaiming that Athens rejects any memory of the Cimonian political period. The historical destiny of Theseus consists of periods of splendor and periods of eclipse Cleisthenes had removed him from the list of eponymous heros;[165] Cimon, the "new Theseus," gave him a marvelous opportunity for revenge by establishing him as the founder of the city[166] — these were reasons enough for the demos to banish him again to purgatory. He emerged definitively in the fourth century, among the Atthidographers, for whom his period marks the beginning of history in the strict sense,[167] or in the *Helen*, in which Isocrates conspicuously restores to him deeds that the epitaphioi had deprived

* Isocrates, *Panathenaicus* 170.

him of.* But before this triumph, the catalog of exploits was generally seen as a sign of a long, significant eclipse. Thus the democracy seems to have achieved a double objective: to put in the forefront the human community of the Athenians and to repudiate the policies of a leader whom it had ostracized.

The mark of the 460s is even more obvious if we consider the significance of the mythical wars, to which the orators devote a section. The struggle against the barbarian is of course well represented in the catalog, since, apart from the war of Eumolpus, the war of the Amazons, the mythical model of the Persian Wars,† prefigured the invasion and defeat of the Persians on the walls of the Poikile,‡ as in the funeral oration; but the other two traditional exploits show Athens at war with Greeks, defending the Heraclidae against Eurystheus's Peloponnesians and forcing Creon to give back the bodies of the "Seven against Thebes."

For the authors of the epitaphioi, these two episodes are an opportunity of recalling this generosity, this compassion for the weak and oppressed,§ which both tragedy and rhetoric agree are a principal feature of the Athenian character. That the tragic writers exalt this generosity** whereas the orators pretend to criticize it††

* Isocrates, *Helenus* 16–38 and above all 31–37.
† One might compare Lysias 4–6 (war of the Amazons) and *Menexenus* 239d–240a (Persian invasion).
‡ Pausanias 1.15.2–3: the Amazons and Marathon.
§ With the exception of Pericles, who touches on the theme but takes a position of self-interest, all the epitaphioi treat this topos: Gorgias, DK, 82 B 6, p. 285, ll. 15–16; Lysias 14, 22, 67; *Menexenus* 242b5; Demosthenes 7, 11, 28; Hyperides 5.
** Aeschylus: *Eumenides, Eleusinians;* Euripides: *Medea, Heraclidae, Herakles, Suppliant Women;* Sophocles: *Oedipus at Colonus.*
†† The best example is Plato, *Menexenus* 244e4–245a4 (Athens incapable of self-ishness). See also Andocides 3.28; Isocrates, *Panegyricus* 53; and Euripides, *Heraclidae* 150–77 and *Suppliant Women* 321 and 576–77. Only Cleon is perhaps serious in his criticism of Athenian compassion (Thucydides 3.37.1–2 and 40.2–3).

cannot conceal the essential facts that all are dealing with the same topos and that the project is obviously the same: to show that Athens is fighting on the side of right.* Because they cannot tolerate a Greek who violates a Hellenic law,† the Athenians take up arms to force Creon to submit; because they welcome the suppliant Heraclidae,‡ they feel obliged to punish their persecutors. Thus generosity leads to a sort of perpetual military activism,§ and militant compassion becomes belligerency. Gorgias, who understood this very well, in his epitaphios characterizes the Athenians as "devoted to those whom fate strikes unjustly, terrible toward those whom fate unjustly rewards," "violent toward the violent, moderate toward the moderate."[168]** In interpreting these mythical exempla, we must not, therefore, reduce them to variations on pity: in the epitaphioi, Athens is promachos, and only war gives it an opportunity of affirming its arete. So it is not enough to pay attention to the identity of the suppliants; even more important is that of the punished persecutors, or in other words, the defeated enemy. To give this enemy the name Pausanias is to ignore Eurystheus's Peloponnesians or Creon's Thebans, mythical ancestors of very real adversaries whom Athens had to confront more than once after 462, when it broke with Sparta. It is also to forget Isocrates's proposed interpretation of the myths of the catalog in the fourth century: "Of the Greek cities, the greatest, our own excepted, were then and still are Argos, Thebes, and Lacedaemon. We see how our ancestors defeated all the others: to defend the defeated Argives, they gave orders to the Thebans when they were the proudest; to defend the children of Herakles, they defeated the Argives and other Peloponnesians in battle."†† Whether or not it is

---

* A theme developed above all by Lysias: 6, 10, 12, 17, 46, 61.

† Lysias 9. Cf. Euripides, *Suppliant Women* 311, 526, 538, 561, 671.

‡ Isocrates brings together the themes of the Heraclidae and of Adrastus under the heading *hiketeiai*.

§ Euripides, *Suppliant Women* 576–77.

** DK, 82 B 6, p. 286, ll. 3–4 and 7.

†† Isocrates, *Panegyricus* 64.

in the interest of his argument, the rhetor thus reveals here the profound significance that the myths of the catalog had assumed for almost a century. Similarly, nothing suggests that the Athenian city waited until 431 to indulge in that "war of the myths" that Roger Goossens finds in the tragedies of Euripides at the time of the war of Archidamus.[169]

In fact, in the fifth century, Athens seems to have used the mythical episodes systematically as a foundation and justification for its relations, amicable or hostile, with three great cities, Argos, Thebes, and Sparta. From this point of view, the episode of the Heraclidae serves as a double warning to Sparta, since "the Peloponnesians of that time" were defeated there,* and since the contemporary Peloponnesians, the descendants of the Heraclidae, were implicitly presented as ungrateful, forgetful of Athens's acts of kindness toward them. Indeed, when the tension between the two cities was at its height, the orators and tragic writers did not refrain from making the moral of the story perfectly clear: composed after 430, Euripides's *Heraclidae is* simply a long indictment of Sparta;[170] and Lysias's epitaphios, animated by deep hatred of Spartan hegemony, takes pleasure in recalling that in protecting the children of Herakles without knowing "in what situation they might find themselves later," the Athenians were merely obeying their thirst for justice and glory.† The Theban episode finds its full significance in the light of Athens's interventionist policy. Between the two versions, pacific or bellicose, of this affair, both depicted on the tragic stage of the fifth century, the epitaphioi deliberately chose the bellicose version.[171]‡ This is hardly surprising: as a military speech, the funeral oration speaks only of military exploits. Furthermore, such a choice had to be made after 459, at a time when Athens, in alliance with Argos, was trying to

---

* Lysias 13, 15. Cf. Herodotus 9.27; Xenophon, *Memorabilia* 3.5.10, and Pausanias 1.32.6, who refers to "the first war between Athenians and Peloponnesians."

† Lysias 13. See also 14 and 15. Isocrates, *Panegyricus* 62, is even more explicit.

‡ Pacific version: in Aeschylus's *Eleusinians* (Plutarch, *Theseus* 29). Bellicose version: in Euripides's *Suppliant Women* (for the *logoi-rhōmē* alternative, see 25–26).

weaken Theban power by intervening in favor of the Boeotian minorities.* The writers of the fourth century would not hesitate in turn to use the mythical punishment of the Thebans when Athenian propaganda or their own political interests required it.[172]†

Thus the catalog of mythical exploits certainly seems to correspond to a period when, definitively renouncing any Panhellenic action, Athens was trying to justify its struggle against certain Greek cities in terms of the absolute necessity of defending others' liberty.‡

We can detect still another trace of the same atmosphere in this mythical catalog — a negative trace, since it involves yet another silence. The catalog, which is just as important for what it leaves out as for what it includes, conspicuously omits the Trojan War. It would hardly be surprising — a purely Athenian speech had no need of a theme with Panhellenic connotations§ — if one of the texts inspired by the tradition of the funeral oration included this episode among the exploits of the catalog.** One might add — although it does not change anything — that, although they do not include participation in the Trojan War in the catalog of legendary Athenian exploits, some of the official orators refer quite freely to this illustrious expedition, which was regarded as the greatest military undertaking of the past.

However, the orators rarely use the Trojan epic as anything

* Cf. *Menexenus* 242a–b.

† Isocrates, *Panegyricus* 54–65 and *Plataicus* 53; Xenophon, *Hellenica* 6.5.46.

‡ It is not irrelevant that this theme is absent from Pericles's epitaphios. All the other speeches present it: for example, Lysias 9 and 68; *Menexenus* 239b1–2, 242a, 242b5, 243a1, 244b–d, 245a1–4; Demosthenes 1.18.23; Hyperides 4, 5, 10, 16–17, 24, 34.

§ Cf. Thucydides 1.3.1. Isocrates uses it quite naturally when he wants to advocate the union of all the Greeks against the barbarians (*Panegyricus* 158, 159), but since the *Panathenaicus* is purely a eulogy of Athens, it carefully omits an episode that gives the city only a minor role (189).

** Herodotus 9.27 (oration of the Athenians at Plataea).

more than a foil to bring out the valor of the Athenian combatants.* It is certain that use of this polemical comparison dates from the fifth century. In 439, Pericles compared the expedition of Samos, which "in nine months had subjected the first and most powerful of the Ionians," with the ten years of effort that Agamemnon had needed to take a barbarian city.† This parallel, which Ion of Chios attributes to the excessive pride of the strategos,‡ can be seen rather as a wish to glorify Athens and the Athenians at all costs. It was a rhetorical move, of course, but this proud agon between present and past no doubt had its place in the epitaphios of Samos.[173] Was it not out of a wish to denigrate the Trojan War that the same Pericles, in the speech that Thucydides attributes to him, declares that the city has "no need of a Homer to exalt it"?§ It is difficult in this downgrading of Homer to distinguish between what may be attributed to Pericles and what to Thucydides; but the audacious antithesis that so scandalized Ion of Chios is enough to prove that it was Pericles who took the initiative and anticipated the historian.[174] It has been supposed that the orator was criticizing an already-established tradition, in which praise of Menestheus was obligatory. But even if this were the case, the subject of the debate was certainly not of purely rhetorical importance; the liveliest ideological struggles often crystallize around mythical themes, and the adherents and opponents of the Cimonian policy no doubt confronted each other by means of the Trojan War more than once during the fifth century. From the time of Cimon, the exaltation of the heroes of the Homeric epic** had served to advocate the pursuit of the Panhellenic struggle against the Persians, and it was precisely around the eulogy of Menes-

---

* Demosthenes 10; Hyperides 33, 35, 36. See also Isocrates, *Panegyricus* 83 and *Evagoras* 65.

† Plutarch, *Pericles* 28.7 (= *F.Gr.Hist.*, 292 [Ion of Chios] F 16).

‡ Plutarch, *Pericles* 28.7 "Ion relates how the defeat of Samos gave him immense, extraordinary pride."

§ Thucydides 2.41.4.

** For Polygnotus's *Ilioupersis* at the Poikile, see Pausanias 1.15.2.

theus that the epigrams of Eion are ordered. Of course, in 439 the exile and death of Cimon, the peace of Callias, and the ostracism of Thucydides, Melesias's son, had long sanctioned the abandonment of this policy,[175] but there were still enough Cimonians in Athens to regret the good old days when the enemy was Persian and not Greek;* in this climate, it was expedient to depreciate the siege of Troy to the advantage of that of Samos. However, we can go still further back and link this polemical comparison with the decade that saw Athens's abandonment of a Panhellenic past and the adoption of a hegemonic present. Pausanias is perhaps transmitting the durable memory of the epitaphios of the dead of Drabescus when he compares the Trojan War, "undertaken in common accord by all the Greeks," with the expeditions that the Athenians "are carrying out alone,"[176]† and it is not irrelevant that in this purely Athenian series the expedition to Thrace is the first — and only — historical undertaking mentioned.

The rejection of the Trojan War cannot, then, be dissociated from the other gaps in the catalog, which have already been interpreted as so many rejections of the past. Because the Trojan adventure had no place in the history of an Athens that was immemorially Athenian, the orators rejected it; and in that exclusion, we see an echo of the upheavals that in the second quarter of the century profoundly affected Athenian politics.

There remains, of course, the problem posed by Herodotus's text: does the presence of the "combats joined at Troy"‡ in the list of their exploits that the Athenians drew up at Plataea mean that there were epitaphioi that exalted this Panhellenic theme? The question may very well have presented itself to the ancients; the manuscript tradition, at least, tried to get around what must have seemed like an anomaly, for certain manuscripts substitute *hērōikoisi* (heroic actions) for *Troikoisi* (the Trojan cycle).§ In fact, it is

* Plutarch, *Pericles* 29.6.
† Pausanias 1.29.5.
‡ Herodotus 9.27.20.
§ *Troikoisi:* A B C P; *hero:* D R S V.

quite useless to correct the text, for from the point of view of the economy of that narrative the mention of the Trojan War would be justifiable in Herodotus: not only did the historian never challenge the importance of the legendary expedition, which he saw as a prefiguration of the Persian Wars,* but the reference to this episode is perfectly relevant in the context of the Greek coalition against the Persian invader. It is therefore not impossible that, transposing the funeral oration from the Periclean period to the time of Plataea, Herodotus thought it expedient to add a Panhellenic coloring that was oddly missing from the epitaphioi that he heard. To do this, he had only to replace Eumolpus's war with the war against Priam: after all, whether Thracian or Trojan, the enemy was still a barbarian. We might even detect in the text some indication that Herodotus is intervening in order to alter an already-established tradition. The same can be said of the austere brevity with which the Athenians allude to this collective exploit, just before rejecting the validity of those catalogs of noble deeds.† Mentioned at the end of the list, this theme is treated with discretion, not to say reluctance; between "We gave in to no one" and the insistence with which Athens claims the honor of defeating the Amazons,‡ there is perhaps a gap between the acceptable treatment of a theme and a heterogeneous addition.

Apart from this single exception, all the epitaphioi reject the Trojan War, and this is a significant rejection, given that every Greek city saw its participation in the Trojan adventure as the normal beginning of its national history.§ Considered from this point of view, the funeral oration again confirms Athenian originality.

Thus the silences in the oration accord with its explicit statements. In the structure of the obligatory passages of the funeral oration, it is tempting to see the mark of the 460s. At least, the

---

* Herodotus 1.3ff.

† *Ibid.* 9.27.21.

‡ *Ibid.* 9.27.18.

§ Pausanias 2.4.2, 25.5, and 30.10 (Argolis); 4.3 (Messenia); 8.6.1–3 (Arcadia).

state of our evidence does not allow us to go back further, toward some hypothetical original funeral oration: leaving all conjecture aside, then, we must conclude that there was a close link between the oration and the democracy of Ephialtes and Pericles, which gave the epitaphios logos the definitive form in which it has survived.

With a view to placing the funeral oration more firmly in the context of fifth-century Athenian politics, I shall conclude by trying to specify the place occupied by this oration, which is both military and democratic, in the struggle openly waged by Athens after 461 against a large part of Greece.

First, it was an ideological struggle: any weapon was acceptable in the contest for hegemony, and contrasts with antagonistic political models generally played an important part in it. Thus it is not irrelevant that the Athenians offered their democratic system as a model.* Indeed, fearing the contagion of Athenian activism on the Messenians,† the Spartans themselves were inciting them to rise up starting in 462 — unless Thucydides is projecting back to an earlier time the mentality of 430. And to a greater extent than the real "imitations" of the democracy of Cleisthenes and Pericles, which in any case were few and far between, ideological propaganda helped promote the Athenian example.[177]

But this conflict also had its military side. Faced with the solid hoplitic reputation of the Lacedaemonians, Athens had to give credence to the rumor of its noble exploits. Just as the Parthenos supplanted the ancient Polias,[178] a victorious Athens no doubt preceded more than once a civilizing Athens; and although the two figures competed on the tragic stage, the orators of the demosion sema hardly had the choice.[179] Thus the funeral oration could on occasion become part of the war machine against Sparta. Everything encouraged this potential: its character as an institutional eulogy of Athenian arete, its catalog of erga, and the

* Thucydides 2.37.1: *paradeigma.*
† *Ibid.* 1.103.3.

insistence with which the epitaphioi celebrated native Athenians, the just defenders of the soil that had produced and raised them.

During those war years, the tone of the epitaphioi was no doubt often bellicose, and the best proof of this is Pericles's epitaphios. Of course, to stress everything that makes it a war speech goes against the traditional interpretation, which makes this logos a humanistic exaltation of the fatherland of all culture; but a close examination shows that for Pericles, Athens is first of all a model of political and military arete. Not only does the orator devote a long section to the military worth of the Athenian people,* but even when he evokes the Athenian love of the arts and sciences, he does so only in passing.[180]† His aim is not so much to exalt in the city the "prytaneum of science" or to present the citizens as the most learned of the Greeks‡ as to establish Athens's absolute difference,§ that "intelligence in war"[181] that is the polis's strength.** In the epitaphioi, arete is primarily military: an examination of a passage of the *Panegyricus* leads to the same conclusion. After a long eulogy of the intellectual superiority of Athens,†† Isocrates defends himself for praising these qualities in Athens, "being too embarrassed to exalt her for her deeds in war."‡‡ Thereafter the orator returns to the normal pattern, unfolding the catalog of Athenian exploits in the manner of the epitaphioi that he has explicitly taken as his model.§§ Conversely, when he wants to advocate peace, Isocrates has to go against the theme of the epitaphioi.*** Thus, when they borrow the form and topoi of the

* *Ibid.* 2.39.

† *Ibid.* 40.1.

‡ Prytaneum of science: Plato, *Protagoras* 337d4–6. The most learned of the Greeks: *ibid.* 319b3–5.

§ Thucydides 2.40.3: *diapherontos.*

** *Ibid.*: *kratistoi.*

†† Isocrates, *Panegyricus* 47–50.

‡‡ *Ibid.* 51.

§§ *Ibid.* 74.

*** Isocrates, *Panathenaicus* 36, 41, 43, 49–50.

funeral oration, the Athenian writers use them as a weapon, as Xenophon does in his *Memorabilia* when he tries to denigrate Thebes by praising the warrior qualities of Athens in terms reminiscent of Pericles's epitaphios.*

But to situate the funeral oration in its time, the last word belongs to historians, or, more precisely, to the historian who in the fifth century turned an attentive ear to the national traditions of the Greek cities. So, leaving our fourth-century sources, we shall return to Herodotus, seeking in his writings, through the echo of the epitaphioi, the specific intentions of the Athenian official oration.

I have already referred several times to a speech delivered at Plataea by the Athenians, during a conflict over prestige that prefigures the real confrontation between the Greeks. It is a crucial text, which must be read at two levels. In the narration, it adapts itself without difficulty to very particular circumstances; thus the episode of the Heraclidae provides the Athenians with a ready-made response to the claims of the Tegeates.† However, only a comparison with the epitaphioi reveals the range of themes that make up this speech. Although it is relevant to recall at this precise moment Athens's relations with the Heraclidae, the same cannot be said for the Theban episode, and it may seem surprising that in the context of a struggle against Persia, the defeat of the Amazons, the mythical paradigm of the defeat of the barbarians, is not developed at any greater length. The Athenians are especially loquacious about the noble deeds that, in mythical times they performed against Greeks. Are we to think that this was how the epitaphioi, which Herodotus transposed even more faithfully than has generally been believed, wanted it? This speech of the Athenians contains not only the catalog of exploits but also the essential topoi of the exordium of the funeral oration, adapted to the needs of the moment.‡ Should we add, criticizing the recourse

---

* One might compare Xenophon, *Memorabilia* 3.5.4 and Thucydides 2.39.2.

† The Tegeates (Herodotus 9.26) boasted of defeating the Heraclidae.

‡ *Ibid.* 9.27.3–5 (two occurrences of the logos/ergon antithesis) and 6 (the compulsory nature of the oration).

to myth,* that Herodotus's Athenians sound much more like contemporaries of Pericles than like participants in the Persian Wars?

Because he is recounting what the cities say of themselves,[182] Herodotus gives voice to the national topoi.† He even goes so far as to take them into account when he shows the enemies recognizing the valor of Athens, as in an epitaphios,‡ or when he declares that the Athenians have saved Greece.§ Without laying too much stress on the well-founded reputation for pro-Athenian bias that these passages have earned him since Antiquity,** we can safely observe that in his quest for local traditions, Herodotus could not fail to come across the funeral oration. Conversely, however, it is not irrelevant that this narrative, the "Athenian" part of which is consciously inspired by the tradition of the epitaphioi,[183] is dominated by a view of the world in which agon rules instead of hegemony. It might be doubted whether this agon really came into effect after the fall of the tyrants,†† pitting against each other powerful Lacedaemonia and the Athenian democracy:[184]‡‡ this may have been a "gross anachronism,"[185] by which the historian transposed the climate of the Pentecontaetia to the year 500. But for our purposes the most important fact remains that of the interdependence between funeral oration and hegemonic rivalry: an interdependence, perceptible throughout the

* *Ibid.* 9.27.23–24: "Enough has been said of ancient exploits."

† For example, for Sparta: Herodotus 7.104 and 228 (obedience to the law); for Athens: 5.82 (the olive tree), 6.106 and 7.161 (autochthony), 6.137 (Athenian magnanimity), 6.112 (bravery of the hoplites at Marathon), 8.55 (the rivalry between Athena and Poseidon).

‡ Herodotus 7.10.

§ *Ibid.* 7.139, which may be compared with a quite similar passage in Lysias's epitaphios (45).

** Plutarch, *On the Malignity of Herodotus* 26.

†† Herodotus 5.91.

‡‡ *Ibid.* 5.97: "Athens, of all cities, was the most powerful"; cf. *ibid.* 5.98; 6.109; 7.10, 32, 157–61; 8.2–3; 9.102 (and a large part of the account of Plataea).

text, between an official speech and a political climate, between topoi and ideological struggle.

There is a certain justice in this: because it uses the funeral oration, written history helps to elucidate it. It does so, it is true, in an indirect and partial way. It is not enough to assign a historical context to the oration, any more than it is enough to insert it into a practice or tradition; and we cannot forget the fundamental issue that, throughout this search for origins, has emerged in all its complexity: that of the function of the epitaphioi, a eulogy in honor of the dead or an address for the benefit of the living, an educational homily or a war speech? As if it had too great — or too small — an object, the funeral oration seems to correspond to all these definitions. Starting from this perplexing multiplicity, we shall continue to examine the oration with a view to discovering its purpose.

CHAPTER TWO

The Address to the Dead and

Its Destination

To assign the funeral oration an object and an effect may well be an ambitious project, given the many obstacles in its way.

If the epitaphioi are so many war speeches addressed to other cities, we should use the official speech and the city's relations with "the others" to throw light on each other. In fact, when, in Herodotus or Thucydides, the Athenians set out to explain or to justify their actions with regard to other cities, when, before an assembly of Greeks, they proclaim their rights, they have recourse to the themes of the epitaphioi. But the real function of the funeral oration is nevertheless difficult to determine: what effects might be expected of a speech when the real relations, which for a Greek were expressed in battles, deprived words of any efficacy? And what might be said to an adversary temporarily transformed into a listener in the course of a speech?

If, on the other hand, the oration is for internal consumption and confines its area of influence to the frontiers of Attica, the question of its effect is no simpler. Of course we may compare the funeral oration with the speeches attributed by the historians to strategoi exhorting their troops before a battle, and in many respects the *stratēgikoi logoi* seem to have been inspired by the speeches delivered in the Kerameikos. But there is a considerable difference between a speech delivered before a battle by way of encouragement and a eulogy of the dead, even if it includes an exhortation to the living. In the first case, the words are delivered immediately before action, and thus are aimed at an immediate effect; in the other, they take place after the action, and any effect they are to have must be long-term, in the lifetime of the city itself. Thus, unlike the *stratēgikos logos*, which mixes topoi and the concrete analysis of a situation, the funeral oration does not go beyond generalities.

Thus any inclusion of the funeral oration in a systematic classification of types of speech proves difficult. Since they end with an exhortation and have so much in common with political speech, the epitaphioi cannot be placed in the purely ornamental category of *logoi epideiktikoi;*[1] But despite the similarity that Aristotle points out between eulogy and counsel,[*] we cannot reduce a speech that is essentially devoted to the celebration of Athens and the Athenians to a *logos sumbouleutikos.*

Confining themselves to a restrictive definition of the efficacy of a logos, scholars have shown little interest in the funeral oration as a genre and have preferred to deal with individual epitaphioi: that of Gorgias, which Vinzenz Buchheit declares to be "epideictic in form, symbouleutic in function,"[2] or that of Hyperides, which owes the fact that it is the only truly complete epitaphios to its immediate political purpose.[3][†] At most, they have assimilated the funeral oration to an epideictic speech, linking it to a genre that, since Aristotle, has been considered to have had no object. If, for each logos, the listener is an end[‡] — since there are as many oratorical genres as there are audiences[§] — it is not irrelevant that the person hearing an epideictic speech is defined as a spectator,[**] characterized by passivity and reduced to the role of a lover of fine phrases, whereas the symbouleutic speech is addressed to

---

[*] Aristotle, *Rhetoric* 1.9.1367b36.

[†] Hyperides 2: "It is just to praise our city for the resolution [*proairesis*] that it adopted."

[‡] Aristotle, *Rhetoric* 1.3.1358a7–b2.

[§] *Ibid.* 1358a36–37.

[**] *Ibid.* 1358b6: *theoros.*

members of an assembly,* entrusted with decision making. So this definition of the epideictic genre, taken up again and developed by theorists after Aristotle, is not incompatible with Martin P. Nilsson's dismissive statement to the effect that "the importance of the funeral oration in political life was practically nil."[4]

Is the funeral oration, then, a genre without an object, a logos that, by its own admission, never attained any ergon? In this sense, Pericles's epitaphios would seem exemplary, for after proclaiming the superiority of ergon over logos,† it reverses the order of values by substituting for the soldiers' real grave, initially exalted as ergon,‡ a purely symbolic monument (*taphos*).§ Henry R. Immerwahr rightly observes that throughout this epitaphios, the term *ergon* is gradually deprived of any material reference, as if, in contact with speech, any reality gradually fades away; but should we follow him to the extent of agreeing that such an "abstraction," though particularly clear in this epitaphios, characterizes the funeral oration as genre in general?[5] And how are we to interpret this abstraction: as an inherent, inevitable part of a genre too cut off from the realities of political life, or as an indelible mark imprinted on speech by a particular stage in social thought?[6]

The historian's task, then, is to determine, without ignoring whatever might make the funeral oration a speech without object at every moment of its history, the effect or effects intended by the epitaphioi. If each oration is intended to be efficacious here and now, the desired effect is not necessarily always the same or always obtainable.[7] And if the funeral oration has several different aims, trying to win support for a particular strategy or being content to confirm accepted values, it is because it is rooted both in the evolution of the city and in its own, at first sight paradoxical, destiny.

---

* *Ibid.* 1358b5: *ekklesiastes.*
† Thucydides 2.35.
‡ *Ibid.* 2.35.1.
§ *Ibid.* 2.43.2–3.

The Terrain of a Strategy: From De Facto Hegemony to the Hegemonic Speech

From the outset, an epitaphios was similar to a speech justifying the right of Athenians to hegemony,* but the fundamental ambiguity of the genre lies in this very resemblance. How could a eulogy for the dead delivered in Athens be addressed to the other Greek cities? In the funeral oration, we are never quite sure to whom the city is speaking, to itself or to "the others"; this opposition is one of the leitmotifs of the epitaphioi.†

Of course, the very nature of the ceremony implies that the city recognizes the existence of "the others": in war, each polis is confronted by a threat from the outside, and by solemnly burying those citizens who have fallen in battle, the Athenian community is not simply honoring its own but taking cognizance of the casualties it has inflicted on the enemy. Thus conflict is given its *de facto* consecration even if, in the event of a serious defeat, the orators deny that the enemy has anything to do with the city's misfortunes.‡

As adversary, "the other" is an absentee, whose silent presence is presupposed by the entire ceremony; as ally or mere foreigner, he is invited to the funeral, as spectator and listener if not as interlocutor. So we should give the other a more precise form, throwing light on the oration's aim by an examining its public.

Athenians and foreigners* were equally free to attend the funeral, and the epitaphioi echo the information given by Thucydides.[8] It is to "the whole crowd, Athenians and foreigners,"† that Pericles addresses his lesson on Athens; Demosthenes interrupts one passage to appeal to the benevolence of those who, among his audience, are *exō tou genous*;[9]‡ and finally, in the *Menexenus*, the

---

* Cf. Herodotus 9.27.6–8 and 30.

† For example, Thucydides 2.40.4 (the many); Lysias 44 (the others); *Menexenus* 237b7 (the others); Demosthenes 8 (the other Greeks); Hyperides 7 (other peoples).

‡ *Menexenus* 243dS: "It is our own divisions and not others that triumph over us."

* Thucydides 2.34.4.

† *Ibid.* 2.36.4.

‡ Demosthenes 13.

foreigners who are with Socrates come, like him, to listen to the orator.* Who were these xenoi? To regard them simply as metics would be to ignore the insistence with which these texts present the solemnities as open to all.† They must have been, then, all those foreigners who happened to be in the city at the time, all those drawn to Athens by the *hiera kai hosia* where one could "see and hear."[10]‡ There was even a very strong wish that xenoi be present because of the military character of the ceremony: did not Athens pride herself, in the most famous of the epitaphioi, on the openness that guided her military policies?§ But let there be no mistake: beneath the democratic mask of openness, it is easy enough to glimpse a desire to impress foreigners, allies, friends, and real or potential enemies. In the context of agonistic relations, any warlike act, whether the departure of the Athenian expeditionary corps to Sicily or the collective funeral, turned into a "demonstration of power and greatness for the benefit of other Greeks"** and presupposed the actual participation of a public in holiday mood.†† In short, for Athens, the funeral oration must be "a way of deluding oneself about foreigners and allies."[11]

But the funeral oration also bears witness to the fact that every Greek city of the classical period had uneasy relations with the outside world. Intended to have an effect on others, it was nevertheless delivered in Athens to the glory of the citizens of Athens, and after declaring that he will speak as much for foreigners as for astoi, Pericles restricts his exhortation and consolation to Athenians alone, to parents and children, companions and wives. Nor does Plato fail to stress those things that make the funeral strictly an Athenian event: in the prologue to the *Menexenus*, Socrates, after mentioning the presence of xenoi, seems to forget the fact

---

* *Menexenus* 235b3–4.
† Thucydides 2.34–4.
‡ Xenophon, *Poroi* 5.4.
§ Thucydides 2.39.1.
** *Ibid.* 6.31.4.
†† *Ibid.* 6.31.1.

and goes on to accuse the oration of "praising Athens before Athenians";* and, referring to the funeral procession in the exordium, he makes no mention whatsoever of foreigners.† This omission is telling: is it then, that "other" that Athens would like to convince; or rather, as the *Menexenus* suggests, was his presence necessary to the city only so that the latter could admire itself in others' eyes?

Such a relationship certainly runs the risk of being more imaginary than real, which would confirm a study of the characteristics attributed to "the others" by the epitaphioi: the ally, like the enemy, plays the role of foil, necessary but with no personality of his own.

First of all, the ally — or rather, the subject, since the funeral oration originates in an imperialistic city, if not actually in the empire. The epitaphioi, it is true, refrained from using the term *hupēkoos* (subject),‡ and it is hardly surprising, for a eulogistic speech could not affect the cold lucidity that Thucydides attributes to his orators§ or that the demos showed in its decrees.[12]** But on the other hand, the relative scarcity of the term *summachos* (ally) is surprising. It is certainly found in Lysias's epitaphios, which in the early fourth century makes an apologia for the lost empire,†† but it is strangely absent from the passage that Pericles, at a time when Athens was at the height of her power, devotes to the city's foreign policy. This passage is both realistic and aristocratic,[13] and, by means of what James H. Oliver calls the "dialectic of *charis*,"[14] it reduces others to a position of indebtedness,

* *Menexenus* 235d; Aristotle refers to this passage twice: *Rhetoric* 1367b8–9 and 1415b32.
† *Menexenus* 236d6.
‡ A single occurrence: Thucydides 2.41.3.
§ Theme of the empire-tyranny: *ibid.* 2.63.2 (Pericles); 3.37.2 (Cleon); 6.18.3 (Alcibiades).
** Cf. *IG*, I², 27 and 28 a, referring to "cities subjected to the power [*kratos*] of the Athenians."
†† Lysias 55.

though they are referred to as friends.* Forced to leave all initiative to Athens and laden with its benefits, these "friends" had no alternative but the weakness of the debtor† — rather like Euripides's Herakles, described in the last lines of the tragedy as "following Theseus like a boat being towed by another."‡ Indeed the epitaphioi describe allies as grateful debtors or suppliants whose entreaties have been granted, and in their descriptions of the battles they omit all mention of auxiliary troops, so that the glory does not have to be shared with summachoi.§ All greatness is solitary, and Athens would much rather have suppliants, on whom it may lavish its compassion, than effective allies.[15]**

In the epitaphioi, "the other" takes many different forms, but he always plays the same role in relation to Athens: that of an inferior, even a subordinate. Either the others are regarded as a colorful crowd of immigrants, metics†† even in their own countries, whose natives are only too pleased to stress their inferiority; or they are invited to gather around Athens, or even to merge with her. According to circumstances, they are called on to benefit from the city's openness or to regard the death of an Athenian soldier as their own bereavement.‡‡ The striking image in Lysias's epitaphios of personified Greece, cutting off her hair to show her grief for the citizens of Athens all the more clearly, is the best example.[16]§§

---

* Thucydides 2.40.4. Compare with 1.32.1, 33.1, 34.3, and 42.2–3; cf. also 1.9.3.

† *Ibid.* 2.40.4.

‡ Euripides, *Herakles* 1424.

§ Cf. Thucydides 2.39.2 and Lysias 24 ("they believed that a victory that they could not win alone would also be impossible with the help of their allies").

** Lysias 23: "They did not expect their allies ... to come to their help; instead of owing their salvation to others, it was up to them, they believed, to save the rest of Greece." For the theme of pity, see *ibid.* 14, 67, 69.

†† *Menexenus* 237b4–5 (immigrants, metics); Demosthenes 4 (immigrants, titular citizens but comparable to adopted children).

‡‡ Thucydides 2.39.1; Lysias 60.

§§ Lysias 60.

Usually they exist only as spectators of Athenian valor; the epitaphioi are content to recall that the city meets with universal admiration* and that even its enemies are enthralled by its greatness.†

So, at most, it may be admitted that an ally was merely a subject (hupēkoos), since all conflicts were resolved in admiration,
for, as Aristotle declares, "it is as if there were a common accord,
if even those who have to suffer from something praise it."[17]‡ This
theme, therefore, is essential to the representation of Athens, and
those who pour scorn on it in passing,§ as Isocrates does, still
make abundant use of it.**

Nevertheless, we sense what imaginary satisfactions are implied in such an idea; in the absence in the real world of that
enthusiastic gratitude that it imagines in the oration, the city
invents perfect enemies and allies who are always content. This
is how the Athenians dream their relations with others, and in
counting on posterity to be sympathetic, they duplicate the real
audience with an audience to come.†† But we may just as easily
interpret these appeals to posterity as the purest expression of
Athenian narcissism: in being so convinced of its future glory, was
not the city wrapping itself still more tightly in its insularity? By
aiming at an indeterminate future in this way, one runs the risk of
misunderstanding the existing balance of power; by refusing others any reality, the Athenians slumbered in the satisfying certainty
of their own exemplariness, losing all vigilance toward those

---

* Thucydides 2.39.4 and 41.4; Lysias 20, 26, 41, 47, 66, 67, 69; *Menexenus*
237c6, 237d1–2, 241c8–9; Demosthenes 4; Hyperides 18 (all of Greece will
come on a pilgrimage to see the work of these men), 29, 35.

† Thucydides 2.41.3. Cf. Lysias 44 (Athenians considered worthy of hegemony,
by friends and enemies); *Menexenus* 243a5–7 (Athenians more admired by their
enemies than others by their friends); Demosthenes 21.

‡Aristotle, *Rhetoric* 6.6.1363a1ff.

§ Isocrates, *Antidosis* 300.

** Isocrates, *Panegyricus*.

†† Thucydides 2.41.4 ("we will be admired by all, in the present and in the
future"); *Menexenus* 241c8–9.

underestimated foreigners. No doubt the balance of power had changed in the fourth century, often forcing the Athenians to be content with narcissistic satisfaction. However, it is not impossible that the oration, addressed by Athens to itself as much as to others, had this dual destination from the outset. This is, of course, only a hypothesis, but it throws light both on the history of the variations of the funeral oration and on its conservatism. The remarks above already stress the paradoxical situation of an oration that claims hegemony over others while being addressed primarily to Athenians.

The first anomaly, though not the least, is the strange silence in the epitaphioi regarding Athenian imperialism, which in its reality and myths alike the orators "forgot" or concealed during both the great days of *archē* and those somber years of the fourth century when Athens lived on regrets and memories.

Deaf to the concrete evidence of arche, the epitaphioi are equally impervious to its mythical background. Inviting the allies to take part in the Great Panathenaeas as colonists,[18] the imperialist city was presenting itself as the metropolis of Ionia, and from the mid-fifth century on Ion, naturalized an Athenian, eclipsed the national heroes, the eponyms of the Cleisthenean tribes, in the League's propaganda.[19] Tragedy becomes the echo of Ionian legend. In exalting Ion's descendants, Euripides justifies in turn the empire by colonization and colonization by myth,* just as Isocrates does a few years before the creation of the second maritime confederation.† The *Atthides* of the fourth century follow a similar tendency when, to the traditional intervention of Theseus against the Amazons and in support of Adrastus, they add a war against the Minoan thalassocracy, Athens's first — and mythical — maritime expedition.[20] On the other hand, nothing of the kind is to be found in the epitaphioi; they confine themselves to the wars with Peloponnesians and Thebans and are concerned

---

* Euripides, *Ion* 1582–88.
† Isocrates, *Panegyricus* 34–37 and 122.

with the settlement of a region only to use autochthony as a weapon against the inhabitants of the Peloponnesus, who are presented as immigrants on their own soil. To explain this silence, must one claim that the imperialist representations in fifth-century epitaphioi disappeared from their counterparts of the next century? To imagine such a development would be to underestimate the conservatism of the genre. Furthermore, if such passages were an integral part of the funeral oration, Lysias, who wanted to use the oration in rebuilding the empire, would have been careful not to omit them in his account of the mythical exploits, which is one of the most complete that we possess. Thus it is tempting to conclude that the funeral oration was able, in the full flow of imperialism, to ignore the myths of arche. Is it possible that the empire was a reality alien to the world of the funeral oration?

Pericles's epitaphios confirms this hypothesis all the more tellingly in that the oration was — or is supposed to have been — delivered in a city that was "still in full flower."* Praise of the empire seems to have played a quite secondary role; only much later does the orator refer to it,† and the power of the city‡ appears only as the ultimate verification of the greatness of Athens, as the conclusion of an already-complete development.§ Therefore, any reader of Thucydides experiences a certain embarrassment in accounting for this phenomenon. Although Jacqueline de Romilly, showing that for the orator the power of the city is the result and proof of Athenian merits, can, *in extremis*, assign to the epitaphios a place in the general theory of imperialism,[21] Hermann Strasburger believes that the oration has something ghostly about it;[22] finally, Hellmut Flashar considers such a development a luxury, since, without the imperialist component, the figure of the Athenian citizen is already sufficient in itself,** so that he feels

---

* Thucydides 2.31.2.
† *Ibid.* 2.40.4 and 41.2–4.
‡ *Ibid.* 2.41.2.
§ *Ibid.* 2.41.1: "To sum up, I say that the whole city is an education for Hellas."
** *Ibid.: to sōma autarkes.*

some difficulty in integrating this text into the perspective of a "Machtideologie."[23]

Indeed, for the orator, the empire is merely the *sign* of a deeper, more durable reality, namely, the greatness of Athens. Of course, he uses such unequivocal terms as *hupēkooi*, *archetai*, and *sunkatoikisantes*, and the power of Athens is the fundamental *ergon* that validates the whole eulogy. But although he uses the verbal form *archetai*, Pericles does not call the empire *archē*, preferring *dunamis*, whose sense is much broader. And the verb *sunkatoikizein*, with which the passage closes, far from indicating a colonizing act, assumes a figurative sense by virtue of the direct object attributed to it: what the Athenians are founding are "commemorative monuments" of good and evil things (*mnēmeia kakōn te kai agathōn*).[24*] Now, the orator has just declared that the true monument is a trace in men's memories and not a material building; so we must regard these *mnēmeia*, which refer to no tangible realization of Athenian imperialism, as memories of fine victories or noble defeats, as signs of arete. And when he declares, "We have compelled every land and sea to open a path to our daring,"[†] Pericles certainly characterizes the incessant activity that is peculiar to imperialist Athens, but he also does much more (or much less), for *pasa thalassa kai gē* is merely a generalization, intended to prove the scope of Athenian arete rather than to describe the empire, while daring, the conquering virtue, is seen here primarily as a mark of courage. Finally, the declaration that the whole world, even one's subjects, acknowledges the valor of the city is a topos and certainly seems chimerical when compared with the Athenians' frank admission at Melos that nothing is to be expected of subjects but hatred.[‡] More important than the eulogy of the empire, then, is the essentially aristocratic preoccupation with glory, and the orator establishes quite clearly that the memory of Athens is already independent of the survival of its empire.

* *Ibid.* 2.41.4.

† *Ibid.*

‡ Thucydides 5.91.1.

To this astonishing text we might add the passage that Pericles devotes to Athenian prosperity: "Because of the greatness of our city, the fruits of the whole earth flow in upon us so that we enjoy the goods of other countries as freely as our own."* This declaration has often been quoted but has seldom been subjected to detailed examination; it has traditionally been regarded as an apologia for "the commercial predominance of Athens and of the activity of its port."[25] No doubt such a reading is quite possible, especially because Pericles's sentence, in both its theme and its terms, is joined by many other discussions of the "economic imperialism" of Athens. The comic writers, such as Hermippus, take great delight in listing at length the commodities that flow in to Piraeus from every region of the world.[26]† Aristophanes pours scorn on the imperialist pretensions of the demos whose entire distinction consists in getting Greece to contribute to its welfare.[27]‡ Pseudo-Xenophon, who also refers to the influx of commodities from every part of the world to the same market, goes on to declare that "only the Athenians are capable of gathering into their own hands the wealth of Greeks and barbarians";§ and, following him, the writers of the fourth century, first Isocrates, then Xenophon, exalt Athens's maritime and commercial vocation.** The kinship of all these texts with the epitaphios is obvious, and yet the "imitations" of the epitaphios by Hermippus or Aristophanes, by pseudo-Xenophon or Isocrates, are unfaithful in that they develop the letter while misinterpreting the spirit of the oration.

Indeed, far from listing commodities or countries, far from exalting Piraeus and the black barks coursing the sea routes, Pericles keeps to the most apparently neutral term possible. Of course Athens "watches the arrival of goods from every country"

* *Ibid.* 2.38.2.
† Hermippus, frag. 63 Kock (*Phormophoroi*).
‡ *Wasps* 520.
§ [Xenophon], *Constitution of the Athenians* 2.7–11.
** Isocrates, *Panegyricus* 42; Xenophon, *Poroi* 1.7–8.

(*epeserchetai ek pasēs gēs ta panta*), but the term *epeserchetai,* which is not even specified by *ek thalassēs,* as in the oration of Archidamus at the debate in Sparta,* certainly does not in itself imply maritime traffic; at most it indicates importing, the introduction of a commodity from abroad.[28] Carried to this degree, abstraction becomes omission — and without any doubt deliberate omission: if, referring to the prosperity of Athens, Pericles makes it neither the condition of Athenian power[29] nor the corollary of mastery of the seas, it is because he sees it, as Edouard Will puts it so well,[30] as an extra, something given in addition to compensate for greatness (*alla megethos tēs poleōs*). Whereas pseudo-Xenophon sees "everything flow into the same market, thanks to the empire of the sea,"† and Isocrates sings the praises of Piraeus, "invention of Athens"[31] and "market [*emporion*] in the midst of Greece," Pericles integrates the prosperity of Athens into the theme, which is dominant in his speech, of the self-sufficiency of the city;‡ thus the other is assimilated by Athens even in its products. It is hard to imagine a finer definition of the "subsistence economy" that characterized the Greek cities of the classical period.[32] It is true that "the *civic* ethic, which has its source in the aristocratic ethic, showed a prodigious capacity for resisting economic realities."[33] But it is not irrelevant that an epitaphios provides such striking evidence of it.

Was the funeral oration an imperialistic speech, then? There is no simple answer to this question. No doubt Pericles's audience saw it as fulfilling that function despite everything in the oration that makes it a denial of empire.[34] Thus the strange strategy by which the epitaphios makes understood what it refuses to say outright is probably no accident, and to convince ourselves of this, we need only compare it with the last of the speeches that Thucydides attributes to Pericles. On the one hand, we have the serene, lucid declaration that "arche is the same as tyranny" and, on the other,

---

* Thucydides 1.81.2: "they will bring by sea what they need."
† [Xenophon] 2.7.
‡ Thucydides 2.38.2.

131

pride "that no subject has ever complained that his masters do not deserve to rule."* Must we speak here of contradiction? The coherence of Pericles's political statement and of Thucydides's historical reflection is such that we cannot stop short at this solution, and the existence of a similar gap between Pericles's first oration, centered on the mastery of the seas, and the epitaphios, which ignores this basis for Athenian power,† suggests that even within this account Thucydides opposes two types of discourse, at once irreconcilable and complementary: in an epitaphios, one does not speak of empire as one does in a political speech. If there is a contradiction, then, it stems from the imperialist city itself, which in the speeches of the ekklesia, in the decrees, and at the Panathenaea[35] proclaims its *kratos* over the allies but in the orations at the Kerameikos disguises dynamis as arete.

So it would be too simple to declare that when confronted by the empire and its problems, the Athenians developed "no justification, no ideological cover."[36] This would be to forget that in the fifth century, the funeral oration fulfilled this function perfectly. At the official funeral, Athens was on show — before Greece, before itself — and, renouncing the frank lucidity of the debates in the assembly, the orators transformed the empire into a manifestation of Athenian excellence. Examination of a fourth-century epitaphios confirms this hypothesis; trying to use the funeral oration in the service of the imperialist propaganda that developed from the earliest years of the century, Lysias explicitly touches on the lost maritime empire.‡ However, the evocation of Athenian greatness has precedence over that of its power. The defense of arche is ultimately very limited, much less developed than in Isocrates's plagiarism of it,§ and, referring to the Athenians as "guides of the cities,"** the orator reminds us that the essential

---

* Thucydides 2.63.2 and 41.3.
† *Ibid.* 1.143.4–5; 2.38.2.
‡ Lysias 55: "They commanded the sea for seventy years."
§ *Ibid.* 55–56; Isocrates, *Panegyricus* 101–109.
** Lysias 57.

theme of the funeral oration is not empire but hegemony.[37] More specifically, arche is called *hegemonia* and in support of Athens's domination the orators expound on the man; meets for which Athens is in the first rank of all cities.

So the funeral oration will henceforth be studied as "hegemonic speech." Without ever equaling the fastidious determination with which, in the *Panegyricus*, Isocrates concludes, by virtue of Athenian superiority, that Athens has the right to govern Greece, the epitaphioi, of which Lysias's oration is a perfect example, share the same point of view.* The history of Athens, champion of freedom and justice, provides them with a pretext for claiming the preeminence of the city over the other Greeks,† and they tirelessly list the innumerable acts of bravery performed by the Athenians‡ and set out the "proofs" of the city's superiority.§ Even if we suppose that the oration was not addressed directly to the Greeks, it must at least, by reminding the Athenians that they have always been preeminent in arete, have revived in them the courage necessary to lay claim to the first rank by arms.** In fact, for anyone who tries to reconstruct the history of the funeral oration, the speech does seem to have assumed these two functions successively.

The concrete, precise political purpose of Isocrates's orations has been contrasted with the empty literary variations of the official orators.[38] To do this is to forget that the first part of the *Panegyricus is* easily reduced to a sort of epitaphios.[39] During this first half of the speech, Isocrates is preoccupied with advocating the hegemony of Athens, and he would probably not have borrowed

* Isocrates, *Panegyricus* 20, 21, 22, 25, 37, 57, 66, 71, and so on.

† Lysias 47 ("everyone judged them worthy of hegemony over Greece"), 57, 59 (proof to the contrary: "when hegemony passed into the other camp"), 60.

‡ *Ibid.* 43.

§ Thucydides 2.39.2, 41.2, 41.4, 42.1; Lysias 28, 47, 63, 65; *Menexenus* 327c8 and d8, 237e5–6, 238a4, 244b1; Demosthenes 5.

** This is the meaning that Xenophon attributes to the praise of Athens (*Memorabilia* 3.5.8).

his form from the funeral oration if the epitaphioi had not already in the fifth century assumed a hegemonic function — even if only as a rhetorical *model*. Herodotus's and Thucydides's histories provide indirect proof: reconstructing the speech delivered by the Athenians at the debate at Sparta, Thucydides seems indeed to have drawn on the tradition of the funeral oration, just as Herodotus had for the speech of the Athenians at Plataea.[40] These examples are enough to attest to the vitality of the funeral oration, a paradigm of the *logos hēgemonikos*.

Of course, lacking any epitaphios dating from the Pentecontaetia, historians of the oration find themselves in a paradoxical situation, forced to deduce the model from its imitations; but this is not a sufficient reason to give up any attempt to locate the outlines of the hegemonic speech in Thucydides. As a presentation by Athenians of the power of Athens, the oration, while seeking to provide a basis for a superiority* and to bear witness to its grandeur,† never completely loses the character of a speech of glorification; of course, declaring that "our city deserves to be spoken of,"‡ the Athenians wish to encourage the Spartans and their allies to support the right side,§ but their formula also recalls that the funeral oration, Thucydides's model, is essentially a eulogy. Their oration is also similar to an epitaphios in that it presents a historical excursus: although the Athenians displayed the same reticence as Pericles toward mythical exploits and, like him, refused to refer to them,** they took good care not to omit an account of the Persian Wars, for, despite the familiarity of such a reference,†† and although the listeners were well acquainted with

---

* Thucydides 1.73.1.

† *Ibid.* 1.73.3: "What we shall say will have value . . . as testimony and as an indication you will thus see against which city . . . you will have to measure yourself."

‡ *Ibid.* 1.73.1: "Our city is worth talking about."

§ *Ibid.* 1.73.3.

** *Ibid.* 1.73.2: "Why should I speak to you of events in the remote past?"

†† *Ibid.*: "As for the Persian Wars . . . it must be rather tiresome to keep bringing them up."

the facts,* the recollection of this exploit represented, for the orator of the city, both an advantage and a necessity.† The function of the catalog of exploits is therefore perfectly clear here: although recalling the merits of Athens may convince the enemy that its hegemony is well founded and that its power is a real danger, the oration may well have obviated the need for a demonstration of strength, perhaps even for a war. It may even have silenced the enemy; proclaiming that their intention is not to engage in an argument,‡ the Athenians react to a given situation but also reveal the profound nature of the hegemonic oration, *a speech without a reply*, intended to arouse in its listeners both submission and respect. Thucydides's readers have not failed to observe that the coexistence of justification and threat within the same speech looks like a contradiction.[41] In fact, this contradiction, which is inherent in the very notion of hegemony — superiority exerted over equals — characterizes every catalog of exploits and is in no way peculiar to that page in Thucydides. The problem lies elsewhere, namely in the inevitable gap that emerges between the aim of the oration and its actual effect. It is unlikely that recalling the merits of the hegemonic city ever avoided a war, and in Sparta, as at the Kerameikos, the Athenians' oration was merely a monologue: the Spartans retired to deliberate, convinced of Athens's guilt,§ and from then on the enemy did the talking, whether for or against war.

But whatever doubts we may express concerning the actual effectiveness of the oration, the use made of it in the fifth century presupposes the existence of an other who needs to be convinced and conveys a certain confidence in the persuasive power of the logos. The situation was different in the fourth century: after the defeat of 404, Athens finally lost its hegemony, and the orators strove above all to be heard by their fellow citizens. So, while

* *Ibid.*: autoi xunistē.
† *Ibid.*: anankē legein (compare with Herodotus 9.27).
‡ Thucydides 1.73.1: *antilogia*.
§ *Ibid.* 1.79.2.

retaining the form and theme that had been dictated by its original destination, the funeral oration was now addressed above all
to the Athenians. Not that it gave up on effectiveness entirely:
Lysias's epitaphios certainly has many of the features of a symbouleutic narrative.

Let us pause for a moment and consider this oration, which
was probably delivered between 394 and 386 and which is first in
the chronology of fourth-century epitaphioi. With their tendency
to the hypercritical, nineteenth-century scholars challenged its
authenticity, but with arguments so feeble that they invalidated
the thesis they sought to establish.[42] Readers in Antiquity were
not so severe toward an oration whose eloquent peroration, at
least, they appreciated. Moreover, Isocrates's and Plato's many
imitations of this text in the *Panegyricus* and the *Menexenus* — obvious plagiarism in the first case, subtle parody in the second[43] —
strongly suggest its attribution to Lysias. Of course, two delicate
questions remain: was the oration ever delivered, and if so, by
whom?[44] But perhaps this is a false problem. If the metic Lysias
could not be entrusted with this official mission, there was no
law against his writing an epitaphios — for someone else to deliver or for his own greater glory in a prestigious genre.[45] Now,
although written orations, which were increasingly common in
the fourth century, much to Plato's indignation,* abandoned the
persuasiveness of living speech, they did not abandon any intention of influencing the public. So we shall finally render to Lysias
what is probably the work of Lysias and has in fact never ceased to
play this role. This being so, we have not wasted our time in a
pointless digression, since it was important to the demonstration
to base our argument on secure foundations. Far from regarding
Lysias's oration as a formal exercise, I shall regard it as a dated
document.

Composed during the Corinthian War, the epitaphios tries to
support the earliest attempts to reconstruct the empire by contrasting the brilliant image of Athenian arche with the somber

* Plato, *Phaedrus* 257e–258a.

description of Lacedaemonian hegemony.* In this context, it is true, the declaration that Athenian hegemony is well founded constitutes wishful thinking, a timeless, almost ornamental flourish, for it balances a passage dominated by regret for the past. This is not enough to deny it all effectiveness: is not the call to return to the past a central theme of Athenian politics in the fourth century? It can be viewed as a sign of malaise, but it was also the only argument capable of arousing the city's somewhat dampened ardor. Lysias's epitaphios belongs precisely to that narrow margin between repetition and renewal that characterized both the second maritime confederation and Demosthenes's political struggle or the final mobilization of Athenian forces in the siege of Lamia.

After 404, then, such were the limits of the hegemonic discourse, and such was also its effectiveness. Thus the claim of hegemony, which is purely symbolic after Chaironeia, recovers all its relevance in 322. Although Demosthenes's epitaphios is an admission of disaster† and is content to recall briefly the vanished days of Athenian superiority,‡ the slogan *eleutheria kai hēgemonia* is not an empty one in Hyperides's oration,§ at a time when the demos was reminding the Greek cities that, as in the past, Athens would do her duty "for the salvation of the whole of Greece,"** in the name of a better future.[46]††

Between these high points of Athenian history in 392, 338, and 322, the gaps in the corpus do not allow us to reconstruct a consistent history of the hegemonic theme in the funeral oration. Perhaps the backward-looking topos often made a stronger impression than the exhortation to action. But however incomplete it

* Lysias 56–57 (Athenian arche); 59 (Lacedaemonian hegemony).

† Demosthenes 23–24.

‡ *Ibid.* 10 and 24.

§ Hyperides 10–11, 14, 16, 19, 24–26.

** Cf. Diodorus 18.10.3.

†† Hyperides 14: "On the foundations laid by Leosthenes the men of today are striving to build the work of the future."

may be, the corpus reminds us that between these two sides of the same policy there is balance, even coexistence.

The hegemony of Athens for the freedom of all the Greeks: against all the lessons of experience, but also and above all against Spartan propaganda, which turned 403 into year 1 of Greek freedom, this theme had a difficult time in the funeral oration. So certain historians, sensitive to the constant repetition of the formula *eleutheria tōn Hellēnōn*, have sought to attribute to the oration effectiveness in the propaganda campaign for the Hellenic union. If Georges Mathieu is to be believed, Lysias's epitaphios, "though written on the occasion of a war between Greeks and intended above all to praise Athens, in line with the rules of the genre . . . is inspired by a feeling for Greek unity."[47] Others have regarded the *Menexenus* as a pamphlet written in favor of that unity.[48] Last, we must examine Isocrates's use of the funeral oration in the *Panegyricus*, without forgetting the Panhellenic character traditionally attributed to Gorgias's epitaphios,* written in the late fifth or early fourth century — and this last hypothesis, though rarely advanced, seems to be more satisfying, for at this time the union of the Greeks was evoked in many of the orations.

But it is not easy to turn an epitaphios into a Panhellenic speech, for the two logoi are quite separate, as much through the circumstances in which they took place as through the orator who delivered them. The first was spoken by an Athenian politician at the end of a year of war between Greeks, the second by a cosmopolitan individual, a Sophist or rhetor, on the occasion of a Panhellenic truce;[49] and the exaltation of Athenian difference hardly lends itself to the advocacy of the sacred union. It has rightly been stressed that the theme of the services rendered by Athens to Greece was simply a mask for Athenian nationalism.[50] This might not be a conclusive argument, for it is of the very essence of Panhellenism to seek to graft the union of the Greeks onto the hegemony of one city.[51] But after all, it may well have been an impossible task to reconcile in

* DK B 5 b (Philostratus, *Life of the Sophists* 1.9.5).

the same speech an appeal to concord and the systematic denigration of "the others," who were inferior by nature.

Philostratus praises the skill of Gorgias, who, while developing in the epitaphios the same themes as in the *Olympicus*, avoids using the word "concord" between the Greeks;* but over and above the Sophist's talent, this silence reveals the incompatibility between the funeral oration and Panhellenism. Either one writes an epitaphios, in which case one must proscribe the term *homonoia*, or one has Panhellenic intentions, in which case one must subvert the traditional themes of the funeral oration, which is transformed into a threnos on the wars between Greeks.[52]

Furthermore, the Sophist could allow himself certain liberties with an Athenian genre. Lysias's epitaphios is a better illustration of the necessary limits of "Greek patriotism" in the funeral oration: the orator praises the Athenians for being able to give up their former enmities and to run to the assistance of the Corinthians. But it would be pointless to seek in that statement anything other than a polemic against Sparta, whose selfishness accentuates the eternal generosity of the Athenians† and justifies in advance the struggle against Greeks in the name of the freedom of those same Greeks,‡ referred to in terms very similar to those of the *Menexenus*. By the same token, this resemblance encourages us to doubt the supposed originality of the epitaphios delivered by Socrates, and it is hardly surprising that the advocates of the Panhellenic significance of the *Menexenus* feel a certain embarrassment when confronted by this dialogue. As a hymn to Greek freedom, it is no more than a pastiche of Lysias's epitaphios,§ and the *Menexenus* might therefore be read as an ordinary epitaphios were Plato's intentions not revealed in the irony with which he pushes the topoi of the oration to the point of absurdity.

Finally, a study of the *Panegyricus* illustrates the limits and

* *Ibid.*
† Lysias 67.
‡ *Ibid.* 68.
§ *Menexenus* 242a7, 242b6–7, 243a.

difficulties of a Panhellenic use of the funeral oration; employing quite naturally a sort of epitaphios to claim the hegemony of Athens, Isocrates is forced to abandon this form as soon as he advocates a sharing of power between Athens and Sparta. Thus the text, which juxtaposes epitaphios and Panhellenic speech, has a clearly composite character, the two elements being linked together only by one of those palinodes in which Isocrates specialized:* the same words change meaning from one part to the other, the "we" referring to the Athenians in the "epitaphios" and to the Greeks in the "Panhellenic speech," and it may be that neither the funeral oration nor Panhellenism gains much at the orator's hands. Isocrates's palinode should probably not mislead us: as an Athenian speech the *Panegyricus* is intended to be read by Athenians, and Isocrates turns out to be less concerned with the future of Greece than with that of the city. In this sense, the Panhellenic speech is merely a camouflage for the hegemonic speech.[53] But, conversely, what in spite of everything is Hellenic in the *Panegyricus* alters from the beginning the epitaphios-like themes used in it. We can compare Isocrates's text with Pericles's epitaphios, but in addition to the resemblances we must stress the profound difference in inspiration between the two speeches whereas Pericles praises the demokratia,† Isocrates exalts the ancient politeia established by the original Athenians;‡ and far from offering the democratic system as a universal model, he attributes to Athens the creation of the first constitution, an undifferentiated matrix from which every political form may emerge. Pericles sees the civic festivities as the necessary compensation for the labors of the exemplary city,§ while Isocrates turns Athens into a permanent *panēguris,*** that is, the seat of a perpetual Panhellenic ceremony.††

* Isocrates, *Panegyricus* 128–29.
† Thucydides 2.37.1.
‡ Isocrates, *Panegyricus* 39.
§ Thucydides 2.38.1.
** Isocrates, *Panegyricus* 46.
†† *Ibid.* 44.

And although for the rhetor Athens is above all else a benefactor, for the politician she is a warrior whose first aim is to be imitated; proposing Athens as a model, Pericles insists on its uniqueness, whereas Isocrates turns it into a symbol, the focal point of all Hellenism and all civilization.

A war speech cannot with impunity be transformed into one of those harangues on peace so dear to the fourth century. Conversely, the funeral oration can be made to serve Panhellenic propaganda only by being linked with the requirements of Athenian nationalism: as a warrior community, the city of the epitaphioi may lay claim to the honor of fighting for the salvation and freedom of the Greeks, but on the express condition that it occupies pride of place in that struggle — like the Homeric heroes, the Athenians fought *en promachois*.

Thus from its birth the funeral oration bears the mark of the agonistic spirit that in the fifth century characterized relations between Athens and the other important cities and to which the work of Herodotus bears witness.

The agonistic coloring of the oration is, then, merely the last but not the least aspect of this complex relationship that Athens maintains with the others and that is reflected in the funeral oration's becoming a strategy, that is, a means of approaching the enemy from a distance.[54] The funeral oration corresponds to a certain vision of the world of the cities, dominated by both *isotēs* and *eris* (equality and rivalry).[55] It was a world in which equality ought to reign, for by right each polis was as worthy as another, and the struggle for superiority acknowledged no precedence among any; referring to the others uniformly as *hoi alloi*, the oration does not seem to distinguish between great and small, just as Herodotus found it quite natural to compare the Athenians with the Tegeates. But in fact a hierarchy of power had grown up, and in the funeral oration Athens isolated a few cities in order to compare them with herself; for eris, which sets equal against equal,*

---

* Hesiod, *Works and Days* 24–26.

141

also presupposes that the adversaries are worthy to confront each other.[56]

By referring to war constantly as an agon,* the funeral oration bears the trace of that struggle for prestige, and when he makes the Lacedaemonians the *antagōnistai* of the Athenians,† Isocrates is not really innovating but simply developing what existed in the epitaphioi, explicitly or implicitly. The funeral oration consistently gives a name to the antagonist: Sparta. And if there is a locus proper to that opposition between the two "model cities" that has always structured and continues to structure any reading of classical Greek history,[57] the funeral oration is that locus — or one of them. We are familiar with the role played in Pericles's epitaphios by the opposition between Sparta and Athens,[58] which is tacit at first, then is made more explicit when the orator turns to the chapter on war — only at that moment is the adversary named.[59]‡ But to see this agon, which actually existed in 430, simply as a theme based on circumstance would be to misunderstand the astonishing persistence of the agonistic motif throughout the history of the genre. Although Demosthenes and Hyperides no longer name an antagonist that has all too obviously withdrawn from the fray, works close to the funeral oration, such as those of Lycurgus and Isocrates, have no such scruples. The account of the Persian Wars in *Against Leocrates* is dominated by eris, as if the symbolic rivalry, projected into the past, assumed even greater importance once the actual historical situation was less suitable ground for an agon.§ As for the *Panathenaicus*, it presents a critique of Sparta and its legend that has been regarded as the most comprehensive in all of Greek literature.[60] Like the authors of the epitaphioi, the orator tries to

* *Agōn:* Thucydides 2.42.1 and 45.1; Lysias 55; Demosthenes 20 and 25 (cf. 30). *Agonizomai:* Lysias 34; Hyperides 17, 18, 19, 20, 23, 38. *Synagonistai:* Hyperides 24 and 39.

† Isocrates, *Panegyricus* 73 and 85; cf. 91.

‡ Thucydides 2.39: from "our opponents" (1), there is a transition to "Lacedaemonians" (2).

§ Lycurgus, *Against Leocrates* 108.

glorify Athens at the expense of Sparta. This approach is not new: it had already been well used in the fifth century, and Isocrates himself made abundant use of it in the *Panegyricus*. But in 380, as in 430, the ideological struggle against the Lacedaemonians, Athens's principal adversaries or the possessors of hegemony, derived from a precise political point of view: is the anti-Lacedaemonian orientation of Athenian politics around 340 enough to explain the resolutely agonistic character of the *Panathenaicus*?[61] In fact, the oration had its reasons, which at this point were essentially rhetorical; declaring that praise is best set off against a background of comparison, Isocrates treats the agon as a rule or device of praise; if you want to praise a city, you must compare it with a worthy rival.* Thus an opposition that was born out of struggle is emptied of meaning to the point of becoming a literary device.

Perhaps the theme of the agon revealed a secret strategic weakness from the outset. Indeed it seems that Athens could best establish her identity only by proclaiming her superiority on the very terrain on which the Spartans had established their own: that of war, and land-based war at that. If, confronting the Lacedaemonians, whom the whole of Greece recognizes as *andreiotatoi* (the bravest),† the Athenians win the prize for bravery,‡ their superiority is unchallengeable. Before being taken up and developed by Lycurgus or Isocrates,§ this syllogistic reasoning was widely used in the fifth century and especially during the Peloponnesian War. This is how, in the *Heraclidae*, Euripides tries to persuade the Athenians that they are the strongest people on earth;[62] and Pericles's epitaphios is, as we have seen, dominated by this agon, in which Athens will easily be a match for the Lacedaemonians, the journeymen of the art of war.** We still do not know, however, if any audience was convinced by these passages; where propaganda

* Isocrates, *Panathenaicus* 39–40; cf. *Panegyricus* 73.

† Lycurgus, *Against Leocrates* 105.

‡ Isocrates, *Panegyricus* 72.

§ Lycurgus, *Against Leocrates* 105; Isocrates, *Panathenaicus* 175.

** Thucydides 2.39.

is concerned, only effectiveness counts, which would easily make up for the hazardous character of the syllogism. If we are to judge by the incredulity with which the Greeks learned that at Sphacteria homoioi had surrendered to Athenian troops,* we can only conclude that no Athenian propaganda was enough to undermine the reputation of the Spartan hoplites.† Once more, then, it is likely that the evocation of the agon with Sparta served only to galvanize Athenian energies — more than once — and to flatter the city's self-esteem. In venturing onto the other's terrain, one is using a double-edged weapon: at best, one convinces oneself and forgets the real disproportion of the forces involved; at worst, one is content with an imaginary victory that can always conceal a secret fascination with one's opponent's merits.

To convince others and to convince oneself: these two aims do not necessarily overlap, and more than one study of the epitaphioi has revealed the vanity of the hegemonic ambitions of which the funeral oration bears the trace. Confronted by the lesson of the facts as well as by its own logic as an agonistic speech, the funeral oration probably never found a better public than the Athenians to whom it was addressed. Such, no doubt, is the inevitable fate of any agonistic strategy. However, this study of the epitaphioi is not therefore useless, for it reveals the paradoxical continuity of Athenian foreign policy: never overtly imperialist, incapable of being truly Panhellenic, but always eloquent when exalting the primacy of Athens, the funeral oration becomes the faithful echo of the same single policy to which the city never ceased to declare its attachment, even against the current.

From hegemony to hegemonic dreams: the funeral oration was ready to assume the role bequeathed by the vicissitudes of the fourth century, that of an educator, constantly reminding the citizens that their patriotism must serve the superiority, past and future, of the hegemonic city.

* *Ibid.* 4.40.
† Cf. Euripides, *Andromache* 724–26.

The *"Fine Death"* or the Impossible Development
of a Bios Politikos

At once a eulogy of worthy men, an honor accorded the dead, and a stock of instructive examples,* the funeral oration is, both for Lysias and for Pericles, a lesson in civic morality intended for the living.† It is a one-dimensional lesson in which the virtue of the citizen is canceled out by the valor of the soldier, in which military activity is offered as a model for civic practice. This strict ethic is suggestive of the original time of the hoplitic phalanx rather than a reflection of the military organization of Athens in the fifth century, based as it was on the political organization of the city.[63] In this first discrepancy, which is essential to the oration, one might discern the irreducible gap that any society maintains between its material structures and its official, systematized values. But when, in the fourth century, the development of professionalism profoundly altered the old equivalence between soldier and citizen, the gap ran the risk of becoming a flagrant anachronism. Because it was so completely bound up with the city, the funeral oration could not entirely ignore these problems. The following paragraphs try to chart the proper course of the oration between the fixity of a conservative form and the innovations found in certain epitaphioi.

The aim of Pericles's exhortation or of Adrastus's speech in *The Suppliant Women* is to urge the survivors to accept the same fate as the citizens being eulogized. This amounts to exhorting the citizens to die for the city, whatever euphemisms are used to disguise the appeal.‡ Is the eulogy addressed to death? This is how Dionysius

---

* Lysias 3: The Athenians' exploits are commemorated "by words in the eulogies of men of courage, by the honors conferred upon them on such occasions as this, by the lessons to be found for the living in the exploits of the dead."

† Thucydides 2.42.1: *didaskalia*; cf. Euripides, *Suppliant Women* 914.

‡ Thucydides 2.41.5: "Every one of us who has survived would naturally exhaust himself in her service." Compare with 2.42.4 (*pathein*) and with the epigram of the Argives at Tanagra (*pentho[s d'etlasan]*), Meiggs-Lewis 35.

of Halicarnassus understood it, when he contrasted the Roman laudatio funebris that crowned a fine life with the Athenian funeral oration that places arete in death.[64]* I do not intend to say much about the very real relevance of Dionysius's observations on the laudatio funebris. It is true that the Romans honored the living man in the dead, even when they borrowed the formulas of the funeral oration. Thus, when delivering the funeral oration for the soldiers of the legion of Mars, Cicero applied the Athenian oration to ends that were quite obviously alien to it — but Rome can serve only as a counterexample here.[65]† So, without following Dionysius of Halicarnassus in his search for the best funeral oration, we shall take him as a guide in the study of the epitaphioi, for despite his partiality he did perceive the paradoxical aim of the Athenian speech to the dead: the city celebrates the citizen only because he is dead; only then has he shown the valor and merit that are attributed posthumously to him in the formula *anēr agathos genomenos*, which is endlessly repeated in the epitaphioi.

In linking arete, the "verbal noun" of which the phrase *agathon gignesthai* is merely an elaborate formula,[66] with military behavior, the funeral oration places itself in a very ancient hoplitic tradition of which Tyrtaeus was the poet, and a number of resemblances have been found between individual epitaphioi and particular elegies by Tyrtaeus.[67] In characterizing military valor, the term *anēr agathos genomenos* can easily come to refer to death in battle. Not every death, however: although death must be as natural for the warrior as the rays of the sun,§ hoplitic morality ordains that it should be accepted and not sought. Herodotus's

* Dionysius of Halicarnassus, *Roman Antiquities* 5.17.5–6.

† Cicero, *Fourteenth Philippic* 25–35.

‡ For the formula in the strict sense, see, for example, Tyrtaeus 9 D 10 and 20: *anēr agathos gignetai en tōi polemōi*. For more exact comparisons, see Tyrtaeus 9 D 28–33 (Gorgias); 6 D 6 (Hyperides 3), 9 D 32 (*ibid.* 34), 9 D 29–30 (*ibid.* 27), 9 D 27 and 41–42 (*ibid.* 31). Finally, Lysias 24 seems like a transcription into prose of elegies 6 and 7.

§ Tyrtaeus 8 D 4.

anecdote concerning Aristodamus, the best Spartan warrior at Plataea but deprived of honors by his fellow citizens because he quite obviously aspired to death, is proof of this.* In all the Greek cities, this term is applied to the "fine death,"† to the sacrifice accepted by the citizen: the epigram of Thermopylae refers to the dead as *agathoi*,‡ and this designation seems to be a technical term in the funerary inscription of Thasos;[68] but at Athens, in and through the funeral oration, it assumes unparalleled breadth of reference. It is no accident that Aristotle, expressing an idea similar to the one developed by Phaedrus in the *Symposium*, considers the "fine death" to be the central theme of any eulogy.§

Thus, in according the supreme praise only to the dead, the city is more demanding of its members than the epic or aristocratic ethic was of the noble. Of course, in Homer or Pindar honors are heaped on a fine death, but death is not the only source of all valor. Pindar prefers athletic achievements to military ones, and when he celebrates the "hurricane of battle," the poet does not attribute less valor to the living than to the dead warrior.** Similarly, accepting the dangerous existence of the combatant, the Homeric hero also — indeed primarily — chooses a life in which, he knows, substantial benefits will go hand in hand with risks, in which *geras* is no less important than *kleos*.[69]†† It is true that he owes it to his arete to lead such a life; but this valor, the attribute of an elite, has already been acquired and will merely be confirmed by further deeds. The Homeric hero *is agathos*. On the other hand, the term *agathon gignesthai* implies that the citizen's arete is not an immanent quality. In a city, no one is an aner

* Herodotus 9.71 (Aristodamus is in a state of *lyssa*).

† *Thanatos kalos, kalos teleutan,* or *apothneiskein:* see *Menexenus* 246d2, Demosthenes 1.26 and 27; Hyperides 27.

‡ Diodorus 11.6.1. 6: *andres agathoi*.

§ Plato, *Symposium* 179a–b; Aristotle, *Rhetoric* 1.3.1359a5.

** Pindar, *Isthmians* 7.25ff.

†† *Iliad* 12.310–21. Compare with Lysias 14: "Without expecting any other benefit [*kerdos*] than glory."

agathos by essence; he must become it. This is already apparent in Tyrtaeus's elegies and in Simonides's famous ode to Scopas,[70] but without reducing all valor to a fine death: although he sings of the agathoi of Thermopylae, Simonides is well aware of the cost of a more positive arete, which finds its field of action in the city, and though exalting the greatness of the warrior who falls in battle, Tyrtaeus refuses the valorous survivor neither glory nor honors.[71]* In its extremism, the funeral oration goes much further than this: if, as a passage in Hyperides's epitaphios suggests,† one is truly an *anēr* only in death,[72] a fine death has all the characteristics of an initiation — a fearful initiation in which death no longer has anything symbolic about it, in which *thanatos is* a transition but also a beginning and end, in which one is born into a new status only by renouncing forever he condition of the living creature.

However, we must not look to the epitaphioi for a romanticism of annihilation The funeral oration is immune to aesthetic giddiness; it knows nothing of the "black death" or of the glorious pathos that Tyrtaeus associates with the fall of the young combatant.[73] By a "fine death" is meant a glorious death, and the lesson of the oration is summed up in an austere precept of civic morality: "the idea that a man who has died bravely has done everything that may be expected of him";[74] he has "his share, the finest of all," as Pericles puts it.‡ Reared by the city, he has given proof of the reason for its existence;§ he has also, in a more immediate sense, defended freedom.

But what confers on the citizen's death its eminent valor does not belong to the order of actions or deeds: in the epitaphioi, the action is effaced, as is the very fact of death of which *andres agathoi genomenoi is* an elliptical euphemism. Declaring that memory

---

* Tyrtaeus 9 D 35–42. Cf. Callinus 1 D 19.

† Hyperides 29: "Once, in their childhood, they were devoid of reason; now they have become men of heart [*nun de andres agathoi gegonasi*]."

‡ Thucydides 2.43.1.

§ *Ibid.* 2.41.5.

"is to be attached more to the decision than to the act of the dead," Pericles shows that the essential thing lies not in the ergon but in the intention that motivates it.[75]* So the hierarchy of civic values must be assumed by each citizen, deciding in a lucid act of will that happiness lies in freedom, and freedom in courage.† Such a formulation belongs to a long civic tradition, apparent in the early fifth century in the epitaph of the Tegeates, praised for wanting to leave their children a free city,‡ in terms that are taken up again by all the epitaphioi.§ The eulogy, then, is addressed above all to a will, which is a choice: the dead have chosen between their lives — always reduced to the physiological dimension** — and the city. This decision is particularly developed in Plato, since it gives rise to a prosopopoeia of the dead, which serves as an exhortation;†† but the theme itself appears to be essential to the funeral oration: each orator devotes a special passage to it, marked by a more elaborate style. Thucydides makes it the most important element in the eulogy of the citizens.*** In Lysias's epitaphios, the decision to die is the linchpin of the account of Marathon, the first "historical" exploit.[76]† In Demosthenes, the mythological excursus of the Eponyms, generally regarded as a strange innovation, is primarily a way of treating this central theme.‡ Gorgias's fragment of an epitaphios is also ordered around a decision,§ which becomes

* *Ibid.* 2.43.3.

† *Ibid.* 2.43.4.

‡ *Anthologia Palatina* 7.512: *boulonto*.

§ *Boulomai*: Thucydides 2.42.4; Lysias 62; Demosthenes 1. *Hairoumai*: Lysias 62; *Menexenus* 246d2; Demosthenes 26, 28, 37; Hyperides 3 (*proairesis*), 40. *Ethelō*: Demosthenes 27, 37; Hyperides 15.

** *Sōma*: Thucydides 2.43.2; Demosthenes 27; Hyperides 15. *Psuchē*: Lysias 24; Demosthenes 28. *Bios*: Lysias 71; Hyperides 26.

†† *Menexenus* 246d1–248d6.

‡‡ Thucydides 2.42.2–4.

§§ Lysias 24–26.

*** Demosthenes 27–31.

††† Gorgias DK, B 6, p. 285, 1. 7: *prokrinontes*.

an acceptance of combat, and therefore of death. Finally, Hyperides's epitaphios is nothing other than the eulogy of a determination that he calls *proairesis*,* the active decision that for his contemporary Aristotle becomes the central concept of ethical reflection.[77]†

Proairesis, to borrow a term that, though much later, corresponds perfectly to its object, is therefore a positive value, whose importance is manifested not only in catastrophic situations or in accounts of defeat, as Demosthenes's epitaphios and Diodorus's passage on Thermopylae might lead one to believe.‡ Indeed, it is to this determination to die that the Athenians, if Lysias's epitaphios is to be believed, owed the victory of Marathon, because, "without reasoning on the dangers of war, they were convinced that a glorious death leaves behind one the eternal renown that is associated with valor."§

Thus, opposed to the reasoning that weighs the danger, the decision is immediate and as if innate in each Athenian. But we must be quite clear what the words mean. This decision is not the action of a subject endowed with a "power of self-determination that is proper to him"; It is not a private opinion, but rather the combatant's personal acceptance of a social imperative.[78] What the citizen-soldier finds in himself is the civic norm (*nomizontes*), a sense of the community — hence the unanimous enthusiasm that drove the small troop of Athenians to confront much greater numbers. So it is hardly surprising that, when characterizing this decision, fourth-century orators such as Demosthenes, Hyperides, and Lycurgus tend to resort more to *ethelō* than to *boulomai*.** This linguistic reference may be seen as a significant choice

* Hyperides 3.40.

† See Aristotle, *Nicomachean Ethics* 1111b5ff.

‡ Diodorus, 11.11.2 (the valor of the combatants must be judged, not by results, but by their *proairesis*).

§ Lysias 23–24.

** To the examples cited in n. § on p. 149 might be added Lycurgus, *Against Leocrates* 107.

— a choice of consent against inclination, of the will of reason against the will of impulse — involving a whole conception of the actual share the subject assumes in his decision. The lesson is clear: at this crucial moment of the *krisis* in which the Athenian renounces life, it is the city that decides through him.

In fact, like that of Herakles, the favorite theme of the classical period,[79] the choice of the Athenian in the funeral oration is determined through and through by agencies external to the subject: trained to acquiesce in the values of the city, to cherish *kalon* and to avoid *aischron*, could the citizen hesitate when the alternative offered was between *kalos* and *mē kalos*?* It does not matter that on the positive side there was death; this is what the funeral oration endlessly repeats. Aristotle, in his treatment of the epideictic genre, sums up the spirit of the oration thus: "Those acts that one does not perform with self in mind are beautiful or at least preferable [*haireta*]; those that one performs for one's country, in contempt of one's own interest, are absolutely good."†

This choice must be renewed before any battle. Thus Herodotus regards as superior to the others Themistocles's speech, which, exhorting the Greeks before Salamis, begins by setting up a sort of balance sheet in which good is contrasted with evil, and concludes that it is necessary to choose the better.‡ Herodotus elucidates the funeral oration perfectly, since, for the historian as for the orators, all morality is based on these conventional criteria that are the values of the city.[80] As in the epitaphioi, any account of battle is preceded by a decision, always the same but nevertheless always memorable: that of Leonidas at Thermopylae dominates the description of the battle, and that of Callimachus of Aphidna leads into the Athenians' victory at Marathon. Of course, Leonidas is a king and Callimachus a polemarch: but these titles, far from making them exceptions, make them authentic representatives of their city, whose fate reflects that of all the Spartan or Athenian citizen-

---

* Plato, *Menexenus* 246d2.

† Aristotle, *Rhetoric* 1.9.1366b35–38.

‡ Herodotus 8.83.

soldiers. Just as each combatant must make his own decision to die, so the decision to join battle rests on them alone: Leonidas chose for the Spartans; and Callimachus, the eleventh symbolic person, cast the decisive vote in a debate in which the strategoi were divided.* However, in each case, the alternative is presented to the warrior *from the outside*: it is an oracle that incites Leonidas to choose, or rather to accept, death,† and Miltiades plays a similar role for Callimachus, weighing the pros and cons before leaving the polemarch face-to-face with his choice.[81]‡ In battle, each will die *anēr genomenos agathos*,§ the death of the citizen-soldier.

Thus, from the histories to the epitaphioi and from great men to combatants in the ranks, the fine death is the model of a civic choice that is both free and determined. The funeral oration ignores the exemplary characters that the historian was happy to isolate in the solitude of their decision; but to all the anonymous dead it attributes the same choice and the same end, so that their example may inspire emulation among the survivors;** it must remind the Athenian citizens that a glorious death distinguishes a man from the rest of humanity, which awaits its fate passively.†† So the verb *apothnēiskein* is kept for a death that is submitted to,‡‡ as opposed to the death of the andres agathoi, in which the element of chance has been reduced as far as possible.[82]

However, the Athenian public is given a hard lesson here, for in this traditional representation of the fine death, the citizen is totally dispossessed of himself. It is as if, in the funeral oration,

* *Ibid*. 6.109.19: "There are ten of us strategoi and we all hold different opinions [*dicha*]."
† *Ibid*. 7.220.
‡ *Ibid*. 6.109.25–26.
§ *Ibid*. 6.114 and 7.224.
** Thucydides 2.43.4.
†† Lysias 79.
‡‡ Lysias 24: "It fell to them, they thought, to share death [*apothanein*] with all men but to be valorous [*agathois einai*] with the few."

the city were trying to deprive the existence of each citizen of any meaning, reducing it — as we have seen — simply to its biological dimension. From this fact, the gap is widened between the reality of hoplitic combat, in which the life of the citizen is the most valuable of assets,[83] and the orations at the Kerameikos, which, in the manner of Tyrtaeus,* urge the citizens not to spare their lives, perceived, in the final flash of the decision, as alien assets.† It is in the abandonment of self that one becomes an aner agathos, as if all that one possessed were one's death.

Thus, in its most official expression, Athenian patriotism may be reduced to the ideal of devotion, and we would do well to refrain from deciding if submission to the city or the modern alienation of the state is the more restrictive imperative. So I would not accept without reservations Yvon Garlan's views on the essentially realistic character of patriotism in the ancient world.[84] Of course, the citizen-soldier certainly saw the defense of his family or property as "the visible, immediate purpose of the combat," and, by linking paternity and military valor so closely together,[85] the city admits that ardor in battle is nourished by private interests; but at the solemn hour of the collective funeral, the funeral oration offers the citizen no other family but the city, no other land but one's country.[86]

In short, the aner agathos is denied his uniqueness but is nevertheless glorious, dead to the life of mortals but still living in men's memories; and, like the epitaph of Potidaea,‡ the epitaphioi contrast the loss of the body with the attainment of eternal glory for each individual.§ This renown is conferred by a speech in which the names of the dead have been replaced by a

* Tyrtaeus 6–7 D, vv. 14 and 18; 8 D, v. 5. Compare with Lysias 25 and Demosthenes 27.
† Lysias 24: *psuchē allotria.*
‡ *GV* 20 (= *IG*, I², 945), 11–12: "Putting their life [*psuchē*] in the balance, they exchanged it for valor [*aretē*]."
§ Thucydides 2.43.2; cf. also *ibid.* 3. Lysias 24, 79, 81. Demosthenes 28, 32, 36. Hyperides 25, 42. Gorgias, DK, B 6, 1.5; ll. 16–17.

list of Athenian exploits: the agent has truly disappeared in his act.

So in an epitaphios there is no praise of the lives of the citizens; what is praised in them is always the proairesis, that is, ultimately, the fine death. It seems, then, that although there is a civic death, the oration rejects any introduction of a "citizen's life," just as fifth-century history, that other civic genre, rejects biography.[87] "Reared in the virtues of the ancestors, they knew upon becoming men [andres genomenoi] how to preserve that inheritance of glory and to show their own valor."* This brief summary of the normal career of the citizen is edifying, for the phrase that characterized the attainment of manhood is very close to the one that designates death.[88] So we can now understand the importance that the eulogy had in the city: the dead had no other life than that of Athens. The indispensable passage on autochthony stood for place of birth, the eulogy of the politeia replaced upbringing, and the deeds of their ancestors replaced their own action, since their own exploits were rarely discussed in a separate passage.[89] *There is no life but that of the city.*

However, certain epitaphioi seem to reveal an effort to constitute, even within the immutable genre of the funeral oration, the category of a properly civic way of life, of which the oration was the eulogy; they did not diminish the fine death, but saw it as the necessary culmination of a fine life. Of course, these attempts seem destined to remain isolated in a genre that does not readily lend itself to them. But they correspond very well to two moments in the history of the city, reflecting successively the Sophists' questioning of the "old Athenian upbringing" so dear to Aristophanes and the hypertrophy of private values proper to the fourth century.[90]†

So we shall try to retrace the history of these innovations, without concealing the fact that such a history goes hand in hand with the constant reminder of the permanence of the

* Lysias 69.
† Aristophanes, *Clouds* 961.

most traditional values. The ultimately conservative character of the funeral oration is all the more remarkable in that, in everyday political practice, the city took care — and had done so for a long time — not to confine arete to the sphere of war. Of course, the official texts do not, like the private epitaphs exalting a *chrēstē gunē*, go so far as to attribute arete to women;[91] but the term *andres agathoi* is in no sense reserved for the dead. Although in the late fifth and the fourth century, some public or private inscriptions persist in giving this term its military sense, the decrees of the demos reflect a much more realistic conception of valor, which they identify with *euergesia*, and henceforth apply the term *andres agathoi* to the living — proxenoi or citizens, *euergetai* who often showed their benevolence toward the city without going so far as to sacrifice their lives for it.[92*] In their own way, the literary works testify to this evolution; the title of *anēr agathos*, which Herodotus reserves for glorious combatants, is applied in Thucydides to any virtuous citizen, even to any good man.[93] But what future was there for new representations in so traditionalist a genre as the funeral oration?

Perhaps it was left to the Sophists to try to alter the funeral oration. When praising the dead, Gorgias refers to them as *andres*, men who were fully men.[†] The use of military topoi and the distinction, maintained throughout the fragment, between *anthrōpos* and *anēr* suggest at first the virile sense of the term "warriors." But the warrior virtues seem to be particularly conventional in Gorgias, for when evoking them, the Sophist uses stereotyped formulas that contrast with the stylistic innovations of the beginning of the fragment, where the topoi have been reworked to the point of seeming to some to be the expression of original thought. Without taking a position with regard to this "originality,"[94] I will simply note that

---

* For example, *IG,* I², 59, 9 (427–26); *IG,* I², 103, 7–8 (412–11); *Sylloge*³, 108, 6 (410–409). Compare with Andocides 2.18; Lysias, *Against Agoratos* 63; Aeschines, *Against Timarchus* 118.

† DK, 82 B 6: *andrasi.*

Gorgias's aner is not to be reduced entirely to the classical type of
the Athenian citizen-soldier. If *ekektento ... tēn aretēn* really means
simply, as most commentators think,[95] "they *had* a divine gift,
valor," are we to understand that for the Sophist valor may exist
before death? Other factors might suggest such an interpretation.
To begin with, the Sophist attributes to the men who had died qualities that were traditionally presented as Athenian, of course, but
that the orators usually attributed either to the Athenians of the
past or to the living. Respect for the unwritten law, a happy combination of doing and saying, benevolence toward the weak, a love of
justice, and other civic attitudes are seen here as proper to those
andres. Last, praising the dead for having often (*polla*) preferred
benevolence to rigor and the correctness of reasoning to the decision of the law, Gorgias exalts a form of behavior that resembles at
least as much the choice of way of life as the decision to die. Reconciling in them the traditional qualities of the city and the criteria
of existence proper to the Athenian elite,[96] Gorgias's Athenians are
exemplary as much in their lives as in their deaths.

But the Sophist does not go any further and preserves the
essential features of the civic representations. This collective portrait, made up of an accumulation of pure social virtues, never
renounces the values of the community — which is the basis of
Plato's criticism of it, as he reverses one of the formulas of the
epitaphios to accuse the orators of neglecting individuality.*

Such a reproach cannot of course be directed at Euripides,
who, in The Suppliant Women, has Adrastus deliver several eulogies in the form of a funeral oration. But it would be pointless to
see this as a criticism of the collective eulogy.[97] This transformation was made necessary by the close bond between tragedy
and the mythical universe in which only unique personalities
emerge; but those portraits that give the heroes of epic such a
curious image quite simply reflect "those virtues that are most
indispensable to the greatness of Athens and to the normal functioning of its democratic institutions.[98] They are types of citi-

* *Menexenus* 235a1.

zens or metics,* and are all characterized by their relations to a polis,†with the exception of Tydaeus, who is presented as a specialist in war. This was no doubt a highly significant exception within a eulogy of the civic virtues and has been seen as an ancestor of the debate on ways of life. Are we to understand that Euripides is criticizing the value placed on the fine death as a criterion for all merit? There can be no doubt that we must see in these civic, peaceful portraits a polemical intention against Aeschylean tragedy, which, in *Seven Against Thebes*, represented the same heroes as purely military.[99] But beyond poetic eris, the criticism becomes more general, and in a tragedy that, while comprising a battle, condemns the very principle of war, Euripides seems to be protesting against the meaning that the epitaphioi give to the expression *anēr agathos*. From the outset, Theseus has rejected any account of exploits,‡ urging Adrastus to present the dead only in terms of their past lives. The "fine death" is treated no better; the death of Evadne, which must be regarded as a pure suicide, not a useful end like that of Macaria in the *Heraclidae*, may well be a caricature. Evadne may exalt her own glory and valor, but the chorus — integrated from this point on into the civic world — sees nothing but horror in this useless exploit.§

However, one does not easily attack the values of the funeral oration, and Euripides's ambiguous position is revealed in all its complexity in the conclusion he attributes to Adrastus. After describing the life led by his companions in time of peace, Adrastus declares, in a phrase whose Sophistic aspect has been noted,[100] that it is possible to teach courage.** Every epitaphios no doubt sets out to be a lesson in courage and civic devotion, and on this

---

* *Suppliant Women* 892 (Parthenopaeus as exemplary metic).

† *Ibid.* 871 (Capaneus), 878–79 (Eteoclus), 887 (Hippomedon), 893 and 897 (Parthenopaeus).

‡ *Ibid.* 846–56.

§ *Ibid.* 1072 (*deinon*); note also the ambiguity of *ekbaccheusamena* (1001).

** *Ibid.* 913–14 (*hē euandria didaktos*) and 917. One might add that Hippomedon's eulogy (881–87) forms part of the military preparation.

point Euripides does not wish to distance himself too overtly. But the eulogies delivered by Adrastus are inspired by a less narrow conception, in which courage is merely one element of life in the city. Should the funeral oration, then, triumph *in extremis*?

It would be unwise to draw conclusions about the evolution of the genre based on *The Suppliant Women* or Gorgias's epitaphios. These two texts reveal the same effort to redefine arete within a funeral oration; but the Sophist and the tragedian were not subject to the same constraints of the genre as the official orators. So they could innovate in their definitions of arete, insisting on the exemplary character of a fine life. However, there is no evidence that these innovations did not remain isolated and that the orations actually delivered in the Kerameikos did not continue to concern themselves with the fine death. This, at least, is what seems to be suggested by Pericles's epitaphios, in which critical rigor accords perfectly with the classical definition of arete; the orator, though recognizing the difficulties attached to the traditional conception of valor, nevertheless concludes by completely justifying it: "And it seems to me that such a death as these men died gives proof enough of manly courage, whether as first revealing it or as affording its final confirmation."[101]*

Thus, while echoing the debate on the definition of arete (identified with the fine death or crowning a fine life), Pericles recalls the arguments of this debate only to reject them, by taking responsibility (*dokei moi*) for the traditional view of valor, which he bases on the topos, abundantly represented in his epitaphios, of the opposition between private and public.† Declaring that courage in the service of the fatherland effaces the memory of a lackluster life, the orator answers in advance the kinds of criticisms raised by Plato.‡ So the problem is no sooner posed than resolved by the traditional answer: it is not certain whether the reflections of the Sophists did much to undermine the certainties of the funeral oration.

* Thucydides 2.42.2.
† *Ibid.* 42.3.
‡ *Menexenus* 234c4: "even if one is worthless [*phaulos*]."

The crisis in public values in the fourth century offered a greater threat to the genre, which had already been damaged in its essential representations. Freed from the austere civic framework in which the democratic city had enclosed it in the fifth century, death was once again and more than ever a private affair. In the Kerameikos, the family tombs surrounded the poluandria on all sides, and in the Athenian cemeteries the private stelae offered an individual wisdom of moderation and domestic virtues: the epitaphs declare that virtue is practiced throughout a life and that arete, even if military,[102]* always goes hand in hand with *sōphrosunē*.[103] No view could be more alien to the funeral oration, and yet many an echo of it is found in Demosthenes's epitaphios. The orator seems to be constantly tempted to grant a positive status to the past lives of the dead, that "long habit of virtuous occupations," which he sees as the origin of their final act of devotion.† Thus from the beginning of the oration he declares that they had already acquired glory in their lives;‡ by attributing to them a fine birth, a good upbringing, and an honorable life, he acknowledges in them other virtues besides andreia and, in addition to *andres agathoi* calls them virtuous (*spoudaioi*), which suggests a quite Aristotelian idea of practical, active, and zealous wisdom.§ The rest of the oration confirms these first impressions; the orator bases its development on the chronological order of the life of each individual, citizen and private man, from childhood** suggested by the personal memories of his close relatives.†† Demosthenes finally declares that military bravery, far from being a pure revelation, is merely confirmation of valor that has previously

---

* *GV* 1564 (*IG*, II/III², 6859): the epitaph has the form of an invocation to omnipotent Wisdom (Potnia Sophrosune), daughter of Aidos of the great heart, whom the dead Kleidemos honored at the same time as Arete, victorious in war.

† Demosthenes 27.

‡ *Ibid.* 2.

§ *Ibid.* 3.

** *Ibid.* 15.

†† *Ibid.* 16. The same idea is found in *Menexenus* 237a4.

been demonstrated.* The significance of arete is no longer exhausted in that of andreia, merit is no longer limited to knowing how to die well; what, in Pericles, was the object of a question that was soon set aside appears here quite overtly. But as if, in an epitaphios, any innovation had to be accompanied by a strengthening of traditional values, the orator seems to see no contradiction in later devoting some particularly lengthy passages to the fine death.

Conversely, Hyperides, the author of the least conformist of the epitaphioi, gives arete a purely military sense[104] and rejects any education that would not have as its sole end the training of citizen-soldiers ready to die: "Shall I say in what self-restraint and temperance [en pollēi sōphrosunēi] their childhood was nourished and formed, as some have known it? But everyone, I think, knows that our aim in rearing our children is that brave men result [andres agathoi gignontai]."†

This attack on mistaken predecessors who have tried to give a history of arete in which sophrosune has its place not only is a conspicuous indirect proof of the authenticity of Demosthenes's epitaphios[105] but also cuts short any new definition of valor, and from the courage of the dead the orator concludes that Athenian education is of good quality.

Thus each epitaphios seems both to serve as a barrier to new ideas and, for a time, to reflect them. Such "innovation" on a precise point is coupled with a solemn reaffirmation of classical values. Conversely, without realizing it, the orator who in certain respects is the most conformist will introduce heterogeneous elements into the funeral oration: though traditionalist on the subject of the fine death, Hyperides's epitaphios is also essential evidence for the beginning of the individual eulogy in the late fourth century.

Indeed, although he reminds us that the warrior's death is

* Demosthenes 17: "For all virtue [arete], I say, and I repeat it, the beginning is understanding [sunēsis] and the fulfillment is courage [andreia]."
† Hyperides 8.

the absolute criterion of valor, Hyperides does not apply with
the same fidelity as his predecessors the schema that made it
the culmination of a deliberation, followed by a choice and
an act. He proceeds to a sort of division of labor in which only
the strategos, endowed with both proairesis and andreia, fully
deserves the title aner agathos. Hyperides certainly praises the
city for taking a decision, but he hastens to add that it was
Leosthenes who inspired that decision; as for the soldiers, they
were left, from the outset, with nothing but courage, the carrying out of orders, and death.[106]* This is as much as to say, as
Aristotle declares in a famous passage, that the strategos is the
army's greatest asset.† This comparison is all the more applicable
in that Hyperides discusses the same idea a second time, placing
all initiative and all noble decision on the side of the leader,
and acceptance of a victorious death on the side of the soldiers.‡
How could one be the source of one's own actions when one
is deprived of *bouleutikon*? At a time when another epitaphios
reduces proairesis to an imitation of the exemplary proairesis of
the Eponyms,[107] when Aristotle insists that only the "dominant
part" decides,§ the citizen has merely to comply with the will of
the *hēgemōn*.** It is not until the end of the oration that, definitively born as andres agathoi and welcomed to the underworld
by the heroes of the past,†† the Athenians are finally praised for
their choice.‡‡

Such a subversion of the criteria of the funeral oration is easily
explained: we know of the ever-increasing importance acquired

* *Ibid.* 3.

† Aristotle, *Metaphysics* 4.10.1075a.

‡ Hyperides 15: "Wisdom in decision making is the responsibility of the strategos; but victory in combat is the work of those who agree to put their lives in
danger."

§ Aristotle, *Nicomachean Ethics* 3.3.1113a7.

** Hyperides 3.

†† *Ibid.* 28–29 and 35–39.

‡‡ *Ibid.* 40.

by exceptional individuals from the end of the fifth century. Although the first signs of this were visible at Delphi, that "place of propaganda,"[108] where the so-called base of the navarchs was initially a monument to the glory of Lysander,[109] in 322 such practices had long been accepted at Athens, and if Diodorus is to be believed, Leosthenes was given a hero's funeral.* This statement has been challenged and Hyperides says nothing explicit on this subject, consumed as he is with indignation at the enemy's excessive indulgence in heroization.† But he is himself profoundly affected by these new representations reducing part of the operation to a struggle for influence between Philip and Alexander on the one hand and Leosthenes on the other,‡ he replaces the history of cities with that of great men, and his refusal to yield to the fashion for individual genealogies, as opposed to autochthony, the common birth of all Athenians,§ begins to look like a rearguard action. In fact, in his epitaphios individual praise constantly competes with the classical themes of the funeral oration, and this has been seen as the sign of "a profound modification of democracy," since it means a change in "the essential character of a genre that it had created for its own satisfaction."[110]

Hyperides praises in Leosthenes only the strategos chosen by the city to lead its national forces;** although he briefly mentions the leader of the mercenaries,†† he prefers to ignore anything that might make his hero look like an adventurer, or even an outsider, and reveal the Lamian War as a *misthophorikos polemos*.[111]‡‡ By this silence, the orator safeguards both the civic character of the oration and its democratic inspiration.[112] Nevertheless, the figure of Leosthenes dominates the very structure of the epitaphios; each

---

* Diodorus 17.13.5.

† Hyperides 21: that is, of the general Hephaestion.

‡ *Ibid.* 13.

§ *Ibid.* 7.

** *Ibid.* 11.

†† *Ibid.*

‡‡ Dexippus, *E.Gr.Hist.*, frag. 33 D.

new passage begins with the great man's name.* Consequently, the citizens are henceforth designated as "the others"[113]† and, even in the tomb, become mere auxiliaries,‡ bound to their leader by personal ties. Thus, unlike Leonidas, summoned by Simonides to testify for the anonymous combatants,§ Leosthenes transforms his fellow citizens into mere witnesses of his own valor. Although Hyperides declares that "to praise Leosthenes is also to glorify the other citizens,"** his protests look very much like denial. Pericles apologizes for prolonging the praise of the city by showing that he has already begun that of the dead; now the praise of an individual stands for that of the citizens. It is not certain that they have gained more reality by this approach, for they are now eliminated from the expressions traditionally applied to them: for "they carried off the victory" Hyperides substitutes "he carried off the victory."†† The city hardly gains more from this exaltation of the strategos: of course it needs him,‡‡ as Greece needs the city; but soon it is no longer to Athens but to Leosthenes that Greece has to give thanks.§§

After obstinately refusing to grant the citizen a bios politikos, was the funeral oration condemned to decline into edifying biography? In the absence of any epitaphioi after 322, it is difficult to give a definite answer. However, to explain the role that fell to Leosthenes in Hyperides's oration, we do not need to invoke the

---

* Hyperides 1 (prologue), 3 (exposition of the subject), 6 (reference to the eulogy of Leosthenes), 10 (opening of the eulogy); 15 (transition to the eulogy of his soldiers), 24 (beginning of the *makarismos*), 35 (welcome of Leosthenes in the underworld).

† *Ibid.* 1, 6, 15 (twice), and elsewhere.

‡ *Ibid.* 24 and 39. In 36, they are burial companions.

§ Diodorus 11.11.6.

** Hyperides 15: "Let no one suspect me of not taking other citizens into account and of glorifying Leosthenes alone," and so on.

†† The singular (11, 12) is found alongside the plural (15, 18).

‡‡ *Ibid.* 10: "Our city needed a man."

§§ *Ibid.* 14.

fatality of an irreversible evolution, for the exceptional circumstances that in 322 surrounded the civic funeral would in themselves be enough to account for the exaltation of the strategos.
No doubt the funeral oration was threatened, but no more or less
than the city itself. And if the growing fashion for the personal
eulogy finally overtakes it, it continues, on the other hand, to
influence those eulogies in their themes and aims: the encomiums
of Evagoras, Agesilaus, or Gryllus are still eulogies addressed to
the dead, so powerful is the model of the epitaphioi. It would
therefore be dangerous to fall into the trap of evolutionism and
posit, from Thucydides to Hyperides, a continuous progression
from the funeral oration to the individual encomium.[114]

A study of the representations of death and immortality in the epitaphioi leads to similar conclusions. Indeed, just as a bios politikos
tried to develop on the immutable terrain of civic arete, so, without the theme of immortality ever being profoundly altered, we
see death, as an inevitable and incommensurable reality possessing
every civic value, assume an increasingly important place both in
the epitaphioi and on the Attic stelae of the fourth century.

    The aim of consolation in every epitaphios is to transmute the
parents' grief into pride. Pericles does not depart from this framework, and many commentators have been indignant at the cold-
ness of his argumentation. The epitaphioi of the next century
dwell more readily on consolation. Just as the stelae of the late
fourth century favor the moving theme of the old father absorbed
in contemplation of his dead son,[115] so Lysias dwells at length on
the despair of the relatives whom nothing can appease and by
which the individual suddenly sees himself as alien to a city whose
greatness has been the cause of his misfortune,* while Demosthenes shows the living dominated by the memory of the dead,
whose trace they see everywhere.†

    A similar tendency to stress emotion animates those stelae in

* Lysias 74 and 76.
† Demosthenes 16.

which "death weeps in others" and Lysias's epitaphios, in which we may detect a certain narcissism of mourning, when the orator states that "those citizens who survive are right to weep over the dead, to moan over themselves, and to pity their kinsmen."[116]* And it is only in the next sentence, incidentally in the form of a relative clause, that the civic motivation of the dead is mentioned.[†] The balance between public and private has suddenly become precarious. In the fifth century, the expression of personal feelings was channeled into, almost sublimated in, a civic demonstration; in the next century, individual suffering seems to have become respectable in Athens and in the epitaphioi. This development, already apparent in Lysias's oration, in which the measures taken by the city are simply a feeble compensation for the distress of individuals, culminates after Chaironeia in a city "filled with tears and mourning" that makes the grief of individuals its own.[‡]

Could it be that the polis is no longer the necessary center of all cohesion? Curiously enough, the orators seem to "naturalize" the city at the same time that they borrow its values. To express the feeling of death, they resort to a political vocabulary; thus death becomes a supreme *isonomia*, and the mortal condition, from which no one escapes, is the only real community.[§] The private epitaphs of the fourth century bitterly recognize this universal law in which men's time disappears;[**] but it is significant that during the same period the collective epitaphs of the Kerameikos[††] and the epitaphioi also submit to that law the andres

* Lysias 71.

† *Ibid.*: "[those men] who, putting valor above everything, have abandoned life."

‡ Demosthenes 32.

§ Lysias 77: "[We know] that death is a common [*koinos*] thing for the worst and the best of men; it has neither contempt for the wicked nor admiration for the good, but gives itself to all equally [*ison … pasin*]." Cf. *GV* 1653 (fourth-century private epitaph): "The common law [*nomos koinos*] for all men is to die."

** *GV* 1654 (early fourth century). Cf. *GV* 596, 931, 1889.

†† See the epigram of Chaironeia quoted by Demosthenes, *De corona* 289.

agathoi, reduced to the common lot,* although for them the dogma of immortality always arises like a *deus ex machina*.

In this domain, too, it would be pointless to conclude that some irreversible development had taken place; with all the weight of civic tradition, the fine death resists the omnipotence of the implacable *daimōn* that presides over human destinies.† Thus, after reducing the death of citizens to a "natural accident," Lysias's epitaphios resolutely returns to the canonical distinction between natural death and death chosen in the name of a noble cause.‡ At most a balance is struck, within the fine death itself, between choice and chance, between proairesis and fate.§ Thus a division of responsibility is set up: in the natural order, the last word goes to the deity; in the human, civic sphere of honor, the dead alone have decided their fate.** Between the all-powerful daimon and a mankind that transcends human nature, the balance is unstable, of course, and always liable to be broken at the worst times of defeat,†† as in the days following Chaironeia, when the city acceded to the decisions of the daimon and made Tyche (Fortune) the presiding genius of the fine death.[117]‡‡ But if Demosthenes gives the greater share of responsibility to the deity in his epitaphios, he does not do so unreservedly:[118] the agathoi still retain their glory, which conquers death.

In short, the traditional representations are maintained, as is shown in Hyperides's epitaphios, which resolutely runs counter to that of Lysias, declaring that the memory of valor will on every occasion conquer the sense of pain.§§ While making a few inroads

* Lysias 77; Demosthenes 37.
† Lysias 78.
‡ *Ibid.* 77–79.
§ Hyperides 13.
** Demosthenes 37.
†† *Ibid.* 21; see also 19.
‡‡ See the epitaph of Chaironeia (Tod, 176) and Demosthenes, *De corona* 192, 200, 208.
§§ Compare Hyperides 30–31 with Lysias 74.

into the funeral oration, individual emotion fails to undermine the official representation of immortality accorded the citizen-soldier by the city, and it is impossible to stress too much this remarkable fidelity to the laws of the genre, even though in the same period the private epitaphs tended, on the contrary, to cheapen eternal glory, which they generously accorded to all and sundry.[119]

Some have seen in Hyperides the original expression of a more personal view of immortality. The orator, refusing to regard the slain combatants as dead, declares that they have exchanged their lives for an eternal order,* in a "second birth."† But although we can acknowledge that such an expression is of interest, we must also note that it hardly departs from the most traditional view of civic immortality.[120] Far from being like the exploits of the Indo-European warrior,[121] the beginning of new life, this second birth — as becomes clear in the rest of the text amounts to nothing more than the attainment by the dead of the status of andres agathoi,‡ which guarantees them an eternal, if collective, existence in the civic memory,§ their only chance of survival and only posthumous resting place. Quite naturally, the orator marks out the territory of memory that the city owes its dead,** and without bothering to reserve for Leosthenes and his companions the residence that their eminence might seem to call for, he is content to dispatch them to the underworld, although he does accord them an honorable welcome there.†† In all these respects, Hyperides remains faithful to the tradition that, from Tyrtaeus on, accords the aner agathos immortal glory, the supreme honor that is sufficient in itself to distinguish the valorous citizen from the ordinary dead with whom he will have to consort

* Hyperides 27. Cf. Demosthenes 32.
† Hyperides 28.
‡ *Ibid.* 29.
§ *Ibid.*
** *Ibid.* 30.
†† *Ibid.* 35–39.

in Hades.* So I do not believe that we should look here for the sign of a new conception of immortality.[122]

Imperishable because civic, the glory that Hyperides promises the dead is certainly the same that all the official orators exalted from the tribune of the demosion sema. Without ever using the term *athanatos*, Pericles accords to the citizen the praise that does not grow old;† in a series of oppositions characteristic of his style, Gorgias guarantees these dead mourning that will never die;‡ Plato contrasts the glory of courageous men with the chimerical dream of immortality;§ Demosthenes declares that in dying for the city, one exchanges the brief instant of life for immutable renown;** while Lysias, after giving due prominence to quite human feelings about death, follows the others and declares that the only immortality lies in valor.†† In this brief summary of an astonishingly homogeneous corpus, Hyperides's epitaphios is in good company.

Thus no real variation appears from one oration to another, and, in their austere orthodoxy the epitaphioi even seem unaware of that "celestial immortality" in the ether that in 432 the city had officially promised the dead of Potidaea.[123]‡‡ It is not that the orators do not sometimes distance themselves from the dogma of civic immortality, but they challenge the very notion of immor-

---

* Tyrtaeus 9 D 31–32: "Neither the noble glory nor the name [of the warrior] ever dies, but, in going under the ground, it becomes immortal." Compare also Hyperides 27 (those who are not dead) and 35 (in Hades) with Simonides 121 D ("the dead, they are not dead, since, from on high, the brightness of their valor removes them from Hades's realm").

† Thucydides 2.43.2.

‡ DK, 82 B 6 (on the *pothos*).

§ *Menexenus* 247d5–6: "It is not immortality that they wanted for their sons, but valor and glory."

** Demosthenes 32.

†† Lysias 78–79.

‡‡ *GV* 20 (= *IG,* I², 945, v. 6): "The ether has received their souls and the earth their bodies." Cf. Euripides, *Suppliant Women* 531–36 and 1140.

tality without ever questioning its civic content. Far from trying to invoke some beyond, they try to reduce the — already quite limited — element of the unknown. So this rationalizing reticence seems to be inherent in the civic genre, perhaps from the beginning, certainly from 439. Declaring that "although nature wants us to weep over them as mortals, their valor demands that we sing them as immortal,"* Lysias expresses not so much the rationalism of an *Aufklärer*[124] as fidelity to a current of thought[125] that stretches from the epitaphios of Samos — in which, from a comparison of the honors paid the dead with those one gives the gods, Pericles concludes that it is possible to call citizens immortal[126]† — to that of Demosthenes, who uses the same analogical reasoning to make them the familiar spirits of the gods below,‡ or else to the last sentences that have been restored to us of Hyperides's oration.§

Such a unity of representation cannot be the result of mere chance. At most it is possible to observe in the later epitaphioi a more moving presentation of the theme. Thus, reviving notions associated with myth, Demosthenes's epitaphios promises the citizens who have died "the same rank as the brave men who have preceded them into the Islands of the Blessed."** But with regard to the classification of immortal beings, the orator has only the vaguest of notions: he confuses the status of the familiar spirits of the gods of the underworld with that of the inhabitants of the Islands of the Blessed, forgetting that these islands, reserved for heroes after their deaths or even during their lifetimes, are traditionally situated at the outermost limits of Ocean,†† the kingdom of Kronos, not of Hades.[127] Everything suggests that these "innovations" are purely metaphorical and that the orator himself is

* Lysias 80: "as immortals … for those who have fallen in war are worthy of the same honors as the immortals."

† Stesimbrotus of Thasos (= Plutarch, *Pericles* 8 and 9).

‡ Demosthenes 34.

§ Hyperides 43.

** Demosthenes 34.

†† Hesiod, *Works and Days* 171–73; Pindar, *Olympians* 2.76–79.

aware of this: in his conclusion, he prudently confines himself to an evocation of glory, the only tangible reality, because the only one accorded by the city.

From Pericles to Demosthenes and Hyperides, the city, then, takes complete charge of the death of its citizens. As *eudaimones* the dead may expect no other felicity than the enjoyment of eternal renown. Of course the orators of the fourth century seem to vacillate between a purely civic definition of happiness in death[*] and a more popular view, illustrated by Herodotus and by the tragic writers,[†] for whom the dead man is happy to be delivered from the trials and tribulations of life, from illness and old age.[128] But in Lysias, as in Hyperides and even Demosthenes the civic eudaimonia of a fine death always prevails in the end.[129‡] Confronted by every deviation, the polis has the last word in the funeral oration, whether we explain this phenomenon by the passive resistance of traditional values or by the deliberate nature of the oration.[130]

It is not that the funeral oration is unaware of the internal development of Athens; on the contrary, this development has repercussions for the oration, as we have seen. But throughout its history, it remains faithful to the same representations. The image of the fine death is not dethroned by the various sketches of a concept of civic life, and the traditional idea of immortality is not really affected by the crisis of the fourth century. Could it have been otherwise? The fundamental shift that made a eulogy of Athens out of an address to the dead does not accord the dead citizen any other representation than that — in many respects imaginary — representation of the city, the only fixed point around which the oration is organized. However, one does not always move without a break from the city to the dead, from the time specific to Athens to the actual time of the funeral. And although

* Pericles's death: Thucydides 2.44.2.

† Herodotus 1.30–33; see Aristotle's discussion, *Nicomachean Ethics* 1.1100aff.

‡ Lysias 78–79; Demosthenes 33; Hyperides 42–43.

it is true that certain immutable values and shifting representations coexist within the same epitaphios, it is important to study
the image that time acquires in a speech in which duration penetrates only imperfectly.

Timescale and the Development of the City

For the citizens who have died in battle, the history of Athens is
an existence more real than their own lives. Must we, then, conclude that the totality of time belongs to them forever? The
funeral oration has already been characterized as one that surveys
all time, mythical as well as historical, in the catalog of exploits,[131]
and thus seems to obey the Aristotelian definition of the epideictic genre to which the *Rhetoric* assigns not only the present but
also the past and the future;* now, examining these three "parts"†
of time and favoring the one that both divides and unites all temporality,‡ Aristotle establishes a double link between this genre
and the temporal chain as a whole.[132]

Yet, far from presenting a regular chronological sequence, the
historical excursus of the oration always comprises times of
strength and times of weakness. It is as difficult to establish a single temporal line common to all the epitaphioi as to see the presence of all moments in time within the same oration. Of course
the history of Athens is dominated through and through by the
greatness of the city, but never more so than in those times of
strength in which all its reality seems to be concentrated. It
would be pointless to inquire how the Athenians could be satisfied with so incomplete a history, for this would be to endow
them with an abstract, modern view of temporality as a measura-
ble continuum, a view quite alien to the Greek experience of
time,[133] in which quality was far more important than number, in
which living memory was worth more than all the archives, in
which *chronos* was not so much an object of science as the subject,

* Aristotle, *Rhetoric* 1.3.1358b17–20.
† Aristotle, *Physics* 4.10.218a4 (*merē*).
‡ *Ibid.* 13.222a17–29 (concerning the present).

171

sometimes a savior, sometimes a destroyer, of human actions.[134] It would also be to forget that a Greek city was interested in its past only to justify or magnify its present and much preferred the mythical past, which it could always reinterpret, to the more recent past, which was still too close. For example, Theseus's "historical" career merges with the history of Athens and is gradually enriched by the experiences of the city, while that of Cleisthenes begins and ends with the reform that bears his name.[135] To study time in the epitaphioi amounts, then, to studying the representation that Athens makes of itself, for in order to conceive of time, the polis uses no other norm than itself: it is in time, and time is concentrated in it. So according to the temporal sequence that an epitaphios gives it in preference to all others, the figure of the city, projected into the past or exalted in the present, will be more or less current but will always remain the only stable reference.

Each period invests a temporal moment with its aspirations and values: the fifth century promotes what the fourth century conceals; thus it seems impossible for the time of Pericles and that of a fourth-century orator to be in harmony.

As a contemporary of Herodotus and Thucydides, for whom history is, though in different ways, above all that of the present,[136] Pericles deliberately refuses any collusion between the city and mythical time. We know that for him the siege of Samos was easily equal to that of Troy,* and when, in the epitaphios of 431–30, he rejects the evidence of the poets,† it is impossible to distinguish between the convictions of the rationalist statesman and those of the historian telling the story of the greatest war that Greece had ever known.‡

The orators of the fourth century, on the other hand, had to

---

* Plutarch, *Pericles* 28.7.

† Thucydides 2.41.4.

‡ *Ibid.* 1.1.2 and 21.2 (the Peloponnesian War more important than earlier ones), 21.1 (poets lacking credibility), 10.3 and 11.3 (the Trojan War inferior to present-day wars).

reckon with the previous century; so they tended to see any new action as a mere imitation of earlier ones.* For example, Isocrates's conviction, whether sincere or pretended, that the past must be repeated leads him to advocate a return to the ancestral regime to solve the present problems of the city for "it is clear that . . . the situation that existed for our ancestors will be reproduced for us, since the same policies always necessarily result from similar actions."†

This idea, which underlies the fourth-century funeral oration, is brought out by Plato in his epitaphios, in which Marathon is the radiant model of which every future event ought to be a copy and of which innumerable many imitations were already to be found in the history of Athens.[137]‡ Finally, if we go still further back to the most distant past, we find the legendary exploits, the time of myth that does not always have the same function either. For Herodotus's Athenians, myth was molded on the most recent history, and the defeat of the Amazons was merely a prefiguration of that of the Persians at Marathon. In Lysias's epitaphios, on the other hand, everything has already been set up in a legendary past, and history seems to verify the myth within a temporality in which actions correspond to one another in a nontemporal manner.[138]§

So the epitaphioi are certainly not in agreement as to when the great moment of the polis occurred, for the city, though remaining recognizable as itself from one oration to another, sometimes appears as a tangible reality, embodied here and now, and sometimes as an ideal model, but one belonging to the past or to the future rather than to the present. By the same token, these variations affect the destination of the address to the dead. Indeed, according to the temporal sequence that it adopts, an epitaphios sets out to celebrate the greatness of the dead of the year or, on the

---

* Even if these acts were mythical; see Demosthenes 27–32 (excursus on the Eponyms).

† Isocrates, *Areopagiticus* 78.

‡ *Menexenus* 240e1–6.

§ Lysias 17–20.

contrary, to turn them into pale imitations of the Athenians of the past. It is true that "in linking it firmly with the past, we hope to make the present more lasting, to secure it and so prevent it from escaping and becoming itself the past";[139] but in trying to "secure" it, the fourth-century epitaphioi run the risk of never giving any reality to the dead they celebrate. To justify his silence on the events of the last decade, the orator of the *Menexenus* declares that it would be useless to say more about "events that concern neither a distant past nor other men than the present generation."* In other words, he is organizing his narrative according to the living gathered in the Kerameikos who have no wish to hear yet again of episodes that they already know only too well; but, this being the case, he sets such a value on the past that the citizens who have died are deprived of all the glory of their exploits.

The time of the city, the time of the citizens, the time of the dead: from Pericles to Hyperides, the epitaphioi tried to articulate these three periods, in systems in which coincidence is rarer than divergence. A study of these systems should help us to determine, in each oration, the degree of existence attributed to the city, the citizens, and the dead.

What makes Pericles's oration a coherent whole is this choice of a single unit of measure: everything — the greatness of the city, the dynamism of the citizens, the exemplary character of the dead — is determined by the experience of the present generation.† So the chronological divisions are not intended to establish a strict equivalence between the duration of the three periods mentioned: our ancestors, our fathers, ourselves.‡ In the guise of a genealogy, the three generations mark out the three great stages in the history of Athens. The first leads from the discreet reference to autochthony to the even more allusive reference to the Persian Wars; it sets up the essential elements and makes a development possible. The

---

* *Menexenus* 244d2–3.
† Thucydides 2.36.3.
‡ *Ibid.* 2.36.1–2.

second sees the birth and organization of arche, mentioned here as a historical acquisition. The third, which we should no doubt see as beginning at the latest with Pericles's advent to power, transforms what was a promise into a reality and gives the city its telos. But it is as if the past had been awaiting the present from the very beginning. By making, as it were, the generation of the *pateres* parenthetical, the epitaphios presents the ancestors as having handed down the land of Attica to Pericles's contemporaries,* and suggests that the fathers acquired the empire not for themselves but for their sons, who alone give each reality its full meaning.† Thus each period is linked directly to the culmination of the process. Ancestors have rarely been eclipsed to such an extent by their descendants. Conservatives would call on the men of today to show themselves worthy of their ancestors; in Pericles's quietly audacious oration, however, the ancestors have the honor of producing such a posterity, which in itself sums up a whole history of Athens. The past is elucidated by the present, as if the model of Pericles's city had from the outset determined the progress of the polis toward its culmination. The present, then, becomes a paradigm, a model in space, since Athens is worthy of imitation by the other peoples,‡ a model also in time. Does the genealogical image conceal, in fact, the biological, quasi-teleological schema of a growth, the growth of Athens, that progressively develops its phusis?

It would be tempting to think that such a view left hardly any more room for the future than for the past: since the development that has led to the present is complete, has not the process come to an end? In certain respects, the oration can be interpreted in this way. Declaring that as of this moment Athens has done enough to win immortality through its dead,[140]§ Pericles leaves little to the invention of his successors. As a result, a great deal has been said

* *Ibid.* 2.36.1.

† *Ibid.* 2.36.2: "They added to what they had been given the whole of the empire we now possess."

‡ *Ibid.* 2.37.1.

§ *Ibid.* 2.41.4.

about the symbolic character conferred on the epitaphios by its situation in the chronology of Athenian history and of Thucydides's work: delivered at the end of the first year of war but reconstructed by the historian after 404, it seems in fact to be an anticipatory farewell to a world, the "epitaphios of Athens," a moving prelude to the account of the war.[141] Of course, the catastrophe of 404 inevitably gives it such a meaning after the fact, both for Thucydides and for his readers, and it is difficult to resist the teleological temptation of interpreting 430 in terms of 404. But if we consider the epitaphios only as a purple passage essential to Thucydides's work, we forget that there is no evidence that the oration actually delivered by the statesman was not like the one attributed to him by the historian — in which case it was certainly invested, both by the orator and by his audience, with a quite different significance. By exalting the city's present, he would ensure its future. It was a risky enterprise, of course, and one that tended toward the loss of any sense of temporality: if one overvalues the present, in what terms can one still conceive of the past and the future, except to absorb them into an excessively drawn-out present? We know what happens to the past in the epitaphios. Where the future is concerned, Pericles's strategy is more subtle: by integrating the future into the present and the unknown into the known, the statesman may have been trying not so much to conquer the eternal as to confirm the present, not so much to transcend time as to dominate it. When it confronts the Peloponnesian War, Athens tirelessly — even aggressively — annexes the future to its present: it is precisely what the Corinthians say at the debate at Sparta, contrasting Lacedaemonian conservatism with Athenian dynamism;* and, again, it is in the name of this dynamism, in the exhortation of his epitaphios, that Pericles invites the living to confirm the glorious present by their future actions, so that the city may survive in all its brilliance.†

Finally, we should not forget that the orator's aims belong to the

* Thucydides 1.70.7.
† *Ibid.* 2.43.1.

sphere of practical politics: at the end of the year of war, on the eve of new battles, the oration must attest to the cohesion of the community and help strengthen it. So the time of the city must be made to coincide with that of the citizens, dead and living. For Pericles, there could be no more distance between the city and the dead — praise of whom is expressly derived from that of the polis — than between the living and the dead, the first measuring their bravery against that of the second. Such, then, is the meaning of the Athenian present: it fixes a fine image that defies all setbacks in advance, but above all it must make the unity of the city unassailable.

The epitaphioi of the early fourth century display no such certainties and make no attempt to reconcile all temporalities in a present that is open to action. Defeat and disunity have created a chasm between the real city and its ideal image, and in Lysias and Plato, whose orations are more or less contemporary, the emphasis is on "yesterday," even on "long ago," as if Athens were now living on its past.[142]

Pericles tries to unite the city, its orator, and its citizens by making a "we" the subject of the eulogy.* The third person certainly occurs when praise is given to the dead,† but this distance can be reduced to the inevitable one that separates a living creature from the dead. In the fourth-century oration the harmony seems irremediably broken, and the epitaphios tries, with success, to link the timeless time of the city with that of the orator, engaged in a perpetual agon with his predecessors; that of the public to whom he is speaking, living men immersed in the present; and the glorious eternity that characterizes the dead. If we consider this new distribution of time from the outset in all its complexity, we may finally observe that the dead are implicitly divided into two groups, since the orators say a great deal less about the dead of the day (*hoi nun thaptomenoi*) than about the Athenians of former times (*ekeinoi*), situated in a distant past and alone worthy to serve as models to the living.

* *Ibid.* 2.36–41.
† *Ibid.* 2.41.5: *hoide.*

177

Thus in Lysias, who celebrates the Athenians of former times above all, and in Demosthenes, who speaks after the defeat of Chaironeia, the history of Athens is no longer recounted in the first person. There is the time of the city — that of past exploits — and another, that of the living, the present with its difficulties and even disillusions, within which it is still permissible to say "we" when, in the consolation, the orator associates himself with the collective mourning.* But this exception confirms the rule: the reverence of the living for the Athenians of former times, forever undefeated and seen as possessing every quality, now prevents them from being able to identify themselves totally with them, and it is not without irony that Plato reserves the "we" for the periods of distress in which identification is easier.† The dead whom the oration is supposed to celebrate no longer find their place in this shattered temporality, but pale and fade away before those who preceded them in the Kerameikos, symbolically ahead of them even in death. The orator of the *Menexenus* declares that the praise is addressed to all who lie in the demosion sema and who, since earliest times, have given their lives for the city.‡ This enables him to say nothing about the actions of the recent dead, except that they had a fine death — certainly insufficient information for providing a name to the battle in which they lost their lives. Thus any reference to present events disappears and the effects of this show in the oration, which is stripped of any content except Athens's incessant monologue concerning its past. But Lysias's epitaphios is in many respects just as timeless; the soldiers who fell at Corinth are given no more than a few vague sentences,§ and in any case the oration is not specifically addressed to them, for they have to share the eulogy with all the dead of the Kerameikos.**

* Lysias 75–77.
† *Menexenus* 243d.
‡ *Ibid.* 246a5–6.
§ Lysias 67–70: the dead of Corinth; 4–16 and 20–66: Athenians of the past.
** *Ibid.* 1, 20, 54, 64: *hoi enthade keimenoi andres.*

In this effacement of the present, it is possible to see the atmosphere of the Athens of 390, when the most audacious initiatives already seemed burdened with the weight of the past. But this past has been cleansed of its dross. Since the greatness of Athens has taken refuge it, the orator is selective, exalting the exemplary episodes and devoting all his talent to avoiding any mention of the Peloponnesian War and the final defeat. As the price of this silence, the oration forgets for a moment to push back the greatness of Athens to some distant past and returns to its hegemonic function to claim the city's preeminence.* But this claim, deliberate and programmatic, is strangely timeless: the "must" turns it into a ritual protestation, and the city is established in eternity with an unchanging image.

Everything is in place for the dead to become merely a link in the endless chain of the Athenian generations, the context of which is no longer chronos but *aiōn*, which Emile Benveniste describes as "a force that is one and yet double, transitory and permanent, exhausting itself and being born again in the course of the generations, disappearing in its very renewal, and surviving forever through its ever-renewed plenitude."[143] Not only were their lives not their own, but compared with those of their ancestors, they are generally thought of as a historical incident — a necessary incident, for there must be citizens if the city is to last forever, but an essentially repetitive one.

So circumstances must lend themselves to such an effacement of temporality: a gloomy situation is disguised without too much difficulty, but a catastrophic event undermines fine generalizations† and prevents the orator from concealing the present in all innocence. Thus Demosthenes's epitaphios seems to refer hastily to the combatants of the past in order to move on speedily to address his homage only to those who died at Chaironeia.‡ As if

* *Ibid.* 57: "That is why Athenians must … be the guides of the cities."
† Lycurgus, *Against Leocrates* 42 (concerning Chaironeia: *metabolē*).
‡ Demosthenes 12.

nothing had happened between the Persian Wars and 338, a sentence condenses all the events of that period into a vague "until time brings us to the present generation."* However, there is nothing comparable with Pericles's certainties. The time evoked by the orator is the all-powerful chronos of the epitaph of the dead at Chaironeia,[144][†] and for the first time in an epitaphios it is not the Athenians who preside over the course of history but time. The account of the greatness and decline of Athens now becomes a rapid cliché: "Furthermore, checking all acts of selfish aggrandizement among the Greeks themselves, assigning themselves to each station where justice was arrayed, they went on bearing the brunt of all dangers that chanced to arise."[‡]

However, the orator does not cast all of the past into oblivion; only strictly historical events are subjected to this treatment, whereas legendary exploits are normally mentioned.[§] No doubt this rejection of the recent past may be explained by the conviction, which underpins the epitaphios that the history of Athens has finally ended, and with it that of Greece of which the combatants at Chaironeia were the last hope.[**] This pessimistic view of the future has aroused the mistrust of certain historians, who, believing that the Greeks did not perceive at once the extent of their defeat, are inclined to see an anachronism in such an interpretation of the facts and therefore see the oration as the later work of a rhetor.[145] But it is always dangerous to succumb to the fever for hypercriticism: If the epitaphios must be declared apocryphal because it likens the catastrophe of Chaironeia to some cosmic cataclysm,[††] are we also to declare inauthentic one of the few surviving fragments of the "epitaphios of Samos" because in

---

* *Ibid.* 11.

† *GV* 27 (Tod, 176): [o Chron]de pantoion thnēto[is panepiskopē daimōn].

‡ Demosthenes 11.

§ *Ibid.* 8.

** *Ibid.* 23–24: "As soon as the breath left each of their bodies, the honor of Greece vanished."

†† *Ibid.* 24.

it Pericles "compared the city robbed of its youth to a year that has lost its spring"?[146]* No one has ever thought seriously of doing so.[147] So this does not seem to be reason enough to condemn the epitaphios. On the contrary, from the *Fourth Philippic* to *De corona*, everything suggests that in the aftermath of Chaironeia Demosthenes's reaction was to refrain from comforting himself with illusions as to the nature of the peace granted by Philip; and if the Athenian people chose the orator whose sorrow accorded best with their own to deliver the funeral oration,† it is very likely that the "authentic" epitaphios was indeed a sort of threnos with no view of the future.[148] It is no accident that Lycurgus makes the image of Greek freedom being buried‡ the center of the fictional epitaphios that he addresses in 331 to the dead of Chaironeia.§

So we have to accept the obvious and agree that in the epitaphios the time of Athens is considerably reduced. Because they possess neither the brilliance of the mythical exploits nor the sad immediacy of the recent defeat, the battles of the fifth and fourth centuries lose much of their reality, and a gap opens up between the legendary past and the present. The history of Athens comprises, therefore, three high points — that of myth, that of Marathon, and, despite everything, that of Chaironeia — and two low points, the most recent past and the future. If we consider that the last of the high points, the present, was a disaster, it can be said that in fact the past dominated the funeral oration, but only on condition that it was as far away as possible. Conversely, "if this monumental method of surveying the past dominates ... the past itself suffers wrong. Whole tracts of it are forgotten and despised; they flow away like a dark, unbroken river, with only a few gaily colored islands of fact rising above it."[149] According to this principle stated by Nietzsche, the eulogy ultimately tries, then, to identify the dead of Chaironeia with their mythical

* Aristotle, *Rhetoric* 1.7.1365a31–33 and 3.10.1411a1–4.

† Demosthenes, *De corona* 285–88.

‡ Lycurgus, *Against Leocrates* 50: cf. Demosthenes 23–24.

§ Lycurgus, *Against Leocrates* 46–51.

ancestors:* in order to be faithful to the city's founders, the citizens of the ten tribes can only die glorious deaths, and this death is a return to the sources of Athens. Through death, the destiny of the city disappears: history disappears, the past justifies the present, and the present returns to the most distant past. Such a spirit certainly seems to have presided over the funeral, in which the antiquarian eulogy of the Eponyms responds to the backward-looking character of the monument of Chaironeia, as reconstructed by Bradeen.[150]

However, the short-lived success of an organized policy of resistance ought to have revived the prestige of the present. Hyperides, an earnest democrat and a courageous politician (his abortive plan to free the slaves who had taken part in the defense of the city is an example), wanted his epitaphios to mobilize the energies of the citizens at a time when the death of Alexander seemed once again to offer Athens a future.

Thus the orator deliberately rejects any reference to the past, explaining his decision at the outset with a firmness reminiscent of Pericles's epitaphios.† And the rest of the oration never disavows this initial rejection. Such an attitude is easily explained: a self-satisfied evocation of the exploits of former years would be not only useless but dangerous, for in a city used to venerating its past, the shadow of famous triumphs might eclipse the achievements of today's combatants, who, more than any catalog of exploits, have realized the topos of the struggle for Greek freedom.* Inserting a picture of the present in the epitaphios† — itself a remarkable innovation — Hyperides wants to show that for once, the Athenians of the present are really what, in other orations, the Athenians of the past were: the mortal enemies of all despotism and defenders of right and law.‡ So the orator is not afraid to

* Demosthenes 12.
† Hyperides 4.
* *Ibid.* 16.
† *Ibid.* 20–23.
‡ *Ibid.* 20 and 23.

resort to a certain exaggeration and declare that no other campaign has better displayed the valor of the troops.* And although
he in turn takes up the agonistic comparison between the Athenian soldiers and the heroes of the Trojan War,† he rejects any
explicit comparison between the Lamian War and the Persian
Wars. Now, this parallel, which came back into favor among the
orators in 322,[151] seemed almost obligatory when Hyperides
delivered the epitaphios: two victorious battles had been or were
supposed to have been fought, one near Plataea, the other in the
region of Thermopylae.[152] The first is simply referred to as having
occurred "in Boeotia."‡ The second is mentioned, it seems, only
to enhance the present eulogy by implicitly devaluing the combatants of 480, about whom Hyperides maintains a provocative
silence;§ and the censorship of the name Leonidas, which is necessarily bound up with Thermopylae, allows the substitution of
"Leosthenes" for "Leonidas." The orator frees himself sufficiently
from the idolatry of the past to apply word for word, to the soldiers of the Lamian War the eulogy that the other epitaphioi
reserved for the combatants of 480. To them alone is given the
credit for fighting for the finest cause, for mounting tiny forces
against an all-powerful enemy, for taming that arrogant adversary,
for bringing freedom to Greece and glory to their country; last,
the Athenians of 322, believing "that in the sense of honor lies
true strength and in courage the importance of an army," hold
to the reasoning that Lysias attributed to the legendary troops
of Marathon.**

It might be objected that by their deaths these exemplary
Athenians already belong to the past. No matter. A convinced
optimist, Hyperides declares that the link has already been made
and that "on the foundations laid by Leosthenes, the work of the

* *Ibid.* 23; see also 19.
† *Ibid.* 33–35.
‡ *Ibid.* 11.
§ *Ibid.* 18.
** *Ibid.* 19.

future is already being built up to."* Thus the last of the epitaphioi looks forward confidently to a future to be conquered, and this final appropriation of temporality by Athens is more important than the orator's silences or "political shortsightedness."[153]

Thus, in their shifting relationship to the Athenian experience of time, the epitaphioi bear the trace of the city's evolution; but in their variations, they never entirely depart from a number of main themes peculiar to the genre. Seldom does an oration accord the same time to the dead whom it must celebrate as to the city that it exalts. In fact, the funeral oration seems haunted by a model of *timelessness* that every epitaphios, even the most resolutely innovatory, displays, despite the orator's efforts.

The fourth-century orations are obviously the best example. At a time when the Atthidographers, engaged in a concrete political struggle, accorded an ever-greater place to historical time and especially to their own period,[154] the interest accorded the past by an epitaphios may have been proportional to the efficacy of the funeral oration.

The case of Pericles's epitaphios is more complex; but, though insisting on the significance that it assumed in 430, scholars have not concealed the fact that to open up the present to the immortality of memory is to render eternal the image of the city, and thus to make possible all timeless interpretations of the term *tēs Hellados paideusis.*† Pierre Vidal-Naquet characterizes Thucydides's time as oscillating between the eternal and the changing: is this not also the double temptation of the epitaphios?[155] Pericles's present seems very like Aristotle's "timeless kernel of time...an unalterable form of temporalization."[156]

No oration illustrates better than Hyperides's the perpetual pull between time and eternity. In it, the eulogy of the dead comes back into its own, but that of the polis tends to disappear as if *dead and city could not both be the center of an epitaphios.* Indeed,

* *Ibid.* 14.
† Thucydides 2.41.1.

Hyperides uses the traditional themes of the prologue only to dismiss the encomium of the city, which was regarded as too long for the circumstances,* and unlike Pericles, who apologized only afterward for the length of such a passage,† he takes *kairos* as a pretext to confine himself to a mere summary of Athens's qualities.‡ And even in so few words, he represents the city in a very uncivic way, for in comparing it to the sun he integrates it into the order of the universe.§ Thus, though always conceived of as a center, the polis is a center no longer for itself but for cosmic space. The Platonic cast of such a comparison has been noted;[157] It would not have surprised Diogenes Laertius, who counts the orator among the philosopher's disciples.** But we must go further: just as much as Plato in the *Laws*, Hyperides overthrows Cleisthenean values by inscribing the city in cosmic space and time.[158] In the late fourth century, when the cult of Chronos finds its place in the threatened world of the cities, Hyperides does not escape the influence of the categories of his era, and his epitaphios immediately places itself under the patronage of time, the universal witness of all noble deeds.†† Thus the actions of the dead Athenians will find their true place in the infinite *aion*.[159]‡‡

However, because he does not forget his concrete political aim, the orator is able to distinguish between the time of the city and the time of the citizens. Although the polis is definitively immobilized in timelessness,§§ the citizen enters eternity only after a fine death; because he is a living being, his own action is

---

* Hyperides 4: "The time available to me is insufficient and the moment [*kairos*] unsuitable for long speeches [*makrologein*]."

† Thucydides 2.42.1.

‡ Hyperides 5.

§ *Ibid.*

** Diogenes Laertius, *Lives of the Philosophers* 3.46. See also [Plutarch], *Lives of the Ten Orators* 848d.

†† Hyperides 1.

‡‡ *Ibid.*

§§ *Ibid.* 5: "Our city does not cease [*diatelei*] to punish evildoers."

inscribed in a creative, dynamic present. Thus, although the last epitaphios testifies to the threats weighing on the city almost as a state of its very being, there is more to this ultimate corrosion of temporality. How, in addressing the living, is one to speak of the city, both present and past, and of the dead, of the present but also already of the past? Lysias, Plato, and Demosthenes solve this problem only at the cost of a rupture in temporality, which either sought refuge within the confines of a glorious past epoch or merely disintegrated into neutral, gray moments; nor did they escape the temptation to inscribe the city, the dead, and the living on three temporal axes, forever dissociated in the present of political experience. Confronted in turn by the same difficulty, Hyperides tried above all to save the cohesion of the civic corpus beyond death. But more than all the others, he produced a gap between an immobile time and a human time of action and courage.

The funeral oration is the prism of Athens's relations with "the others," the dead, and itself, and the history of the genre throws light on a number of difficulties: the difficulty of relating to "the others," the refusal to grant citizens anything other than a fine death, the tricks used to harmonize the time of the city and the time of men. Studied from these three points of view, the funeral oration shows an ever more imaginary insertion of the city in a time that is ever more timeless. So we have been forced to adopt a double reading, one that ignores neither the historical development of a genre tied to the city nor the relative stability of a form that from one century to another always returns to Athens the same image of itself.

To answer the question of the efficacy of the oration, raised at the beginning of the chapter, we must therefore formulate it in other terms: perhaps the funeral oration does not have an immediate effect on a given set of political circumstances, but it helps to confirm, even to imprint on the memory, a certain image of Athens. Although no epitaphios ever was enough to convince the Greeks of the justness of Athenian hegemony, the constant reiteration of the city's hegemonic pretensions in the epitaphioi did a great deal to assure the success of the Athenian version of the Persian Wars. Although Athenian citizens continued to value life and to curse their officers,* they were nonetheless shaped by the noble ideal of the fine death. And although the oration is always threatened by timelessness, it nevertheless establishes an official history that confirms the community in the direction that it has chosen.

* Aristophanes, *Peace* 1171.

CHAPTER THREE

The Athenian History of Athens

To study the epitaphioi in chronological succession, we must not only locate within the oration the many traces of permanence and transformation that, for us, constitute the history of Athens; we must also reveal the broad outlines of an ideal Athenian politics, whose realism often proves paradoxical: in this sense, it probably has no other locus than an official form like the funeral oration. But in order to function in the collective imagination, such a politics nevertheless had coherence and reality, in that it offered Athenians the unchanging lesson that they had to draw from the city's shifting affairs.

Whatever the real power of Athens may have been in the Greek and Mediterranean world, and whether the dead were victors or vanquished the funeral oration reminded Athenians that in its many acts, diverse situations, and vicissitudes, the city remained one and the same. This "historical account" of events that leads from the city's origins to the last year of war, the direct cause of the present ceremony, is not, therefore, strictly speaking, a history. But we still have to examine, in the narrative's form itself, the techniques that make it possible for the oration to present always the same satisfying version, effacing the problems that a critical study reveals.

Selections from an Immobile Narrative

If the Greeks of the classical period could conceive of history only as partial and limited in space and time,[1] the "territory of the historian"[2] is not necessarily bound by the frontiers of a city but may embrace the whole of Greece, and even that part of the barbarian world that one fine day was to go to war with the Greeks. The *Hellenica* may be local history,[3] but what are we to say of the catalogue of Athenian exploits? Of course, the funeral oration may extend its view to all the lands and seas where Athenian valor has distinguished itself,* but the norm remains, for Lysias, for Pericles, and for Demosthenes, the Attic land,* the land of the city. It is all a question of degree, even in particularism, and there is a considerable difference between "the cities of men"† and "the city."‡

Does this mean that for the Athenians all history has its locus in Athens? Jacoby tends to believe this when, comparing the *Atthides* with Ionian historiography, whose aim is Hellenic, he declares: "For the Athenians, history is the history of their city, and they wrote it because they were making it and as long as they were making it."[4] Such a statement deserves to be verified outside those specifically Athenian histories, the *Atthides*, or the catalog of exploits. Without undertaking a systematic investigation, which is beyond the bounds of this study, we might note that Athens certainly seems to have annexed to its own advantage certain events belonging to a common history of all the Greeks and to have transformed them into topoi of its own history. Thus the Athenian writers tend to transform the second Persian War, a war of the Hellenic coalition, into a mere epilogue of the Athenian victory at Marathon. This tendency is apparent in Xenophon, whose double status as Laconophile and author of the *Hellenica* ought to protect him from seeming Athenocentric. When, in his first speech as strategos in the *Anabasis*, Xenophon reminds the Ten Thousand of the noble deeds of their ancestors, it is hardly surprising that he refers to the second Persian War; it enables him to congratulate his men for having already shown themselves

---

* Thucydides 2.41.4; Lysias 2.
* Thucydides 2.36.1: *chōra;* Lysias 5(*chōra*); Demosthenes 8: *gē.*
† Herodotus 1.5: *astea anthropon.* Cf. Thucydides 1.1.
‡ *Hēdē hē polis:* see, for example, Lysias 5, 6, 16, 21.

worthy of their ancestors when confronting the descendants of
Xerxes's soldiers at Cunaxa.* It is more surprising to see him devote a fairly long passage to the purely Athenian victory of
Marathon, given that Dorians were in a majority in his audience.
Perhaps the young Xenophon, a character in a historical novel,
eludes the vigilance of Xenophon the historian. Perhaps it is difficult, however much he may be a friend of the Lacedaemonians, to
forget the Athenian version of history. or perhaps we should
impute this anomaly to the very genre of the speech delivered: a
strategos's speech always presents enough topoi that are shared
with an epitaphios so that the speaker may draw inspiration from
the catalog of Athenian exploits included in the funeral oration.[5]
No doubt this example does not in itself prove the necessarily
patriotic character of all history written by the Athenians, but it
shows that this catalog of noble deeds is the very model of Athenian national history.

Athens is always in the forefront; this is both necessary and
good, for if ever it were to disappear from the stage, the mecha-
nism would jam: the triumph of others is the advent of a "history
for evil" in which the world no longer follows its normal course.[†]
Athens, then, is the agent of history, of a history that the orators,
faithful to the Greek definition of that notion but also to the military character of the oration, conceived of in terms of war and
erga: thus the epitaphioi recount nothing more than a series of
campaigns, more or less linked together by the formula "and
then," which allows one to glide delicately over the exact causes
of a conflict.[6‡] So for us this is merely a monotonous collection of
exploits whose significance is always the same: history is broken
up into so many instances of bravery. This tendency is particularly
apparent in the Platonic pastiche of the funeral oration, which

* Xenophon, *Anabasis* 3.2.11–14: Marathon (11–12), second Persian War (13),
the Ten Thousand and their ancestors (14).

† Lysias 55–57.

‡ See especially *Menexenus* 242c3. Cf. also *ibid.* 241d1, 242a6, 242e5, 243e1,
244b4, and Lysias 27, 44, 48.

multiplies the *meta tauta* and enumerates the wars without attending to divisions that had already been accepted: tradition knows of two Peloponnesian wars; the *Menexenus* tells of three.* For the orator of the epitaphios, who must produce the proof of Athens's unchallenged excellence, the proliferation of examples is a good thing, for the thesis is verified all the more. And whereas the *Atthides* try to present a continuous history of Athens, this concern was probably alien to the funeral oration, which is content to recall innumerable instances of Athenian valor† since "the beginning of men."[7] So the orators inscribe the history of Athens in a much broader timescale than the historiographers,[8] without even bothering to fill the empty periods like authors of chronicles,[9] for the perennial nature of Athenian merit is enough to give coherence to the narrative. In the historical excursus of the funeral oration, we find not the unfolding of a continuity but the repetitive and exemplary enactment of a single arete.

The rule is confirmed by apparent exceptions that show in their paradoxical way the unity of Athenian merit. Thus although war is by definition the activity of the andres, citizens and combatants, the funeral oration does not completely ignore courageous acts performed by women, the young, or the elderly, so long as these anomalies reinforce the glory of Athens. Women, of course, must not desert their nature by showing courage (andreia), and the Amazons are monstrous because they violate this rule;[10] but for Athenian women, the prohibition can be lifted. Referring to the daughters of Leos, who "acted like men,"[11] Demosthenes views their behavior less as a transgression than as an exemplary demonstration of arete.‡ This approach is especially evident in the account in Lysias's epitaphios of the war of Megara,§ in which, in the absence of citizens old enough to serve,** young and old

* *Menexenus* 242e5.
† Cf. the theme "they showed their valor."
‡ Demosthenes 29.
§ Lysias 49–53; cf. Thucydides 1.105.4–6.
** Lysias 49.

decided to face danger alone* and, under Myronides's leadership, won a brilliant victory.[12]† When reserve troops wage a war alone and go on the attack, the world is already upside down;[13] but what made this battle an exemplary exploit was the particular status of the combatants: neōtatoi and presbutatoi not only were on the margins of citizenship‡ but were not true warriors at all, and andreia ought not to have been their lot.[14] The orator, however, states unequivocally that they possess arete, either from experience or from nature;§ and the identity of Athenian merit, far from being weakened by such a paradoxical situation, is strengthened by it, as this contrasted picture, opposing two antithetical age-groups — on the one hand, veterans who know how to command and, on the other, young emulators, capable of obedience — shows.** In their bodies, they fall short of or have gone beyond a norm, but strength of soul makes them pure Athenians.†† Thus, before separating young and old once again and sending them back to their usual vocations,‡‡ the orator uses a cleavage within the city to show, even at the heart of difference, the unity of Athenian valor.[15] Despite its "historical" character, such an exploit transcends the time of history and takes its place in aion, since its only function is to recall the permanence of the Athenian principle, eternally renewed from generation to generation. In the funeral oration, each generation is merely the temporary embodiment, destined always to end in a fine death, of the city, which, like the olive tree, its symbol, replaces falling leaves with new shoots.[16]§§

---

* Ibid. 50. Monoi obviously assumes a new sense: usually citizen-soldiers confront the enemy monoi; the improvised warriors are here doubly alone, as Athenians and as reserve troops.

† Ibid. 52.

‡ Cf. Aristotle's crucial text, Politics 3.1.1275a17.

§ Lysias 51 (empeiria/phusis).

** Ibid.

†† Ibid. 53.

‡‡ Ibid.: paideia for the young, an advisory function in the boule for the old.

§§ Plutarch, Quaestiones convivales 723ff.

Although repetition, in which time disappears, is one characteristic of myths,[17] the meta tauta of Lysias or Plato cannot sustain
the illusion for long. The funeral oration uses the language of
temporal succession, but it functions in it in an almost metaphorical way which brings the narrative of exploits close to a mythical
narration.[18]

In fact, this type of narrative has highly complex relations with
myth, and the presence in the epitaphioi of legendary exploits and
even of myths enumerated as such — the war of the Amazons,
autochthony — deserves consideration.

The funeral oration does not, of course, relate those myths for
their own sake. In appropriating them, it reduces them to their
simplest expression and transforms them into educational paradigms: the virtues of the city must be attested in some immemorial way. This is certainly how Isocrates sees it when he declares
that he has "adopted this distant starting point" to show that the
object of his eulogy was superior from the beginning,* or Lycurgus, for whom Athens is great because it was the model of
heroism from earliest Antiquity.† Now, in the fifth and fourth centuries, myth was no longer understood as an original narrative
form; devalued by a rationalist criticism that contrasted the rigor
of logos with the illusory brilliance of muthōdēs,[19] it preserved all
its authority as a paradigm: thus in Plato "it is naturalized with the
status of a philosopher,"[20] and he writes in the Critias the mythical
history of the city of the Republic.[21] Myth is necessary because it
is the absolute example, contemplation of which takes the place
of education by inducing the citizens to act well.‡ But its presence at the beginning of the catalog is required above all so that
it may confer its own characteristics on the historical narrative
that follows: in the Menexenus, Plato pretends to refer to mythical exploits only to reject them, but in doing so, he shows that
in moving through myth, the orator still wishes to transform

* Isocrates, *Panathenaicus* 120.
† Lycurgus, *Against Leocrates* 83.
‡ See *ibid.* 100.

each exploit into a legendary account — hence his rivalry with the poets.*

So the distinction that we have so far maintained between legendary war and historical war is fully meaningful only for a modern.[22] Rarely do the epitaphioi refer to the transition from the time of legends to the time of Marathon as a break; on the contrary, the official orators go so far as to suggest that all Athenian exploits have some *mythos* about them, something that, in their somewhat vague terminology, is related at once to poetry by its form and to heroic deeds by its content.† When Demosthenes distinguishes the noble exploits that have already been raised to the rank of myth from those, closer to himself in time, that have not yet been so transformed,‡ he only appears to be obeying rationalist demands. In fact, the orator, who is quite willing to mix the arete of the Eponyms§ with that of the Athenians at Chaironeia, declares quite simply, following Plato (whom he is imitating), his wish to go beyond the poets by stealing from them a subject that they were hitherto supposed to have ignored. Similarly, in the Panegyricus, Isocrates points out the extent to which his account is made up of muthodes only to justify the mixture of legend and fact in the development of his argument.** Finally, although Lysias creates a de facto separation between the time of the ancestors and the time that begins at Marathon, nothing in his work suggests that he treats these two series of exploits differently.[23]†† We are far from the methodological barriers erected by Thucydides or even by Herodotus against the accounts of the poets. It is even likely that the funeral oration was never really affected by the

* *Menexenus* 239b–c.

† Demosthenes 9.

‡ *Ibid.*

§ *Ibid.* 29.

** Isocrates, *Panegyricus* 28 and 30.

†† Lysias 20: the evocation of the *progonoi* refers to *to palaion* (4–16); that of their descendants announces the narrative of exploits performed since Marathon.

exigencies of the historians; although the characteristics studied here are primarily those of fourth-century epitaphioi, there is ample evidence that the oration contained them at least *in potentia* in the century before. Refusing to repeat earlier epitaphioi, Pericles must reject both mythical exploits and recent wars, whose equivalence was already postulated in the epigram of Elon.[24]

Whether mythical or paradigmatic, the history of the epitaphioi is characterized, then, by a certain unity of tone: a unity obtained at the cost of various techniques of reconstruction and concealment, which, though present in all the historical developments of Athenian eloquence, are particularly clear in the funeral oration. So there is no departure from the sphere of the mythodes, since such techniques are those of ceremonial productions for a temporary audience that are heard and forgotten, which Thucydides contrasts with his own historical discourse, a ruthless enemy to fantasy.[25]*

Of course, the orators tend to select episodes likely to please the public; thus the Persian Wars are a favorite theme. This is not so of the Peloponnesian War, which Demosthenes mentions only once in his entire oeuvre, and even then only to recall that Athens never abandoned a fight.† It is true that a symbouleutic speech may choose its examples, whereas an epitaphios cannot do so entirely and must use a number of tricks to conceal or attenuate the existence of defeats among the erga, for defeat breaks the fine thread and upsets all values accusing Leocrates of having, by his behavior, "sullied a glory accumulated over the centuries" and despoiled the ancestors of their ancient renown,‡ Lycurgus shows that paradigmatic history is always threatened by the real — present or past — which, assuming the form of a failure, may in a moment destroy the glory of the city. Even a reminder of some disaster remote in time is dangerous: since each episode, as a paradigm,

* Thucydides 1.22.4.

† Demosthenes, *Against Androtion* 15.

‡ Lycurgus, *Against Leocrates* 110.

contains the whole history of Athens, one lost battle can cause everything to collapse.

It is still possible to silence an isolated episode or one whose meaning is debatable: whereas the orator of the *Menexenus* indulges in the luxury of mentioning Tanagra to exalt Oenophyta all the more at a later point,* Lysias says nothing about either battle. It is more difficult to keep silent about the Peloponnesian War; however, the *Menexenus* deals with the difficulty by circumventing it, and again each defeat is eclipsed by a victory. Thus the success at Sphacteria definitively illustrates Athens's superiority over Sparta[†] and overshadows in advance the extremely discreet announcement of the disaster in Sicily;[‡] in an even more striking way, the orator dwells at length on the victory at Arginusae, which forms a kind of pause before the reference to the final defeat.[§] However, it is just about possible to avoid any account of the operations; thus Lysias, faithful to the attitude already adopted concerning Tanagra, proceeds to a new and much more disturbing ellipsis.[**]

But it is impossible to silence the final failure: a defeat of such magnitude must therefore be transformed into a new proof of the greatness of Athens. So the advocates of silence and the specialists in half-truths are forced to resort to the same paradoxes and to declare, like Lysias's epitaphios, that "their valor was also demonstrated in adversity";[††] disaster then becomes a catastrophe for the victors, and the true defeated are not those one thinks,[‡‡] since the power of Athens was the salvation of Greece.

---

* *Menexenus* 242a6–b5. It is true that Plato presents the battle of Tanagra as indecisive, whereas Thucydides regards it as a Lacedaemonian success (1.108).

† *Menexenus* 242c–e.

‡ *Ibid.* 242e–243a.

§ *Ibid.* 243c–d.

** Between the last words of 57 and the first of 58, there ought to be an account of the war.

†† Lysias 58.

‡‡ *Ibid.*: "a terrible disaster, both for us who were defeated and for the rest of the Greeks."

There are two possible ways of presenting the enemy when transforming a defeat into a paradoxical proof of valor. One is to make him more powerful than he actually was. By means of this exaggeration, failure appears almost normal; thus the epigram usually associated with the defeat at Tanagra gave the *kudos* to the Athenians who had confronted most of Hellas.* However, Athenian pride usually refused to admit that defeat was imputable to the strength or valor of the enemy. Declaring that the Athenian fleet could be destroyed only by the incompetence of a commander or by the will of the gods, Lysias chooses the second attitude.† What he says is reminiscent of the epigram of Coronea,[26]‡ in which the enemy is replaced by a vengeful demigod at the same time, he announces Demosthenes's accusations against the Theban commanders, who were alone regarded as responsible for the disaster at Chaironeia.§

In fact, in order to keep the initiative, rather than acknowledge that the city's enemies had any effect on events, Athens preferred to explain their successes by its own shortcomings. When, during the debate at Sparta, the Corinthians declare that on several occasions the Lacedaemonians have owed their success not so much to their own actions as to mistakes made by the Athenians, they are really giving an Athenian version of the facts.[27]** "The Athenians succumbed only to the blows that they gave themselves through their own internal conflicts":†† thus concluding his praise of Pericles, Thucydides adopts a quasi-official explanation for the defeat of 404, attributing the victory of the Lacedaemonians, who did not expect it, to the city's internal dissensions. Athens, then, *has been defeated only by itself*: such, in Lysias's epitaphios, is also

* *IG*, I², 946 (= *Anthologia Palatina* 7.254).

† Lysias 58.

‡ *GV* 17, v. 3–4 (opposition between the power of the enemies and the intervention of a demigod).

§ Demosthenes 22.

** Thucydides 1.69.5; cf. 1.144.1.

†† *Ibid.* 2.65.12.

the final interpretation of the ultimate defeat, reached at the end of an argument that is as specious as it is elaborate.*

This interpretation is logical from an Athenocentric point of view. Plato understands this very well and, in his epitaphios, ends his account of the war with a sophistry in which, without innovating, he is content to say through the funeral oration what it dared not state openly: since Athens has not been defeated by an enemy, the ultimate defeat does not matter; and going back to the last Athenian victory, the *Menexenus* immortalizes it in order to declare that Athens won the war.† Athenian solipsism has obviously been forced back here to its last defenses, and by praising the city for vanquishing itself, the epitaphioi must have attracted the irony of a philosopher for whom the most shameful defeat is that which one inflicts on oneself.‡ It is true that the task was difficult, since it was necessary to preserve the glory of Athens, defeated in a lackluster battle and humiliated through owing its survival to "others." Thus the orators had to divert attention away from the military operation to the city's internal divisions.

An honorable defeat is simpler to describe: the funeral oration may then employ all the resources of hoplitic morale to transform a real defeat into a symbolic victory.[28] The orators declare that the essential thing is not to have retreated;§ the dead, andres agathoi genomenoi, are said to have been victorious because they did not give in to the victors, and the oration implicitly concludes with the glory going to the city. Honor is saved at the cost of an argument whose paradoxical character is not always lost on the orator using it.**

This argument served first to glorify the unchallenged valor of

* Lysias 65.

† *Menexenus* 243d.

‡ Compare *Menexenus* 243d7 ("it is we ourselves who have both defeated and been defeated by ourselves") and *Laws* 1.626e2–3.

§ Lycurgus, *Against Leocrates* 48.

** *Ibid.* 49 ("To tell the truth, though it may seem a paradox [*paradoxotaton*], the simple truth [*alethes*] is, they died victorious").

the combatants of Thermopylae. Although it appears for the first time in Lysias's epitaphios, which was to inspire both Isocrates and Ephorus,* and although Herodotus does not make explicit use of it in his account of the battle, it is likely to be of an earlier date: could this argument have invented a speech as hostile to Sparta as the funeral oration? In any case, the renown of Leonidas's companions gave this argument legitimacy, and the epitaphioi soon turned it into an Athenian theme applied by Demosthenes and Lycurgus to the defeat at Chaironeia. Demosthenes's epitaphios in particular excels at this subtle task of reversal and displacement. The existence of victors and vanquished is denied as soon as it is affirmed.† The orator proceeds to a redistribution of these two statuses that, in the guise of according the dead of both camps an equal share of honor, places the Macedonian and the Athenian survivors on an equal footing, thus depriving the enemy of the real victory.‡ For a time, then, there is only life on one side and the fine death on the other; but this is a false balance, and the fine death draws all the positive values to itself. Compared with those who have done everything to win success and have fallen in the attempt, the survivors cut a poor figure; they have no will — the dead have taken everything and left them with nothing but chance.§ By the end of this passage, the living are left with nothing but tyche (fortune),** good for some, bad for others, and it becomes impossible for the enemy to vaunt such a success.††

Thus reconstruction of an ideal victory is performed here by the eulogy of the proairesis of the dead, which makes the passage

---

* Lysias 31. Cf. Isocrates, *Panegyricus* 92; Diodorus (= Ephorus) 11.11.4.

† Demosthenes 19: "It is the inevitable fate of battles that on one side there are victors, and on the other defeated."

‡ *Ibid.*: *nikan* (victory) is contrasted with *kratein* (brute force).

§ *Ibid.*: "Among the living, victory is decided according to the will of the god [*daimōn*]."

** *Ibid.* 20.

†† *Ibid.* 21 (enemies owe their success not so much to their feats of arms as to some disconcerting twist of fortune).

on the Eponyms a mythical orchestration of the theme of victorious defeat. To praise the dead for their choice is also, and above
all, to avoid any examination of the specific policy that led to the
real defeat. There is no reason to be surprised by or indignant
about this. The funeral oration is intended to give Athenians an
image of their unity; how, then, could it evoke an ideological
struggle taking place within the city?[29] How could Demosthenes
have taken the opportunity to attack Aeschines when the epitaphioi attempted to transform even civil war into a demonstration of concord?*

The Athenian history of Athens, then, forms a satisfying whole at
the cost of innumerable paradoxes that this study seeks to illuminate. The orator is both assisted and constrained by a preestablished model and a certain number of topoi or fixed formulas, a
framework through which any event must pass. So when the narrative confronts some inglorious episode, it is immediately transformed so as to be assimilable; and the terminology is never more
stereotyped than in these filter-passages.

   Let us take, by way of example, a passage from the *Menexenus*
that, though fiction, is more real than any of the orations actually
delivered. To evoke the Sicilian expedition, the orator presents
in succession (1) a reference to the fine death and a recollection
of the honors due to citizens who have fallen in battle, (2) a reminder of the trophies, (3) Athens's vocation as liberator, (4) the
city's traditional piety;† he then briefly mentions the failure of the
undertaking — though discharging the city of all responsibility.
Almost immediately after mention of the fatal word "failure"
(*edustachesan*), a new topos is introduced, this time with a remarkable development, namely, that of the recognition paid to
Athenian valor by her enemies.

   Woven out of paradoxes, silences, and compulsory representations, the catalog of exploits invariably looks like a *selection*.

---

* *Menexenus* 243e.
† *Ibid.* 242e6–243a7.

Indeed it could not be otherwise: the only author of an epitaphios who has the audacity to reject any account of *erga* is also the only one who allows himself the luxury of balancing references to successes and to reverses.* Even then, his formula is so brief and general that the reverses are lost in the ultimate elaboration of his praise of the city.

With a funeral oration, then, Athens establishes herself in a history whose privileged instrument is rhetoric. The reaction of a Thucydides, developing his own account of the Pentecontaetia against the official version of the facts,[30] remains an isolated one. Isocrates, the master of the fourth-century historians, borrows from the *epitaphioi* their methods and modes of exposition, and this double authority — that of an official speech and that of a master of political rhetoric[31] — will determine the form and purposes of the historical genre. A single example is enough to demonstrate this point. Renouncing the scruples of Thucydides, who saw the battle of Tanagra as an Athenian defeat, Ephorus, like Plato, turns it into a battle with an uncertain outcome, and then interpolates between Tanagra and the success at Oenophyta, thus doubled in advance, a brilliant victory unmentioned by historians† that may owe its existence solely to the invention of the author of an epitaphios who has substituted for Tanagra an episode more worthy of Athens.[32] The funeral oration won the day, reintroducing into historiography the "fantastic" elements that Thucydides wanted to proscribe forever. Is it possible at the end of this survey, to use the word "history" for those accounts in which all evolution disappears so as to repeat forever the same victory? To characterize this immobile movement, one is tempted to call the funeral oration "quasi-history," which for Collingwood comprises both myth and "theocratic history."[33]

However, the funeral oration cannot be so easily reduced to "quasihistory." Although the temporality of the catalog of exploits is similar in certain respects to that of myth, the rhetorical form

* Thucydides 2.41.4: *mnēmeia ... kakōn ... kai agathōn.*
† Diodorus 11.82.4.

of the account belongs to a quite different register from that of mythical logic, which is polysemous and overdetermined; and unlike theocratic history, which reveals divine will at work in the world of men, the epitaphioi, which are entirely devoted to the epiphany of Athenian virtues, only rarely allow the gods to intervene in human affairs, as when, for example, it is convenient to attenuate a defeat by depriving the enemy of the prize of his victory.* In these ways, the funeral oration belongs without any doubt to the same cultural age as the burgeoning historiography.

Like the historical genre, which from its very beginning took as its object men's actions,[34] the funeral oration stresses human exploits whose exceptional nature provides both orators and historians with material and criteria for selection.[35] To a greater degree than history, the funeral oration, which declares itself to be the city's memory, is a "survival operation against time, which destroys all."[36] But here the resemblance between the catalog of exploits and fifth-century historiography ends. The purpose is not the same for the two types of narratives: one is a triumphant litany, and the other is a genre that defines itself as an investigation. Unlike the historians, who choose their topic only when certain of the validity of the documents they will be using,[37] the orators show little concern to base their arguments on dependable evidence, preferring to avail themselves of venerable mythical traditions† and to shelter, in the end, behind the greatness of Athens: the authority of the city provides the basis for an account that, in turn, confirms the city in its idealized view of itself. Unlike historiography, the funeral oration does not seek, does not ask questions; it knows already and says what it knows.

Even more characteristic is its relation to time: not only does the funeral oration constitute no serious chronology and thus is opposed to the *Atthides*, whose basic target it is;[38] not only does it assign no temporal limits;[39] but by anchoring the city in the

---

* Apart from Lysias 58, one might cite Demosthenes 19 and 21 (*daimōn*).

† Demosthenes 4: "The noble origin [*eugeneia*] of those men has been universally recognized from time immemorial."

immemorial past of autochthony, it carries to an extreme the profound indifference shown by Herodotus toward any precise dating.[40] Furthermore, this strange history excludes by definition the possibility of any change, thus refusing the very mode by which the Greek experienced the historical process.[41]

The epitaphioi do, however, accommodate themselves to catastrophic changes, provided that they affect the enemy, definitively crushed like the Amazons* or miraculously led, like the great king in the early fourth century, to place his salvation in the hands of the Athenians alone.[42]† Because the Athenians are bearers of meaning,[43] because their history unfolds under the sign of coherence,‡ the funeral oration must ward off the forces of destruction by throwing them well beyond the frontiers of Athens. When it is impossible to deny that the city, too, has known a cruel reversal, the horizon broadens inordinately, and the Athenian vicissitudes become a cosmic catastrophe, plunging the whole of Greece into darkness.§ As the light of the civilized world, Athens retires from the stage only by depriving her enemies' victories of any meaning, by defining them as *chalepē tuchē* — the ill fortune of Athens.**

There is a single actor, the Athenian principle, but innumerable extras. To a far greater degree than history, this immobile narrative takes after both catechism and military preparation. And if the final exhortation of the speech invites the survivors to imitate the valor of the dead, it is because the orator, in reciting the catalog of exploits, has given the citizens the most official of lessons. Thus the funeral oration has its place in Athenian paideia,††

* Lysias 5: "They denied their earlier reputation." Section 6 concludes this episode by again stressing the reversal.
† *Menexenus* 244d6–e1.
‡ Lysias 43: "Their good fortune accorded with the dangers they had incurred."
§ Demosthenes 24 (*skotos*); Athens, light of the civilized world, *ibid.* ("just as if the light of day were removed from this universe of ours"); cf. Hyperides 5 ("like the sun . . . our city").
** Demosthenes 21.
†† Cf. Lysias 3.

that vast educative complex comprising institutions and cultural models that from childhood to death took charge of the citizen, molding him by constantly reminding him of civic values.*

No doubt it was a diffuse education, and not a unified educational system: we know that the democracy found indoctrination of the Spartan type repugnant — the Athenians liked to recall that they led an unconstrained life,† and perhaps the opposition between Sparta and Athens was more than a cliché in this respect. But although it did not organize education, the city was not unconcerned either about the functioning of schools[44] or about the behavior of adults, who were continuously trained by a generalized education that was expressed at every stage in civic life, from the ephebia to the meetings of the assembly in which the citizen underwent his political apprenticeship, and in the ceremonies (Panathenaea, Dionysia, or public funerals), intended to reactivate official values. Because they always repeated the same thing, with all the resources of persuasive eloquence, the epitaphioi played an important part in this civic chorus: on their school benches, children learned by heart selected passages from the great poetic works, "eulogies of ancient heroes"‡ that aroused in them a desire to emulate; the catalog of exploits was the equivalent, in prose and for adults, of these versified lessons.[45] There was no fundamental difference between the edifying Achilles, offered as a model for Athenian youth, and the exemplary Athenians, the heroes of the historical catalog. The same system of representations by which the city lived and which we must designate as the official ideology of Athens[46] extracted from the Homeric epic examples that still had real meaning§ and made Athenian history a repetitive gesture, in which the battles of the present copied those of the past and foreshadowed exploits to come.

Thus the funeral oration assumed its educative function by

---

* Plato, *Protagoras* 325c6–7.

† Thucydides 2.39.1.

‡ Plato, *Protagoras* 325e–326a3.

§ Aristophanes, *Frogs* 1034–36 (Homer the educator). Cf. also 1054–55.

anchoring the city in an unchanging temporality. But by linking the present of Athens to its past and future, it also played the role of a history. It is quite obvious that beneath its official form, the Athenians experienced change in the mode of repetition, and once we accept that it was vital for the community to imitate itself, we can no longer challenge the notion that a repetitive future is truly a future or refuse the name of history to that account of "old exploits forever new."* So, without requiring the catalog of the epitaphioi to conform to the rigor of historiography, we must take seriously the single, contradictory effort by which the orators stopped time at the very moment when they were making it the framework for a strengthening of the city; such is the way, the only way, of *ideological history*.

The Geste of Athens

In attempting to embellish each episode, the orators comply with the rules of the genre, since only "fine actions" are fit material for the eulogy;† but they also seem to obey a more hidden requirement that they turn the city at war into a heroic confraternity.

Inscribing each event in aion,‡ the catalog of exploits tends to represent the Athenian combatants of the past in a way that relates them to the warriors of legend. Such a transfiguration, however, does not call into question the importance and depth of the hoplitic representations in the funeral oration: the fine death, the center of the speech, is by definiton a civic death. But if, dedicated to the combatants of the present the epitaphioi concentrate in themselves purely civic values, at another less conscious level they form a link with legendary themes: the further back one goes into the past, the more the narrative of the actions is duplicated by a sort of heroic gesture, a collective gesture, since the solitary heroes of myth have been excluded from the oration.[47] This stealthy reappearance of myth is not the smallest paradox of the funeral oration.

* Lysias 26.
† Aristotle, *Rhetoric* 1.9.1367a17: *kala erga*.
‡ Demosthenes 6: *di'aiōnos*.

Heroic legend divides the world of war into two opposed and complementary camps presided over by Dike and Hybris respectively. To every "wild" warrior is opposed a just warrior; among the gods, Ares and Athena form an antithetical couple.[48] Perpetually engaged in just wars against the ever-threatening excesses of impious adversaries,[†] the Athenians, whom Plato sees as the first armed disciples of the goddess,[‡] are obviously on the side of *dikē*, and in Lysias's epitaphios — of all the orations the one that stresses most the legality of Athens's struggle[§] — the catalog of exploits opens with the war in which, in very ancient times,[**] Athenians fought the daughters of Ares[††] and ensured Dike's triumph over Hybris.

As a way of opening a catalog of exploits that are both legendary and hoplitic, the example is well chosen, for it tells of the victory of order — that of the Athenian city, a club for just men and warriors — over absolute disorder, represented by the men-women.[49][‡‡] It will be remembered that the most traditional views of feminine arete dominate the few passages that the funeral oration deigns to devote to women: a brief but deeply felt speech by Pericles,[§§] addressed *in extremis* to the widows of war, references by the orators to the protection that the city will have to accord to those weak creatures — wives, perpetual minors,[*] or sisters destined for honorable marriage[***] — an indignant description of the

---

[*] Hybris in the legendary wars: Lysias 9 (Theban cycle) and 14 (Eurystheus and the Peloponnesians); Demosthenes 8 (Theban cycle). Hybris in the historical wars: Demosthenes 28; Hyperides 20 and 36 (the hybris of the Macedonians). Cf. Isocrates, *Panegyricus* 80.

[†] Plato, *Timaeus* 24b6–7. In the *Menexenus* (238b), the orator declares that the gods have trained the Athenians for "the acquisition and the use of weapons."

[‡] Lysias 6, 10, 12, 14, 17, 22, 46, 61, 67.

[§] *Ibid.* 4: *to palaion.*

[**] *Ibid.*

[††] *Iliad* 6.186 defines them as *antianeires* (equal but opposed to men).

[‡‡] Thucydides 2.45.2.

[§§] Lysias 75.

[***] Hyperides 27.

outrages inflicted by impious enemies on the women and girls of Greece.* In a military speech, which uses *aretē* and *andreia* without distinction to designate the highest worth, there is little room for a female virtue, except to define it as the reverse of male virtue. Thus, after reminding the sons and daughters of the dead that the first imperative for the aner is always to go beyond himself,† Pericles asks the women not to prove inferior to their natures:‡ phusis, a starting point for men, is, then, for women, an end, inscribed in them as a norm. Similarly, the word *doxa* has meaning only in a male world in which renown is the highest reward; female glory — a contradiction in terms — consists on the contrary in not being spoken of.[50]§ In the circumstances, it is of the utmost importance that the Athenians should have defeated the Amazons, erecting an eternally impassable barrier between male *eupsuchia* and female phusis.

Initially, Lysias presents the Amazons in their monstrous superiority. In the world of brute physical strength, they are *monai, prōtai*, dominating others. Warriors against nature, they have substituted the most male activity for their female phusis,** which enables them to beat men on their own ground; *gunaikes* in body, they are andres in soul, an aberrant version of the *sōma/psuchē* antithesis. At least this is the reputation they had acquired among obscure, undifferentiated peoples, whose only dimension is war.†† But though powerful by their deeds, they do not possess the logos that celebrates warlike exploits; logos is to be found entirely at Athens, a civilized polis, whose glory reaches them. It was a desire for glory, then, that threw these warrior-women against the city,‡‡ and the second act of this story sees the collapse of their audacity;

---

* *Ibid.* 20 and 36.

† Thucydides 2.45.1.

‡ *Ibid.* 2.45.2: "if you do not show yourselves to be inferior to what is your nature."

§ See Plutarch's commentary on this passage, *Virtues of Women* 242c.

** Lysias 4.

†† *Ibid.* 5.

‡‡ *Ibid.*

as if the Athenians were the touchstone of arete, the women's usurped reputation dissolves upon contact with them.* The order of the world is reestablished: the Amazons had never met anything but andres; when faced by andres agathoi, they were returned, body and soul, to their female natures.† But their madness‡ brings on them a punishment reserved for the race of bronze: total extinction in death, without leaving a name.§ This anonymous death which heightens the now-immortal renown of Athens,** justly punishes them for usurping the name of warriors and coveting others' land.

The orator may now pass from the picture of Athens the terrible to that of Athens the benevolent,†† contrasting an inglorious end with the glorious funeral of the Seven against Thebes.‡‡ Beyond rhetorical oppositions, we must see in this the two sides of the same figure of glory and justice: ever warlike, like the divinity that protects it, the redoubtable city, as embodied in the Athena Promachos at the entrance to the Acropolis, may be as reassuring as the chryselephantine Virgin of the Parthenon, armed, but in repose.

Henceforth all defensive wars will see the punishment of impious invaders,§§ and every offensive expedition will save the oppressed from unjust domination.*** The fine image is in place, and all the more so since the legendary dimension is necessarily present in the narrative, through the obligatory eulogy of Athenian autochthony.

---

* *Ibid.* "They denied their earlier reputation."

† *Ibid.*: "They found before them men of heart; their souls were no longer above their sex."

‡ *Ibid.* 6: *anoia*.

§ *Anonymon*; cf. Hesiod, *Works and Days* 154 (the bronze men).

** Lysias 6.

†† Cf. Gorgias: "violent toward the violent, moderate toward the moderate."

‡‡ Lysias 7–10.

§§ Account of the Persian Wars: Lysias 29 and 37; *Menexenus* 240d.

*** Lysias 57 and 68.

The myths of autochthony are often an integral part of a military gesture;[51] the ephebic oath invokes the Cecropid Aglauros, and the land that the ephebe swears to protect is the hero's nurse (Kourotrophos), as well as the bearer of fruit (Karpophoros). In the funeral oration, however autochthony, a patriotic and civic myth embodying the unity of the Athenian community,[52] is a political symbol even more than a military theme: the just wars of the city cannot be compared with the destructive hybris of those sons of Earth known as Spartans or Giants.[53] So, praising the Athenians for being born from their soil, the epitaphioi try above all to bring out their nobility,[54]* which finds expression in the frequent opposition between the vulgar mass and the elite of the autochthones.†

The orators, then, use *eugeneia* and *autochthōnia* interchangeably,‡ believing, with Aristotle, that "for a people or a city nobility is autochthonous or ancient origin";[55]§ and although they are sometimes content simply to mention the antiquity of the race,** they usually prefer to expatiate on the particular relationship that unites the Athenians to their land, establishes their origin on law,†† and makes them the only authentic Greeks.‡‡ The reminder

* *Ibid.* 20; *Menexenus* 239a7; Hyperides 7.

† Lysias 17 (the Athenians/the polloi).

‡ Demosthenes 4: eugeneia opens the passage on autochthony, and in 3 the orator has denied that andreia was the only value and devoted a passage to fine birth.

§ Aristotle, *Rhetoric* 1.5.1360b31ff.

** Thucydides 2.36.1 (permanence of the Athenian principle on Attic soil); Lycurgus, *Against Leocrates* 83 (antiquity of Athens). Herodotus (7.161) combines the two themes: "We who represent the most ancient people of Greece and who, alone among the Greeks, have never migrated."

†† Lysias 17; Demosthenes 4 contrasts "the others," condemned forever to be merely "adopted children," with the Athenians, "citizens of legitimate birth"; the same opposition is found in Lycurgus (*Against Leocrates* 48), transposed from sons to fathers.

‡‡ Plato, *Menexenus* 245d1.

of autochthony is, of course, a linchpin of Athenian external propaganda: according to the needs of the moment, the purity of an unalloyed birth provides the basis for hegemony* or the city's hatred of barbarians.† This theme must also have played a role in internal political struggles, if we note the insistence with which Herodotus reminds his readers that the Alcmaeonidae, unlike the Tyrannicides, the Peisistratids, or Isagoras, were of pure Athenian race.[56]‡ But the reference to autochthonous birth is above all an ideal support for Athenian narcissism, for it gives the Athenians an aristocratic image of themselves. Benveniste reminds us that the Greek notion of liberty, constituted on the basis of "growth" — growth of a social category or of a community — originally referred to the sharing of a common origin,[57] and, whatever the deeper reasons for the decree of 451–50 were, the limitations on Athenian citizenship had a great deal to do with strengthening the citizens, awareness of being of pure lineage.[58] In short, autochthony is *the Athenian myth par excellence:* reference to it is always intended to diminish the other Greeks in an imaginary victory of the one over the others, of the true over the false.§

Autochthony, then, is for the orators an essentially noble theme, and although some of them are inclined to relate the Athenians' andreia to their status as sons of the Attic earth, it is through the expedient of nobility that they rediscover this ancient link. Declaring that the memory of their legitimate origin alone allowed the Athenians of Chaironeia to measure up to the most courageous,** or passing quite naturally from the exaltation of

---

* For example, Herodotus 7.161.

† Plato, *Menexenus* 245d.

‡ Herodotus 5.62 (the Alcmaeonids); 55 and 58 (Harmodius and Aristogiton); 65 (the Peisistratids); 66 (Isagoras).

§ Lycurgus (*Against Leocrates,* 100) cites in support of his thesis the famous fragment of Euripides's *Erechtheus,* in which the poet contrasts tbe polis (v. 5) with the "other cities" (v. 8) and nominal citizenship with real citizenship (v. 13).

** Lycurgus, *Against Leocrates* 48.

211

"unparalleled nobility" to that of unmatchable valor,* Lycurgus and Herodotus seem to echo Gorgias's epitaphios, which attributes to the Athenians "innate Ares."† Only its nobility arms Athens in the service of justice, and Lysias can declare: "They attributed to their race and soil the valor that they showed against the barbarians of Asia."‡

So the funeral oration is the locus of the proclamation of Athenian "nonprofessionalism"[59] in military matters, finding its most extended expression in Pericles's epitaphios but referred to in all the orations. Lysias contrasts the defeatism of the enemy with the quiet determination of the aner agathos.§ Similarly, Pericles declares: "Our confidence is based little on preparation and stratagems, but rather on the valor that we draw from ourselves at the moment of action."**

Such a declaration may be explained, in the precise context of 430, as a way of "masking beneath fine phrases ... the relative weakness of the land army";[60]†† but the consistency with which the authors of the epitaphioi echo Pericles suggests that we should go beyond this initial representation, which is overly bound up with a particular set of circumstances. The epitaphioi never attribute any role to techne in Athenian military activity,‡‡ because, in presenting the Athenians as aristocratic warriors, the funeral oration serves a double purpose: while concealing *de facto* the maritime war, which requires very extensive training,[61]§§ it makes itself explicitly a war machine against Sparta, since, faced with the arduous "breaking in" of the Lacedaemonians,[62] Athenian courage

---

* Hyperides 7–8.

† DK, B 6, p. 286, l. 11: *emphutos Arēs*.

‡ Lysias 43. Cf. Euripides, *Heraclidae* 297–328.

§ Lysias 8.

** Thucydides 2.39.1.

†† A weakness stressed by pseudo-Xenophon, *Constitution of the Athenians* 2.1.

‡‡ The only exception is *Menexenus* 238b5, where the word *technai* covers indeed a much wider field than military activity.

§§ Cf. [Xenophon], *Constitution of the Athenians* 1.20.

is presented as a fact of nature. Thoroughly imbued with *agoge* (training),[63] the Spartan citizens are homoioi only insofar as they have already proved their valor through the many tests to which they have been accustomed.[64] Did the Athenian citizen, on the other hand, discover his valor on the battlefield? This is certainly what the epitaphioi suggest, describing the manifestations of arete as so many epiphanies.* One is born into valor in being born an Athenian, and the *Menexenus* refers to the city quite naturally as the phusis of the combatants,† but danger serves to reveal this innate bravery. So Pericles sets about denying the need for any upbringing involving painful training.‡ We now understand why the funeral oration is reluctant to devote a special passage to paideia, even by reducing it to the sphere of military activity. Thus the convergence of these passages attests once again to the unity of the genre and cannot be regarded as an indication of the reality of Athenian life. How could a topos closely bound up with Athenian self-celebration teach us anything about the existence or nonexistence of an ephebia in the time of Pericles or Lysias? So we must abandon any attempt to interpret it in realistic terms in the manner of Wilamowitz, who, at the mere mention of the word *ephēbia*, "shook his head," refusing to admit that military education was compatible with a free mode of life.[65] A comparative study of the epitaphioi enables us, on the contrary, to see in this topos the expression of a wish: the orators are trying to transform the citizen-soldiers into aristocratic warriors and are willing to find room for paideia only by annexing it to autochthony.§ Thus what is no doubt a timid concession to reality brings about a powerful return of imaginary representations. Of course Pericles refuses to base Athenian phusis on a mythical foundation, but opposing nature to teaching, he situates himself in the purest

---

* *Menexenus* 237b1–2: *apephēsanto;* 243c142: *ekphanēs;* Hyperides 23: *enephanisen.*

† *Menexenus* 237a6.

‡ Thucydides 2.39.1.

§ *Menexenus* 237b3–c5; 237c6–238a7; 238b1–6; Demosthenes 3; Hyperides 7 and 8. Cf. Thucydides 2.39.4.

tradition of aristocratic thinking, the one that reserves true glory to hereditary heroism and disdains acquired, and therefore necessarily imperfect, virtues.* On the one hand, ease; on the other, laborious, inelegant effort.†

Ease is not, of course, attributed solely to the citizens' behavior as warriors;‡ it is at work as much in everyday, private life§ as in a taste for fine things** and for Pericles is a fundamental feature of the Athenian character: under the name of flexibility,†† it turns complexity into a graceful unity.[66] But the main thing is that the reconciliation between nobility and the civic sense occurs initially in courage.[67] On this point, there is agreement among all the epitaphioi. Although Pericles's sole purpose is the depiction of the Athenian mode of being,‡‡ the elements of this portrait are found among the other orators, scattered here and there in the narrative of exploits.[68] Through this conception of courage, the funeral oration, which presents the warrior side of Athens, is imbued with aristocratic values.

The noble wishes above all to be different, for "extraordinary actions those that belong only to us, are the finest,"§§ and the oration sets out to establish this absolute difference, whether it states it at the outset in the eulogy of autochthony, as is usually the case, or postpones for a time any statement of it. In this respect, Pericles's epitaphios provides the most complete example of the transition from an implicit opposition*** to an overtly declared difference, which is turned into a weapon: "the others"

* Cf. Pindar, *Nemeans* 3.40ff.
† Thucydides 2.39.1.
‡ *Ibid.* 2.39.2 and 39.4.
§ *Ibid.* 2.37.3: "that tolerance that governs all our private relationships."
** *Ibid.* 2.40.1: "We cultivate the beautiful in simplicity."
†† *Ibid.* 2.41.1.
‡‡ *Ibid.* 2.36.4: "[I shall show] what principles of conduct [*epitēdeusis*] have brought us to this situation."
§§ Aristotle, *Rhetoric* 1.9.1367a25–26.
*** Thucydides 2.37.1: *hoi pelas*; 38.2: *tōn allōn anthrōpōn*.

become the adversary,* and the appearance of the verb *diapherein* at the beginning of the passage on war leads to the use of the verb *kratein*.† In and through war, difference becomes superiority.‡

But this difference need not always be expressed in action. It has become a state of fact, a deeply rooted nature. In Pericles, this is expressed by the use of the perfect tense,§ which "presents the author as possessor of accomplishment.[69] We now understand why Pericles has replaced the narrative of exploits with a definition of the warrior nature of Athens: any act is merely a consequence of the Athenian character, each war a mere realization of the fundamental principle.[70]** But in their own way, the fourth-century epitaphioi, except that of Hyperides, also make the city an *essence*, by attributing to it a collection of ideal actions. On the whole, the funeral oration rests on the idea that the city has already done enough for everything to attest to its greatness, since the reverses suffered by Athens confirm the reputation that she gained during the days of her power.††

The Athenian citizen, then, is that "rather proud man" whom nothing can diminish,‡‡ that is, a man in whom the self-sufficiency of the city is embodied;§§ as *sōma autarkēs*, he unites the various aspects of Athenian behavior.*** Through this definition, which crowns the eulogy of the city, Pericles's epitaphios, without departing from the central themes of the funeral oration, explains its profound significance: like the other orations, it aims to define an Athenian essence; but instead of basing the uniqueness of

* *Ibid.* 2.39.1: *tōn enantiōn.*

† *Ibid.* 2.39.1–2.

‡ *Ibid.* 2.40.3: from "we distinguish ourselves" to "we have the firmest hearts."

§ *Ibid.* 2.40.4: "For merit, we are the opposite [*enēntiōmetha*] of the many."

** *Ibid.* 2.36.4 (*epitēdeusis*) and 41.2 (*tropoi*).

†† Lysias 57–58.

‡‡ Thucydides 2.43.6.

§§ *Ibid.* 2.36.3 (*polis … autarkēstatē*).

*** *Ibid.* 2.41.1.

Athens on its mythical autochthony, it founds the superiority of Athenian man in the very autarkic and hegemonic nature of the historical city.

In doing so, Pericles's epitaphios reveals the full extent of Athenian intentions in 430: the city, whether or not aware of having reached its zenith, lays claim to exemplariness and proposes a perfect model of humanity, thus renouncing Solonian wisdom, which, born of a time of crisis, held that no man can unite everything within himself.* It may be that in this statement Pericles criticizes the idea of a statesman of the past, just as Thucydides takes the opportunity of rejecting Herodotus's ethics. But this is not the main point declaring that this ideal, which is impossible for all others, has been realized at Athens, where in each individual opposites are reconciled, the orator confidently returns to the most ancient aristocratic ideal.[71] It is a harmonization of reputation and reality,[†] Of essence and action,[‡] of audacity and reasoning,[§] of doing and saying.[72][**] This essential unity stated several times in the epitaphios and developed by Gorgias in an important passage,[73][††] is in fact the unity attributed in the *Iliad* to the hero who is "as skilled in talking as in acting."

Warrior virtue and *euboulia:* these two qualities, which "sketch a sort of ideal portrait," are embodied in the *kouroi* of the epic as in "so many rejoinders,"[74] and the archaic Sparta sung by the poets,[‡‡] the land of weapons and Muses, also tried to embody them. In granting them to Athens the orators and dramatists

* Herodotus 1.32.
† Thucydides 2.41.3 and 42.2; cf. Lysias 22.
‡ Thucydides 2.39.1; cf. Lysias 43.
§ Thucydides 2.40.3: *tolma* and *logismos*; cf. Lysias 42, concerning Themistocles.
** Thucydides 2.40.2. Cf. Lysias 40: "They won in valor, both in council and in the perils of battle."
†† DK, B 6, p. 285, 1. 9 and p. 286, 1. 3: the law of the andres is "to speak or to keep silent and to carry out what one must do." "They had doubly used ... their resolution and their energy, the first in deliberation, the second in performance."
‡‡ Terpander, Pindar, and Alcman, cited by Plutarch, *Lycurgus* 25–26.

transform the citizens into epic heroes;[75] but by the same token, they attack the prestige of Sparta, thus deprived of all *gnōmē*.* Even supposing that we should, with certain historians, see in this harmony of doing and saying an idea dear to Pericles rather than a topos of the funeral oration,[76] we must still admit that it has profoundly influenced the funeral oration, as is apparent not only in Gorgias's epitaphios but also in those of Lysias, who endows the valorous Athenians with the acuity of giving good advice; of Demosthenes, who combines his eulogy of andreia with praise of sophrosune; and of Hyperides, in which Leosthenes surpasses Themistocles in courage and wisdom.† If Pericles's epitaphios seems to function as a model, it is because it is the completed expression of the noble ideal exalted in the funeral oration.

Through the funeral oration, Athens and the Athenians make themselves into paradigms, and these perfect Athenians described by the Spartan in the *Laws*‡ are the fruit of the ceaseless work carried out in the orations on the multifarious notion of nobility. Brought together in the funeral oration, noble deeds of an eminent nature illustrate and verify an arete always identical with itself; the valor of the Athenians is revealed in each battle but is always beyond its venous historical manifestations.[77] Valor is the eminently aristocratic last word of the catalog of exploits and of the funeral oration as official celebration of Athens.

---

* Thucydides 2.40.2–3; Lysias 46: "Instructed by this speech, they understood that they were unjust and were taking wrong decisions." Cf. Isocrates, *Panathenaicus* 161.

† Lysias 46. Demosthenes 3 and 17 (*synesis, andreia:* "On both points these men were different"), 18 and 30 (Cecrops characterized by *synesis* and *alke*); Hyperides 38: *andreia kai phronēsis.*

‡ Plato, *Laws* 1.642c7–9.

CHAPTER FOUR

"As for the Name...
It Is Called a Democracy"*

An analysis of the narratives of the funeral oration reveals —
inevitably, it seems — a striking contradiction: how can a speech
that has been seen as a *practice* proper to democracy display, both
in its representations and in its language, so many aristocratic
characteristics? The problem is all the more crucial in that the
praise of democracy, the vital kernel of the praise of the polis, is
an essential element of the genre. The necessary existence of this
passage, conceived as the imprint of the political system on the
oration, seems likely to be the most useful guide in an effort to
establish the role of the funeral oration in the history of the Cleisthenean city.[1]

In its narratives, however, the funeral oration turns out to be
an aristocratic discourse. It is true that constituting as it does a
heroic achievement by Athens in its struggle with rival cities, the
catalog of exploits bears the mark of an agonistic spirit and that
the profusion of noble representations may be accounted for by
the paradoxical relation between the city and "others."[2] But if the
vocabulary of the elite is not confined to the sphere of foreign policy, if it also imbues the praise of democracy, then the phenomenon has far-reaching implications. Once again the contradiction
seems to have affected not only the oration but the city itself.

* Thucydides 2.37.1.

219

Our approach so far has required us to seek in the epitaphioi, through the eulogies of democracy, the relationship maintained in the funeral oration between the city and that system of government. For, if there is a constitution that may be said — according to a formula dear to Greek Antiquity — to be *psuchē poleōs* (the soul of the city),* it is democracy, which has been regarded by the ancients and the moderns as the very principle of classical Athens. Does the funeral oration renounce aristocratic representations in praising this constitution? Is there a democratic way of speaking about democracy? These are the important questions that we must now confront.

The Practice and Theory of Democracy

For anyone trying to reconstruct the Athenian theory of democracy, the epitaphioi are invaluable aids, in that they present an ordered eulogy of the political system. According to A.H.M. Jones, they even seem to constitute the most reliable source for such an investigation.[3] Believing that he has found in Pericles's epitaphios the expression of a democratic spirit contradictory to Thucydides's political views, and regarding Lysias's oration as a summing up of democracy for the use of the crowd,[4†] Jones concludes that the funeral oration is the privileged locus of democratic theory.

On the other hand, if we are to believe Klaus Oppenheimer, Pericles's epitaphios, insofar as it is mainly a portrayal of the Athenian constitution (although this observation might be extended to all the eulogies of democracy found in the epitaphioi), "is simply an *Athēnaiōn politeia*."[5] Since the word *politeia* may refer to three very different literary forms,[6] it should be pointed out that Oppenheimer is not thinking here of a scientific politeia, a genre that did not really exist before Aristotle, or a philosophical politeia: the funeral oration does claim, of course, to present the best constitution, the *aristē politeia*, but it regards as already achieved here and now what philosophy seeks to construct or de-

---

* CE. Isocrates, *Areopagiticus* 14 and *Panathenaicus* 138; Plato, *Menexenus* 238c1.
† Lysias 18–19.

spairs of finding anywhere but in Utopia. The eulogy of democracy clearly belongs to political politeia.[7]

Such an identification, however, has its difficulties. To begin with, if Jacoby is to be believed, this genre of literature, used in the fifth century by extreme right-wing Athenian circles, then in the following century by the moderates, was always bound up with criticism of democracy, never with its praise or defense.[8]

Furthermore, Pericles's epitaphios, by its sheer scope, goes well beyond the bounds of a politeia, unless we interpret that term broadly as "way of life."[9] At the beginning of his oration, Pericles distinguishes between the constitution (*politeia*), on the one hand, and the practice (*epitēdeusis*) and spirit (*tropoi*) of Athens, on the other;* nevertheless, flanked from the outset by these two terms, the notion of constitution is gradually contaminated, not to say destroyed by them,† and from a eulogy of the constitution Pericles seems in the end to arrive at a praise of the Athenian *nature*. If it is true that Athenian democracy scarcely had time to elaborate its own theory, the representations that passed for theory having resulted from its struggle with other political systems,[10] it might be that the definition of democracy as a phusis was originally a polemical concept, forged in the political battle against those supporters of oligarchy who believed that because the constitution was historically datable, it had an artificial, even contingent character. This may not be a decisive argument; but it is a sign that requires interpretation. Pericles's epitaphios and the funeral oration in general have sufficiently complex relations with an Athenaion politeia that we must acknowledge this issue, even if we have no ready answer to it. But to define the funeral oration as a means of presenting a theory of democracy raises a number of problems.

To begin with, it may be that the presence of a eulogy of democracy within a fixed form turns the entire passage into a topos,

---

* Thucydides 2.36.4.

† *Ibid.* 2.41.2 (there is no longer any question of Athenian tropoi).

which seems to contradict the development of a theory. Aware of this difficulty, Jones himself observes that such eulogies are often no more than "banal generalities."[11]

Indeed, the depiction of the constitution is usually general enough to cover any form of polis governed by law and not by force.[12] This is so in a passage in Lysias's epitaphios in which the orator praises Athenians for always obeying the supremacy of law and the teachings of reason.[*] Perhaps democracy acquired these general definitions from the long history of its relationship with *isonomia*.[13] Yet the epitaphioi sometimes give the impression that the representation of Athens is more important in them than that of democracy, so that even when the oration can be regarded as implicitly democratic, it is *primarily Athenian* in its language: the orators may deprive Theseus and the other legendary kings of any share in the mythical exploits, but in attributing these deeds to the Athenaioi and not to the demos, they do not go as far as Isocrates, who cannot be suspected of democratic sympathies.[†]

Last, and most important, all the epitaphioi might be expected to possess the criteria of democracy, criteria that are not an invention of the moderns but might be taken from the inscriptions and various writings of the historians, philosophers, tragic writers, and orators.[14] Yet on many such criteria — and by no means the least important — the funeral oration preserves a strange silence.

One of the first known references to the term demokratia — *dēmou kratousa cheir hopē plēthunetai*[‡] — combines an affirmation of the sovereign power of the demos with a recognition of majority law, based on the equality of the citizens.[15] Equality, the target of those opposed to the political system, is obviously for the democrats a positive principle,[16§] especially in the form of *isē-goria*: this term, which might be translated as "equality in the

---

[*] Lysias 19.

[†] Compare Lysias 7 and Isocrates, *Panathenaicus* 170.

[‡] Aeschylus, *Suppliants* 604; the text evokes "the law of the popular ballot in which the majority prevails."

[§] Cf. Euripides, *Suppliant Women* 404–408 and 433–41; *Phoenissae* 535ff.

agora"[17] and which includes the right of every citizen to address
the assembled people, is for Herodotus the very symbol of democracy, or, to be more precise, the most suitable word to describe
the Cleisthenean constitution* — and it is in defending *isēgoria*
that Protagoras shows himself to be a theorist of democracy.
Though mentioned once in Demosthenes's epitaphios (and even
there outside the actual eulogy of democracy),† isegoria *is* curiously absent from the other orations. Of course, the absence of a
term regarded in the late fifth century as old-fashioned may not
be surprising;[18] but is that a reason for the very *notion* of equality
in speech to be almost ignored in the epitaphioi? Indeed, although
what is most like a reference to isegoria is found in the passage
that Pericles devotes to the use of speech, the allusion remains
vague;‡ the orator insists not so much on everyone's *right* to
speech as on one's civic, rational *duty* to use the logos. Similarly,
although liberty is well represented in the funeral oration,§ *parrhēsia*, the freedom of speech that was the invention of fifth-century Athenian democracy and one of its major presuppositions,[19]
makes no more than very discreet appearances in the epitaphioi.
The only text that explicitly refers to this is the oration attributed
to Demosthenes, and here it is associated with *aischunē* (the sense
of honor), a term that suggests *aidōs*, the aristocratic virtue that
parrhesia had supplanted.[20] In any case, freedom of speech is
regarded here not so much from the point of view of political life
as from that of the city's military activities.

Finally, misthophoria and the drawing of lots, which for both
ancients and moderns constitute the essential characteristics of
Athenian democracy,[21] are totally ignored in the epitaphioi. This
omission may be understandable in the case of the drawing of
lots, "the most vulnerable... and most widely attacked feature"
of the system,[22] and perhaps also the most difficult to defend;

* Herodotus 5.78.
† Demosthenes 28 (Theseus, inventor of *isēgoria*).
‡ Thucydides 2.40.2–3.
§ *Ibid.* 2.37.2; Lysias 18; *Menexenus* 239a2.

even Jones does not manage to produce a single text that offers any real apologia of it; indeed it is probably not an accident due to the "poverty of our information,"[23] and the silence that surrounds this "cardinal institution" is more than disturbing. But the absence of any explicit mention of misthophoria in so complete a passage as that of Pericles must be regarded as significant.

Conversely, arete, the essential principle of government by the elite, seems to hold an important place in the epitaphioi. According to Gregory Vlastos, the insistence on arete, typical of the texts of Thucydides and Plato, seems to distinguish the epitaphioi delivered by Pericles and Socrates from the other orations, which give a more orthodox representation of democracy.[24] But this is still an optimistic view, one that a study of the epitaphioi of Lysias and Demosthenes hardly confirms. Of course, Pericles's speech* — followed and even carried further by the *Menexenus*† — specifically suggests the idea of an aristocratic democracy; but to various degrees, all the epitaphioi present the anomaly of defining democracy in nondemocratic terms.

There are several ways of approaching such a paradoxical situation, but the problem is formidable: if the funeral oration, a creation of fifth-century democracy, provides a distorted image of that system, it may be feared that this contradiction lies much more in the system than in the oration. This raises the general problem of whether there existed in Athens a *democratic* theory of democracy.

We may, like Jones, be content to declare it "curious that in the abundant literature produced in the greatest democracy of Greece there survives no statement of democratic political theory," and then try to reconstruct this theory, lost to us as the result of a series of unfortunate accidents.[25] True, the only texts genuinely inspired by democratic thinking are those of the fourth-century orators, who, in the excitement of the moment, failed to expatiate on the basic principles that, for them, needed no expla-

* Thucydides 2.37.1.
† Plato, *Menexenus* 238c7–d2.

nation. But does this mean that we do not have to explain why "all the writings of publicists, all the works of political philosophy that we possess express, in varying degrees, oligarchical sympathies"?[26] Jones believes he has found serious support in the epitaphioi, but in fact he cannot use them without considerably distorting the texts. Thus he regards the *Menexenus* as "a statement of democratic principles,"[27] whereas Plato aims on the contrary to reveal the inanity of the aristocratic pretensions of a system that he regarded as at best an unfortunate hybrid. Thus a rigorous reading of the epitaphioi must probably renounce any attempt to find this undiscoverable democratic theory of democracy.

But if the most official of the Athenian orations does not present an organized democratic theory, perhaps we should give up any attempt at reconstructing such a theory and interpret the obstacles encountered by Jones as so many proofs of its nonexistence in fifth- and fourth-century Athens. Following Louis Gernet,[28] M.I. Finley seems inclined to accept this conclusion: there are plenty of "notions, maxims, generalizations, but they do not add up to a system."[29] Is this phenomenon to be explained by a sort of bad conscience on the part of the democrats, who, fearing to reveal a partisan attitude, diluted the specificity of their constitution in a mass of heterogeneous elements? Or is it because the Athenians identified democracy with life itself,[30] and life has no theory? Are we to conclude that the democrats preferred action, which was urgent and necessary, to writing and reflecting on politics, which seems to be suggested by Cleon's hostility to any intrusion by intellectuals in affairs of state?*

Finley does not really choose among all these hypotheses, although he lays special stress on the last explanation and confirms this position in his book *Democracy Ancient and Modern*. "The philosophers attacked democracy; the committed democrats responded by ignoring them, by going about the business of government and politics in a democratic way, without writing treatises on the subject."[31] Such, it would seem, was the distribution

* Thucydides 3.37.3–5 and 38.

225

of tasks between opponents and partisans of the system — polemics and writing pamphlets on the one hand, unconcerned choice of action on the other.

So the democrats acted and did not write. But to point out a fact is not to elucidate the causes of such a situation. We must still explain why, in fifth- and fourth-century Athens, the choice of a way of life and a type of action was not accompanied by a theoretical justification of that way of life and that action: why, when faced with written pamphlets, which is what the oligarchic *politeiai* were, the democrats did not in turn become writers to defend democracy against what were often violent attacks. Perhaps the system was so secure that they felt no need to resort to indirect, written intervention. Perhaps, too, we should go further and examine the status of writing in the Athenian democracy, a status closely bound up with that of education.

Athens: the intellectual center of Greece;* the Athenians: "half-educated," as Finley puts it.[32] Perhaps we can mitigate this exaggerated contradiction by recalling that the demos, the overwhelming majority of which possessed the rudiments of education — reading and writing[33] — largely relied on the lessons of experience, learning its political role at the assembly sessions,[34] whereas "the sons of the rich, sent to school earlier than the others, left it later.† Of course, those wealthier classes also provided the Athenian system with not only its leaders — at least until 429 — but also its opponents,[35] and the silence of a Pericles on matters of theory cannot be accounted for by some cultural obstacle. The explanation must be sought elsewhere, namely in the general attitude of the Athenian democracy of the fifth and perhaps also of the fourth century to writing.

Observing that Pericles "left no writing, apart from his decrees," Plutarch reminds us of the need to distinguish between two kinds of writing: an *instrumental* writing, which serves to convey the laws and decrees of the assembly, and a *theoretical*,

---

* Plato, *Protagoras* 337d6 ("the prytaneum of science").
† *Ibid.* 326c5–6, and more generally 325c6–326e6.

reflexive writing, which is made concrete in texts.* We know that
the first, which permitted the demos to exercise effective control
over its magistrates and sanctioned political decisions, was essential to democracy,[36] whose written laws were its very foundation.[37†]
But insofar as any decree is presented as a faithful transcription of
an assembly session,[38] its writing is totally subordinated to the
logos,‡ the sole motive force of political action, to which it brings
at most the durable addition of publicity. Writing is democratic in
that it makes popular support for a persuasive speech permanent.
Is it still so when, as a synonym for theoretical elaboration, it is an
action? Or, to pose the problem in other terms, *who* writes in
Athens? By failing to pose this crucial question clearly enough,[39]
scholars generally forget that the Athenian writers were not
among the ranks of the democratic leaders. If we except the
poets, tragic or comic, whose plays were primarily intended to be
acted, foreigners who passed themselves off as Athenian writers,
Sophists whose democratic polis was the sphere of action par
excellence, and historians such as Herodotus and Hellanicus, for
whom the history of Greece or of the cities was not to be written
without that of Athens; and if we except the case, frequent
enough in the fourth century, of the speech written down after
the event, we must conclude that only those who, for one reason
or another, took no direct part in the affairs of the city devoted
themselves to the activity of writing. An exile such as Thucydides;[40§] opponents, such as pseudo-Xenophon and the authors of
politeiai; an Isocrates, who, according to tradition, "kept apart
from public life because he had a weak voice and a shy character";** a Plato, whose abortive political experiences had led him
to theoretical speculation†† — all were, necessarily or by choice,

* Plutarch, *Pericles* 8.7.
† Euripides, *Suppliant Women* 433–34.
‡ Plato, *Phaedrus* 258a9–10 (*logos sungegrammenos*).
§ Thucydides 5.26.5 (the leisure of the exile).
** [Plutarch], *Life of the Ten Orators* 4.4–5.
†† Cf. the seventh letter, 324c, 325a5 and b1, 325e1–2, 331d.

citizens who were *apragmones* (inactive), if not *achreioi* (useless),* in a city that preached participation in public life and condemned aristocratic leisure.† Conversely, if Plato is to be believed, "those who have most power in the city ... blush to write speeches or to leave after them writings in their own hands, for fear of the judgments of the future and of being called Sophists."‡ This statement, presented as a true description of a widely held opinion,§ applies in the first instance to Athens and to Athenian politicians:[41] was not Plutarch merely echoing it when he observed that although Pericles did not write, he took the greatest care with his speeches?**

If we are to draw any conclusion from these convergent facts, it might be that Athenian democracy distrusted writing — or, what amounts to the same thing, never used it — as an instrument of theoretical reflection: only speech was really respected in the political sphere of Athens, and this is hardly surprising. Was not logos — a mode of direct, effective intervention — "the political tool par excellence"[42] as much as a place of egalitarian exchange? This circumstance might explain the nonexistence of a *written* theory of democracy. But every historian of Greece knows that one must look in the speeches for what is not to be found in the written works,[43] and as a result the statements and omissions of the funeral oration take on an added significance. Indeed, if democracy has no weapon but logos, where might one better seek a coherent eulogy of the system of government than in this official oration? It is to be found neither in legal pleas nor in political speeches: in the fever of action, orators scarcely had time to offer their fellow citizens a reflection on the political practices of Athens, and this is not what their audience expected of them. The funeral oration, on the other hand, serves as a pause, after battle, before new actions, and the public expected from the orator a formal eulogy of democracy. If, then, it

---

* To use the terms of Pericles's epitaphios (Thucydides 2.40.2).

† Cf. *ibid.* 5.26.5 and Plato, seventh letter, 331d5 (the sage's *bēsuchia*).

‡ Plato, *Phaedrus* 257d5–8.

§ *Ibid.* 257d4–5.

** Plutarch, *Pericles* 8.6–7.

is really impossible to find in it an organized form of democratic thinking, such a phenomenon must be interpreted for itself. We shall now try to understand the reasons for this disturbing absence.

The study of the funeral oration should, then, try to determine whether the oration was merely the symptom of a malaise that was deeply rooted in the city and that translated, on every level, into the absence of properly democratic reflection, or whether, on the contrary, this phenomenon is to be explained by the very nature of the funeral oration, a military speech that the general spirit of the eulogy and the noble connotations of battle forced to move solely within the sphere of aristocratic representations. In either case, we will endeavor to situate the funeral oration in the context of an evolution of the Athenian representations of democracy: the problems are not the same for the time of Ephialtes as for that of Cleon or, still less, for that of Lysias and Demosthenes, and it may be that our general understanding of the eulogy of democracy is influenced by the fact that we possess no epitaphios written before 430.

An examination of the various "anomalies" presented by the epitaphioi in their eulogy of democracy is therefore necessary; it will enable us to trace a possible evolution from one oration to another or to confirm, in this sphere, too, the unity of the genre.

Eulogy of Democracy, Aristocratic Representations

There are two ways of presenting democracy in terms that are not strictly democratic: either the orator, like Pericles, proposes arete as its fundamental principle, or he gives it a nontemporal constitution with a quasimythical origin, as in Lysias's epitaphios. We shall study these two attitudes in turn, different versions of the same attempt to protect democracy from the criticism of its opponents — a dangerous undertaking, for it risks undermining the originality of the system.

I am not of course claiming that Pericles's epitaphios possesses *no* democractic features — such a position would be untenable. On the contrary, Pericles very quickly, at the beginning of a sentence, makes a brilliant reference to liberty in its double form, public and private,* which all writers, both opponents and supporters of democracy, recognize as the very basis of the system;† respect for law, another democratic characteristic, is identified with rational fear, *deos*,‡ and after referring to obedience to the magistrates in words that are fairly close to the official formula of the inscriptions, § the orator stresses the importance of Athenian legislation in matters of justice.[44] The reference to the city's "openness" is, for Pericles, an opportunity for stressing that "our city is thrown open to the world and we never ... debar anyone from learning or seeing anything,"** a feature that has been seen as essential to any polis[45] but that finds its most perfect expression in a democratic constitution. Last, devoting a fairly long passage to the democratic theme of equal political competence for all, the orator recalls that in Athens wealth and poverty are defined not in terms of prestige or dishonor,[46] but as two contingent situations both subordinate to the duty of acting in and for the city;†† so, after declaring that the same person may concern himself both with his own affairs and with those of the state,[47] Pericles finally identifies a refusal to take part in public life as a sort of political parasitism. In these three closely linked points, it is easy to recognize three essential characteristics of democracy: the practice of the liturgies, the Athenian revaluing of work — the limits of which should not conceal its profound originality[48] — and, above all the cate-

---

* Thucydides 2.37.2: "And not only in our public life are we liberal [*eleutheros ... politeuomen*], but also as regards our freedom of suspicion of one another in the pursuit of our daily life."

† Aristotle, *Politics* 6.1317a40 (liberty, the fundamental principle of the democratic system). Political liberty: Euripides, *Heraclidae* 411–24; [Xenophon], *Constitution of the Athenians* 1.8. Liberty in private relations: [Xenophon], *Constitution of the Athenians* 1.10–12, Plato, *Statesman* 303b1; Aristotle, *Politics* 6.1317b11–12.

‡ Thucydides 2.37.3.

§ *Ibid.*: *tōn ... aiei en archei ontōn akrasei.*

** *Ibid.* 2.39.1.

†† *Ibid.* 2.40.1–2; wealth and poverty: 40.1; the union of private and public affairs, definition of the parasite-citizen: 40.2. Cf. also 2.37.1, where a term is copied from the official formula that opens the debates of the ekklesia: *echon ti agathon drasai tēn polin.*

gorical imperative for everyone to participate in civic affairs.[49]

Concerning himself more with the epitedeusis of Athens than with politeia in the strict sense, Pericles does not, of course, provide an exhaustive exposition of the democratic constitution. In a few very general formulas in his epitaphios, we can only just detect remote allusions to the ekklesia or the *heliaia*, and it is not certain whether the orator ever refers — even indirectly — to the Cleisthenean boule of the Five Hundred,[50] an essential organ of democracy.[51]* However, this silence does not constitute an anomaly, for praise is given first to the *spirit* of the system.

But there are more disturbing silences, statements that sound less democratic. To begin with, there are the very terms in which Pericles defines democracy.† Apart from the fact that *pleiones* (the majority) might sound both more precise and more limiting than *polloi* (the many)‡ and especially *pantes* (all),§ the term *oikein es* is worthy of attention. Vlastos rightly remarks that it would be wrong to translate it, as most editors and commentators do, simply as government *of* the people.[52] Of course, the term is sufficiently vague to allow — even to encourage — us to slide in this direction. However, this is not what the expression says: in fact it refers to government *for* the people, and the demos is viewed as a beneficiary of the system rather than as a sovereign people.** It

---

* Aristotle, *Politics* 6.1317b30; cf. also 4.1299b32 and 38.

† Thucydides 2.37.1: "Our system is called a democracy because it serves the interests [*oikein es*] not of the few [*oligoi*] but of the majority [*pleiones*]."

‡ Lysias 56: in the allied cities, the Athenians "did not consider it just that the many [*polloi*] should be enslaved to an oligarchy [*oligoi*]"; cf. Herodotus 3.80 ("it is in the many that everything resides").

§ Lysias 18 (democracy as "liberty of all"); cf. Thucydides 6.39.1 (oration of Athenagoras, leader of the Syracusan democrats): "I say that the word *people* designates a complete whole and the word *oligarchy* only a part."

** There is an instructive comparison with Euripides, *Suppliant Women* 406 ("the people reign"), whose formulation involves no ambiguity. See also the precise definition given by Aristotle, *Politics* 5.1310a28–29 (two criteria of democracy: the sovereignty of the majority — *to pleion kurion* — and liberty) and 6.1317b9–10.

231

would be pointless to see this as some oversight or mere stylistic device on Thucydides's part; as Vlastos observes very clearly, "the idea of the masses engaging in the actual business of government ... is suppressed throughout the whole of this speech."[53] The term is intentionally ambiguous, and it may be no accident that the term demokratia, which refers to the power (kratos) of the people, does not occupy the central position in the sentence.[54]

With this process of distortion, by which the democratic element is stated, but in a context that profoundly alters it, we come to an essential characteristic of the eulogy of democracy in this epitaphios. It is all there, and yet, reading the text closely, we realize that the orator is saying something quite different from what he seems to be saying.

As we have seen, Pericles insists that the Athenian citizen could participate in political life while managing his own affairs or practicing a profession; in fact, however, things are more complicated than they seem at first. The orator develops this idea in two different forms,* and it would be naive to think that he is merely repeating himself. If one is attentive to the gap between *epimēleia*, an active concern for political life, the administration of the city's affairs, and mere decision making (*gnōnai*); if one translates *pros erga tetrammenois* as "the workers";[55] if one is attentive to the subtlety involved in the use of a negative form such as *mē endeos*, then Pericles is in fact saying something quite different, which might be translated more or less like this: "It is possible for the same individual to concern himself both with his private affairs and with public affairs, like those who devote themselves to an understanding of political questions."[56]

But such a translation, which is both evasive and too clear, still does not completely explain a difficult and ambiguous text. Indeed it ignores the many difficulties that have faced scholars trying to dispose of the term *heterois* (others)[57] and forgets that no *official* orator, even one enjoying the prestige of Pericles,

* Thucydides 2.40.2: *Eni te tois autois ... kai heterois.*

could recognize so overtly the existence in Athens of "two classes." More subtly, Pericles is probably saying two things at once. He certainly recognizes that everyone has political competence, but he does not exclude the possibility that it is different for the two categories of Athenians: those who concern themselves, with equal vigilance, with their *oikos* and the city;[58] and those who practice a profession that does not prevent them from taking decisions in the assembly, where the multiplicity of their activities is merged in a *political* unity. In doing so, Pericles replies to the criticisms of the oligarchs, for whom "work will always prevent a poor laborer, even an educated one, from attending to public affairs,"* and his answer is specifically democratic; but he also supports a division of tasks that effectively leaves the aristocrats with access to the principal positions of responsibility in the city. However, the passage is subtle enough for each part of the audience to understand what it wants to understand:[59] "the exercise of various trades does not prevent one from acquiring sufficient knowledge of political questions" (the version for the "half-educated" crowd); or "the others, the workers of every kind are after all quite capable of arriving at correct decisions" (the more secret meaning, decipherable by the cultured elite). The democratic criterion is expressed in a formulation with a double meaning: in a single passage, the orator speaks to two audiences, which democracy tries to treat as a single civic body, and whose fine ambiguity preserves unity in the text of the epitaphios.[60]

A similar distortion limits the role of law in the oration. Declaring that the law secures equality to all alike in their private disputes,"† Pericles makes room for these two fundamental criteria of democracy, laws and equality. But in reality he limits the efficacy of the *nomoi* to the sphere of private relations, which deprives the notion of isonomia of any meaning, making it unrecognizable and antiquated.[61] In fact, being always either below or above the political world, laws do not occupy in the epitaphios

* Euripides, *Suppliant Women* 420–22.
† Thucydides 2.37.1.

233

the central place usually assigned them in civic life, since, after limiting their intervention to the regulation of private transactions the orator further dissolves their specificity by integrating them into a larger whole, that of the *nomima*, or venerable ancestral customs.[62] Distinguishing between two kinds of laws, "those that are ordained for the protection of the injured and those unwritten laws that bring upon the transgressor admitted dishonors,"* Pericles does not really mention the written laws, which were the basis of the democratic system:† they are only implicitly understood as such,[63] in opposition to the unwritten laws, the *agraphoi nomoi.* Conversely, the presence of these agraphoi nomoi is in itself a significant phenomenon. We know how much the Greek aristocratic tradition mistrusted written laws;[64] and certain fourth-century Athenian writers' exaltation of the unwritten laws‡ must be seen as a conservative act, whether or not they are referring to Sparta.§ Of course, as Edmund Büchner observes, Pericles does not really criticize written legislation,[65] which indeed his argument presupposes, and Gorgias goes much further, praising the dead for the many instances in which they preferred correct thought and speech to detailed points of law,** by virtue of that nomos, both religious and political,†† that is the observance of *kairos.* But even so, the presentation of unwritten laws as an essential characteristic of Athenian democracy deserves attention, especially if, as some scholars believe, it is a general tendency of the funeral oration.[66] By referring to "Draconian laws" when speaking in the courts or in the assembly,‡‡ the fourth-century orators present this first written code as one of the glories of

* *Ibid.* 2.37.3.

† Demosthenes, *Against Timocrates* 5 (laws — and written laws — as the essential contribution of democracy); 75–76 (*nomos* opposed to *oligarchia*).

‡ Isocrates, *Areopagiticus* 41; Plato, *Republic* 425b7–8 and d6–8.

§ Cf. Plutarch, *Lycurgus* 13.4.

** DK, 82 B 6, p. 285,11. 7–8.

†† *Ibid.* 2.8–9: *theiotatos kai koinotatos nomos.*

‡‡ Demosthenes, *Against Aristocrates* 51; *Against Leptines* 158; *Against Timocrates* 211.

Athens:[67] could the funeral oration be resolutely deaf to historical experience?

We may also wonder about the significance of that "admitted dishonor" (*aischunē homologoumenē*) that punishes the transgression of unwritten laws. Perhaps the use of this term corresponds, like the addition of *aidōs* to *dikē* in the myth of the *Protagoras*,* to a desire to introduce, beside "the observance of rules for themselves, . . . a more private, more personal feeling":[68] the aischune of the unwritten laws would temper the rigor of the written norms, just as aidos makes *dikē* less rigid. But the word *aischunē* conveys more than a nuance: there is something of an echo of the archaic societies in which "everyone feels that he is being watched by others."[69] Indeed, "shame," like the notion of aidos, to which it is closely related,[70] designates the weight of public opinion,[71]† and its evocation is a reference back to the most ancient aristocratic ethic.[72] Thus a passage that opens with fear (*deos*) ends with *aischunē*, and even though the orator is careful to separate these terms in a sort of chiasma, the binomial *deos/aischunē* suggests the pairing *aidōs kai deos* — a very ancient pairing‡ that came back into fashion in fifth-century tragedy[73] and, in the form of *phobos/sebas*, governed the praise of the Areopagus in *The Eumenides*.§ Could it be that the Areopagus, despite the orator's subtle precautions, is more present in the epitaphios than the boule? The question is important, even if it must remain open.

If we come back now to Pericles's first definition of the Athenian constitution, it is hardly surprising that the orator uses the antithesis between *kaleisthai* and *pephukenai* to characterize democracy as a *name* that the reality of the system greatly exceeds.[74]** We may believe that such a definition shows that Pericles is on the

* Plato, *Protagoras* 322c2, c4, d1, d5.
† Cf. Lysias 25 (at Marathon, the Athenians were more afraid of the shame incurred at contravening their own laws than of external danger).
‡ *Iliad* 15.657–58; *Hymn to Demeter* 190.
§ Aeschylus, *Eumenides* 690–91, 697–98, 700.
** Thucydides 2.37.1.

defensive;[75] the word demokratia still appears as a sort of formal concession. De Romilly believes that we should not see in this text "oppositions in the strict sense, . . . each point of view rectifying and complementing the preceding one in such a way as to suggest the very harmony of the system."[76] But without going as far as the scholiast, who believes the orator is saying that Athens, though nominally a democracy, is in fact an aristocracy, we are nevertheless forced to understand this sentence as an opposition between an *onoma* and its ergon, even if — according to Thucydides's own custom — the antithesis is only half explicit.

The text, then, may be read as Vlastos reads it: "To be sure (*men*), our constitution, being government for the people, is called 'democracy'; but (*de* adversative, scaling down still further what Athenians would associate with this word), while (1) on the one hand (*men* concessive: in this respect no opposition to *dēmokratia keklētai*, from the point of view of laws we have equality in litigation, yet (2) on the other hand (*de* strongly adversative, the real opposition to *dēmokratia keklētai*, from the point of view of titles each is preferred according to our esteem for him (i.e.) (a) not so much for his class as (b) for his excellence."[77]

Thus arete carries the stress of the sentence, and once isonomia is relegated to the sphere of private relations, *worth* becomes the only measure of political life: to *kata tous nomous* is opposed *kata tēn axiōsin*, and by this means emulation and affirmation of personal merit are reintroduced.[78] In Platonic or Aristotelian language,* we might say that to arithmetic equality, the norm of private relations, is opposed a sort of geometric equality, the principle governing accession to responsibility.[79] By placing *ap' aretēs protimatai* at the culminating point of the period, does the orator wish, as Vlastos says, to suggest that Athenian democracy is an "aristocracy of talent"?[80] Such an expression requires some qualification. Although he uses the term arete, Pericles avoids the word *aristokratia*,[81] which refers explicitly to a system in which Athens

* Aristotle, *Politics* 6.1317b3–4 (equality in terms of number/equality in terms of merit).

would not recognize itself.[82] No doubt he is simply trying to gain recognition for the aristocratic spirit of Athenian democracy, which "never entirely turned its back on the aristocratic ideal ... always preserving an area of public activity in which the excellence of the few could have free rein."[83]

It was legitimate, then, to define this "area of public activity" in which arete had its role to play; but it is as if the epitaphios reduced the whole of Athenian political life to that privileged sphere in which election distributed the honors. If one has to defend democracy against those critics who see it as the system in which the laborer lays down the law,* in which "the poor and the people enjoy more advantages than the nobles and the rich,"† can one do so only by concealing what is essential in democratic practice? In fact, we shall seek in vain in the epitaphios for any mention of the nonelective responsibilities whose granting depends democratically on the drawing of lots,‡ and which nevertheless constitute a service, sanctioned by misthophoria. Furthermore, no passage is devoted to that direct, egalitarian exercise of citizenship represented by attendance at the ekklesia, any more than to the strict supervision of its magistrates by the sovereign demos.§

Of course, Pericles is careful to distinguish the arete appreciated at Athens from its oligarchic homonym, which is bound up with birth or fortune:[84] "It is not so much membership in a particular category as merit that brings one honors; conversely, poverty does not prevent a man, capable in every respect of serving the state, from doing so because of the obscurity of his situation."[85]** In its rejection of the social criteria on which oligarchic systems are based, democracy thus becomes the refuge of the

---

* Plato, *Protagoras* 319b–d; Xenophon, *Memorabilia* 1.2.9; *Dissoi logoi,* DK, 90.7.

† [Xenophon], *Constitution of the Athenians* 1.2.

‡ However, the drawing of lots is central in Herodotus (3.80, the oration of Otanes) and hinted at in Euripides's *Heraclidae* (36).

§ Herodotus (3.80), on the other hand, gives plenty of room to these two elements, listed after the mention of the drawing of lots.

** Thucydides 2.37.1.

THE INVENTION OF ATHENS

pure aristocratic *principle*.[86] But the detailed arguments given by the orator are clear only in appearance.

Thus the formula *ouk apo merous to pleon . . . e ap' aretēs* has often proved an embarrassment to the commentators. Some, refusing to accept — or failing to explain — the absence of the drawing of lots and the rotation of responsibilities,* have interpreted *apo merous* as an allusion to those missing democratic criteria.[87] But these are desperate attempts failing by lack of realism or by ignorance of the strategy of the oration: could an official orator be so clumsy as to deny overtly, before the assembled people, the very bases of democracy?[88] In fact, the epitaphios is no more concerned than any of the other known forms of speech with the drawing of lots or the rotation of offices. But as de Romilly and Vlastos have realized, *meros*, which normally designates a section of society,† here refers to membership in a category or class, and Pericles deliberately avoids using a more precise term, such as *ploutos* or *genos*;[89] the vagueness of the term allows every social category to profit by it.

But there is another, much more serious ambiguity in this formula, one that has not received much attention from the commentators:[90] it would have been useful to stress how the orator, at the very moment when he denies the importance of social criteria in the recruitment of magistrates, surreptitiously reintroduces these same criteria. Indeed, *ou . . . to pleon . . . ē . . .* is not the exact equivalent of *ouk . . . alla . . .*, and declaring that the selection is carried out *less* on the grounds of belonging to a particular category than in terms of merit, Pericles implicitly recognizes that the place occupied by an individual in the hierarchy of Solon's property-based electoral groups is not irrelevant.[91]

Finally, when Pericles declares that poverty is not a handicap, he seems to be aiming at two contradictory targets at the same time: to state an egalitarian principle and to recognize implicitly the exis-

---

* Unlike Euripides, *Suppliant Women* 406–407 (and Aristotle, *Politics* 6.1317b3–11).
† Euripides, *Suppliant Women* 241: *meros* (social class); cf. 238: *meris* and 244: *moiron*. Cf. also Thucydides 6.39.1: *meros* = social class (twice).

tence of a hierarchy of prestige within the city. Of course, democratic equality distinguishes between *axiōma*, social consideration,
rank, and *axiōsis*, the assessment by Athenians of one of their number, an assessment that sees, beyond the obscurity of a poor citizen's
situation, his real worth — this is a crucial point. But *axiōma* is also
an echo of *axiōsis*, and the very construction of the sentence (*oud'
au*: nor, conversely) indicates that we have not left the sphere of the
assessment of merit, the sphere of elective responsibilities in which
prestige is a determinant factor;* in what form could the poor man,
by definition deprived of social consideration (*axiōmatos aphaneiai*),
"serve the state"?[92] It would be pointless, then, to seek in that sentence, as some historians have done, an allusion to misthophoria.[93]
On the contrary, everything seems to suggest that the orator continued to identify democracy with arete while constantly covering
up the traces that might expose this strange identification.

But in Antiquity, one reader was not taken in by the appearances
subtly constructed by Pericles and Thucydides: Plato, taking pleasure in refuting democracy in the very midst of praising it, makes
the words that Pericles avoided stand out[94] and thus exposes what
the epitaphios merely hinted at, while stressing the incoherence of
his hidden intentions. The opposition, which is no more than suggested, between the name and the reality of the system is developed here in a mass of antitheses;† a single formula (*met' eudoxias
plēthous aristokratia*) is enough for Plato to transform arete into
aristokratia, thus showing that the role of the crowd is one of
approval and undermining the definition that he has just given;‡

* As is emphasized by *hos hekastos en toi eudokimei*.
† *Menexenus* 238d1–2: "Some call it [*kalei*] democracy, others whatever name
they please, but it is in reality [*tēi alēthēiai*] government by the elite with the
approval of the crowd."
‡ Similarly, in 238d4–5, Plato begins by declaring the kratos of the crowd
("power in the city belongs essentially to the crowd": *enkrates to plēthos*) only to
reduce this power in the end by declaring the "best" as leaders (the crowd gives
them *archai kai kratos*, magistracies and power).

how can one imagine an aristocracy based on *eudoxia plēthous?* Even then, the crowd must have a good doxa (opinion).

Even more specifically, a passage in the *Menexenus* refers ironically to the opposition between *apo merous* and *ap' aretēs.* Praising Athens for being "an aristocracy with the approval of the crowd," Socrates offers by way of proof the fact that it had kept kings; "sometimes," he says, "they have held this title by birth and sometimes by election."* Although the phylobasileis have been recognized as kings *ek genous,* the "elected kings" have posed a problem: attempts have been made to see them as archon kings and then, by extension, as all the archons.[95] But could Plato be committing the gross error of including the appointment of magistrates by drawing lots under the heading of election? This "error" must be taken as intentional. Substituting *hairetoi* for *aretē* by means of a pun, Plato "forces" and elucidates the text of Pericles's oration once again: the transformation of magistrates appointed by lots into elected magistrates enables him to bring out the process by which, while denying birth as a criterion of access to responsibilities,† the orator deliberately conceals the lot in order to valorize the election alone.[96]

By subjecting the oration to this critical reading, Plato was no doubt attacking Thucydides, Pericles, and the funeral oration at one and the same time; but ever since, all readers of the epitaphios have been aware of the aristocratic character of this eulogy of democracy, a character that does in fact pose a difficult problem: if it is true that Pericles's government contributed, more than any other, to giving a solid base to Athenian democracy, how can one explain the gap between his oration, as reconstructed by Thucydides, and his actual political practice? Many historians have stressed the size of this gap. One might be surprised that the statesman who broadened access to the magistracy should here restrict isonomia to private relations.[97] The absence of any allu-

---

* *Menexenus* 238d2–4.

† *Ibid.*: *ek genous* forms with *hairetoi* the same pair as *apo merous* with *ap' aretēs.*

sion to misthophoria, which, in opening up participation in the affairs of the city to all, is the target of reactionary attacks, is no less strange.[98] Must this anomaly be imputed to Pericles? Should we hold Thucydides responsible for it? Or is it quite normal in an epitaphios? No other known epitaphios contains a eulogy of misthophoria, a fact that de Romilly misjudges when she declares that "the idea of *misthos* may well have figured in the passage."[99]

We may dismiss from the outset the hypothesis that under Pericles's government, Athens did not really enjoy democracy. It is true that Pericles exercised *de facto* authority, but only within the democratic institution;[100] and, anyway, to declare that democracy exists only when every "great man" has disappeared amounts to saying that this political system did not exist until 428, a claim that cannot be seriously sustained.[101]

Are we to think, then, that this gap is the trace left by the historian on the politician's oration? If so, we must set the historical Pericles against Thucydides's character, which allows us not to impute the aristocratic nature of the passage in the epitaphios to the constraints of the funeral oration as a genre. Thus, for Helmuth Vretska, the epitaphios, though seeming to praise democracy, is simply a commentary on the well-known sentence "Athens, though in name a democracy, was in fact ruled by her first citizen";[102*] and, for Goossens as for Francis Cornford, who sees Pericles as the embodiment of Athenian *timē*,[103] everything is explained by the rapid development, after the politician's death, of a "Pericles legend."[104]

I shall not try here to conceal the close link that binds the epitaphios to the whole of Thucydides's work,† but especially to the first two books and to the other two orations attributed to Pericles in them, or to the portrait that the historian draws of the statesman by way of a funeral oration: certain statements in the epitaphios are obviously echoes of things said in the orations of

---

* Thucydides 2.65.9.

† Compare, for example, 3.42.2 (Diodotus) and 2.40.2 (Pericles), 3.67.6 (Sparta as *paradeigma*) and 2.37.1 (Athens as *paradeigma*).

the Corcyreans and Corinthians.* Pericles's last oration often plays a revealing role in relation to the epitaphios, developing what was only suggested in it† or saying openly what had not been said in it at all;‡ and, in the insistence with which Thucydides stresses that prestige was the "first citizen's" only power base, we may see the direct application of the passage on axiosis.§ Nevertheless, it is also true that by its abstraction, which contrasts strongly with the realism of Pericles's other speeches, and by the place it gives to *timē*,[105] the epitaphios enjoys a sort of autonomy in the general economy of the oeuvre, and it has been possible to see a "uniqueness" in the "very presence" of this oration,[106] dominated as it is through and through by aristocratic representations. It is therefore reasonable to believe that while reconstructing the oration according to the overall perspectives of his own text, Thucydides did not incorporate the epitaphios in his *History* by chance: it was no doubt essential to his project of writing down what the orator had actually said — or what the genre made him say.

But many clues suggest that Pericles did in fact deliver a speech quite similar to the literary epitaphios. After reminding us of everything that links this text to the historian's thought, de Romilly observes that the ideas expressed are nevertheless those of the politician and that they accord perfectly with the climate of opinion at the beginning of the Archidamian War.[107] Likewise, Victor Ehrenberg believes that it is possible to attribute to Pericles the idea that citizens must be "in love with Athens,"[108]** and Bernard Knox reminds us that in the Periclean period the relationship of the Athenians to their city was one of veneration.[109] Finally, and above all, there is a disturbing resemblance, often

---

* Athens, the allies, and *charis*: 1.33.1–2 (oration of the Corcyreans); 2.40.4 (epitaphios). Athens, Sparta, deeds, and reputation: 1.69.5 (oration of the Corinthians); 2.41.3 and 42.2 (epitaphios).

† *Pasa thalassa kai gē*: 2.41.4 (epitaphios); 2.62.2 (last oration).

‡ Memory: 2.41.4 (epitaphios); memory and decline: 2.64.3 (last oration).

§ Compare 2.37.1 and 2.65.4 (*pleistou axiōn*), 8 (*axiōma* and *axiōsis*).

** Thucydides 2.43.1: *erastas ... autēs*.

remarked on, between the agon of *The Suppliant Women* and Thucydides's text, which is an argument in favor of the thesis that the oration *or its themes* belong to an earlier period than the tragedy, insofar as Euripides seems to systematically make explicit what in Pericles remains implicit: thus there are passages on private disputes between citizens,* on participation by the poor in public life,† on the connection between freedom and being able to serve the state.‡ It is doubtless correct to believe that the two writers were drawing inspiration from a common source, in fact from the epitaphios actually delivered by Pericles.[110]

Thucydides's mark is to be sought, then, in the register of expression accorded to the whole work, rather than in the content and strategy of the oration. Fidelity to the genre, to the circumstances, to the content and spirit, if not to the very letter: does not such a reconstruction conform to the broad principles laid down by the historian in the celebrated methodological account in book 1?[111]§

But if we regard the epitaphios as a speech by Pericles before being a text by Thucydides, the aristocratic character of the passage on democracy takes on a new significance: in giving such an image of the political system that he had helped to strengthen, the politician had to submit, as an official orator, to the influence of a genre dominated by aristocratic representations. A study of the most "original" epitaphios leads to that of the funeral oration: the individual oration attests to the spirit of the genre.

At other times, with other orators, a different strategy served the same purpose. In the fourth century, the ennobling of democracy consisted in pushing back its founding to mythical times. Of course, democracy, a historical acquisition and the context of the oration, ought to be "the only title of Athenian glory to derive its legitimacy solely from the present" and not from the past.[112] But in Lysias or

---

* *Ibid.* 2.37.1; Euripides, *Suppliant Women* 433–36.

† Thucydides 2.37.1 and 40.1–2; *Suppliant Women* 420–22, 424 (*axiōma*), 433–34.

‡ Thucydides 2.37.1 (end)–2; *Suppliant Women* 438–39.

§ Thucydides 1.22.1.

Demosthenes as well as in Hyperides, the funeral oration ignores not only the historically datable character of the system (Cleisthenes is never mentioned, any more than the Peisistratids)* but also its development and its transformations. In this respect, it differs from the fourth-century *Atthides*, which turned the historical and chronological description of the Athenian constitution into a political weapon.[113] And whereas in Herodotus the term *hoi Athēnaioi*, after being applied in a neutral way to the city of Athens, is, from book 5 on, more and more often associated with democracy and with the demos as a political force,[114] the funeral oration knows no such progression. The term *hoi Athēnaioi* seems immutable in the epitaphios, perhaps because the Athenians are seen as constituting a demos from the beginning; but by the same token, democracy becomes as essential a component of Athens as it is alien to history.[115]

Plato recognized this feature of the funeral oration very clearly. According to him, the orators' tactic was to say that the Athenian system of government had always been the same from the beginning,[†] which allowed them to bring together "the war dead, all the ancestors . . . and [the Athenians] still alive,"[‡] so that democracy, stretching back into the past, became a "fine constitution" (*kalē politeia*),[§] identical with itself, now and long ago. This would prove, if there is need to, that in the *Menexenus*, Plato criticizes not only Pericles's epitaphios,[116] which praises democracy here and now, but also, more generally, the funeral oration of his time, and with it all the panegyrics of Athens, in which the state derives its glory not from itself,

---

* On the other hand, as we have seen, Demosthenes makes Theseus the founder of isegoria (28).

† *Menexenus* 238c5–7: "It was then the same system as in our own day, the government by the elite which governs us today and which has always remained from those distant times." Compare with Isocrates, *Helenus* 37 (concerning Theseus: *eti kai nyn*).

‡ Compare *Menexenus* 235a4–6 (criticism of the funeral oration) and 238c2–4 (Socrates's oration: "our forebears and the men of today, including the dead present here").

§ *Ibid.* 238c2–3.

but — very aristocratically — from the exaltation of the ancestors.

By linking democracy to the theme of autochthony,[117] the Athenians were of course suppressing the period of the tyrants,[118] but they did not seem to see the paradox inherent in making Athens a *progressive* city *from birth*; thus the topos of autochthony masks the historical awareness that Athens might have had of itself.[119]

More than any other text, Lysias's epitaphios is evidence of the ambiguity of such an approach. In it, the eulogy of democracy is grafted onto that of autochthony,* presented as a proof of nobility, since the Athenians are opposed by birth to the lowly multitude.† Thus democracy, the rule of law,†† is a consequence of the legitimate§ — and therefore noble — origin of the Athenians, by virtue of an implicit reasoning, brought out by Plato in the *Menexenus*, that deduces political equality from equality of origin** or establishes a link between the disparate origin of the other cities and the systems of inequality that reign there.†† Once again, faithful to his tactic, the philosopher is not content to make what seem to be clear allusions to the text imitated,‡‡ but makes it say openly what he would suggest discreetly.

It is not only in the temporal unfolding of the text that demokratia, annexed to autochthony§§ and flanked by noble exploits,*** is linked to eugeneia, but also, in absolute terms, the time of myth

---

* Lysias 17: autochthony; 18–19: democracy.

† *Ibid.* 17.

‡ *Ibid.* 19 (*nomos*).

§ *Ibid.* 17: *hē ... archē tou biou dikaia*.

** *Menexenus* 239a3–4; cf. also 238e1–2.

†† *Ibid.* 238e2–4: "The other cities are made up of populations of different origin and of unequal elements, which accounts for the inequality of their governments."

‡‡ *Pantodapon:* cf. Lysias 17 (*pantachothen*); *turannides kai oligarchiai:* cf. Lysias 18 (*dunasteias*).

§§ The orator in 20 links democracy to the heroic exploits by *phuntes kalōs kai gnōntes homoia*, which further emphasizes the link between good birth and good politeia. Cf. *Menexenus* 239a7.

*** Lysias 16: the Heraclidae; 20: Marathon.

is for the orator the moment of democracy. In other words, it has no origin; it is immemorial: "They were also the first and only ones *of that time* who abolished kingdoms among themselves and established democracy.* *En ekeinoi tōi chronōi* refers either to the first birth of the autochthones, that is, to the origin of humanity[†] — or, beyond the passage on autochthony, to the period of the great mythical exploits.[‡] So there is, to say the least, a tension between myth and history in this passage. The orator presents the institution of democracy as a sort of historical fact, as is evident in the use of the aorist *katestēsanto*, but he locates it in a sufficiently vague past for Athens to become the *protos heuretēs* of democracy.

However, the orator's democratic sentiments can hardly be in question. Demokratia is not, for him, as in Pericles's epitaphios, a name but a fact,[§] which in its uniqueness is opposed to the multiplicity of despotic systems.** That he uses the word without hesitation or reservations brings out even more clearly the contrast between this passage and the corresponding one in the *Panegyricus*,[††] in which Isocrates, though clearly drawing his inspiration from Lysias's text, whose main points he repeats, alters whatever struck him in this text as being too democratic: everything is there except the term demokratia itself, for which he substitutes *politeia*.[‡‡] This vague expression, referring equally well to oligarchy as to democracy[§§] and suggesting the blessed time when neither oligarchy nor democracy existed,*** allows him to remain vague about the form of state he claims to be describing. On the other hand,

* Lysias 18.
† *Prōtoi*: the Athenians are therefore doubly so — by nature and in the sphere of the city's life — and this term indicates both superiority and anteriority.
‡ Indeed, *prōtoi de* corresponds to *polla men* (exploits).
§ Compare Lysias 18 with Thucydides 2.37.1 (*onoma ... dēmokratia*).
** Lysias 18: *dunasteiai/dēmokratia*.
†† Isocrates, *Panegyricus* 39.
‡‡ Lysias 18 (*dēmokratian katestēsanto*); Isocrates 39 (*politeian katestēsato*).
§§ Cf., for example, *Panegyricus* 16.
*** *Panathenaicus* 119.

Lysias, who makes democracy a reality and calls it by its name, is not afraid to list its essential criteria: freedom, which the orator, moved by a democratic optimism, gives to all,* not just to a majority;† a community of hope in danger,‡ which Plato might also grant to democracy, although he refuses it to oligarchies;§ law, referred to several times as the norm of the system;** the logos's educational role of deliberation and persuasion.†† Finally, opposing the world of violence to the political sphere,‡‡ the orator adopts the tone with which Aeschylus, at the time of Ephialtes, exalted the power of the people in *The Suppliants*,[120]§§ and takes up the democratic declaration that Athens was the first civilized city.[121]*** The identification made in the epitaphios between democracy and civilization recalls the myth of Protagoras rather than the developments of the theme in the Panegyricus,††† in which civilization exists without democracy, or in the *Helenus*,‡‡‡ in which Isocrates attributes to Theseus what for Lysias was the work of the Athenians.

Yet once again there are discordant elements, for this democratic passage sometimes uses a vocabulary that is much less so. When Lysias praises the Athenians "for entrusting to law the task of honoring the good and punishing the wicked,"§§§ he is referring

---

* Lysias 18.

† Cf. Thucydides 2.37.1 (*pleiones*).

‡ Lysias 18.

§ Plato, *Republic* 8.551d–e.

** Lysias 18 (three occurrences of *nomos*).

†† *Ibid.*: *hupo logou didaskomenous.*

‡‡ *Ibid.* 19: on one side, to rule by force; on the other, to determine right by law, to persuade by reason, and to obey in practice those two powers (democratic reconciliation of action and speech: cf. Thucydides 2.40.2–3).

§§ Aeschylus, *Suppliants* 365–75, 605–22, and elsewhere.

*** Lysias 19: "It is fitting only to wild beasts [*ergon thērion*], they thought, to rule by force, but it fell to men to determine right by law."

††† Isocrates, *Panegyricus* 39.

‡‡‡ Isocrates, *Helenus* 35.

§§§ Lysias 19.

to the theme of Athens as champion of right, but the division of the world into *kakoi* and *agathoi* — terms that Pericles carefully avoided* — would not be out of place in the mouth of an oligarch such as pseudo-Xenophon or a moderate such as Isocrates: it is in this way that in the *Areopagiticus*, Isocrates opposes "bad democracy" (that is, democracy), which grants the same thing to good and bad alike, to "good democracy" (that is, the constitution of the ancestors, which was democratic only in name), which *honors and punishes each according to his merit*.† In fact, the tone of this passage suggests not so much democracy as Solonian *eunomia*, which, in drawing up "laws that were the same for the wicked man as for the good applied strict justice to both,"[122]‡ and, even more than Solonian eunomia Spartan eunomia.§ But nothing suggests that Lysias was trying to free *kakos* and *agathos* from the aristocratic values traditionally associated with these terms in order to give them a new meaning in some "democratic" attempt at redefining values; and in any case, it is doubtful whether it is possible to say something new with the same words. In order to exalt the law democratically, must the orator, then, use an archaistic language, the same one that the adversaries and critics of democracy used quite naturally?

Though a similar process, liberty, an eminently democratic theme is identified with homonoia,** the slogan of the Athenian moderates, abundantly used by Andocides, Isocrates, and Xenophon.[123]†† It is true that under the influence of moderate politi-

---

* Thucydides 2.37.3.

† Isocrates, *Areopagiticus* 21–22, which contains the pairs of opposites good/bad, to reward/to punish.

‡ Solon 24 D 18–20 (= *Constitution of Athens* 12, 14).

§ Cf., for example, Plutarch, *Lycurgus* 27.5.

** Lysias 18: "They considered the liberty of all to be the supreme concord [*homonoia*]."

†† Andocides, *On the Mysteries* 106, 108 (Marathon); Isocrates, *Against Callimachus* 68; Xenophon, *Memorabilia* 3.5.16; finally, it is not insignificant that in defending a citizen accused of antidemocratic intrigues, Lysias appeals to *homonoia* 25.20).

cians such as Archinus,* the great achiever of national reconciliation, the restoration of 403 gave this word a democratic stamp: so Lysias's use of this term in 392 is understandable but nevertheless perplexing, for it attests to the ease with which democracy adopted a vocabulary that was not specific to it.

Does the eulogy of democracy in the funeral oration always have a composite character, then? An examination of the "historical" passages in the epitaphios, which are alien to the actual eulogy of the political system, allows us both to confirm and to qualify this impression.

To defend the fifth-century empire, the orator feels obliged to maintain the thesis that the Athenians systematically implanted democracy in the cities.[124]† He therefore draws an unambiguous distinction between the interest of the many and that of the few,‡ as a democratic reader might well do.[125] On the other hand, evoking the greatness of the men of Piraeus, who "rose up to defend democracy,"§ "as incapable of giving up any of their rights as of wanting more than others,"[126]** he declares unequivocally that in acting thus, "they were obeying not the constraints of the law, but the persuasion of nature, jealous of imitating in new battles the ancient valor of their ancestors."†† Thus a strange gap has been created between democracy, defined as the rule of law and of educative logos,‡‡ and its defenders, guided by phusis, for whom the realm of nomos was a constraint. Are we to understand that agathoi andres, even if they be the most convinced democrats, can know no other law than their (good) nature? Or that the emotional charge contained in the word *stasiasantes* has frightened the

* Aristotle, *Constitution of Athens* 40.

† Lysias 56.

‡ *Ibid.* (*oligoi/polloi*).

§ *Ibid.* 61: *huper tēs dēmokratias stasiasantes.*

** *Ibid.* 64.

†† *Ibid.* 61. Cf. Thucydides 2.39.4 ("with courage deriving not so much from law [*nomoi*] as from character [*tropoi*]").

‡‡ Lysias 19.

orator, urging him to deck out these democrats with the most conventional virtues, so as to make people forget that they were at first "resisters"? But in distinguishing between phusis and nomos, according to an antithesis that the aristocratic tradition would not disavow,[127]* Lysias is not content to borrow the values of the *aristoi*. Like a pupil of the Sophists playing at turning the civic oration against itself, he associates law with compulsion (*anankē*)[128] and nature with persuasion (*peithō*) and subverts the opposition between *bia* and *peithō*, the regulating principle of Greek political thought.

Eulogy of democracy, justification of empire, exaltation of the democrats of Piraeus: a comparison of these three texts is instructive, for it allows us to appreciate the function of aristocratic representations in the funeral oration and the extent to which they color the oration. The empire is to be reconstructed in a real struggle that will require the mobilization of all democratic energies against the Lacedaemonian hegemony: so the opposing forces are named unambiguously. On the other hand, to exalt the combatants of Piraeus, the orator borrows an aristocratic vocabulary, and noble values seem to be entirely appropriate, not only because these democrats have already become paradigmatic figures but also because one does not evoke civil war without "going so far as to alter the usual meaning of words in relation to acts, in the justifications that one gives them.† Halfway between these two strategies, but closer to the second than to the first, the eulogy of democracy names the great principles that govern Athenian political practice, but endows the system with noble qualities and anchors it in the imaginary time of origins.

In the final analysis, the Athenians are for Lysias agathoi before being polloi. Of course, the orator evokes the struggle of the many against the oligarchs, but he prefers to dream of a city held together by the agreement of all its members, "noble in origin,

---

* Cf. Critias, DK, 88 B 22: "A noble character [*tropos chrēstos*] is more dependable than law [*nomos*]."
† Thucydides 3.82.4.

noble in feeling." So, even more than Pericles, he frequently borrows the vocabulary of the oligoi, a language, it is true, that is quite specious in the mouths of those same oligoi, for, as Thucydides remarks, "aristocracy" is not the reality of oligarchy, but at most its ideological cover.* However, this is not reason enough for democracy to take over such phraseology in turn.

We must now ask whether the eulogy actually addresses the real object to which it is supposedly dedicated. Under the name of democracy and in an unconscious way, are the orators not praising an imaginary, or at least ideal, city, without tensions or factions? In this sense, and in this sense only, the oration may be called ideological, since it expresses what the city wants to be in its own eyes rather than describing what it is in reality.

It has been said that "at all times... the Polis is at once a reality and an ideal";[129] it should be added that in the process of its formation, this ideal ignored actual political divisions. Finley recalls the strange process by which the word *stasis*, which, etymologically, designates nothing more than a political "position," took on such pejorative connotations as to acquire the meaning "sedition." As Finley points out, the explanation of this phenomenon is to be found not in philology but in Greek society, which refused to accept that the choice of a policy might legitimately depend on class considerations or interests and assigned the state timeless, universal objectives.[130] We should even go further: this study forces us to recognize that such an attitude is not only attributable to writers hostile to democracy; when the official orators suppress such contested institutions as the misthophoria or the drawing of lots, when they set the city in the eternity of a stereotyped image[†] or turn Athens into a phusis that nothing, not even the institution of the political, can touch,[131] they also help to

---

* *Ibid.* 3.82.8 (*aristokratia sōphrōn* is, as a designation for oligarchy, *onoma euprepēs*).

† We need only recall Hyperides 5, already studied in Chapter Two. Cf. also Isocrates, *Panegyricus* 52, and *Menexenus* 224c3.

transform democracy into a beautiful, harmonious whole. This representation of Athens may be a composite one (and may, by that fact, expose itself to Plato's mockery), but it wishes above all to be reassuring and from such a perspective *stasis* is an evil, absolute evil.

In the early fourth century, however, Lysias and Plato devoted, in their epitaphioi, a passage to the civil struggles at the end of the previous century; no doubt it was as difficult to ignore them as it was, for the restored democracy, to forget completely that the city had been divided in two. To exalt the unity of the city without remaining silent about internal dissensions was a paradoxical task, which spurred official eloquence on to all manner of ruses. So we shall come back once again to those passages in which the political strategy of the funeral oration is revealed in all its complexity.

When they imagined another Athens, a nondemocratic Athens, or when they criticized the real Athens, the conservative writers had no difficulty in accounting for *stasis*: it was enough to impute responsibility for it to democracy, or to its leaders* — which often amounted to the same thing. Thus, bringing together in the *Memorabilia* the main elements of a eulogy of Athens, Xenophon characterizes the city both by the "mutual friendship" that ideally governs the relationships between its members† and by a quasi-endemic state of division, which in fact sets citizens in opposition to one another;‡ but it requires only a good leader for everything to return to order.§ Thus the criticism of the democratic leaders, who are made solely responsible for division, resolves the contradiction easily: without *stasis*, a parasitic evil grafted onto the good nature of the city, Athens would always be victorious.**

---

* Cf., for example, Aristophanes, *Knights,* passim; Euripides, *Suppliant Women* 423–25 (words of the Theban herald); Aristotle, *Constitution of Athens* 28.
† Xenophon, *Memorabilia* 3.5.2.
‡ *Ibid.* 16–17.
§ *Ibid.* 5 and 21.
** Compare Thucydides 2.65.7 and 11–12.

Quite obviously, the democratic funeral oration does not have this process at its disposal; but it draws widely on the repertoire of arete and makes an aristocratic democracy the very symbol of unity. That is why the episode of the civil struggles is the only one mentioned in the whole of Athenian internal history. Thus Lysias sees the democrats of Piraeus as the true representatives of Athenian unity, uniquely preoccupied with the salvation of the city,* and in the *Menexenus* the civil war becomes a paradoxical expression of fraternity.[132] The inclusion of this episode, in which dissension turns into friendship, thus appears necessary, if we take into account the function of the oration: the funeral oration wants to be the political expression of the city as a whole, and to ensure the cohesion of Athenians against others, it must first proclaim it to the Athenians themselves. Is not the peculiarity of the epideictic oration, which was always bound up with traditional values, to "strengthen a disposition to action by increasing adhesion to the values that it exalts"?[133]

Devoting a passage to *stasis*, the fourth-century epitaphioi thus only appear to break the prohibition of "recalling the evils of the past,"† by which the restored democracy tried to remove from the collective memory of Athens any memory of its fratricidal dissensions. In reality, the funeral oration evokes the civil struggles only to deny them the better.‡ But is to deny stasis not also to refuse any democratic meaning to the struggle of the democratic "resisters"? Such a serious question goes beyond the funeral oration; so let us briefly digress in order to examine more closely what, in 403–402, was the actual attitude of the Athenian demos to its saviors.

Before transforming the "heroes of Phyle" into edifying paradigms for official orations, the restored democracy seems to have shown some embarrassment about them. It was not difficult to

* Lysias 64; see also 62–63.
† Aristotle, *Constitution of Athens* 39.6.
‡ *Menexenus* 244a7: "It is neither evil nor hatred that makes them lay hands on one another, but these evil times."

give them an honorary decree, engraved on a stela for the edification of posterity.[134] It is noteworthy, however, if the version in
Aeschines is correct,* that the term demokratia was not used on
that occasion. On the other hand, we know that the concrete
measures taken in favor of those men were extremely timid, since,
supporting Archinus against Thrasybulus, the demos refused to
open citizenship to all those among them who were not Athenians: the Athenian people did not wish to share its newly regained
privileges with "everybody who had come back from Piraeus,
some of whom were well known to be slaves";† besides, by their
very existence, those heroic combatants no doubt reminded the
Athenians of things they would rather forget. But the dead themselves, whether or not they were citizens, seem to have constituted an embarrassing exception for the city though buried at the
Kerameikos,‡ they were badly integrated into the glorious cohort
of the combatants of the past. This is apparent in the decree of
Theozotides, whose stone has recently been discovered in excavations of the Agora, and which laid down what honors were to be
accorded the sons of the fallen. The decree tended to limit these
honors to the sons of citizens. This is how we must understand
the restrictive clause "all those Athenians who have died a violent
death" (ll. 4–5) and the mention of the patronymic and demotic
of each of the orphans:[135] it was an attempt to isolate the group of
official war victims. But, not content with granting its solicitude
parsimoniously, the demos meant also to remind everyone that it
was conferring a special favor on the democrats and their sons by
treating them as it normally treated war victims and orphans
brought up at the city's expense (*kathaper tōn en tōi polemōi:* ll.
16–17; *kathaper tous orphanous:* l. 9). Killed by other Athenians,§
"fallen under the oligarchy while bringing help to democracy" (*en
tēi oligarchiai boēthountes tēi dēmokratiai:* ll. 5–6),[136] these citizens

* Aeschines, *Against Ctesiphon* 190.
† Aristotle, *Constitution of Athens* 40.2.
‡ Lysias 64 (citizens); 66 (foreigners).
§ *Menexenus* 244a3.

succumbed to "the war that is the most frightful, the most painful, the most sacrilegious, the most odious to gods and men."* Of course, they had not provoked it; on the contrary, their glory lay in their having put an end to it by fighting against fellow citizens who had become enemies.[137] Faithful to the democratic spirit of the ephebic oath, they restored to the city its greatness.[138]† However, their deaths transgressed *de facto* the opposition between *stasis* and *polemos*, the norm of all organized political life,‡ thus creating an exceptional situation.[139] So it is probably no accident that the vocabulary of the decree breaks with the traditional language of the collective funerary epigrams, epitaphioi, and other honorary texts in which death is never presented as *biaios thanatos* (violent death); similarly, whereas *andragathia* (ll. 8–9) normally designates the fine death, the much less canonical term *euergesia* (ll. 6–7), which was usually used in the late fifth century to honor a stranger,[140] widens the distance between democracy and the benefactors who had contributed to restoring it.

Often the inscriptions "reveal what their authors could not or would not say."[141] Thus only this long detour via the *realia* could help us determine precisely the relationship between the funeral oration and the reality of Athenian political life, in this case a *stasis* and its effects. The following conclusions may now be drawn: the funeral oration does not ignore the practical problems confronting the citizen, but its specific task is to efface or absorb them by displacing them to another level, and only a study of these displacements enables us to guess what was at stake in the debates of the ekklesia. Thus in his epitaphios, Lysias gives those Athenians who had died for democracy the same praise he gives to their

* Xenophon, *Hellenica* 2.4.22 (oration of Cleocritus).
† Lysias 63 evokes ll. 9–11 of the ephebic oath ("I shall not let the fatherland diminish but shall hand it on greater and stronger than I have received it, whether alone or with all"). For the respect paid to oaths, cf. Lysias 62: "They had as allies oaths and treaties."
‡ Cf. above all Aeschylus, *Eumenides* 859–66 (opposition between *Arēs emphulios* and *thuraios polemos*).

ancestors, who died defending the city, as if this equivalence had never been a problem. But he cannot repress with impunity the malaise caused by *stasis*;[142] to achieve this goal, the democratic Lysias has to deny some of the most specifically democratic values and to treat the democrats of Piraeus as *agathoi* not only in the military but also in the social and political sense. To efface *stasis* was to efface what was really at stake in the political struggles.

Thus democracy emerges strangely transformed from its treatment by the funeral oration. An aristocratic definition, a return to mythical times, a paradoxical exaltation of the unity of the civic body: the orators could choose among these methods, but they could also use them simultaneously, for the fundamental purpose was always the same, to make the democractic city that *pasa polis* whose unity Pericles exalted* in tones whose purity has been praised for stifling "even so much as an echo of political dissensions."[143] Thus it is hardly surprising that the demos, the sovereign persona of the polis and guardian of kratos, is absent from almost all the epitaphioi.† In the catalog of military exploits and in the eulogy of democracy, a funeral oration knows no other agents than "the Athenians," and this use of *hoi Athēnaioi*, which is quite appropriate in the context of foreign relations among communities, looks like a substitute in a passage on the political system that constitutes the originality of Athens.

In and through the funeral oration, democracy becomes, then, a name to describe a model city. Of course, Pericles's epitaphios conforms much more to the harmonious image that the classical tradition has made of democracy and to the identification, implicit in some historians, of any polis with the democratic polis.[144] But by now it has become clear that there is no gap between the orations of Thucydides and Plato, the close kinship of which is

---

* Thucydides 2.41.1; cf. Euripides, *Erechtheus* (in Lycurgus, *Against Leocrates* 100, v. 16), and Plato, *Menexenus* 241e7.

† The sole exception: Hyperides 27 and 39; one might add two uses of *plethos*: Lysias 66 and *Menexenus* 238d4.

not open to question, and the other epitaphioi. We still have to decide why the funeral oration gives this aristocratic or watered-down image of democracy. Is it obeying constraints internal to it, those of a military oration that based democracy on the very values that bound together the hoplitic phalanx?* Does it show that democracy accepted, in addition to certain aristocratic values, the language of the aristocracy? Or does it reflect the influence of a development in Athenian political thinking?

The Implicit Agon

If it is true that the thought of Protagoras, a Sophist and a foreigner to the city, is the nearest thing to a reflection on democracy,[145] it can be said with some semblance of certainty that Athens had no theory of democracy that was both *systematic* and *Athenian*. However, it is not impossible to determine the position, or successive positions, adopted toward this political system by the other literary genres, such as history or tragedy. To do so, we can gather together the scattered lineaments of a *democratic thought*, if not a *theory of democracy*, for the fifth century; but in the following century, the trace of this thinking becomes less certain, despite the abundance of reference by the orators to democracy. The following paragraphs sketch the broad outlines of this development before relating the funeral oration to it.

According to Otto Schröder, the custom of praising democracy seems to have been a direct outgrowth of the Persian Wars: having experienced the conflict with Persia as a confrontation between despotism and freedom the Athenians became aware of the greatness of their constitution.[146] In 472, in *The Persians*, Aeschylus contrasts the irresponsibility of a monarch with democratic accountability† and, in a couple of lines, affirms the liberty

---

* Compare the formula *mia gnōmē,* which in Lysias characterizes the unity of the Athenian community in combat (13, 17, 24), with the definition of *eleutheria* in the same epitaphios (ll. 11–12 and 15–16 of the ephebic oath). Similarly, compare Thucydides 2.37.3 with ll. 11–14 of the ephebic oath.

† Aeschylus, *Persians* 213–14.

of Athenian citizens.* However, these amount to no more than dispersed and fairly general statements that may equally well apply to
the notion of isonomia, and it is not until *The Suppliants*, in 464,
that a concept of democracy and a democratic terminology begin
to develop. This transformation was probably the result of political
struggles at the time of Ephialtes, but it is important that at that
precise moment tragedy vigorously took the side of demokratia.[147]

A similar enthusiasm, in which we can recognize the spirit of
Pericles's time, animates Herodotus's historical work. I have
already cited the text in which the citizens' conquest of freedom,
with everything that it involves, especially the Athenian "activism"
that was no longer to be denied, is clearly associated with the
growth of Athens's external power.† This is an essential text, for,
apart from the fact that it sees democracy as a historical acquisition occurring in a process of development,‡ it attests to a pre-
vailing reflection on what Herodotus still calls *isēgoriē:* "The
excellence of equality is not to be found in an isolated case, but in
a general way."§ Thus, for the historian, the democratic system
and the tendency to hegemony seem to go hand in hand. Nevertheless, although Herodotus expresses admiration and sympathy
for this dynamism and although he attributes to the Lacedaemonians of the late sixth century the firm resolution to put an end
to Athens's expansion,[148] his praise of Athenian democracy is
not accompanied either by denigration of Spartan eunomia[149] or
by the use of aristocratic values or vocabulary. Eugène Napoleon
Tigerstedt observes that the historian does not seem to be more
interested in the contrast between isonomia and eunomia than in
the opposition between oligarchy and democracy, which was nevertheless contemporary with his work. Are we to attribute this
indifference to the subject chosen by Herodotus? If the Persian
Wars were primarily a confrontation between despotism and

---

* *Ibid.* 241–42 (liberty opposed to the servitude of those who have a master).

† Herodotus 5.78.

‡ Cf. *ibid.* 5.91: "Ideas of glory came to the Athenian people and it grew."

§ *Ibid.* 5.78.

freedom, then Athens and Sparta were on the same side in this struggle; the historian rejects any long digression on the later break between the two cities,* and it was no doubt this attitude that enabled him to adopt such an original and clear position with regard to democracy. Indeed it may have been that the ideological struggle between Sparta and Athens ultimately prevented the constitution of a democratic doctrine that was positive and not merely polemical and defensive. In this case, it is not surprising that the work of the foreigner from Halicarnassus, of the citizen of Thurii, has elements of a purely democratic thought that are not found in the work of the Athenian historian of the Peloponnesian War.

Can it be said that from Herodotus to Thucydides — and perhaps, too, from Aeschylus to Euripides — democracy ceased to offer a model for political thought?

For Herodotus, the history of the cities is that of decisions, and on the Greek side there was no battle that was not preceded by a genuine debate: various opinions had to be expressed before the best carried the day, for, according to the optimism then reigning, the best always did win the day. This strictly political schema is Greek, of course, and contrasts with the false deliberations of the barbarians. But it is even more specifically Athenian, if we take into account the Lacedaemonians' aversion for summoning an assembly in which their allies might express their claims:[150†] it may well be, then, that Athenian democracy was once again the model for politics. But nothing of this kind is found in Thucydides, where certain debates, such as the one that preceded the expedition to Sicily or the first assembly held to discuss Mytilene,‡ could lead to a catastrophic decision: the city no longer dominated the political manipulation of language that had been its strength. The process by which any assembly split into two opposed groups before taking a decision was for Herodotus "a

* Herodotus 8.3.
† *Ibid.* 9.6–10.
‡ Thucydides 3.36.2 and 6.8–26.

good division," the mainspring of history and the condition for a balanced political life. In Thucydides, this becomes the first stage of *stasis*: division is no longer the — ever provisional — moment of debate, but an undermining of the city.* Similarly, political language is no longer the rational instrument of deliberation, but breaks up into words, often seductive, always deceiving,† including, perhaps, demokratia. From this point of view, it does not ultimately matter whether Pericles's epitaphios was faithfully reproduced or was the direct expression of Thucydides's thought: the historian had no alternative but to support a speech that erases the specificity of democracy in order to make Athens the very model of the united polis.

The break between Aeschylus and Euripides may be less clear. However, the eulogy of democracy in *The Suppliant Women*,‡ the most elaborate ever written by Euripides, falls short of the democratic conviction shown by Aeschylus in his tragedy of the same name: whereas in Aeschylus the demos is sovereign, since it is the only authority able to solve the dilemma of King Pelasgus,§ in Euripides it is no longer all-powerful except in name, reduced in fact to approving decisions already taken by Theseus, from whom it derives everything, even its liberty and political equality** — *The Suppliant Women* probably marks a turning point in Euripides's relationship to the Athenian democracy: the eulogy of democracy, though apparently systematic, is more moderate in that play than the more diffuse praise in the *Heraclidae*,[151] and although Euripides is careful to put the attack on the demagogues into the mouth of the Theban herald, the criticism is nonetheless expressed††and accords well with Theseus's exaltation of the middle class.‡‡

* Cf. *ibid.* 3.82.
† *Ibid.* 3.82.4 and 8 (*onoma euprepes*); 5.89 (*onomata kala*).
‡ Euripides, *Suppliant Women* 403–56.
§ Aeschylus, *Suppliants* 483–85 and 517–23.
** Euripides, *Suppliant Women* 349–55.
†† *Ibid.* 412–16; cf. also 232–37.
‡‡ *Ibid.* 238–45.

Thus, like Pericles's epitaphios, *The Suppliant Women* seems to anticipate the events of the late fifth century, which certainly brought victory to the democracy, but to a democracy that may well be regarded as embalmed. Of course, the attacks on democracy still did not abate, even if they were now situated at a higher level of theoretical elaboration in Plato's writings; but on the side of the democrats, we can discern no attempt at a systematic ordering of the arguments in defense of the Athenian system. Not a single fourth-century orator does not claim allegiance to it — Aeschines as well as Demosthenes, Isocrates as well as Hyperides* — but they are far from ready to defend it in reality. The logical consequence of this reversal, well described by J.A.O. Larsen,[152] was the proclamation of Demetrius of Phalerum, who, in establishing a plutocracy at Athens, declared that he had improved democracy.[153] Thus we will not follow the meanderings of fourth-century political thought, since no innovation occurred in the development of a coherent, positive theory of democracy.

Given this admittedly schematic outline of some stages in the development of Athenian political thought, we can now try to situate the funeral oration as a genre within it.

To decide whether the genre evolved, we would need a complete temporal distribution of the epitaphioi. However, not only do we have no oration before 430, but it is not even certain that the first epitaphios in our list — that of Pericles — does not bear the mark of the years after 404. Once again, this text may well impede a study of the genre, so we must look to the vocabulary, structure, and function of the other epitaphioi for more definite evidence.

Using an antithesis that is not peculiar to the funeral oration but is widely represented in it, the epitaphioi often draw a contrast

---

* Aeschines, *Against Ctesiphon* 6 and Isocrates, *Areopagiticus* 71, to confine oneself to suspect statements, which those of Demosthenes and Hyperides are not.

between *dēmokratia* and *dunasteia*.* Are we to see this as the distorted memory of an earlier state of the oration, or did democracy not yet define itself in opposition to oligarchy, a system that, like itself, emerged out of isonomia yet had no other enemy but despotism or tyranny, forms of power that were entirely alien to it? To advance this thesis, we would have to be able to date the substitution of the second antithesis for the first. However, it can be said that during the fifth century the *dēmokratia/oligarchia* opposition, which may definitively be pinned down to 430, gains prevalence over the *isonomia/turannis* antithesis,[154] though without altogether replacing it. The political struggles of the Ephialtes period no doubt had quite a bit to do with this.

But perhaps between these two antitheses there existed, in the immediate aftermath of the Persian Wars, an intermediary stage, characterized by the *dēmokratia/turannis* opposition, an opposition familiar to Aeschylus and taken up later by Herodotus. Does the presence of the *dēmokratia/dunasteia* opposition in the fourth-century epitaphioi allow us to declare that the eulogy of democracy bears the mark of its period? It would be very difficult to do so: far from making *dunasteia* a mere synonym of *turannis*, Demosthenes's epitaphios links this system with the power of the few;† and when Lysias contrasts *dunasteia* with the community of hopes in danger and the liberty of Athenian public life,‡ his target seems to be oligarchy rather than tyranny.[155] At most, the term *dunasteia*, which is broader or vaguer than *oligarchia* and *turannis*, maintains a certain confusion between these two political systems. Now, although the Cimonian period is one of transition, this does not mean that it is certain that it was characterized by confusion; it would be more tempting to see it as a stage in which

---

* Lysias 18: *dunasteias,* and Demosthenes 25: *hai dia tōn oligōn dunasteiai,* which may be compared with *Menexenus* 238e4: *anomaloi politeiai, turannides te kai oligarchiai.* The convergence of these texts makes very likely the reconstruction *despoteias* or *dunasteias* in Hyperides 5.

† Demosthenes 25. Same association in Isocrates, *Panegyricus* 105–106.

‡ Lysias 18.

262

two systems of values, two antagonistic modes of political thought, emerged, sometimes coexisting, sometimes in conflict. The advocates of democracy, whether they already called the Athenian political system by that name or whether they referred to it as an isonomia or isegoria, certainly seem to hold to the demokratia/tyrannis antithesis[156]* and exalt the power of the people in language that owes nothing to the values of the aristoi and in which the master/slave opposition — that of Aeschylus, which Herodotus later took up, against the current but with superb conviction† — predominates. The friends of Cimon, on the other hand, were more concerned to exalt the aristocratic battles fought by the city — and to conceal the victories of the oarsmen[157] — than to define the originality of a politeia whose development already seemed dangerous.[158] There was little room in such a climate for the conjunction, found in certain epitaphioi, between aristocratic values and the *dēmokratia/dunasteia* opposition, which may be a later phenomenon. Indeed the term *dunasteia* does not appear in the common political vocabulary before the end of the fifth century; it was then frequently associated with oligarchia, and it was used in this sense in the next century by Lysias and Demosthenes. In reality, *dunasteia* bears the mark of the troubled times that followed the failure of the Sicilian expedition, when the much-feared tyrants merged with the oligarchs,[159] as we saw under the Thirty. *Dunasteia* refers to everything in oligarchy that was most opposed to the rule of law, which links it to tyranny,‡ but it would be risky to conclude from this that the presence of the word *dunasteia* refers to a period in which democracy had no other enemy but tyranny.

It is not that the funeral oration completely ignores the opposition between liberty and tyranny, to which the epitaphioi of

---

*Aeschylus, *Suppliants* 365–75, opposes democracy to the absolute power of one man.

† Aeschylus, *Persians* 241–42; Herodotus 5.78.

‡ Thucydides 3.62.3. Similarly, Thucydides 6.89.4 is late evidence, to be seen in the specific context of Alcibiades's plea.

Lysias, Plato, and Hyperides refer;* but the passage in the *Menexenus* may easily be reduced to variations on the *dēmokratia/dunasteia* antithesis, since Plato contrasts tyrannies and oligarchies with a system that he sometimes calls democracy and sometimes aristocracy;† and of the three orators, Hyperides is the only one for whom this opposition characterizes the real power relations between Greeks, since it suddenly becomes relevant in the struggle between Athens and the Macedonians, "the tyrants of Greece."[160]‡ On the other hand, tyranny is not, in Plato and Lysias,§ an urgent threat for Greece, but a particular case of the servitude inflicted by the great king on the cities he had subjected:** tyrannis is opposed to eleutheria as Asia is to Greece,†† while the *dēmokratia/dunasteia* antithesis concerns the Greek cities alone.

Now, in this sphere of ideological struggle, in which antagonistic models confront each other as in military operations, the funeral oration is primarily a matter between Greek cities: as military speeches, the epitaphioi transform the battles into so many competitions, but as political speeches they tend more to oppose similar, rival cities than fundamentally heterogeneous adversaries — Sparta and Athens, rather than Athens and the barbarian world — and, where an epitaphios might appear to be holding to the bia/nomos antithesis, an attentive reading will again reveal a rivalry between Athens and Sparta.[161]

Declaring difference against a background of resemblance: the explanation for this fundamentally agonistic strategy is no doubt to be found in the struggle for influence between Sparta and

---

* Lysias: see below, footnotes §, **, and ††; Plato: *Menexenus* 239a2–3; Hyperides: 18, 20, 25, 39.

† *Menexenus* 238e4 and 238c7–d2.

‡ Hyperides 39.

§ Lysias 57 and 59.

** *Ibid.* 21, 41, 57, 59; cf. *Menexenus* 239d6–240a3.

†† Lysias 21, 27, 47.

Athens that, far from affecting only the narrative of military exploits, also structures the political part of the speech. By endowing democracy with aristocratic features, the funeral oration tries in fact to deprive oligarchy of the representations behind which this system shelters, and thus to fight the *oligoi* on their own ground. Of course, the equivalence thus established between Sparta and the oligarchy would still have to be demonstrated at the institutional level but that is not the problem. For us, it is enough that the equivalence should have been self-evident for the Greeks: no doubt the seed was already there when, in 462, the Spartans sent away the Athenian contingent, whose audacity and revolutionary spirit they feared.* In any case, we know the role it played in the second half of the fifth century and above all during the Peloponnesian War.† In fact, in Pericles's epitaphios, oligarchy contrasted from the outset with the democratic system,‡ is identified throughout the oration with Sparta, which was its living embodiment: well before the orator overtly attacked the Lacedaemonians on their own ground, that of military behavior,§ every auditor (or reader) of the epitaphios had recognized Sparta in that "other system" characterized by mutual suspicion in everyday life and mistrust of the outside world.**

Though crucial in the fifth century, this opposition begins to lose its meaning in the next century, to such an extent that it becomes a rhetorical antithesis between Athens, the symbol of democracy, and "the oligarchies." The most obvious example is provided by Demosthenes's epitaphios,†† and the anachronistic character of such an attitude at a time when the real enemy was no longer Sparta but the Macedonian monarchy suggests how profoundly the oration had been marked by the struggle against

* Thucydides 1.102.3.
† *Ibid.* 3.82.1.
‡ *Ibid.* 2.37.1: *mē es oligous all' es pleionas oikein.*
§ *Ibid.* 2.39.2.
** *Ibid.* 2.37.2 and 39.1.
†† Demosthenes 25.

oligarchy. To free oneself from it, one had, no doubt, like Hyperides, to rid oneself at the same time of the eulogy of democracy,
which he no sooner touched on than he abandoned.*

However anachronistic it may have been after Chaironeia, the
agon remained in Demosthenes's time a constant in the funeral
oration. Thus after identifying democracy with "valor"[162]† like his
predecessors,‡ the orator launches into a violent diatribe against
the oligarchies for being incapable of developing in their citizens
any feeling except fear. This enables him to limit all noble aspirations to the democratic parrhesia: basing this freedom of speech
on the sense of honor, that aischune which Pericles associated
with unwritten laws,[163] Demosthenes endows democracy with
the aristocratic values of the few.[164]§ Similarly, painting a contrast
between the behavior of democrat and oligarch before that form
of agon called war,** he refuses the latter any respect for the
hoplitic ideal†† and any fear of blame,‡‡ in order to attribute these
feelings to the democrat.[165] It is not that the orator systematically
ignores the specific criteria of democracy,§§ but he much prefers
to attribute aristocratic features to it, which he then turns against
the oligarchy; thus parrhesia becomes "true speech,"*** which

---

* Hyperides 5.

† Demosthenes 25: "It was above all their political system that was the cause of
their zeal."

‡ Thucydides 2.37.1; *Menexenus* 238c4; Lysias 20.

§ Demosthenes 25: *deos, aischunē;* 26: *parrhēsia.*

** The word is in *ibid.* 25.

†† *Ibid.*: "Each man saves his life with lightness of heart."

‡‡ *Ibid.*: "knowing well that in bending one's masters . . . even if one had committed the blackest indignities, one would receive no more than a light reproach."

§§ The orator contrasts the omnipotence of a small number of magistrates (hoi
kyrioi) with the sovereignty of the community in a democracy (*pantes*); declaring that the mere individual (*homonos*) may cause dishonor by revealing the
behavior of a citizen, he insists in his own way on the rights of the individual in
Athens.

*** *Ibid.* 26.

apportions blame or praise to the combatant.[166] The fine death is not far away.[*]

A study of Lysias's epitaphios leads to similar conclusions: if, essentially opposing the political logos to brute force, the orator seems to take up a position at the — more general — level at which liberty confronts despotism, he does not for all that ignore agon, and we have seen how he tried to make nobility of behavior a characteristic of Athenian democracy. But it is again in Pericles's epitaphios that the agonistic character of the eulogy of democracy is most clearly perceptible. The orator prudently rejects in advance any explicit comparison between the Athenian system and other constitutions, since he denies that Athens copies other cities and declares that it is an example and not an imitator.[†] But it would not be difficult to interpret this prefatory declaration as a denial.[167] The beginning of the epitaphios consists of a paradoxical working out of the double wish that animates Athenian democracy: Athens wants to present its constitution as unique — and any allusion to other systems will therefore be by way of polemics — but it also wishes to annex the enemy's values to itself. This explains the hesitations and the use of negative formulas to define democracy: the orator wishes to propose an example, but it is as if he were beginning by answering the accusations of some absent interlocutor. This in no way means that the oration is conciliatory:[168] it is, or at least it is intended to be, an attack;[‡] as such, it occupies some of the enemy's positions only in order to defeat him the more soundly.

But it is a dangerous strategy, for it risks depriving democracy of its specific characteristics. We have already noted the absence of any reference to misthophoria. Even more astonishing for a modern is the silence of all the epitaphioi on the democracy's maritime vocation. The sea is not absent from Lysias's epitaphios: it testifies to Athenian bravery and skill at Salamis;[§] it is at stake in battle and

---

[*] *Ibid.* 26–27.

[†] Thucydides 2.37.1.

[‡] See the attacks against Sparta in 2.37.2 and 39.1.

[§] Lysias 38 and 42.

in arche;* but when it is a question of praising democracy, the autochthonous Athenians no longer relate to anything but their land, which is seen as both a mother and a fatherland.† The rejection of the maritime dimension is even more complete in Pericles: we are not told whether it was by land or by sea that the goods of the entire world came to Athens,‡ and the fleet, referred to only once in a passage on land warfare,§ seems to have no autonomy. In short, the man of insular strategy who at other times was quite capable of exalting the maritime experience of the Athenians** forgets in the epitaphios whatever is not related to hoplitic warfare and in order to proclaim the originality of Athens on the Spartans' ground denies the naval techne that everyone recognizes as the city's.[169]

As if it were impossible to glorify in the same oration techne and arete — the city of oarsmen and the city of hoplites — the funeral oration, presenting democracy as the only constitution capable of creating true agathoi, rejects maritime Athens at the same time.[170] But in this rejection, the official orators go even further than conservative writers such as Sophocles and Aristophanes. Of course, *Oedipus Rex* is probably not the symbolic enactment of Athenian imperialism that Knox sees it as,[171] and the exceptional character of the eulogy of Athens's maritime glory in *Oedipus at Colonus* has rightly been pointed out.[172][††] But the important point is still that in his last tragedy, Sophocles is not afraid to include in the same praise the indomitable olive tree, which is both nurse and warrior,[173] and the good oar, fit for the

---

* *Ibid.* 41, 48, 55, 57, 59; in 41, the orator even applies to the victory of Salamis the hoplitic, terrestrial topos of the confrontation between the few and the many. Nor is the sea absent from the *Menexenus:* see especially 240a–241c and 241d6–e2.

† Lysias 17: *tēn autēn ... mētera kai patrida.*

‡Thucydides 2.38.2.

§ *Ibid.* 2.9.3. Similarly, in 41.4, *pasa thalassa kai gē* tends more to show the limitlessness of Athenian audacity than to evoke specific operations.

** *Ibid.* 1.142.5–9.

†† Sophocles, *Oedipus at Colonus* 707–19.

hands of Athenians. Aristophanes defines the city as the "country of Triremes,"* and without making him an advocate of Athenian maritime policy,[174] we must not underestimate his real sympathy for the "people of the oarsmen."†

Aristophanes is no more a convinced democrat than Sophocles. Would it be necessary for him, then, to adopt a critical position on democracy in order to perceive its reality?[175] It is tempting to think so when we remember that the most trenchant statement of the Athenian equation between the sea and democracy is found in pseudo-Xenophon. Declaring that "it is true that at Athens the poor and the people enjoy greater advantages than the nobility and the rich, since it is the people who sail the ships and give the city its power,"‡ he brings out — in his own way, which is that of an oligarch — what no orator seems to have dared to say in an epitaphios, namely that the empire is the base of the fifth-century democracy. Similarly, his definition of the system leaves out neither the drawing of lots nor isegoria,§ and in many respects this pamphlet may be seen as *the realistic underside of Pericles's idealistic oration.*[176] To limit ourselves to a few examples, we may recall that he explains the distribution of offices by the interests of the people, whereas Pericles explains it in terms of arete;** that he attributes not to some phusis but to a deliberate policy the Athenian nonprofessionalism in matters of hoplitic warfare;†† but that, conversely, he is quite prepared to make the maritime experience a sort of second nature for the Athenians.‡‡

Clearly *The Constitution of the Athenians* does not contain the one and only truth about the Athenian democracy, a truth that the

---

* Aristophanes, *Birds* 108; cf. also 145.
† Aristophanes, *Acharnians* 162–63.
‡ [Xenophon], *Constitution of the Athenians* 1.2.
§ *Ibid.*
** *Ibid.* 1.3.
†† *Ibid.* 2.1.
‡‡ *Ibid.* 1.19–20.

epitaphioi strove to conceal. The choice of the oligarchic politeia instead of the democratic funeral oration no doubt satisfied a desire or a need that was more philosophical than historical: the desire to arrange a disconcerting reality into a system, the "desire to overcome all contradictions."[177] Although the oligarch shows a marvelously systematic understanding of the Athenian democracy, the partisan passion that animates this false system distorts the ambiguities of Athenian democratic practice. Thus pseudo-Xenophon sees a sort of class dictatorship in Athens,* which democracy never was in the classical period; declaring that the Athenians "always favor the bad to the detriment of the good,"† he forgets what Pericles was well placed to know, namely the part played by "honest people" and the great families in the government of the city. So we must resign ourselves "to reading pseudo-Xenophon from the point of view of the Periclean funeral oration."[178] But the pamphlet fills in the silences of the epitaphioi, silences that it reveals at the same time to be omissions. Because he takes up position on a solely political and non-agonistic terrain, because his very practical aim is the seizure of power and not universal admiration, the pamphleteer brings out what the democratic orators, perhaps out of fear of giving their constitution a partisan image carefully efface. But even though the political system described by pseudo-Xenophon is not the democracy of the fifth century, he is sometimes quite capable of stating clearly what it is based on. Because he distinguishes between moral analysis and practical political judgment, this oligarch sees what constituted the strength of Athens.[179] Thus, in proclaiming "I do not praise the Athenians for choosing this political system...but, given the fact that they have decided thus, I intend to demonstrate that they handle their constitution skillfully and are right to do many things that other Greeks regard as political mistakes,"‡ he

* *Ibid.* 1.8 (the people prefers a state in which it is free and governs to a well-governed state in which it is enslaved).
† *Ibid.* 1.1.
‡ *Ibid.*

gives to the coherence of Athenian politics, which he regards as *systematic*,[*] a proof that no epitaphios provides.

The study of this politeia, then, serves as a counter-proof: the funeral oration cannot be regarded as presenting a real *"constitution" of the Athenians*, for it does not assume the totality of the democracy; it cannot do so, engaged as it is in an agon of nobility.

Although it has now been verified, the fundamentally agonistic character of the epitaphioi has not yet been really explained. We shall try to do this with the help of the double finality of the funeral oration, which, like the official discourse, is both a civic institution and a literary genre.

On the level of the constraints proper to a genre, a comparison of the funeral oration with that other civic literary genre, tragedy, proves fruitful. It seems that in transposing the realities of the present into a mythical perspective, tragedy expresses more faithfully than the funeral oration the broad characteristics of Athenian democracy. We have already stressed the importance that Aeschylus accorded to the sovereignty of the popular assembly and to the responsibility of the magistrates; we have noted the place given to maritime power in *Oedipus at Colonus*. We shall now dwell at somewhat greater length on the work of Euripides, that increasingly moderate democrat, whose expression is sometimes more audacious than his intentions.

Like the funeral oration, Euripidean tragedy places the personal liberty of the citizen in the forefront;[†] like the funeral oration, it draws inspiration from the city's official formulas.[‡] Like it — and more so — it exalts isegoria;[§] but it is not averse to alluding to the drawing of lots, although it does so discreetly.[**] Further-

---

[*] The references are legion: 1.1, 2, 3, 4, 6, 7, 8, 10, 11, 12, 13, 14, 15, 16; 2.1, 9, 16; 3.1, 8, 10.

[†] Euripides, *Heraclidae* 411–13 and 423–24.

[‡] *Ibid.* 1019; *Suppliant Women* 438–39.

[§] *Heraclidae* 180–83; *Suppliant Women* 440–41.

[**] *Heraclidae* 36.

more, Euripides puts into Theseus's mouth a eulogy of democracy whose kinship with Pericles's epitaphios we have already remarked on, but that nonetheless contains two essential elements that are omitted or undervalued in the oration: the rotation of offices, the basis of the people's sovereignty,* and written laws, the city's commonwealth,† which are opposed to "tyranny."

The funeral oration and tragedy do not assign the same position to democracy, do not conceive of it in terms of the same system of oppositions. Comparing democracy and oligarchy, the funeral oration stresses — if only to reject it — the antithesis between the many and valor, whereas tragedy, engaged in the great debate on servitude and responsibility, prefers to contrast democratic liberty with despotic constraint. Thus the demokratia/tyrannis antithesis, so dear to Aeschylean tragedy, still coexists in Euripides with attacks on oligarchy, during the early years of the Peloponnesian War.‡ But it may be precisely this choice that enables us to explain the more "democratic" character of tragedy: forging a link between the mythical universe and the political world while maintaining the tension between myth and polis,[180] tragedy seeks the strong oppositions between true contraries linked by a relation of polarity, whereas the funeral oration wishes to affirm an *absolute difference*, without any counterpart and, so to speak, constituted by *a single term*. Tragedy, that of Aeschylus as well as that of Sophocles and Euripides, compares despotism, the power of another age, and the free polis, of which democracy is the best example: thus against the Egyptian herald it sets up Pelasgus, just as it quells the insolence of Creon or his representative, the Theban herald, via the mouth of Theseus. Thus the political logos, the only one worthy of that name, faces up to force. True, there are "ambiguities and reversals," since the political logos does not conquer force without recourse to arms;§ but, con-

---

* *Suppliant Women* 406–407.

† *Ibid.* 430–31: *nomoi koinoi;* 443 (written laws).

‡ *Heraclidae* 411–13 and 423–24; *Suppliant Women* 399–403.

§ Aeschylus's *Suppliants* opens and closes with a threat of war, *Oedipus at Colonus* and Euripides's *Suppliant Women* describe the armed confrontation between Athenians and Thebans.

versely, it gives freedom of speech to the opposing force: thus Theseus allows Creon's ambassador to speak. This is the essential point:
tragedy involves by its very nature *an opposition of two voices*, an
agōn logōn whereas the funeral oration is a discourse that expects
no reply.

The agon logon of *The Suppliant Women* is instructive in this
regard. It sets up an opposition between democracy and oligarchy,
for beneath the mask of tyranny the true target is quite obviously
the Theban regime of 424 and not Creon's mythical monarchy.[181]
But the opposition is explicit, embodied in the play: the Theban
herald, presented as a talker who is spoiling for a fight,* is allowed
to develop his criticism of democracy unimpeded and takes full
advantage of it, listing in turn the orators who "puffed up" their
audience for some private profit,† the lowly origin of the demagogues,‡ the chaotic conduct of the city, and the incompetence of
the masses§ — the usual clichés of antidemocratic thought. We may
agree with Goossens that the herald's diatribe is a ruse by Euripides
to put "quasi-oligarchic views" into the mouth of an antipathetic
character, but we are nevertheless forced to acknowledge that such
a tactic purifies the eulogy of democracy of any heterogeneous elements.[182] Indeed, since the criticism of the democratic system has
already been made by someone else, Theseus can choose his arguments in such a way as to present a eulogy of democracy that contains no reservations, or reservations so discreet that they may be
regarded as negligible;[183] and his task is incomparably easier than
that of the orator of an epitaphios, who, compelled to exalt democracy, justifies it before attacks that he does not name and thus tends
inevitably to integrate the enemy's values into his speech.

* *Suppliant Women* 427–28: "Since it was you who challenged me to this debate,
listen: you have provoked me to this assault of words [*hamillan ... logōn*]."
† To puff up: *ibid.* 412; cf. also 423–25; compare with Plato, *Gorgias* 518e–519a
(theme of unhealthy swelling up). Private profit: *Suppliant Women* 413; cf.
Thucydides 2.65.7.
‡ *Suppliant Women* 424: *poneros;* cf. Aristophanes, *Knights* 186.
§ *Suppliant Women* 417–20; cf. Herodotus 3.81 (oration by Megabyzus, advocate
of oligarchy).

Of course, the funeral oration presupposes the confrontation of two antagonistic models, and in it democracy is defined *against* another form of constitution. But whereas in tragedy two heterogeneous worlds oppose each other in two antithetical speeches in which each thesis finds its counterpart, the agon of the funeral oration does not have an antilogical structure:[184] far from weighing the pros and cons, the funeral oration tries to avoid the debate by never overtly allowing the enemy to speak. But there is no true winner in this game: undermined from the inside by aristocratic values and representations, the official oration on democracy ultimately has no language of its own at its disposal. In tragedy, it is an open struggle between rival speeches (*hamilla logōn*); the funeral oration is a truncated agon, a diptych with one of its panels missing.

What has appeared so far to be proper to the genre might, in the final analysis, be imputed to the political system itself and its internal contradictions. Having experienced how difficult it is "to demonstrate the existence of an antagonistic system of values, formulated by and for the lower social classes, rejecting aristocratic values, and substituting for them the values of labor and economic activity," most historians agree in recognizing that "aristocratic values had no rivals" in ancient Greece.[185] We must go further and stress the gap, omnipresent at Athens, between social relations broadly favorable to the demos and the dominant ideological system, which always accorded privileged status to arete and agathos, without managing — or without really trying — to give these terms a new content. A.W.H. Adkins has devoted an important study to this permanence of aristocratic values in the democratic assembly and law courts,[186] and there is no need to go over the same ground. But without going so far as to declare, with Plato, that the Athenians openly recognized aristocracy as the best political system, we may wonder why democracy was unable to forge a specific language for itself. Is this to be explained by a political and social structure that, from the Cleisthenean reform on, integrated the Eupatridai into the democracy without radically breaking with the old, aristocratic Athens[187] and that, despite an audacious redefinition of the political and military rights and duties of the citizen,[188] went on regarding the land as the only honorable "visible good"?[189] Or, conversely, are we to seek in the originality of the Athenian system of government the paradoxical reason for its theoretical conservatism?[190] It is not always easy to acknowledge an innovation to the outside world, even when, within the city itself, the *graphē paranomon*, a permanent threat, reminds one that "it is worst of all if we do not stand firm by any of our decisions."*

No doubt the permanence of aristocratic values in Athens can be imputed to two kinds of reasons, and we should see this as a phenomenon profoundly rooted in democratic practice: the anomalies of the funeral oration derive as much from this gap, inherent in the Athenian democracy as from the character of the oration, an institutional speech that could in no way distance itself from the political experience that underlay it.

We may now treat the funeral oration as a form of democratic discourse despite its contradictions and perhaps even because of them. In the absence of any theory of democracy, the epitaphioi present a eulogy of the political system; an aristocratic eulogy, in the absence of a democratic theory. If the Athenians, more inclined to claim originality than to accept all its consequences, did not forge their own language; if they preferred the seductions of speech to the rigor of writing, these are *facts*, which must be accepted as such without the anachronistic luxury of regret that it is so. Old words to describe new institutions: no doubt, in the classical period there was no other way of speaking of the Athenian system. The funeral oration, therefore, is democratic in that it preserves the official orthodoxy against all attempts at absorption or distortion, of which the most characteristic, in the fourth century, is that of Isocrates. In the final stage of this survey, a comparison between the epitaphioi and Isocrates's fictional speeches,

---

* Thucydides 3.37.3 (oration by Cleon).

which say a great deal about democracy but in fact have very little to do with it, proves instructive.

The democracy of the epitaphioi has been compared with the "constitution of the ancestors."[191] The comparison is not invalid, insofar as Isocrates often took the funeral oration as the schema for his speeches; thus, after describing the mirage of the *patrios politeia* and accepting, on certain conditions, the restored democracy of the fourth century, the *Areopagiticus* ends in the form of an epitaphios.*

But Isocrates addresses this eulogy quite unambiguously to ancient Athens,† that is, in reality, to the pre-Cleisthenean city, an approach that was already evident in the *Panegryicus*.‡ In 380, Isocrates proceeded with circumspection, since the Athenian public's attachment to democracy was strong enough that he did not dare to attack it head-on. Indeed he always avoided being regarded as an opponent of it.§ Of course, he rejects, in a quite conscious way, a system that in his view bullies property owners, and in that stand he is radically opposed to the method of the funeral oration, which, in idealizing the present democracy, tends to efface all differences; but he conceals this refusal behind ever more "democratic" protestations. Thus, in the *Panathenaicus*, he ends by making the patrios politeia a "democracy of the best,"** although he has previously defined it as anterior to any democracy.†† But nowhere else is the dissociation of the reality from the name of democracy carried as far as in the *Areopagiticus*. First Isocrates heaps ridicule on the thing without calling it by its

* Isocrates, *Areopagiticus* 20–55: *patrios politeia;* 60–71: the present democracy compared with oligarchy; 72: *eugeneia;* 74: autochthony; 75: Amazons, Thracians, Peloponnesians, and Persian Wars; 76–84: conclusion and resumption of themes.
† *Ibid.* 76.
‡ *Panegyricus* 75–81.
§ *Peace* 14; see also *Areopagiticus* 60.
** *Panathenaicus* 131.
†† *Ibid.* 119; this constitution is defined only in opposition to the *monarchiai* and to savage life.

name,* which he wishes to keep for his own political ideal; then he reintroduces the word demokratia while drawing a contrast between the democracy of the present and that of the past.† This time, the trick comes off: the real system may be denied to the benefit of a constitution that, without needing to be democratic anymore, becomes the "true democracy," that of the past.‡ Obviously this system, existing only in its author's imagination, is a "counterimage" of the real democracy, in relation to which it is defined. Isocrates claims to be revealing the true face of a bad politeia hiding behind a seductive vocabulary,§ but when it comes to defining the criteria of the good constitution, he can come up with nothing but negations,** his only innovation — stated at last in a positive proposition — being to ask for the co-optation of magistrates from among "the most competent people.††

So, attacking democracy with its own weapons, since he has come up with a "more democratic selection than the drawing of lots,"‡‡ Isocrates reverses procedure adopted by Pericles. The one tried in the epitaphios to transform democracy into aristocracy; the other would like to get an aristocracy, even a plutocracy, accepted as democracy. Pericles pushed Athenian arete to the forefront: so, without overtly denying those elements that were far too democratic, he was content to omit them. Isocrates is trying to give reality to the myth of a democracy of the ancestors, but he is thereby forced to present himself as more democratic than democracy. On the one hand, omission; on the other, overstatement: a curious game in which ergon and logos never coincide. However we should not be taken in by all this. The official orators embellish the Athenian constitution or keep silent about certain

---

* *Areopagiticus* 13.

† *Ibid.* 15.

‡ *Ibid.* 16.

§ *Ibid.* 20.

** *Ibid.* 21.

†† *Ibid.* 22.

‡‡ *Ibid.* 23. The same argument is found in the *Dissoi logoi* 7.5–6.

of its aspects only because they are attached to it, and Pericles's silences and the aristocratic praise of the men of Piraeus in Lysias are more democratic than Isocrates's exaggerations. Isocrates's real viewpoint is to be found not in his protestations of democratic orthodoxy but, from the *Panegyricus* on, in his substitution of *politeia* for demokratia.* That substitution allows him to rid himself at the same time of all the strictly political categories whose triumph was celebrated by Aeschylus and Herodotus and which, in Pericles and Lysias, functioned as the phusis of Athens.[192]

We must not, then, look for a theory of democracy in the funeral oration. The epitaphios provides democracy with a certain way of speaking of itself, even in a language that it did not invent: the funeral oration must praise democracy and can do so only in noble language. These are the constraints imposed both by the political structures and by the genre.

But from this point of view, too, Pericles's epitaphios seems to dominate the other orations, and the frequent references to it in this chapter have been necessary to show that, far from constituting an exception, this epitaphios only develops more brilliantly the thought of other orations. It is now impossible either to regard it as the only good example of the eulogy of democracy or to contrast it with other, more properly "democratic" epitaphioi. Neither an isolatable document of its genre nor an isolated exception in the midst of more traditional orations, Pericles's epitaphios attests, on the contrary, to the unity of the funeral oration. The objection that this text tended to block any overall study of the Athenian oration to the dead, discussed from the beginning of this book, is thus refuted. We can now study the funeral oration as a genre.

---

* *Panegyricus* 39.

CHAPTER FIVE

The Funeral Oration
as Political Genre

An ossified genre condemned to disappear, banal works that have nothing to teach us because they say nothing original: there are a number of commonplaces that must be dealt with once the unity of the funeral oration as a genre is sufficiently established. It is not that we must rush to the defense of an unjustly criticized form; but it is not certain that those who present the funeral oration as a "false genre"[1] — in relation to what truth? — are posing the problem correctly.

It is true that from one epitaphios to another, the funeral oration changes little. This immobility has in itself taught us a great deal, by leading us to determine with precision those aspects of Athenian civic experience that must necessarily feature in the oration and those that are excluded from it by an equal necessity. Thus we have been able to reconstitute a chain of representations, passing through certain compulsory "points of presence,"[2] which have made it possible by the same token to identify the principal "absent words,"[3] operations to which the epitaphioi lend themselves, like any text and perhaps more than any other kind of text, by virtue of the permanence of their content. For this first reason, it would be pointless to go no further than to remark on the "banality" of the oration. Furthermore, it is by no means obvious that we can legitimately apply to a genre that is also an institution criteria of appreciation more suited to a literary work: we shall return to this point.

Just as pointless, but more dangerous, because more subtle, is the idea that as a form using topoi, the funeral oration was already a doomed genre, moribund from its very inception. Certainly the funeral oration seemed to disappear or at least dwindle after 322. But does this mean that the disappearance was inevitable? Such an inference seems to jump too quickly from fact to necessity. On the contrary, everything goes to show that in Hyperides's time the funeral oration seemed in no way doomed to die the fine death of a genre made of topoi, simply through the exhaustion of its content: the crisis of civic values had failed to shake Athenian orthodoxy in the epitaphioi in any lasting way, and the epitaphios logos was not really threatened by the encroachments of the individual eulogy, since it still served as a model for those individual act of praise.[4]

With tradition looking very like immobility and the topoi like repetition without content, it is tempting to identify repetition with routine. Some historians have adopted these overhasty identifications, thereby abandoning any attempt to integrate the two most remarkable epitaphioi of the corpus, those of Pericles and Hyperides, into a study of the genre. The tendency is either to treat them as "exceptions," the only ones worthy of interest, and to banish the other orations to the darkness that favors mediocrity, or to deny the constricting character of the genre, doomed to a proliferation of more or less successful individual instances, depending on the personality of the orator.[5] But it is not impossible to reason differently when we realize that a balance between innovation and tradition is reestablished within each epitaphios by means of a sort of self-regulation. Thus in Hyperides's oration, each isolated invention is balanced by an excessive orthodoxy in the traditional passages. Should we not see this renewal of convention as the resistance of a genre that uses topoi like so many antibodies against the intrusion of any heterogeneous element? If the orators know what must be said and what must be silenced; if, scrupulously respecting certain compulsory themes, the most innovative of them submits to the rules of the genre, it is not impossible that such a permanence attests in its own way to the real vitality of the funeral oration: vitality made up of resistance to the changes taking place in Athenian society, one that is paradoxical only for those who misunderstand the forces for self-preservation at work in any community.

Again, Pericles's epitaphios seems to present a more serious obstacle to the study of the genre: in comparing the other epitaphioi with this oration, historians tend to contrast the more accomplished model with its pale imitations, and those who regard this text as representative of the fifth-century funeral oration then conclude that a process of ossification set in during the next century, in the funeral oration as in many other fields. However, an attentive examination of the epitaphioi leads us to modify this first impression considerably: in his oration, Pericles is quite obviously attacking those of his predecessors, whose oratorical tics and set passages he is pretending to reject. Is not this the best proof that the genre was already fixed, if not ossified, in the fifth century? If so, then we must support George Kennedy, for whom the genre reveals "almost immediately a highly formulated form."[6]

In the absence of ancient documents, it seems impossible to verify the assertion that "the traditional funeral oration led the way toward a traditionalism in all of [Athenian] literature."[7] But if we are to determine the status of the funeral oration as logos, we must study this very traditionalism, for although the presence of topoi may seem like a fault in the oration, to maintain this purely normative point of view is not a good method. The topoi are the raw material of every epitaphios, and the unity of the genre is constructed out of these "commonplaces," which therefore cannot be treated as misplaced or contingent ornaments.[8] On the contrary, we should study the topoi for themselves, acknowledging their primary function, which is to provide the oration with both material and limits. Their inflexibility then ceases to be an obstacle and becomes a valuable aid to a historical understanding of the oration, since, tirelessly reproducing the same conceptual structure of one of the earliest forms of Athenian prose, they offer a sort of inventory of what may have been the mental equipment[9] of eloquence before the triumph of rhetoric.

A Limited Originality

The repetitive nature of a form based on topoi is initially seen as a limitation and largely accounts for the criticisms of certain epitaphioi if not always of the funeral oration as a whole, from Antiquity on.* Many modern scholars have repeated these criticisms, blaming the "monotony" of the oration on its decorative, that is, ultimately epideictic, status.[10] They thus follow the tradition of the rhetoricians, inherited from Aristotle, who in the *Rhetoric* draws no distinction between epitaphios and egkomion,[11] and classify the funeral oration in the epideictic genre, of which, as a subdivision, it is supposed to possess every aspect.

Thus, among moderns, the funeral oration of the fifth and fourth centuries suffers from the same general disaffection with which the Latin rhetors of the imperial period treated all works written for state occasions.[12] Contrasted with political and legal debates, true combats in which two adversaries sought to win the audience's decision on controversial matters, regarded as more repetitive than inventive, based more on display† than on argument, the epideictic genre was relegated to a purely formal function by Roman theorists, who, like Quintilian, saw its purpose not as the "uplift" attributed to it by Aristotle,‡ but as a formal search for aesthetic qualities.[13] The genre was never really to recover,[14] but that is another story, one that does not, and perhaps never did, concern the funeral oration of classical Athens. How could these late theorists teach us anything about a civic oration that had long since lost its *raison d'être* when they were writing?

The first misinterpretation of the meaning and import of the funeral oration is more or less contemporary with the oration itself, since it should be attributed to Aristotle, whose classificatory and normative thought, triumphant in Antiquity, still dominates all modern analyses of the history and function of Greek

---

* Thus Dionysius of Halicarnassus regards Demosthenes's epitaphios as "empty and puerile" (On *the Style of Demosthenes* 1095).

† Quintilian, *Institutio oratoria* 3.8: *tota ostentationis.*

‡ Aristotle, *Rhetoric* 1.3.1358b27–28.

prose. Aristotle witnessed, if not the decline of the funeral oration, which was still in use when he was writing his *Rhetoric*, at
least the end of a historical development that, as far as the oration
for public occasions was concerned, was leading from the civilization of the logos to that of the written word.[15] So he declares,
"The style of the epideictic genre is the one best suited to being
written down, for its proper object is reading," and he goes on to
contrast the *lexis graphikē* with the *lexis agōnistikē*,[*] the latter
being proper to speeches that were actually delivered — a distinction that was to influence later theories of the *genos epidetktihon*.
Of course, one might claim that in formulating this definition
Aristotle is thinking not of the funeral oration but principally of
the works of Isocrates.[16†] But this is yet another way of avoiding
the real problem: while making innumerable allusions to the epitaphioi, is Aristotle aware of what differentiates them from the
fictitious "orations" of Isocrates? Does he accord enough importance to the profoundly political meaning that these logoi assumed
at a time when Athens was making history?[17] If we agree with
Buchheit that for Aristotle the only kind of eulogy was an individual one, then we must accept the obvious fact that one may
include the funeral oration, a necessarily collective eulogy, in the
general theory of the epideictic genre only at the cost of misunderstanding its specificity.[18]

Scholars to use the term "epideictic genre" to designate a whole
to which the funeral oration belongs only imperfectly or after the
event. The address to the dead, the official consecration of the
omnipotence of speech in Athens, has at the outset very little to
do with school exercises, even though it was gradually annexed by
them.[19] Of course the epitaphioi inspired many of Isocrates's orations, but the mania for commentary, proper to Isocrates, was
quite alien to them. Shall we note finally that the funeral oration
became a mere aesthetic manifestation when some epitaphioi,

* *Ibid.* 3.12.1414a18–19, 1414b24–25, as well as 1413b4.
† *Ibid.* 1414b25–27.

whether actually delivered like Pericles's or fictitious like Gorgias's and perhaps Lysias's, were published as writings? But this practice was quite unknown to the first orators, whose speeches are cruelly unavailable to the historian.[20] This absence corresponds to the fact that in Athenian society at that time, speech, though highly valued — and perhaps for that very reason — was not to be reduced to literature, individual orations were relatively interchangeable, and the orator was primarily a politician.

The funeral oration as we know it resembles a logos epideiktikos in its stylistic concerns,[21] and the theme of rivalry between the orators, which was to be so popular in orations for state occasions, is common in the epitaphioi. But the civic character of the funeral oration prevents us from applying to it Aristotle's definitions of the epideictic genre. In these definitions, the polis is singularly absent: "neither citizen nor judge," the listener is a mere spectator, "drawn there solely by the pleasure of seeing an artist in speech at grips with the difficulties of his profession."[22] Nor can we object that the last sentence of the oration, always devoted to dismissing the audience, is addressed to a passive crowd. In reality, this ritual formula does not imply that the listener is a mere spectator. On the contrary, it first invites him to participate in the ceremony, which would be incomplete without his laments.[23]*

It is not enough, then, to see the funeral oration as an epideictic speech. An institution of the city cannot be confused with the invention of a rhetor, and the epideictic genre therefore seems more like a neighboring genre than like a larger whole. It is not in Aristotle's inevitably classificatory thought, but in a study of the funeral oration itself, regarded as a fixed form and as a genre made up of topoi, that we must look for an answer to the question of its status.

Can a "speech-spectacle" be merely decorative? To what extent does a fixed form force all thought content to become a topos, and so prevent any invention? Perhaps there is no other answer to

* Lysias 81. See also Thucydides 2.46, *Menexenus* 249c6–8, Demosthenes 37.

these questions than to examine the most rhetorical of the epi-taphioi, that of Gorgias. Considered successively an archetype[24] and an example, declared by some to be devoid of meaning and by others to be rich in thought, it has, more than all the other epi-taphioi, been the object of conflicting interpretations, all of which, however, tend to forget that it is at the same time a text by Gorgias and an epitaphios, and all of which fail to link these two facts together.

Many scholars have seen the oration as a manifesto for a Sophist education, "clearly bearing the mark of a definite individ-ual";[25] and, without spending more time accounting for the form chosen by Gorgias, they turn this text, regarded as "the funeral eulogy of accomplished citizens, whom the Sophists have edu-cated,"[26] into a "decisive document for the study of the rhetor's ethics."[27] Such a reading would be acceptable if it did not fail to treat the oration as an epitaphios, that is, as one version among others of the funeral oration genre. But in ignoring this character, scholars risk interpreting a topos as original thought.

Declaring that the epitaphios is only an assemblage of received ideas,[28] historians of the epideictic genre adopt the opposite atti-tude. To those who regard the epitaphios as the most representative text of Gorgias's style or who think that the Sophist has unfailingly influenced the form of the funeral oration, they reply that this form had essentially been established by the mid-fifth century and that, far from modifying it, Gorgias first had to subject himself to it.

But these approaches risk underestimating the unique charac-ter of Gorgias's oration: for the citizen of Athens, the composition of an epitaphios was an obligation that could not be shirked once one had been appointed to deliver it;* for the Sophist Gorgias, on the other hand, it was a conscious choice. Everything seems to separate the civic genre of the funeral oration and the Sophist's method. But with its antithetical form[29] and its conventional thought, the funeral oration provided Gorgias with material that was both restricting and flexible: restricting, because it imposed

* Thucydides 2.35; *Menexenus* 236e1; Demosthenes 1.

certain themes and words; flexible, because it lent itself to stylistic effects and provided a stock of thoughts that were all the more effective because they were traditional. The excessive number of antitheses and the use of recognized values must, then, be explained by a double reference, to Gorgias and to the funeral oration; and this double reading must necessarily take into account the constraints of the genre and the Sophist's innovations.

In order to avoid the most serious misinterpretations, we must treat this text above all as an epitaphios. Thus the formula *ouk apeiroi emphutou Areōs* (they were not without experience of the innate Ares),* which Vollgraff considers unacceptable in a public speech,[30] seems in no way out of place in the military context of an epitaphios: has not the orator previously praised the Athenians for being "violent toward the violent"?† Similarly, the term *enopliou Eridos* (armed contention)‡ seems to embarrass certain commentators. But if, considering the funeral oration a unitary genre, we compare Gorgias with Pericles§ or Lysias, we discover that for the Athenians war is doubly eris — not only by definition but also in the second degree, when the adversary is, like Sparta, a specialist in the military art — and there is no need, in translating this term, to import into the epitaphios the notion of a "competition with oneself."[31] Finally, in praising the Athenians for being "pious toward their parents through the care" that they lavished upon them,** the orator is probably not congratulating them on respecting the "catechism of the Sophists,"[32] but reminding his listeners that to take care of parents was an obligation for the sons; and he declares, anticipating the consolation, that after their death the city will take over their task.†† It can be seen from these few examples that it is not always necessary to appeal to the Sophist's

* DK, B 6, p. 286, ll. 10–11.
† *Ibid.* 1. 7: *hubristai eis tous hubristas.*
‡ *Ibid.*, ll. 11–12.
§ Thucydides 2.39.
** DK, B 6, p. 286, ll. 13–14: *hosioi pros tous tokeas tei therapeiai.*
†† Cf. Thucydides 2.46.1; Lysias 75; *Menexenus* 248e4–249c3.

virtues to elucidate the epitaphios. This would be to forget that as a general rule Gorgias works on topoi, bringing to them no other modification but a new arrangement, and it sometimes happens that a term may be identified as the superimposition of several traditional themes. Thus *to praon epieikēs tou authadous dikaiou prokrinontes* (setting greater store by the gentleness of equity than by the harshness of the law)* turns out on analysis to be a combination of two antitheses dear to the funeral oration and functioning here on several levels: that of *epieikēs* and *dikaion* is banal† but might already cover the opposition, explicitly formulated later,‡ between written and unwritten law; that of *praon* and *authades* reminds us that against insensate pride the Athenians are on the side of the weak and the oppressed. But it also suggests that before being "violent toward the violent," they are good at seeking agreement: this aspect, which is stressed by Euripides,§ is not neglected in Lysias's epitaphios.** The raw material, then, is not new, and Gorgias's epitaphios borrows commonplaces from other orations; his originality consists in juxtaposing them, which enables him perhaps to go beyond them. At this stage of the analysis, it may not be out of place to interpret the whole of the formula as a relativistic declaration inspired by the ethic of kairos.[33] But, again, this interpretation yields its full interest only if we realize that the Sophist, an opportunist in form as well as incontent, has turned to the advantage of his own thought themes proper to the funeral oration. This is not the first time that Gorgias has done this: did he not, in the exordium of the *Helenus*, pile up the greatest possible number of *idées reçues*, with the sole purpose of reworking them and transforming them by juxtaposition?†† But in tackling the funeral oration, he was attempting a much more delicate exercise:

* DK, B 6, p. 285, ll. 6–7.
† Cf., for example, Herodotus 3.53.
‡ DK, B 6, p. 285, ll. 7–8.
§ Euripides, *Suppliant Women* 347–48.
** Lysias 7 (to the Thebans, the Athenians "began by sending heralds").
†† DK, B 11, 21.

it was a question no longer of playing with opinions gleaned from different sources but of appropriating a fixed form to which he had first to subject himself.

So every reader of the epitaphios must be aware of this phenomenon of superimposition by which a topos is overlaid by a new form and a new content. But the topos remains recognizable, and the "innovations" do not fundamentally undermine the funeral oration. Is the orator praising the Athenians for being *aphoboi eis tous aphobous, deinoi en tois deinois* (intrepid toward the intrepid, redoubtable to the redoubtable)?* We must see in it both the qualities of the aner agathos and the Sophists' valuation of kairos; to isolate the military dimension would be to flatten the text, and to cling only to the opportunistic aspect of the formula would give an erroneous interpretation.

A survey of one last example will allow us to determine the limits within which an epitaphios may have meaning. "Can I speak as I wish, and desire the norm?"† the orator exclaims in a sort of *captatio benevolentiae*. If we compare this passage with other epitaphioi, we can recognize in it two commonplaces found in any exordium.[34]‡ But we may also compare this text with other fragments by Gorgias and show that it contains a reflection on the logos proper to the Sophist himself.[35] However — and this is the essential point — in order to elucidate this text, we must always proceed by comparison: whether we see it as a mere application of the topoi of the funeral oration or find in it ideas already developed elsewhere by the Sophist, we must refer to other works in the same series. As an epitaphios, the oration acquires its full meaning as an example of a genre; as an epitaphios written by Gorgias, it is the application of ideas worked out in other texts: it

---

* *Ibid*. B6, p. 285, l. 8.

† *Ibid*. ll. 2–3.

‡ To be able to speak: cf. Thucydides 2.35.1; Lysias 54, *Menexenus* 239c1–2, Demosthenes 1, 12 (what rhetoric was to call *excusatio propter infirmitatem*). To want the norm: cf. Thucydides 2.35.1–2; Lysias 1; Demosthenes 1; Hyperides, 2.23 (= *difficultas verbis facta assequendi*).

is not in this oration but in the *Helenus* that a theory of kairos is to be found. The funeral oration cannot, then, be twisted to suit just any purpose and seems to play no other role than that of an inert support for an already-constituted thought.

This oration is a curious text indeed, one in which all new thought may be reduced to a received or already-formulated idea, in which all formal invention follows an already-established model: thus what is generally regarded as the purest statement of the Sophist's thought[36]* still sounds strangely like the declarations of some other epitaphios.[37]† This lack of autonomy in the oration is explained by the characteristics of the genre: one may try to alter its contents from the inside, but one cannot use it to say something new. To borrow what Milman Parry said of Homer's poetry, one might suggest that in the funeral oration, "there may be traces of a certain originality, but it is an originality that consists only in rearranging the words and expressions of tradition without important modifications."[38] This does not mean that nothing can be said in this genre: it is, of course, not an easy undertaking, and the constraints may lead an orator to contradict in his epitaphios what he may have said in other circumstances.[39] But Gorgias comes through this test with flying colors; he satisfies the requirements of both the genre and his own thought, and this example proves that theorists have too often confused the "already said" with the "pointless," deducing from the genre's limited originality its total vacuity.

On closer study, then, Gorgias's epitaphios reveals a certain "originality," which, though limited, is not always a matter of mere decoration. In order to show that this conclusion is not based on an isolated case, we will now examine a number of texts that are not usually recognized as anything other than ornamental. This is the case of the exordiums of the epitaphioi, in which, more than

* DK, B 6, p. 285, 1. 9 and p. 286, 1. 1: *to deon en toi deonti kai legein kai sigan kai poiein.*

† Cf. Thucydides 2.40.3; this is the topos of the harmony between logos and ergon, which Gorgias develops so fully later (*kai dissa askēsantes*, and so on).

elsewhere, there is an abundance of topoi and in which commentators have delighted in pointing out the trompe-l'œil antitheses and their empty, wearying repetitiveness.

At the same time, we might also consider the nature and function of the topos. The ambiguity of this term, which has gradually taken on, in addition to its initial meaning, the much broader one of "cliché," "stereotype," might seem to suggest that there is no interest whatsoever in an assemblage of commonplaces. But without being so bold as to give the topos a definition that not even Aristotle's *Topica* contained,[40] we may regard it less as just an empty medium* than as the witness of the agonizing — and eternal — question posed by rhetoric, namely, "what is to be said?,"[41] or as a sign of the problems facing a given oration in a particular historical context; for, before being frozen as so much rhetorical padding or as quasi-automatic formulas, the topoi were ideas or representations proper to a particular society[42] and, as such, were mainly of interest to the historian trying to discover the "framework of a mentality."[43]

This is certainly how the topoi of the exordiums strike one; in them is inscribed the reflective relationship of the work with itself, of the orator with his activity: a relationship to the genre, to the object of the oration, to the public, to other orators, to the city.[44] Thus the exordium, a reserve of everything that has to be said and left unsaid, is itself a "topic." Scholars are right to stress the importance that such openness has in an epideictic discourse; but this topic turns out to be particularly crucial to the funeral oration, a strictly codified form of speech: it necessarily precedes the understanding of any epitaphios, so much so that commentators seem incapable of judging the genre according to other criteria than those stated in the exordium in the form of topoi.[45]

We shall therefore study the exordiums at two levels. First we shall survey the content to determine the problems that confront the oration and must be resolved if it is to be anything other than vain words. We shall then show that the topos, though a limitation, is also the material whose arrangement gives the civic oration its form.

* Aristotle, *Rhetoric* 2.26.1403a17.

The Problems of a Logos Politikos

If Plato is to be believed, the author of an epitaphios owes it to himself to refuse any agon with the poets. Thus the author of the *Menexenus*, dismissing in a formula of *praeteritio* any account of mythical exploits, declares: "The poets have already sung magnificently in verse and displayed their valor to all the world; if therefore we were to try in turn to glorify the same subjects in simple prose, we might seem to occupy only the second rank."* It is an ambiguous refusal, since in reality the epitaphioi do not refrain from exploiting themes presented here as strictly poetic. Does Plato want to suggest that this protest hides an ardent desire to rival poetry? Whatever the truth may be, this opposition between *mousikē* and *logos psilos*, this conflict between poiein and legein,† seems to be a necessary theme of the exordium in a funeral oration. Some would no doubt interpret it as a sign of the very real influence exercised by poetry on epideictic prose after Gorgias, if Aristotle is to be believed.‡ I am inclined to see it instead as a trace of the period in which the funeral oration appeared, well before the establishment of rhetoric,[46] well before Gorgias and the Sophists gave Greek prose a new form, in that transitional period when "prose begins to replace poetry as the most serious vehicle of thought."[47] It is true that, defying the opposition between rhetoric and poetry constitutive of the Aristotelian system,[48] the funeral oration seems by its very nature to hesitate between legein and poiein, since, having the duty to strengthen in each Athenian a conviction that is both private and collective, it sets out to use whatever may charm its audience — alliteration, repetition, or puns, to mention only a few of the poetic figures used.[49] But the opposition between mousike and logos concerns not so much the form of the oration as the fundamental rivalry of two genres having antagonistic functions. We may see it as a reminder of the special status of the funeral oration, which, born of lyric poetry and in competition with it,[50] uses poetic themes but reinterprets them

---

* *Menexenus* 239b7–c2; cf. Thucydides 2.41.4; Demosthenes 9.
† Lysias 2.
‡ Aristotle, *Rhetoric* 3.1.1404a24–26.

from a resolutely political perspective.[51] Hence the full meaning of the topos of the agon with the poets: the prose oration must necessarily define itself against the versified speech that it simultaneously resembles and opposes.

A study of the exordiums confirms the preceding analysis. Evoking the need to get the correct measure of the oration and to give memorable acts their share of glory, the orator tirelessly repeats topoi that seem to have been borrowed originally from lyric poetry. But in the funeral oration, they are inverted: where the poet declaims his certainty, the orator expresses his anxiety. These are in each case traditional, compulsory declarations; but it is significant that the relationship to speech changes sign from one genre to another: from being positive in poetry, it becomes, in the funeral oration, negative and constricting.

A triumphant poetics, confident of its value, animates the work of Pindar: "associated with the victorious athletes" whom he is celebrating,* the poet receives his own share of the glory that he gives them,† and each ode tends to become an auto-celebration of all-powerful speech.‡ The author of an epitaphios likewise seeks to bathe himself in the glory that he attributes to the Athenians;§ but this is a secret purpose, which only Plato's malice brings to light and which is hidden behind a number of complaints — fear of being overwhelmed by the scope of the task,** anxiety when faced with

---

* Pindar, *Olympians* 1.115b.

† Pindar, *Isthmians* 1.45. To the valiant, works of every kind; to the poet, words.

‡ *Olympians* 6 is a good example of this: from the myth of family origins and the eulogy of the virtues of the conqueror's race, Pindar moves to the glory of his own fatherland and to "the charming flower of its hymns."

§ *Menexenus* 236a6: *epainon eudokimein*.

** Cf. Lysias 54 ("it is not easy for one man to describe in detail the dangers that so many others have incurred") and Thucydides 2.35.1 ("the reputation of many would not have been imperiled by one man and their merits believed or not, as he speaks well or ill"). Compare with the facile offering (*koupha dōsis*) of the poet (Pindar, *Isthmians* 1.45).

the abundance of the material,* regret at not having the necessary time† — as if, in order to win, the orator had to pretend to be defeated in advance,‡ as if speech, instead of saving deeds, endangered them.§

It is certainly the status of the word that is in question; the poet who hopes both to dominate the logos and to dominate by it, is opposed to the orator, who fears he may not master speech. Pindar's poetry is based on the perfect coincidence of ergon and logos, of victory and the ode. Celebrating athletes and sharing in their glory, the poet models his art on the exploits that he exalts, adopting the "equestrian mode" to crown Hieron, winner of the horse race,** and comparing himself to the skillful javelin-thrower who hits the target as closely as possible.†† But these comparisons are not mere metaphors; they are made necessary by the connaturality of poem and deed. Are not all talents equally the gift of the gods, eloquence as well as physical strength?‡‡ To celebrate a winner, Pindar must also win a victory and, making himself an archer,§§ project the arrow of proud words far enough to outstrip his rivals and reach the target.*** Even more than an athlete, he is, so to speak, the agonothete of his own poem, which becomes "a fine struggle in words,"

* Demosthenes 15; Hyperides 4 ("it is not easy for one orator to do justice to so many great actions").

† Lysias 1 and 54; Hyperides 4. Many variations on this theme are found in the *Menexenus*: 239b6 (insufficient time for the oration), 234c5 and 235c9 (lack of time to prepare the oration), 246b1–2 (the whole of time would not be adequate).

‡ The battle is lost in advance: see Lysias 54 ("what speeches, what time, what orator would be capable of revealing the valor of the men who lie in this place?").

§ The comparison is instructive between Pindar (*Nemeans* 8.31ff: the fine renown with which the dead may be *succored*) and Thucydides 2.35.1 (when entrusted to a single man, the arete of the dead *may* lose all credit).

** Pindar, *Olympians* 1.100ff.

†† *Nemeans* 9.55.

‡‡ *Pythians* 1.42.

§§ *Nemeans* 6.27.

*** *Pythians* 1.43ff.

rich in "twists" and "woven words."* Molded upon its object, the poetic logos is therefore also an ergon. It is so even in a double sense. It is not only an act but also a monumental masterpiece destined to outlast the ephemeral deed that it exalts:† "Its facade, illuminated with a pure light, will proclaim and will get men to repeat ... the illustrious victory."[52]‡ In reality, such a proposition destroys the balance that has been set up between deed and word: the deed is *only* ergon, the word is *also* ergon; the word therefore dominates all possible acts, which need it in order to exist fully. Declaring that no noble deed can dispense with its logos§ and that valor, "praised by men of talent, ... increases,"** Pindar proclaims the force of "the living word which is the power of life and in which positive values are manifested."[53] The said is therefore superior to the done; for Pindar, as for his contemporary Heraclitus, the logos, "glory among men" and "vision of reason,"[54] represents all value.

The ergon/logos opposition is just as fundamental to the funeral oration; central in the exordium, it frequently also structures later passages. But this time, the logos declares itself inferior to reality (ergon) — and by this term we must understand the rest of the ceremonial as well as the wartime acts of the dead.

This movement is particularly apparent in Pericles's epitaphios, in which the deceptive charm of poetic language is rejected in the name of factual truth,[55] a truth identified with the power of Athens.†† But the criticism is aimed not only at the poetic logos; it seems to be directed against all speech, since the orator's first words are a regret "that to men whose valor has been expressed in acts" one is not content to pay "equal homage in acts."‡‡ Thus the most famous of the speeches uses the logos against itself, disavowing it or at least declar-

* *Nemeans* 4.93–94.
† *Ibid.* 6.4.
‡ *Pythians* 6.5–14; cf. *ibid.* 7.1–4 and *Olympians* 6.1–4.
§ Cf. *Olympians* 10.109–15; *Nemeans* 6.29–30.
** *Nemeans* 8.40ff.
†† *Thucydides* 2.41.4.
‡‡ *Ibid.* 35.1.

ing it superfluous from the outset. It is an ambiguous criticism, especially since this deprecation of speech is a topos used by all the orators and enables them in the end to find a suitable exordium — that is, perhaps, to conceal the very real difficulty of speaking at all.

Even when criticizing the logos, the orator seems at first to be embarrassed by the sheer excess of ergon. By this term, he designates simultaneously the presence of the tomb before which the ceremony is taking place; the *reality* of the deed accomplished, that is, the "fine death" of the Athenians; the already-constituted *material* that he must use all over again; and the noble deeds of Athenians of all times, whose greatness and number defy all verbal description. Ceremony, present deeds, the city's glorious past — the speech certainly does not lack a subject; on the contrary, it seems to be threatened by an overabundance of material or a hypertrophy of reality.* It might be possible to speak of past deeds, which provide the orator with well-known passages, easy enough to turn out because already well signposted; but recent acts, those of the dead of the day, silence him. When confronted by them, when forced to treat the subject imposed upon him by the circumstances, Demosthenes appeals to the powerlessness of speech: "I praise, but *here I am now face-to-face with the acts themselves and I do not know where to begin. Since they all surge in upon me at the same time, I feel unable to choose from among them.*"† No doubt he must give the same sense to the anaphora *ergōi . . . ergōi* by which Pericles stresses the uselessness of words.‡ Of course, Pericles is more radical than Demosthenes in his criticism of the oration, since he asks himself not where he can begin but why he should begin at all. However, both express in their different ways the same difficulty: will the logos be able to account for the real?

Thus each exordium seems to weigh once again on the respective value of what is seen and what is heard[56] and concludes — definitively or temporarily — that visible homage must have primacy

* Lysias 2: *aphthonia.*
† Demosthenes 15.
‡ Thucydides 2.35.1.

over praise, or at least that the latter poses the greater difficulty. In the preliminary statement of his epitaphios, Lysias denies that words can perform the task that has been accorded him by the decision of the city: "Citizens present at this funeral, if I believed it possible to express in a speech the valor of the warriors who repose in this place, I would have to complain that I have been given so few days' notice to address you."*

The proper action of the oration would ideally consist in evoking (dēlōsai) the noble deeds of the dead. But the logos is perceived as irreducibly heterogeneous to all ergon, a negative certainty that is expressed by the unreality of the present ("if I believed…"). This is especially so because before any words are spoken, the deeds have already been made visible† by the inhibiting presence of the funerary monument, in which the remains of the Athenians (ton enthade kei-menon) are gathered together and which, giving its name to the cer-emony,‡ concentrates all the attention of the public on itself (paron-tes epi tōide tōi taphōi). Since this spectacle already has its spectators, how can the orator, who has only words at his disposal, show (logōi dēlōsai) anything new? Such an expression presupposes a rivalry between sight and hearing: on the one hand, a direct, two-term rela-tionship between a public and the immediately perceptible ergon of the tomb; on the other, an infinitely more complex relationship among the orator, the listeners, and the actions of the dead, which runs the risk of giving rise to many different assessments of reality.§

The funeral oration, which must evoke the erga of the past and which takes place after the most recent ergon, namely, the burial of the dead, is doubly *words after deeds*. At least this is how it pres-ents itself, in a speech that fears being nothing more than a speech, and the orators do not fail to declare their defiance toward speech while delivering the epitaphios, as if they were forced "to fall back

---

* Lysias 1.

† Thucydides 2.34.6 (the orator begins only *after* the dead have been covered with earth).

‡ *Taphos* refers to the funeral as well as to the tomb.

§ Cf. Thucydides 2.35.2.

on speech in order to escape the fascination of things and upon things in order to escape the fascination of words."[57] But by this very fact they repeat, without knowing it, a certain attitude toward speech that belongs to the transitional period when the classical city was gradually moving away from its archaic models. Without forgetting that the topoi are an aide-mémoire, a stock of reified contents, preestablished material allowing the orator to speak, we shall therefore treat them also as crystallizations of the ambiguity inherent in a genre that came into being in a period when the role of speech was itself undergoing change.

Is the "logos of man," as Clémence Ramnoux thinks, "an invention of the age of culture that saw the flowering of the funeral oration and the victory ode"?[58] Even if these two genres were strictly contemporary, which is by no means evident, the victory of secularized speech was interpreted in very different, if not opposite, ways: in contrast to Pindar's certainties, the funeral oration is characterized by the affirmation — admittedly just as stereotyped — of the weakness of speech. Thus it adopts toward the logos one available position at a particular moment in the long history of the relations between the done and the said. Complementarity of act and word in the Homeric world,* the disturbance of this balance in archaic society,† and finally, in the fifth century, total separation: if these are, broadly speaking, the essential stages of this long evolution, studied by Felix Heinimann, the funeral oration belongs to a time when the divorce between logos and ergon had well and truly already occurred.[59]

But to be aware of this distance does not necessarily mean that we must accept the total devaluation of the logos in favor of the ergon, as Cleon does,‡ and we will not rush to declare that from

* For example, *Iliad* 9.443.

† For example, Solon, frag. 8 D, 7ff. (*gloss* and *epe* are contrasted with *ergon*).

‡ Thucydides 3.38.4; this paragraph is constructed entirely on the opposition between logos and ergon ("spectators of words and listeners of deeds, giving more credence to the account heard than to the event seen with your own eyes").

then on *all* speech has lost its value. In most cases, the logos, political as well as philosophical, serenely assumes a position "apart," and although it abandons the performative statements of magico-religious speech[60] to become an instrument of persuasion, deliberation, or discussion, it gains by being, in the world of the cities, the "all-powerful master," celebrated by Gorgias[61]* that, in Thucydides's taut style, orders the real that it seeks to dominate.[62] Far from always being a source of anxiety the experience of the heterogeneity of words and things may help the orator to establish the discourse in an autonomous reality.[63]

In this "process of secularization,"[64] the democratic funeral oration occupies a paradoxical position, and the topoi of the exordiums give the impression that the genre accepts with difficulty its break with archaic expressions of glory. Delivered in Athens, where the "speech-dialogue" reigned, it nevertheless does not preside over any decision or deliberation, but follows action instead of preceding it and seems quite willing to present itself as a mere supplement. Nor does it have the efficacy of magico-religious speech, even though it seems to come close to it insofar as, being the city's Catalog and Memory, it is a modern "speech about ancient times."[65] But unlike the poet, invested with a divine, all-powerful mission, who must account only to the Muses, the orator, a member of the city and appointed by it to carry out an official, compulsory task, knows that he must win the agreement of his audience.[66]†

Of course archaic poetry did not deliberately ignore the whole problem of persuasion. Proclaiming that he must observe the criterion of relevance in his words, for "nothing is more painful to the citizens, in their innermost hearts, than praise of the merits of others,"‡ Pindar is inclined to acknowledge the truth in the law

* DK, 82 B 11 (= *Helenus*), 8: *logos dunastes megas.*
† Demosthenes 14: "The persuasive virtue [*peithō*] of orations also requires the goodwill [*eunoia*] of the listeners."
‡ Pindar, *Pythians* 1.82–84; cf. *Olympians* 5.16 and 6.7; *Pythians* 7.19 and 11.29 and 55; *Nemeans* 8.21–22; *Paeans* 2.54.

laid down by Pericles, by which "incredulity is born with jealousy."* Even so, Pindar, more than Pericles or Demosthenes, risks arousing envy in his public, since he praises to the clouds an individual, his deeds, his family, and his name,† whereas the official orator exalts anonymous, interchangeable citizens before other citizens. But the poet has full confidence in *charis* (grace) "to give credence to the unbelievable."‡

Such certainty is unknown to the orator, a politician whose words have no other sanction than the consent of his assembled fellow citizens.[67] So Pericles is led to work out a psychology of the listener to an epitaphios, as a being endowed with pathos.§ If he is to be believed, the oration confronts a double difficulty: even if the orator overcomes the epistemological obstacle posed by the difficulty of establishing the truth,** he must still fulfill a precise demand made by his audience.†† The listener is not only attentive to the widening gap between erga and logos when the eulogy falls short of the actions it celebrates, but in his assessment of the oration he introduces an ideal image of himself that must not be called into question,‡‡ lest the living become jealous of the dead. The detractors of the funeral oration, such as Plato, observed that Pericles raises a false problem, since, through the dead, it is in fact the living who are being praised;§§ but they forget — or pretend to forget — that a certain *captatio benevolentiae* is necessary in any case: in expounding the problems of the oration — and only thus — the orator seeks to convince the audience that,

---

* Thucydides 2.35.2. Cf. Gorgias, DK, B 6, p. 285, l. 14 (*anthrōpinos phthonos*).

† Pindar, *Pythians* 11.29.

‡ Pindar, *Olympians* 1.30–34.

§ To borrow an Aristotelian formulation of this idea: see *Rhetoric* 1.2.1356a14.

** Thucydides 2.35.2: in this matter, "belief in the truth is hard to confirm."

†† *Ibid.*: "The friends of the dead who know the facts may well think that the words of the speaker fall short of his wishes and knowledge."

‡‡ *Ibid.*: "When he hears of anything that exceeds his own abilities, he may, out of jealousy [*phthonos*], suspect exaggeration."

§§ *Menexenus* 235a2–5 and 236a5–6.

far from delivering a solitary speech, he is the spokesman of a collective opinion. Aristotle understood very clearly that this was the function of the exordium when, referring to Plato's criticism of the funeral oration, he declared: "In the exordia of the epideictic genre, one must make sure that the listener imagines that he has some share in the praise."*

Every epitaphios, then, must shelter behind an exordium in which is expounded once and for all the difficulty in finding the right degree of praise. Pindar was aware of this problem: he knew that human speech, proud of its new strength, could play a dangerous game with praise; but his belief in an inspired poetic logos ultimately removed the difficulty.[68] The orator, on the other hand, is left with the fear of being powerless to equal reality by his words. "It is difficult to find the right tone,"† says Pericles, and Lysias echoes him when he declares that it is impossible to equal acts with words.‡ But is it really a question of acts? The reality before which speech declares its powerlessness, and whose incommensurable value it must always begin by conjuring up, is ultimately not the dead but the city, omnipresent and demanding, both a public and the object of praise.

The inadequacy of words to express deeds is, of course, only a threat, skillfully used to excuse in advance any faltering passage.[69] But even so, it may be that the oration is actually *inhibited* by the overriding *need* — in order to reach its declared object, the actions of the dead — *to pass through the city*, its real object. Thus, unlike the poet, who can always abandon too long a passage on the victorious athlete's fatherland, the official orator cannot avoid expatiating on the city,§ even at the risk of relegating to second place the deeds that his oration is supposed to be celebrating. In Pindar, there is sometimes not enough time for praise of the city; in Pericles and Lysias, the citizens lose out. Speaking of Athens, in the

* Aristotle, *Rhetoric* 3.14.1415b28–32.
† Thucydides 2.35.2.
‡ Lysias 1. Cf. Demosthenes 1.
§ Thucydides 2.42.1–2.

name of Athens, and to Athenians, the orator takes refuge behind the all-powerful authority of the city, reminding his listeners that the form of the oration itself is not free.* In short, as Henri-Etienne Caffiaux remarks, "it even seems that the state wanted to immobilize it in these suitable forms . . . condemning it to having to repeat what had already been said."[70] And when the funeral oration ceases to claim that it is a patch and to regard itself as a patrios nomos, a custom instituted by the ancestors, it is still the city that the oration discovers in itself, the city that it turns into a reality as natural and as ancient as the race of the autochthones. Thus nothing has been left to chance, since the ancients decided both that a speech had to be made† and the way in which it was to be done.‡

So the city influences the oration by imposing norms on it, but above all by imposing itself on it as the single, universal authority on all logos. However, this constraint is counterbalanced: a codified speech is also within its limits, a facile speech. As nomos and topoi, the funeral oration preexists every epitaphios, and the orator often seems to have evoked the difficulties of the oration only to prove all the more his fidelity to the city. This is probably the explanation for the movement of Pericles's exordium, in which the "criticism" of the funeral oration is resolved in ultimate submission.§

Were the problems raised only so that a rapid, formal solution of them might be presented in the oration? This is what Plato suggests, opening the exordium of the *Menexenus* with a condensed and resolutely idyllic version of the relation between speech and actions, the orator and his public.** But all the other orators tend

* Lysias 1. Cf. *Menexenus* 237a–b; to the question "What sort of speech will this be?" the orator has two answers: (1) the city wants it thus; (2) the city will be the subject of the oration.

† *Menexenus* 236e1.

‡ *Ibid.* 236b4.

§ Thucydides 2.35.3: "However, since our ancestors have set the seal of their approval upon the practice, I must obey the law."

** *Menexenus* 236e1–3: "Thanks to a fine oration, fine actions deserve of those who have performed them remembrance and homage by the audience."

to do the same, though in less expeditious ways. In this respect, the exordium of Lysias's epitaphios is exemplary: it removes all the difficulties that it first evokes. It is enough for the orator to recall the innumerable orations made before his own[*] for the preliminary statement on the impossibility of matching deeds with words to be forgotten:[†] one may speak of acts when others have already spoken of them. In this way, the logos takes on the reassuring appearance of fact: there are works of discourse, and on this terrain the orator may already proceed to the reconciliation of saying and doing, by claiming the interdependence of the poetic poiein and the rhetorical legein,[‡] united in the same celebration of the Athenians of all time.[§]

Furthermore, through having been celebrated in earlier epitaphioi, the valor of the Athenians has become material for the discourse, and the superabundance of their deeds is transformed into an inexhaustible stock of themes ready to be used in speeches and already "put into words."[**] Logos and erga are now allied, and the oration may be worked out without any discontinuity from acts that have been turned into topoi. Last, in a final form of reconciliation on the very field of operations, the laments of the enemies become hymns to Athenian valor:[††] the deeds have already, spontaneously, given birth to their own praise.

After these short-lived anxieties, a definitive certainty settles in, which must be developed by the orator: only the Athenians realized in themselves the balance between logos and erga, so that

---

[*] Lysias 2 (agon with earlier orations).

[†] *Ibid.* 1.

[‡] *Ibid.* 2.

[§] *Ibid.*: "The material offered by their valor to poetry and eloquence is so rich that, after inspiring so many masterpieces, far from being exhausted, it still leaves enough to be said by newcomers."

[**] *Ibid.*: *tosauten ... aphthonian pareskeuasen he touton aretē.* (Compare with Demosthenes 12: "The bravery of those men itself shows us the number of exploits that are within our grasp [*procheira*] and that are easy enough to list."

[††] Lysias 2.

if Pericles is to be believed, "there are few Greeks of whom it may be said as of them, that their deeds matched their words."*

How could this reversal take place? An examination of the structure of the text gives us the key: the reconciliation of acts and words is always proclaimed after the praise of the city, explicitly designated as *hē polis* and has been made possible only by the substitution of the city for the acts of the dead as the object of the oration. Pericles's declaration is situated precisely at the transition that leads from the praise of Athens to that of the dead Athenians,† and Lysias also places *hē polis* between the divorce and the reconciliation.‡ The eulogy of the dead proved difficult. The detour via the city displaces the problem: the constricting character of the oration becomes proof of the benevolence of Athens, which wants its orators to win favor with the audience;§ the dead are forgotten, and we find ourselves once again with the living, gathered together for the same civic ceremony. At the same time, the "I" of the orator disappears, at least as the subject of the sentence;** *hē polis* takes its place as the origin of every act and every decision; and the orator, exonerated in advance from being only a repeater, is integrated into the body of his predecessors.†† Thus words are no longer directly confronted with the deeds that they must celebrate, but become a social activity. Last and most important, the function of the epitaphios is no longer to match the deeds of the dead but to vie with other orations, those of earlier orators. This is an essential consequence of the city intervention into the exordium and one

---

* Thucydides 2.42.2.

† In 2.42.1, Pericles justifies the length of the passage on the city and announces that he is about to praise the dead; in 42.2, he affirms the cohesion of the Athenians and the polis and declares that there is a balance between deeds and words.

‡ Lysias 1.

§ *Ibid.*

** We move from *ei … hēgoumen* to *hē polis hēgoumenē*; the "I" is now relegated to the role of complement (*hē polis moi dokei*).

†† Lysias 1: from the isolated orator we have moved to the orators, all docile executants of the city's orders.

that is explicitly stated by Lysias: "My speech will certainly concern those men; however, it is not with their actions that it will compete, but with the orators who have celebrated them before me.[*] The fundamental shift from the dead and their deeds to the orators and their works has been accomplished; but it was already being prepared for in the wordplay *tōn enthade keimenōn / tōn enthade legontōn*. Thus everything in the text converges to the same end: to reject the impossible rivalry between the oration and the fine death — for death, even a civic death, still preserves something irreducible — and to choose a terrain in which the confrontation takes place between equals. Human speech might not be strong enough to compete with the actions of the dead, but as civic logos it is now in competition with all other similar speeches. Of course, the funeral oration does not go as far as Gorgias, for whom "it is not beings that we reveal, but a discourse that is other than reality."[71][†] It seeks on the contrary to reconcile logos and ergon; but to effect this reconciliation, it must accept, if even as a temporary stage in the reasoning, that what is essential happens between logi.

Thus each epitaphios is engaged in an agon with all the others; and well beyond the gymnastic, hippic, and musical competitions included in the official program of the funerals, there continues from one celebration to another an endless agon epitaphios that puts the orations in conflict with each other. Speech is no longer alone but takes its place, temporally as well as spatially, in an institutional whole. In that never-ending competition, no winner is declared, but no orator forgets to measure himself against his predecessors,[‡] which is a guarantee of survival for the genre.

---

[*] *Ibid.* 2: *Homos de ho men logos moi peri toutōn, ho d'agōn ou pros ta toutōn erga alla pros tous prōteron ep' autois eirēkotas.*

[†] DK, 82 B 3, 84.

[‡] Even if, like Pericles, he denies wishing to join in the game, or if, like Demosthenes 10, he pretends to be conscientiously imitating his rivals. Clearly it is Isocrates who, in the *Panegyricus*, develops the theme most fully (4–10 and especially 13–14: criticism of the usual exordiums and their topoi; but before criticizing the exordiums, he obeys the rule that requires mention of the agon).

The topoi of the exordiums attempt, then, to reduce all possible gaps between the oration and its object, between the orator and his audience, between the orator and his reputation, justifying them in advance, in case they should emerge, by the omnipresent power of the city. Plato certainly seems to have understood this, and when he refers to the funeral oration and related orations as *logoi politikoi*,* we must no doubt understand this term in the broad sense of "speech of the city." Thus this brief survey of the exordiums, which has led from the crisis in secularized speech to the institutionalized rivalry of the epitaphioi, has demonstrated not only its difficulties but also the facility of a form of speech that is civic through and through.

An Oration Consisting of Topoi

When we first examined the genre, the topoi appeared to be so many knots of resistance, protecting the funeral oration against the introduction of any external element, any heterogeneous thought, but, by this very fact, confining each oration within its own autonomy: not everything can be said in an epitaphios, and what is said binds it to all the other examples.

Accordingly, we have postulated that the topoi limit expression because they are themselves the repetitive expression of something, and we have looked for what, concealed within these "knots," resists any attempt to modify the oration. A study of the exordium, in which each epitaphios, presenting itself as both unique and traditional, recalls the great feature of the genre, has revealed that the topoi of the funeral oration are bearer of a single meaning, a single invading sign: the city. As such, they are a rule in the sense of both a command and a method.

But the nature of the topoi is to elude all definition, for although they constitute a rule, they are also *material* for the oration,

---

* *Menexenus* 249e4. Dionysius of Halicarnassus takes up the expression on the subject of the *Menexenus* (*On the Style of Demosthenes* 1027): the *Menexenus* is the most powerful of the "political orations"; cf. Cicero, *Orator* 44: *orationem popularem*.

half thought, half form. They are so many repertoires of words, formulas, and ideas, preexisting every oration like a canvas, or, to be more precise, like a sort of *zero degree of the epitaphios*, and their existence attests to the possibility of speaking once again in order to say the same thing.* We should even go much further: it is insofar as they are already the raw material of so many epitaphioi that they provide the orator with a precious aid in the agon in which he competes with all his predecessors.

This is hardly surprising: where topoi are concerned, there is no literary property, a bourgeois notion unknown to the ancient world, and it would be pointless to look for the "first inventor" of the topoi. They do not belong to whoever used them first, or even to the last orator to use them, but, forever going back into circulation after use, they are really at the disposal of all.

As such, they correspond to a use of words that is both agonistic and egalitarian: they are the democratic instrument of that ever-renewed agon epitaphios by which, from one age to another and in honor of all the Athenian dead, the orators appointed by the city vie with one another.

It may be objected that the term *agōn is* used here only in a metaphorical sense, since at each ceremony only one oration was delivered.[72] Of course, the declaiming of an epitaphios was not part of the regular competitions among professional encomiographers that took place in the Hellenistic and Roman periods. But it is also impossible to treat this institutional, civic form of speech as a mere occasional "hearing," as a particular case of the *epideixeis* that were given, from the fifth century on, by rhetors on the occasion of a panegyric. Of course, no agonothete presided at this competition, which had no other context than the temporal succession of all the epitaphioi; and of course the rivals against whom the orators dreamed of measuring themselves sometimes belonged to

---

* Isocrates knows this very well; in the *Panegyricus* (74) after mentioning the difficulty of "speaking last," he acknowledges that there is enough material left for him to make an oration.

another period. But although Demosthenes vies with Pericles[73] and the orator of the *Menexenus* expresses the fear that he may rank second to the poets,* all the official orators nevertheless believed that they were taking part in an agon. Apart from the extract from Lysias studied above, a curious passage in Demosthenes's epitaphios offers proof of this. After comparing his mission with other civic services such as the organization of a competition — an example not chosen at random — the orator lays down the conditions that will enable him to win reputation and favor (*doxan . . . kai charin*), which gives him the opportunity of listing in a moment the whole vocabulary of the agon.† Clearly, not all the orators enjoyed the success of Pericles, who, according to Plutarch, was "garlanded with crowns and bands by women, like a winning athlete," for his epitaphios of Samos;‡ but all sought renown§ by erasing the previous orator from people's minds: was not this an eminently agonistic relationship? Finally, it is not self-evident that Lysias and Plato did not include their own epitaphioi in the *agōnes . . . mousikes pases* or in the *agōnes . . . sophias*** that they mention in the list of festivities.[74]

It is in the context of this quasi-institutional rivalry of the orations that we may understand the functioning of the topoi. The funeral competitions of the epic promised the winner a reward among the *xuneia keimena*, "well arranged at the center," which had become "common objects . . . available for a new personal appropriation."[75] The ever-open agon in which the epitaphioi were engaged from one ceremony to the other brings the orator no other prize than flattering renown; but in a way, the topoi of the funeral oration also play a role as objects in common, though not as a reward but as the instruments of speech. While an oration

---

* *Menexenus* 239c1–2.

† Demosthenes 13–14.

‡ Plutarch, *Pericles* 28. 5. An interesting comparison, if it is not the anachronistic indication of a Hellenistic reinterpretation of Pericles's "glory."

§ *Menexenus* 236a6.

** *Ibid.* 249b6; Lysias 80.

lasts, they are offered to the orator as material for his speech, that is, as means of winning renown. Lysias declares that the material *offered* to poetry and eloquence by the valor of the dead is an inexhaustible source of epitaphioi;* it would be better to say that the topoi, the agreed-upon expression of predetermined acts, are, in the strict sense, the *place, common to all*,[76] in which, from one oration to another, a competition takes place, among orators who are equals,[77] since all are equally invested with the confidence of the people. Each one, coming in turn to take up the same position, which is both honorary and civic, on the speaker's platform of the demosion sema, knows, in his ephemeral superiority, that he is neither the first nor the last. Rather than compare this succession of interchangeable orators with the state competitions of the Hellenistic period, then, we should compare it with some such civic institution as the rotation of offices, the very basis of the functioning of the democracy.[78] So all the orations are of equal value, all expressing to the same degree collective representations in a preestablished form.

The topoi, then, are the units, common to all the orations, in themselves impersonal and so to speak collective, of the funeral oration, the civic speech of Athens, in the fifth and fourth centuries. Moreover, these topoi do not disappear with the funeral oration but are tirelessly used again and again in the fastidious eulogies of the Hellenistic and Roman periods, composed by scholars eager to curry favor with those in power. They are, however, no longer the democratic instrument of a civic speech. They become the tool of rhetoric, "that privileged technique ... that allows the ruling classes to guarantee their *ownership of speech*."[79] Perhaps this development was already beginning in the fourth century among those orators, "infatuated with wordspinning" and power, whom Plato attacks in the *Phaedrus*.† But those whom the people appointed to deliver the funeral oration were still, like Demosthenes and Hyperides, representatives of the

---

* Lysias 2.

† Plato, *Phaedrus* 257e1–2 and 258b10–c1.

demos — and not among the "learned personages" ironically referred to by Plato* — and their topoi remained above all civic.

A constricting but inert form, the topos was unavoidable but pliant,[80] freeing the orator in advance from any need to seek originality, insofar as the funeral oration was an institutional form of speech. It was doubly an institution: It was an organized social practice possessing a precise function, and it was also a codified genre, anterior to each of the productions that constituted it and on which it imposed its rules. Although in art genre may be regarded as a method of classifying works *a posteriori*, nothing is further removed, perhaps, from the spiritual world of the classical city than the notion of a work of art as "a creation manifesting the aesthetic will of an artist";[81] it is far more accurate to define the civic genres as quasi-institutional models of logos. In fact, the epitaphioi, in which nothing is left to chance, resemble one another like so many slightly varying copies, and although historians of rhetoric usually make the funeral oration the first example of artistic prose, this genre fits ill under the heading "literary works." It should be added, once again, that the very concept of literature, in the sense in which we understand it today, is a modern one, born of the breaking up of classical forms,[82] and we can speak of a "literature of the fifth century" only by a sort of homonymy. Unsuitable as a description of civic tragedy and eloquence, the term "literature" is better suited to the intellectual climate of the Hellenistic world, which delighted in the rhetorical charms of the public lecture[83] and in which the subtleties of a hermetic poetry and the refined accents of a lyricism of sincerity were born.[84] It would apply perfectly to the triumphant aesthetics of the Greco-Roman world of the second century A.D., which, under the name "new rhetoric," absorbed and regulated all speech and finally killed eloquence with declamation.[85]

But the city of the classical period, marking all public speech with a civic imprint, protected — or sought to protect — the oration from such "deviations"; neither a pure lecture nor a field of exper-

---

* *Menexenus* 234c4–5: *andrōn sophōn.*

iment, the funeral oration remained like itself. A new thought always tends to dictate its own form, even to destroy previous forms: thus those who, like Agathon, tried to introduce into tragedy fictions born of their own imaginations did not so much renew tragedy as bring about its decline.[86]* Still, the tragic genre was freer than the funeral oration; containing something like a ferment of individuality, the tragedies were "written works, literary productions individualized in time and space, none of which has strictly speaking a parallel."[87] Should we admit, then, that it is paradoxically to the protection of its topoi that the funeral oration owed its ability to survive? This is a curious case of the resistance of conformism, for although "Sophocles's *Oedipus Rex* is not one version among others of the Oedipus myth,"[88] each epitaphios is certainly a version of the funeral oration.

It is precisely here that the limited but real facility of the genre lies: each orator may take up the challenge of tradition and calmly forge a new epitaphios in which he proceeds to a new arrangement of the usual topoi. This amounts of course to no more than minute variations:† sometimes it is enough to alter the meaning of a word, the modality of a verbal form. When Pericles stresses the danger of basing the merits of a whole group on a single individual,‡ or when Lysias declares that "it is not easy for one person to recount in detail the perils undergone by many men,"§ the idea is absolutely identical in both versions; in the topos, the difference is introduced solely within the verb *kinduneuesthai*, which in Thucydides is endowed with a derivative meaning and an auxiliary function and which finds its true meaning again in Lysias. Thus the funeral oration is constituted in a perpetual forward-and-back-

---

* In the *Poetics* (1451b18ff.), Aristotle reminds us that everything in the *Anthos* was the fruit of Agathon's imagination.

† Compare, for example, Thucydides 2.41.4 (*pasan ... thalassan kai gēn esbaton*) and Lysias 2 (*oute gēs apeiroi oute thalattes oudemias*).

‡ Thucydides 2.35.1.

§ Lysias 54.

ward movement: from one epitaphios to another, the same themes are taken up and developed or concentrated, and often only a different arrangement of the same elements enables us to distinguish one epitaphios from another. But the essential thing is that the distinction may be made, for the agon is played out between small differences rather than between radically heterogeneous forms.

Thus from oration to oration, the topoi change slightly, undergo various arrangements, and produce new wholes, so that it is difficult to list them or even to delimit them with any degree of rigor. Both fixed and mobile, assuring the genre a real immobility and a superficial movement, capable of entering into so many combinations, they acquire a — relative — plasticity. So a study of the topoi cannot confine itself to those interminable recyclings so dear to scholars of the late nineteenth century.[89] For the same reason, any quantitative examination based on the drawing up of a frequency table is a risky business. Such a method is certainly not without interest, but it must be based on truly rigorous criteria. In any case, it runs the risk of proving inadequate if it treats the topoi as mere monads. Finally, it stops at describing or observing; although Pericles's oration, while presenting a criticism of the norms of the funeral oration, nevertheless conforms perfectly to the genre, it is not enough simply to observe this fact, even with the help of calculations that aim at precision: this phenomenon still needs to be explained. To account for the traditional, or at least conformist, character of the epitaphioi, one must previously have decided what the nature and function of the topos are, which we have done above.

Only then can we reach a conclusion: insofar as the topoi are units — necessary, but interchangeable — of civic speech, originality in the funeral oration has no other means of expression than through them. If one regards them only as the symptom of a malaise, one will speak of orations *with topoi*; but if they really are, as I believe, the material and condition of existence for the epitaphioi, one will define the funeral oration as a discourse *consisting of topoi*. A few examples will demonstrate the modalities of its functioning, in the epitaphioi of Pericles, Hyperides, Lysias, and Demosthenes.

311

Pericles sets out to keep his distance from earlier orators;* but an examination of his oration reminds us that there was nothing specifically original in this project, that it is impossible to escape the necessities of the agon even when, by a supreme refinement, one pretends to reject combat by taking up a position beyond words, in the domain of erga. After carrying out this proud distancing act, the orator is quick to go back on his words. What else could he do? Whereas his predecessors were in the habit of praising the practice of the funeral oration, Pericles inverts the topos, questioning the relevance of such a practice; or rather — for his subtlety, doubled by that of Thucydides, knows more indirect tricks — he introduces doubt into it by intertwining it with the traditional opposition between saying and doing. Thus the nomos, sometimes presented as the unity of an act and a speech† and sometimes placed on the side of acts alone,‡ finds itself, by an unexpected reversal, entirely on the side of speech.§ More characteristic still is the working of the commonplace of the inadequacy of words in describing acts. Gradually explaining the meaning of a topos that he has avoided stating in its simplest form** but that he develops in snatches, Pericles sets it *playing upon itself*. He even divides it, since to the relation between logos and erga he adds a new, three-term relation among the orator, the listener, and acts. Thus he makes a commonplace look like a new thought. But, conversely, he never ceases to exploit the inevitable material that the genre imposes on him. Here the topoi assume an essential function, since they enable the funeral oration to ward off all attacks in advance by criticizing itself from within. A similar observation might be made about the epitaphios of Hyperides, another appar-

---

* Thucydides 2.35.1: *hoi men polloi . . . emoi de . . .*

† Only by Thucydides, it is true: 2.34.1 (introduction to the chapter on the ceremony) and 7 ("thus this funeral takes place" also refers to the declamation of the funeral oration).

‡ *Ibid.* 2.35.1.

§ *Ibid.* 2.35.3.

** To be found in Lysias 1: *logon ison paraskeuasai tois . . . ergois.*

ently anticonformist orator. But whereas Hyperides allows himself a few facilities, setting up false commonplaces* in order to
reject them with the help of authentic topoi,† Pericles, using only
the accepted material, belongs in fact to a purer tradition.

It becomes clear, then, that Pericles uses topoi, even though he
challenges them — which enables him to use them all the same,
but in a more insidious way. Of course, he handles them with
enough intellectual rigor to make us forget their status as commonplaces: thus the ergon/logos opposition, far from being a
mere rhetorical trick, is constantly questioned and assessed throughout the oration,[90] so much so that some scholars have regarded it
as the true subject of the epitaphios.[91] But although he fills those
malleable forms known as topoi with content, Pericles refrains
from rejecting them; the same themes recur throughout the history of the funeral oration and its most distant‡ or degraded§
forms. The fact that there are brilliant successes and uncertain
results in no way undermines the universality of this rule.

The topoi allow the orators to overcome the double obstacle that
might be presented by the greatness of the victory won by the
dead — or the extent of their defeat — and the renown of earlier
orations. Thus it is by weaving commonplaces together that the
exordium of Lysias's epitaphios moves by a series of displacements.

The traditional and debilitating affirmation of the inferiority
of the oration in relation to its object is transformed into the
complaint, still as acceptable but also more limited, that the orator has not had enough time to prepare his speech;** the topos of

---

* Hyperides 6: after the traditional question "Where shall I begin my oration?" (cf.
Menexenus 237a2), the orator touches on autochthony by a detour ("Am I going to
expatiate on each man's family?" is a false question in the funeral oration).

† So the answer is, "This, I imagine, would be rather naive," and in 7 the orator
gives the theme of noble autochthony the most complete formulation.

‡ Such as the oration of the Athenians at Plataea (Herodotus 9.27).

§ Such as certain heterodox passages in Hyperides's epitaphios.

** Lysias 1.

inadequacy has given place to that of brevity. Then Lysias uses the distinction between the ceremony itself and the oration to substitute for the public at the funeral, gathered together in a ritual commemoration, another audience, a much more profane assembly, whose attention is diverted from the dead to the orators. At the same time, the context attributed to the oration contracts, and the whole of mankind, called upon at first as witnesses, gives way to the polis, a milieu much more familiar to the orator, who as a good Athenian does not forget that, compared with the city, the whole universe is as nothing. With the appearance of the polis, the initial grievances are transformed into acts of grace, for there is no epitaphios in which recriminations on the difficulty of the task are not turned into an exaltation of the wholly benevolent city.* Thus, finally giving up any ambition to reach its object, speech becomes an intransitive activity, and the central shift occurs, in which a competition between orators takes the place of the impossible agon between words and deeds.† From this point on, everything is finally sorted out: it is not the orator who is providing a speech, but the material that provides itself, arete having become the substance of earlier orations; and although one might fear that eternity would not suffice for the immensity of the task, this docile material, a true *deus ex machina*, is more than enough for a flowering of new orations. This time the exordium really has come to an end and mankind may reappear, summoned to support the eulogy of the Athenians with its tears.‡

It is impossible to imagine a better summary of the topoi of the exordium: nothing in this passage is the result of invention, everything has already been said. But this summary is at the same time the beginning of an oration, that is, a text that has both a meaning and a progression. All the orators use the topos of the inadequacy of words to describe acts and the topos of the rivalry between orations, but the solution that makes the second the

* Cf., for example, Demosthenes 1 and 2.
† Lysias 2.
‡ *Ibid.: para pasin anthrōpois.*

THE FUNERAL ORATION AS POLITICAL GENRE

denouement of the first is original and reveals some awareness of the function of the funeral oration. Lysias is not alone in considering Athenian valor, reified into accounts of noble deeds, a sort of ever usable *procheiros logos*;* but he is alone in using this commonplace to suggest that in the agon between epitaphioi, the oration already exists before itself.

It is possible, then, both to speak in topoi — since none of the commonplaces of the exordium is being neglected — and to say something through a new arrangement of these topoi.[92] This is a fundamental law, and the statement of it might serve as conclusion to this study. But we must also take into account the methodological implications of such an observation, which reopens the question of the authenticity of an epitaphios. If the funeral oration is nothing but topoi, it makes no sense to infer from the abundance of commonplaces used by an orator that his oration is inauthentic[93] and to declare indignantly that one cannot attribute to the elegant Lysias or to the proud Demosthenes productions so "unoriginal" as the epitaphioi that bear their names.[94]

To prove that Demosthenes's epitaphios is an exercise of some later school, Jan Chaillet draws up a list of its "borrowings": this group of words is an imitation of a passage of the *Menexenus*;† certain paragraphs are reminiscent of *De corona*;‡ others copy passages out of Lycurgus, Isocrates, and Hyperides.[95]§ But none of these remarks bears examination. To begin with, it is audacious, to say the least, to condemn the epitaphios attributed to an orator for similarities to an authentic oration by the same orator; one can only conclude that anything can serve to prove the inauthenticity of a text, since other criticisms reproach the author of the

---

* Cf. Demosthenes 12.

† *Ibid.* 14: *ploutos, tachos, ischus;* Plato, *Menexenus* 246e3–5: *ploutos, kallos, ischus.*

‡ Demosthenes 14: cf. *De corona* 227; Demosthenes 18: cf. *De corona* 20.

§ Demosthenes 10: cf. Isocrates, *Panegyricus* 83; Demosthenes 19: cf. Lycurgus, *Against Leocrates* 49, and Isocrates, *Panegyricus* 92; Demosthenes 33 and 34: cf. Hyperides 43.

epitaphios for failing to develop the thesis of the plea *De corona*.[96] The other comparisons are no more convincing: if the presence of a similar third group in two orations proves that the second is the work of a forger,[97] then a great many of the orators are forgers. Furthermore, one can always say that Demosthenes copies the *Panegyricus* because he compares the combatants of the Persian Wars to the heroes of the Trojan War; but that proves nothing about the authenticity or inauthenticity of the epitaphios, unless one accuses Hyperides's clearly authentic epitaphios of being false because, like Pericles, he uses this comparison to the glory of the warriors of the present.* Finally, the idea that death puts an end to the miseries of the human condition is banal enough to be borrowed from tragedy, which repeats it tirelessly, and not from some shamelessly plagiarized epitaphios. It is pointless to add further examples; all such comparisons prove nothing.

Of course it is possible to show, by more relevant juxtapositions, that the author of the epitaphios was well acquainted with Pericles's oration[98]† and especially with the *Menexenus*,‡ whose topoi he seems to amalgamate into a mosaic. But even here there is need for caution: If one is looking for resemblances, there is not a single passage of an epitaphios that does not refer to all other epitaphioi, in an echolalia that would be vertiginous if we possessed all the orations ever delivered. In a civilization in which, even in the fourth century and despite the progress of the written word, the transmission of culture was essentially oral, the topoi remained in the memory of every Athenian and every orator, at the disposal of all and impossible to attribute to an author.[99] In these circumstances, is it reasonable to conceive of the composition of an epitaphios in terms of plagiarism or to imagine that Demosthenes would be content to copy out word for word the orations that we happen to possess? How, in this generalized pastiche, could one separate the authentic from the inauthentic?

* Hyperides 36: cf. Plutarch, *Pericles* 28.7.
† Demosthenes 6 certainly seems to be referring to Thucydides 2.35 and 36.
‡ Demosthenes 8–9 seems to be a gloss on *Menexenus* 239b3–c7.

Such an operation is doomed to failure. A comparative study cannot, then, solve the problem, and only the presence of gross anachronisms in an epitaphios would allow one to relegate it definitively to the category of the false and the pastiche.[100]

A study of the genre cannot neglect any of the known epitaphioi. Our objective here is not to pass an aesthetic judgment on productions that are often of unequal quality. Each epitaphios is, of course, the result of *work* and of a study of form, whose success is not always guaranteed. In isolating the function of the epitaphios within the genre rather than judging it by modern literary criteria, I have tried to show how ill founded is the identification of a discourse made up of topoi with some notion of "empty speech." The funeral oration certainly may seem to some to be a genre without object, but it is not the topoi that threaten it with dissolution.

Of course a topos gradually wears out, becoming ever less significant as it freezes into stereotype. But this wear and tear speaks above all to the history of the funeral oration's posterity.[101] In the classical period, the topos, the civic norm in which to speak straightforwardly of Athens, was the seal by which the city authenticated the oration. As official speech, the funeral oration lacks autonomy and permeability: it is not a very literary genre, if by that term one means its ability to subject itself to external changes and thereby integrate them; it is, in the strict sense, a *genos politikon*. The political element in it often appears to be colorless, lacking in tension, fanciful, pale. But to be surprised at this is to ask too much of an official speech, whose close link with democracy is more significant than the emptiness of its theoretical contents. As a genre born of the city and totally invested by it, the funeral oration perished with the final defeat of that city; when set "free," the topoi no longer referred to any reality. Is it, then, a genre without object? This term applies not to the classical funeral oration but to the forms in which it outlived itself in the Hellenistic period.

Destiny of a Civic Genre

Certain representations survive the society that gave them birth. The same may be said of the Athenian myth, if we are to believe Plutarch, who explained Sulla's furious attack on Athens by the wish to compete with the old reputation of the city that, by 86 BCE, had become no more than a shadow of its former self.* Sulla, it is true, spurned the Athenian parliamentarians, who, coming up with no realistic proposition, were content to exalt the mythical deeds of their ancestors;† but after sacking the city, he spared those who were still alive there, in the name of the glory of the ancient Athenians. Plutarch's own preoccupations played a part in this account, of course, and it is hardly surprising to observe something like a resurgence of the topoi of the funeral oration in this guardian of the past. However, if any credit is to be given to the speech delivered by the spurned ambassadors, the kinship of the themes evoked — Theseus, Eumolpus, and the Persian Wars — with those of the epitaphioi certainly seems to suggest that even when reduced to the status of "a sham polis,"[102] the city continued to base its policies on the old commonplaces. This at least is how Strasburger interprets this text when he declares that for more than six hundred years, the same topoi appeared virtually unaltered in the writings of the Athenian publicists who inspired Plutarch.[103] Could the image of Athens have resisted, better than Athens itself, the consequences of the defeats of 338 and 322? Reading one of the amphictyonic decrees of the second century BCE, in which the Athenians are emphatically praised,‡ one would be forgiven for thinking so, since Athens was now perpetuated beyond the narrow limits of the city, throughout the Greek world — a result unhoped for in the fifth and fourth centuries.

Does this amount to a permanence of the civic representations in the Hellenistic and Roman periods, the conquest of the whole of Greece and of the Roman conquerors by these strictly Athen-

* Plutarch, *Sulla* 13.1.
† *Ibid.* 13.5 and 14.9.
‡ *Sylloge*³, 704 E, ll. 11–12: *ho demos ha[pantōn tōn en anthr]opois agathōn archēgos.*

318

ian topoi? However attractive such notions may be, they require considerable qualification. Not all the topoi of praise that formed the web of the funeral oration when, alone or with other cities, Athens made history survived the Lamian War, which saw the collapse of Athenian hopes.[104] The military topoi, the most important ones, those that gave the hegemonic oration its meaning, fell into the background or were revived on the occasion of some resurgence of patriotism; they enjoyed no more than an illusory or at best symbolic survival. Others survived, deprived of their meaning, like the praise of democracy — increasingly harmless,[105] since the Athenians counted their "liberators," Antigonus and Demetrius,[106] among the eponyms — or modified, like the eulogy of autochthony, which no longer formed the basis of the military originality of the city but remained an Athenian myth, to become eventually the most worn of all the Greek myths.[107]*

Of course, at the end of the fourth century the "restored democracy" tried to live off its past glory, but military glory was no longer called for, and the Athenians now preferred to lay claim to their eminent cultural superiority in terms reminiscent more of the *Panegyricus* than of the funeral oration, more of Isocrates than of Pericles or Lysias.[108] Athens became the universal benefactress, and the list of services that she had rendered mankind grew longer and longer. There was now nothing to oppose the spread of this new image, which was finally accepted in the second century BCE; was not the cultural glory of Athens the counterpart of its political and economic insignificance? It already seemed a long time since Alexander, victorious on the Granicus, had honored Athens through Athena, dedicating three hundred panoplies on the Acropolis.[109] For the Diadochi, once the last vague desire to resist was forgotten, Athens was nothing but a cultural center, which they were quite willing to treat as a "venerable museum of Hellenic traditions."[110] In short, never had Athenian propaganda been so accepted by the Greek world as a whole.

* Cf., for example, Pausanias 9.1.1: even the Plataeans claimed the honor of being "autochthonous in origin."

It may be that this process became irreversible only when the Athenians lost all hope of reconquering their independence by force of arms. Indeed, between the Lamian War and the Chremonidean War, the military topoi of the funeral oration came back into fashion on several occasions, during the struggles against the Macedonian kings. This was probably also the case at the time of the expedition that, under Olympiodorus's leadership, "delivered Athens from the Macedonians"* at the beginning of the third century. According to Pausanias, who almost certainly transcribed the official version of the text, the Athenians, imbued with the memory of their ancestors and "aware of the change that had occurred in their credit," would have armed the volunteers, including the old men and adolescents, who, as worthy emulators of the companions of Myronides, fought gloriously.† But more than any other episode, the Chremonidean War bears the trace of this patriotic exaltation nourished on the great themes of the past. Animated by the hatred of tyranny, the decree of Chremonides takes on the tone of Hyperides's epitaphios to stigmatize the injustice, impiety, and despotism of the enemy,‡ and, in declaring war on Antigonus Gonatas, the Athenian people began by evoking its prestigious past, expatiating on famous deeds, in which the struggles for liberty also took the form of a fine rivalry between Athenians and Lacedaemonians,§ allies and competitors, as jealous of their personal glory as of Hellenic independence.** Thus, roused to fight for Greek independence, the Athenians returned in 267–66 to the military topoi of the funeral oration. Every historian is aware of the limitations and ambiguity of the policies of Chremonides, who believed he was resuscitating the Hellenic and Athenian past,¹¹¹ even though he was serving the interests of Ptolemy, praise of whom was strangely mixed in the decree with

---

* Ibid. 1.26.2.

† Ibid. 1.26.1 (memory of the ancestors, the intervention of the old men and youths).

‡ Sylloge³, 434–35, ll. 33–34. Cf. ll. 15–16 on one-time enemies.

§ Ibid., ll. 9–12 and 35.

** Ibid., ll. 13–14.

praise of the ancestors.* Unaware of the weakness of their position, the Athenians saw this war as an opportunity of regaining
the city's former independence — it was, in a sense, their last
chance.[112] It is hardly surprising that with the final defeat, which
destroyed these anachronistic hopes, the ancient themes of the
celebration of Athens faded away for so long. If the death of
Philochorus marks the end of the *Atthides*,[113] the military topoi
stood up no better than political history to the defeat of Athens
and underwent a long eclipse after 260, they faded away, reap-
pearing only occasionally.

Between 267 and 262, these topoi no doubt underwent a purely
artificial resurrection; indeed, it is quite likely that they had
already become pure form, without content and without proper
application, since, from the time that Athens ceased to be the free
democracy in which the funeral oration had come to birth, all
traces of this civic discourse that formed the web of the classical
period disappear. As far as we know, the last authentic epitaphios
to have survived is that of Hyperides.

Does the year 322, then, mark the end of the funeral oration as
well as that of the independence of the city with which it was so
closely bound? If so, then the Athenians would appear from 322
onward to have abandoned a form that had become empty with
the loss of their liberty. The question is important, but we lack
information that would enable us to answer it with any certainty.
However, we should be on guard against an overly facile schema-
tization: the funeral oration probably did not die a violent death
but gradually fell into decline. Even though we have no proof
of this, it may well be that epitaphioi were delivered at the funeral
of those citizens who had died fighting against Lachares, against
the Macedonians, or alongside the Romans, those citizens who
were buried in the Kerameikos and whose tomb Pausanias saw.†
Perhaps, too, the Epitaphia of the Hellenistic period, symbolic

* *Ibid.*, ll. 16–19.
† Pausanias 1.29.10 and 14.

commemorations of all the Athenian dead of the past,[114] involved the delivery of orations, although we do not know whether such orations were regarded as real epitaphioi or whether they formed part of the many literary competitions included in the agon epitaphios.[115] For the Roman period, the evidence of Menander of Laodicea seems conclusive: every year, he declares, the Athenians spoke a logos epitaphios in praise of their dead.* But it is not certain whether this very general sentence, more like a timeless definition than a piece of historical information, may really be applied to the third century CE, as several scholars have claimed.[116]

Even supposing that we accept this view, such evidence does not prove that the funeral oration really survived without interruption or that it was invested with the same civic significance as in the classical period. To begin with, we have no information concerning the existence of epitaphioi between the fourth and the second centuries BCE, and it is also tempting to believe that the funeral oration made a symbolic reappearance only in the Roman period, when Athens was luxuriating in archaizing commemorations. And even if it continued without interruption, benefiting indirectly from the prestige enjoyed in the Hellenistic period by the encomium in all its forms,[117] it is probable that in a civilization in which politics had taken on a new meaning, the old civic oration had lost much of its significance. Finally, even if epitaphioi were delivered continuously, no tradition — literary or historical, epigraphic or papyrological — informs us about these orations, which might have been quite simply repeated.† Furthermore, the time of the civic funeral oration had well and truly gone; in the Hellenistic and Roman periods, the term *epitaphioi logoi* designated above all innumerable school exercises, intended to praise some exceptional individual in a standard series of some thirty

---

* Menander the rhetor, *Peri epideiktikon*, in *Rhetores graeci*, vol. 3, p. 418: "Among the Athenians, one calls an epitaphios the oration delivered each year over the war dead."

† For example, the repetition of the epitaphios in the *Menexenus*, according to Cicero, *Orator* 151.

predetermined passages:[118]* there were a great many of these, but most were preserved in the indirect evidence of the theorists.[119]

So, to pose the question of the Hellenistic posterity of the collective civic oration, we must leave the domain of the epitaphios logos and make a detour via a form that, since Isocrates, had borrowed from the funeral oration a particular way of praising Athens and the Athenians and turned it to its own advantage: the Panathenaic oration, which had a great vogue under the Roman Empire.[120] That of Aelius Aristides, who, in the opinion of Menander the rhetor, was the best possible model of the eulogy of a city,† provides us with a finished example and, because it allows us to make a useful comparison between the epitaphioi of the classical age and the literary works of the rhetors, gives us the ultimate counter-proof necessary to the study of the civic genre: a certain image of Athens still animates this long declamation, but it is a flat, diluted image. Furthermore, as a eulogy of Athens, the oration is necessarily without an object, since it is Rome — which the rhetor exalts in another encomium — and not Athens that, for Aristides as for his contemporaries, gives human history its full meaning. So the epitaphioi of Lysias and Demosthenes regain their full political significance by being compared with the *Panathenaicus*.

An abstract oration on a symbolic city that is no longer a polis except in name: this is how we might define Aelius Aristides's *Panathenaicus*.

From the exordium, everything is predictable: the *Panathenaicus* resembles an epitaphios, using all its topoi, even though the rhetor pretends to challenge the use of these worn-out themes.‡

---

* Cf. Menander's *Peri epideiktikon* or the plan given by Theon (*Rhetores graeci*, vol. 2, pp. 109ff.).

† The *Panathenaicus* is Menander's main reference in the chapters devoted to the eulogy of a city (*Rhetores graeci*, vol. 3, pp. 346ff.): see especially p. 350, l. 10, and p. 360, ll. 8–10.

‡ Aelius Aristides, *Panathenaicus* 3.

And yet the topoi are scarcely recognizable, cut off from their original function, for the great opposition between logos and erga no longer animates them. Any reference to acts or to a reality that might equal the oration has disappeared: *there is nothing left but logos*,[121] the single pole around which the declamation is organized. The topos of the inadequacy of speech in the face of acts is therefore unrecognizable and pointless, since, transposed into rhetorical terms, it merely evokes the possible inferiority of one form (schema) in relation to its argument (logos).* Athens is that argument: it no longer has anything real about it, but, already constituted as a literary theme, it *is* discourse. Indeed, it is as nurse of the sciences and letters that it is praised,† and, setting out to exalt the Athenian tradition of the logoi, language has really no difficulty in matching a subject that is homologous with it.‡

This initial disappearance of the ergon is confirmed throughout the oration by the transformation to which the now purely formal topoi are subjected. Thus Aelius Aristides takes up the temporal division, observed by all the epitaphioi, by which the history of Athens is split into three periods, that of the ancestors, that of the fathers, and the present; but this division, excessively drawn out, no longer has any function but to relegate to the past any history of acts. Indeed, the account of the exploits covers only two periods, that of the *progonoi* — that is, as in Isocrates, mythical times§ — and that of the pateres, which begins with Cleisthenes and ends with the defeat at Chaironeia:** these ages saw the ideal of Athenian excellence realized *in acts*. The third period, which for Pericles

* *Ibid.*: *schēma phauloteron tou logou.*
† *Ibid.* 2.
‡ *Ibid.* 5.
§ *Progonoi*: ibid. 43–74 (from the divine foundation of the Areopagus to the Cleisthenean reform); cf. Isocrates, *Panegyricus* 64 (the affairs of the Seven against Thebes and of the Heraclidae), 69 (struggle against the Amazons), 75–81 (the Athenians before the Persian Wars), and *Panathenaicus* 123–48 (from the birth of the autochthones to the tyranny of Peisistratus).
** Aelius Aristides, *Panathenaicus* 74–138 and 145–224.

was the time of dynamism and for Lysias that of emulation,* approximately corresponds to the present of the rhetor, since it is organized around the reign of Hadrian,† but it can boast of no victories except the purely peaceful one of the Athenian logos, the benefactor of all humanity.‡ Thus, for Aelius Aristides, *the time of acts was past*; the logos replaced the act, and all the anomalies of the exordium were clarified.

But this new distribution, which turns acts into a temporary, imperfect stage, is highly significant. In a passage whose importance has been stressed by James H. Oliver,[122] the rhetor declares that Athens's true empire is not the historical, political one, limited in space and time, which the city had won in the fifth century thanks to its triremes,§ but an unlimited, universal empire, that of philanthropia and wisdom.** Not only does this passage have no parallel in the public speeches of the classical period, but it represents a profound shift in values: whereas in Pericles's epitaphios everything converged on the city, which made the goods of the whole earth its own,†† the Athens of Aelius Aristides, losing all specificity, becomes a sort of *commonplace of Hellenism*; a moral, beneficent power, the quintessence of human nature and the common center of the Greek world,‡‡ it is animated by a quite Stoic love of civilized humanity. So, depriving the topos of autochthony, by which the city once affirmed its difference, of any polemical character, the rhetor declares that the land of Attica, mother of man, has belonged from its origin to all Greeks.[123]§§ They seem to

---

* Thucydides 2.36.3; Lysias 61–69.

† Aelius Aristides, *Panathenaicus* 225–34: Hadrian and the Antonines in general.

‡ *Ibid.* 225–30.

§ *Ibid.* 227 ("what I call the great Athenian empire does not amount to two hundred triremes").

** *Ibid.* 230 (the hegemony of education and knowledge).

†† Thucydides 2.38.2.

‡‡ Aelius Aristides, *Panathenaicus* 274 (the prytaneum of science, the center [*hestia*] of Greece, the complete image of human nature).

§§ *Ibid.* 25–26.

be the same words, the same topoi, but in being used in this way, they have lost all but metaphorical meaning. The same goes for the arche: whereas the true empire, the humanist empire whose advent is lauded by Aelius Aristides, has always existed *in potentia*,* the military, political power that for the Athenians of the classical period constituted reality itself is interpreted after the fact as a stage in an educational process and becomes an epiphenomenon, at most a premonitory sign. The *Panathenaicus* ultimately deprives Athens of its history, turning it into a civilizing panacea.

Substituting a Panhellenic Athens for the hegemonic city of the epitaphioi, the rhetor belongs to the Hellenistic tradition that saw Athens as "the semidivine benefactress of Greece."[124] Of course, the writers of the fifth century were not averse to celebrating Athens as the mother of civilization: several tragedies presented this image;[125†] and although the funeral oration, a war-oriented speech, always subordinated it to the warrior image of the city, it did not ignore it completely.‡ But neither the tragic writers nor the orators dissociated the birth of civilization from the emergence of a political world:§ civilizing Athens certainly was, as a polis; as *Hellados paideusis*,** she sought above all to be a school of political conduct. On the other hand, the Hellenistic period made concrete the triumph of the edifying cultural image: as soon as the city was no longer a danger to anybody, the whole Greek world was quite willing to praise a merely symbolic primacy.[126] Thus, without disappearing, the eulogy of Athens changed profoundly:

* *Ibid.* 227.

† Sophocles's *Triptolemus* is lost, but *Oedipus at Colonus* bears the trace of these concerns. The references in Euripides are legion: examples include the great eology of Athens in *Medea* (824–45), *Trojan Women* (799), *Ion* (1433: eulogy of the olive tree), and *Suppliant Women* (29ff.: Athens hierophant of the corn).

‡ Lysias 19: *thēria/anthrōpoi*.

§ This association is particularly clear in the passage from Lysias quoted above in which civilization and democracy go hand in hand.

** Thucydides 2.41.1.

having become a literary work, it was no longer delivered as an epitaphios but was composed by a rhetor in search of some brilliant declamation; or, as a fictional discourse attributed to an imaginary character, it provided the historian with a juicy morsel. As proof we have the resonant eulogy of the Athenians that Diodorus attributes to Nicolaus of Syracuse* and that, inspired by Ephorus or Timaeus,[127] tells us a great deal more about the mood of the Hellenistic world than about the state of mind of a Sicilian in 413 BCE. Its author is no longer an Athenian orator entrusted with an official mission, but a Greek, a foreigner to the city that he is praising. So hegemonic pretensions give way to thanksgiving, military power to beneficence, warlike deeds to liberal emulation.† As a cultural and spiritual center,‡ Athens was now thought of more as a *town* — a university town[128]§ — than as a polis. So its relationship to discourse and its status in the eulogy changed: it was no longer a collective subject entrusting one of its members with the task of reflecting back to it in a civic speech the image of itself that it wished to authenticate. Rather, having become a literary theme and material for a declamation, it was in the position of an object[129] and lent itself easily to the philosophical and cultural purposes of Aelius Aristides, who brandished it as the very symbol of Hellenism against the combined threats of the barbarian world and Christianity.

It is hardly surprising, then, that the strictly political themes of the eulogy of Athens undergo a veritable subversion in this *Panathenaicus* dating from the second century CE. Of course, it is no

---

* Diodorus 13.20–27.

† They are evoked at length in Aelius Aristides but become symbolic of another, peaceful victory. They are briefly evoked by Diodorus (25.1–2) but are not essential to the argument.

‡ Diodorus 13.27.1.

§ In Isocrates, Athens is already designated as *astu tēs Hellados* (*On the Team* 27; *Antidosis* 299, in which the other cities become townships, *komai*). Isocrates discusses the theme of education at length in the *Panegyricus* (cf. 50: "Those who were his disciples become masters for others").

longer a question of praising democracy, which has become one element among others of the Athenian political system and which, as such, receives a brief, vague, diluted treatment.* Declaring, as Isocrates had done, that the Athenians gave the world every possible type of constitution,† the rhetor is eager to make ancient Athens the model of the mixed constitution, a harmonious mixture in which, however, aristocracy dominates.‡ Endowed with the constitution of the ancestors, the gift of Athena, approved by Apollo,§ the city, is governed by the happy conjunction of the virtue of the Areopagites and the goodwill of the people. Isocrates would not have imagined a more idyllic picture of a city that had ceased at last to be synonymous with democracy: for the Cleisthenean division of the demos into demes and tribes** one could now, without betraying contemporary reality, substitute a division into phylai and *genē*.[130]††

Thus the Panathenaic discourse had definitively supplanted the funeral oration in the Hellenistic world before both began to be favored by Western culture, which, to discuss Athens, freely borrows themes from these two orations. However, the *Panathenaicus* won the battle in the liberal humanities insofar as it made Athens, the visible embodiment of logos, an intermediary between the gods and men,‡‡ a cultural symbol.§§ Artistic, peace-

---

* Aelius Aristides, *Panathenaicus* 266.

† In the *Panegyricus* 39, Isocrates declares that the Athenians gave men laws and constitution; Aelius Aristides develops and expands this idea (*Panathenaicus* 263: "Thus all models of constitutions found their origin there"), which seems like a topos of Hellenistic rhetoric (cf. Menander, *Peri epideiktikon*, p. 360).

‡ *Panathenaicus* 262–63; cf. 265 (*tēn krasin tōn politeiōn*).

§ *Ibid.* 40 (Athena), 261 (Apollo).

** Isocrates (*Panathenaicus* 145) speaks in terms of demes and tribes, for in order to please the Athenians, the constitution of the ancestors must not stray too far from the political reality that they know.

†† Aelius Aristides, *Panathenaicus* 261: Apollo gave the Athenians the tribes and the *genē*.

‡‡ *Ibid.* 271–74.

§§ *Ibid.* 222: *to sumbolon tēs Hellados*.

loving Athens, "a public made up entirely of connoisseurs,"[131] was no doubt one aspect of the complex reality of the fifth century, but this image acquired predominance only in and through the Hellenistic culture[132] and not, as has all too often been believed,[133] in Pericles's epitaphios; through the voice of its most "enlightened" statesman, the city of the fifth century wished above all to be a fighting polis: *different, rather than universal.*

Between the funeral oration and the *Panathenaicus* of the Hellenistic and Roman periods there is, then, a rupture; and although Aelius Aristides aims at taking his place in the oratorical agon in which the best eulogy of Athens must triumph, he is unable to understand the unity of a civic oration of which he is the heir only in appearance. Thus, declaring that no one has ever before gathered together in a single speech the innumerable aspects of Athenian superiority, he lists the many genres among which the eulogy seems to him to have been scattered — the poetic eulogy of the city as the friend of the gods, the account of the wars between Greeks and barbarians, the presentation of the constitution, the epitaphios logos to the memory of the dead* — without seeing that this last discourse encompassed all the others in the classical period.

Conversely, the Hellenistic eulogy, far from presenting the unity conferred on speech by civic inspiration, "is broken up into a loose succession of brilliant pieces juxtaposed according to a rhapsodic model."[134] No longer possessing anything but a decorative function, the account of noble deeds escapes from the pre-established framework of the topoi and blossoms into *ekphraseis.*[135] Thus the recollection of the Peloponnesian War and especially the Persian Wars, a favorite theme of the rhetors, gives rise to full-blown narrations, swarming with detail: these fragments of anthology, of terrifying length, in which the use of ellipsis in describing acts is no longer expected, spare us nothing. No longer does any selective principle govern an oration in which a place must be found for *everything,* from the ideal geography of Attica to the passing evocation of Socrates or of Xerxes observing the

* *Ibid.* 4.

battle of Salamis from his throne.* Thus the orator no longer even tries, as Isocrates did, to conceal the fictitious character of the oration. The *Panathenaicus* is so long that it would take two days to get through it: an excellent pretext to compose two exordiums instead of one.† But in this rhetorical game, the unity of the eulogy of Athens has long since been forgotten.

This detour via the Hellenistic encomium has wandered from the funeral oration only to further illuminate its character as a civic genre, which, once deprived of its vital reference to the polis, loses its significance. Although the history of the genre ends with a sort of "loss" of the oration, this is the failure less of the funeral oration itself than of the city as a historical structure. If the novelties of the last known epitaphios, that of Hyperides, are the sign of a change in civic relations and not of some fatality within the oration, if the eulogy of Athens survives only by dilution, then it becomes obvious that the funeral oration died not because it was a genre consisting of topoi but because democracy itself perished. And the verbose resurgences of the Hellenistic and Roman periods were incapable of reanimating it: civic in its function as well as in its themes, it derived everything from the democratic city, including the contradictions that have so often been observed in the epitaphioi.

So it is hardly surprising that, in what modern scholars — and perhaps the ancients as well — considered to be its repetitive, monotonous form but one perfectly adapted to its role as a self-celebration of the city, the funeral oration remained, throughout the classical period, an Athenian model of speech on Athens, if not the very model in relation to which the other civic forms of discourse had to define themselves when they took Athens as their subject.

---

* The ideal geography of Attica: 8–24; Xerxes: 127; Socrates: 251.
† First exordium: 1–6; second exordium: 139–41.

CHAPTER SIX

Under the Spell of an Ideal

Throughout this study, I have tried to elucidate the funeral oration and the Athenian city of the classical period in light of each
other. As the historical product of an expanding community, the
oration can find its status only when situated in the political and
military life of the democratic city. But, conversely, an analysis of
the epitaphioi has enabled us to discern, in the repetitions and
behind the silences of the funeral oration, the version that, from
the fifth to the fourth century, official Athens wished to give of its
relationship to others, to history, to the political system that gave
it its strength and prestige. Closely dependent on a particular set
of historical circumstances but guardian of a tradition, and therefore conservative, the funeral oration maintained with the Athenian city an osmotic relationship that prevented it forever from
achieving the autonomous, specific existence that would have
made it a real literary genre.

But it also gained in authority what it lost in originality: as an
expression of the official ideology, it imposed schemata that no
Athenian of the fifth or the fourth century was able to escape.
The funeral oration was the obligatory canvas or, to use Saussure's
terminology, the mannequin on which many Athenian orations
about Athens were molded in the classical period.[1]

In the last part of this book, I shall try, then, to define the
unquestionable fascination that the funeral oration seems to have
exerted over the Athenians: the immediate effect of the speech on

its audience — as far as this may be reconstructed, thus giving a content to the narcissistic ecstasy depicted in the *Menexenus* — but also the less direct effect on the relationship between the city and other "classical" genres. Without going back to the relationship of kinship and mutual tension that both linked and opposed tragedies and epitaphioi, we shall examine that equally complex relationship that links the genre made up of topoi with ancient comedy, the faithful and distorting mirror of the city. Nor can historiography escape this investigation, for, devoted as ever to recounting wars, but always attracted by a comparative study of constitutions, it is certainly likely to meet the funeral oration on both counts.[2] We have seen the importance that the funeral oration acquired in Herodotus as an implicit schema for the passage on Athens;[3] but we must ask the same questions of the work of Thucydides, whose reputation for a scientific approach may not have been completely immune to the fascination of the logos epitaphios. Finally, philosophy itself did not remain different to the tone of the funeral oration, as the work of Plato shows trying to exorcise the spell of the oration by means of pastiche and to give a truly noble Athens a history that would be worthy of her, the philosopher borrowed from comedy the effective weapon of parody and tried to reconcile eulogy and history.

To characterize the effect of the funeral oration on its audience, to assess the influence exerted by the epitaphioi on writers who like Aristophanes, Thucydides, and Plato, were not unconditional admirers of democracy:[4] these two approaches are complementary in that they recognize the importance of a patriotic discourse powerful enough to impose a certain idea of the city.

When the Abstraction of Athens Prevails over the Athenians

After deciphering in the topoi, the web of the epitaphioi, the omnipresence, covert or overt, of the city, is it possible to carry the investigation still further, to treat the funeral oration not as a text but also as a form of speech, characterized by a certain type of efficacy? In fact the historian of ancient rhetoric must find his situation difficult when, at the end of long textual analyses, he senses the truth of the Greek adage that, when written down, a speech lacks the essential quality — life* — and, being unable to assess the impact of a speech on its audience, is forced to reconstruct in a conjectural way the *psuchagōgiē* that, for the Athenians of the fifth and fourth centuries, was the principal function of rhetorical art.† Unless, that is, other texts provide something like living evidence of the immediate effect of the logos: in this respect, the prologue of the *Menexenus* is a valuable aid in our understanding of the funeral oration, since, intended to explain how to understand the epitaphios that is to follow — and all the epitaphioi delivered in Athens — Plato describes with some irony the reactions of the public assembled in the demosion sema.

According to Plato, no Athenian could resist this oration, so expert were the orators, described from the outset as *sophoi*, in spellbinding the souls of their listeners.‡ The funeral oration, then, is a piece of sorcery (*goēteia*), that is, deception,§ which relates it to the speeches of the Sophists, so skilled at "pouring bewitching words into one's ears [*dia tōn otōn tois logois goēteuein*], at presenting fictions [*eidola legemena*] and thus giving an impression of the true."* Indeed, the description of the oration as *goēteia* refers explicitly to the theory of the logos enunciated by Gorgias,† and, because it belongs among those forms of speech whose power of illusion is exalted by the Sophist,‡ Plato regards the funeral oration as dangerous. It is pernicious above all as a eulogy (epainos), puffing up the public to which it is addressed with vain self-importance, because, like all eulogies, it abandons from the outset any attempt to model itself on the truth of the

---

* Plato, *Phaedrus* 264c2–6; Gorgias thought the same when celebrating the omnipotence of the logos: cf. *Helenus* 8–10 (DK, B 11).

† *Phaedrus* 261a8–b3; cf. Plutarch, *Pericles* 15.2.

‡ *Menexenus* 235a2–3, sophoi: 234c5 (cf. 235c5: dexioi).

§ Cf. *Republic* 3.413c4.

* *Sophist* 234c4–7.

† Cf. *Helenus* 10 (DK, 82 B 11).

‡ Compare *Menexenus* 235a2–3 and Gorgias, *Helenus* 14.

object it is celebrating and endows it with every possible imaginary greatness and beauty.* Of course, the dead are praised, but
formally; the orators, blurring the frontiers between life and
death, address the eulogy to the city and to the living — a distortion of the oration that is adopted in turn by Socrates, when, following Aspasia, he delivers the epitaphios:[5] "They celebrate the
city in many ways, they glorify the war dead, all the ancestors who
have preceded us and ourselves, who are still alive."† So the political consequences of this amalgam, which enables the living to
identify with the andres agathoi whose funeral the city is celebrating, are serious, since, like Socrates, every Athenian takes the
praise to apply to himself‡ and immediately transforms himself
into an epic character, "instantly imagining himself to have become greater, nobler, and more handsome."§

No doubt the funeral oration did produce such "fantasies in
speech" that did not easily vanish in contact with reality.** At least
this is what Plato seems to be suggesting, portraying the listeners,
that is, the entire community, as plunged into sudden lethargy,
into a waking dream. It is a dangerous illusion, not only because
of the lightning rapidity with which the charm of words operates
but also because of the extent of its grip. Indeed, it is hardly surprising that the Athenians should succumb to it: what reality
could satisfy them more than this praise that so ennobled them?††
Stranger still was the effect the oration produced on foreigners
who also succumbed to its charms.‡‡

Thus the funeral oration's persuasive force knows no limits,
and under the admiring gaze of foreigners,§§ a gaze that confirms

* Cf. *Symposium* 198d2–3 and d8–e1.
† *Menexenus* 235a3–6.
‡ *Ibid.* 235a7.
§ *Ibid.* 235b1–2.
** *Sophist* 234e1–2.
†† *Menexenus* 235a7.
‡‡ *Ibid.* 235b7–8.
§§ *Ibid.* 235b3–5.

him in his borrowed being, the citizen poses for posterity, adopting a noble attitude, riveted to the spot as if paralyzed.[*] Moreover, to the loss of movement are added new symptoms, lust as clearly characterized, which complete this clinical examination of the effects of the oration. Thus, for the Athenian who identifies with the dead, the sense of time passing also disappears to be replaced by an agreeable impression of immortality that, for Socrates lasts for "more than three days."[†] Finally, like Pericles's words, which according to Eupolis, left their barb in the wound,[‡] the funeral oration like the sound of the flute, echoes for a long time in the memory, penetrates and leaves a mark — in short, changes the listener[§] — and Socrates himself has great difficulty in awakening from it "on the fourth or fifth day" and regaining possession of himself.[**]

A journey outside time, a loss of self: the ecstasy induced by the funeral oration is very like that experience of the timeless that Plato calls "anamnesis." But this resemblance conceals a profound opposition: It is not enough to escape time, for one must also know how to unite one's soul with the divine[6] and not with that deified simulacrum that is the Athenian ideal. Far from being identified with salvation-bringing anamnesis, the narcissistic ecstasy is, in Plato's view, a drug for which there is no antidote except a return to reality, the most primary form of reminiscence. Moreover, this return is not easy, for the funeral oration possesses a formidable capacity to induce oblivion, that is, for the philosopher, death.[7] Although the oration says a great deal about immortality, the eternal glory promised by the city is merely a parody of the "fine risk" of the *Phaedo*.[††] Every epitaphios misleads the Athenians, since, living in dream in the Islands of the

---

[*] *Ibid.* 235b1: *hestēka.*

[†] *Ibid.* 235c1.

[‡] *Eupolis*, frag. 94 (Kock).

[§] *Menexenus* 235c1–2.

[**] *Ibid.* 235c3.

[††] The first words of the ironic eulogy of civic death (*Menexenus* 234c1) seem to be a sarcastic echo of the declarations of the *Phaedo* (114d6).

Blessed* — an honor by definition reserved for the few† — they are claiming for themselves while still alive a residence that can only be posthumous.[8] By means of this final feature, which the philosopher has no doubt borrowed from some Aristophanes-like comedy[9] but which acquires its full meaning in Plato's own thought,‡ the criticism becomes clearer. To the error of temporality (conceiving of oneself as if one were no longer) and to the offense against truth (taking oneself for a hero or a just man) is added a serious misunderstanding of spatiality: one forgets, if not that one is on earth, at least where one is.§

Thus the funeral oration has abolished the frontiers that separate reality from fantasy and, by focusing excessively on Athens, which it turns into a spectacle** or a mirage, it ends by displacing Athens from itself and substituting for the real city the phantom of an ideal polis, a utopia.[10] Citizens of nowhere, the dazzled Athenians are enthralled by the hollowest of all fantasies.

Such an analysis is inseparable from the overall criticism of the oration developed by Plato in the *Menexenus*. The philosopher has his reasons for subjecting Socrates to the power of the funeral oration: Socrates is no ordinary Athenian, even if at first reading everything seems to suggest that he is.†† Later we shall examine this strange confrontation, the outcome of which is crucial. Furthermore, many elements of this criticism make sense only in the essential context of Plato's thinking: although in the *Menexenus*

---

* *Menexenus* 235c4–5.

† Hesiod, *Works and Days* 171.

‡ *Symposium* 179e2–3 and 180b5 (Achilles sent by the gods to the Islands of the Blessed); *Gorgias*, 523b1–2 (only the just man dwells in the Islands of the Blessed after his death); *Republic* 7.519c5–6.

§ *Menexenus* 235c4.

** The foreigners accompanying Socrates find it *thaumasioteran* (*ibid.* 235b6–7): Athens is a *thauma*.

†† The use of "we" (*ibid.* 235a2; 235a5: twice) suggests that Socrates is reacting as an Athenian.

the funeral oration exerts its power over individuals who, in order to rediscover themselves, must divest themselves of the noble personage with whom they had identified,[11] for Plato it is an opportunity to remind us that in this world there is no task but the quest for oneself. Last, by identifying the orators with Sophists, the philosopher is aiming his criticism, beyond the funeral oration, at the illusion-ridden, deceptive rhetoric against which, from the *Gorgias* on, he had been waging a large-scale offensive.

But the prologue of the *Menexenus*, in which a veritable pathology of the listener of the epitaphioi is worked out, is not of concern only to the historian of Platonic thought. In denouncing the fascination that the epitaphioi exert over the Athenians, this text brings to the study of the oration valuable evidence that is both a description of symptoms and a diagnosis: the funeral oration totally seizes its audience because it doubly avoids the obligation to praise the dead, by redirecting the praise to the community of the living and by making the city more "admirable." It may be objected that this is one and the same shift. This is not, however, what the text itself says: on two occasions, the eulogy of the Athenians and the eulogy of the polis are juxtaposed and distinguished.

1. The orators hypnotize men's souls by celebrating the city and by confusing life and death, past and present, in an amalgam from which the living alone benefit.*

In celebrating the city, one is led to celebrate all the generations that have successively given it existence: the dead of the year, the ancestors, and the living, linked together, as is normal in an enumeration, by the conjunction of additive coordination *kai* (*tous teteleutēkotas...kai tous progonous...kai autos hēmas*). But in the very structure of the sentence, the eulogy of these three groups of citizens is distinguished from praise of the polis: the use of two different verbs, themselves linked by the repetition of *kai* (*kai tēn polin enkomiazontes...kai tous teteleutēkotas [kai...kai] epainountes*), turns the eulogy of men into something quite other than a redundancy or the developed version of *kata pantas tropous*.

* *Ibid.* 235a2–5.

337

Bound together by a close and, so to speak, natural relationship, andres and polis, praise of the city and eulogy of the citizens, constitute nevertheless two stages in the oration. To name and exalt the city does not mean that one does not have to list the groups of citizens. Thus Plato surreptitiously introduces a difference between andres and polis; it is not easy to give content to this distinction, but we must admit that it is there in the letter of the text.

2. Assuming the eulogy to be directed toward himself, Socrates swells with pride, and his behavior arouses the admiration of the foreigners, an admiration that also extends to the city. But the text is less limpid than it at first seems.* Here again the repetition of *kai* distinguishes and unites two objects of wonder. But are we to translate this, as readers of Plato often do: "For they seem to have the same impression *of me as of the rest of the city*, which they judge to be more admirable than before"?[12]

Of course there is an opposition in Plato's work between the individual Socrates, concerned essentially with the solitary or dialectical quest for truth, and the city of the Athenians, a community in which public values reign. But what can be the meaning of the opposition between Socrates and "the rest of the city": on the one hand Socrates, on the other the community minus Socrates?[13] Such arithmetic recalls the mistake of the crane, according to which the *Statesman* drew a distinction between the "genus crane" and the rest of the animal world, in order to glorify itself the more.† What is at issue here is not a correct or incorrect division, but Athens and the Athenians, and everything in the text suggests that Socrates reacts both as an individual and as an Athenian, faithful to his principles, since throughout Plato's work he constantly refuses to live outside the city, or even to conceive of himself outside it.[14]

In fact there is another way of understanding this passage, namely by giving *allos* an adverbial meaning — for which, indeed, there are precedents in Plato‡ — which this adjective readily assumes

* *Ibid.* 235b5–7.
† *Statesman* 263d.
‡ *Cf. Gorgias* 473c7–8; *Symposium* 191b; *Phaedrus* 232e; *Republic* 520b.

when used in the second part of a pair.[15] *Kai pros eme kai pros tēn allēn polin* then means: "of me, but also of the city." On the one hand Socrates, a citizen of Athens, though in his own original way; on the other the city, taken as an object of admiration and regarded, in its widest sense, as a singular entity much more than as a human community. The foreigners do not admire "all the other Athenians"; they admire the city; the unity of Socrates corresponds to the unity of the city.* The text allows both readings, but if we had to choose, we should prefer, against the traditional interpretation, more comfortable in that it disturbs no received ideas,[16] the second reading, which conforms more to the general sense of the dialogue[17] and to the overall movement of Plato's thought, even though, because it is less immediately clear than the first, it raises a disturbing question: what is a polis that is not first conceived of as a community?

Praise of the human community *and* praise of the city: it is probably this strange distinction that Plato reads in the epitaphioi. The historian of ancient Greece, used to taking the Greeks literally when they speak about themselves and for whom therefore the adage *andres gar polis* (for a city consists of its men)[18†] constitutes the most precise definition of any city,[19] would no doubt consider such a distinction pleonastic — or strictly Platonic. However, we will try to throw some light on this cumbersome duality by a study of the epitaphioi, showing that the term *hē polis* (the city) does not have the same meaning in the funeral oration as in the political acts of the Athenian community, as they were expressed in the decrees of the ekklesia or described by the historians.[20] So, leaving the prologue to the *Menexenus*, a valuable but ultimately highly allusive piece of evidence insofar as it is content to suggest a gap between andres and polis, we shall submit the epitaphioi to a new examination.

---

* Suggested by the use of the singular: *sēmnoteros* (235b4), *thaumasiōteran* (235b6–7).

† Thucydides, 7.77.7; cf. Aeschylus, *Persians* 349; Herodotus 8.61; Philochorus (*F.Gr.Hist.*, 328, 2 a: *astu* designates the urban center, *polis* the citizens).

The relationship between the praise of the city and that of the citizens is in theory reversible, and in *The Acharnians*, when the representatives of the allies exalt the people "crowned with violets" and call Athens "the brilliant one," they have only one aim, namely to flatter the Athenians as a whole.* But our study of the funeral oration has already undermined this satisfying equivalence: having characterized every epitaphios as an act of collective praise, we have been obliged to renounce the term "oration to the dead" in order to reveal the lineaments of an "Athenian geste," of which the Athenians themselves are merely the very gifted executants.[21]

By its very existence, the funeral oration attests that the city owes its glory to the devotion of its citizen-soldiers.† So the epitaphioi are not slow to boast, as do the poets, of the merits of the brilliant, well-run city‡ or of the place,§ characterized by its central situation, mild climate fertility, and excellent produce:** the Athenian man, the autochthonous citizen and just warrior, is the only product of the soil of Attica that they praise.[22] Similarly, when they insist on the unity of the city, the epitaphioi seem to be expressing, in their own way, the strictly Greek homology of the civic community and its army of citizens, since they attribute to the polis the unshakable unity that holds the hoplitic phalanx together.[23]

If we examine the texts more closely, however, we discern in the very form of the orations something like a tension between the use of *hoi Athēnaioi* and that of *hē polis*, or rather between

* Aristophanes, *Acharnians* 634–40.

† Thucydides 2.42.2: "The features of our city that I have praised owe all their beauty to the merits of these men."

‡ Astu is mentioned only in passages on the civil strife of 404–403: *Menexenus* 243e5. The same goes for Piraeus (*ibid.* and Lysias 61) and for the walls (Lysias 63).

§ Even in the account of an invasion, *chōra* often gives way to *polis:* cf. Lysias 5.21, 32.

** An apparent exception is *Menexenus* 237b6–238b6 (imitated by Demosthenes 5); but this passage is in fact centered on autochthony.

"the Athenians" (the dead and valorous ancestors), "us" (the living), and "the city" (constituted by these two groups and transcending both).

Among these three objects of praise, parallel or competitive, there is an often complex interplay that makes it possible for the orator to glide from one to another: this is what happens in Pericles's epitaphios. The community of the living, expressing itself through the orator, accords to itself every homage from the very outset, as is shown by the use of the first-person plural,* and although the dead are absent from this great movement of self-celebration, the relation between "the city" and "us" seems at first to be one of perfect reciprocity. The Athenians have placed the city in a state of self-sufficiency, and, conversely, each Athenian, a microcosm of the city, presents a high degree of individual self-determination;† *hē polis* is alternatively the object of Athenian effort and the source of great benefits for all its members.‡ The power of the city, acquired by virtue of Athenian qualities, is evidence of the Athenians' valor:§ can one imagine a more circular relationship? So, when Pericles justifies himself for "speaking at length about the city," declaring that the eulogy of the polis gives its most striking foundation to the praise of the dead,** it is in relation to the dead that he seeks to excuse himself. Indeed, he devotes to them only a brief passage, which opens with the observation that the essential has already been said and ends with a reaffirmation of their total subordination to the city;†† the living, on the other hand, have no reason to take offense at a lesson in Athenocentrism that has flattered their narcissism.

---

* Thucydides 2.36–41; for a few examples of this use of "we," see 36.3, 37.1, 38.1, 39.1, 40.1, 41.4.

† *Ibid.* 2.36.3 and 41.1.

‡ *Ibid.* 2.39.1.

§ *Ibid.* 2.41.2.

** *Ibid.* 2.42.1.

†† *Ibid.* 2.42.2 and 43.1: "So these men conducted themselves there in a manner befitting the city."

And yet things are more complicated: when the orator names *hē polis*, he is referring to a reality that transcends all Athenians, dead as well as living. "I have sung a hymn to the glory of the city":* there can be no doubt that this term, rare in Thucydides,[24] must be attributed to Pericles himself, who, as Knox remarks, proposed for the veneration of the Athenians no other god but the city.[25] In inviting his fellow citizens to contemplate day after day the power of the city and to fall in *love* with her,† the statesman widens still further the gap between the citizens and the city, which is offered to their adoration as the most beautiful of spectacles,[26] sole object of all desire,[27] transcendent and so to speak deified.[28] Although the balance between the living and the dead is now reestablished to the benefit of the latter, presented as models to their compatriots because, in a supreme act of allegiance, they have offered their valor to the city,‡ Athens is nevertheless, for both, the sole principle of all life. But in reality this eminently Periclean theme[29] is implicit from the beginning of the oration, where on two occasions, at the end of a long passage in the first-person plural, *hē polis* gathers up all glory for itself alone;§ and it is again *hē polis* that at the end of the oration calls on the bereaved parents to procreate new citizens, or that solemnly assumes responsibility for the rearing of orphans.** The orator is subtle, and his last word concerns the community of men.†† But is this a way to bridge the gap that has been deliberately created between the polis as a community and the all-powerful polis, object of veneration and love?

* *Ibid.* 2.42.2: *tēn polin humnesa.*
† *Ibid.* 2.43.1.
‡ *Ibid.*
§ *Ibid.* 2.39.4: "The city is worthy of admiration" (conclusion of ch. 39, which begins with "We distinguish ourselves"); 41.1: "In brief, I dare declare: our city as a whole is a living lesson for Greece" (ch. 40 begins and ends with a verb in the first-person plural).
** *Ibid.* 2.44.3 and 46.1.
†† *Ibid.* 2.46.1: *andres aristoi politeuousin.*

According to Knox, this process of abstraction,[30] by which the word *polis* designates an entity superior to every human group and endowed with a sort of autonomous existence, characterized one period only, that of triumphant imperialism.[31] However, an examination of the other epitaphioi — which, with the exception of Gorgias's fragment which is solely devoted to the andres, also give the city and the word *polis* a predominant role — makes it possible to modify this statement.

In Lysias and in Plato, the dead are shadowy figures, and at the very moment when praise should crown their sacrifice, the andres are replaced by the city. The catalog of exploits certainly involves the Athenian combatants — *hoi Athēnaioi* — but when battle is fought and victory won thanks to the fine deaths of the citizens, the orator "forgets" them and attributes all the glory for the military undertaking to *hē polis*. This shift, by which the city collects all the fruit of the battle fought by men, is apparent in several places in the *Menexenus*.* It is flagrant in Lysias's passage on the struggle against the Amazons: at the end of a battle in which the Athenians behaved like a confraternity of just warriors,† *hē polis*, the true *deus ex machine*, wins eternal renown.‡ A benevolent, omnipresent power, sole safeguard of combatants in difficulty,§ the principal subject of all action** and all decision,††

---

* *Menexenus* 241e–242a: after the account of Plataea, Eurymedon, and the Egyptian campaign, and the eulogy of the warriors (241e2–3), the conclusion accords the city all the merit for this battle (241e6–7); the equivalence between polis and andres is implied, but the city soon becomes the only character (242a2 and especially 242a5–6). In 242c5, we see a distribution of roles: the function of conquering falls to the Athenians, but the Greeks show ingratitude to the city.

† Lysias 5.

‡ *Ibid.* 6: one passes from "the valor of our ancestors" to "the immortal memory of the city."

§ *Menexenus* 242e6–243a5.

** Lysias 16, 34, 65; *Menexenus* 243c2, 243d1–4, 244d4–245b2 (in which no action is attributed to the andres).

†† *Menexenus* 244c4 and 244e5.

343

the city credits itself with all merit for the deeds of the dead.*

Yet is such a fact enough to prove that in the funeral oration, the equilibrium between men and the city is fragile? To accept such a view would be to forget that in the term *andres* we must include the citizens whose funeral is being celebrated, the Athenians of former times, and those still living today. Since these three categories of Athenians do not occupy the same position in the oration, the exaltation of the polis may well encroach on the praise of the dead without thereby wronging the other two groups. Thus the occurrences of *hē polis* in the *Menexenus*, which become increasingly frequent as it moves into the account of recent events, threaten only the dead, deprived of a glory that the epitaphios ought to accord them. They in no way eclipse the reputation of the Athenians of former times, to whom the orator leaves full command of their glorious past.† As for the living, they are associated with the celebration of the city, as is indicated by the use of "we" in the passage on the Corinthian War,‡ and their self-esteem is no doubt fully satisfied.

Does the equivalence between men and the polis, implicitly denied when these men are dead, regain its full significance when the subject is "we who are still alive"? Plato's epitaphios seems to suggest this conclusion when, from one sentence to another, it substitutes "we" for *polis*.§ However, we must again beware of overhasty conclusions that are in no way corroborated by the other epitaphioi. Neither Lysias nor Demosthenes praises the city in the first-person plural; while recognizing that the interests of the city go hand in hand with those of the living, Demosthenes distinguishes between polis and *hoi zōntes*** and, in addressing the

* *Ibid.* 243c1–2 ("it is then that one sees the energy and valor of the city shine"), where *aretē poleōs* is substituted for *aretē andrōn*.

† *Ibid.* 240a–241e5 (account of the Persian Wars in which *polis* makes no appearance).

‡ *Ibid.* 243d5–7, e2; 244a6, b1–4, c3–4, 6, 8; 244d3–4; 245b7, c5, e2–8.

§ *Ibid.* 244c4–9.

** Demosthenes 36 ("the entire city and the living"). Cf. 32, in which *hoi zōntes* designates parents (*oikeioi*).

bereaved relatives, appeals to family unity as much as, if not more than, to civic cohesion:[32] political life has temporarily given way to tears and mourning.* Last, when Lysias uses the collective "we" in his final consolation, he speaks in the name of the vast human community of mortals as much as in the name of the political community.† In suggesting that one may in certain cases use "the city" and "we" interchangeably, is not Plato putting the reader on the wrong track? In reality, what matters for him here is to illustrate one of his criticisms of the funeral oration by showing that in the address to the dead, the living take the lion's share: that is why, in the *Menexenus*, "we" and "the city" are synonymous in the present, and only in the present. But the philosopher does not forget that the supreme danger of the funeral oration is that it makes the city the attractive object of narcissistic — and therefore necessarily passive — investment. So after establishing the identification of "we" and "the city," the orator "forgets" the Athenians in order to devote a long passage to the relations between Athens and the great king in which *hē polis* alone occupies front stage.‡ The meaning is clear: when the orators depart too far from reality, the living forget themselves, absorbed in identification with "the city," sole agent, sole source of all decisions.

If "the difference between the singular and the plural consists of the fact that one considers the object sometimes as a unity, sometimes as a plurality,"[33] it is not irrelevant that when confronted with enemies, always considered in their plurality, Athens is usually referred to in the singular, as *hē polis*.§ But, even more clearly, it is a unity in relation to the plurality of its members: significant in this regard are the passages that the orators devote to the honors accorded by the city to the dead and to their families. Lysias is something of an exception when he declares that all

* *Ibid.* 32.

† Lysias 77–78 (mortals) and 75–76 (the city).

‡ *Menexenus* 244c4–d1 and 244d2–245b2.

§ *Ibid.* 244b4–7. Cf. Lysias 21 and 24 (opposition between "divided Greece" and "unanimous resolution" [*mia gnōmē*] of the Athenians).

Athenians, collectively and individually, assume responsibility for the parents, children, and wives of the victims.* For Pericles and Hyperides, Plato and Demosthenes, the duty to honor the dead by appointing the orator, taking charge of raising the orphans, and "entrusting the highest magistracy with the task of protecting the relations of citizens fallen in the war" lies with *hē polis*.† Benevolent to its own‡ and to foreigners who, like the metics in Thrasybulus's army, fought for her,§ the city plays, "with regard to the dead, the role of heir and son; toward sons, that of father; toward the relatives, that of guardian, without ceasing at all times to lavish every form of solicitude on all."** Its omnipresence and its multiform character make the polis an entity; the orators, refusing to list the plurality of citizens, conceive of the city first of all as *a unity*.

It might be objected that this is merely a fact of language that goes well beyond the funeral oration: though one of the collective nouns that, when used in the singular, agree with a verb in the third-person[34] or even first-person plural,[35] *polis* is more often used with a verb in the singular. Thus by generally treating the polis as a unity, the epitaphioi are repeating the same choice, one after the other, and it is not in the syntax of the funeral oration that we must seek the originality of the genre. The choice of subject, on the other hand, is an entirely significant act. In choosing a certain subject (in this case, the polis) over some other subject ("the Athenians" or "we"), the orator is not speaking at random; on the contrary, in his way of conceiving of the relationship between the city and citizens, he is engaging the entire Athenian community, which, gathered together in an assembly, has elected him to deliver the appropriate words. *Polis* is the *name* by which the community refers to itself in order to celebrate itself, even if

---

* Lysias 75–76.

† Demosthenes 2, *Menexenus* 242c2 and 249b3–6; Demosthenes 1, Lysias 1; Thucydides 2.46.1, Hyperides 42, *Menexenus* 249a2–b2; *Menexenus* 248e8–249a2.

‡ Lysias 1: *pronooumenē*. *Menexenus* 248e5–6 (*epimeleia*).

§ Lysias 66.

** *Menexenus* 249b7–c3.

it allows itself to fall under the spell of this term, transformed into an autonomous entity. The symbolic satisfaction that they derive from the evocation of the city saves the Athenians from actually having to think of the city as a community or even as a collection of heterogeneous human groups.[36]

Furthermore, we should hesitate before declaring, with Finley, that the Athenian democracy was immunized against any form of ideological allenation.[37] Attentive to the various connotations, ancient and modern, of the word "democracy," Finley contrasts classical Athens, as ignorant of political apathy as of *raison d'état*,[38] with the modern democracies masking beneath appeals for social consensus the gap that separates the masses from the political class. No doubt from this point of view one is justified in believing that no break between "'we,' the ordinary people, and 'they,' the governmental elite"[39] existed in Athenian political life: keeping a close watch on its magistrates, the demos may not have felt deprived of power. But although it exercised power in fact, the demos seems to have been deprived of it in the official oration to the benefit of the entity *hē polis*: not content with substituting *hoi Athēnaioi* for *ho dēmos*, the orators also substituted the city for the citizens (both the dead, *they, hoi Athēnaioi*, and the living, *we*). Thus a gap is opened up between the Athenians, the zealous agents of a process that transcends them, and the city, the model that inspires action. Although in the word *polis*, as used by the authors of the epitaphioi, unity certainly wins over plurality, *hē polis*, an effective signifier, imposes a meaning before any analysis of its content, and in the funeral oration the Athenian community unconsciously abandons the collective democratic initiative that gave it its originality.

Examining the phenomenon of derivation that subordinates *politēs* to *polis*, Benveniste observes, at the level of language, the city's primacy over the citizen: the city, "abstract body, state, source and center of authority, exists of itself; it is embodied neither in a building, nor in an institution, nor in an assembly; it is independent of men."[40] Such unorthodox observations challenge many received ideas;[41] however, they accord perfectly with the process of abstraction by which, in and through the funeral oration, the Athenians defined themselves in a relation of satisfied dependence on their polis.[42]

Neither study of the word *politēs* nor examination of the occurrences of the word *polis* allows us to state general conclusions concerning the actual nature of the Greek city or even of the Athenian city. No more than language is the oration a mirror of society,[43] and the entity *hē polis* does not reflect the real functioning of the Athenian city. But political experience is made up of such imaginary relationships as the one that the Athenian community has, in the funeral oration, with the abstraction that represents it: "the city" is only a name, but pregnant with significations, possessing a powerful effect on the Athenian public. When confronted by the reality of an imaginary formation, the historian must try to understand its how and why.

In elucidating the process that, within a military oration, transforms the combatants into stage extras, we must first remember that abstraction is a fundamental characteristic of the funeral oration, as I have emphasized many times throughout this study. Thus the epitaphioi deal with only the most exemplary national myths of Athens and are content to keep only a few elements, which are always endowed with the same meaning.

When they wished to affirm their identity, to base their claims in a conflict, or to immortalize a victory, the cities usually resorted to the authority of the gods or heroes who protected them: thus an inscription at Selinus lists the divinities to which the city owed its victory.[44] Similarly, in the conflict at Plataea against the Athenians, the Tegeates called on the hero Echemus,[*] and for Pindar the praise of the city involved a eulogy of the heroes who once honored it. The Athenian city did likewise, erecting the bronze Promachos on the Acropolis so that Athena should attest to the power of the polis, erecting a monument to the Eponyms in the Agora, and entrusting those same Eponyms with the

* Herodotus 9.26.

task of seeing that there was an Athenian presence in the Panhellenic shrine at Delphi.[45] However, the funeral oration is marked
very little by this politico-religious dimension: by virtue of a religious prohibition,* and for reasons that concern the secular character of the oration, the orators do not mention the names of the
Olympian gods and, with the exception of Demosthenes, do not
accord the eponymous heroes the central role that is theirs in
national tradition.[46] As we have seen, the mythical exploits are
attributed to the Athenian community in combat, and the synoe-
cist Theseus has no place in an oration that ignores individuals.[47]
Finally, as it is exalted in the funeral oration, autochthony is neither characteristic of unique heroes nor the distinctive mark of
warrior brotherhoods more or less integrated into the social body.[48]
The autochthonous Athenians have loyalty neither to Cecrops nor
to Erechtheus nor to Erichthonius,† but, born of the Attic soil, they
are descended only from themselves,‡ and autochthony, extended to
the community as a whole,§ cementing internal cohesion,** and proclaiming to the outside world the identity of the polis, must be regarded as the central myth of the funeral oration — but is it still a myth?

Thus, freed from the great authorities — divine or heroic — by
which community apprehends itself through worship, the oration
may devote itself entirely and *without mediation* to Athens and to
the Athenians, to the city and to its men. In the funeral oration,
the Athenians, interchangeable and anonymous, are so many
replicas of a single, implicit model, that of the hoplite, whose
constricting ethic they observe: in the epitaphioi, there are no
oarsmen or archers, only Athenians. This lack of differentiation is

---

* *Menexenus* 238b2–3; Demosthenes 30 and 31.

† The only mention of Cecrops and Erechtheus: Demosthenes 27 and 30 (without any precise reference to their character as autochthones).

‡ Cf. Thucydides 2.36.1 (permanence of the Athenian principle on the chora).

§ Demosthenes 4.

** Plato attributes the reconciliation of 403 to "the real kinship that produces
... a secure friendship, based on the community of race" (*Menexenus* 244a1–3):
autochthony is the basis for the unity of the city.

no doubt democratic; above all we may, with some confidence, impute it to the "similarity" proper to the hoplitic phalanx. But does equality necessarily mean identity? To make a living city, is it enough to gather together "similar individuals," faceless homoioi? Aristotle did not think so* and criticized the Platonic city, which, ever more unified, forgets to remain a plurality and regresses toward the individual.† To absorb multiplicity in unity is also the objective of the orators, and because they are perfectly interchangeable, the Athenians of the epitaphioi tend ultimately to give way to the unity-polis.

To declare that the military character of the oration helps to shift the eulogy of men toward the city is, then, only superficially paradoxical, and the collective funerary epigrams of the fifth century broadly corroborate this conclusion.

Characterized by its unity, strengthened by the lack of differentiation among its members, the city exalted by the orators is a perfectly satisfying construction for the minds of the listeners, in that it ignores all the internal tensions of the historical polis. Indeed, the funeral oration is not content, as Plato suggests, to praise dead and living indiscriminately, but, blurring all frontiers, removes the principal cleavages — age-groups with sometimes vague limits or social categories opposed to one another by their way of life or their interests — that might threaten the cohesion of Athenian society. Because the exemplary citizen-soldier is an adult, there is little room for the young or the old in the epitaphioi.[49] Lysias evokes those warriors of fortune only to relegate them at once to their specific activities,‡ and all the orators exhort the young to become in turn andres§ and invite the old to show themselves worthy of the andres whom they have engendered.** Thus, whether relegated to the frontiers of andreia or merged in

* Aristotle, *Politics* 2.2.1261a23–24.
† *Ibid.* 1261a16–18.
‡ Lysias 50–53.
§ Thucydides 2.45.1.
** *Menexenus* 247d4–e1; Thucydides 2.44.4.

the category of andres, young and old do not disrupt the homo-
geneity of the Athenian warrior group. Because they move in the
pure ether of an ideal politics, the orators can also ignore the fact
that there are rich and poor in Athenian society. Pericles certainly
pays some attention to the diversity of social conditions, but his
purpose tends to reduce any antagonism in the city or, for that
matter, within Athenian man himself:[50] in the homogeneous
world of an ideal political life, the opposition between *ploutos* and
penia is blunted and transformed into a harmonious cooperation
in the service of the same values.* The operation obviously has a
double purpose: by suppressing internal differences, to present to
foreigners the image of a unity that no external intervention can
infringe, and to convey the assurance that all *stasis* will ultimately
be resolved in a joyful fraternal fusion.†

Thus, whether they simply evoke the name of the city or
define it in long passages, the orators are aiming at an effect of
unity. *Hē polis* absorbs plurality in an abstract singularity; contradictions and diversity in the social body are suppressed in the
notion of city. Seeking "to establish from noble struggle … the
nonexistence of the multiple,"‡ the funeral oration makes the city,
as signifier and signified, the political expression of the One, and
this quasi-Parmenidean aim attests that the conflict between the
one and the multiple, a philosophical topos, was also the subject
of an ideological struggle in Athens.

But the historian must be careful not to succumb in turn to the
spell of the One. As the product of an official oration, the entity of
the polis is only one of the possible forms of imaginary relationship
between the Athenian community and itself. To define its proper
sphere of influence, we must compare the city of the epitaphioi
with some of the official representations in which the Athenian
city explicitly mentioned itself in the fifth and fourth centuries.

* Thucydides 2.37.1 and 40.1–3.
† *Menexenus* 243e5–6.
‡ Cf. Plato, *Parmenides* 127e8–10.

351

Blessed with the hypostasis of a city without extent and without diversity the Athenians also delighted in enumerating the many components of the polis, as is apparent in the frieze of the Panathenaea, a figurative representation of the city that is as official as its oratorical evocation. From the demosion sema to the Parthenon, Athens finds a spatial dimension and, in the long movement of the procession, becomes a community once again. In its most concrete form, a polis was, in the funeral oration, a confraternity of similars; on the other hand, listing the "dissimilar elements" that make up Athenian society — citizens, metics, and slaves; men and women; youths, adults, and old people; soldiers, priests, and magistrates — the frieze provides a definition that is Aristotelian before Aristotle,* or perhaps quite simply democratic.[51] Must we, then, set up an opposition between the realism of the visual representation and the abstraction of the auditory evocation? This would be to forget that the ionic frieze is not a realistic document for the use of later historians[52] — many of its elements make such a treatment impossible; examples include the excessive importance accorded to the cavalry to the detriment of the hoplites,[53] the stylization of space, and the purely aesthetic effects of contrast.[54] So the city of Phidias, though closer to the real polis than to that of Pericles or Lysias, also influence has its share of fantasy.

But between these two contemporary, competing models of the city there exists all the distance that separates a product of logos and a work of art intended to be seen. On the one hand is what the epitaphios of the *Menexenus* calls "naked speech" (*logos psilos*),† on the other the continuous frieze whose unfolding presents itself as the replica of the real progress of the procession. The term *logos psilos* obviously refers to prose, the political language that tends to win a certain autonomy in relation to reality, a philosophic language proper to thinking in general, abstract terms.[55] The oration, however, is naked not only because it is deprived of the charms of poetry but also because, reduced to its own re-

* Aristotle, *Politics* 3.4.1277a5–6: "The city is made up of dissimilar elements."
† *Menexenus* 239c1.

sources, it knows that it is cut off from its object. In addition, in evoking the city, the funeral oration has difficulty avoiding abstraction: in the most "concrete" of the epitaphioi, that of Hyperides, the polis remains pure allegory.[56]* By unwinding the image of the Panathenaic procession around the *sēkos* of the Parthenon, the sculptor, on the other hand, has at his disposal matter and space, and his work has no difficulty suggesting the density of reality and the living diversity of the city.

Citing as proof the *pompē* that ends the *Eumenides* or the epiphany of Athens at the end of *Knights*,† critics might object that it is in the works of language that the city preserves its human density and its spatial dimension. Aeschylus's intentions are clear: when the spectators gather, thus associating themselves with the procession formed in the orchestra in honor of the Eumenides, the Athenian community as a whole experiences the concord so much celebrated by Aeschylus. Aristophanes's verse is more difficult to interpret: in this ambiguous text in which Athens is both the home of Demos‡ and a revered power,[57] in which the "vestibule" of Demos is also that of the Acropolis, we are reduced to conjectures about what the spectators actually saw. When, through the sausage seller, the poet invites the audience to greet with the ritual shout the appearance of ancient Athens,§ what theatrical effect are we to imagine accompanying the word *phainomenaisin?* Although Athens is solemnly invoked and invited to show Demos in all its new splendor,** its epiphany is not that of an anthropomorphic presence. Unlike Peace, a deity who has descended among men in a perceptible, not to say desirable, form and with whom, through Hermes, one may converse,†† the city is in no sense a deified entity; but by invoking it in the plural under the noun *Athēnai*, the

---

* Hyperides 5.

† Aeschylus, *Eumenides* 1021–47; Aristophanes, *Knights* 1323–34.

‡ *Knights* 1323 and 1328; for *ta propulaia*, see 1326.

§ *Ibid.* 1318 and 1327.

** *Ibid.* 1329–30.

†† Aristophanes, *Peace* 560 and 520; 497–98, 582–83, 617; 657–705.

poet reminds his listeners that Athens is primarily a community. No doubt, then, despite the reservations of scholars, we must identify ancient Athens, the home of Demos, perceived through the Propylaea, with the Acropolis, which, for the city, is a vital center, at once religious, political, and artistic. So it is quite likely that in support of these lines, Aristophanes offered for the contemplation of the Athenians the splendors of an Acropolis that presented to the spectator a very real polis.[58] Without claiming to exhaust the riches of a text in which many notions of the city are superimposed on one another, we can at least say that in Aristophanes, the evocation of the polis probably associated the pleasure of seeing with that of hearing: an important conclusion, even if we shall never know what forms the staging actually took.

Thus, in Aeschylus as in Aristophanes, the city is endowed with a perceptible presence — whether it deploys its multiplicity in a procession or is symbolically concentrated in one of the shrines of its civic space — and, far from undermining my analyses, these examples serve as counterproofs in that, compared with the entity of the polis, an abstract product of the oration, they show that a certain material presence of the city is inseparable from *representation*, plastic or theatrical.

The polis-entity, on the other hand, is abstract through and through, and, being addressed to an imaginary without image, it exists in opposition to figurative abstractions, which are based on a certain type of representation. In the funeral oration, the city is faceless, which differentiates the oration from all the official personifications of the Athenian community represented by its poliad deity or delegating its power to allegories of Demos or Demokratia. In the fifth and fourth centuries, the Athenians found it natural to represent their city by the figure of Athena, who appears in many reliefs surmounting decrees of alliance or proxenia.[59] By thus identifying the authority of the polis with that of the deity, they did not conform to a widely attested Greek practice; playing on the homonymic relationship that links the name of Athens with that of the goddess, they adorned their community with the form and power

354

of a religious presence. By calling on Demos and Demokratia to represent her, the Athenian city set out after 403 on another path, one that led to philosophical allegory and to statues of personified concepts. It was a more abstract path; even when deified,[60] Demokratia probably never had the presence of Athena, rich in the many aspects of an official religion. However, as anthropomorphic entities associated with the city's gods and heroes, in the Agora or in official documents, Demos and Demokratia take their place among the great figures of national tradition and, in the form of bas-reliefs, paintings, or statues, offer a material support for the imaginary. Demos — sometimes represented alone* but more often in association with Athena[61] or Demokratia, as in the famous painting by Euphranor† or on the heading of the law of 337–36 against tyranny[62] — and Demokratia, celebrated in 332–1 and 331–30 by a public sacrifice,[63] were, in the second half of the fourth century and perhaps in the late fifth, the object of an unquestionable reverence that has perhaps too readily been identified with a cult established at the time of the democratic restoration of 403.[64] The personification of Demos or the Poleis, widely attested in ancient comedy and especially in Aristophanes, in no way implies the existence of a cult, and in giving life to the Demoi or to Democracy and Aristocracy, formidable purveyors of intoxication,‡ Eupolis and Heniochus are simply obeying a general tendency of the Greek linguistic system in which "the word is power."[65] But whether or not they were deified, these entities had certainly passed from the theatrical stage to the political and symbolic stage of the Agora. For us, the essential point is that the words demos and demokratia officially took shape on being established at the heart of the civic space.

Thus, without systematically examining the corpus of personified abstractions, we have at our disposal a valuable element for comparison in our investigation of the polis-entity. Between the

---

* Pausanias 1.3.5: on the Agora, Lyson's statue of Demos.

† *Ibid*. 1.3.3: Theseus, Demos, and Demokratia.

‡ Heniochus, frag. 5 Kock.

many figures that embody Athens and the city of the epitaphioi, we find again, in another mode, the gap that separates abstraction from representation. Whereas sculpture gives a face and a body to incorporeal entities, the funeral oration tends to suppress the living multiplicity of Athenians to the advantage of the unity of an abstract polis. No face, it seems, must come between the orators and the men whom it is their duty to celebrate: the funeral oration does not mention the name Athena[66] and sets out to neutralize both demos and demokratia. Also, when the orators prefer *hē polis* to *hoi Athēnaioi* and blur all the differences that give the city not only its complexity but also its very existence, the phenomenon deserves attention. The epitaphioi use only words: but does that fact explain why the single word *polis* should suppress the concrete plurality of the city?

One last feature distinguishes the polis-entity from the personified abstractions dear to the fourth century, most of which were portrayed as female: in the funeral oration, *hē polis* easily assumes a male role, adopting toward the orphan the role of the father and behaving like a son toward the dead.* This is hardly surprising: in this military, civic, and therefore male oration, no female element may assume a decisive function and autochthony may even serve as an etiological myth for this exclusion of women. In his epitaphios, Demosthenes deprives women of their share in the procreation of citizens and gives it to the land of the city, "the original fatherland."† Thus the bilateral character of kinship is apparently preserved, but at the cost of a flagrant imbalance, since patrilineal filiation, which gives each Athenian his identity, coexists with a collective undifferentiated filiation that makes all Athenians interchangeable sons of the fatherland. Mother of all citizens, father of war orphans, *hē polis* seems to transcend the

---

* *Menexenus* 249a4–5 and 249b7–c1.

† Demosthenes 4: "It is not only to a father that their birth may be traced, but collectively to the whole of their ancestral land, of which they are acknowledged to be the autochthonous sons." Later Demosthenes defines the Athenians as "citizens, the lawful issue of their fatherland."

distinction between male and female.[67] Removed from all representation and faceless, the city of the epitaphioi is therefore also without gender.

Is it possible, toward the end of this analysis, to assign a period to this entity that is the vital, but imprecise and secret, center of the funeral oration?

At first the answer appears to be no, given the static nature of the oration from Pericles to Hyperides, all the orators accord *hē polis* an autonomous existence, even though some, such as Lysias, try to maintain a balance between men and the city. But when examined more closely, the field of action accorded the city shifts between 430 and 322: Pericles makes the polis reality itself, whereas Hyperides relegates it, omnipotent but distant, to the heaven of fixed entities. It is nevertheless incumbent on the orator to pay homage to it before exalting the figure of the leader, which was much more current in 322; but this homage sounds like a concession. If we also recall that in according the city an essential place in the *Menexenus*, Plato is really attacking Pericles's epitaphios, the concordance of clues leads us to date the acme of this process of abstraction to the second half of the fifth century. Let us keep in mind that all the conditions favorable to the abstraction of the city were combined in the Athens of the late fifth century. Whereas the period of the Persian Wars was marked, as Herodotus's history attests, by the equation between men and the polis, the age of the empire was for Thucydides, as for his contemporaries, that of the dynamis of Athens. Because, having placed their confidence in Themistocles, they knew that two hundred ships filled with troops were enough to constitute the city,* Herodotus's Athenians had no need to call on *hē polis* to claim the rank that was their due.† But when Thucydides's contemporaries wanted reassurance about their power, they turned

---

* Herodotus 8.61.

† *Ibid.* 7.161 and 9.27: compare with Thucydides 1.73.1 ("Our city deserves to be spoken of").

to the tragedies, which reminded them that "many are the works of the city and many its triumphs."* In Euripides and Sophocles, as well as in Lysias's epitaphios, it is the authority of the polis that the suppliants address: in the theater as in the Kerameikos, one can never speak enough of the city.[68]

Against the excessively assertive statements of Knox, we must stress the permanence of the abstract model of the city in the epitaphioi. I have tried here to give back to this abstract city its origin, without forgetting that the time of ideological formations is that of "la longue durée."

One thing remains to be said if we wish to give this veneration of the city its full historical specificity. To show how, from the fifth century and particularly in the funeral oration, the city was transformed into an omnipotent entity imposing itself on the listeners as Unity itself, I have stressed everything in the epitaphioi that tends to suppress the human plurality that makes up the polis. Nevertheless, in the epitaphioi abstraction does not entail a complete break with reality. This becomes clear if we compare the entity dear to the funeral oration with the Hellenistic hypostases of the city characterized by verbal inflation or allegorizing overstatement. The Athenians of the classical period distinguished between the official oration and political practice: assigning a time and a place to the city's self-celebration, they did not encumber the decisions of the assembly with nonsensical epithets, as the Hellenistic cities all too readily did in their most minor decrees; in the Athenian decrees of the fourth century, "the city" is neither *lamprotatē* (the most brilliant) nor *prōtē endoxos* (first in reputation).[69] Moreover, even the epitaphioi performed the eulogy of the city in very precise conditions: as if the orators dared not address directly to the city the eulogy ultimately accorded it, *hē polis* usually intervenes only after the mention of some Athenian exploit, which it crowns and to which it lends the weight of its authority while robbing it of its glory. A great deal of stress has been laid on the indefiniteness of the polis-entity; but it should also be remembered that this indefinite-

* Euripides, *Suppliant Women* 576–77.

358

ness, which is not necessarily synonymous with vacuity, prevents any transformation of the city into allegory, thus protecting it against a form of representation whose counterpart is often a political void. When, in the fourth century, Demokratia takes shape and is installed on the Agora, has not the term demokratia already become, on the lips of moderate politicians, a hollow word?

Far from undermining earlier arguments, these remarks draw the fleeting outlines of the abstraction of the city, remembering that the funeral oration is the product of a cultural age in which all reality still found its model in the polis. Omnipresent but without fixed form, the polis in the epitaphioi is what Adam Parry calls a "social abstraction":[70] an autonomous entity with restricted liberty and one that has not lost all reference to the human experience that it designates. By interrupting the account of the Peloponnesian War in order to insert Pericles's epitaphios, by defining the funeral oration as logos politikos, Thucydides and Plato show that the break between the abstraction of the city and the real Athens was not complete.

To grasp more fully the characteristics of the polis-entity, we have been led to contrast it with figurative representations, which imply a certain presence of the city here and now. But we must resist the anachronistic temptation to place all reality on the side of representation: this would be to attribute a universal validity to the modern hierarchy of the five senses in which sight has primacy over hearing.[71] But although nascent historiography assessed the respective value of what is seen and what is heard, it is not certain that in Athenian political practice, dominated by logos, sight had the upper hand.[72] So we cannot be content, with Glotz, to seek in the ephebic oath the reassuring certainty that the city to which the Athenian devoted himself body and soul was not "an abstraction ... but something concrete that he [saw] every day with his own eyes."[73] If the Athenians were indeed fanatics for praise, those lovers of fine words on whom Aristophanes pours such scorn also knew, like their favorite orators, how to make the city the first to be "written in capital letters." Like the city and the laws of the *Crito*, which ultimately have no existence except the persistent one of a voice,[74]* the city of the epitaphioi had no need of concrete representation to exercise a decisive influence on the Athenian public. Perceived through the immediacy of hearing, it was "inscribed in the heads" of the citizens;† the product and principle of the oration become schema of thought: a "certain idea" of Athens, or, better still, an *ideal*.

This faceless, genderless city resists analysis by modern readers: how are we to grasp its indetermination without constantly running the risk of forcing it, even betraying it? But to the Athenians, on whom it exerted a direct influence, it gave a language in which to speak of Athens; so it is possible to monitor its effect on Athenian writers who, like Thucydides and Plato, devote most of their thought to the "classical city," giving it more or less deliberately the name Athens and unity as its essence. Accordingly, we shall seek in the writings of Thucydides and Plato no longer direct information about the funeral oration but the trace of a secondary effect of the logos.

Eulogy and History

Eulogy and history: on one hand, "the Athenian history of Athens," with its amplifications, its silences, and its edifying purpose; on the other, a historiography conscious of the austerity of its task, that of Thucydides, who, rejecting the charms of the fantastic,‡ tries to accumulate a store of useful, trustworthy knowledge.[75] The match seems altogether unequal. Thus, according to Strasburger, who expresses the most widely held opinion, between the pompous inflation of the epitaphioi and the sobriety with which Thucydides expresses his admiration for Athens, there is the unbridgeable gap that separates science from partisan passion — reason from myth.[76]

In expounding the principles of his history, in the famous methodological exposition of book 1, Thucydides himself gave some credence to this interpretation of his work, inviting his readers, present and future, to cast off the abusive totalizations indulged in

* Plato, *Crito* 54d2–5.
† This Platonic metaphor is implicit in the *Menexenus* 235c2.
‡ Thucydides 1.22.4.

by the orators, a species by definition suspect. For the historian, there is no implicit agon that necessarily ends with the symbolic defeat of the absent adversary but equal attention is paid to the opposing forces. Indeed, Thucydides's chosen subject is not Athens but — explicitly and from the first lines of his work — the military process that brought the Athenians into conflict with the Peloponnesians.* Whereas the orators exalt heroic deeds, the historian wishes to study a mutual relationship, and the rejection of any embellishment,† the logical consequence of this initial project, inevitably sets history against the epitaphioi.

Of course the funeral oration is not the only target of this critical rigor: by banishing all fantasy from his history, Thucydides is taking on all forms of oral expression — eloquence or poetry[77] — and not attacking explicitly the authors of epitaphioi, who are subsumed in the much broader category of mistaken predecessors, poets, or logographers. But, with its form consisting of accumulated embellishments and its purpose amounting to little more than flattery, the eulogy is strangely like the muthodes, and when he accuses the logographers of trying above all to seduce an audience, Thucydides treats them as mere orators.‡ It is true that in the late fifth century "the spoken word still dominated the written word,"[78] and, Greek literature being destined on the whole for public reading,[79] every prose writer had to be an orator from time to time. Thus, when he contrasts history, an eternal acquisition, with an ephemeral oratorical performance,§ Thucydides no doubt has in mind the public declamations of a Herodotus. However, the criticism also extends to the funeral oration: is not it, too, an *agonisma?*** Finally, even if the historian did not explicitly attack the authors of the epitaphioi in book 1, there is a strange

* Thucydides 1.1.1.
† *Ibid.* 1.21.1 (on the poets); cf. 10.3 (on Homer).
‡ *Ibid.* 1.21.1 and 22.4 (*akroasis*).
§ *Ibid.* 1.22. 4: opposition between *ktēma es aiei* and *agonisma es to parachrēma*.
** For Lysias, an epitaphios is an agon (2), and in Plato the orator "enters the lists" (235d6 *agōnizetai*).

similarity between this polemical definition of history and the accusations that, in the epitaphios of book 2, Pericles formulates against the ephemeral seductions of encomiastic eloquence:* the same terms, the same thought, and perhaps the same target.

Between history and epitaphios, then, there seems to be an essential incompatibility, and a comparison of the two modes of discourse seems only to have widened the gap between them.

And yet, between theory and practice there is an immense gap, through which the funeral oration is reintroduced into Thucydides's work. To begin with, the banished muthodes reappears, though only in the more muted form of the "drama," to structure the web of the text; Cornford, sometimes with a certain exaggeration, demonstrated this.[80] Second, Athens is not a neutral figure in Thucydides: A.W. Gomme and Henry R. Immerwahr even go so far as to declare that the historian has made her the "hero" of his work.[81] Last, and above all, the historian, far from undervaluing the funeral oration, made an epitaphios a keystone of his text.[82]

This may be obvious enough, although it should be observed that it does not appear as such to all readers of the epitaphios, less preoccupied with the function of the oration than with its manner of insertion into the text as a whole. Now, if we bear in mind that the oration functions at two levels — that of the narrative content, in which it is a speech delivered by a statesman in a particular set of circumstances, and that of the structure of the work, in which it assumes its place in an intelligible ordering — we realize that, while probably remaining faithful to most of what Pericles said, it also represents for Thucydides a symbol of the greatness of Athens, destined to ward off in advance any account of its failure. This perspective throws light on the homological relationship that has often been observed between the epitaphios and the work as a whole:[83] a logos attests in advance to the ergon as a whole, and there is not a single word of Pericles that does not find its echo in Thucydides's narrative.

This raises a question: in spite of the methodological intransi-

* Compare 1.22.4 with 2.41.4.

gence of its author, does not Thucydides's history reveal, despite itself, despite its author, a secret fascination for the one, omnipotent city of the epitaphioi? Of course, like Pericles, Thucydides challenges the topoi of the oration,* and in writing the history of the Peloponnesian War, he clearly intended to put an end to the narcissism of all the Athenian histories of Athens. But when one tries to define the character of the peoples, it is not easy to reject the portrait of Athenian man laid down in the funerary oration. When one sees unity as the end of every polis, how can one avoid the city of the epitaphioi, the Athenian model of unity? One does not rid oneself of the funeral oration so easily: this is what is revealed by the analogy between the epitaphios of book 2 and the history as a whole.

Furthermore, we cannot see the similarities between the historical narrative and the eulogy as merely a matter of chance: the same conception of the memory as depository of greatness,[84†] the same way of seeing Sparta from the Athenian point of view,[85] the same explanation of the ultimate defeat of Athens,‡ in a passage in which the necessary unity of the polis is contrasted with the deleterious multiplicity of the leaders, a source of division.§ Of course the influence of the eulogy on history is not always as immediately perceptible, but at various stages in the narrative we can decipher, in the web of the text, a reference to the funeral oration in a complex mode that ranges from attraction to rejection. Thus the oration may be regarded as one of the models in relation to which historical inquiry must situate itself, if only negatively. This relationship is never simple; nor is it enough to elucidate the meaning of the text. But when, drawing lessons from a war that is no longer an agon but a "violent master,"** the Athenians renounce "fine words" and cease to base their acts on their logos,

* Thucydides 1.73.2, cf. 2.36.4.

† See, for example, *ibid*. 1.10.2 (*kleos*) and 2.11.9 (*doxa*).

‡ Compare *ibid*. 2.65.12 and *Menexenus* 243d4–7.

§ Thucydides, 2.65.

** For *agon,* cf. 1.70.1 (speech of the Corinthians) and 2.42.1 (epitaphios); *biaios didaskalos*: 3.82.2.

that is, on the ideal of the Athenian character,* we can read between the lines the death certificate of something — a type of political, military behavior, a model of the city — that found its place in the funeral oration: the debate about Melos shows indirectly the extent to which, in the first books of the history, the official logos of Athens still played the role of an ergon.

From the first book, certain passages turn out, it is true, to be resistant to the influence of the Athenian tradition. Such is the case with the account of the Pentecontaetia, animated by the wish to distance itself from the catalog of the epitaphioi:[86] indeed, the elliptical dryness of this excursus accords with such a purpose, and Thucydides's history seems to avoid any relationship, negative or positive, with the history of the orators.

The archaeological passage is governed by a much more complex strategy. Here, as in Pericles's epitaphios, everything is organized in terms of the present, whose reality, that of Athenian power (*dúnamis*),† effaces all renown deriving from the past.‡ But although they obey the same conception of time, these two texts are fundamentally opposed in purpose, as history is opposed to eloquence. Like the historian, the orator rejects the mythical no-man's-land, thus falsely placing himself in opposition to the national tradition of Athens that presents city life as an Athenian invention that came to birth with the autochthones.§ But in proposing a few dates,**

---

* Compare 1.73.1 (oration of the Athenians at Sparta: "the noise [*logos*] that is usually associated with us," 2.42.2) (epitaphios: "There are few Greeks for whom words [*logos*], as much as for them, would find an exact equivalent in deeds [*erga*]"), and 5.89 (Melian debate: *onomata kala*).

† Archaeology: 1.9.1, 13.5, 14.1, and especially 15.1–2. Epitaphios: 2.41.2, 41.4, and 43.1.

‡ The thesis is formulated in 1.1.2 ("nothing loomed large in it, wars no more than the rest"); cf. also 1.21.2. Compare with Pericles's epitaphios (2.41.4).

§ On this level, Lysias's epitaphios (19) meets the Atthidographic tradition (Philochorus, *F.Gr.H.,* 328 F 2a and b).

** Thucydides 1.12.3 (migration of the Boeotians and Dorians); 13.3–4 (construction of four ships for the Samians and first naval battle).

Thucydides leaves Athens and tries to reconstruct a universal, intelligible process of development, in accordance with his requirements of scientific rigor. Against the official orators, but also against Pericles, who takes the city as his sole object, the historian sets out to describe the formation of a whole called Hellas,* in which ancient Athens has only a minimal place.

Greece, it is true, has only the past: the present belongs to Athens, and the passage on the first ages of Greece is meaningful only outside itself, in the power of Pericles's city. But in Thucydides's work, Athens has more than one face; there are at least two cities, which, like the real and the paradigm, sometimes coexist and sometimes are mutually exclusive. Depending on whether the necessities of the narrative are emphasizing its activism or its valor, the imperialist polis is a tyrant-city or a city of arete, and democracy, which from the Athenian point of view is the government of the best by themselves, is seen in other circumstances as a formidable ferment of subversive agitation.† From one passage to another, a redistribution of roles tends to take place between these two cities; in this way, the Archaeology gives Athenian power its material, concrete, that is, maritime, dimension, whereas the oration sees it as an immanent greatness, an extension of the Athenian character.‡ The thing that brings the two texts together is also what separates them: the Archaeology culminates in an epiphany of Athenian dynamism,§ but this dynamism is maritime, and, concealed in the epitaphios, the imperialist complex — urban fortifications + wealth + fleet[87] — is here the very motive force of history. In developing his general theory of maritime power, Thucydides inevitably distances himself from a traditional form in which greatness belongs to the city by its very essence.

To distance oneself from something is not, however, to condemn

* See esp. 1.3.1 and 3.

† Tyrant-city, city of arete: compare 1.69.1 (or 2.63.2, 3.37.2 and so on) and 2.40.4; democracy of the best and *neōteropoiia*: see 2.46.1 and 1.102.3.

‡ Compare 1.15.1–2 and 2.41.2.

§ 1.23.6 (*alēthestate prophasis*).

it to oblivion, and the eulogy remains on the horizon of the history. Indeed, the Archaeology is implicitly determined in a polemical relationship with the tradition of the funeral oration. It is a negative relation, of course, since, basing the Athenian principle on reason, the history corrects the embellishments of the oration and uses the topoi of the narration only to challenge them. Thus Thucydides does not completely reflect the topos of autochthony, but he carefully avoids using the term and, against all the idyllic clichés, characterizes Attica by its sterility. The infertility of the soil guarantees internal stability and unity of settlement,* so that here again we find themes dear to the panegyrists: the identity of the race,[†] political unity,[‡] already miraculously preserved, and Athenian hospitality.[§] Every polemic has its ambiguities, and we should not be too surprised at these few concessions to the national traditions of Athens. But there is more to it than that: insofar as in his choice of topic Thucydides does not abandon all criteria of valor — the Peloponnesian War is the greatest crisis ever known,[**] a conflict between two powers at full strength[††] — the Archaeology contributes to the eulogy of the present by providing a proof *a contrario.*

Though adopting a different way from that of the funeral oration, this passage prepares in its own fashion the ground for the epitaphios. Conversely, the epitaphios, an exemplary presentation of a model,[‡‡] is linked to the narrative of the first two books as a paradigm to the reality. Throughout book 1, the reality of Athens takes on shape and strength: a necessary result of the historical development reconstructed in the Archaeology, Athenian power is designated as the real cause of the war and dominates the debate of

---

* 1.2.5: "However far one goes back Attica's barrenness accounts for the absence of internal rivalries, for its inhabitants have always remained the same."
† Cf. *ibid.* 2.36.1; *Menexenus* 237b6.
‡ Thucydides 1.2.5: *astasiaston.* Cf. the theme of homonoia in Lysias.
§ 1.2.6.
** 1.1.2 and 21.2.
†† 1.1.1.
‡‡ 2.37.1: *paradeigma.*

Sparta, as much in the contrasting portrait that the Corinthians draw of the two adversaries, to the advantage of Athenian dynamism, as in the introductory speech and apologia delivered by the Athenians before the Spartans' final decision. In book 2, before the plague arrives and overthrows all values,[88] before evolution toward an uncertain future makes a process of breakdown possible* and brings defeat and internal struggles,† the epitaphios makes the involvement of the Athenian principle in war fully intelligible‡ and exalts the present by opening up the prospect of eternity.§ Thus, far from providing the anthologies with a purple passage that is easily separated from its context, the epitaphios is thoroughly bound up with the beginning of the work, which it helps to order by its very presence. But it remains an essential touchstone throughout the narrative, at least until the experience of Melos renders it invalid.

Beginning in book 3, it is true, the great themes of the funeral oration are subjected to rough treatment. *Stasis* is eating away at the cities, forcing the citizens to contravene the normal laws of war[89] and political life, and although Athens is temporarily spared this evil, it is no longer the model of civic unity that the epitaphios exalted: by calling for the assistance of the Athenians, the demos of the cities is not so much seeking a model as trying to defeat an enemy.** In short, the universal recognition of Athenian greatness has given way to tactical, fragmentary alliances. But in book 5, the Athenians themselves give up any attempt to conform to the ideal that they were claiming to embody: the Melian debate, a turning point in the Athenian theory and practice of imperialism,[90] is also the point at which the funeral oration as model of discourse and political argument is definitively rejected.

Renouncing everything that is not realpolitik, Athens must divest herself of the halo of glory and generosity with which she

---

* Evoked not in the epitaphios but in 2.64.3 (Pericles's last speech).

† Already referred to in 2.65.

‡ 2.36.4.

§ 2.41.4.

** This is particularly clear in 3.27.3 (at Mytilene).

bedecked herself in the epitaphioi. She still expects others to acknowledge her prestige, but she now prefers that this take the form of hostility since friendship has become synonymous with weakness;* and although the Athenians still allow themselves the aristocratic luxury of serenely confronting the risk of defeat,† they no longer evoke the immortal renown that will survive them.[91] Therefore they announce that they will no longer have recourse to "fine words" (*onomata kala*),‡ and by this term are meant the usual topoi of self-justification. However, the Athenians are not only renouncing the commonplaces but also repudiating the very practice of the uninterrupted oration in favor of a fake dialogue,§ under the pretext that it "would provide long, unconvincing passages."** But for Thucydides as well as for Plato, the uninterrupted oration is by definition a political speech;[92] thus it is a civic mode of the logos, in both its form and its content, that the Athenians are rejecting in abandoning the funeral oration.

We may therefore read in Thucydides's text, if not a theory, at least a history of this rejection. The agonistic world of the epitaphioi presupposed that Athens confronted rivals who were — at least *de jure* — similar;[93] but the Peloponnesian War disturbed the balance, or, more precisely, the ideal of balance, and it was left to the now-inferior Melians to accept point by point the reasons of the stronger.†† So the eulogy to which the funeral oration is related is repudiated; an eminently justified form of speech in book 2, the eulogy becomes in book 5 empty, useless words, "seductive arguments without refutation."‡‡

---

* 5.95.

† 5.91.1 and 2.

‡ 5.89; similarly, in 111, honor becomes an *onoma epagōgon*, which overcomes and betrays anyone who allows himself to be led by words.

§ 5.85.

** 5.89.

†† *Ibid.: hoi asthēneis.*

‡‡ 5.85.

From this point on in Thucydides's work, all trace of a collusion between history and the eulogy gradually disappears, in a world dominated by force and division.

Thus Euphemus, the Athenian envoy to the assembly of Camarina, ignoring or criticizing the topos of the funeral oration, rejects any justification of empire that is based on "fine words."* In the sphere of external relations, the reminder of the Persian Wars and the theme of the struggle for liberty give way to an exposition of well-understood interests. Similarly, the passages on Athenian political life no longer reveal any attempt to identify an aristocratic democracy with a city characterized by unity. When the army of Samos arrogates to itself the title demos† and declares itself in favor of democracy,‡ the break is complete between *hē polis* — which in fact no longer deserves this name§ — and *to stratopedon* (the army),[94]** and preservation of the unity of the city will require the intervention of Alcibiades, that same Alicibiades who, in earlier times, was not afraid to contrast "democracy, that well known madness," with the good regime that ensured the city's greatness and freedom.†† Personal opportunism has caused Alcibiades to renounce the ideal of Pericles's oration before the Spartans, but after him no other Athenian orator exalts that ideal. In short, although the themes of the funeral oration make fleeting appearances in the narrative,‡‡ the oration itself is no longer a model for discourse on Athens.

In subjecting Thucydides's work to this investigation, I have made no claim to be carrying out a systematic study of the text or

---

* 6.83.2.

† 8.86.8.

‡ 8.73.5 and 75.2.

§ In 8.76.3, the soldiers believe that "the city" consists only of a minority; in 76, *hē polis* is as much a political as a geographic definition.

** 8.76.1 (and the entire chapter in general).

†† 6.89.6.

‡‡ In 8.96, the opposition between the Athenians and the Lacedaemonians is like a faded memory of the speech of the Corinthians in book 1.

exhausting the meaning of such subtle pages: that would be to succumb to the imperialism of the funeral oration. So this investigation is deliberately limited: believing with Immerwahr that it is important to determine the relationship between history and the eulogy according to Thucydides,[95] I have tried to decipher, in the web of the narrative, another history, that of the funeral oration and of the representations that are bound up with it. In Thucydides, of course, lucidity prevails over fascination, and this other history is that of a defeat. But the fact remains that Thucydides thought fit to give a place to the history of the logos in his account of the erga, and that in pursuing the most rigorous thought that any Athenian has devoted to the Greece of the cities, the historian encountered the city of the epitaphioi as one of the specific representations of Athens.

Even Plato's philosophical history cannot avoid defining itself in relation to the funeral oration. Of course the author of the *Menexenus* and the *Statesman* shows no indulgence toward the seductive accounts that mislead the crowds instead of instructing them.* But when, in the *Timaeus* and the *Critias*, he "brings to life" the city of the *Republic*† and compares it with other states with a view to testing its paideia,‡ his eulogy of it is evidence of a complex relation with the funeral oration and with the polis of the epitaphioi.[96]

To this animated model the philosopher gives no other name but Athens. Of course, he is referring to an earlier Athens, to Athens in the past, but the choice of a name cannot be taken lightly. Is there, then, no other appellation worthy of the Socratic city? In fact, the prologue of the *Timaeus* suggests that once again, in his paradoxical way, Plato is playing with the ambiguous attraction that, throughout his work, Athens exerted over him. To celebrate the model city, one must be more than simply "expert in speech making," and the Sophist, a skillful orator but a wanderer

* *Statesman* 304d1.
† *Timaeus* 19b8.
‡ *Ibid.* 19c7.

without a city, is rejected from the outset:* only a citizen may assume this glorious task. The Platonic orator is therefore Athenian; but this orator is called Critias, and if this is Critias the oligarch, he is of all the Athenians the most heretical. This special status allows him, against the secular and political orthodoxy of the funeral oration, to play with another orthodoxy, the prestigious and possibly immemorial orthodoxy of the myths: so he is far from omitting the names of "Cecrops, Erechtheus, Erichthonius, Erysichthon, and those other heroes before Theseus,"† by which he anchors his narrative in the mythical tradition of the city. Similarly, when the orator declares that present-day Athens retains some remnants of its ancient fertility‡ or that the present shape of the Attic promontory is to its earlier form what a skeleton is to a body,§ he seems concerned to link, even if in a degraded relationship, the very defective Athens of his own time to its earlier model. The city of the present has lost all memory of its perfect prototype, but the myth of the earlier Athens responds precisely to the need to keep the name while rejecting its present reality.

"The citizens that you had imagined were in truth, we would say ... Our ancestors":** thus Critias, receiving from Timaeus the nature of man, from Socrates the nature of the citizen,†† and mindful of the *palaios logos*‡‡ that his ancestor Critias got from Solon,§§ will populate the Socratic city with Athenians of former times, after subjecting them, before the court made up of the protagonists in the dialogue, to a sort of philosophical *dokimasia*.***

---

* *Ibid.* 19e2–5.
† *Critias* 110a.
‡ *Ibid.* 110e6–7.
§ *Ibid.* 111b4–7.
** *Timaeus* 26c8–d3.
†† *Ibid.* 27a5–b1.
‡‡ *Ibid.* 21a8.
§§ *Ibid.* 27b1–2.
*** *Ibid.* 27b3–4.

"And henceforth we will speak of them as fellow citizens and Athenians":* out of this genesis and by the detour of an "ancient history," *a certain Athens* may become the embodiment of the city.

To achieve this aim, one will have had to shift one's perspective, leave Athenian space and the time of civic history and traverse the long distance to find Athens in Saïs,† but also gather around Socrates, the killjoy of the real polis, Timaeus, the philosopher of Locris, Hermocrates, the Syracusan statesman and inveterate enemy of Athenian imperialism, and Critias the "tryant," the mortal enemy of democracy — all of them strangers to Athens or hostile to the historic city.[97] Such is Plato's oblique approach to Athens.

But by means of this detour Athens, the ever-decentered center of Platonic discourse, is a paradigm, and in a double sense: the term designates for the philosopher both the example from which reflection may rise to the model and the model that enables thought to understand the real world.[98] Now, in Plato's work, Athens certainly seems to assume the function of an example that might at the same time, in certain conditions, be a model. As a perceptible example, it helps reflection on the polis to constitute itself on the basis of it and against it; but it is still the reality that, magnified, distanced, mythified, animates the model.

The Athenian polis becomes an archetype of the city only by losing all historical reality, and Plato alone is qualified to make this paradigm speak. Delivered on the day of the Cureotis,[99]‡ the third day of the Apaturia, the festival of the phratries, before three assembled generations, the true discourse on Athens is anchored in a genos, the right to deliver it being a privilege that Plato may have owed to his family's link with the exemplary Solon.§ This family affair takes us outside the civic context in which the

---

* *Ibid.* 27b5–6.

† *Ibid.* 27e.

‡ *Ibid.* 21b4 and 7: *paides;* 21b4: *pateres;* 21c: *gerōn.*

§ Dropides, Critias's great-grandfather and Plato's ancestor, was a relation of Solon's (20e1–2).

funeral oration takes place, and a gap opens up between the philosophical discourse on Athens and the official discourse. Distance, however, does not mean indifference, and, without ever explicitly evoking the funeral oration, Plato refers tacitly to the logos politikos: he brings it into question by delivering a counter-eulogy of the city.[100]

No doubt this is a polemical reference: whereas the discourse of ancient Athens is prepared and delivered around Socrates, the funeral oration seems at first to be definitely rejected, on the grounds that it perpetrates error. The orator's mere choice is enough to mark the gap. To deliver an appropriate eulogy, the city appoints an Athenian who enjoys its favor;* similarly, the panegyrist of the *Timaeus* must be "capable of delivering the eulogy of those men and their city in the correct way.† But the resemblance is merely apparent, for the criteria of choice are very different in each case. Far from being a topos of the exordium, the measure of the eulogy in the *Timaeus* is a moral as well as an intellectual imperative, since it is a matter of praising the Socratic politeia. If Socrates, who is not or does not wish to be a politician, declines to give an opinion,‡ as he is so fond of doing, at the moment of delivering an uninterrupted speech, this is not an episode to be brushed aside lightly: it means that the choice is a serious matter. So various categories of possible orators are considered and rejected in turn. There remains the small group of Socrates's interlocutors, who alone are capable of assuming this task because they are all both philosophers and politicians§ — and Critias more than all the others, for his speech already bears the seal of the past.**

Furthermore, Critias is an Athenian; but in order to widen the gap between philosophical praise and the official oration, the

* See Thucydides 2.34.6.
† *Timaeus* 19d2.
‡ *Ibid.* 19d1.
§ *Ibid.* 19e8–20a1.
** *Ibid.* 20d2.

speech about ancient Athens must be marked from the start by
otherness in relation to present-day Athens, whose citizens,
reduced to a state of perpetual youth, are ignorant of everything
concerning their real origin.* That is why the first orator in the
long succession of narratives resuscitated by Critias is a foreigner,
an old Egyptian priest living in an old country where time stands
still.† On this occasion, we really are a long way from the funeral
oration and from the Athens of the fourth century.

And new differences arise, which we will list more briefly.

Between the two kinds of publics and the two discourses, we
find the gap that separated the orators. The audience, or successive
audiences, of the logos or Athens, a genos assembled for a festival
of the phratry or a banquet of friends in the middle of which
Critias makes his speech,‡ has nothing in common with the mixed
assembly of citizens and foreigners attending a state funeral.[101]

As for the speech, it is in many respects the opposite of an epitaphios. Whereas the funeral oration has the rather easy task of
praising the public that is being addressed, Critias's account, presenting an unknown Athens to a demanding audience, is a difficult form of discourse.§ So, unlike the epitaphioi, a speech all
ready to be delivered,** the logos of Athens is postponed for as
long as it takes to remember it.††

Last, because he repeats a priest's account, originally delivered
on the occasion of a festival, the speech on ancient Athens claims
to be a revelation‡‡ and is explicitly placed under the patronage of
the gods; whereas Pericles — or Thucydides — addressed a hymn to

---

* *Ibid.* 23b1–2. And this apostrophe is addressed to Solon, whose compatriots
are in a sense the primordial seed (23c1): can the same be said of Plato's fellow
citizens?

† *Ibid.* 22a–b.

‡ *Critias* 112e10.

§ *Timaeus* 20d8.

** *Menexenus* 235d1–2

†† *Timaeus* 26a1–3.

‡‡ *Ibid.* 27b4–5: *emēnusen*.

the city, Critias — or Plato — sings a hymn to the deity: to praise the city is also, even primarily, to celebrate Athena.[*] An autonomous entity, the city of the epitaphioi tended to have no origin other than itself; the Platonic Athens, on the other hand, is rooted in a privileged relationship with the divine, and only to the Athenians of former times does the epithet *theophileis* (beloved of the gods), brought into disrepute by the orators of the fourth century,[†] "really" apply, since they are "related" to the gods,[‡] whether they are the foster children and pupils[§] or owe their lives to them.[**] If human history derives all its value from divine intervention,[102] then ancient Athens, like the philosophical Sparta of the *Laws*, has over the real city the superiority of the model over the copy.

So, telling the true history of the polis,[103] the Platonic discourse on Athens is presented as the only real eulogy, endowed with all the qualities that, in the *Phaedrus*, the philosopher attributes to the animated logos.[††] Like it, the eulogy is living and is alone capable of giving life to a theoretical model that would otherwise retain the silent immobility of painted creatures.[‡‡] Also like the living logos, it is linked with memory:[§§] as the story of the story of a story, it has used writing only so that it may finally be inscribed in ineffaceable characters in the soul of an Athenian.[104***]

Thus the philosophical reader, accustomed to the subtle interplay of difference and similarity, can discern, between the funeral oration and the logos of early Athens, the gap that separates

[*] Compare Thucydides 2.42.2 (hymn to the city) and *Timaeus* 21a1–2 (hymn to the goddess). Critias repeats the act of the Egyptian priest dedicating the narrative to Athena (23d6–7).

[†] *Menexenus* 237c8 (*theophiles*), 237d1; Isocrates, *Panegyricus* 29 (*theophilos*).

[‡] *Critias* 109c10; *Timaeus* 24d1–3.

[§] *Timaeus* 24d5–6.

[**] *Ibid.* 23c1–2; cf. *Critias* 109d1.

[††] *Phaedrus* 264c2–3.

[‡‡] *Timaeus* 19b6–7.

[§§] *Critias* 108d2: great invocation to the goddess Mnemosyne.

[***] *Timaeus* 26c3–4. Compare with *Phaedrus* 276a5–6.

deserved from erroneous praise, even when they are strangely similar: Critias's speech, which initiates the story and gives the action, is, like the funeral oration, an account of war deeds. But the demands of philosophical history require that military operations be the expression of an effective opposition between two antagonistic principles: the struggle of Athens against Atlantis is actually "the realization ... of an ideological difference."[105] Hostile to the civic orators who, unable to detect Athens's real enemies, devote themselves to an account of the struggles between the Greeks, Plato entrusts Critias with the task of praising an "honorable war,"* between Greeks and barbarians, between the land principle and the sea principle.[106]

From the perspective of strict Platonic orthodoxy, then, the funeral oration must be regarded as a counterfeit of the true discourse on Athens. But historians are not expected to participate in the philosophical game to the extent of misunderstanding the influence that the funeral oration has exercised on the philosopher, perhaps without his awareness. Indeed, not only does the palaios logos of the *Timaeus* have strange resemblances to the epitaphios of the *Menexenus* — and many a reader of Plato has been taken in by this[107] — but, in its essence and in its history, the Platonic city irresistibly suggests the city of the epitaphioi. Characterized like it by unity,[108] the polis of the philosopher, like that of the orators, knows none of the mistakes and difficulties of earlier humanity; in Plato as in Lysias, the autochthonous Athenians are born simultaneously into existence and into the bios politikos.[109]† And if, when he depicts the city in repose, Critias gives the andres who constitute it the lion's share, the glory of the military exploits goes, in the *Timaeus* as in the epitaphioi, to *hē polis*, whose unity victoriously confronted the plurality of its enemies. Similarly, the irremediable oblivion into which the deeds of the

---

* *Timaeus* 20b4–6.

† Compare *Critias* 109d1–2, *Timaeus* 23b–c, and Lysias 17–19, *Critias* 112e3–5 and Thucydides 2.36.1.

autochthonous kings, the military leaders of ancient Athens, have fallen makes it possible to attribute all ergon to the city.*

So some comparison is required between these two very unhistorical "histories" of Athens,[110] announced in similar terms,† moved by an identical wish to save an exemplary city from oblivion,‡ and which, by this common project, become a celebration of a polis that is both well governed and courageous in battle.§ As far as the constitution is concerned, the two discourses are opposed, since the Athens of the *Timaeus* and the *Critias* is concerned very little to be a democracy, but the similarity of their deeds in war makes us forget this divergence soon enough. We need only compare the account of the noble deeds of ancient Athens with the evocation of the Persian Wars in the funeral oration: activated like the Persian invasion by hybris,** the expedition of the Atlantians who also threatened both Europe and Asia,†† is for ancient Athens —as for the city of Themistocles and Miltiades—an opportunity to reveal her exceptional valor‡‡ and to attract universal admiration. "First at the head of the Hellenes, then necessarily alone, abandoned by the others, having come through the supreme dangers, she vanquished the invaders, erected the trophy, and... freed all the peoples." In this summary,§§ as stereotyped and elliptical as those of the epitaphioi, there is not a single element that Plato does not borrow from the Athenian tradition. Of course,

---

* *Critias* 109d2–4 and 110a6–b4.

† Compare the announcement of the subject in *Timaeus* 20c5–6 with *Menexenus* 239a8 and Lysias 3 and 20.

‡ For the act of remembrance, cf. *Timaeus* 21a1 and Lysias 3; *Menexenus* 238d9, 239c5, 239d4, and elsewhere; Demosthenes 6; Hyperides 4.

§ The qualities of primitive Athens (*Timaeus* 23c4–5: "The city was of all cities the most valiant in war and in every respect the most law-abiding") correspond to the two passages of the epitaphioi: *erga, politeia*.

** *Timaeus* 24e3.

†† *Ibid.* 24e3–4; cf. *Menexenus* 239d1–2.

‡‡ *Timaeus* 25b6–7.

§§ *Ibid.* 25b8–c6.

philosophical history should obey a strict chronology; in fact it reverses it completely, substituting for the ill-fated succession of events that, in the fifth century, led from Marathon to Salamis and to the maritime empire* a sequence that begins with the hegemony and culminates in the necessary isolation of ancient Athens — as if Marathon, instead of being a beginning, were an end. By this reversal, the philosopher orients history in the right direction and allows the land to triumph over the sea. But the Athenian history of Athens remains nevertheless the only material of this new construction, because Plato merely redistributes elements that were already securely anchored in the civic tradition of the eulogy of Athens. Finally, if we add that the very principle of a reconstruction of history is not alien to the funeral oration,[III] the philosophical undertaking no longer seems as heretical as it believes itself to be.

Does this mean that Plato also succumbs to the fascination of the funeral oration? The philosopher precluded an interpretation of this type by stressing on several occasions the dangerously "slippery" character of resemblances.[†] If one accepts the presuppositions of the Platonic analyses, one will conclude, despite the many resemblances that link the philosophical logos of Athens to the funeral oration, that these two discourses are radically opposed both in object and in function: the philosopher exalts an Athens that never existed only to give life to a theoretical model; the orator addresses to his misled fellow citizens the expected eulogy that will confirm them in their error. The *Menexenus* acquires its full significance from the gap between these two forms of discourse. But if we recognize that for Plato human history is never unambiguous, we need not be surprised at the ever-open confrontation, from the *Menexenus* to the *Timaeus* and the *Critias*, between the philosophical model and the official ideal of the city, two rival but similar discourses. Given the astonishing developments by which philosophical history defeats civic history on its own ground, we

* Cf. *Laws* 4.706a — 707d.

† See the *Sophist* as a whole and in particular 231a6–8.

are compelled to ask: was not Plato himself caught in the trap of the play of the Same and the Other?[112] Was he able to resist the temptation of "the eulogy of an unreal past," a mode of discourse to which he nevertheless denies all validity in the *Laws*?*

This question will remain open: Plato has been cited here only as a privileged witness of the hold exerted by the funeral oration over the Athenian thinkers of the city, however subtle they may be. Beyond their differences, "objective" history and philosophical history at least come together when they speak of Athens or of the polis, in the same wish to silence the funeral oration or to compete with it: in a polemical or ambiguous way, they have a relationship to that form of discourse, perhaps because both take it seriously, believing that it offers an access to Athens that, however inadequate or dangerous, nevertheless has meaning and effect. Furthermore, an adversary who is already in place is probably not exorcised so easily.

Comic Parody and Platonic Pastiche: Two Antidotes Against a Fascination

Perhaps the only way of ridding oneself of the funeral oration would be to *put it at a distance*, by showing behind its fine words the inanity of certain grandiloquent propositions: humor is liberating,[113] and there can be no doubt that such a distancing would free the Athenians from Athens — provided that the Athenian citizen was able to wrest himself from the charms of narcissism.

By its nature and by its object — the risible, which is "part of the ugly"† — comedy seems destined to empty of their meaning the fine words of the inner theater of Athens. Within the necessarily narrow limits established by its status as an Athenian genre, it actually fulfills this role with regard to tragedy, and it is to be expected that it would also attack the funeral oration, peopled as it is like tragedy with "larger-than-life men."‡ Everything seems to

* *Laws* 3.686b–687d.
† Aristotle, *Poetics* 1449a32–33.
‡ *Ibid.* 1448a17–18.

suggest this: its character as an institutional parody, the freedom with which it can play on words and on the multiple registers of language, and its public — the same Athenian demos that the funeral oration confirms in its private convictions and that only comedy can bring back to earth.

Yet ancient comedy never attacks the funeral oration explicitly. Is this strange reticence to be explained by the repugnance felt by the comic authors toward evoking the death of their fellow citizens?[114] In no case must this silence be attributed to indifference: the comic poets have too many grievances against the official ideology to be content to ignore it, and, without attacking the funeral oration head-on, they adopt an indirect strategy that ridicules the essential themes of the oration one by one.

Between the funeral oration, a military speech that situates valor in death, and Aristophanes's comedy, keen to denounce any bellicosity, the relationship can only have been one of irreconcilable hostility. Unconvinced by the theories that made the peasant the prototype of the soldier, Aristophanes, a friend of country people, rejects any exaltation of the hoplite,[115] preferring to the fine death the struggle waged by each individual "to save his own skin."[116]* In the same spirit, Aristophanean comedy tries to defuse the patriotic tirades of tragedy; *The Acharnians* presents the critical, pacifist obverse of the *Heraclidae*;[117] Dicaeopolis, the antihero who is determined "to save his own skin,"[118]† is resolutely deaf to all the glorious topoi on which Macaria bases her conduct.‡ But Aristophanes is not content to attack — once again — Euripidean tragedy; perhaps he also takes on the military institutions themselves: summoning as witnesses of rediscovered peace "the vines, the young fig trees, and plants of every kind,"§ is he not reversing the ephebic oath, a hoplitic oath transformed, in peasant fashion, into a hymn to Peace?[119] Last, Aristophanes usually likes to ridi-

---

* Aristophanes, *Frogs* 190: literally, fighting "to save one's meat."

† Aristophanes, *Acharnians* 357.

‡ Euripides, *Heraclidae* 518 and 533.

§ *Peace* 596–98. Cf. *Acharnians* 995–99.

cule the official version of Athenian history, and when, like all the other comic writers of the fifth century, he makes fun of the political harangues and the flights of fine words on Marathon,* it is highly likely that the funeral oration is included in this overall condemnation of war oratory.

As praise of Athens, on the other hand, the epitaphioi are much more overtly attacked. Whereas Pericles's epitaphios invites the Athenians to fall in love with the city, Aristophanean comedy tries to put them on their guard against the trap of using such a passionate vocabulary in political life.[120] Of course the authors of the epitaphioi do not declare their love to the people outright, as the demagogues do,† but for Aristophanes the worst demagoguery lies perhaps in making the citizens in love with themselves through the love they have for the city.

A resolute enemy of all unconsidered praise,[121] the comic poet therefore attacks any eulogy of Athens that flatters the citizens' latent narcissism.‡ One must, at any price, protect the Athenians from the delights of smugness; so, in the parabasis of *The Acharnians*, Aristophanes offers himself as an antidote to such excessive praise: without unduly flattering his compatriots, he will teach them the best.§

But one still has to get oneself heard by this Demos that prefers unconditional praise to lessons in morality. Because laughter, which frees one from fascination, is the most effective weapon of criticism, the comic poet has no other strategy by which to educate than ridicule. One must make the Athenians laugh at the praise that they are so happy to address to the city and to the democratic system, both on the tragic stage and on the speaker's platform of the demosion sema. Thus, when Eupolis, after challenging

* *Knights* 782. Cf. Hermippus, frag. 81 Kock.
† *Acharnians* 143; *Knights* 732–34 and 1340–44.
‡ Aristophanes, *Acharnians* 370–72 ("I know our country people, I know what pleasure they take in hearing the city and themselves praised [*eulogein*]"). Compare Pericles's use of *eulogia* (Thucydides 2.42.1).
§ *Acharnians* 656–58.

isegoria, pretends to congratulate the polis for giving rights to "a very poor specimen of a man,"* it is difficult not to evoke in counterpoint the declarations of Pericles or of Theseus in *The Suppliant Women*.[122†] An epitaphios, a patriotic tragedy: of these two very Athenian genres, which is the target here? It is difficult to decide, but this example may remind us that without inventing a new strategy, the comic writers knew how to use against the funeral oration the redoubtable weapon that they had forged against tragedy, namely parody.

Tragedy remains the principal target of ancient comedy; this is quite clear in Aristophanes, for whom parody is often synonymous with paratragedy.[123] But the poet also knows how to make fun of the eulogy of Athens by reducing the praise to a few high-flown words. Let us, then, examine the relationship that is established in parody between laughter and praise.

Instead of making a frontal attack on an official oration that the Athenians were fond of, the comic poet, with cunning intelligence, turns against themselves this "strong discourse" and its dominant topoi. He has his reasons for adopting such a strategy. The task of the official orator is easy, since no praise seems excessive to an audience that he is confirming in its ideal being.[‡] All he has to do, then, so as not to offend this collective narcissism, is banish from his discourse all praise of an individual. To get himself heard by this Demos, which is both the audience and the principal object of the comedy,[124§] the comic poet must, on the contrary, use indirect means. Finding himself necessarily in a contradictory — if not oppositional — position with regard to the values currently revered by the people,[125] he cannot attack head-on so haughty an audience as the Athenian demos, or at least he must

* Eupolis frags. 291–92 Kock.

† Thucydides 2.37.1; Euripides, *Suppliant Women* 437 and 441–42.

‡ This is the reproach addressed to him by both Aristophanes (cf. *Acharnians* 369–74) and Plato (*Menexenus* 235d4–7).

§ *Knights* illustrates this definition in exemplary fashion by making Demos the central character of the comedy.

make it believe that he cannot do so, which amounts to the same thing. So Aristophanes turns attention away from the demos by innumerable attacks on individuals who otherwise would never have entered posterity. But this is the least of the tricks available to comedy. There are other, more subtle ones, by which it sheltered behind official discourse in order to mock it the more effectively. Like Cratinus and Eupolis, Aristophanes does tell the Athenians what he has to tell them, but by the path of paradox: through an astonishing reversal, praise becomes the weapon of criticism. To reach his target, he sometimes has only to defuse the eulogy by taking it at its word. Thus, in *The Acharnians*, he gives concrete meaning to the adjective *liparai*, and the "brilliant Athens" of Pindar becomes "gleaming" Athens. What spectator could still take pride in an adjective "suitable to sardines"?[126]* Similarly, by substituting *karpousthai tēn Hellada* (making use of Greece) for *karpousthai ta tōn allōn anthrōpōn* (*agatha*) (enjoying the goods of the whole world),† Aristophanes transforms a quasi-autarkic enjoyment[127] into plunder on a vast scale and reveals the reality of the imperialism behind the abstractions so dear to Pericles's epitaphios.[128]

Thus the funeral oration reappears, but led astray, diverted from its primary function to the benefit of comic ridicule, and it becomes easier to understand why Aristophanes and Eupolis wrote so many caricatures of the eulogy of Athens: *by turning it against itself, they neutralized it.* This is often the role of comic parabasis.[129]

In this way, the anapests of *Knights* follow a eulogy of the Athenians of earlier times that could well appear in an epitaphios.‡ But no sooner delivered, the praise turns, contrary to all the norms of the funeral oration, into an attack on present-day democracy. Confiscated by the knights, who alone defended the city and the national gods without pay§ and who offer themselves

---

* *Acharnians* 639–40.

† Compare here *Wasps* 520 and Thucydides 2.38.2.

‡ Aristophanes, *Knights* 565–68.

§ *Ibid.* 576–77 (an echo of 566, devoted to the fathers).

as the only true servants of the state, the eulogy unmasks the corrupt strategoi of the Athens of 424.* Similarly the invocation to Pallas that opens the second half-chorus† — the fervor of which is unequaled except by that of the great chorus in *Clouds*‡ – serves as a prelude to the mock-serious eulogy of the horses.§ The latter replaces the praise of the knights but definitively robs the restive strategoi of all honor, showing them to have been less zealous in their duty than these noble animals.**

However, parody never lacks ambiguity, and in ancient comedy the eulogy of Athens is not always a caricature. It is permissible to praise Athens provided that the reference is to the past: a pretext for great speeches Marathon is also for Eupolis the symbol of a virtuous city, that of Miltiades and Myronides.†† Similarly, whereas in *The Acharnians* Aristophanes ridicules the brilliant Athens, crowned with violets, to which Pindar sings his praises, he exalts it at the end of *Knights*‡‡ deserving of condemnation when addressed to the present-day city, praise becomes meaningful when addressed to the old Athens.§§ Thus, with a touch of cynical humor, he can praise Demos as "worthy of the city and of the trophy of Marathon."*** A fragment of the *Georgoi* shows that Aristophanes was also capable of celebrating the autochthonous city††† with exemplary fervor. Thus the comic poet did not refrain altogether from praise, provided there was good reason for it: in such

* *Ibid.* 573–76.

† *Ibid.* 581–94.

‡ *Clouds* 299–313.

§ *Knights* 595–610.

** Compare the behavior of the strategoi in 576 and that of the horses in 602–604.

†† Eupolis, frag. 90 Kock (*Demoi*).

‡‡ *Knights* 1329.

§§ *Ibid.* 1327.

*** *Ibid.* 1334.

††† Aristophanes, frag. 110 Kock (*Georgoi*): "Dear city of Cecrops, issue of your own soil, I salute thee, brilliant country, breast of a valorous earth."

a case, praise, delivered in the unreal mode, tried to provoke the people to a healthy indignation and a return to the past.*

Accordingly, it is not easy, in a comic eulogy of Athens, to distinguish between the respective shares of the comic and of the eulogy. A half-chorus of *Wasps* is proof: the Athenian Wasps, calling to their aid autochthony, themes of civic responsibility and courage, the memory of the Persian Wars, the topos of the universal recognition of Athenian merit, and the claim of the right to arche,† certainly seem for a time to speak for the city, just as their leader expresses himself in anapests on behalf of the poet.‡ Of course Aristophanes is not taken in by the Athenian old men, even when they declare their intention of pursuing the parasitic hornets:§ proud of their sting, the Wasps remain more pettifoggers than warriors, and their last word is for the triobol.** But in a half-chorus, Athenian autochthony has been celebrated in a splendid mixture of humor and patriotism.

Thus not only does Aristophanes use topoi that he vigorously condemns when the orators use them, but in his work parody is not always easily distinguishable from seriousness.[130] Is this because one could not turn the praise of Athens against itself with impunity? The *Birds* certainly seems to bear this out; there the burlesque eulogy, the reactionary themes, and the satire on the official funeral†† lead to the creation of an ideal city that is ultimately —

---

* Thus, on two occasions in *Wasps*, Bdelycleon uses an epitaphios theme to shake Philocleon. In 678, the reminder of the sufferings of war contrasts with the miserable status of the demos, and in 710 the name Marathon punctuates the description of happiness, impossible under the demagogues.

† *Ibid.* 1060–90; autochthony: 1076; courage: 1076; civic spirit: 1076–77; Persian Wars: 1081–83 (Marathon) and 1086–87 (Salamis); topos of Athens recognized by the others: 1089–90; claim of the right to arche: 1098–1101.

‡ *Wasps* 1015–59.

§ *Ibid.* 1114–21.

**Ibid.* 1121.

†† *Birds* 36–38: burlesque eulogy; 44: *topon apragmona* (reactionary criterion: cf. Thucydides 2.40.2); 395ff.: satire on the official burial.

like any utopia — nothing more than the obverse of the real polis.[131]* This city, praised for being another Athens, an Athens that knows "Quietude,"† is nevertheless constituted solely in relation to the Athenian model,[132]‡ since it must still defend itself against the accusation of slipping into aristocracy and since the mere idea of calling it Sparta is rejected with horror.§ Cloud-Cuckoo-Land, the anti-Athens, nevertheless preserves all the features of the real city, since it experiences bitter political struggles** that accord ill with the patronage of the goddess Hesychia.

Comic fiction aims at reversing roles and making a new model from the copy: men — Athenians, of course — become for a time the zealous imitators of the birds,†† becoming metics of the new polis,‡‡ a paradoxical situation for Athenians. But to express the universal admiration aroused by the aerial city, Aristophanes finds no other language than the one that the epitaphioi wear out celebrating the city. Not only does this new Athens realize the secret project of Pericles's epitaphios in delivering men forever from Laconomania,§§ but this brilliant city, immediately endowed with the highest renown,*** arouses in its admirers the love that Pericles professes for Athens.††† This is now a legitimate passion no doubt: nevertheless, the reappearance of the vocabulary of passion, the Athenian use of which was ridiculed in *Knights*,

* *Birds* 725ff.: everything that is shameful in Athens is beautiful for the Birds.
† *Ibid.* 1320.
‡ Thus, in the prayers, the name of the inhabitants of Chios is joined with that of the inhabitants of Cloud-Cuckoo-Land, just as it is with that of the Athenians in the decrees (*ibid.* 878–80).
§ *Ibid.* 124–25 and 815.
** *Ibid.* 1583–84.
†† *Ibid.* 1276ff.
‡‡ *Ibid.* 1319: *metoikein.*
§§ *Ibid.* 1280–81. Compare 1285 (the Birds are universally imitated) and Thucydides 2.37.1 (the Athenians are a model and not imitators).
*** *Birds* 826, 921, 957, 1277.
††† Compare Thucydides 2.43.1 and *Birds* 1279 and 1316.

constitutes a phenomenon that is ambiguous, to say the least.

There is, then, only a narrow gap between eulogy and parody, and the relationship between ancient comedy and the topoi of the funeral oration is not exempt from all fascination. However, despite these inevitable ambiguities, parody constitutes perhaps the only possible critical attitude for an Athenian confronted by the praise of Athens, in that it plays with the narcissistic mirage. So it is in comedy that Plato seeks an effective weapon, when he devotes a dialogue to demystifying the funeral oration.

The philosopher is greatly indebted to ancient comedy, not only for a number of images[133] but also for a method to undermine, or at least achieve distance from, the eulogy of Athens, as the prologue to the *Menexenus*, with its fairly obvious references to Aristophanean comedy, makes clear.

To begin with, Aristophanes's definition of the bad eulogy as praise addressed rightly or wrongly to the city and to the citizens by an impostor* might serve as an epigraph to this Platonic dialogue. Furthermore, in accusing the epitaphioi of flattering the Athenians in order to transport them in imagination to the Islands of the Blessed, the philosopher borrows a passage from *Wasps* in which the chorus, charmed by Philocleon's words, declares that it has "grown while listening to them and imagined myself to be *dikast* in the Islands of the Blessed."† Of course, Plato changes register, substituting the atmosphere of the demosion sema for the pettifogging coloration proper to Aristophanes; but, like the comic poet's, his attack is directed mainly at Athenian narcissism: Socrates feels confirmed in his being by the oration, just as the old men are by Philocleon's words. In fact, there is not a single element that Plato does not borrow from Aristophanes: the exhaustible character of the speech of self-celebration,‡ the depiction of the illusions

* *Acharnians* 372–73.

† *Menexenus* 235a6–b3 and 235c4–5; *Wasps* 636–41.

‡ Compare Aristophanes 636–37 ("as he knew how to say everything without omitting anything") and Plato 235a3–4 ("they celebrate ... in every way").

of grandeur that overcome the audience,* the euphoric effect of eloquence,† the imaginary voyage to the Islands of the Blessed.‡ This last feature is the most important of all, for its presence in both texts shows that Plato plagiarized Aristophanes quite explicitly and deliberately.[134] For Plato as for Aristophanes, the Islands of the Blessed are the final stage of the voyage of death or the non-place of Utopia. But the philosopher also knows that the comic writers are fond of playing on the many uses of *makar* (blessed). When they do not figure in comic expressions in which death is a source of humor,§ *makar* and its derivatives frequently govern mock-serious ceremonies, such as the marriages that conclude Aristophanes's plays,** and exalt — ironically or seriously? — the city or the demos.††

Thus Plato ridicules the funeral oration with the words of comedy. From the opening of the dialogue, he borrows from the comic poets the weapons of parody, and this strategy is deliberate: parody is the only effective weapon against the mirage of the epitaphioi. But Plato goes further than Aristophanes and systematically carries the comics' fragmentary, ambiguous criticism of the oration to its logical conclusion. Thus we return to the *Menexenus*, seen not only as a dialogue on the funeral oration but also as the only work of the classical period devoted explicitly to exorcising the official oration.

---

* "I grew on hearing it" (637–38): see *Menexenus* 235b1–2 ("I remain under the spell when listening to them, imagining myself at once to have grown taller").

† The pleasure of listening to the orator (641) is the general theme of the prologue of the *Menexenus* (for example 235b7–8).

‡ *En makarōn nēsois dikazein* (639–40) is transformed into *en makarōn nēsois oikein* (235c4–5).

§ *Knights* 1151; cf. Plato, *Hippias Major* 293a.

** *Peace* 1333, *Birds* 1721 and 1759; for the relationship between *makar* and the divine or magic, see also *Knights* 1387, *Plutus* 655, *Clouds* 307, *Peace* 780 and 1075, *Birds* 222, 702, 703, 899.

†† *Thesmophoriazusae* 1112: "O happy [*makarios*] people, O fortunate land" (but the servant woman who is speaking is drunk); cf. also 558: "Happy [*makaria*] is the city and forever" (when women finally have power); *Wasps* 5550: "What happiness, what felicity can be greater than that of a dikast?" *Knights* 157: "happy Athens."

Against the funeral oration, Plato sets up Socrates; against the official oration, the man who, among the orators of the fourth century, breaks the charm of all the civic celebrations.[135] We must now elucidate the meaning of this confrontation that brings these two parties together in a trial in which only Socrates speaks, since the funeral oration itself borrows his voice, but in which the Athenian oration is tirelessly questioned. Abandoning all his principles, Socrates delivers a logos politikos in the *Menexenus*, and this circumstance, unique in Plato's work, indicates the importance of what is at stake: if he has chosen the funeral oration as his target, it is because in the epitaphioi the city recognizes itself as it wishes to be. The *Menexenus*, then, is a minor dialogue only for those who fail to see in the funeral oration its character as civic discourse. We will not reopen the debate concerning its authenticity,[136] which a more demanding reading of the text might have avoided. Here we shall simply elucidate the method by which Plato rejects the funeral oration in and by his words, subjecting to the corrosive force of irony the solemn identity of an oration whose relationship with Socratic speech is one of opposition, if not of absolute otherness.

Retaining in his definition of the funeral oration only its character as epainos,* Socrates attacks it as a eulogy: a eulogy without surprise, since the orations are as interchangeable as the orators, pseudo scholars always ready to crank out yet another composition.† Thus from the outset, Plato reveals his intention of attacking the funeral oration by means of its own themes: by insisting on the absence of improvisation in the orations,‡ he is not content to echo the ideas of Alcidamas, the theoretician of *autoschediazein*,[137] but he utterly destroys the well-known topos of the

---

* It is first included in the category of *kalon* (*Menexenus* 234c1), and Socrates insistently exhausts the semantic field of *epainos* in order to define it: 234c4, 234c5, 234c6, 235a3, 235a6.

† *Ibid.* 234c4–6.

‡ *Ibid.* 234c5–6: the orators "do not praise at random but in speeches prepared well in advance."

shortness of the time allowed to prepare it. So Socrates can declare that in the epitaphioi, praise is not accorded indiscriminately (*ouk eikei*). Does this mean, however, that the funeral oration conforms to the imperative assigned to good eloquence in the *Gorgias:* never to speak at random but always to have a particular aim in mind?* To believe this would be to allow ourselves to be misled by the use of the same term in both texts.

Here begins a subtle game in which the funeral oration, already set in contradiction with its own topoi, is compared with fine eloquence only to be rejected all the more thoroughly. Perhaps the author of an epitaphios imitates the good orator, but he does so badly: the first bases his words on an ideal model; the second seeks above all to shine and, with little concern for the truth, conforms only to the conventions of the genre. Accusing the civic orators of "giving to each person the qualities that belong to him and those that are foreign to him," Plato takes delight in writing a pastiche of Gorgias's epitaphios,† and this borrowing is not the result of mere chance: in the philosopher's eyes, the funeral oration is an instance of bad rhetoric, symbolized by the Sophist and attacked in the *Gorgias.* Moreover, the criterion of good eloquence has been applied to it only derisively;[138] *ouk eikei* must be read as an antiphrasis and it is *eikēi epainounton* that must be understood: prepared entirely in advance, the oration has no trace of improvisation, yet it distributes its praise at random.

As eulogy, the funeral oration falls, then, under the general criticism of the epainos or encomiastic genre[139] as it is formulated in the *Symposium.* But whereas the fine eulogy‡ is opposed, like a caricature, to the true eulogy,§ the funeral oration is entirely on the bad side, since on two occasions it is termed *kalos epainos.* Not only does Socrates reproach the orators for "praising beautifully"; the epitaphios he delivers also refers to itself as a fine

---

* *Gorgias* 503d6–7.

† *Menexenus* 234a1. Compare with the first lines of Gorgias's epitaphios.

‡ *Symposium* 198d8.

§ Or to the truth of the eulogy (*ibid.* 198d7).

eulogy.* The presence of this simple expression at the heart of the oration invalidates any attempt to take it seriously.

The fine epitaphios takes pride in the deceptive seduction of a highly colored language.† This systematic search for the fine effect, which Isocrates, followed by Aristotle,‡ considers necessary in the encomiastic genre, is for Plato the very sign of the pernicious vacuity of language that derives its beauty only from words.§ *Nothing but words*: that, for Plato, is the fundamental vice of the funeral oration. This redundancy is contrasted, throughout the philosopher's work, with a "Socratic style," which knows no law but the demands of truth.[140]**

Like every eulogy, then, the funeral oration is in opposition to Socratic speech. But through both its effects and its function, it sins against truth even more dangerously than other forms of eulogy. Indeed, if all erroneous praise is reprehensible in that it maintains its public in error, the funeral oration, strengthened by its status as official discourse, exercises its pernicious influence on the whole Athenian polis. Thus the criticism of the epitaphioi achieves its true dimension, for what is at issue here is essentially politics. In attacking the funeral oration, Plato is again taking on Athenian democracy, and in one of its most solemn practices. Democratic is the rule that gives the poor man a magnificent tomb and accords a fine speech to the commonplace man redeemed by a fine death.[141]†† Democratic also is the collective character of the epitaphioi: for all, the same destiny, for all, the same oration; and against this egalitarianism the advocate of geometric equality protests. Furthermore, democratic is the interchangeable character of the orators and that rotation of offices by virtue of which the epitaphios is delivered in turn by all the

---

* *Menexenus* 234c6 and 239d5.

† *Ibid.* 235a2.

‡ Isocrates, *Evagoras* 8 and *Panathenaicus* 246; Aristotle, *Rhetoric* 3.1416b25.

§ *Phaedrus* 234e7–8.

** Cf. *Apology* 17b7–c2 and *Symposium* 199b4–5.

†† *Menexenus* 234c2–4.

politicians in sight.[142] Finally, delivered to all equally, this oration, as a political speech, knows no distinctions, and thus sets itself in opposition to Socratic speech, which is concerned with difference and singularity.[143]

In this criticism of the funeral oration, there is more than a mere denunciation of democracy. Opposed in their aims, the funeral oration and the Socratic dialogue are strangely similar in the effect of bewitchment that they produce on their audience,* and the two fascinations have too much in common not to be in competition. In the *Menexenus*, the funeral oration seems to win: is not Socrates the enchanter subjected to the charms that he usually exercises over others? But this reversal of roles is really no more than a theatrical effect and thus probably the result of a conscious plan that we should examine.

The narcissistic ecstasy into which Socrates is plunged reveals in the first instance the disturbing power of a speech capable of immobilizing and filling with imaginary content an individual who wishes to be as empty and infertile as a midwife. This is not a unique case: on several occasions in Plato's oeuvre, Socrates, before speaking himself, pretends to have been transported, even possessed, by someone else's speech, including those of Protagoras, Agathon, Lysias, Anytus, Meletus, and Lykon.† In fact, therefore, it is a procedure intended to indicate in advance the irreducible difference between two types of speech. But in the hierarchy of the speeches criticized by Socrates, the funeral oration, officially assured of the unanimous assent of the citizens, occupies a special place; consequently, it has a right to an unusually long commentary, in which its similarities with Socratic speech are clearly suggested. These similarities are ignored by those who, wishing to preserve at all cost the absolute difference of the Socratic figure, insist only on the opposition between two modes of discourse.[144]

* As the laments of Meno (*Meno* 80a3) and Agathon (*Symposium* 194a4) show.

† *Protagoras* 328d3–7; *Symposium* 198a–c; *Phaedrus* 234d1–6; *Apology* 17a1–3.

We must study these similarities if we wish to appreciate the profound difference between the two kinds of speech.

The similarity becomes clear in all its complexity if we compare the text of the *Menexenus* with one of the principal passages in the *Symposium*, namely Alcibiades's praise of Socrates. Socrates delivers a poisoned eulogy, of the epitaphioi, and Alcibiades praises the Socratic figure in an ambiguous way: Socrates the charmer responds to Socrates charmed.* Both instances are examples of rhetorical effect, the extraordinary effect exercised on an exceptional public — Alcibiades is no more an ordinary listener than is Socrates — and, by way of verification, on an undifferentiated, anonymous audience, made up of strangers and idlers, the crowd of Socrates's interlocutors.† Socrates is a flutist without a flute, who enchants "without an instrument, with naked words"‡ but the funeral oration, also made up of naked words, is, in its resonance, flute music as well.§ Like the funeral oration, Socrates, to get hold of his listeners' minds, must first take possession of their ears.** So, through innumerable variations on the theme of speech and hearing, the two texts sketch out a pathology of the effects of the logos,†† characterized by the lightning suddenness‡‡ with which the listener is transported into ecstatic enthusiasm.§§ In fact, the result is much the same, or at least might be so: having become *gennaios* (noble), Socrates is immobilized on the spot in a dream of immortality; Alcibiades, for his part, dreams of "lying down beside this character

* Socrates bewitched: *Menexenus* 235b1 (*kēloumenos*); Socrates the charmer: *Symposium* 215c1 (compared with Marsyas, whose flute spellbound — *ekēlei* — whoever heard it).

† *Menexenus* 235b5–6; *Symposium* 215e2–3; both contain the expression *ta auta paschein*.

‡ *Symposium* 215b8 (*ouk auletes*) and 215c8 (*psilois logois*).

§ *Menexenus* 239c1 (*logoi psiloi*) and 235c1–2 (*enaulos*).

** *Ibid.* 235c2, *Symposium* 216a1 and 216a7.

†† *Paschein: Menexenus* 235b6; *Symposium* 215d8, d9, e3, e5.

‡‡ *Menexenus* 235b2 and 5; *Symposium* 215d6.

§§ *Symposium* 215d8.

and growing old there"* and must summon all his energy to tear himself away from this nascent paralysis. Both experiences end in a difficult awakening. But the resemblance then turns into opposition: Socrates comes back to himself; Alcibiades loses himself.†

The imposture of the funeral oration revealed in this comparison lies not so much in the immediacy of its effect[145] as in its uncertain duration: its action is both long and short, since in the end it dissipates; it is even more ephemeral than the gardens of Adonis.[146]‡ Alcibiades's flight, on the other hand, shows that Socratic speech operates at a different level. So as not to allow an immediate effect to be transformed into a lasting action, avoiding conversion to the *bios philosophikos* and repeating in reverse the apologue of Herakles,[147] Alcibiades takes off like a slave in flight.[148]§ To the funeral oration, with its power of oblivion, is opposed Socrates's speech, which awakens the Athenian from his satisfied sleep, revealing the void beneath the fine appearance. Whereas the orators awaken to an imaginary nobility, Alcibiades is filled with shame before Socrates alone,** and this brilliant politician perceives servile dispositions in himself†† and quickly understands that life ought no longer to be livable for him.‡‡ Since, to escape Socrates, one has no other choice but flight, the opposition becomes more precise and more varied: Socrates may recover from hearing an epitaphios, but his words, and his alone, no one forgets. This difference is fundamental.

Yet the dissimilarity does not win an unambiguous victory, for a new series of links, more secret and more tenuous, woven between the *Menexenus* and the *Symposium*, continues to connect

* *Ibid.* 216a8.

† *Menexenus* 235c3; *Symposium* 216b5.

‡ *Phaedrus* 276b3–5 (the gardens of Adonis last for at least eight days).

§ *Symposium* 216b5: *drapeteuo.*

** *Ibid.* 216b2, 3, 6.

†† *Andrapododos diakeimenou* (*ibid.* 215e6) is precisely opposed to *gennaios diatithemai* (*Menexenus* 235a7).

‡‡ *Symposium* 216a5.

the funeral oration to Socratic speech. Indeed, from one text to the other, a confrontation, sometimes explicit, sometimes simply suggested, but always legible, operates between Socrates and Pericles, between the "energumen,"[149] whose words disturb, and the politician, whose speeches inflate the self-importance of his audience in an unhealthy way.*

It is in Menexenus that, unknown to himself, this confrontation first takes place. Bearing the same name as one of Socrates's sons, Menexenus does not understand that his name ought to lead him to wisdom,[150] but, like Alcibiades, of whom he is a pale copy,[151] he wants to run Athens and abandons "education and philosophy"† — much more naively, it is true, than Alcibiades, for whom the rival poles of philosophy and politics are explicitly embodied in Socrates and Pericles — a difficult struggle between two kinships, spiritual and physical.

But one figure links these two texts more closely still: Pericles, both evoked by and invoked against Socrates. Pericles is undoubtedly one target of the *Menexenus*, in which Socrates names him twice, as a pupil of Aspasia and as the author of the epitaphios of which he uses fragments;‡ indeed, as a number of reminiscences and allusions show,[152] the epitaphios that he delivers in Thucydides is a model and a foil for the Platonic text.[153] In the *Symposium*, on the other hand, when Alcibiades contrasts Socrates with the traditional orators, Pericles is the only one he allows to emerge from the anonymous crowd of "other good orators";§ perhaps he is already present in the person of "the first-class orator" whose words are powerless to counterbalance those of Socrates.**

Of course, the kinship that links Pericles to Alcibiades counts

---

* *Gorgias* 515b–d and 518e3–5.

† *Menexenus* 235a5.

‡ *Ibid.* 235e7 and 236b5–6.

§ *Symposium* 215e4. Compare with *Menexenus* 235e5–7 (Pericles, among the *agathoi rhetores* trained by Aspasia, is "the first of Greece").

** *Symposium* 215d2; in the *Phaedrus*, Pericles is cited as a perfect example of the political orator (269e1–2).

for much in this ambiguous reference, both eulogistic, since Pericles is the only one capable of opposing Socrates, and depreciative, since his speeches can do nothing against this devil. But there is more to it than this: in Pericles, it is the political orator that is being attacked — he whose speech was a sting,* he whom the Athenians, as the comic writers show on many occasions, regarded as the symbol of all eloquence past and to come.† More precisely, he is the author of two epitaphioi[154] and the one who, for his oration at Samos, was crowned as he descended from the speaker's platform‡ as Socrates is crowned by Alcibiades. Thus, alone in being cited against Socrates because he alone is capable of producing in his audience an effect that, though incommensurable and inferior, is nevertheless similar, combining the eloquence of an exceptional orator and the power of every epitaphios, Pericles is no doubt that first-class orator whose "other speeches"§ sought in vain to measure up to Socrates's speech. If this reading of the *Symposium* is correct, if for "the first-class orator" we may substitute the name Pericles, then perhaps the "other speeches" are essentially epitaphioi; in which case, the funeral oration, silently evoked outside the *Menexenus*, is designated as *allos logos* in relation to Socratic speech. Other — that is, both different and similar, and therefore in competition.

The funeral oration does not simply compete with Socratic speech in its effects; it also speaks the same language as Socrates; both discuss virtue and immortality. The whole morality of the funeral oration may be condensed into the synonymy of *thanatos* and *aretē*: the orators call the soldier's death virtue and Aspasia is content to apply their criteria when, after praising the dead for not abandoning their posts, she accords them the title of andres agathoi and presents them as models of virtue (*aristoi*).** But the

* Eupolis, frag. 94 Kock; cf. *Comica adespota* 10.
† Eupolis, frags. 95–96.
‡ Plutarch, *Pericles* 28.4–5.
§ *Symposium* 215d1–2.
** *Menexenus* 246b4–6.

substitution of *aretē* for *thanatos* is particularly pernicious in Plato's eyes, since he is trying, through Socrates's teaching, to give the term *agathos* another meaning than "devoted to the polis" or "dead in battle."

It is not that one must abandon one's devotion to the city; Socrates's life would be sufficient proof to the contrary. Despite original aspects of his teaching that were to weigh heavily in the final judgment of the Athenians,[155] he was on the whole faithful to the principal civic norms.[156] Similarly, faithful to the Socratic example, Plato criticizes Athens without ever rejecting her, and although, in the *Laches*, he challenges the hoplitic definition of war, he does not for a moment envisage relieving the warrior of the *Republic* from his duty to die at his post. But long before writing the *Laws*, in which he reserved the highest posthumous honors for the euthynoi alone,[157]* the philosopher considers true praise a serious matter, crowning a fine life and not only a fine death.† Therefore, he must denounce false resemblances[158] by attacking Athenian practice on its own ground; in a society in which praise is accorded only to the dead, the height of error still consists in attributing it to oneself during one's lifetime. One then feels invested with an incomparable dignity, but this dignity, which is merely a matter of outward show, contrasts strangely with the usual mode of being of Socrates the Silenus, grotesque in appearance but filled with inner wisdom — a not very "spectacular" model of *kalokagathia*.[159]‡ Plato gives a name to this void surrounded by solemnity: paralyzed by illusions of grandeur, Socrates is *semnos*.§

Sēmnos is an apparently praiseworthy term, but in reality it is charged with pejorative overtones, and every *sēmnotēs* seems ambiguous, even if it is that of a god.[160] This term is known to tragedy and history,[161] but it is particularly dear to the language of

* *Laws* 2.922a and 12.947b–e.
† Cf. *Republic* 10.607a4; *Laws* 7.801e6–10.
‡ Cf. *Symposium* 216d5–7 and 221e–226a6.
§ *Menexenus* 235d4 and 235b8.

comedy, in which it designates the caricature of greatness, grand airs, pride.[162] The negative connotation of *semnos* and of its derivatives (*semnos, semnunein, semnunesthai*) is clear in Plato: in twenty-nine uses of these terms, there are up to twenty-eight that are ironic or pejorative,[163] which leaves very little margin for a really positive meaning. For the philosopher, semnotes reveals the outcropping of some moral and dialectical defect in external behavior: ignorance, deliberate rejection of correct discrimination, or the inability to distinguish correctly between the same and the other, the true and the false. The deficient person wishes to be different and, as it were, of a superior essence; he takes himself for something other than he is, and this imaginary importance is expressed in a stiff, formal manner, frequently associated with self-importance (*chaunotēs*).* So it would be risky to take at face value the sudden "access of grandeur"[164] that seizes Socrates when he hears an epitaphios: confirmation comes from comparing this bogus majesty with some other Platonic examples of semnotes.

Immobilized by the orators' words, Socrates remains petrified and serious, like the Parmenidean Being, which the Sophist describes as "without a life or force of its own, solemn [*semnos*] and sacred,"† and which makes possible nothing but repetition.‡ This insipid solemnity passes off grand airs for greatness, and, without seeing that Socrates is *giving himself airs*, the strangers immediately accord him more importance than before. Semnos, Socrates believes himself, like all his fellow citizens, to be superior to the rest of mankind and struts about before the xenoi, committing the same error in discrimination as the crane who, in the *Statesman*, opposes the "genus crane" to the rest of the world in order to glorify himself all the more:§ is not the aim of the funeral oration to render the city "more admirable" (*thaumasiotera*) by opposing it to the rest of mankind?

A dignity nourished on the tirelessly reiterated account of the

* For example, in *Theaetetus* 175b4 or *Sophist* 227b6.
† *Sophist* 249a1.
‡ *Parmenides* 128e3.
§ *Statesman* 263a7.

ancestors' exploits, Socrates's semnotes is ridiculous. To give oneself such airs is to condemn oneself to saying nothing new, to always repeating oneself, just as the writing and the painted beings of the *Phaedrus*, who meet every question with a solemn silence that is composed of sempiternal repetition of the same answer.[165]* Similarly, Socrates, having become semnos, can only repeat his greatness, his nobility, and his beauty, over more than three days, and this pitiful self-importance is a mirror of the hollow splendor of the oration.

In attributing an attack of semnotes to Socrates the listener-to-epitaphioi, Plato designates the funeral oration as a source and locus of semnotes: to produce such a transformation in the subtlest of Athenians, the oration must contain a good dose of redundant majesty.

But the figure — strange in Plato's work — of semnos Socrates not only helps to denounce the emptiness of the epitaphioi. It is also used to less obvious ends, in the service of Socrates's interminable apologia that carries through from one dialogue to another: it becomes a war machine against an adversary, Aristophanes, whose vocabulary Plato borrows without acknowledgment in order to neutralize it the better. *Semnos* is not only a word deriving from the comic register; in it are concentrated all the accusations that Athenian comedy, represented principally by Aristophanes, launches against Socrates. Characterized, like all philosophers, by pretentious gravity, Socrates walks the streets of Athens with an air of importance that Aristophanes finds extremely irritating† and that the comic writer Callias accuses him of passing on to his disciples.[166]‡ Plato replies to these attacks in the *Symposium* with a mock-serious portrait of the diabolical Silenus.[167]§ But he also responds to them

---

* *Phaedrus* 275d6.

† Aristophanes, *Clouds* 362–63. Socrates is serious and important like the clouds, which are also *semnai* (265, 291, 314, 364).

‡ Callias, frag. 12 Kock (*Pedetai*). Euripides, proud of his "Sophist education," is full of contempt for his fellow citizens, mimicking in this Socrates's behavior.

§ *Symposium* 215b, 216e, 221d–222a (*semnos* inverted into *geloios*).

indirectly in the *Menexenus*, by substituting the arrogance of a speech for that of an individual: Socrates is not semnos by himself, and therefore could not puff up his disciples with a false grandeur that he himself did not possess; he becomes semnos only temporarily and under the effects of the epitaphioi whose gravity he borrows.

By thus shifting the accusation onto the funeral oration, Plato achieves a double purpose: he defends Socrates against Aristophanes, but without abandoning his criticism of the epitaphioi. On the contrary, he demonstrates irrefutably that vainglory is not only an effect but also a fundamental characteristic of these orations. From the outside, semnotes has passed *inside the funeral oration*, characterized as *semnos logos*.

In this term, we should no doubt see yet another of Plato's borrowings from the language of comedy.* However, it fell to the philosopher to elaborate the concept of *semnos legein*, or "worthy mode of speech," to characterize the false grandeur of the speech of praise,† a genre whose repetitions and stylistic devices are intended solely to allow the speech to praise itself and the orator to display his talent.‡

The funeral oration does not escape this rule, and Socrates proceeds to a systematic questioning of the topoi of the exordium, in which he sees nothing more than a determination to make use of anything to glorify oneself. So, for the edification of the overcredulous Menexenus, always disposed to take the orators literally, he turns each topos against itself, thus reducing it to nothing: the constrained, forced improvisation of which the orators complain gives place to the recitation of previously written speeches;[168]§ the fear of lacking material loses all meaning given the essential facility of a speech that praises its own public;** last, the theme of the *phthonos*

* *Semnos logos*: Crates, frag. 24 Kock on tragedy; Aristophanes, *Wasps* 1174; Euripides, *Hippolytus* 957. Cf. also Aristophanes, *Frogs* 1005 and 925.
† *Phaedrus* 243a1 and 258a1 and especially *Symposium* 199a2–3.
‡ *Phaedrus* 235a7 (critique of Lysias's oration).
§ *Menexenus* 235c8–10 and d1–2 (reprise of 234c5–6).
** *Ibid.* 235c8 and d5–7.

is revealed as useless coquetry. The author of an epitaphios is in no danger of wounding the amour propre of his listeners by exaggerated praise of others, as Pericles claims;* and if it is true that "one cannot tolerate unlimited praise of a third party," the funeral oration in no way risks wounding the sensibilities of the public, since, having shifted from the dead, the praise is addressed essentially to the living and to the city. In these circumstances, anyone can acquire renown[†] — for this is the orator's sole aim. At the same time, the speech finds its place in the world of appearances,[‡] the world in which one takes topoi for the truth, in which a simulacrum of the city is passed off as the polis.

One last feature helps to designate the funeral oration definitively as semnos logos. Because it feeds on conventions, the funeral oration is repetitive, and each epitaphios becomes a copy conforming to a genre that from one incarnation to another, knows no difference and always mechanically produces the same effect on the listener.[§] In fact, when Menexenus asks, "What would you say if it fell to you to speak?" Socrates replies, "Nothing from deep down within me";[**] he thereby stresses the uselessness of resorting to invention in a domain in which all the themes are known in advance and in which it is necessary to imitate previous orators. So Socrates becomes in turn an orator only by repeating a speech following Aspasia, who herself was content to repeat Pericles's epitaphios. The lesson of this chain of repetitions is clear — or seems to be: as an assemblage of "scraps of epitaphios stuck together,"[169][††] the funeral oration never imitates anything but imitations;[170] it is an imitation of itself.

But this interpretation does not exhaust the meaning of the Platonic text, for it ignores one very obvious and very strange

* Thucydides 2.35.2.

† *Menexenus* 235a5–6: *eudokimein.*

‡ In 235d7, the orator's project is to *appear (dokein)* a good orator.

§ *Ibid.* 235b1: *hekastote.*

** *Ibid.* 235e1–236a8.

†† *Ibid.* 236b6.

fact: Socrates is imitating not a male but a female orator. If silence is as necessary and natural to woman as logos is to man, a woman cannot deliver a speech without profoundly disturbing the order of things. Aristophanes knew this: to assemble the women of Athens, he disguises them beforehand as men* and identifies speaking well with manly speech.† Thus it is highly likely that Plato is again using the resources of comedy here, and Menexenus's astonished admiration brings out the oddity all the better: "Aspasia is very lucky, according to you, if she — a woman! — can compose such speeches,"‡ that is, as the rest of the text shows, "political speeches."§ The introduction of a feminine element into an eminently male procedure is yet another way of discrediting the funeral oration. Of course, Menexenus is not actually convinced of the real identity of the orator;** of course, as Socrates is delivering the epitaphios, Aspasia is completely forgotten; but the part that she has played in the elaboration of the speech is enough to show that the funeral oration is merely a deceptive imitation of what a true logos politikos would be. It is a dangerous imitation and one that resembles the model as much as Aspasia resembles Diotima.[171] So this speech must be exorcised by the ironic, restless otherness of the Socratic figure: such is the role of pastiche.

To hunt out the semnos logos hidden in the funeral oration, Socrates uses two methods in succession: apparent eulogy and pastiche. In the first case, a false eulogy of the funeral oration presents Socrates as suffering from this speech; in the second, delivering an epitaphios after Aspasia, Socrates does everything to distance himself from the genre.

Under cover of praising the funeral oration, Socrates begins by

---

* Aristophanes, *Thesmophoriazusae* 119–23: to perorate (*lalein*), one puts on a beard.
† *Ibid.* 149 (*andristi* = *kalos*).
‡ *Menexenus* 249d3–5.
§ *Ibid.* 249e4.
** *Ibid.* 236c6 and 249d–e1.

attacking it; against the spirit of seriousness there is no other weapon but play;* for Plato, play is an authentic form of the serious.[172]†Like the comic poets from whom he borrows most of his techniques, the philosopher maintains an ambiguous relationship with the eulogy, criticizing it as a traditional form but using it extensively in order to ridicule while pretending to exalt. Thus the ironic eulogy of the funeral oration ridicules it from the outset.[173]‡ Only irony can deflate the self-importance of those in authority: to the funeral oration a speech that creates a sense of importance, there is no other possible antidote than Socrates the Silenus.

Likewise, when Socrates himself begins to speak after suffering from the paralyzing power of the funeral oration, we must again see the pastiche as a *serious game*. Indeed, delivering one of those epitaphioi whose false importance has just been denounced, Socrates "plays" or pretends to play§ at being an orator, in a cunning mimesis that still misleads many modern readers because his apparent fidelity to the genre.

Surely to write a pastiche of an author is to presuppose that he is present whole and entire on every page, ever identical with himself through the diversity of his texts. Saturated with topoi, the pastiche, a "truer" copy than the original, usually attacks an already well known form of expression benefiting from the consent of the social body and seeks to deprive it of any future by showing it to be immutable through its various manifestations. At least it tries, by taking up position on its own ground, to deprive it of its official grandeur: thus, through *paratragodia*, comedy plays with tragedy. Plato, who gathers together and appropriates all the literary genres of his time, makes great use of pastiche:[174] imitating Agathon or Lysias, he immobilizes their speech, drawing attention to their style and, ironically, giving it its most complete

* *Ibid.* 235c7: "You always mock the orators."
† Cf. *Laws* 7.803c–e, in which *spoudaios* may be read as the antithesis of *semnos*.
‡ Plutarch, *Pericles* 24.7.
§ *Menexenus* 236c8–9.

form. He uses the same strategy to attack Athens by means of his official eulogy.

In this way, however, he also reveals a double inferiority. There is the inferiority of all the orators, beaten on their own ground, which their most fervent admirer is forced to concede: Menexenus acknowledges Socrates's talent, just as Phaedrus is forced to abandon the idea of a competition in which Lysias would be the victor.* Then there is the inferiority of the epitaphioi in relation to that of Socrates — and, it is tempting to add, *the inferiority of the oration in relation to itself* and its intentions, for the pastiche introduces doubt into the unrelieved seriousness of an epitaphios.

One must look for the mark of Plato not so much in the content, which is that of the traditional funeral oration, as in the presence of such terms as *dokein* and *phainesthai*, which undermine the statement that follows them, exposing the oration as a parody. If democracy were really an aristocracy, as the orator claims, would one confer authority on those who "on every occasion have *seemed* to be the best"?† Indeed, it would be difficult to accept that a *sophia* or an arete recognized as such by public opinion deserves, in Plato's eyes, to be offered as a model.

It would be pointless to try to see the Platonic epitaphios as a "reasonable funeral oration";[175] I would therefore oppose all the "serious" readings of the *Menexenus*, even though they are based on a tradition going back to Antiquity.[176] The epitaphios is neither a hymn to the ideal Athens of the philosopher, nor a Socratic model of the genre, nor a speech on peace, nor a political pamphlet intended to promote a Platonic counter-program, nor a reflection on death and immortality.[177] To take seriously the content of the epitaphios is to ignore the unity of the dialogue — which becomes truncated into two opposing "parts" — and the true question posed in it, that of the value of the Athenian funeral oration. Worse still, one looks for the mark of Plato where one should see only the systematic application of the topoi of the

* *Ibid.* 249e1–2; *Phaedrus* 257c1–4.
† *Menexenus* 238d5–8.

genre — exaltation of arete, praise of autochthony,[178] the opposition between Athens and the other Greeks. Through ignorance of the rules of pastiche, such a reading always ends by attributing to the philosopher ideas that he has constantly and consistently attacked throughout his oeuvre: how could Plato seriously praise Athens for having been the object of a quarrel between the gods,* vaunt the democracy that sees contemporary Athenians as good,† or glorify the combatants of Salamis without some ulterior motive?‡ Reconciling in the same admiration Marathon and Salamis, aristocracy and democracy, the city of the olive tree and the city of the sea, the Athens of the *Menexenus* is in Plato's eyes a bad mixture and not the first sketch for the primitive Athens of the *Timaeus* or the *Critias*.

Finally, to try to find the sign of its serious character in the form of the oration is a hopeless undertaking, for the epitaphios delivered by Socrates contains all the faults that Plato attributes to rhetoric: the outline pedantically announced in the exordium and followed by a dogmatic application,§ the search for pitiful proofs to support some scanty or questionable idea,** the enumeration of exploits or qualities placed end to end.†† More like the inflated productions of Lysias or Agathon than the dialectical flights of Diotima, Socrates's epitaphios runs counter to all the demands of true philosophical rhetoric as defined in the *Phaedrus*, and it cannot be seen as one of the first examples of this good rhetoric.[179] Of course the speech has had its admirers, and Menexenus's enthusiastic approval was matched by that of the Athenians

---

* *Ibid.* 237c8–d1; compare with *Republic* 2.378e4 and *Critias* 109b2 (the gods are above the discord that men attribute to them).

† Compare *Menexenus* 238c2–4 and *Timaeus* 23c1.

‡ Compare *Menexenus* 241a–b and *Laws* 4.706b–d, 707c (Salamis, "shameful victory").

§ Compare *Menexenus* 237a–b and *Symposium* 195a (Agathon's speech).

** Cf. *Menexenus* 237c8 and d8 and *Symposium* 195a–b1.

†† Compare *Menexenus* 237b2 and c7, 237d2, 238a6 with the criticism of Lysias's oration (*Phaedrus* 235b2–3, 238d4–5).

of Cicero's time.* But in these imprudent enthusiasms we may discern the effect that a successful pastiche has on an audience definitively misled by the official oration of Athens.[180]

This analysis of the interpretations of the *Menexenus* reveals the traps of the semnos logos, since the reader gets lost in the serious game of pastiche. In fact, like Socrates's first speech in the *Phaedrus*, the epitaphios is an example of "the way in which he who knows the true may, *by turning words into a game*, mislead his listeners."† Menexenus accused Socrates of "playing with the orators."‡ But this was only the first stage in an ironic game with the political speech: by playing the orator, Socrates played with his audience, both present and future.

Only a critical reading, attentive to the inversions he uses to bring his enemy down while borrowing the latter's own weapons, can outwit Socrates's ruses. Plato wanted to exorcise the oration of Athens by allowing it to speak, and through that ambiguous prosopopoeia of the city he turns the funeral oration against itself.[181] The funeral oration is conquered only by an epitaphios on condition that it is Socrates who delivers it.

Such was the project of the parody. We are still left wondering about the real efficacy of such a strategy. In about 380, Plato no doubt thought he had finished for good with the eulogy of Athens. The confrontation between the *Menexenus* and the *Critias* and the strange similarity linking philosophical eulogy and the official logos of Athens would, however, be enough to prove that there was probably no final victory over the fascination. But this is hardly surprising: like the comic poets, whom he subtly echoes, the philosopher had not completely armed himself against ambiguity. At least we can see in the *Menexenus* the most sustained effort by an Athenian to distance himself from the city of the epitaphioi: that is why we have spent this much time on the very Athenian agon between philosophy and the imaginary city.

* Cicero, *Orator* 151.
† *Phaedrus* 262d1–2.
‡ *Menexenus* 235c7.

CONCLUSION

Imaginary* Athens or the
Invention of the City

Not content with identifying themselves with Athens, the Athenians invented Athens. The Athenian experience of the city cannot be reduced to the empiricism of the political experience so readily attributed to the Greeks; in the polis, as the Athenians of the classical period understood the term, the imaginary occupied a greater place than is usually believed

Of course, gathered together at the Pnyx or sitting in the democratic courts, the Athenian demos did experience, from day to day, the identity of the civic community and the "state," a Greek dogma of which Athens provides the historians of Antiquity with a choice illustration.[1] But for Athens to become this model of polis, the Athenians had already produced, for their own use, something like an ideal, well beyond the sum of concrete experiences that made up their political life.

The cause has been understood at least since Hegel: "The

---

* "Imaginary" is the usual way of rendering the French *imaginaire*, both as adjective and as noun. As a noun, *l'imaginaire* was given wide currency first by Sartre, then by Jacques Lacan, who incorporated it in a triad with the *réel* and the *symbolique*. From French psychoanalysis, where it corresponds roughly to Freud's "fantasy" but with a more flexible use, it has spilled over into other domains, notably social theory, as in "social imaginary." It is in this sense that it is used here, in reference to the city's "self-image," how it sees itself in fantasy, with a large element of idealization and wish fulfillment. — TRANS.

consideration of the State in the abstract ... was alien to them
[the Greeks]. Their grand object was their country in its living
and real aspect; *this actual* Athens, this Sparta, these Temples,
these Altars, this form of social life, this union of fellow-citizens,
these manners and customs."[2] Immersed in the concrete immediacy of the polis, the Greeks seemed to have had no other relationship with the city than one of experience or habit, without
distance or reflection: the experience of the life of the citizen,
which according to Xenophon, consists in Athens in "taking part
together in the ceremonies ... of the cult, dancing in the same
choruses, attending the same schools, serving in the same ranks"*
— in short, the ordinary life of the community.

It remains to be proved that for a community there is no alternative but the one between abstract thinking and pure immediacy.
Between "the abstraction of a state" and the perfect adequation of
society to itself, is there no room for any other idea of the polis?

If the Athenians made more of Athens than Athens, if there
was an Athenian way of conceiving of the city in which *hē polis*
was irreducible to "this Athens" — or to the Athenians, or to civic
life, or even to politeia,[3] and still less to Athena[4] — this is a phenomenon worth studying, despite the inevitable inadequacies of
the modern concepts at our disposal[5] and the temptation to transpose effects of discourse into images. Careful to locate in democracy the lineaments of "the political work of art," Hegel saw the
beautiful as the natural milieu of Athens, the very foundation of
the citizens' adhesion to the polis but also of our own adhesion to
Athens,[5] and in fact "external appearances"[6] (and, most urgently,
the spectacle of the Acropolis) have helped to concentrate in
Athens much of the prestige of the "Greek city." But for whoever,
beyond visual effects, is interested in the mental operation, in the
discursive constitution of an exemplary polis, the funeral oration
is the locus par excellence of this invention of Athens. This does
not mean that the public funeral was its only stage; but having
survived the silence that has engulfed a large part of the Athenian

* Xenophon, *Hellenica* 2.4.20.

logos, the official oration is for us the irreplaceable vehicle of the Athenian imaginary of the city.

On the horizon of the oration is an ideal. *Hē polis*, an immobile prime mover, is the irreducible kernel of meaning; opaque like everything appertaining to origin, but the source of all value, the city presides over the celebration of the Athenians, beyond the unbridgeable gap that separates the dead from the living in the funeral. Against this background is ordered a whole series of gaps, not only between "reality" and the oration (the gap between the dead of the demosion sema and the interchangeable andres agathoi of the epitaphioi, between arche and its exaltation in the form of hegemony, between democratic practice and the city of arete exalted by the orators) but also, within the oration itself, between the experienced time of the city and aion, which always tends to have the last word (the gap between the moment of battle and the eternity of the fine death, between the repetitive listing of battles and the exemplary geste of warlike valor; the resistance set up by the topoi of the eulogy to the many interventions of the lament).

Parallel among themselves, these gaps seem to be basic to the oration; so it is important to study them step-by-step, before attempting to define the ungraspable entity that the polis is in the funeral oration. If we must, in the last resort, interpret these gaps, we may invoke a causality internal to the genre, the official oration, conservative in essence, whose function is to ensure the permanence of the city, confronting the other in war and threatened in its very being by the death of its men. We must note then, that the genre is allowed only a limited freedom: as a discursive institution, it is protected by its topoi against all innovations arising from changes in Athenian society, but strictly bound up, both in its history and in its function, with the fate of the democratic city, the funeral oration cannot claim the autonomy that characterizes a literary genre. As the bearer of orthodoxy, it duplicates the reality of the political and military life of Athens, not without distorting it but without ever questioning it, as tragedy, for example, was to do.[7] However, it is precisely this resistance to innovation — whether we call it stability or immobility — that must be questioned in the oration: indeed the function of the funeral oration seems to be to maintain unchanged a certain paradigmatic idea of what Athenian valor is. We must go even further and try to relate a practice of discourse to the overall organization of Athenian society: because polyrhythmy[8] and the gap between representations and material structures are pertinent features of any ideology,[9] we have already on several occasions designated the funeral oration as an ideological discourse.

Two sets of reasons make it difficult to speak of ideology in a strict sense. One is that, blithely forgetting that a concept loses all relevance when divorced from the thought that produced it, common usage today has borrowed the term and trivialized its meaning, applying it indifferently to any "system of ideas" and no longer, as Marx meant it in *The German Ideology*, to the "dominant thoughts" — that is, to the thoughts of the dominant class, or rather, to the "ideas" that this class elaborates "of its domination."[10] No doubt one may reject such a reduction, as I have tried to do throughout this study; but one is never certain of having successfully resisted the solicitations of the dominant language that makes the word "ideology" the key word of ideology. For historians of ancient Greece, there is a second difficulty: because the concept of ideology is intimately bound up with a particular state of society (in short, with the institution of bourgeois civil society), it is not self-evident that it may legitimately be used of an Athenian discourse. Some scholars, at least, have hesitated to do so, even going so far as to deny that there is any place for ideology in ancient Greece;[11] and the "open franchise" whereby the Athenian demos accommodated itself to being a "minority elite" seems at first sight to support their view.[12] So it is time to justify the use of this word here by considering the question of ideology in ancient society.[13]

If the most general property of an ideological discourse is to *conceal* the internal divisions of a society, then the funeral oration functions, for the Athenian citizens, as an ideology when it suppresses, within the civic army, the difference of status between

combatants or when it makes the Athenian democracy the fatherland of arete. Whether it silences misthophoria, the rotation of
offices, and the drawing of lots; whether it deprives democracy,
grafted onto autochthonous origin, of any history; or whether it
transforms *stasis* into a manifestation of unity, the funeral oration
is trying to deny the existence of any division within the city. In
this role, then, it is even more Platonic than Plato, who, to ensure
the unity of the polis and the *homoiotes* between warriors, was not
afraid to banish certain categories of inferior citizens to the
periphery of the city.

In the epitaphioi, the city, by its very essence, has no periphery: those "strangers within,"[14] that is, the metics and the slaves,
are ignored by the official oration with a consistency that cannot
be accidental. In fact, Athenian — and, more generally, Greek —
thinking about the city does not always observe the same silence:
from myth to philosophy, the anthropological thought of the
Greeks repeatedly declared that the fully human world of the city
rested on certain exclusions,[15] and even the moral protests of the
Sophists and the tragic poets never denied slavery as an institution. On the contrary, although the funeral oration tacitly conveys
an idea of exclusion, the authors of the epitaphioi show little
interest in dwelling on this subject,[16] even in the eminently ideological mode of denial;[17] in the oration, there is no external world
except "the others," that is, the Greeks, who were in reality "the
same," with whom it was worth competing. But it is noteworthy
that on this point the oration adopts a new camouflage, concealing the realities of the empire behind the prestige of hegemony,
due to the Athenians as the sign of general admiration.

In short, the funeral oration has the effect of masking, at two
levels, the question of power within and outside the democratic
city: kratos of the people, transformed in Pericles, Plato, and Lysias
into an appreciation of valor; and kratos exercised over Greeks,
transformed into a prize for bravery, as if the world of the epitaphioi
knew no relationships except agonistic ones. But one would look
in vain for any allusions, clear or masked, to slavery. It is as if it
did not exist or, at least, as if the slaves, those outcasts of the city,

constituted the underside of the oration:[18] *logos* and *erga* (politics and war) are key words in the funeral oration, and the Athenians never met with slaves in either terrain — one met only one's neighbor.

It is not, therefore, a universal definition of the human that we are looking for in the Athenian official oration, in which the fine death separates forever the anthropos, sunk in matter, from the aner, who was able to dominate his perishable body and his mortal condition and enter the eternity of memory.[19*] The orators are in no way trying to elaborate an anthropology, even in the form of a hierarchy at the summit of which a fully human man would be identified with the soldier-citizen; their project is rather to widen the gap between andreia and the human condition.[†] Of course, the epitaphioi are not averse to calling on the whole of mankind, a public subjugated by admiration, to witness the spectacle of Athenian arete;[‡] thus, in Lysias, the whole world is present at the battle of Salamis, and in this untragic universe tears of pity soon give way to the feeling that the Athenians are triumphing over all men.[§] But in Lysias and the other orators, it is ultimately between Greeks that everything is played out,[**] since only Greeks rival each other in valor. At the end of the competition, the rivalry continues in the form of imitation, and Athens willingly agrees to educate the others by its example: but only Greeks are admitted to the school of Athens,[††] and the lesson is one not of philanthropia but always of arete, and of Athenian arete. From Pericles to Hyperides, the same postulate animates the epitaphioi: between Athens and the others, the difference is not, will never

* Cf. Lysias 81.

† *Menexenus* 242a3–4: the city met "the fate that men [*anthrōpoi*] are pleased to inflict on success: envy."

‡ Lysias 26, 66, 67, 71 (see also 41 and 57); *Menexenus* 239a8; Demosthenes 4.

§ Lysias 40.

** *Ibid.* 42–43.

†† Thucydides 2.41.1 (cf. *Menexenus* 241c2) throws light on 2.39.1. For "philanthropical" readings of these texts in the Roman period, see Aelius Aristides, *Panathenaicus* 230 and 274 (Oliver) and Flavius Josephus, *Against Apion* 262.

be, reducible. To be this model of Greekness that it intended to present to the Greeks, the city had first to be its own model. So the official orators are not concerned with the claim to universality that was to lead Aelius Aristides to make Hellenistic Athens "the complete image of human nature";[20] they sought rather, in exalting the absolute uniqueness of the polis, "to put Athens in the superlative."[21] Such is, in the epitaphioi, the aim of the passages on autochthony. For the Athenians, it is a matter of being able to claim not so much descent from the first man as the honor of having been born, andres by origin, from the Attic earth, already constituted as a civic land;[22] thus the oration suggests that the Athenians have never imitated anyone but themselves, in a repetitive but homogeneous time.

Now, it is precisely in this claim to a uniqueness that is both eternal and dating back to the most distant origins that the gap between the funeral oration and modern ideological discourses emerges. In bourgeois society, in which it exercises a dominant role (and perhaps already in its first "birth" in late-fourteenth-century Florence), ideology was intimately linked with a conception of the universal that, in an immense denial, concealed class opposition, immediately recognizable beneath the rights of man and the imperatives of the general interest.[23] Every conception of humanity tends to be accompanied by the belief in an advent or, rather, a reestablishment of the universal, to be embodied (or re-embodied) at last after a dark age: thus the men of the Renaissance and the French Revolution appropriated their history by identifying themselves with the ancient Romans, as if one coincided with oneself only by splitting.[24] There is nothing of this kind in the funeral oration, in which the Athenian history of Athens is pure plenitude, ever-renewed coincidence of the city with itself in the revelation of arete: since Athens exists and since its andres are autochthonous, the world has never been empty.

At this point, we may be better armed to answer, through the funeral oration, the question of ideology in an ancient society. At least I shall try to elucidate in what sense and within what limitations the Athenian official oration seems to me to function as an ideology.

A study of the funeral oration alone shows that it is simplistic to declare that "in ancient Greece, with its open exploitation of slaves and foreign subjects, there would be little scope for ideology in the Marxist sense."[25] To begin with, it is not certain that one can think in the same terms about "domination" over the Greeks and "exploitation" of slaves; these two types of subjection did not, for the Greeks, necessarily belong to the same level of servitude. Otherwise it would be surprising that the vocabulary of slavery, perfectly neutral when referring to a socioeconomic reality, becomes highly pejorative in the sphere of political relations as soon as it plays the role of a metaphor of imperialism or even of oligarchy.* Now, the funeral oration, which deliberately ignores the neutral meaning of the word, just as it ignores the reality of mercantile slavery, continues to place servitude metaphorically on the side of the barbarians or the oligarchic regimes, yet strives on the other hand to transpose onto the agonistic terrain of hegemony all power exercised by Athenians over other Greeks. Perhaps the debates of the ekklesia actually reflected the undisturbed pragmatism usually attributed to them, but the fact remains that the official oration had to distance itself from reality; and if it is true that "an ethical system that leaves room in itself for mercantile slavery is not sapped by the imperialist submission of other states,"[26] our study of the epitaphioi suggests that the Athenians did not accommodate themselves in all circumstances and in all uses of the civic logos to exercising (or even to having exercised) a "tyranny" over other Greeks. In this denial of the power relations that Athens twice tried to establish; we have an eminently ideological attitude.

If this conversion of power into pure prestige does constitute a crack in Athenian "realism," the silence observed by the funeral oration on the subject of slaves might suggest that there was nothing to be said about it in an official oration, or at least that in

---

* Persian imperialism: Lysias 21, 41, 46, 57, 59, 60; *Menexenus* 240a2–4 and elsewhere. Macedonian imperialism: Hyperides 17 and 20. Oligarchy: Lysias 59 and 64; *Menexenus* 239a2–3.

ancient Athens slavery was situated, in relation to the logos, in the greatest possible exteriority: the exteriority of the fact in relation to speech. So we will not interpret this silence as a deliberate — and successful — attempt to conceal at all costs the question of exploitation: if this were the case, the epitaphioi would no doubt, here and there, carry traces of this operation; no discourse can conceal reality altogether, without some slip, without some displacement. Thus I do not believe that the official orators tried for one moment to conceal an exploitation that, in any case, they were probably incapable of conceiving as such.[27] In fact their silence brings us back to a much more general omission: the oration suppresses whatever does not belong to the sphere of war or politics, that is, everything that allows the city to ensure its own subsistence, from the work of the slaves to the commercial role of the metics, from the artisans to the importation of wheat.[28] Those were matters for the ekklesia.* The demosion sema was not concerned with them; at best, the orators preferred to believe that the Attic soil had itself produced the wheat and oil, whereas the gods had provided the Athenians with their first weapons.†

But speech comes into its own as soon as the oration devotes itself to celebrating the Athenian political system. Without concerning myself with seeking confirmation of the dominant status of politics in the Greek city, I have tried to decipher the aristocratic vocabulary used by the orators to praise democracy. In official, clearly democratic speech, such language cannot be regarded as a contingent phenomenon; we may see it as proof that "aristocratic values were without rival" in the Greek cities.[29] Given the constancy with which the epitaphioi suppress the most democratic features of the politeia under the declared dominance of arete, it seems clear that democracy never acquired a language of its own. To confer the prize for excellence in citizenship on the citizens of Athens,‡

---

* Aristotle, *Constitution of Athens* 43.4: the *kuria ekklesia* deliberates *peri sitou*.

† Wheat and oil: *Menexenus* 237e6–238a7; Demosthenes 5. Weapons: *Menexenus* 238b6.

‡ Thucydides 2.46.1.

perhaps it was necessary to forget that, lacking their own language, all the democrats had at their disposal, at least in Greece, were a few ringing slogans and a few key words, such as "sharing" (of power and land).* I am especially inclined to believe that this aphasia was the price that Athenian democracy paid, for two centuries, for the political equilibrium that allowed it to forget that in most of the Greek cities, a ceaseless struggle for the conquest of power continued to set rich against poor. And when, distracted by its dream of a single, indivisible city, an epitaphios conceals the gravity of the civic struggles of the late fifth century behind its eulogy of the "common kinship" that makes all Athenians part of one great family,† it is impossible to doubt any longer that the oration had an ideological function.

Thus, at two levels — war and politics — power relations are transposed in the funeral oration into relations of competition within the homogeneous milieu of arete, and the lesson of the oration is certainly the same in both cases: all valor, all worth, is concentrated in the city, whether it is turned outward or seen from within. Given that in the Greek cities all social relations were mediated through war and politics, it is not surprising that this double agency is also, in the Athenian official oration, the very locus of ideology. In advancing this proposition, we must give up any attempt to import into ancient Greece an unmodified modern concept of ideology. Above all, we must abandon the idea that when faced with mercantile slavery, the city always had in reserve an articulated discourse, whether it involved cynical acceptance of reality or, conversely, self-justification: posing the issue in these terms, we would forget too quickly that no society is so transparent to itself that the social relations on which it is based emerge in all its discourses.[30] If, on the other hand, we accept that in some societies not all the contradictions are consistent with one another, then we must also accept that the most official civic logos was unable to take into account the material

* See Plato, *Republic* 8.557a2–6, and Aristotle, *Constitution of Athens* 40.3.
† *Menexenus* 243e.

structures that enabled the polis to function, but that, against the background of this silence, it worked to preserve from all tension the city of the citizens — the only reality, because the only value, in the eyes of the Greeks.

It is from this perspective that we must consider the question of ideology in ancient Greece. Yet we have not really finished with the question of ideology in the funeral oration: although, to characterize the many discernible gaps that the historian finds between logos and ergon throughout a study of the oration, I have tried to use the concept of ideology in a relevant way, I have preferred to use the noun of the imaginary to designate the process by which, in the oration, an ideality of the polis, both opaque and dominant, is constituted. I must now explain this choice.

Although we have found in the funeral oration several operations by which Athenians concealed from themselves the objective data of reality, we cannot grasp the full meaning of the oration by seeing concealment as its sole function, its sole effect. The concept of ideology is closely linked with other, more vague or excessively simple notions — duplicity, mystification, cosmetics, the mask, illusion — and, whether it owes this cumbersome list of associations to its history or to the terms in which it was first formulated, it was not always easy for it to separate itself from them. We can get rid of duplicity without too much difficulty, and of the simplistic idea that a dominant class manipulates mystification in full awareness of its own interests. The same does not go for the problematic of illusion, a more subtle notion that raises formidable questions as soon as it is applied to an ancient society:[31] Illusion for whom? In relation to a reality that is largely constructed by us? In relation to what awareness or to what knowledge? In relation to which observer who possesses this knowledge and can use it correctly? Perhaps the historian, armed with the distance that separates him from his object, or the philosopher, skilled at tracking down *eidola*. But unless one unquestioningly accepts the Platonic critique of the political genre, can one reduce the funeral oration to mere "trompe-l'oeil"?[32] This is what Pericles's epitaphios has probably been for historians who have treated it as a simple, unbiased description of Athens, and for the historian in quest of *realia*, this is what the funeral oration as a whole may be as well: because it is the result of a process of idealization, the city of the epitaphioi is of no use to him, worse than that, it blurs all the traces of "objective understanding."[33] And yet, however uncomfortable it may be, this blurring does not allow us to conclude that for the Athenians this polis was merely an illusion. An institutional illusion is still a fact, and insofar as it produces representations and insofar as it develops a language to speak about Athens, the funeral oration must be regarded as an integral part of Athenian political practice: no doubt the epitaphioi tend to autonomize *hē polis*, but if the Athenians conceived of themselves as a city through the mediation of this entity, it is certainly a political act that they are performing in listening to the oration.

Because this operation interests me in itself, I have refused to engage in the interminable tracking down of illusion. So in conclusion, I will not ask whether the Athenians were aware of idealizing the city; this would be to ignore that every mental operation is largely opaque to itself. Instead, designating under the term "imaginary" all the figures in which a society apprehends its identity,[34] I have tried to elucidate the functioning of this kernel of irreducible and totalizing signification to which the funeral oration gives the name "city."

As if, outside politics, it were not possible to give the universe an overall meaning, there is in the oration no reality that must not be inscribed in the civic order. Thus, proclaiming that their autochthonous birth gave the Athenians "both a mother and a fatherland,"* Lysias's epitaphios, in a few words, represses "nature" to the advantage of a purely political symbolism. Without really being rejected, myth is exhausted, reduced to its zero degree — the story of the birth of Erichthonius gives way to the collective origin of the Athenians — and *Gē-Mētēr*, the primordial power to solitary births, gives way to the civic land or, more precisely,

* Lysias 17.

to the couple *mētēr kai patris*, which suggests a bilateral kinship, the very same that in Athens, beginning with Pericles's law, defined citizenship. Only death does not allow itself to be tamed by the city; against all the laws that accord arete the lion's share in the distribution of honors, "it has neither contempt for the wicked nor regard for the valorous."* But because in the fine death it is still the city that conquers nature, the political oration seeks to go beyond the common fate of humanity, and it is significant that the Athenians chose the setting of the public funeral to reaffirm the omnipotence of the polis: to replace the man with the citizen even in death is certainly the ultimate achievement of the civic imaginary.

Thus, in the funeral oration, the city ensures, in imaginary terms, its grip on reality, and the Athenians invent Athens. For their own use. Or for us. Who knows?

But we still have to decide what we mean by this "for us." At this stage, we can no longer naively believe that the message is addressed to us. Could we "really" be in the minds of the orators, when nothing can provide us with immediate contact with the Athenian oration? On the contrary, in my effort to reconstruct the effect produced by the funeral oration on its public, it has not escaped me that it is I who have reconstructed it. By gradually locating in the epitaphioi the expression of a certain idea of Athens, I was no doubt looking for what would enable me to understand the oration, and it is equally likely that I have found what the oration is for us,[35] in the light of our own preoccupations and the methods at our disposal to examine the documents.

This does not mean that this is the last word on the funeral oration or that I am claiming an exhaustive understanding of it. Nor does it mean that what I have seen in the text was not there. Others have said it better than I: "History is inhabited by the strangeness that it seeks, and it imposes its law on the distant regions that it conquers in the belief that it is bringing them back to life."[36]

---

* *Ibid.* 77. The city, on the other hand, is able to distinguish between agathoi and kakoi: see Hyperides 5 and Lysias 19.

The first reading made of the epitaphioi by the scholars of the Hellenistic period — by Aelius Aristides and the many rhetors who, in their collections of *progumnasmata*, referred to the funeral oration[37*] — already functioned in this gap between the present and the past. Whether they based a general theory of the eulogy on a particular passage of Pericles's epitaphios or whether they sought in the funeral oration their own ideal of a universally beneficent Athens, they always find human nature in the oration: because, in paideia, anthropos has gained ground over aner, because *humanitas* has been built up on the ruins of andreia, because a politico-military "virtue" is still too close and already too distant an ideal for them to be able to recognize its importance, they diverted for centuries the reading of the genre into a humanist perspective. But the fact is there: despite a generally distorting interpretation, when they resort to the funeral oration in order to make Athens a model and the praise of Athens — or the epitaphios logos — the model of praise,[38] they do, in their own way, bring out the essential lesson of the oration.

Was I any better armed to read the oration? It would be more accurate to say that I had other weapons: my relationship to the "classical city," which I see as both an ideal type and a historical figure of the history of ancient Athens, and my interest in "the imaginary institution of society," an interest that is concerned with our cultural horizon as a whole. Perhaps I have brought out in the funeral oration an imaginary city very like the classical city of our own imaginary. But in refraining from treating the oration as a "description" of reality, remembering that in the democratic city there was already a gap between logos and ergon, this reading begins to undermine any notion we may have had of an Athens always homogeneous to itself. In giving the paradigmatic city a specific place and a specific voice, I have gone some way to restoring the strangeness to all the other forms that Athens has assumed.

* Theon, *Rhetores graeci* (Spengel ed.) 2.63.110 (on Pericles's epitaphios: Thucydides 2.45.1) and 68 (epitaphioi of Plato, Thucydides, Hyperides, and Lysias).

Notes

PREFACE TO THE SECOND EDITION

1. Eric Alliez asked me to edit this abridged version in order to publish the book in Brazil, and while his arguments managed to convince me at the time, the project had initially been suggested to me by Miguel Abensour, who had wanted to publish a "short" version of *The Invention of Athens* in the series he edits [Critique de la politique, published by Payot — TRANS]. I would like to express my warmest gratitude to both of them.

2. Here, too, I am grateful, and very pleased, that the book did find this audience of patient readers, some of whom were known to me while many were not.

3. I am grateful to the Editions de l'Ecole des Hautes Etudes en Sciences Sociales for allowing this somewhat shorter version to coexist with the complete text.

4. Thus no changes were made to certain developments that I would have liked to illuminate with readings of works published after this book was written. I am thinking especially of the books by Reinhard Stupperich, "Staatsbegräbnis und Privatgrabmal im klassischen Athen" (Ph.D. diss., Münster, 1977); Christoph W. Clairmont, *Patrios Nomos: Public Burial in Athens During the Fifth and Fourth Centuries B.C.* (Oxford: B.A.R., 1983); and Ian Morris, *Death-Ritual and Social Structure in Classical Antiquity* (Cambridge, UK: Cambridge University Press, 1992); as well as Michel Nouhaud, *L'Utilisation de l'histoire par les orateurs attiques* (Paris: Les Belles Lettres, 1982). Nor was I able to take into account certain articles, such as Simon Goldhill's on the Great Dionysia ("The Great Dionysia and Civic Ideology," in John J. Winkler and Froma I. Zeitlin [eds.], *Nothing to Do with Dionysos?* [Princeton: Princeton University Press, 1990], pp. 97–129), which would now lead me to complete, if not to modify, my discussion of the civic honors granted to war orphans.

5. See Chapter Six, where the imaginary without image is presented not as the only possible figure of the city but as one important figure among others.

6. And one that was supposed to be autonomous — which should make one cautious when applying to images any analysis based largely on the examination of the productions of *logos*. I have explained my position on the notion of image and its use in "Repolitiser la cité," *L'Homme* 97–98 (1986), pp. 239–54.

7. This quotation is from Jean-Pierre Vernant's preface to Claude Bérard et al., *A City of Images: Iconography and Society in Ancient Greece*, trans. Deborah Lyons (Princeton, NJ: Princeton University Press, 1989), p. 8 [trans. modified]; see also p. 7, on the "overly literary idea of the ancient world, and of Athens in particular, that classical studies have presented," as opposed to the "great importance" of imagery.

8. That is no doubt how we should understand Gregory Nagy's distrust of this notion; after playing a major role in creating the conditions of possibility for these investigations, today he prefers, as an anthropologist, to use the concept of "occasion" or of "occasionality."

9. I am thinking of the works of Yan Thomas; see especially "L'Institution civile de la cité," *Le Débat* 74 (1993), pp. 22–44, as well as "L'Institution de la majesté," in *De l'Etat: Fondations juridiques, outils symboliques* (Paris: A. Michel, 1991), pp. 331–86, and "*Imago naturae*: Note sur l'institutionnalité de la nature à Rome," in *Théologie et droit dans la science politique de l'Etat moderne* (Rome: Ecole Française de Rome, 1992), pp. 201–27.

10. And ashes are equivalent to "dust" for the parents of the dead, as is stated superbly in a *stasimon* from Aeschylus's *Agamemnon*, in which Ares exercises his profession of "gold-changer" on bodies that have been permanently transformed (ll. 437–42).

11. This model, expressed in and through the funeral oration, supposes an official ideology that has no place for the notion of a "fine" life; it is in this framework and only in this framework that I maintain that the notion of *anēr agathos*, or rather — since it is usually used in the plural — of *andres agathoi*, implies the *death* of the citizen (for a contrary view, see Christian Meier, *Die Rolle des Krieges im klassischen Athen* [Munich: Stiftung Historisches Kolley, 1991], p. 47 n. 131).

12. This means that the Athenian "fine death" is a beginning — the beginning of a long history in Western civilization (see Jean-François Lyotard, *The Differend: Phrases in Dispute*, trans. Georges Van Den Abbeele [Minneapolis: University of Minnesota Press, 1988], pp. 99–100)—and not an end.

13. See "The Spartans' 'Beautiful Death,'" in *The Experiences of Tiresias: The Feminine and the Greek Man*, trans. Paula Wissing (Princeton, NJ: Princeton University Press, 1995), pp. 63–74.

14. See Jean-Pierre Vernant, "La Belle Mort et le cadavre outragé" and "*Pantà kalà*: D'Homère à Simonide"; both texts were reprinted in *L'Individu, la mort, l'amour: Soi-même et l'autre en Grèce ancienne* (Paris: Gallimard, 1989), pp. 41–79 and 91–101.

15. Perhaps first of all because, as Bénédicte Gros has correctly observed (in her master's thesis at the EHESS, June 1993), "it is always by killing and never by dying that one gains *kleos*." For a critical point of view on "epic fine death," see Pietro Pucci, "Banter and Banquets for Heroic Death" in Andrew Benjamin (ed.), *Post-structuralist Classics* (London and New York: Routledge, 1988), as well as Nicole Loraux, "Le Point de vue du mort," *Poésie* 57 (1991), pp. 67–74.

16. Nicole Loraux, *The Children of Athena: Athenian Ideas About Citizenship and the Division Between the Sexes*, trans. Caroline Levine (Princeton, NJ: Princeton University Press, 1993); originally published in France in 1981.

17. See "Les Bénéfices de l'autochthonie," *Le Genre humain* 3–4 (1982), pp. 238–52, and "Gloire du Même, prestige de l'Autre: Variations grecques sur l'origine," *Le Genre humain* 21 (1990), pp. 115–39.

18. I will not mention here the details of the debates that arose concerning particular points in *The Children of Athena*, which are presented in the postface to the second edition of that book (1990) [included in the translation cited above — Trans].

19. The degree of citizenship granted to the women of Athens is one of the most bitterly disputed questions. See, for example, Cynthia Patterson's discussion (in "*Hai Attikai*: The Other Athenian Citizens," in Marilyn Skinner [ed.], *Rescuing Creusa, Helios* 13 [1986], pp. 49–67) of my assertion in *The Children of Athena* (which I still maintain) that "female Athenians do not exist."

20. See, for example, Barry S. Strauss, "The Melting Pot, the Mosaic, and the Agora," in J. Peter Euben, John Wallach, and Josiah Ober (eds.), *Athenian Political Thought and the Reconstruction of American Democracy* (Ithaca, NY: Cornell University Press, 1994).

21. This was one of the questions raised at the conference "Greeks and Barbarians," held at Cornell University, April 23–25, 1993 — questions formulated in terms that inextricably mingle the American good conscience with the Western bad conscience.

22. See for example, "Thucydide et la sédition dans les mots," *Quaderni di storia* (1986), pp. 95–134; "Le Lien de la division," *Le Cahier du Collège International de philosophie* 4 (1987), pp. 101–24; "De l'amnistie et de son contraire," in *Usages de l'oubli* (Paris: Seuil, 1988), pp. 23–47; and "Reflections of the Greek City on Unity and Division," in Anthony Molho, Kurt Raaflaub, and Julia Emlen (eds.), *City-States in Classical Antiquity and Medieval Italy* (Ann Arbor: University of Michigan Press, 1991), pp. 33–51. See also *The Divided City: On Memory and Forgetting in Ancient Athens*, trans. Corinne Pache with Jeff Fort (New York: Zone Books, 2002) — TRANS.

23. Namely that of Moses I. Finley — who, it is true, often pronounced rather hasty judgments — in a note in *Politics in the Ancient World* (New York: Cambridge University Press, 1983), p. 125 n.7.

24. See, for example, Josaih Ober, *Mass and Elite in Democratic Athens* (Princeton, NJ: Princeton University Press, 1989), pp. 290–91.

25. See Chapter Four, pp. 257–78.

26. See "La Démocratie à l'épreuve de l'étranger (Athènes, Paris)," in Roger-Paul Droit (ed.), *Les Grecs, les Romains et nous: L'Antiquité est-elle moderne?* (Paris: Le Monde, 1991), pp. 164–88.

27. Including the book edited by Marcel Detienne, *Les Savoirs de l'écriture en Grèce ancienne* (Lille: Presses Universitaires de Lille, 1988). On Athens, see also Rosalind Thomas, *Oral Tradition and Written Record in Classical Athens* (Cambridge, UK: Cambridge University Press, 1989).

28. This position was developed and specified a bit further in the conclusion of "Solon et la voix de l'écrit," in Detienne (ed.), *Les Savoirs de l'écriture*, pp. 126–29.

29. To the few titles already selected from an abundant bibliography we can add Pierre Vidal-Naquet, *Politics Ancient and Modern*, trans. Janet Lloyd (Cambridge, UK: Polity Press, 1995).

30. See Nicole Loraux and Patrice Loraux, "*L'Athēnaíōn politeía* avec et sans Athéniens," *Rue Descartes* 1–2 (1991), pp. 57–79.

31. A choice that is often implicit, however, and about which I no doubt should have been clearer, especially since the essential part of the corpus of the funeral oration dates from the fourth century.

32. Mogens H. Hansen, for example, in *The Athenian Democracy in the Age of Demosthenes: Structure, Principles, and Ideology*, trans. J.A. Crook (Oxford: Blackwell, 1991).

33. Despite Josiah Ober and Barry S. Strauss ("Drama, Political Rhetoric, and the Discourse of Athenian Democracy," in Winkler and Zeitlin [eds.], *Nothing to Do with Dionysos?* p. 241), I continue to believe that *homonoia* is not, in post-403 Athens, a "central democratic virtue"—the same authors (p. 243) also speak of "survival" in relation to the fourth-century democracy, using a word with heavily charged implications—but a key concept of the "moderate" thought that triumphed at the time.

34. In English in the original—TRANS.

35. The qualifier *sunetos* is used to characterize the listeners who possess this capacity, which no doubt would not displease Thucydides, whose penchant for *sunesis* is well known.

36. On the *ainos*, see especially Gregory Nagy, *The Best of the Achaeans: Concepts of the Hero in Archaic Greek Poetry* (Baltimore: Johns Hopkins University Press, 1979), pp. 238–42, and *Pindar's Homer: The Lyric Possession of an Ancient Past* (Baltimore: Johns Hopkins University Press, 1990), pp. 314–38, as well as "Theognis and Megara: A Poet's Vision of His City," in Thomas J. Figueira and Gregory Nagy (ed.), *Theognis of Megara: Poetry and the Polis* (Baltimore: Johns Hopkins University Press, 1985), esp. p. 24: a mode of poetic discourse that is unmistakably understandable only to its intended audience.

37. Garry Wills, *Lincoln at Gettysburg: The Words That Remade America* (New York: Simon and Schuster, 1992); I thank Stephen White for bringing this work to my attention; see esp. ch. 1, "Oratory of the Greek Revival," and app. 3, in which (p. 212) the author mentions the genre's influence on John F. Kennedy's inauguration speech, an influence that I sensed but that, due to a lack of information, I mentioned only in passing (Introduction, n.25).

38. I have also designated this configuration as the "ideal of the city."

39. Ober, *Mass and Elite*, p. 291 n.75.

INTRODUCTION: A VERY ATHENIAN INVENTION

1. A comparison between the *epitaphios logos* and the *laudatio funebris* (see pp. 76–77) allows us to appreciate the distinction between *polis* and *civitas*; thus it mainly concerns those who, like Henri Marrou, refuse to see the "ancient city" as anything other than an *Idealtypus* (report in the *Neuvième Congrès des Sciences Historiques* [Paris: A. Colin, 1950], vol. 1, pp. 327–29).

2. See Pierre Bourdieu's analysis of the celebration speech in *Actes de la recherche en sciences sociales* 5–6 (1975), esp. the quotations from Nietzsche on pp. 5 and 67.

3. *Kechēnaioi*: "Citizen-flycatchers" according to Jean Taillardat's translation (*Les Images d'Aristophane: Etudes de langue et de style* [Paris: Société d'Edition les Belles Lettres, 1965]), or "idler-ians" (according to Hilaire van Daele [CUF, vol. 1, p. 134]). To tell the truth, this play on the words *Athēnaiōi* and *kechēnaioi* is difficult to translate if one does not want to miss the comic effect of *paranomasis*. On *kechēnaioi*, see Taillardat, *Les Images d'Aristophane*, pp. 264–67.

4. On whether this nomos is to be understood as law or custom, see Martin Ostwald, *Nomos and the Beginnings of the Athenian Democracy* (Oxford: Clarendon, 1969), pp. 175–76.

5. On the impossibility of determining precisely the frontier between the symbolic and the functional in an institution, see Cornelius Castoriadis, *L'Institution imaginaire de la société* (Paris: Seuil, 1975), pp. 159–77.

6. See Marcel Detienne, *The Masters of Truth in Archaic Greece*, trans. Janet Lloyd (New York: Zone Books, 1996).

7. Generally the orators prefer to use *teleutan*, as is apparent in Thucydides and Plato. The use of *apothanein* is interesting in the epitaphios attributed to Lysias: often reserved for enemies or defeated allies (6, 10, 31), this verb also designates death as a natural necessity (14) and as the common fate of mankind in contrast to the victorious death of the elite (24).

8. To parody a Lacedaemonian apothegm that was not intended to spare Athens: *en Athenais panta kala* (Plutarch, *Lacedaemonian Apothegms*, 236b–c); see Georg Peter Landmann's commentary in "Das Lob Athens in der Grabrede des Perikles (Thukydides II, 34–41)," *MH* 31 (1974), pp. 65–95 (quotation p. 83).

9. Using the grammatical terms of modern French, one might say that in the funeral oration the Athenians live in the future perfect.

10. Felix Jacoby, *Atthis: The Local Chronicles of Ancient Athens* (Oxford: Clarendon, 1949), pp. 73–78.

11. Phanodemus, Lycurgus's collaborator in the policy of national restoration, wrote his *Atthis* in a spirit very close to that of the epitaphioi, as Jacoby observes (*F.Gr.Hist.*, vol. 3, supp. A, p. 325); but most Atthidographers pay little attention to the funeral oration.

12. See the remarks by Arnaldo Momigliano in his report to the Congress of Italian Historians (Perugia, 1967): "Prospettiva 1967 della storia greca," *RSI* 80 (1968), pp. 5–19 (esp. 9 and 17).

13. *The Philosophy of History*, trans. J. Sibree (New York: Dover, 1956), pp. 255–56.

14. A. Havelock, *The Liberal Temper in Greek Politics* (London: Cape, 1957), pp. 16 and 19.

15. This work, published simultaneously in Geneva, Paris, and London, contains a translation of the orations of Pericles, Plato, and Lysias, as well as fragments of the epitaphioi of Gorgias and Hyperides and Cicero's eulogy of the soldiers of the legion of Mars (*Fourteenth Philippic*); its introduction, "Essai sur le discours funèbre," contains many judicious remarks (see esp. pp. 8 and 28–31).

16. As Landmann reminds us in "Das Lob Athens," p. 65; the relevant passage was 2.37.2 (exaltation of liberty).

17. On the Hegelian *Heimatlichkeit*, the ancestor of this tendency in interpretation, see Dominique Janicaud, *Hegel et le destin de la Grèce* (Paris: Vrin, 1975), pp. 144 and 166.

18. Ulrich von Wilamowitz, *GT*, vol. 1, p. 205. Wilamowitz, on the other hand, seems to be immune (because of his conservatism?) to the mirage of Pericles's epitaphios, to which, if I am not mistaken, he makes no reference in *Aristoteles und Athen* (Berlin: Weidmann, 1893).

19. The *Menexenus*, studied in German schools in the 1880s (see the works by Theodor Berndt, F. Roch, and O. Perthe drawing up in 1888, 1882, and 1886 the program for the gymnasiums of Herford, Gorz, and Bielefeld), was officially made part of the French program for the *programme seconde* on October 1, 1896: hence a proliferation of school editions between 1897 and 1900.

20. On the historiography of this German problem, see Konrad Gaiser, *Das Staatsmodell des Thukydides: Zum Rede des Perikles für die Gefallenen* (Heidelberg: Kerle, 1975), pp. 17–18; see also Landmann, "Das Lob Athens," p. 94 (on Hellmut Flashar's work: "so wird Perikles zu Hitler"). French scholarship followed the movement at some distance, especially after the First World War; see P. Girard, "L'Année a perdu son printemps," *REG* 32 (1919), pp. 227–39 (on the epitaphios of Samos and the "young lives sacrificed" during the First World War). For a Swiss contribution to this debate, see the strange article by W. Deonna, "L'Eternel Présent: Guerre du Peloponnèse (431–404) et guerre mondiale (1914–18)," *REG* 35 (1922), pp. 1–62 and 113–79 (on Pericles's epitaphios and the superhuman pride of the German Reich).

21. A.W. Gomme, writing as a "sentimental" individual moved by Pericles's epitaphios. "Concepts of Freedom," in *More Essays in Greek History and Literature* (Oxford: Blackwell, 1962), p. 147.

22. Landmann, "Das Lob Athens, pp. 65 and 92.

23. Hegel, *Philosophy of History*, p. 261; see Janicaud, *Hegel et le destin de la Grèce*, pp. 183–84. Gustave Glotz (*La Cité grecque* [Paris: Michel, 1968], pp. 153–54) speaks of "commentary" on Athenian ideals and thinks that the oration does not, in the end, distort reality too much (p. 155)—a view that leads him to read 2.37.1 as the privileged expression of Athenian equality (p. 141).

24. On Athenian democracy (conceived as a synonym of "Greek democracy") as a model and telos of the city in Hegel, see Janicaud, *Hegel et le destin de la Grèce*, p. 167. For Glotz, "the end of the Greek city" coincides with the fall of Athens (*La Cité grecque*, pp. 389–99).

25. Apart from Bruni's imitation of the epitaphios, one might cite John F. Kennedy's probable imitation in his inaugural address. Metaxas's prohibition of the text is also a sort of reading.

26. On Bruni's *Funeral Oration*, see Hans Baron, *The Crisis of the Early Italian Renaissance: Civic Humanism and Republican Liberty in an Age of Classicism and Tyranny* (Princeton, NJ: Princeton University Press, 1966), pp. 412–30: Bruni imitates Thucydides in his description of Florentine institutions, glosses *paideusis Hellados* in a long eulogy of Florence as protectress of arts and letters, and transforms Nanni Strozzi into the embodiment of the ideal citizen-soldier.

27. On fraternity, see Glotz, *La Cité grecque*, p. 153; on correct balance, see *ibid.*, pp. 155–56.

28. The "character of Athens," writes Hegel in *Philosophy of History*; Pericles intended to exalt the character of the Athenians, and there is a significant nuance here. On the neglect of politeia, see Janicaud, *Hegel et le destin de la Grèce*, p. 170: the constitution is secondary in relation to *Sittlichkeit*.

29. Not only does Hegel deal with ch. 40 (love of the beautiful) before ch. 39 (courage); he also constantly distorts the text, even though he follows it closely. Thus *tolman te hoi autoi malista kai … eklogizesthai* (the conjunction of contraries) becomes "*despite* this courage, we are aware of what we are doing"; and in the final formula, Hegel adds *in extremis* "a bold courage."

30. On the "youth" of Greece, one might cite, apart from Hegel (*Philosophy of History*, pp. 225ff.), Marx's remarks in the introduction to A *Contribution to the Critique of Political Economy*.

31. George Grote examines Pericles's epitaphios in vol. 4 of *A History of Greece* (London: Murray, 1862), pp. 265–75. See also Arnaldo Momigliano, "George Grote and the Study of Greek History," in *Studies in Historiography* (London: Weidenfeld and Nicolson, 1966), pp. 56–74, esp. 65.

32. Grote considers the nomos in relation to the epitaphios of Samos (*History of Greece*, vol. 4, p. 170) and the choice of Pericles as a political act (pp. 170 and 265); the stamp of Pericles (pp. 266–67) does not entirely conceal the impersonality of the genre (p. 267).

33. He quotes the passage on the constitution extensively but without commentary; he refers to 2.39.2–3 on p. 273.

34. See especially *ibid.*, pp. 271–72 (cf. pp. 159–60).

35. *Paideusis Hellados* becomes "a normal school of energetic action" (p. 160) see also pp. 267, 270 ("the picture of the Athenian commonwealth in its glory") 272 ("positive impulse"), and 273 (on Athens's multifarious activities).

36. "Comfortable": see *ibid.*, p. 272, and Momigliano, "George Grote," p. 62.

37. See Grote, *History of Greece*, vol. 4, p. 271.

38. In one example of distortion, in *eleutheros . . . politeuomen* he translates *te . . . kai* as "not merely . . . but also" (*ibid.*, p. 268); for the overvaluing of Athens, see *ibid.*, p. 273, and Momigliano, "George Grote," p. 70.

39. For Hegel, virtue is the principle of democracy (*Philosophy of History*, p. 251), as it is for Montesquieu, by whom he was certainly inspired (cf. Janicaud, *Hegel et le destin de la Grèce*, pp. 56 and 169–71) and who was probably referring to Pericles's epitaphios. (see Pierre Vidal-Naquet, "Tradition de la démocratie grecque," introduction to *Démocratie antique et démocratie moderne*, by M.I. Finley [Paris: Payot, 1976], p. 26). For Glotz, see *La Cité grecque*, p. 141.

40. With Grote one might link Havelock, *Liberal Temper*, pp. 147, 414, and passim, and A.W. Gomme, *Commentary*, vol. 2, p. 111.

41. In their treatment of Pericles's declarations on the Athenian personality unified in its diversity and autonomous in its adaptability (2.41.1), Hegel stresses unity ("in a democracy the main point is that the character of the citizen be plastic 'all of a piece,'" *Philosophy of History*, p. 255) and Grote diversity, which he sees as an exaltation of man's multifarious character (*History of Greece*, p. 271).

42. See the methodological considerations of Michel de Certeau in *L'Ecriture de l'histoire* (Paris: Gallimard, 1975), p. 44.

43. Exorcising the prestige of certain texts is a never-ending task: thus Felix Jacoby, struggling against the overvaluation of Pericles's epitaphios, ends up underestimating the interest of the genre as a whole and even the specialty of the funeral, which he would like to merge into the ritual celebration of all the dead during the Genesia, see *"Patrios Nomos:* State Burial in Athens and the Public

Cemetery in the Kerameikos," *JHS* 64 (1944), pp. 37–66, and "*Genesia*: A Forgotten Festival of the Dead," *CQ* 38 (1944), pp. 67–75.

44. Nobody, however, has thought to imagine a speech given by Dio.

45. According to Jacoby, this is "the first example of a real funeral oration published by its author" ("*Patrios Nomos*," p. 57). Moreover, although it is certainly the first, it is probably also the last and only example, since Jacoby does not accept the authenticity of the texts attributed to Lysias and Demosthenes.

46. In contrast, the identification of the elements of epitaphioi scattered throughout Herodotus's work has never presented a problem, for Herodotus does not enjoy the same reputation for seriousness.

47. This argument is advanced by all who plead for the authenticity of the texts. For Lysias, see Jules Girard, "Sur l'authenticité de l'oraison funèbre attribuée à Lysias," *RA* (1870), and Walz, *Der lysianische Epitaphios*; for Demosthenes see Johannes Sykutris, "Der demosthenische Epitaphios," *Hermes* 63 (1928), pp. 241–58, G. Colin, "L'Oraison funèbre d'Hypéride, ses rapports avec les autres oraisons funèbres athéniennes," *REG* 51 (1938), pp. 209–66 and 305–94; and Max Pohlenz, "Zu den attischen Reden auf die Gefallenen," *Symbolae Osloenses* (1948), pp. 46–74.

48. Without entirely ignoring questions of authenticity, I shall therefore raise them only as they appear necessary to a study of the genre; I shall avoid entering into any dispute in which no argument is more convincing than the opposing one and, renouncing for the time being any doubts about the authenticity of a speech I shall speak of Lysias and Demosthenes, and not of [Lysias] and [Demosthenes].

49. Examples are the Athenians' speech at Plataea in Herodotus 9.27 and in the debate with Sparta in Thucydides 1.73ff.; the definition of a eulogy of Athens in Xenophon's *Memorabilia* 3.5; Isocrates's *Panegyricus* and *Panathenaicus*; and esp. Lycurgus's *Against Leocrates*.

50. The formalist temptation is long-lived. See, for example, sixteenth-century collections of state speeches (such as the fourth volume of Willem Canter's edition of Aelius Aristides [Baser, 1566]) and the eighteenth-century collections (such as Abbe Auger, *oeuvres complètes d'Isocrate* [Paris, 1781], vol. 2, which presents epitaphioi and eulogies by Sophists, preceded by "Réflexions sur les éloges des anciens Grecs et sur les nôtres").

51. Marx posed the question in these terms in *The German Ideology;* but if there is little chance of arriving on earth when one comes from heaven, the

reverse operation seems to be no easier, and Marx's famous passage provides no instructions as to how it is to be done.

52. This is a risk not entirely avoided by M.I. Finley in *Democracy Ancient and Modern* (New Brunswick, NJ: Rutgers University Press, 1973), pp. 50–66; see Chapter Two, p. 132.

53. Without the American excavations of the Agora, how would we know that the Athenians waited until 430 or 425 to erect a monument to the Cleisthenean eponyms that was worthy of them? See T. Leslie Shear's remarks in *Hesperia* 39 (1970), pp. 219–22, on the rhythm proper to ideological systems, see Georges Duy, "Histoire sociale et ideologies des sociétés," in Jacques Le Goff and Pierre Nora (eds.), *Faire de l'histoire*, 3 vols. (Paris: Gallimard, 1974), vol. 1, pp. 148–49.

54. On the inertia of mentalities, which turns the history of mentalities into "the history of slowness in history," see Jacques Le Goff, "Les Mentalités: Une histoire ambiguë," in *Faire de l'histoire*, vol. 3, pp. 76–94 (quotation pp. 81–82).

CHAPTER ONE: THE FUNERAL ORATION IN THE DEMOCRATIC CITY

1. Felix Jacoby, *"Patrios Nomos*: State Burial in Athens and the Public Cemetery in the Kerameikos," *JHS* 64 (1944), p. 55: "an item of the program." The same attitude leads Jacoby to declare that "Thucydides did not attach much importance to this official speech" (p. 57 n.92). Has his interest in the ceremony kept him from seeing that Thucydides's excursus is oriented entirely to the funeral oration? See Chapter One, p. 46–47.

2. Ulrich von Wilamowitz, *GT*, vol. 1, p. 205.

3. See Marcel Detienne, *The Masters of Truth in Archaic Greece*, trans. Janet Lloyd (New York: Zone Books, 1996), pp. 103–106.

4. This is an obligatory theme of the exordium: see Chapter Five, pp. 292–97.

5. Thus, for example, the absence of any debate in a practice such as ostracism would require a long commentary.

6. Pericles mentions the fostering of children (2.46.1), but parents have a right only to exhortations: the orator, it is true, thinks first of the eternity of the city, and the future is more important to him than the past.

7. On the street of the tombs, many holes that correspond to the wooden stakes of this tribune suggest a temporary scaffolding rather than a permanent monument. See K. Gebauer and H. Johannes, "Ausgrabungen im Kerameikos," *AA* 51 (1936), col. 208, and Dieter Ohly, "Kerameikos-Grabung, Tatigkeitsbericht 1956–61," *AA* 80 (1965), cols. 309–10.

8. On the funerary law of Thasos, see Jean Pouilloux, *Recherches sur l'histoire et les cultes de Thasos*: E. de Boccard, (Paris 1954), vol. 1, no. 141, pp. 371–80. This inscription has also been studied by Franciszek Sokolowski (*Lois sacrées des cités grecques: Supplément* [Paris: E. de Boccard, 1962], no. 64) and published by the Institut Fernand-Courby in *Nouveau Choix d'inscriptions grecques* (Paris, 1971), no. 19, pp. 105–109. Together with Rhodes (Diodorus, 20.84), only Thasos has a nomos as complete as and as close to Athens's, and the possibility of an imitation is not to be excluded.

9. A few famous examples are the dead of Thermopylae and Plataea and the Theban combatants of Chaironeia, all buried on the battlefield. For more detail, see Jacoby, "Patrios Nomos," pp. 42–44; A.W. Gomme, *Commentary*, vol. 2, p. 94; Donna Kurtz and John Boardman, *Greek Burial Customs* (London: Thames and Hudson, 1971), pp. 246–47 and 257.

10. Cf., Herodotus 6.111 and Pierre Vidal-Naquet, "La Tradition de l'hoplite athénien," in Jean-Pierre Vernant (ed.), *Problèmes de la guerre en Grèce ancienne* (The Hague: Mouton, 1968), p. 165.

11. The city described here by Thucydides is that of the 430s and also the ideal city of Pericles's epitaphios. In more troubled times, during the patriotic reaction of the 330s, attendance at the ceremony, though not a legal obligation, would have been regarded as proof of civic spirit. Thus Leocrates's absence from the funeral for the dead of Chaironeia condemned him in Lycurgus's eyes (*Against Leocrates* 45).

12. On *xenoi* designating allies in fifth-century texts, see Philippe Gauthier, "Les *Xénoi* dans les textes athéniens," *RFG* 84 (1971), pp. 44–79. Between the obligation to attend the Panathenaea and the complete freedom that obtained for the funeral procession, there is a considerable and noteworthy difference.

13. The orator is chosen by the people, after deliberations by the boule, which proposes a *probouleuma;* see *Menexenus* 234b4–10 and Demosthenes, *De corona* 285. It goes without saying that the final decision rested exclusively with the assembly.

14. This should be seen not as a topographical indicator — Thucydides does not even name this cemetery — but as a *qualitative* one.

15. For Olivier Reverdin (*La Religion de la cité platonicienne* [Paris: E. de Boccard, 1945], p. 116), prophylactic measures were less severe on account of the state of preservation of the ashes, which would explain the discrepancy. An explanation of this type turns out to be inadequate for phenomena related to a

functional analysis; for similar cases, see Claude Bérard, *Eretria*, vol. 3, *L'Héroôn à la porte de l'Ouest* (Berne: Francke, 1970), pp. 30 and 52. For the aristocratic character of prothesis, see Louis Gernet and André Boulanger, *Le Génie grec dans la religion* (Paris: Albin Michel, 1970), p. 245.

16. Cypress wood is not subject to decay (Theophrastus, *History of Plants* 5.42; Pliny, *Natural History* 16.213 and 223); a noble material (Plutarch, *Pericles* 12.6), it was used in the construction of palaces (*Odyssey* 17.340) or temples (Pindar, *Pythians* 5.39; Pliny, *Natural History* 16.215; cf. Pausanias 8.17.2). For the cypress as the Tree of the Dead, in Greece as in Rome, see Pliny, *Natural History* 139, and above all Plato, *Laws* 5.741c6–7: "a memorial inscribed in cypress." The main points on this subject are collected in the article "cypress" in *RE*.

17. See Pouilloux's remarks on the *kēdeuein mē exestō* of the funerary law of Thasos in *Recherches*, pp. 375–76.

18. Wilamowitz, *GT*, vol. 1, p. 204; Henri Jeanmaire, *Couroi et Courètes: Essai sur l'éducation spartiate et sur les rites d'adolescence dans l'antiquité hellénique* (Lille: Bibliothèque Universitaire, 1939), pp. 133–44 (the ephebes at the Kerameikos) and 313ff. (the link between the Kerameikos and Theseus's exploits).

19. Cf. Homer A. Thompson, "The Panathenaic Festival," *AA* 76 (1961), cols. 224–31. The procession for the Panathenaea probably gathered in the Kerameikos, left from the Pompeion (situated just inside the Dipylon), and crossed the Agora diagonally (on the link between the Agora and the cult of the dead, see *ibid*. col. 228).

20. Pausanias's declaration (1.29.4: "stelae that make known the name and deme of each individual") is, unless this is a complete mistake, as Gomme believes (*Commentary*, vol. 2, pp. 96–97), at least the generalization of an exception. Indeed perhaps Pausanias described not so much what he had seen as what he had read in Diodorus's work, as Jacoby believes ("*Patrios Nomos*," pp. 40–41 and 47).

21. Among others, the famous "monument of Sicily," which is still being sought and has never been positively identified, either by A.E. Raubitschek, *Hesperia* 12 (1943), or by E. Mastrokostas, *AE* (1955), pp. 180–202, or by S.N. Koumanoudis, *AE* (1964), pp. 83–86. See the critique of all these attempts in Donald W. Bradeen, "The Athenian Casualty Lists," *CQ* 19 (1969), pp. 145–59, esp. 157–58 (cited hereafter as "Casualty," II). Associated with Pericles's epitaphios, the monument of 431–30 is also the object of much attention: see Raubitschek, *Hesperia* 12 (1943), and Christoph W. Clairmont, *Gravestone and*

Epigram: Greek Memorials from the Archaic and Classical Period (Mainz: Zabern, 1970), which without proof assigns to this monument a decisive role in the sequence of poluandria (pp. 43–45). The first prize goes to Semni Karusu, "Hermes psychopompos," *Ath. Mitt.* 76 (1961), pp. 91–106, who brings together on the "monument of Coronaea" the name of Phidias and Hermès Ludovisi (?), those of Sophocles (for the epigram), and that of Pericles (whose influence would have been crucial).

22. Following Gauthier (*"Xénoi"*) and others, I will henceforth designate these as the "lists of the dead."

23. Felix Jacoby, "Some Athenian Epigrams from the Persian Wars," *Hesperia* 14 (1945), pp. 157–211, repr. in *Kleine Schriften* (Berlin: Akademie, 1961), vol. 1, pp. 456–520, esp. pp. 475–76.

24. The heading is usually in the genitive (see, for example, *IG*, I², 929 and 943, and Donald W. Bradeen, *The Athenian Agora*, vol. 17, *Inscriptions: The Funerary Monuments* [Princeton, NJ: American School of Classical Studies at Athens, 1974], nos. 10, 11, 15, 18, 23 [all volumes in this project of the American School of Classical Studies at Athens are hereafter cited as *Agora*]). There are a few, exceptional examples of headings in the nominative; see Donald W. Bradeen, "Athenian Casualty Lists," *Hesperia* 33 (1964), pp. 16–62 (cited hereafter as "Casualty," I), pp. 22 and 33, and *Agora* vol. 17, no. 1, 1.54 (these three exceptions are quoted in "Casualty," II, p. 147).

25. The monuments of several stelae accord each tribe the same number of columns, whatever its losses ("Casualty," I, p. 45). The incision of grooves on the edge, and even at the center, of a stela was intended to separate the tribes and to give the impression of individual stelae (see "Casualty," I, pp. 21 and 23, and "The Athenian Casualty List of 464 B.C.," *Hesperia* 36 [1967], pp. 321–28). Finally, the differences between one *phulē* and another in *Agora*, vol. 17, no. 23, indicate that each tribe erected its own list independently.

26. According to Wilamowitz (*Aristoteles und Athen* [Berlin: Weidmann, 1893], vol. 2, p. 171), the absence of the patronymic is normal on an official monument, at least in the fifth century, since the Cleisthenean reform wanted "to prevent citizens from calling themselves by their fathers' names" (Aristotle, *Constitution of Athens* 21.4). One might add that the patronymic seldom appears on the lists, even outside Athens: see Johannes Malzer, "Verluste und Verlustlisten im griechischen Altertum bis auf die Zeit Alexanders des grossen" (Ph.D. diss., Jena, 1912), pp. 103–105, and Pouilloux, *Recherches*, vol. 1, p. 377. How-

ever, there was nothing general about the rule; both Samos (Herodotus 6.14.10) and Thasos registered losses *patrothen*.

27. Despite Pausanias (1.29.4), this absence is a relevant feature of the lists, and only the presence of the demotic has enabled A.E. Raubitschek ("The Heroes of Phyle," *Hesperia* 10 [1941], pp. 284–95) to identify an honorific list where Benjamin Dean Meritt (*Hesperia* 2 [1933], p. 154) saw a casualty list. Concerning a similar case (*IG*, II/III², 1951), see Yvon Garlan, "Les Esclaves grecs en temps de guerre," in *Actes du Colloque d'Histoire Sociale, 1970*, Annales littéraires de l'Université de Besançon (*Paris*, 1972), p. 38.

28. On the absence of the demotic characterizing the strategos exercising his functions, see Eugene Schweigert, "The Athenian Cleruchy of Samos," *AJPh* 61 (1940), pp. 194–98, and Marcel Pierart, "A propos de l'élection des stratèges athéniens," *BCH* 98 (1974), p. 127.

29. On financing by the state, see Kurtz and Boardman, *Greek Burial Customs*, pp. 112–21. Excess income was usually diverted to the building of public monuments (cf. M.M. Austin and Pierre Vidal-Naquet, *Economies et sociétés en Grèce ancienne* [Paris: A. Colin, 1972], p. 138). In the case of tombs of *proxenoi*, however, the erection of the stela and the engraving of the inscription were probably left to private initiative: see Werner Peek, *Kerameikos: Ergebnisse der Ausgrabungen*, vol. 3, *Inschriften, ostraka, Fluchtafeln* (Berlin: W. de Gruyter, 1941), p. 28.

30. Cf. Bérard, *Eretria*, vol. 3, pp. 31, 48–55, 66–71.

31. On Thucydides 2.34.4, see Pouilloux, *Recherches*, vol. 1, p. 375. The presence of women at the prothesis and at the tomb was traditional: see Margaret Alexiou, *The Ritual Lament in Greek Tradition* (Cambridge, UK: Cambridge University Press, 1974), pp. 6–7. But this concession to tradition was coupled with extreme severity: indeed, the legislation on the funeral usually allowed close relatives to proceed in the cortege (see Gernet and Boulanger, *Le Génie grec*, p. 137).

32. The funerary law of Thasos, though making provision for a dowry for the daughters of the dead (ll. 21–22), reserves the greatest honors for the *fathers and sons*.

33. At Thasos, on the other hand, the banquet was undoubtedly public, cf. Pouilloux, Recherches, pp. 373–74.

34. See above all Jacoby, "*Patrios Nomos*," pp. 60 and 62, and the similar but more discriminating opinions of Paul Wolters, "Eine Darstellung des athenischen

Staatfriedhofs," *SBAW* (1913), p. 7, and W.K. Lacey, *The Family in Classical Greece* (London: Thames and Hudson, 1972), p. 78.

35. Cf. Louis Robert, "Les Inscriptions grecques de Bulgarie," *Rev. Phil.* 33 (1959), p. 220.

36. On all these points, there is abundant information in Philo of Byzantium's *Mechanics*, published by Yvon Garlan as an appendix to his *Recherches de poliorcétique grecque* (Athens: Ecole Française d'Athènes, 1974): see esp. C 45–48 and 72 and Garlan's commentary, pp. 387 and 393–94 (the point of view is eminently pragmatic).

37. This remark was made by Gertrude Smith, "Athenian Casualty Lists," *CPhil.* 14 (1919), pp. 351–64, esp. p. 355. The sources were collected by O. Jacob, "Les Cités grecques et les blessés de guerre," in *Mélanges Gustave Glotz* (Paris: PUF, 1932), vol. 2, pp. 461–81 (for Athens, pp. 461–64), and A.A.M. Esser, "Invaliden- und hinterbliebenenfürsorge in der Antike," *Gymnasium* 52 (1942), pp. 25–29.

38. *Nouveau Choix d'inscriptions grecques*, p. 108 (on l. 12).

39. *Orphanoi* is how Aristotle and the epigraphic texts designated them, the publication of Theozotides's decree (Ronald Stroud, "Greek Inscriptions: Theozotides and the Athenian Orphans," *Hesperia* 40 [1971], pp. 280–301) confirmed this: lines 11 and 19 support the identification of the orphanoi of *IG*, I², 6, as war orphans.

40. The Athenian texts are completely silent on the fate of daughters of the dead, whereas the funerary law of Thasos makes provision for dowries for them (ll. 21–22).

41. No doubt through a magistrate, as in the case of the parents; "the highest magistracy [*archē*]": *Menexenus* 249a1.

42. According to Otto Schulthess (*Vormundschaft mach attischen Recht* [Freiburg: Mohr, 1886], p. 26), the state was content to pay an indemnity to the orphans' guardians without actually interfering in their upbringing the amount of the payment was probably one obol a day (cf. Stroud, "Greek Inscriptions," p. 290). On the general question of *trophē* as subsistence payment, see A. Willhelm, "Die lokrische Mädcheninschrift," *Jahreshefte des österreichischen archäologischen Institutes* 14 (1911), pp. 163–256, (esp. 217–20); and Edouard Will, "Notes sur *misthos*," in *Hommages à Claire Préaux* (Brussels, 1975), pp. 426–38, esp. 432–35. Paul Girard (*L'Education athénienne* [Paris: Hachette, 1891], p. 23) believes, without offering any evidence, in an upbringing by the state.

43. *Mechri hebes* means not "up to their adolescence" (cf. Jacqueline de Romilly's translation, CUF) but "up to their majority;" on the civic *hebe*, see Jules Labarbe, *La Loi navale de Thémistocle* (Paris: Société d'Edition les Belles Lettres, 1957), pp. 68–70 and 201–202, and Chrysis Pelekidis, *Histoire de l'éphébie attique des origines à 31 avant Jésus Christ* (Paris: 1962), pp. 51–69. It might also be compared with the funerary law of Thasos, ll. 16–17: "when they have attained their majority [*hēlikia*]."

44. Among which one might mention the *proedrie:* cf. Aeschines, *Against Ctesiphon* 154, and the funerary law of Thasos (ll. 13–15).

45. The expression is borrowed from Jean Rudhardt, *Notions fondamentales de la pensée religieuse et actes constitutifs du culte dans la Grèce classique* (Geneva: Droz, 1958), p. 132.

46. Jacoby, *"Patrios Nomos,"* p. 39.

47. Cf. M.I. Finley, *The Ancestral Constitution* (Cambridge: UK Cambridge University Press, 1971), pp. 6–14 and Eberhard Ruschenbusch, "Patrios Politeia: Theseus, Drakon, Solon und Kleisthenes im Publizistik und Geschichtschreibung des 5. und 4. Jahrhunderts," *Historia* 9 (1958), pp. 398–424.

48. On the Cleisthenean framework, see Christos Karusos, *Aristodikos* (*Stuttgart*: Kohlhammer, 1961), p. 41, and M.B. Wallace, "Notes on Early Greek Grave Epigrams," *Phoenix* 24 (1970), p. 102. The polemarch presided over the sacrifices in honor of citizens who had died in battle; are we to see in this the memory of a time when he had not yet lost his authority as a military leader? Following Albert Martin ("Notes sur l'héortologie athénienne," *Rev. Phil.* 10 [1886], p. 26), Pelekidis (*Histoire*, p. 235) and N.G.L. Hammond ("Strategia and Hegemonia in Fifth Century Athens," *CQ* 19 [1969], pp. 111–43, repr. as "Problems of Command in Fifth Century Athens," in *Studies in Greek History* [Oxford: Clarendon, 1973], pp. 356–57) think so. But this argument is not decisive: without necessarily being an "active officer," the polemarch intervenes quite naturally in the religious ceremonies concerning soldiers (for Thasos, see *Nouveau Choix d'inscriptions grecques*, p. 108).

49. The parallel between Athens and the other Greeks is only apparent: although the Spartans of Thermopylae obtained a special inscription, they were buried on the spot and honored by a common decision; Athens, on the other hand, reserved special treatment for her dead and instituted a nomos that was turned toward the future. Thus a Panhellenic decision — the heroic cult of Plataea — is concealed for Athens's benefit. Everything in this text bears the

mark of Ephorus, who was Diodorus's principal source for book 11 (see Otto Schröder, "De laudibus Athenarum a poetis tragicis et ab oratoribus epidicticis excultis" [Ph.D. diss., Göttingen, 1914], and Eduard Schwartz, "Diodorus," in *RE*, 5, cols. 662–704).

50. On the various stages, see Jacoby, "Epigrams," pp. 459 n.15 and 518; on the institution of the nomos, "*Patrios Nomos*," pp. 50–54.

51. The value of Pausanias's information is the only real issue concerning this text, and there is no reason to suppose that it escaped all ideological presupposition. The temporal interpretation of the text, on the other hand, poses no problem (see the editions of Frazer, M.A. Levi, and Ernst Meyer), and there is no reason to seek in it, like Gomme (*Commentary*, vol. 2, pp. 95–97) and Bradeen ("Casualty," II, pp. 154–55), following Alfred Brücker ("Kerameikos-Studien," *Ath. Mitt.* 35 [1910], p. 197), Sebastian Wenz ("Studien zu attischen Kriegergräbern" [Ph.D. diss., Erfurt, 1913], pp. 13–17 and 25), and Schröder ("De laudibus Athenarum," pp. 68–76), some topographical indication: *prōtoi etaphesan is* not a variant of *prōtos ... estin houtos taphos* (29.3) unless one deliberately ignores the difference between an aorist and a present.

52. Except, of course, burial in the Kerameikos and no doubt the epitaphios: cf. Jacoby, "Epigrams," pp. 476–78.

53. Pierre Amandry, "Collection Paul Canellopoulos" (1), *BCH* 95 (1971), pp. 586–626, esp. 623–25.

54. Eugene Vanderpool, "Three Prize Vases," *AD* 24 (1969), pp. 1–5.

55. As Amandry has well shown ("Collection," pp. 615–20).

56. On this development, see Claude Mossé, *La Fin de la democratie athénienne* (Paris: PUF, 1962), pp. 259–86.

57. On the monument of Dexileus (394–93) see Marcus Niebuhr Tod, *A Selection of Greek Historical Inscriptions* (Oxford: Clarendon, 1947), vol. 2, no. 105, and Alexander Conze, *Die attischen Grabreliefs* (Vienna, 1893–1900), no. 1158, pl. 248; on Demokleides, see Charles Picard, *Manuel d'archéologie grecque: La Sculpture*, 4 vols., *IVème Siècle, 2ème partie* (Paris: Picard, 1963), pl. 517, and Conze, no. 623, pl. 122. One might add the monument erected to an unknown man (*GV*, 2043; Clairmont, *Gravestone and Epigram*, no. 28), the epitaphic fragments published by Bradeen (*Agora*, vol. 17, nos. 1029 and 1029a: two individual tombs, the second of which, with a base, was of noble style), and a soldier's tomb made by Praxiteles and mentioned by Pausanias (1.2.3), although this is not an exhaustive list.

58. On cenotaphs, see Bruckner, "Kerameikos-Studien," p. 191. Burial in the demosion sema is postulated by Plutarch's anecdote about Phocion (*On Ways of Praising Oneself* 17: under Phocion's magistracy, no epitaphios was delivered, and all dead citizens were buried in the family tomb).

59. Bérard has raised the objection to me that Dexileus's name, having been mentioned in the inscription of the Hippeis, probably did not appear on the obituary list as well. Of course the list cannot decide this issue: only the first lines have survived. Were the cavalry of 394 buried apart (as Emily Vermeule seems to believe, "Five Vases from the Grave Precinct of Dexileus," *JDI* 84 [1970], p. 98)? I do not believe in the possibility of so exceptional an honor. The tendency to reserve special honors for the cavalry in both the fifth and the fourth century does not exclude burial in the poluandrion. It seems to me that beside the tomb there was room for a semiofficial commemorative monument (a monument erected by the tribe in addition to the official poluandrion?).

60. See Robert, "Les Inscriptions grecques de Bulgarie," pp. 217–19.

61. Gauthier "*Xénoi*," p. 64.

62. On *toxotai barbaroi* as Scythian archers, see Gauthier ("*Xénoi*," p. 64). On the archers at the frontiers of the Greek world, see Louis Robert, *Hellenica*, Volume XI-XII (Paris: Maisonneuve, 1960), pp. 271–75, on Cretan archers in the Greek armies of the fifth century, see Henri van Effenterre, *La Crète et le monde grec de Platon à Polybe* (Paris: E. de Boccard, 1948), p. 43 n.6.

63. See the articles by Garlan ("Les Esclaves grecs," p. 48) and Rachel L. Sargent, "The Use of Slaves by the Athenians in Warfare," *CPhil.* 22 (1927), pp. 202–11 and 264–79. For a military list of slaves at Chios, see Louis Robert, *Etudes épigraphiques et philologiques* (Paris: Champion, 1938), pp. 118–25.

64. Wilamowitz, "Aus Kydathen," p. 85.

65. Personal letter to the author from Philippe Gauthier.

66. *Athēnaiōn* has a dual function: introduced by *de*, it contrasts total Athenian losses with Boeotian losses (*Boiotōn men*), but it also plays the role of a substantive (*Athēnaiōn . . . chilion*) opposed to *psilon de*. Because he has failed to see this double function, A.H.M. Jones (*Athenian Democracy* [Oxford: Blackwell, 1957], pp. 12–13) concludes that *all* the dead were citizens, including officers' servants.

67. Apart from the celebrated debate in Euripides's *Herakles* (151–205), in which the archer, that nonentity (*ouden ōn*) endowed with a trace of courage (*doxa eupsuchias*), is opposed to the hoplite (*anēr*), the only possessor of true

courage, one might mention Aristophanes's highly deprecatory use of the word *toxotēs*; see Jean Taillardat, *Les Images d'Aristophane: Etudes de langue et de style* (Paris: Société d'Edition les Belles Lettres, 1965), pp. 240–41.

68. Is the "obituary of Delion" in Thucydides proof of the exclusion of the psiloi? In fact, Thucydides is not copying an obituary here, but as usual he gives the exact figure only for the hoplites, whose loss alone he considers significant; one might compare this with 2.87.3. Finally, the existence of an individual tomb for a peltast (*Agora*, vol. 17, no. 1028) is not enough to prove that the psiloi were buried separately.

69. P. Vidal-Naquet, "Hoplite athénien," pp. 154 and 174.

70. A single list of the dead bears the word *hopli[tai]* (*Agora*, vol. 17, no. 23, with Bradeen's restoration). But the incomplete nature of this list does not exclude the mention of other categories, as Bradeen stresses ("Casualty," I, p. 33).

71. The epitaph of Mannes the Phrygian, who may have been a freed slave listed as a metic (*IG*, I², 1084), is not enough to prove that metics were buried apart; see Philippe Gauthier, *Symbola: Les Étrangers et la justice athénienne* (Nancy: Université de Nancy II, 1972), p. 114 n.17.

72. A comparison of 4.90.1 and 4.94.1 suggests that for Thucydides *astoi* refers both to citizens and to metics. Thucydides explicitly mentions metics only in very special cases (2.13.7: an exact listing; 2.31.1: the exceptional use of metics as hoplites at the beginning of the war).

73. On Aristophanes's text, see Taillardat, *Les Images d'Aristophane*, pp. 391–93; on the integration of metics into the city, see Gauthier, *Symbola*, pp. 111–116.

74. See Garlan ("Les Esclaves grecs," p. 44). Everything separates the polyandrion of the citizens from that of the Plataeans and slaves: not only the distance between the two tombs — about 1.5 kilometers — but also the funerary modes, with cremation for the citizens, simple burial (a much less costly method) for the Plataeans and slaves; see Kurtz and Boardman, *Greek Burial Customs*, p. 246.

75. This is the meaning of *dokimasia* (1. 5) in Stroud, "Theozotides and the Athenian Orphans," pp. 291–92. The meaning is probably double, verifying both the father's status and the son's legitimacy.

76. Cf. Gomme, *Commentary*, vol. 1, p. 197.

77. See Chapter Six, p. 389–90.

78. Cf. Jacoby, *"Patrios Nomos,"* pp. 61–66.

79. At Thasos, the agon was inserted in the Herakleia; there is nothing to prove that the same applied to the funeral (Pouilloux, *Recherches*, vol. 1, p. 378). For the distinction between the funeral and the annual celebration in Athens, see Kurtz and Boardman, *Greek Burial Customs*, p. 112.

80. The term was coined by Pierre Vidal-Naquet, who concludes that it was indeed heroization ("La Guerre tragique," in *Athènes au temps de Périclès* [Paris, 1965], p. 270).

81. *"Patrios Nomos,"* pp. 39 and 60. See also Wilamowitz, *GT*, pp. 203–204, and C.M. Bowra, *The Greek Experience* (New York: New American Library, 1957), pp. 20ff.

82. Paul Foucart, *Le Culte des héros chez les Grecs* (Paris: Imprimerie Nationale, 1918), pp. 116–20; Erwin Rohde, *Psyché: Le Culte de l'âme chez les Grecs et leur croyance a l'immortalité* (Paris: Payot, 1928), pp. 150 and 549.

83. Cf. Eugen Reiner, *Die rituelle Totenklage der Griechen* (Stuttgart and Berlin: Kohlhammer, 1938), p. 118 ("heros-ähnlichen").

84. On ambiguity, see Angelo Brelich, *Heros: Il culto greco degli eroi e il problema degli esseri semi-divini* (Rome: Ateneo, 1958), pp. 13 and 87ff. The ambiguity has passed into French and English; the Germans are more fortunate and have two terms at their disposal, *Heroen* and *Helden*, which, however, they use interchangeably (see Wilamowitz, *GT*, pp. 203–204).

Heroization and immortality are confused by Roger Goossens, *Euripide et Athènes* (Brussels: Palais des Académies, 1962), pp. 51–52.

85. This is why I do not feel able to include their cult in the ritual of the Genesia, as Jacoby would (*"Patrios Nomos,"* pp. 61–66), whom Gomme criticizes for that reason (*Commentary*, vol. 2, pp. 100–101).

86. See Pouilloux, *Recherches*, vol. 1, p. 378, *and Nouveau Recueil d'inscriptions grecques*, p. 109; on Eretria, see Bérard, *Eretria*, vol. 3, p. 68.

87. On the name in the heroic cult, see Herodotus 7.117. The list of the dead, apart from its military and political function, is justified in the context of a heroic cult; see Jacoby, "Epigrams," pp. 478 and 480. It will be remembered that in *Works and Days*, 154, the hero's *name* distinguishes him from the mass of *nonymnoi* (nameless); cf. Jean-Pierre Vernant, "Aspects de la personne dans la religion grecque," in *MP*, vol. 2, p. 89.

88. On the agon epitaphios as an integral part of a heroic ritual, see Theodora Hadzisteliou-Price, "Hero Cult and Homer," *Historia* 22 (1973), pp.

143–44, and Rudhardt, *Notions fondamentales de la pensée religieuse*, pp. 129 and 157; on the *enagismata*, see Rudhardt, *ibid.*, pp. 129 and 238–39.

89. Pouilloux, *Recherches*, pp. 375–76.

90. On exceptional status and the relationship with the past, see Louis Gernet, "L'Anthropologie dans la religion grecque," in *Anthropologie de la Grèce antique* (Paris: Maspero, 1968), p. 13; on *hōs hērōi* = as to an epic hero, see Nikolaos Michael Kontoléon, *Aspects de la Grèce préclassique* (Paris: Collège de France, 1970), p. 46.

91. Cf. Oddone Longo, "Ad Alceo 112.10 L.P.: Per la storia di un topos," *Bolletino dell'Istituto di Filologia Greca* (Padua), 1 (1974), p. 226.

92. See Kontoléon, *Aspects*, pp. 39–47.

93. *Eudaimon* is a derivative of *daimon*, a "floating signifier" that made little headway in the polis; cf. Marcel Detienne, *De la pensée religieuse à la pensée politique: La notion de daimôn dans le pythagorisme ancien* (Paris: Belles Lettres, 1963), pp. 26–27, 54, 65–66.

94. Goossens, *Euripide et Athènes*, p. 54. On collective, nonpersonal immortality, see Rudhardt, *Notions fondamentales de la pensée religieuse*, pp. 123–24.

95. Cf. Angelo Brelich, *Gli eroi greci: Un problema storico-religioso* (Rome: Ateneo, 1958), pp. 80–82, and Alexiou, *Ritual Lament,* p. 61.

96. Cf. Alain Michel, *Les Rapports de la rhétorique et de la philosophie dans l'oeuvre de Cicéron: Recherches sur les fondements philosophiques de l'art de persuader* (Paris: PUF, 1960), pp. 382–84.

97. Jean-Pierre Vernant, *Les Origines de la pensée grecque* (Paris: PUF, 1962), p. 42.

98. Cf. Octave Navarre, *Essai sur la rhétorique grecque avant Aristote* (Paris: Hachette, 1900), and Vinzenz Buchheit, *Untersuchungen zur Theorie des Genos epideiktikon von Gorgias bis Aristoteles* (Munich: Huber, 1960). Similarly, Alexiou thinks that the funeral oration has its source in a tradition more literary than "popular" (*Ritual Lament*, p. 107).

99. *To thrēnein pepoiēmena* clearly means not "affected laments" (Robert Flacelière) but "versified lamentation"; see Reiner, *Die rituelle Totenklage*, pp. 4–5, and Alexiou, *Ritual Lament*, p. 12.

100. On the *kēdeia/kēdea* link, see Alexiou, *Ritual Lament*, pp. 10–11; on the meaning of the funerary legislations, see Alexiou, *Ritual Lament*, pp. 14–15 and 23, and Gernet and Boulanger, *Le Génie grec*, p. 137.

101. Tettichos's epitaph is related to an epitaphios in many respects and par-

ticularly by v. 4, to which Margherita Guarducci has rightly given a political reading (in the epigraphical appendix to G.M.A. Richter, *The Archaic Gravestones of
Attica* [London: Phaidon, 1961]; the opposite view is found in Richmond Lattimore, *Themes in Greek and Latin Epitaphs* [Urbana: University of Illinois Press,
1962], p. 235). The presence of an appeal for pity is all the more significant in that
it marks the gap between the individual epitaph and the collective epitaphios.

102. This lament probably took place during the annual celebrations in
honor of the dead man rather than at the public funeral: cf. Louis Robert, in
L'Epigramme grecque, Entretiens de la Fondation Hardt, 14 (Vandoeuvres-
Geneva, 1968), pp. 32–33.

103. On this text, cf. Austin and Vidal-Naquet, *Economies et sociétés,* p. 276.
See also Reiner, *Die rituelle Toten Klage,* pp. 49–50, for a comparison with the
funeral of the tyrants of Erythrae.

104. The very structure of the sentence expresses difference: in Thucydides, a temporal succession; in Herodotus, an extended activity, onto which is
grafted a secondary manifestation.

105. On the king as a "disruptive force," see M.I. Finley, "Sparta," in *Problèmes de la guerre en Grèce ancienne,* p. 151.

106. On pothos, see the analyses of Jean-Pierrre Vernant in "La Catégorie
psychologique du double," in *MP,* vol. 2, p. 71, and in a course given at the Ecole
Pratique des Hautes Etudes (Vème section) in 1974–75 on the representation of
the gods.

107. See Marcel Detienne, "La Phalange," in *Problèmes de la guerre en Grèce
ancienne,* pp. 119–42, esp. 127–28.

108. See Herodotus 6.21 (fine imposed on Phrynichus for making the city
weep with his play about the taking of Miletus) and Aeschines, *Against Ctesiphon*
183–86 (Cimon, the demos, and the Hermes of Eion), commentary on the text
by Jacoby, "Epigrams," pp. 508–509.

109. Friedrich Nietzsche, *The Birth of Tragedy,* trans. Walter Kaufmann
(New York: Vintage Books, 1967), p. 43.

110. "Tragischer Epitaphios": Wilamowitz, *Aristoteles und Athen,* vol. 1,
p. 249. The scholiast already saw in this drama an *enkomion Athēnaiōn;* in fact,
there are many allusions to the funeral oration in this tragedy. So I agree with C.
Collard ("The Funeral Oration in Euripides' *Supplices,*" *BICS* 19 [1972], pp.
39–53) that any reading of *The Suppliant Women* as a satire on the funeral oration
is erroneous.

443

111. As Günther Zuntz observes in *The Political Plays of Euripides* (Manchester: Manchester University Press, 1955), pp. 11–25. The tension between threnos and *epainos*, the same that opposes lyricism to the dialogue form within the language of tragedy, enables Euripides to ward off both Aeschylean lyricism and the noncivic forms of mourning.

112. Cf. Alexiou, *Ritual Lament*, p. 107.

113. Only Gorgias will allow himself to subvert the topos by opposing the hymns due to victories over the barbarians and the threnoi due to the victories over the Greeks (Philostratus 1.9.5 = *DK*, 82 B 5 b); but the Sophist, a stranger to the Athenian city, could take the liberty of denaturing the funeral oration by introducing a Panhellenic tone into it (which Isocrates would imitate, *Panegyricus* 158).

114. At the very most, the speaker, evoking ritual lamentations, ends by prolonging the final tones of the lament. Compare Thucydides 2.46.2 (cf. *Menexenus* 249c8 and Demosthenes 37, where the same movement occurs) and Lysias 81.

115. On the language of poetic glory, the essential work is that of Detienne, *The Masters of Truth*, pp. 39–52 and passim.

116. See also Emile Benveniste, *Vocabulaire des institutions indo-européenes* (Paris: Minuit, 1969), vol. 2, pp. 59ff. and 133ff.; Max Greindl, "Kléos, Kydos, Euchos, Timè, Phatis, Doxa" (Ph.D. diss., Munich, 1938), pp. 21ff. and 104ff.; and "Ruhm" in Rüdiger Schmitt, *Dichtung und Dichterprache in indogermanischer Zeit* (Wiesbaden: Harrassowitz, 1967).

117. See Chapter Two, pp. 152–54.

118. On this aspect of poetic speech, cf. Clémence Ramnoux, *La Nuit et les enfants de la nuit dans la tradition grecque* (Paris: Flammarion, 1959).

119. The eulogy of Themistocles (Lysias 42) — very close to the portrait drawn by Herodotus (8.124) and Thucydides (1.138.3) — is an exception that might be explained by the democratic spirit of this epitaphios if Myronides (52) were not also mentioned. It will be observed at least that these great personages belong to the past, which makes it easier for them to avoid the rule of anonymity.

120. Cf. Greindl, "*Kléos,*" p. 160.

121. Karl Jost, *Das Beispiel und Vorbild der Vorfahren bei den attischen Rednern,* Paderborn Studien (1934), p. 249.

122. This question is examined from a rather different point of view in Chapter Six (see pp. 332–51).

123. See Georg Misch, *A History of Autobiography in Antiquity* (London: Routledge and Paul, 1950), vol. 1, pp. 25ff.

124. Detienne, *The Masters of Truth*, p. 46.

125. Distance is a constituent of magico-religious language; fascination characterizes "secularized" poetry as defined by Simonides. Cf. Detienne, *ibid.*, pp. 74–75, 109, 116–17.

126. Jacoby, "Epigrams," p. 475.

127. Cf. Bruno Gentili, "Epigramma ed elegia," in *L'Epigramme grecque,* pp. 54–56.

128. See Prato's commentary (*Tyrtaeus*, p. 135) and Gentili, "Epigramma," p. 55.

129. Cf. Jacoby, "Epigrams," pp. 474–76. The transfer of the bodies into the civic space may be related to this development.

130. See Jacoby, "Epigrams," pp. 510–17, on the *pote* of the epigram of Eion. Much less convincing are the analyses of H.T. Wade-Gery, "Classical Epigrams and Epitaphs: A Study of the Cimonian Age," *JHS* 53 (1933), pp. 71–104.

131. Against A.E. Raubitschek ("Des Denkmal-Epigramm," in *L'Epigramme grecque,* pp. 2–26), Gentili tries to minimize the influence of the epic on the funerary epigram, to the advantage of that of the elegy ("Epigramma," pp. 64–66); but he is himself led to oppose the epic style of the epitaph of a warrior (Arniadas of Corcyra: *GV*, p. 73) to the more prosaic one of a contemporary epitaph, dedicated in the same city to a *proxenos* (Menecrates: *GV*, p. 42); see Gentili, "Epigramma," pp. 29 and 65–66.

132. See my article "Hebè et andreia: Deux versions de la mort du combattant athénien," *Ancient Society* 6 (1975), pp. 1–31.

133. See Chapter Two, pp. 145–70.

134. See, for example, Gauthier, "La Cité," in *Athènes au temps de Périclès,* pp. 27–47. One might add that the regime of Cleisthenes did not immediately find its name, since the very term "democracy" appeared fairly late. Cf. J.A.O. Larsen, "Cleisthenes and the Development of the Theory of Democracy at Athens," in *Essays in Political Theory Presented to George H. Sabine* (Ithaca, NY: Cornell University Press, 1948), pp. 1–16; against this view, see Victor Ehrenberg, "Origins of Democracy," *Historia* 1 (1950) 515–48, who argues in favor of an early appearance of the word demokratia on the basis of a dating of Aeschylus's *Suppliants* that is much too early.

135. Pericles's epitaphios is, it will be remembered, mainly responsible for

the idea that the funeral oration is a later addition to the nomos; but in Thucydides's text, this idea can be attributed only to the critical attitude adopted by Pericles with regard to earlier epitaphioi.

136. On the "Oath of Plataea," see Robert, *Etudes épigraphiques et philologiques*.

137. See Amédée Hauvette, "Les *Eleusiniens* d'Eschyle et l'institution du discours funèbre à Athènes," in *Mélanges H. Weil* (Paris, 1898), p. 170.

138. Wilhelm Kierdorf, Erlebnis und Darstellung der *Perserkriege, Studien zu Simonides, Pindar, Aischylos und den attischen Rednern* (Göttingen: Vandenhoeck and Ruprecht, 1966), ch. 3.

139. On the "epigrams of Marathon," see the bibliography in Meiggs-Lewis (no. 26, pp. 54–57); see esp. the article by Pierre Amandry in *Theoria: Festschrift für W.H. Schuchbardt* (Baden-Baden: Grimm, 1960), pp. 1–9.

140. Cf. William C. West, "Saviors of Greece," *ORBS* 11 (1970), pp. 271–82, esp. 273; the first "epigram of Marathon" is the only solid evidence of Athenian propaganda during the first years of the Pentecontaetia.

141. See Pierre Vidal-Naquet, "Une Enigme à Delphes: A propos de la base de Marathon (Pausanias, X, 10,1–2)," *RH* 238 (1967), pp. 281–302. See also Pierre Amandry, "Athènes au lendemain des guerres médiques," *RUB* (1961), pp. 198–223.

142. Herodotus's account of the Persian Wars gives many examples of the custom of awarding a prize for bravery to the living (8.123) or the dead (Aristodamus, the best Spartan combatant at Plataea, is deprived of honor by his *lyssa*, not by his death; 9.71).

143. On *lampron ergon*, see the commentary by Reginald Walter Macan, *Herodotus: The Seventh, Eighth, and Ninth Books* (London: Macmillan, 1908). It concerns a single combat (cf. 6.92) with challenge, as in the *Iliad* (9.75).

144. When death occurs in exceptional circumstances, Herodotus does not fail to indicate it (see 6.114; death of Cynegyrus); likewise, he mentions any burial place that departs from the norm (9.105: Hermolycus, the best combatant at Mycale, who fell at Carystus, is buried at Cape Geraestus) or follows some earlier usage (1.30: Tellus buried "at the very spot where he fell").

145. Cf. Jacoby, "Epigrams," pp. 458–59, and Werner Peek, *GG*, pp. 20ff.

146. See Jacoby, "Epigrams," pp. 513–17.

147. "The focal point of Athenian political life," according to Homer A. Thompson and Wycherley, *Agora*, vol. 14, p. 92; on the Poikile, see the bibliographical references in *Agora*, vol. 3, p. 31.

148. L.H. Jeffery ("The Battle of Oinoe in the Stoa Poikile: A Problem in Greek Art and History," *BSA* 60 [1965], pp. 41–57) is shocked by the intrusion of a recent historical event in a set of mythical or already legendary exploits, so she tries to link this painting with some mythical war. This is to underestimate the importance of the turning point of the 460s (see p. 102). Furthermore, such a juxtaposition is not without parallel: thus in the fourth century, at the Stoa of Zeus, Euphranor depicted the battle of Mantinea alongside the allegory of Theseus, Demos, and Demokratia (see *Agora*, vol. 14, p. 101).

149. Cf. Evelyn B. Harrison, "The Composition of the Amazonomachy on the Shield of Athena Parthenos," *Hesperia* 35 (1966), pp. 106–33, esp. 128–32 ("that immense panorama of human history").

150. Alone among the orators who dwell on the catalog, Lysias interpolates between the two temporal sequences the obligatory passage on autochthony and democracy. On myth as prehistory, see Martin P. Nilsson, *Cults, Myths, Oracles, and Politics in Ancient Greece* (Lund: Gleerup, 1951), pp. 12–15 and 49–64. In the epitaphioi, one does not even find what Bernhard Abraham van Groningen (*In The Grip of the Past: Essay on an Aspect of Greek Thought* [Leiden: Brill, 1953]) calls a "genealogical no-man's-land" (see, for example, Herodotus's attempt to link the historical character Leonidas with the mythical ancestor Herakles: 7.204).

151. At least as far as the Pentecontaetia is concerned: E. Schwartz (*RE*, 6, col. 14) believes that Ephorus closely followed the catalog of the epitaphioi here.

152. On this subject, see Arnaldo Momigliano, *Filippo il Macedone, saggio sulla storia greca del IV secolo* (Florence: Le Monnier, 1934), and Jost, *Das Beispiel und Vorbild der Vorfahren.*

153. For the first time, unless one considers as a precedent the *rhētra* of Lycurgus, who attributes *kratos* to the demos. But this difficult text has been subjected to many readings, and it should be noted that *kratos* is in any case associated with another word, probably *nikēn* (see Plutarch, *Lycurgus* 6.2 and Tyrtaeus D3a).

154. Hermann Strasburger ("Thukydides und die politische Selbstdarstellung der Athener," *Hermes* 86 [1958], p. 34) believes that the traditional funeral oration confined the eulogy of liberty to the passages on external politics; by shifting the emphasis toward the internal organization of a city, Pericles, it would appear, was making a profound break. In fact, Pericles's ruse consists in rejecting the catalog of exploits; this move allows him to present the eulogy of democracy as an innovation, which it probably was not.

155. This is the strange solution of Hermann Schneider, "Untersuchungen über die Staatsbegräbnisse und den Aufbau der öffentlichen Leichenreden bei den Athenern in der klassischen Zeit" (Ph.D. diss., Berne, 1912).

156. The date of Aeschylus's *Eleusinians*, according to Jacoby, *F.Gr.Hist.*, commentary on 328 F 112.

157. On Erechtheus's end, see Colin Austin, "Nouveaux Fragments de l'*Erechthée* d'Euripide," *Recherches de papyrologie* 4 (1967), pp. 11–67.

158. On Theseus as a creation of the late sixth century, cf. Felix Jacoby, *Atthis: The Local Chronicles of Ancient Athens* (Oxford: Clarendon, 1949), pp. 219ff., and Martin P. Nilsson, "Political Propaganda in Sixth Century Athens," in *Studies Presented to David Moore Robinson* (S. Louis: Washington University, 1953), vol. 2, pp. 743–48.

159. Xenophon (*Memorabilia* 3.5.10), on the other hand, lists these episodes under the general heading "wars of the Theseus period," an interesting expression in a text obviously inspired by the tradition of the funeral oration and which merely emphasizes all the more the strange silence of the epitaphioi with regard to Theseus.

160. Gisela Schmitz-Kahlmann, *Das Beispiel der Geschichte im politischen Denken des Isokrates*, Philologus, supp. 31 (1939), p. 69.

161. See A.E. Raubitschek, "Demokratia," *Hesperia* 31 (1962), pp. 238–43.

162. This is the opinion of James H. Oliver, *Demokratia, the Gods, and the Free World* (Baltimore: Johns Hopkins Press, 1960), p. 30 n.29.

163. Jeanmaire, *Couroi,* pp. 308ff. and 372–75.

164. Theseus is much more authoritarian than Aeschylus's Pelasgus, and his figure makes that of the demos, which in Aeschylus possessed most of the power, look very pale.

165. Cf. Pierre Lévêque and Pierre Vidal-Naquet, *Clisthène l'Athénien: Essai sur la représentation de l'espace et du temps dans la pensée politique grecque* (Paris: Belles Lettres, 1964), pp. 119–20.

166. On Cimon, "the new Theseus," cf. Anthony J. Podlecki, "Cimon, Skyros, and Theseus' Bones," *JHS* 91 (1971), pp. 141–43. On Cimon and Theseus, see, for example, Vidal-Naquet, "Une Enigme à Delphes."

167. Jacoby, *Atthis*, p. 122.

168. Wilhelm Vollgraff, *L'Oraison funèbre de Gorgias* (Leiden: Brill, 1952), p. 55, sees it as "the alarming opportunism of a political chameleon." It would be more reasonable to compare this formula with Lysias 14: "full of compassion for the victims and of hatred for the oppressors."

169. Goossens, *Euripide et Athènes*, pp. 103–105 and 207.

170. In Euripides, the lesson is complete, since, conquered by the Athenians, Eurystheus prophesies the treachery of the descendants of the Heraclidae toward Athens (1032–36); furthermore, as Garlan observes (*Recherches de poliorcétique grecque*, p. 62), the allusion to the mythological devastation of Sparta by Iolaus (740–43) salves the Athenians' wounded pride.

171. The version of the truce was not drawn up only by the Thebans (Pausanias 1.39.2), for it was the theme of Aeschylus's *Eleusinians*. With the exception of Isocrates's *Panathenaicus* and Philochorus's *Atthis* (*F.Gr. Hist.*, p. 328, no. 112), Athenian tradition nevertheless prefers the bellicose version. Like Wilamowitz (*GT*, pp. 205–206), Jacoby (*F.Gr.Hist.*, vol. 3, no. 1, pp. 441ff.) supposes that this unfavorable version was introduced by the author of an epitaphios after the battle of Tanagra (457) or of Coronea (446).

172. We know that with alliance in view, Isocrates chose the pacific version in the *Panathenaicus* (169ff.). Cf. S. Perlman, "The Historical Example: Its Use and Importance as Political Propaganda in the Attic Orators," *Scripta Hierosolymitana* 7 (1961), pp. 150–66.

173. See the pertinent "remarks" by Felix Jacoby ("Some Remarks on Ion of Chios," *CQ* 41 [1947], pp. 1–7; repr. in *Abhandlungen zur griechischen Geschichtschreibung* [Leiden: Brill, 1956], pp. 144–68, esp. 164–65). George Grote was already protesting against the partiality of Ion: "If we possessed the oration actually delivered, we would probably see that it accorded all the honor for the exploit to Athens and to its citizens in general, comparing their action to that of Agamemnon and his army (and not himself with Agamemnon)" (*A History of Greece* [London: Murray, 1862], vol. 4, p. 170).

174. Far from attributing to Pericles a theme deriving from his own historical reflection, could it not be that Thucydides was influenced by the orator in his many deprecatory allusions to the Trojan War (for example, 1.10.3 and 11.3)? The paradox may be argued.

175. In pictorial representations, the subject of the Trojan War may have survived longer: a favorite theme in the early fifth century (cf. Charles Dugas, "A la *Leschè* des Cnidiens," *REG* 51 [1938], pp. 53–59), it is also found on the metopes of the Parthenon, though not, it is true, on the uniquely Athenian pediment.

176. See Jacoby, "*Patrios Nomos*," pp. 47ff., "Some Remarks," p. 165, and "Epigrams," pp. 510–11.

177. Athens served as a model for the practices at Thurii, and perhaps at Elis: for Elis, see Gomme, Andrews, and Dover, *Commentary*, vol. 4, pp. 60–61; for Thurii, see Victor Ehrenberg, "The Foundation of Thurii," *AJP* 69 (1948), pp. 149–70.

178. Cf. C.J. Herington, *Athena Parthenos and Athena Polias* (Manchester: Manchester University Press, 1955), pp. 17–65, and Will, MGO, pp. 556–61.

179. With the exception of the *Menexenus*, in which Plato takes pleasure in developing the theme (237d–238a), the epitaphioi usually have very little to say, even in the fourth century, on the civilizing benefits of Athens: compare the passage in Plato with that of Demosthenes's oration (5), which is a — very allusive — imitation of it.

180. Adam Parry ("Thucydides' Use of Abstract Language," *Language as Action, Yale French Studies* 45 [1970], pp. 3–20) saw clearly (p. 9) that *aneu malakias* sets the primarily military tone of this declaration; thus the orator says that the Athenians may be intellectuals and also defeat the Spartans.

181. On this theme, see Bernard Knox, *Oedipus at Thebes: Sophocles' Tragic Hero and His Time* (New Haven, CT: Yale University Press, 1966), p. 71: the intellectualism of the Athenians perhaps, but the intellectualism of a *hēgemon is* the important point, as Knox understands it.

182. On this subject, see Eugène Napoleon Tigerstedt, *The Legend of Sparta in Classical Antiquity* (Lund, 1965), vol. 1, pp. 82–83, 97–98, 100, 105, and so on; H. Verdin, "Notes sur l'attitude des historians grecs à l'égard de la tradition locale," *Ancient Society* 2 (1970), pp. 183–200; and A. French, "Topical Influences on Herodotos' Narrative," *Mnemosyne* 25 (1972), pp. 9–27.

183. On 7.161–62 (the influence of the epitaphios of Samos), see W.W. How and J. Wells, *A Commentary on Herodotus* (Oxford: Clarendon, 1928).

184. See Henry R. Immerwahr, *Form and Thought in Herodotus* (Ann Arbor, MI: Edwards Bros., 1966), pp. 199–200, 215, 256.

185. The expression was coined by French, "Topical Influences on Herodotus' Narrative," p. 19 (on Herodotus 5.97).

CHAPTER TWO: THE ADDRESS TO THE DEAD AND ITS DESTINATION

1. As Karl Jost saw very clearly (*Das Beispiel und Vorbild der Vorfahren, bei den attischen Rednern*, Paderborn Studien [1934], pp. 249ff.), the funeral oration belongs both to the eulogy, devoted to the heroizing veneration of the dead, and to the political speech.

2. Vinzenz Buchheit, *Untersuchungen zur Theorie des Genos epideiktikon von Gorgias bis Aristoteles* (Munich: Huber, 1960), p. 29; the same idea in George Kennedy, *The Art of Persuasion in Greece* (Princeton, NJ: Princeton University Press, 1963), pp. 156–57.

3. Piero Treves, "Apocrifi demostenici," I, *Athenaeum* 14 (1936), pp. 153–74: Hyperides's epitaphios "combines the celebration of the dead, the defense of the living, and a political speech."

4. Martin P. Nilsson, *Cults, Myths, Oracles, and Politics in Ancient Greece* (Lund: Gleerup, 1951), pp. 87ff.

5. Henry R. Immerwahr, "*Ergon*: History as a Monument in Herodotus and Thucydides," *AJPh* 81 (1960), pp. 261–90, esp. 285–90.

6. For Adam Parry, "Thucydides' Use of Abstract Language," *Language as Action, Yale French Studies* 45 (1970), pp. 3–20, the development of prose as the essential vehicle of man's understanding of the world is duplicated in the fifth century by the mastery of abstraction: this brings us back to the birth of the funeral oration.

7. Insofar as it is *delivered* before an audience, each oration has a function in the city's present, unlike the epigram, which, because it is intended to be read, is addressed perhaps less to contemporaries (as A.E. Raubitschek observes, "Das Denkmal Epigramm," in *L'Epigramme grecque*, Entretiens de la Fondation Hardt, 14 [Vandoeuvres-Geneva, 1968], pp. 3–4) than to generations to come.

8. The translation of *astoi* as "citizens" (Jacqueline de Romilly) is too restrictive: the astoi should no doubt be seen as all the Athenians taken together — citizens and metics; all those living in Athens — as opposed to xenoi, allies or foreigners. To confirm this, see Thucydides 4.90.1 and 94.1 (where *astoi* is the total number of Athenians and metics) and the famous passage in Aristophanes's *Acharnians* (502–508), which depicts the metics as the bran of the city; see Jean Taillardat's commentary in *Les Images d'Aristophane: Etudes de langue et de style*) Paris: Société d'Edition les Belles Lettres, 1965), pp. 392–93, and Philippe Gauthier, "Les *Xénoi* dans les textes athéniens," *REG* 84 (1971), pp. 47–49.

9. Robert Clavaud translates this expression rather oddly as "les personnes étrangères à leurs families"; although *genos* may designate the family in the epitaphios (7), the term is used much more frequently to mean "Athenian birth" (6.27), and the rest of the paragraph shows quite clearly that it refers to a *captatio benevolentiae*. Indeed, in a note (p. 57), Clavaud himself compares this passage with Thucydides 2.34.4.

10. I must thank Philippe Gauthier for making this point to me.

11. Henri-Etienne Caffiaux, *De l'oraison funèbre dans la Grèce païenne* (Valencienness, 1860), p. 55.

12. See Russell Meiggs, *The Athenian Empire* (Oxford: Clarendon, 1972), pp. 152–71.

13. J.T. Hooker ("*Charis* and *Arete* in Thucydides," *Hermes* 102 [1974], pp. 164–69) shows that in this context arete is used both from the point of view of self-interest, which was well understood in Athens, and from that typically aristocratic one of the gift and its reciprocation. Cf. also James H. Oliver, *Demokratia, the Gods, and the Free World* (Baltimore: Johns Hopkins Press, 1960), on the link between charis and arete, and A.W.H. Adkins, *Moral Values and Political Behaviour in Ancient Greece* (London: Chatto and Windus, 1972), pp. 130–31 and 133–39.

14. Oliver, *Demokratia,* p. 109.

15. On the omissions necessitated by such presuppositions, see Nicole Loraux, *The Invention of Athens: The Funeral Oration in the Classical City*, trans. Alan Sheridan (Cambridge, MA: Harvard University Press, 1986), pp. 155–71 (on the account of Marathon in Lysias).

16. The foreigner, it goes without saying, is *Greek*: cf. Gauthier, "*Xénoi,*" p. 44, and *Symbola: Les Etrangers et la justice dans les cités grecques* (Nancy: Université de Nancy II, 1972), p. 9. The epitaphioi use *hoi alloi* (the others) and *hoi alloi Hellenes* (the other Greeks) interchangeably.

17. Are we to see in this passage, as does M.I. Finley (*Democracy Ancient and Modern* [New Brunswick, NJ: Rutgers University Press, 1973], pp. 50–51), the only attempt to be found in an Athenian text to provide the empire with an ideological justification? This would be to misunderstand the scope of the funeral oration's enterprise of idealizing Athenian domination.

18. If, that is, we can accept the restoration [*kathaper apoi*]*k*[*oi*] in *IG*, I^{2,} 63 (Meiggs-Lewis, 69, l. 58). On the significance of the presence of the allies at the Panathenaeas, see Meiggs, *Athenian Empire,* pp. 292–95 and 305.

19. Most of the references are in the article by John P. Barron, "Religious Propaganda of the Delian League," *JHS* 84 (1964), pp. 35–48, esp. 46. Cf. also Nilsson, *Cults, Myths, Oracles, and Politics,* pp. 60–64; A.E. Raubitschek, "The Peace Policy of Pericles," *AJA* 70 (1966), pp. 37–41, esp. 39; Meiggs, *Athenian Empire*, p. 294.

20. Cf. Felix Jacoby, *Atthis: The Local Chronicles of Ancient Athens* (Oxford: Clarendon, 1949), p. 137.

21. Jacqueline de Romilly, *Thucydide et l'impérialisme athénien* (Paris: Société d'Edition les Belles Lettres, 1947), pp. 116–24.

22. Hermann Strasburger, "Thukydides und die politische Selbstdarstellung der Athener," *Hermes* 86 (1958), p. 34.

23. Hellmut Flashar, "Der Epitaphios des Perikles, seine Funktion im Geschichtswerk des Thukydides," *SHAW* (1969), pp. 26ff.

24. De Romilly's translation ("nous avons laissé des monuments impérissables") does not take into account the pun on *sunkatoikisantes.*

25. I owe the expression to Claude Mossé, "Le Pirée," in *Athènes au temps de Périclès* (Paris: Hachette, 1965), p. 87; in that article, Mossé interprets the passage from the point of view of an "indissoluble union between democracy and empire."

26. On this theme, see Meiggs, *Athenian Empire*, p. 264. Mossé ("Le Pirée," p. 85) rightly compares the two texts, without, however, bringing out what distinguishes them.

27. Taillardat (*Les Images d'Aristophane*, p. 418) compares this passage with the epitaphios and shows that, as usual, Aristophanes is parodying an expression dear to the political orators.

28. Cf. Liddel-Scott, s.v. *epeiserkhomai.* In the absence of any reference to the sea, this passage cannot be identified with a variation on Athens's effective insularity; The best translation is therefore the most neutral, for example, that of Henri van Effenterre: "Il nous arrive de tout, et de toute la terre" (*L'Histoire en Grèce* [Paris: A. Colin, 1967], p. 133). See, on the other hand, the precision of the parallel passage in Xenophon (*Poroi* 1.7–8), which includes a triple reference to the insularity of Attica, "like an island," "bathed on all sides," "surrounded by the sea."

29. The theme that Yvon Garlan, citing Thucydides 2.13.2 as support, calls "the chrematistic leitmotif of Periclean thought" (*Recherches de poliorcétique grecque* [Athens: Ecole Française d'Athènes, 1974], p. 51) is completely absent from the epitaphios, which in fact deals here more with prosperity than with wealth.

30. Edouard Will, "Bulletin historique," *RH* 238 (1967), pp. 430–32; cf. also *MGO*, p. 210.

31. M.M. Austin and Pierre Vidal-Naquet, *Economies et sociétés en Grèce ancienne* (Paris: A. Colin, 1972), p. 318.

32. Marx stressed the value placed by the Athenians on self-sufficiency,

which is all the more remarkable in that, according to him, certain texts (such as Pericles's first oration in Thucydides) seem to indicate that the Athenian thought of himself as a "mercantile producer"; but he rightly observes that the point of view of self-sufficiency is always dominant (*Capital* [London, 1974], vol. 1, p. 345 n.1).

33. Will, "Bulletin historique," p. 432. Cf. Austin and Vidal-Naquet, *Economies et sociétés*, p. 128.

34. 1 am using this term in a way similar to that of Freud's *Verleugnung* (cf. Jean Laplanche and J.-B. Pontalis, *The Language of Psycho-Analysis,* trans. Donald Nicholson-Smith [London: Hogarth, 1973], under "Disavowal [Denial]," pp. 118–21).

35. No *Panathenaicus* rivaled the funeral oration in the fifth century, and no official speech of this type existed until later (probably around 118 B.C.: cf. James H. Oliver, *The Civilizing Power*, Transactions of the American Philosophical Society, vol. 58 [Philadelphia: American Philosophical Society, 1968], p. 17), so much so that in order to write the *Panegyricus* and the *Panathenaicus*, fictitious speeches, Isocrates drew on the tradition of the funeral oration, the only official speech. But the festival itself was a demonstration of the kratos of Athens.

36. Finley, *Democracy Ancient and Modern*, pp. 50–51. A more complicated position is found in Meiggs, *Athenian Empire*, p. 385.

37. For the *archē/hegemonia* opposition, see Will, *MGO*, pp. 171–73 (definition of the two notions and bibliography): hegemony implies a certain power in action or direction, empire an authority that is practiced for its own profit.

38. Gisela Schmitz-Kahlmann, *Das Beispiel der Geschichte im politischen denken des Isokrates* (Leipzig, 1939), pp. 81ff.

39. This idea is developed with some persuasive force by Edmund Büchner, *Der Panegyrikos des Isokrates: Eine historisch-philologische Untersuchung* (Wiesbaden: Steiner, 1958).

40. Strasburger, "Selbstdarstellung," p. 24, and de Romilly, *Thucydide et l'impérialisme athénien,* pp. 204ff., while trying to bring out the differences, reveal the kinship between the two texts.

41. Cf. de Romilly, *Thucydide et l'impérialisme athénien*, pp. 204–29.

42. Friedrich Blass, *Die attische Beredsamkeit* (Leipzig: Teubner, 1887), vol. 1, pp. 436ff., whose arguments are far from convincing.

43. An ancient tradition: Theon of Alexandria (*Rhetores graeci*, Spengel, p. 68) cites Lysias's epitaphios among the famous epitaphioi; furthermore, chs.

75–79 of the oration are found on papyrus: see Roger A. Pack, *The Greek and Latin Literary Texts from Greco-Roman Egypt* (Ann Arbor: University of Michigan Press, 1965), no. 1291. Plato's many allusions to Lysias's epitaphios (allusions that will be discussed throughout this book) prove that it antedates the *Menexenus*.

44. Max Pohlenz ("Zu den attischen Reden auf die Gefallenen,") 50 [1948], pp. 46–74) and Georges Mathieu (note on Isocrates's *Panegyricus*, CUF, p. 7) insist on the impossibility of the metic's addressing the Athenian polis; this difficulty caused much trouble to Josef Walz (*Der lysianische Epitaphios*, Philologus, supp. 29 [1936]), an advocate of authenticity, who extricated himself by sophistry, declaring that "Lysias belongs *de facto* to the Athenian community."

45. Lysias as logographer is a frequently formulated hypothesis. On the funeral oration as an attractive genre, see K.J. Dover, *Lysias and the Corpus Lysiacum* (Berkeley: University of California Press, 1968), p. 193.

46. On the contemporary significance of the slogan *eleutheria kai hegemonia*, see Ettore Lepore, "Leostene e le origini della guerra lamiaca," *PP* 10 (1945), pp. 161–85, esp. 185; Lorenzo Braccesi, "L'epitafio di Iperide come fonte storica," *Athenaeum* 58 (1970), pp. 276–301, esp. 286–87; Edouard Will, *Histoire politique du monde hellénistique* (Nancy, 1966), vol. 1, p. 28.

47. Georges Mathieu, *Les Idées politiques d'Isocrate* (Paris: Société d'Edition les Belles Lettres, 1925), p. 27.

48. Cf. Max Pohlenz, *Aus Platos Werdezeit* (Berlin: Weidmann, 1913), pp. 303–305, Piero Treves, "Note sulla guerra corinzia," III, *RFIC* 65 (1937), Charles H. Kahn, "Plato's Funeral Oration: The Motive of the *Menexenus*," *CPhil.* 58 (1963), pp. 220–34; T.T.B. Ryder, *Koine Eirene* (London: Published for the University of Hull by Oxford University Press, 1965), pp. 42ff.

49. Büchner, *Panegyrikos*, p. 6.

50. Cf. Strasburger, "Selbstdarstellung." For the late addition of the panhellenic theme to the exaltation of Marathon, a national victory, see William C. West, "Saviors of Greece," *GRBS* 11 (1970), pp. 275–78. As West rightly observes, Salamis, though more easily assimilated into Panhellenic propaganda, also, indeed primarily, implied hegemony to the Athenians.

51. This idea has been forcefully developed by Arnaldo Momigliano, *Filippo il Macedone, saggio sulla storia greca del IV secolo* (Florence: Le Monnier, 1934), chs. 5 ("Il conflitto degli ideali") and 6 ("I teorici del Panellenismo") cf. also Claude Mossé, *La Fin de la démocratie athénienne* (Paris: PUF, 1962), pp. 431ff., and Pierre Vidal-Naquet's review of Ryder's *Koine Eirene* in *REG* 80 (1967), pp. 613–14.

52. Cf. Chapter One, p. 85 and n.113.

53. Ryder, *Koine Eirene*, pp. 49–50.

54. In its ancient sense, strategy is "the art of making an army maneuver over a theater of operations until the moment when it engages the enemy" (*Dictionnaire Robert*, vol. 6, p. 363).

55. "There is rivalry only between those who resemble each other, who recognize the same values, judge themselves by the same criteria, agree to play the same game" (Jean-Pierre Vernant, introduction to *Les Problèmes de la guerre en Grèce ancienne* [The Hague: Mouton, 1968], p. 21).

56. On the importance of the agonistic ideal in the funeral oration, see Will, *MGO*, p. 429 n.1, and Hermann Strasburger, "Der Einzelne und die Gemeinschaft im Denken der Griechen," *Historiche Zeitschrift* 177 (1954), pp. 227–48 (on *archē* and *aristeia*, pp. 239–40).

57. On this danger, cf. Arnaldo Momigliano vigorously denouncing the "polarization of Greek studies on Sparta and Athens" ("Prospettiva 1967 della storia greca," *RSI* 80 [1968], pp. 5–19, esp. 9).

58. This opposition structures *the oration as a whole*: see Chapter Four, pp. 277–78. Plato had already made this observation in the *Menexenus* (235d3–4) on the funeral oration in general and on Pericles's epitaphios in particular, and it is — quite rightly — a commonplace of all commentaries on the epitaphios, despite the reluctance of some modern commentators to admit it (see de Romilly, *Thucydide et l'impérialisme athénien*, p. 129, and Gomme, *Commentary*, vol. 2, pp. 107, 109–10, 117).

59. See the analyses by Johannes Th. Kakridis, *Der thukydideische Epitaphios* (Munich: Beck, 1961), pp. 36–48.

60. Eugène Napoleon Tigerstedt, *The Legend of Sparta in Classical Antiquity* (Lund, 1965), p. 187.

61. Tigerstedt (*ibid.*) and Momigliano (*Filippo il macedone*, ch. 6) think so.

62. Roger Goossens, *Euripide et Athènes* (Brussels: Palais des Académies, 1962), pp. 209–10. See also Lionel Pearson, "Propaganda in the Archidamian War," *CPhil.* 31 (1936), pp. 33–52, esp. 38–39.

63. See Pierre Vidal-Naquet, "La Tradition de l'hoplite athénien," in *Problèmes de la guerre*, pp. 161–62.

64. Dionysus's "even if one is commonplace in other things" is an allusion to the *Menexenus* (234c4).

65. As Cicero recalls it, Rome was not in the habit of having collective

funerals for soldiers who had died in battle (34); so the orator draws inspiration from the epitaphioi, a debt that he conceals (for example, 31: the eternal glory of the dead, the pain of those close to the dead; 32: the opposition between a short life and eternal memory). However, the eulogy of the dead departs noticeably from the Greek model on several points:

(1) The orator praises the living as much as — if not more than — the dead.

(2) The eulogy is delivered not for itself but in the service of a particular policy, the policy that Cicero has applied and will continue to apply. Thus the orator presents the eulogy as an innovation of which he is the inventor (31 and 33–34): far from being the application of a nomos, the collective funeral stems from an individual proposition (31), adapted to exceptional circumstances (27 and 35); and the eulogy serves as an introduction and background to a *senatus consultum* of which Cicero is the instigator (36–38). Nothing is more alien to the funeral oration, which usually does not lend itself very easily to so precise a political purpose: see Chapter Three, p. 201 and n.29.

66. According to Eduard Schwartz (*Das Geschichtswerk des Thukydides*, p. 351), quoted by Julius Gerlach, "Aner agathos" (Ph.D. diss., Munich, 1932), p. 19. On the military use of arete, see A.W.H. Adkins, *Merit and Responsibility: A Study in Greek Values* (Oxford: Clarendon, 1960), pp. 157 and 169 n.2.

67. The resemblances have been stressed by Werner Jaeger, "Tyrtaios: Uber die wahre *Arete*," *SPAW* (1932), pp. 537–68, and by Tigerstedt, *Legend of Sparta,* pp. 46–50. On Tyrtaeus, see also Bruno Snell, *Die Entdeckung des Geistes* (Hamburg: Claassen, 1955), pp. 238–40; Werner Jaeger, *Paideia: Ideals of Greek Culture,* 2nd ed. (Oxford: Blackwell, 1939), pp. 81–94; W.J. Verdenius, "Tyrtaeus 6–7 D: A Commentary," *Mnemosyne* 22 (1969), pp. 337–55; and the excellent scholarly edition of Carlo Prato, *Tyrtaeus* (Rome, 1968).

68. On *agathoi* as the technical term in the funerary inscriptions, see Jean Pouilloux, *Recherches sur l'histoire et les cultes de Thasos* (Paris: E. de Boccard, 1954), p. 372 ("les Braves"). See also Prato, *Tyrtaeus,* p. 88.

69. See Henri Jeanmaire, *Couroi et Courètes: Essai sur l'éducation spartiate et sur les rites d'adolescence dans l'antiquité hellénique* (Lille: Bibliothèque Universitaire, 1939), pp. 78–79, and Prato, Tyrtaeus, introduction (pp. 22–23 on the "immediate stimuli" of the Homeric combat as opposed to the introspective civic values in the hoplitic battle).

70. Cf. Leonard Woodbury, "Simonides on *Arete*," *TAPA* 84 (1953), pp. 135–63.

71. As Verdenius ("Tyrtaeus 6–7 D," p. 352) and Christopher M. Dawson, "*Spoudaiogeloion*: Random Thoughts on Occasional Poems," *YCS* 19 (1966), pp. 34–76 (on Tyrtaeus 8 D 13), observe. See also Nicole Loraux, "La Belle Mort spartiate," *Ktema* 2 (1977), pp. 105–20.

72. If death is a possible consequence of courage, andreia is the essential property of the aner: therefore, to be truly an aner, one certainly runs the risk of being dead! Whereas in tragedy one is happy only after death, in the funeral oration one is a *man* only after death.

73. In Tyrtaeus, the death of the young warrior belongs to the category of *kalon*, which, however, cannot be reduced simply to aesthetic values as it is by Verdenius ("Tyrtaeus 6–7 D," pp. 338–50) and Walter Donian ("The Origin of *Kalos Kagathos*," *AJPh* 94 [1973], pp. 368–71). For a more subtle interpretation, see Adkins, *Merit and Responsibility,* pp. 163–64, and Prato, *Tyrtaeus,* pp. 87, 98, 100 (on 6–7 D 1, 26 and 30). A few epitaphs in the Kerameikos also stress the youthful brilliance of the fine death: see Nicole Loraux, "Hebè et andreia: Deux versions de la mort du combatant athénien," *Ancient Society* 6 (1975), pp. 1–31.

74. C.M. Bowra, *The Greek Experience* (New York: New American Library, 1957), pp. 37ff.

75. De Romilly's translation of *gnōmē* as "sentiment" renders this opposition very imperfectly.

76. See above, n.15.

77. René-Antoine Gauthier and Jean-Yves Jolif, *Commentaire de l'Ethique à Nicomaque* (Louvain: Publications Universitaires, 1970), pp. 189–206.

78. On all this, see Jean-Pierre Vernant, "Ebauches de la volonté dans la tragédie grecque," in *MT*, p. 73.

79. Cf. Snell, *Die Entdeckung des Geistes*, pp. 325–31, on "the image of the crossroads."

80. Henry R. Immerwahr, *Form and Thought in Herodotus* (Ann Arbor, MI: Edwards Bros., 1966), pp. 308ff.

81. However, whereas Leonidas obeys an oracle, Callimachus allows himself to be convinced by the *peithō* of a speech. The difference may be revealing of everything that separates an oligarchy, in which the speech of the gods prevails, and a democracy, in which the speech is primarily human. These analyses owe much to Vidal-Naquet's seminar on history and tragedy (1971–72).

82. This is no doubt how we should understand a difficult passage in Thucydides (2.42.4), as does de Romilly.

83. Despite Herodotus 7.9 (it is true that the hoplitic battle is described in it by a Persian). For Tyrtaeus, hoplitic discipline limits the extent of the losses (Tyrtaeus 8 D 13). See also the remarks by Garlan, *Recherches de poliorcétique grecque*, p. 275.

84. Garlan, *Recherches de poliorcétique grecque*, p. 70. Careful to stress the equivalence established in Greece between the individual's patriotic ardor and economic activity, Garlan misunderstands a whole dimension of Greek patriotism.

85. See André Aymard, "Paternité et valeur militaire," *RFL* 33 (1955), pp. 42–43 and Yvon Garlan, *La Guerre dans l'antiquité* (Paris: Nathan, 1972), p. 65.

86. A single exception, Lysias 35 ("to do battle at sea for their dearest, for the prizes there at Salamis"), 36, and 39, is of course mentioned by W.K. Lacey (*The Family in Classical Greece* [London: Thames and Hudson, 1972], p. 78), who, insensitive to the exceptionally realistic character of the account of Salamis in Lysias, sees the defense of the family and patrimony as a central theme of the funeral oration.

87. Cf. Arnaldo Momigliano, *The Development of Greek Biography* (Cambridge, MA: Harvard University Press, 1971), pp. 34–38.

88. We know that in civic and civil life *andra gignesthai* designates the attainment of majority, that is, enrollment in the register of the deme (see the references in Chrysis Pelekidis, *Histoire de l'éphébie attique des origines à 31 avant Jésus-Christ* [Paris: E. de Boccard, 1962], p. 51). Thus the same formula corresponds in practice to enrollment in the *lexiarchikon grammateion,* and in the funeral oration to enrollment in the obituary.

89. This schema is obvious to the point of caricature in the *Menexenus.*

90. Cf. Henri Irénée Marrou, *Histoire de l'éducation dans l'antiquité* (Paris: Seuil, 1948), chs. 4 and 5; Will, MGO, pp. 490–91.

91. On *chrēstē gunē*, see Christoph W. Clairmont, *Gravestone and Epigram: Greek Memorials from the Archaic and Classical Period* (Mainz: Zabern, 1970), no. 39 (mid-fourth century).

92. On the "contemporary and practical" character of the expression *anēr agathos* in the proxenic inscriptions, see Arlette Lambrechts, *Tekst en uitzicht van de Atheense proxeniedecreten tot 323 V.C.* (Brussels: Paleis der Academiën, 1958), pp. 142 and 145: the services rendered are always in the present and not in the past. On *anēr agathos* as a synonym of *euergetēs* in the honorific inscriptions of the fifth and fourth centuries, see Eiliv Skard, *Zwei religiös-politische Begriffe: Euergetes-Concordia* (Oslo, 1932), pp. 19–26; but I do not follow Skard when he

extends this analysis to the military use of *anēr agathos* (*ibid.*, pp. 43–44): unlike euergesia, military arete is a duty and implies no distance in relation to the community.

93. On the evolution of the meaning of *agathos* and *aretē* in the late fifth century, see Adkins, *Moral Values and Political Behaviour*, pp. 126ff., and Hooker, "*Charis* and *Arete* in Thucydides*," p. 168.

94. See Chapter Five, pp. 284–89.

95. For example, Eugène Dupréel (*Les Sophistes* [Neuchatel: Griffon, 1948], p. 87), Mario Untersteiner, and Jean-Paul Dumont. Hermann Diels and Walther Kranz see this expression as a mere equivalent of *entheos en autois aretē*. However, a comparison with Lysias 24 is perplexing and would lead us to construe *ekektento* not as a state but as the end of a long development. Nevertheless, whether this arete is a state or an acquisition resulting from previous action, the value of the pluperfect leads us to place arete in the past, that is, in the life of the andres.

96. Cf. Robert Joly, *Le Thème philosophique des genres de vie dans l'antiquité classique* (Brussels: Palais des Académies, 1955), p. 59.

97. Generally speaking, no epitaphios, even a late one, except Hyperides's oration, which indeed protests against such a thing, considers the possibility of praising individuals.

98. Goossens, *Euripide et Athènes*, p. 451; see also Günther Zuntz, *Political Plays of Euripides* (Manchester: Manchester University Press, 1955), pp. 14ff., and C. Collard, "The Funeral Oration in Euripides' *Supplices*," *BICS* 19 (1972), pp. 40 and 44.

99. In the *Phoenissae*, a tragedy of violence, the portraits of the seven leaders are again dominated by war, and even savage war.

100. Eugène Dupréel (*La Légende socratique et les sources de Platon* [Brussels: Sand, 1922], ch. 2) insists on the Sophistic aspect of any question of the *ei didakton* type.

101. I am not quite certain that one must, like the majority of scholars (Classen-Steup, Gomme, Kakridis, Pierre Roussel, Raymond Weil) since Lorenzo Valla and Henri Estienne, interpret the form of the conjunction *te* ... *kai* ... as the equivalent of the alernative *eite* ... *eite*. If one gives *te* ... *kai* ... the much more canonical meaning "at once," the text means: "La fin qui est la leur aujourd'hui montre, je crois, ce qu'est la valeur d'un homme, en un instant révélée pour la première fois et menée à son achèvement dernier" ("the end that is

theirs today shows, I believe, a man's valor, in an instant revealed for the first time and brought to its culmination"). A similar translation was proposed in 1795 by Pierre Charles Levesque, and the fact that it has since been forgotten does not invalidate it. If we adopt this solution, Pericles's phrase becomes the finest expression of the idea that there is valor only in death.

102. See the commentaries by Peek (*GG*, p. 298, no. 80) and Clairmont (*Gravestone and Epigram*, p. 154). Bruno Gentili ("Epigramma ed elegia," in *L'Epigramme grecque*, p. 76) compares this text with Theognis 1183 (personification of Sophrosune). In fact, the lyrical values are reinvested with meaning in the service of a private ethic from the end of the fifth century.

103. The arete/sophrosyne dyad is a very old one and is found on many sixth-century tombs (cf. L.H. Jeffery, "The Inscribed Gravestones of Archaic Attica," *BSA* 57 [1962], nos. 8, 9, 23, 49; and Helen North, *Sophrosyne: Self-knowledge and Self-Restraint in Greek Literature* [Ithaca, NY: Cornell University Press, 1966], pp. 13–23), but it is absent from the collective epitaphs (and from the funeral orations, with few exceptions), whereas the private epitaphs of the fourth century make abundant use of it.

104. Hans Hess, "Textkritische und erklärende Beiträge zum Epitaphios des Hypereides" (Ph.D. diss., Bonn, 1937), pp. 25ff.

105. Hess ("Hypereides," pp. 41–44) discerns here a polemic against the author of the pseudo-Demosthenean epitaphios or against his school. But in that case, we would have to date this text between 338 and 332, and it would be simpler to attribute it to Demosthenes himself.

106. An essential passage in which the orator simultaneously splits the representation of the fine death, attributing proairesis to the city and andreia to the soldiers, and restores unity in the person of the strategos (one must praise "the strategos Leosthenes for possessing both these merits at once").

107. No doubt we should interpret in this way the presence in Demosthenes of the Catalog of Eponyms.

108. I have borrowed this formula from Pierre Vidal-Naquet, "Une Enigme à Delphes: A propos de la base de Marathon (Pausanias, x, 10, 1–2)," *RH* 238 (1967), p. 297.

109. Cf. Jean Pouilloux and Georges Roux, *Enigmes à Delphes* (Paris: E. de Boccard, 1963), pp. 16ff. (and 69, on the "treasure of Brasidas").

110. Jules Girard, *Etudes sur l'éloquence attique* (Paris: Hachette, 1874), pp. 180–233 ("Hypéride et son éloge funèbre"); quotation p. 216.

111. Cf. Lepore, "Leostene e le origini della guerra lamiaca," pp. 176–83.

112. The democratic version of the Lamian War certainly seems to have sheltered behind the political and military figure of the strategos: see *ibid.*, pp. 169 and 175, and Braccesi, "L'epitafio di Iperide come fonte storica," pp. 278–82.

113. "The others," that is, "the rest." Hyperides reserves for citizens alone (16) the praise that he addresses to the soldiers. It is no less significant that in designating them as "citizens," he feels the need to distinguish them from mercenaries, we are not far from the Hellenistic distinction between *stratiotes* (mercenary) and *polites* (citizen-soldier). Cf. Garlan, *Recherches de poliorcétique grecque,* commentary on Philo of Byzantium, *Mechanical Syntax* C 2, p. 376 (see also C 18, 30, 34, and D 13).

114. Buchheit, *Genos epideiktikon*, pp. 71ff.

115. Cf. Knud Friis Johansen, *The Attic Grave-Reliefs of the Classical Period* (Copenhagen: Munksgaard, 1951), pp. 15ff., and Alexander Conze, *Die attischen Grabreliefs* (Vienna, 1893–1900), nos. 1054–58.

116. André de Ridder's (*De l'idée de la mort en Grèce à l'époque classique* [Paris: Thorin, 1897]).

117. If at least *Anthologia Palatina* 7.253 is really linked to Chaironeia. Peek suggests this dating without really taking responsibility for it (*GV*, p. 28), although he rightly believes that such a representation of the fine death accords only with the atmosphere of the late fourth century (*GG*, p. 27).

118. For Johannes Sykutris, "Der demosthenische Epitaphios," *Hermes* 63 (1928), pp. 241–53, and Pohlenz, "Zu den attischen Reden auf die Gefallenen," p. 68, the multiplicity of references to the daimon is proof of the authenticity of the Demosthenean epitaphios; but it is necessary also, with Clavaud (Notice on the epitaphios, CUF, pp. 32–33), to stress the orator's hesitations.

119. On the weakening of *mnēmē athanatos* in the fourth century, see Richmond Lattimore, *Themes in Greek and Latin Epitaphs* (Urbana: University of Illinois Press, 1962), p. 240.

120. Fritz Taeger, *Charisma: Studien zur Geschichte des antiken Herrscherkultes* (Stuttgart: Kohlhammer, 1957), vol. 1, p. 121.

121. Cf. Georges Dumézil, *Heur et malheur du guerrier* (Paris: PUF, 1969), pp. 101–104, esp. the text cited on p. 103.

122. In any case, there is no question here of the immortality of the soul: cf. Erwin Rohde, *Psyché: Le Culte de l'âme chez les grecs et leur croyance à l'immorta-*

lité (Paris: Payot, 1928), p. 430 n.3, and Goossens, *Euripide et Athènes*, p. 51 n.109.

123. On this subject, cf. Rohde, *Psyché*, pp. 464ff.; Franz Cumont, *Lux perpetua* (Paris: Geuthner, 1949), ch. 3; and Goossens, *Euripide et Athènes*, p. 52. Goossens believes that the epigram represents the true thought of Pericles, a disciple of Anaxagoras. See also Lattimore, *Themes*, pp. 27 and 31.

124. Cf. Taeger, *Charisma*, vol. 1, p. 122.

125. On the relationship between these "rationalizing" formulations and the question of heroization, see Chapter One, p. 74.

126. Even so, Pericles still evokes immortality on the subject of the gods, that of the citizens remains to be deduced through analogical reasoning. On the rationalism of this comparison, see Bernard Knox, *Oedipus at Thebes: Sophocles' Tragic Hero and His Time* (New Haven, CT: Yale University Press, 1966), pp. 122-23.

127. On *Olympians* 2, in which Pindar reserves for the *esthloi* alone the privilege of obtaining in their lifetime the residence of the heroes in the Islands of the Blessed, see Jean Bollack, "L'Or des rois: Le Mythe de la *deuxième Olympique*," *Rev. Phil.* 37 (1963), pp. 234-54.

128. On this definition of eudaimonia, see Gustav Lejeune-Dirichlet, *De veterum macarismis* (Giessen: Töpelmann, 1914), pp. 51-53.

129. In fact, these three orators hesitate between two definitions of eudaimonia (cf. *ibid.*, p. 52 n.3): the dead are eudaimones because they have lost their lives for the city, but also because they have been relieved forever of the vicissitudes of existence. But although the two definitions are balanced in Demosthenes, the orator concludes with civic eudaimonia. This movement is even clearer in Lysias and Hyperides.

130. Not until July 1978 did I learn of a study by Oddone Longo ("La morte per la patria," *Studi italiani di filologia classica* 4 [1977], pp. 5-36), which considers some of the documents used here from a rather different point of view. I regret that it is now too late to respond in detail to this very interesting study, which, it seems to me, overestimates the relationship of exchange established in the funeral oration between the city and the citizens.

131. Cf. Chapter One, pp. 99-101.

132. On the Aristotelian analysis of time, see Jacques Derrida, "*Ousia* et *grammè*," in *L'Endurance de la pensée (Pour saluer Jean Beaufret)* (Paris: Plon, 1968), pp. 291-359.

133. I am considering here time as experienced by the individual or the community, and not the time of the philosophers, which, as Claire Préaux has rightly stressed, breaks with the crucial problem of memory and survival ("L'Elargissement de l'espace et du temps dans la pensée grecque," *BAB* 54 [1968], pp. 208–67, esp. 252).

134. In addition to the article by Préaux already cited, see M.I. Finley, "Myth, Memory, and History," *H&T* 4 (1955), pp. 281–302, and Arnaldo Momigliano, "Time in Ancient Historiography," *H&T* 6 (1966), pp. 1–23.

135. See Pierre Lévêque and Pierre Vidal-Naquet, *Clisthène l'Athénien: Essai sur la représentation de l'espace et du temps dans la pensée politique grecque* (Paris: Belles Lettres, 1964), pp. 117–22.

136. See the articles by Finley and Momigliano already cited, in addition to the study by Pierre Vidal-Naquet, "Temps des dieux et temps des hommes: Essai sur quelques aspects de l'expérience temporelle chez les Grecs," *RHR* 157 (1960), pp. 55–80. On Herodotus, see Jacoby, *Atthis*, pp. 119ff.

137. Note the use of the verb *apoblepein,* which always by its essence indicates subterfuge; cf. Victor Goldschmidt, "Le Paradigme dans la théorie platonicienne de l'action," in *Questions platoniciennes* (Paris: Vrin, 1970), p. 83 n.28.

138. The transition from myth to history in Lysias is particularly apparent in 17–20.

139. Claude Lévi-Strauss, "Le Temps du mythe," in *Histoire et structure*, special issue of *Annales ESC* (May-Aug. 1971), p. 537.

140. It is not always necessary to use the dead to immortalize Athens. See Pericles's last speech in Thucydides, where the orator credits the city with *doxa aeimnestos* (2.64.5).

141. This idea is very widespread among specialists in Thucydides and among historians who are interested in the funeral oration, from Wilamowitz (*GT*, p. 205) to Felix Jacoby ("*Patrios Nomos*: State Burial in Athens and the Public Cemetery in the Kerameikos," *JHS* 64 [1944], pp. 56 and 58). Giuseppe Nenci, "Atene, *Paideusis Hellados* (Thuc., II, 41, 1)," *Studi classici ed orientali* 19–20 (1970–71), pp. 450–52, has argued a similar thesis.

142. Lysias's epitaphios is dated to around 391 by Walz (*Der lysianische Epitaphios*) and Treves ("Note sulla guerra corinzia"), Bizos (note on the epitaphios, CUF, p. 43) hesitantly suggests the date 392. The traditionally accepted date for the *Menexenus* is 386 or the years immediately after (cf. notice by Louis Méridier, edition of the *Menexenus*, CUF, p. 82, and S. Payrau, "Eirènika: Considéra-

tions sur l'échec des tentatives panhelléniques au IVème siècle av. J.-C.," *REA* 73 [1971], pp. 24–79, esp. 29–31).

143. Emile Benveniste, "Expression indo-européenne de l'éternité," *BSL* 38 (1937) pp. 103–12.

144. On this epitaph, see Préaux ("L'Elargissement de l'espace et du temps," p. 264), who clearly marks the opposition between Herodotus's time the destroyer and time the savior of 338: in the fifth century, it is the human logos that saves; in 338, time is the only messenger to posterity.

145. Treves ("Apocrifi demostenici," I) sees in what he regards as an anachronism the proof of the apocryphal character of the epitaphios. But one might counter that Hyperides's "sun" of 322 (5) answers Demosthenes's "night" of 338 (24): this comparison, which was suggested to me by Philippe Gauthier, constitutes a proof of the authenticity of the Demosthenean epitaphios.

146. On this Periclean sentence, see the bibliography in my article "Hebé et andreia," pp. 9–11 nn.34–36.

147. Demosthenes is obviously drawing inspiration from Pericles (Pohlenz, "Zu den attischen Reden auf die Gefallenen," pp. 66–67, and Clavaud, notice to the epitaphios, p. 21). It now seems surprising that the "pessimism" accepted in Pericles after a victorious war should have been refused to Demosthenes after a defeat.

148. Cf. Clavaud, notice to the epitaphios, p. 61 n.4 and *REG* 82 (1969), p. 658 (on *Fourth Philippic* 74).

149. Friedrich Nietzsche, *The Use and Abuse of History*, trans. Adrian Collins (Indianapolis: Bobbs-Merrill, 1957), pp. 15–16.

150. Donald W. Bradeen, "Athenian Casualty Lists," *Hesperia* 33 (1964), pp. 55–57.

151. The motif is reactivated by the struggle against a new barbarian, the Macedonian: see Braccesi, "L'epitafio di Iperide come fonte storica," pp. 287–88.

152. In fact, Leosthenes never actually joined battle at Thermopylae; see Colin, CUF, p. 287.

153. On these omissions and this shortsightedness, see Braccesi, "L'epitafio di Iperide come fonte storica," pp. 288–89.

154. Cf. Jacoby, *Atthis*, pp. 111ff.

155. Vidal-Naquet, "Temps des dieux et temps des hommes," p. 69.

156. Derrida, "*Ousia* et *grammè*," pp. 227–28.

157. Cf. Hess (*Hypereides*, pp. 37–40), for whom this is a "Platonic envelope around an Isocratic thought."

158. On Plato, cf. Lévêque and Vidal-Naquet, *Clisthène*, pp. 137–46, and Pierre Vidal-Naquet, "La Raison grecque et la cité," *Raison présente* 2 (1967), pp. 51–61.

159. On aion, cf. Enzo Degani, *Aion da Omero ad Aristotele* (Padua: CEDAM, 1961).

CHAPTER THREE: THE ATHENIAN HISTORY OF ATHENS

1. R.G. Collingwood, *The Idea of History* (Oxford: Clarendon, 1946), pp. 26–28 and 31 for the expansion of the field to the Hellenistic period, see pp. 32–33.

2. I have borrowed this term from Emmanuel Le Roy Ladurie.

3. Collingwood, *Idea of History*, p. 32, defines classical Greek history by its "parochial point of view."

4. Felix Jacoby, *Atthis: The Local Chronicles of Ancient Athens* (Oxford: Clarendon, 1949), p. 73.

5. On the strategikos logos and its role in Greek historiography, see Theodore C. Burgess, *Epideictic Literature* (Chicago: University of Chicago Press, 1902), pp. 195–214.

6. It is true that the study of the distant origins of a war was often pushed into the background by ancient historiography; cf. Arnaldo Momigliano, "Some Observations on Causes of War in Ancient Historiography," in *Studies in Historiography* (London: Weidenfeld and Nicolson, 1966). But the utter contempt of the epitaphioi for any serious causality is no accident.

7. On this notion, cf. Claire Préaux, "L'Elargissement de l'espace et du temps dans la pensée grecque," *BAB* 54 (1968), p. 233.

8. Arnaldo Momigliano, "Time in Ancient Historiography," *H&T* 6 (1966), p. 15, insists on the strict temporal limits within which ancient historiography was written; cf. Collingwood, *Idea of History*, pp. 25–28.

9. On chronography, cf. Momigliano, "Time in Ancient Historiography," p. 16.

10. Cf. pp. 206–208.

11. Robert Clavaud rightly translates *andreia* in this passage as "virilité" (translation of the epitaphios, CUF).

12. Myronides: "a scrapper who left an almost epic memory" (Edouard Will, *MGO*, p. 159). In fact, Myronides is for us only a name, with no other con-

tent than his arete, a favorite theme of the Athenian reactionaries (cf. Aristophanes, *Women in Parliament* 303ff. and *Lysistrata* 801ff.; Plutarch, *Pericles* 16.3 and 24.10). In Thucydides, he is the jewel of the generation of *pateres* (4.95.3) and in Diodorus the symbol of Athenian virtues (11.81.5: "a man of intelligence and action").

13. The "world upside down" is a topos thoroughly examined by later rhetoric: cf. Ernst Curtius, *European Literature and the Latin Middle Ages* (New York: Pantheon Books, 1953).

14. On *neōtatoi* and *presbutatoi*, see Pierre Vidal-Naquet, "La Tradition de l'hoplite athénien," in *Problèmes de la guerre en Grèce ancienne* (The Hague: Mouton, 1968), pp. 163 and 172, "Le Chasseur noir et l'origine de l'éphébie athénienne," *Annales ESC* (Sept.–Oct. 1968), pp. 947–64.

15. The traditional division of social labor into age-groups is studied by Pierre Roussel, *Etude sur le principe d'ancienneté dans le monde hellénique*, in *Mémoires de l'Académie des Inscriptions et Belles Lettres* 43, no. 2 (1951), pp. 123–28, esp. 174ff. On the "young," see Pierre Vidal-Naquet, "Le Cru, l'enfant grec et le cult" in Jacques Le Goff and Pierre Nora (eds.), *Faire de l'histoire*, 3 vols. (Paris: Gallimard, 1974), vol. 3, pp. 145–68.

16. Cf. Marcel Detienne, "L'Olivier: Un Mythe politico-religieux," *RHR* 167 (1970), pp. 5–23, repr. in M.I. Finley (ed.), *Problèmes de la terre en Grèce ancienne* (Paris: Mouton, 1973), pp. 293–306, esp. 294–95.

17. Cf. Claude Lévi-Strauss, "Le Temps du mythe," in *Histoire et structure*, special issue of *Annales ESC* (May-Aug. 1971), p. 537, and Georges Dumézil, "Temps et mythe," *Recherches philosophiques* 5 (1935–36), pp. 235–51. Even more than historiography, the catalog of exploits "preserves from myth the habit of computing by generations" (Henri van Effenterre, *l'Histoire en Grèce* [Paris: A. Colin, 1967], p. 9).

18. Collingwood (*Idea of History*, p. 15) observes that in myth, the language of temporal succession is a metaphor.

19. Cf. Jean-Pierre Vernant, "Raisons du mythe," pp. 195 and 200–203.

20. I have borrowed this term from *ibid.*, p. 214.

21. See Pierre Vidal-Naquet, "Athènes et l'Atlantide: Structure et signification d'un mythe platonicien," *REG* 77 (1964), pp. 420–44.

22. M.I. Finley ("Myth, Memory, and History," *H&T* 4 [1955], p. 283) insists on Antiquity's use of myth taken as history. On the concatenation of historical facts and mythical examples by Athenian orators, cf. Felix Jacoby, "Some Athenian

Epigrams from the Persian Wars," *Hesperia* 14 (1945), pp. 516–17 (a comparison of the poem of Eion and the funeral oration).

23. It should be noted that although he borrows his periodization from Pericles, Lysias orients it in the opposite direction: those who, for Pericles, are "the fathers" in relation to the present generation are, for Lysias, the descendants of the ancestors.

24. Cf. Jacoby, "Epigrams," p. 510 (juxtaposing the mythical paradigm and the historical feat of arms suggests that the recent exploit was worthy of being praised by Homer).

25. On Thucydides and muthodes, see A.W. Gomme, "Thucydides," in *The Greek Attitude to Poetry and History* (Berkeley: University of California Press, 1954), p. 117; Vernant, "Raisons du mythe," p. 201; and Bruno Gentili, "Le teorie del racconto storico nel pensiero storiografico dei Greci," in Bruno Gentili and Giovanni Cerri, *Le teorie del discorso storico nel pensiero greco e la storiografia romana arcaica* (Rome: Ateneo, 1975), pp. 19–45, (esp. 23–28).

26. On this epigram, see A. Cameron, "An Epigram of the Fifth Century B.C.," *Harv. Theol. Rev.* 33 (1940), pp. 97–130. Despite earlier examples given by Cameron (p. 103), the religious interpretation of a defeat does not seem to have been commonplace in Athens; indeed Cameron himself shows that the form remains vague.

27. Roger Goossens (*Euripide et Athènes* [Brussels: Palais des Académies, 1962], p. 111), Eugène Napoleon Tigerstedt (*The Legend of Sparta in Classical Antiquity* [Lund, 1965], p. 137), and Will (*MCO*, p. 300: un "éloge hargneux") saw very clearly that the oration of the Corinthians at Sparta is a eulogy of Athens, all the more effective for being placed in the mouth of her enemies. Hermann Strasburger ("Thukydides und die politische Selbstdarstellung der Athener," *Hermes* 86 [1958]) refuses to credit the topoi of the funeral oration with any influence on Thucydides's work; but this is to ignore the fact that in his own subtle way, the historian emphasizes on several occasions the Lacedaemonians' inability to benefit even from their victories (cf. 8.96, for example), finally making his own the theme of Athens conquered by herself.

28. Obviously, any official history uses similar methods, with the arguments at its disposal: cf. Georges Duby, *Le Dimanche de Bouvines* (Paris: Gallimard, 1973), pp. 191 and 194.

29. Pierre Treves ("Apocrifi demostenici," I, *Athenaeum* 14 [1936], pp. 153–74) believes that the orator is remembering the circumstances in which he was

chosen; but apart from the fact that the word *hairetheis* (13) is in itself more precise than the terms in which the orators usually allude to their election, Treves
forgets that such a development would be misplaced in an oration intended to
strengthen the unity of the city; see on this subject Pohlenz's sound remarks,
"Zu den attischen Reden auf die Gefallenen," *Symbolae Osloenses* (1948), p. 58.
On the other hand, transposed into the Roman context, the Greek funeral oration loses this characteristic; thus Cicero integrates it into the *Fourteenth Philippic* to support his political purpose, in a context of civil war.

30. This is the thesis of Strasburger, "Selbstdarstellung," pp. 20ff.

31. I have borrowed this concept from Benedetto Bravo (articulated in a lec-
ture delivered at Vernant's seminar [Ecole Polytechnique des Hautes Etudes,
Vème section, 1972]), on the status of the intellectual in the Hellenistic world.
On "rhetorical history," cf. Burgess, *Epideictic Literature*, and van Effenterre,
L'Histoire en Grèce, pp. 28–38.

32. Strasburger, "Selbstdarstellung," p. 25, thinks that Diodorus is following Ephorus, whose source is probably an epitaphios. Russell Meiggs, *The Athenian Empire* (Oxford: Clarendon, 1972), p. 12, has also noted this strange
phenomenon of duplication.

33. Collingwood, *Idea of History,* pp. 14–15.

34. *Ibid.*, pp. 18ff.

35. Cf. Momigliano, "Time in Ancient Historiography," pp. 14ff.

36. The words are Momigliano's, *ibid.*, paraphrasing Herodotus 1.1. Cf. also
Préaux, "L'Elargissement de l'espace et du temps," pp. 263–64.

37. Cf. Momigliano, "Time in Ancient Historiography," pp. 14 and 15 (two
criteria of selection: valor and fitness), and Collingwood, *Idea of History*, pp.
25–28.

38. It is true that the two types of narrative do not use the same material: as
written works, the *Atthides*, like any chronology, are based on archives and written documents; as speeches, the epitaphioi draw on a common stock of Athenian
topoi; cf. H.L. Hudson-Williams, "Thucydides, Isocrates, and the Rhetorical
Method of Composition," *CQ* 42 (1948), pp. 76–81.

39. Even Ephorus imposed limits on himself, considering it impossible to
go back beyond the Heraclidae.

40. Cf. Préaux, "L'Elargissement de l'espace et du temps," pp. 234–35.

41. On the *peripeteiai*, catastrophic changes from one state of affairs into its
opposite, cf. Collingwood, *Idea of History*, p. 22.

42. The *Menexenus* presents the great king's sudden change of mind as *to theiotaton pantōn; theiotaton* is to be understood, of course, in the sense of "marvelous, extraordinary," but the choice of the term is not neutral.

43. Declaring that only the Amazons were incapable of learning from their misfortunes, Lysias (6) suggests that for all the other enemies, the Athenians represented a living lesson.

44. See Chrysis Pelekidis (*Histoire de l'éphébie attique des origines à 31 avant Jésus-Christ* [Paris: E. de Boccard, 1962], pp. 31–32 and 62) on the Athenian legislation concerning primary schools.

45. If the majority of Athenians had the rudiments of an education (reading and writing), the text of the *Protagoras* (325d6–326a3), which links the apprenticeship of letters with the lessons in morality to be derived from the great authors, is of crucial importance. On the essentially oral character of Athenian education in the early fifth century and even in the next century, cf. Eric A. Havelock, *Preface to Plato* (Cambridge, MA: Belknap Press of Harvard University Press, 1963), pp. 40–48, and Piero Treves, "*Polis* e *Paideusis*: L'educazione ad Atene," *A&R* 12 (1967), pp. 3–4.

46. Compare with the use made of this term by Georges Dumézil, *Heur et malheur du guerrier* (Paris: PUF, 1969), pp. 11–22. On the extension of the notion of ideology, cf. Georges Duby, "Histoire sociale et idéologies des sociétés," in *Faire de l'histoire*, vol. 1, pp. 147–68.

47. On the solitary heroes mentioned in the orations, see Chapter One, pp. 104–106 (concerning Theseus).

48. See Jean-Pierre Vernant, "Le Mythe hésiodique des races," in *MP*, vol. 1, pp. 25–30, Francis Vian, "La Fonction guerrière dans la mythologie grecque," in *Problèmes de la guerre,* pp. 53–68.

49. On the Amazons, cf. Pierre Vidal-Naquet, "Esclavage et gynécocratie dans la tradition, le mythe, l'utopie," in *Recherches sur les structures sociales dans l'Antiquité classique* (Paris, 1970), pp. 63–80, (esp. 67–68), and S.G. Pembroke, "Two Cases of Matriarchy in the Archaic Greek Tradition" (thesis, Cambridge University, 1966), pp. 41–80. If Herodotus (8.93) is to be believed, the Athenians had a particular aversion for manly women, since, "indignant that a woman should come to wage war on Athens," they wanted to subject Artemis to the same fate as the Amazons (cf. Raymond Weil, "Artémise; ou, Le Monde à l'envers," in *Recueil Plassart* [Paris: Société d'Edition les Belles Lettres, 1976], pp. 221–24).

50. Sophrosune, the sole virtue with which, according to Thucydides's scholiast, women are endowed (in the absence of andreia, *dikaiosyne*, and *phronesis*), consists precisely in knowing how to keep quiet (cf. *Lysistrata*, 508) or in not causing themselves to be talked about (cf. Plutarch, *Virtues of Women* 242c). Let us give the final word to Virginia Woolf: "The chief glory of a woman is not to be talked of, said Pericles, himself a much-talked-of man" (*A Room of One's Own* [London: Penguin, 1945], p. 43).

51. Cf. Vernant, "Le Mythe hésiodique des races," pp. 26ff.

52. On the opposition between Gegeneis and autochthones, cf. Claude Berard, *Anodoi: Essai sur l'imagerie des passages chthoniens* (Neuchâtel: Attinger, 1974), p. 35.

53. Cf. Vian, "La Fonction guerrière dans la mythologie grecque."

54. Louis Gernet ("Les Nobles dans la Grèce antique," in *Anthropologie de la Grèce antique* [Paris: Maspero, 1968], p. 336) reminds us of the aristocratic character of the claim to autochthony; cf. also, by the same author, "La Notion de démocratie chez les Grecs," *Revue de la Méditerranée*, 5 (1948), p. 387.

55. For a definition of nobility see also Aristotle, *On Nobility*, frag. 2, text and commentary by Jacques Brunschwig, in *Aristote: Fragments et témoignages* (*Cinq oeuvres perdues*), under the direction of Pierre-Maxime Schuhl (Paris: PUF, 1968), pp. 81–84 and 88–98.

56. On the political struggles between the Alcmaeonids and the other *gene*, cf. Jacoby, *Atthis*, pp. 149–63.

57. Emile Benveniste, *Le Vocabulaire des institutions indo-européennes* (Paris: Minuit, 1969), vol. 1, p. 323: "The root *leudh* from which *'liber'* and *'eleutheros'* derive means 'to grow, to develop.'"

58. One should distinguish between the practical effectiveness of the decree, which confirmed the political privileges of the Athenian demos, and the Athenians' *interpretation* of it, in which the awareness of belonging to an autochthonous race is paramount: cf. W.K. Lacey, *The Family in Ancient Greece* (London: Thames and Hudson, 1972), p. 100, and Bérard, *Anodoi*, pp. 35–36.

59. I have borrowed this term from Vidal-Naquet, "Hoplite athénien," p. 167. Bernard Knox, *Oedipus at Thebes: Sophocles' Tragic Hero and His Time* (New Haven, CT: Yale University Press, 1966), pp. 72–73, sees amateurism as one of the topoi of the Athenian character as defined by the writers of the fifth century.

60. As Vidal-Naquet rightly observes, "La Guerre tragique," in *Athènes au temps de Périclès* (Paris: Hachette, 1965), p. 261.

61. I cannot agree with Arnaldo Momigliano when he declares that for Thucydides, there is a "close link between the maritime power of Athens and the psychological attitude of the Athenians as it is described in . . . Pericles' *epitaphios*" ("Sea-Power in Greek Thought," in *Secondo contributo alla storia degli studi clasici* [Rome: Storia e Letteratura, 1960], p. 61).

62. Cf. Henri Irénée Marrou, *Histoire de l'éducation dans l'antiquité* (Paris: Seuil, 1948), p. 52.

63. On *agoge*, in addition to the works by Henri Jeanmaire (*Couroi et Courètes: Essai sur l'éducation spartiate et sur les rites d'adolescence dans l'antiquité hellénique* [Lille: Bibliothèque Universitaire, 1937]) and Marrou (*Histoire de l'éducation*), see M.I. Finley, "Sparta," in *Problèmes de la guerre*, pp. 143–60.

64. Jeanmaire (*Couroi*, p. 489) believes that only "the proof of arete" in the agoge constitutes the Spartan citizen, neither right of birth nor purity of blood being strictly speaking required. Marrou offers a modified view: "To receive the *agoge* was a necessary if not sufficient condition for the exercise of civic rights" (*Histoire de l'éducation*, p. 52 n.21).

65. Ulrich von Wilamowitz, *Aristoteles und Athen* (Berlin: Weidmann, 1893), vol. 1, p. 191 (commentary on the text by Pelekidis, *Histoire de l'éphébie attique*, p. 9, and Vidal-Naquet, "Hoplite athénien," p. 167). Did Wilamowitz realize, in dating the creation of the ephebia as late as 336–35, that if the funeral oration did indeed depict the reality of Athens, Hyperides, who was speaking in 322, ought to have renounced this topos?

66. A unity whose elements strangely resemble the noble qualities that Pindar (*Olympians* 14, v. 7) places under the patronage of the Charites. Cf. James H. Oliver, *Demokratia, the Gods, and the Free World* (Baltimore: Johns Hopkins Press, 1960), pp. 103–17.

67. Gernet, "Les Nobles dans la Grèce antique," p. 342: "There is an antinomy between the nature of the city and that of nobility." And a more moderate statement, p. 343: "There is in the citizen a quality of human pride that may claim comparison with the noble."

68. On the notion of "Athenian character" as a topos of the late fifth century, particularly important in Thucydides, cf. Knox, *Oedipus at Thebes*, pp. 67–73.

69. Emile Benveniste, *Problèmes de linguistique générale* (Paris: Gallimard, 1966), p. 200.

70. In Aristotelian language, one might say that for Pericles, difference is

the first entelechy, war being the second entelechy or exercise of this difference. For a definition of these notions, see Aristotle, *De anima* 2.1.412a.22ff.

71. Klaus Oppenheimer (*Zwei attische Epitaphien* [Berlin: Ebering, 1933], p. 14) insists on the formulas by which Pericles expresses this coincidence of opposites in 2.40.2.41.1: *ton auton andra*. *Ton auton andra* refers to the complete character of Athenian man and not to variety in way of life, as George Grote would have it (*A History of Greece* [London: Murray, 1862], vol. 4, p. 271: "an unlimited play of invention and diversity in private activities") and, after him, A.W. Gomme, obsessed, like all the liberal historians, by the idea that Athens is the fatherland of individual liberty ("Concepts of Freedom," in *More Essays in Greek History and Literature* [Oxford: Blackwell, 1962], p. 141).

72. As Oliver has clearly seen (*Demokratia*, pp. 42–43), the theme of accordance between words and actions sets up an opposition between Spartans and Athenians within Thucydides's work (cf. 1.69.5 and 2.42.2). It is not impossible that the idea should have formed part of the battery of various arguments used in the ideological struggle between Sparta and Athens in the second half of the fifth century.

73. I follow Jean-Paul Dumont here (*Les Sophistes* [Paris: PUF, 1969], p. 80 n.1) in suppressing Sauppe's addition of (*kai ean*).

74. Jeanmaire, *Couroi*, p. 33.

75. Emanuel Kienzle ("Der Lobpreis von Städten und Landern in der älteren grechischen Dichtung" [Ph.D. diss., Basel, 1936], pp. 74–75) observes that in Euripides and Aristophanes, Sparta, deprived of the euboulia accorded it by the poets, is no longer defined by anything but war, whereas Athens becomes the ideal place of the harmony between acts and reason. Basing his argument on a comparison between Pericles's epitaphios and Archidamus's speech (1.84.3), Lionel Pearson ("Propaganda in the Archidamian War," *CPhil.* 31 [1936], p. 46) also observes that the funeral oration is a response to Spartan propaganda.

76. Hellmut Flashar, "Der Epitaphios des Perikles, seine Funktion im Geschichtswerk des Thukydides," *SHAW* (1969), pp. 22–23, insists on the relationship between this idea and Pericles's politics.

77. I have omitted the third part of "Chapter Three, "Marathon or Paradigmatic History," which was first published in *REA* 75 (1973) and which expanded the study of the narration of an exemplary event. It can still be read in the first edition of this book.

Chapter Four: "As for the Name . . . It Is Called a Democracy"

1. See Chapter One as a whole, and esp. "The Time of the Epitaphios Logos."

2. See Chapter Two, pp. 122–27.

3. A.H.M. Jones, *Athenian Democracy* (Oxford: Blackwell, 1957), pp. 42–43. Chapter 3, "The Athenian Democracy and Its Critics," pp. 41–72, is the essential reference.

4. *Ibid.*, pp. 43 and 60.

5. Klaus Oppenheimer, *Zwei attische Epitaphien* (Berlin: Ebering, 1933), p. 12.

6. Felix Jacoby, *Atthis: The Local Chronicles of Ancient Athens* (Oxford: Clarendon, 1949), pp. 209ff.

7. As Oppenheimer himself shows, citing Protagoras's *Peri politeias,* Thrasymachus's *Patrios politeia,* the writings of pseudo-Xenophon, and the "constitutions" of Critias. Last, he recalls that at the beginning of the *Constitution of the Lacedaemonians,* Xenophon praises Sparta in terms (*ou mimesamenos tas allas poleis*) that evoke Pericles's epitaphios (*Zwei attische Epitaphien,* p. 12). See also Konrad Gaiser, *Das Staatsmodell des Thukydides: Zum Rede des Perikles für die Gefallenen* (Heidelberg: Kerle, 1975), p. 20 and n.13, who sees in Thucydides 2.46 (*aristoi politeuousin*) proof that Pericles's epitaphios contains the model of an ariste politeia.

8. Jacoby, *Atthis,* p. 211.

9. The distinction between the meanings of "constitution" and "way of life" is borrowed from M.I. Finley, *The Ancestral Constitution* (London: Cambridge University Press, 1971), pp. 7–8.

10. J.A.O. Larsen ("Cleisthenes and the Development of the Theory of Democracy at Athens," in *Essays in Political Theory Presented to George H. Sabine* [Ithaca, NY: Cornell University Press, 1948], pp. 13–14) shows how democracy seems, at every moment of its history, to be defined *against* its opponents. It even takes up the hypothesis, already proposed by Victor Ehrenberg in "Origins of Democracy" (*Historia* 1 [1950], p. 534), that the very name demokratia was given to the regime by its opponents before being assumed by its advocates.

11. Jones, *Athenian Democracy,* p. 43.

12. On "the spiritual world of the polis," see chapter 4 of Jean-Pierre Vernant, *Les Origines de la pensée grecque* (Paris: PUF, 1962), pp. 40–60. In Lysias 19 (rule of law), there is no doubt a memory of Pindar (quoted by Herodotus 3.38 and Plato, *Gorgias* 484b): *nomos ho pantōn basileus.*

13. Cf. Gregory Vlastos, "*Isonomia*," *AJPh* 74 (1953), pp. 337–66; Larsen, "Cleisthenes," pp. 5–13; Pierre Lévêque and Pierre Vidal-Naquet, *Clisthène l'Athénien: Essai sur la représentation de l'espace et du temps dans la pensée politique grecque* (Paris: Belles Lettres, 1964), pp. 27–32.

14. On the subject of the archaic inscriptions, it is useful to recall the law of Chios, which has usually been seen as a constitution of a democratic type (Meiggs-Lewis, no. 8; cf. particularly Victor Ehrenberg, "When Did the Polis Rise?" *JHS* 57 [1937], pp. 147–59, and "Origins of Democracy," pp. 515–48); and in a Corcyrean epitaph (*GV* p. 42: for a proxene), the *damos* is the principal character. Last, some scholars have believed that they could get closer to *akrēston emen* in the constitutional law of Dreros (Meiggs-Lewis, no. 2, published by Pierre Demargne and Henri van Effenterre, "Recherches à Dréros, 11," *BCH* 61 [1937], pp. 333–48; commentary on this point by Victor Ehrenberg, "An Early Source of Polis Constitution," *CQ* 37 [1943], pp. 14–18, and Felix Jacoby, "*Chrēstous poiein*," *CQ* 38 [1944], pp. 15–16) on the qualifying term *achreios* in Pericles's epitaphios (Thucydides 2.40.2; cf. T. Triantaphyllopoulos, "Thucydide et une inscription archaïque de Crète," in *Synteleia: Vincenzo Arangio-Ruiz* [Naples: Jovene, 1964]). But such a comparison between an epitaphios and a constitutional law of the seventh century is dubious to say the least.

15. On the political meaning of the term *kratos*, see Albert Debrunner, "*Demokratia*," in *Festschrift für Edouard Tièche* (Bern: Lang, 1947), pp. 11–24, esp. 19 (commentary by Christian Meier, "Drei Bemerkungen zur Vor- und Frühgeschichte des Begriffs Demokratie," in *Discordia Concors: Festgabe für Edgar Bonjour* [Basel: Helbing and Lichtenhahn, 1968], pp. 4–13 and *Entstehung des Begriffs "Demokratie": Vier Prolegomena zu einer historischen Theorie* [Frankfurt: Suhrkamp, 19701, pp. 45–48). Cf. also James H. Oliver, *Demokratia, the Gods, and the Free World* (Baltimore: Johns Hopkins Press, 1960), pp. 28–29.

16. Cf. Jones, *Athenian Democracy*, pp. 45. (many examples).

17. W.G. Forrest, *The Emergence of Greek Democracy* (London: Weidenfeld and Nicolson, 1966). Will, "Bulletin historique," *Revue historique* 238 (1967), pp. 396–97, accepts this translation with some reservations.

18. Arnaldo Momigliano, "La libertà di parole nel mondo antico," *Rivista storica italiana* 83 (1971), pp. 499–524, observes that isegoria conveys something like a whiff of the past (p. 518).

19. *Ibid.*, pp. 513–18.

20. *Ibid.*, on aidos, p. 517.

21. These two institutions were constantly attacked by pro-aristocratic writers: for the drawing of lots, see *Dissoi logoi* 7 (DK, 90), which is the model for all later attacks (including those of Plato); for misthophoria, one may recall Aristotle's *Constitution of Athens* (24.3 and 27.3–5) and the unanimity of ancient comedy in "blaming all misdeeds on payment for public office" (Jean Taillardat, *Les Images d'Aristophane,* pp. 395–97). Among the moderns, M.I. Finley, *Democracy Ancient and Modern* (New Brunswick, NJ: Rutgers University Press, 1973), p. 68, observes: "Selection by lot and pay for office were the linchpin of the system."

22. J.A.O. Larsen, "The Judgment of Antiquity on Democracy," *CPhil.* 49 (1954), pp. 1–14; quotation p. 7.

23. Jones, *Athenian Democracy*, p. 47.

24. Gregory Vlastos, *"Isonomia politikè,"* in Jürgen Mau and Ernst Günther Schmidt (eds.), *Isonomia: Studien zur Gleichheitsvorstellung im griechischen Denken* (Berlin: Akademie, 1964), pp. 1–35 (see p. 28 n.3).

25. Jones, *Athenian Democracy*, p. 41.

26. *Ibid.*

27. *Ibid.*, p. 42. When he writes that the epitaphios in the *Menexenus* may be used *"with reservations* as a statement of democratic principles," is Jones aware that the phrase that I have italicized in fact destroys his statement? These "reservations" concern the idea, essential in the text, that democracy is a form of aristocracy.

28. Louis Gernet, "La Notion de démocratie chez les Grecs," *Revue de la Méditerranée*, 5 (1948), pp. 385–93: "So whoever would like to look for even so much as a theory of the regime would not find very much, except among its adversaries" (pp. 389–90).

29. M.I. Finley, "Athenian Demogogues," *P&P* 21 (1962), pp. 3–24, repr. in M.I. Finley (ed.), *Studies in Ancient Society* (London: Routledge and K. Paul, 1974), pp. 1–25 (the problem is discussed on p. 9).

30. A.W. Gomme, "The Working of the Athenian Democracy," in *More Essays in Greek History and Literature* (Oxford: Blackwell, 1962), pp. 177–93: "They liked it; it was their life or their political life" (p. 193).

31. Finley, *Democracy Ancient and Modern*, p. 28.

32. *Ibid.*, p. 16.

33. This is demonstrated by E.D. Harvey, "Literacy in the Athenian Democracy," *REG* 79 (1966), pp. 585–635.

34. Cf. Finley, *Democracy Ancient and Modern*, pp. 16–26.

35. *Ibid.*, pp. 70–71: the educated classes are the same as those that show their hostility to democracy.

36. See, for example, Vernant, "Espace et organisation politique en Grèce ancienne," in *MP*, vol. 1, pp. 212–13, and Harvey, "Literacy," esp. pp. 623–27 – the comparison between Sparta and Athens – and 629. Cf. also Russell Meiggs, *The Athenian Empire* (Oxford: Clarendon, 1972), pp. 18ff. and 235, on the link between the radical reforms of Ephialtes and the very marked increase in inscriptions of public interest after 460.

37. Cf. Harvey ("Literacy," pp. 598–600), who bases his argument on a passage in Euripides's *Suppliant Women* (431–37), the public posting of laws, the abundance of epigraphical documents, and the declared hostility of other political systems to written laws; however, the last two arguments are relevant only to "classical Greece": the aristocratic regimes of archaic Greece "invented" the writing down of laws, and there are a great many epigraphical documents to prove this.

38. We know that a decree always began with (1) the *decision* ("it has pleased the council and the people"); (2) mention of the prytaneum, the *epistates*, and the secretary; and (3) the proposition, always presented *as the content of a speech* ("so-and-so has said").

39. Harvey ("Literacy," p. 586) wonders what category of Athenians could read political pamphlets; he does not wonder who could have written them. In this attitude, he belongs to a whole tradition that poses the problem of *reading* in a democracy but not that of writing (cf. the significant title of Frederic G. Kenyon's *Books and Readers in Greece and Rome* [Oxford: Clarendon, 1951]).

40. Very important for us from this point of view is Thucydides's "second introduction" (5.26), which insists on the advantages of exile, since enforced leisure enables one to write. On this problem cf. Henri van Effentere, *L'Histoire en Grèce* (Paris: A. Colin, 1967), p. 10.

41. When Plato writes "in the cities," he seldom means anything other than Athens (cf. *Republic* 487d6: philosophers unsuited to serving "the cities"; *Politics* 298a–300c). The fear of being called a Sophist recalls Cleon's speech in Thucydides (3.38.7). Phaedrus is beyond a doubt this spokesman of Athenian public opinion, in opposition to Socrates, to whom Plato, in an anachronism that is quite typical of him, attributes his own criticism of the graphomania of fourth-century Athens.

42. Vernant, *Les Origines de la pensée grecque*, p. 40.

43. My approach here is parallel to that of A.W.H. Adkins in *Moral Values and Political Behaviour in Ancient Greece* (London: Chatto and Windus, 1972), pp. 125–26.

44. The mention of laws "that give support to the victims of injustice" obviously suggests the topos of Athens the seat of justice, but since what is being referred to here is basically the organization *within* the city, this term must be understood as referring to Athenian criminal law.

45. Vernant, *Les Origines de la pensée grecque*, p. 42.

46. On wealth as *agalma*, cf. Louis Gernet, "La Notion mythique de la valeur en Grèce," in *Anthropologie de la Grèce antique* (Paris: Maspero, 1968), pp. 93–137. Will rightly stresses the extent to which the liturgies preserve a trace of aristocratic ostentation (*MGO*, p. 460). Cf. also Adkins, *Moral Values and Political Behaviour*, pp. 119–25.

47. Gomme, "The Working of the Athenian Democracy," pp. 178 and 187, contrasts this statement with the Platonic idea that a person can practice only one profession at a time in the city (the cultivation of virtue, proper to the citizen, is a profession that precludes any other activity: *Laws* 8.847a). Plato probably had Protagoras in mind, for we know that he supported the thesis defended here by Pericles. On this passage, cf. also Jean Bollack, "Les Sophistes," in *Athènes au temps de Périclès* (Paris: Hachette, 1965), p. 216.

48. André Aymard ("Hiérarchie du travail et autarcie individuelle dans la Grèce archaïque," in *Etudes d'histoire ancienne*, pp. 316–33, esp. 319) has shown the limits of this revaluation. Cf. also M.M. Austin and Pierre Vidal-Naquet, *Economies et sociétés en Grèce ancienne* (Paris: A. Colin, 1972), pp. 125–28.

49. I do not believe that one should, with Finley (*Democracy Ancient and Modern*, p. 81), draw parallels between this passage and the Solonian law on the need to take part in civil struggles (Aristotle, *Constitution of Athens* 8.5): the existence of civil struggles could not be mentioned in an epitaphios as a necessity of political life.

50. In *autoi etoi krinomen ge ē enthumoumetha orthōs ta pragmata* (2.40.2), we may, as Gomme suggests (*Commentary*, vol. 2, p. 123), read a distinction between those who propose (*enthumoumetha*) — *bouleutes*, but also ordinary members of the assembly — and those who decide by voting (*krinomen*). But we may also relate the two verbs to the activity of the assembly, voting a *probouleuma* (*krinomen*) or deciding on one's own initiative (*enthumoumetha*): Classen-Steup, ad loc. The two verbs are general enough to be difficult, if not impossible, to define;

the main point is that the reference here is to the ekklesia. The existence of the heliaia and other Athenian tribunals is postulated by 2.37.1 (*idia diaphora*) and 3. No direct allusion, it seems, is made to the boule, unless the verb *gnōnai* (2.40.2) is associated with the probouleumatic activity (*gnōmē* as an equivalent of *probouleuma* was one of the formulas of fourth-century Athenian decrees, but it also appears in fifth-century decrees). Nevertheless, I am inclined to see this verb as yet another allusion to the ekklesia, which, although it was made up of work-ers of all kinds, was capable of taking satisfactory *decisions* (cf. p. 232 and below, n.55).

51. Cf., for example, Gomme, "The Working of the Athenian Democracy," p. 186. One may remember the many commentaries provoked by the *bole demosie* of the constitutional law of Chios (cf. Christian Meier, "Clisthène et le problème politique de la *polis* grecque," *RIDA* 20 [1973], pp. 115–59, esp. 145).

52. Vlastos, *"Isonomia politikè,"* p. 29 n.1; Edward Bentham in his scholarly edition (Oxford, 1746, p. 104) had already observed that *es* designates the object of administration and not the governing subject.

53. Vlastos, *"Isonomia politikè,"* p. 29 n.1. Vlastos draws a distinction between the activity of government and the act of deciding on various proposi-tions (*krinomen,* 2.40.2; *kritai,* 3.37.4, and so on). It is hardly surprising that, try-ing to reveal what Pericles's epitaphios conceals, Plato returns three times to the term *kratos*: *Menexenus* 238d4, 5, and e1.

54. *Ibid.*: "Had he wanted to make the reader think of the full, literal sense of demokratia, he would have been more likely to put it at, or near, the beginning."

55. This reading was dominant in the eighteenth and nineteenth centuries. See Bentham, p. 107; Johann Christoph Gottleber (*Platonis Menexenus et Periclis Thucydidei oratio funebris* [Leipzig, 1782]), and F. Roger, *Eloges funèbres des Athéniens morts pour la patrie* (who translates it "des hommes de peine"). For the term *ep' ergon trepein,* cf. Lowell Edmunds, "Thucydides 2.40.2," *CR* 22 (1972), pp. 171–72 (overall interpretation of the passage).

56. Translation by Aymard, "Hiérarchie du travail et autarcie individuelle," p. 319. For reasons developed by Aymard, p. 420 n.75, it would be preferable to translate *oikeion hama kai politikon* by "to run both one's household and the affairs of the city."

57. We know that the reading *heterois* presented by the manuscripts has been an embarrassment to those who wanted to see in the epitaphios a profes-sion of democratic faith, and several corrections have been proposed. On the

other hand, neither the scholiast nor the nineteenth-century editors (such as Ambroise Firmin-Didot) ever called this text into question.

58. Bollack ("Les Sophistes," p. 216) observes that for Pericles the state is administered like a household, which means that a position of responsibility is on the side of *oikonomia* and not of techne. Indeed, the resemblance between the text of the epitaphios and *Protagoras* 318e6–319a1–2 is quite striking. Against this view: Johannes Th. Kakridis, *Der thukydideische Epitaphios* (Munich: Beck, 1961), for whom *oikeion* simply denotes private activities. Pericles's ruse — or Thucydides's, or, in any case, that of the funeral oration — is probably *to say both things at once.*

59. Cf. Edmunds, "Thucydides II.40.2."

60. K.J. Dover (*Lysias and the Corpus Lysiacum* [Berkeley: University of California Press, 1968], pp. 54–55) observes that an epideictic speech, because it has to say *ta kairia*, tends to use silence or ambivalence as a compromise between the views of the orator and those of the public, and indeed between the opinions of the various elements in the audience.

61. Gomme (*Commentary*, vol. 2, p. 109: "Cf. the use of *isonomia*, Hdt. 111, 80") is hasty, to say the least. Cf. Helmuth Vretska ("Perikles und die Herrschaft des Wurdingsten, Thuk. II., 37, I," *RhM* 109 [1966], p. 113), who expresses surprise that the orator restricts isonomia to the private sphere; and Martin Ostwald (*Nomos and the Beginnings of the Athenian Democracy* [Oxford: Clarendon, 1969]), who believes that both the term and the notion of isonomia are absent from the epitaphios.

62. Cf. Rudolf Hirzel, *Agraphos nomos* (Leipzig: Teubner, 1900), pp. 21ff.

63. See Ostwald, *Nomos*, p. 58.

64. We must distinguish here between the actual practice of the aristocratic cities of the archaic period and the *tradition* of aristocratic thought as expressed during the classical period. For a critique of the writing down of laws, see Plato, *Phaedrus* 257c–58c (logography), 277d, 274c–75e (myth of Theuth and Socrates's commentary on the myth). On this subject, read also Jacques Derrida, "La Pharmacie de Platon," in *La Dissémination* (Paris: Seuil, 1972), pp. 71–197.

65. Edmund Büchner, *Der Panegyrikos des Isokrates: Eine historisch-philogische Untersuchung* (Wiesbaden: Steiner, 1958), p. 80. In a note, however, Büchner cites with a certain embarrassment the passage (2.39.4) in which Pericles, declaring that the Athenians base their valor on topoi and not on nomoi, speaks like the oligarch Critias (DK, 88 B 22: "A valorous character is more dependable than law").

66. Otto Schröder (De laudibus Athenarum a poetis tragicis et ab oratoribus epidicticis excultis" [Ph.D. diss., Göttingen, 1914]) sees in Aeschylus's *Suppliants* (946ff.) an allusion to these unwritten laws and considers this a theme of the funeral oration. Similarly, Hellmut Flashar ("Der Epitaphios des Perikles, seine Funktion im Geschichtswerk des Thukydides," *SHAW* [1969], p. 20) writes: "The distinction between written and unwritten laws belongs to the traditional repertoire of encomiastic speeches."

67. I am not prejudging here the antiquity of the laws commonly referred to as "Draconian" (on this subject, cf. Eberhard Ruschenbusch, "*Patrios politeia*: Theseus, Drakon, Solon und Kleisthenes in Publizistik und Geschichtsschreibung des 5. und 4. Jahrhunderts v. Chr.," *Historia* 8 [1958], pp. 398–424). For us, the important point is that the Athenians regarded them as such.

68. Gernet, "Droit et prédroit en Grèce ancienne," in *Anthropologie*, p. 181.

69. On the "tyranny of the gaze" in archaic societies, cf. Marcel Detienne, *The Masters of Truth in Archaic Greece*, trans. Janet Lloyd (New York: Zone Books, 1996), p. 155 n.41.

70. Gernet, "Droit et prédroit en Grèce ancienne," p. 181. Cf. Eduard von Erffa, *Aidôs und verwandte Begriffe in ihrer Entwicklung von Homer bis Demokrit, Philologus*, supp. 30 (1937).

71. On this passage, cf. von Erffa, *Aidôs*, pp. 187–90: aischune is social scrutiny, not interiorization of individual shame.

72. On the conservatism of references to aischune and aidos, cf. von Erffa, *Aidôs*, and Bruno Snell, *Die Entdeckung des Geistes* (Hamburg: Claassen, 1955), p. 234. See also E.R. Dodds, *The Greeks and the Irrational* (Berkeley: University of California Press, 1951), pp. 17, 28, 43, on "shame culture."

73. Hans Bengl, "Staatstheoretische Probleme im Rahmen der attischen, Tragödie" (Ph.D. diss., Munich, 1929), p. 53, compares Thucydides 2.37ff. with the *Eumenides* (690ff.), but also with Sophocles's *Ajax* (1073–80: *phobos kai aidōs, deos kai aischunē*).

74. This antithesis was clearly formulated by Xenophon, then taken up by the Sophists and transformed into the *onoma/ergon* or *onoma/pragma* antithesis, as Felix Heinimann reminds us, *Nomos und Physis* (Basel: Reinhardt, 1945), pp. 51ff.

75. Larsen ("Cleisthenes," p. 13) thinks that "this defensive attitude shows that "democracy" is a name used by the opponents of the regime." For Georg Peter Landmann, ("Das Lob Athens in der Grabrede des Perikles (Thukydides II 34–41)," *MH* 31 (1974), p. 80), although Pericles feels the need to defend

democracy, the word is still a class slogan. See also Claude Mossé, "La Démocratie athénienne *justifiée* par Périclès," in *Les Institutions grecques* (Paris: A. Colin, 1967), p. 155.

76. Additional notes to the edition of book 2, CUF, p. 96.

77. Vlastos, *"Isonomia politikè,"* p. 29 n.2.

78. *Axiōsis* is difficult to translate. The use of the suffix -*sis* precludes the passive meaning "dignities, honors." De Romilly's translation, "les titres" (titles), is better in that it refers to the meaning of the verb *axioō* "to evaluate," "to appreciate." Axiosis is the esteem or appreciation in which one holds an individual's merits, his ability to command (in his commentary, Vlastos translates *axiōsis* as "claim").

79. Rich and poor are placed much more clearly on an equal footing in *The Suppliant Women* 433–34 ("rich and poor have the same rights [*dikē ise*]"), concerning which text Bengl ("Staatstheoretische Probleme," pp. 32–34) speaks of "arithmetic equality." On these problems, see F.D. Harvey, "Two Kinds of Equality," *C&M* 26 (1965), pp. 101–46, esp. 101–28.

80. Vlastos, *"Isonomia politikè,"* p. 30.

81. The term *aristokratia* is itself much rarer, and in any case more recent than demokratia, as Debrunner (*"Demokratia,"* pp. 14–15) has noted. On the other hand, arete remains one of the "most powerful value-terms of the society" (Adkins, *Moral Values and Political Behaviour*, pp. 113ff.).

82. *Ibid.* Borivoj Borecky ("Die politische Isonomie," *Eirene* 9 [1971], p. 21) sees very clearly that Pericles does not go as far as Plato, who, in the *Menexenus,* is anxious to harden the positions of the Athenian politician: whereas Pericles says that one *may* display one's abilities, Plato declares that only the best have the right to govern the people.

83. Will, *MGO*, p. 429. On the competitive sense preserved by arete in the late fifth century, cf. Adkins, *Moral Values and Political Behaviour*, pp. 113–18 and 139.

84. Gomme remarks that arete must be understood to refer to "the best," not to "the nobles" (*Commentary*, vol. 2, p. 109).

85. Cf. Adkins, *Moral Values and Political Behaviour*, pp. 105 and 141.

86. Note the presence of the verb *protimatai,* derived from *timē,* a term whose aristocratic coloring is undeniable.

87. *Apo merous* in reference to the drawing of lots or to the rotation of responsibilities (*en merei*): cf. Gomme, *Commentary*, vol. 2, p. 108; Kakridis, *Der*

thukydideische Epitaphios, p. 26; Vretska, "Perikles und die Herrschaft des Würdingsten," p.113; Flashar, "Der Epitaphios des Perikles," p. 18.

88. Vlastos, *"Isonomia politikè,"* p. 29 n.2.

89. No doubt influenced by the scholiast (who glosses *apo merous* by "in terms of nobility"), van Herwerden proposes to change it into *apo genous;* this would be to forget that *ploutos is* implied in *oud' au kata penian*. But to translate it as Mossé does (*Les Institutions grecques*, p. 156), "honors go more to merit than to fortune," is to misunderstand the intentionally equivocal nature of the expression: cf. the Platonic gloss "neither weakness, nor poverty, nor obscurity of birth" (*Menexenus* 238d6) and the remarks by de Romilly (additional notes, p. 96: "The term is intentionally vague; only merit counts and not membership in a particular social category, whatever it may be").

90. Except for the translation by van Effenterre (*L'Histoire en Grèce*, p. 132) and the commentary by Gomme, who discusses this expression, though from a perspective that in my opinion is incorrect (*Commentary*, vol. 2, p. 108).

91. Compare this with a fragment from Euripides (*Erechtheus* 362, Nauck), which links in two apparently contradictory statements the egalitarian fiction and the power of wealth: cf. Roger Goossens, *Euripide et Athènes* (Brussels: Palais des Académies, 1962), p. 473. On the role of wealth in democratic Athens, see Adkins, *Moral Values and Political Behaviour*, pp. 115–24 and 140–41.

92. Adkins, *Moral Values and Political Behaviour*, pp. 105 and 141, on Thucydides 2.37.1.

93. For example, Will, *MGO*, p. 64.

94. Cf. Vlastos, *"Isonomia politikè,"* pp. 30ff.

95. Louis Méridier, edition of the *Menexenus,* CUF, p. 90 n.1; Vlastos (*"Isonomia politikè,"* p. 31) doubts that this is possible.

96. Vlastos, *"Isonomia politikè,"* p. 31: "This could only be a joke. But it brings out the other word Pericles had suppressed: it names elective process."

97. Vretska, "Perikles und die Herrschaft des Würdingsten," p. 113.

98. Finley, "Athenian Demagogues," pp. 20–21, rightly observes that the version according to which Pericles used it to obtain power allows the opponents not to examine the real question of the value of misthophoria.

99. Jacqueline de Romilly, *Thucydide et l'impérialisme athénien* (Paris: Société d'Edition les Belles Lettres, 1947), p. 122 n.2. More recently, de Romilly has rightly pointed out the silence of the epitaphios and of *The Suppliant Women* on the drawing of lots (*Problèmes de la démocratie grecque* [Paris: Hermann, 1975], p. 12).

100. Philippe Gauthier has demonstrated this in "La Cité," in *Athènes au temps de Périclès,* pp. 12–47. Cf. also Will, *MGO,* pp. 262–67.

101. This is more or less what Hans Schaefer thinks, "Besonderheit und Begriff der attischen Demokratie im 5 Jahrhundert," in *Synopsis: Festgabe für Alfred Weber* (Heidelberg: Schneider, 1948), pp. 479–503. On the debate among Berve, Ehrenberg, and Bengtson on the theme "democracy and great men," see Henri Irénée Marrou, *Actes du neuvième congrès des sciences historiques* (Paris, 1950), p. 328.

102. The author, obsessed by this idea, as his title ("Perikles und die Herrschaft des Würdingsten") shows, cares little for the characteristics of the funeral oration as a genre.

103. Francis Macdonald Cornford, *Thucydides Mythistoricus,* 2nd ed. (London: Routledge and K. Paul, 1965), ch. 8, p. 147.

104. Goossens, *Euripide et Athènes,* p. 440.

105. Cf. Cornford, *Thucydides Mythistoricus,* pp. 147 and 149–50.

106. De Romilly, notice to book 2, CUF, pp. xxvff.

107. De Romilly, *Thucydide et l'impérialisme athénien,* pp. 128–30. Cf. also Ostwald, *Nomos,* p. 58 n.1.

108. Victor Ehrenberg, *From Solon to Socrates* (London: Methuen, 1968), p. 263.

109. Bernard Knox, *Oedipus at Thebes: Sophocles' Tragic Hero and His Time* (New Haven, CT: Yale University Press, 1966), pp. 161–64.

110. Goossens, *Euripide et Athènes,* p. 440, certainly notes "the harmony of thought, tone, and even phraseology between Pericles's funeral oration" and *The Suppliant Women,* but he believes he must impute it to the two writers' membership in the same political party, that of the moderates (the same idea is found in Felix M. Wassermann, "Thucydides and the Disintegration of the Polis," *TAPA* 85 [1954], pp. 46–54, who sees in both the epitaphios and *The Suppliant Women* a eulogy of *mesa ton politon*).

111. Without referring to the enormous literature on the problem of the authenticity of the orations in Thucydides, I am taking seriously the methodological account in 1.22.1, especially since for him the systematic comparison of Pericles's epitaphios with the other orations takes the place of verification.

112. Schröder, "De laudibus Athenarum," p. 25.

113. Jacoby, *Atthis,* pp. 75ff.

114. Henry R. Immerwahr, *Form and Thought in Herodotus* (Ann Arbor, MI: Edwards Bros., 1966), pp. 119ff., provides many examples to support this statement.

115. On *Clouds,* K.J. Dover (*Aristophanic Comedy* [London: Batsford, 1972],
p. 111) characterizes Athenian conservatism thus: "The Athenians, however,
tended to play down their own innovations; devoted to their ancestors, conscious
of the continued ghostly presence of those ancestors, they were more inclined to
postulate the existence of a kind of prehistoric democracy on Attic soil than to
claim credit for having devised a political system unknown in earlier times."

116. Cf., for example, Ilse von Loewenclau, *Der platonische Menexenos*
(Stuttgart: Kohlhammer, 1961), and Vlastos, "*Isonomia politikè.*"

117. Cf. Bernhard Abraham van Groningen, *In the Grip of the Past: Essay on
an Aspect of Greek Thought* (Leiden: Brill, 1953), ch. 5 ("Genealogy"). Although
such rationalist authors as Thucydides and Cleidemus, who may have published
his *Atthis* under the title *Protogonia* (cf. Jacoby, *Atthis,* p. 83) in an allusion to the
Athenian claim to autochthony, avoid the *term autochthones,* the *theme* nevertheless shapes any Athenian's representation of the city, and it is significant that the
most democratic of the Atthidographers lays great stress on it.

118. Hermann Strasburger, "Thukydides und die politische Selbstdarstellung
der Athener," *Hermes* 86 (1958), p. 23.

119. A study of the topos of autochthony in Isocrates, *Panegyricus* 24–25,
shows that all "historical" hypotheses concerning the occupation of land (by
expulsion of previous occupants, by settling on deserted land, by the intermingling of several different peoples) are rejected as characterizing the situation of
others, whereas the explanation given of the relationship between Athens and its
land requires the use of "noble" expressions. Finally, in par. 25, the orator
declares that the land is at once nurse, fatherland, and mother, a primal promis-
cuity of man and soil that makes it possible to deny the historical character of the
process of land appropriation. Marx was probably thinking of representations of
this type when, describing the second "pre-capitalist form," he observed that the
recognition of landownership presupposes the existence of the community, a
"presupposition considered as divine" ("A Contribution to the Critique of Political Economy," in *Collected Works* [London: Lawrence and Wishart, 1980], vol. 16
pp. 465–77).

120. See Anthony J. Podlecki on *The Suppliants* (*The Political Background of
Aeschylean Tragedy* [Ann Arbor: University of Michigan Press, 1966], ch. 4).

121. A statement that is found in the *Atthides* and in Philochorus (cf. Jacoby
Atthis, pp. 133–34).

122. Austin and Vidal-Naquet, *Economies et sociétés,* p. 238.

123. I am referring here to a paper on homonoia given by Jacqueline de Romilly at the Centre de Recherches sur la Grèce Antique at Strasbourg University II on Dec. 9, 1971. On homonoia, cf. also Will, *MGO*, vol. 1, pp. 510ff., and, from a perspective centered on Rome, Arnaldo Momigliano, "Camillus and Concord," *CQ* 36 (1942), pp. 112–20, repr. in *Secondo contributo alla storia degli studi classici* (Rome: Storia e Letteratura, 1960), pp. 89–104, esp. 101–102.

124. This problem, linked with that of the tyrant-empire, has been the subject of a lively debate, triggered by an article by G.E.M. de Ste. Croix, "The Character of the Athenian Empire," *Historia* 3 (1954), pp. 1–41, and followed by those of Donald W. Bradeen (*Historia* 9 [1960], pp. 257–69), H.W. Pleket (*Historia* 12 [1963], pp. 70–77), T.J. Quinn (*Historia* 13 [1964], pp. 257–66), and others. However, it should be remembered that the editors of the Athenian tribute lists (*ATL* [1950], vol. 3, ch. 9, "Democracy in the Allied Cities") think they can show that the Athenians did not impose democracy systematically: it is obvious, to borrow an expression from Pierre Vidal-Naquet, that Athens was never at the head of some "internationale of democracies."

125. So strong was the moderate ideology in 392, however, that it thought fit to identify democracy with a superior homonoia (55: concord among the allies thanks to the Athenians).

126. Another unquestionably democratic feature: Lysias praises the men of Piraeus for re-erecting the walls (63). But, as Yvon Garlan has shown (*Recherches de poliorcétique grecque* [Athens: Ecole Française d'Athènes, 1974], p. 97), the "urban defenses + ships + democracy" complex constitutes a "historical bloc" dear to the democratic orators.

127. See Adkins's penetrating remarks (*Moral Values and Political Behaviour*, pp. 106–12) on nomos and phusis.

128. Plato's Callicles makes the same shift when he interprets Pindar (*Gorgias* 482e–84c).

129. Ehrenberg, "When Did the Polis Rise?" p. 158.

130. Cf. Finley, "Athenian Demagogues," pp. 5–6.

131. Although in tragedy a gap is created between the political and the mythical (cf. Jean-Pierre Vernant, "Le Moment historique de la tragédie," in *MT*, p. 16), the funeral oration seems on the other hand to be *an oration without any tragic element*, in which the city projects itself as one, indivisible, and, so to speak, impenetrable.

132. On the civil war in the *Menexenus*, see Chapter Three, p. 201.

133. Cf. Chaïm Perelman and Lucie Olbrechts-Tyteca, *Traité de l'argumentation: La Nouvelle Rhétorique* (Brussels: Editions de l'Université de Bruxelles, 1970), pp. 66–67.

134. The fragments of the stela were published by Meritt, who believed they were the remains of an obituary (*Hesperia* 2 [1933], pp. 151–54), and identified by A.E. Raubitschek ("The Heroes of Phyle," *Hesperia* 10 [1941], pp. 284–95).

135. Cf. Ronald S. Stroud, "Theozotides and the Athenian Orphans," *Hesperia* 40 (1971), p. 291. We shall not consider the discrepancy between the decree, which stresses above all the Athenian quality of the *father*, and Lysias's oration, which poses the problem of the *nothoi*. In fact, verification of legitimacy follows from d[*oki*]*masato* (1. 15), and, after a great many offenses committed during the war against the Periclean law of 451–50, it should be remembered that there was a return to the norm (cf. Louis Gernet in Lysias, *Oeuvres complètes*, CUF, pp. 235–36; Georges Mathieu, "La Réorganisation du corps civique athénien," *REG* 39 [1926], pp. 65–116, esp. 98–104; and Stroud, "Theozotides," pp. 299ff.).

136. This clause has two functions: to stress the exceptional status of the dead and at the same time to recall in what their valor consisted.

137. Lysias's epitaphios, like the decree of Demophantus (Andocides 1.96–97), uses the term *polemios* to designate the citizen who is an enemy of the city, but it does so with numerous precautions: in 61 *pantas polemious* is vague, and in 62 *polemious* refers both to the Lacedaemonians and to *politas*. In fact, Lysias never uses *polemios* directly in the sense of "outlaw" (on this term, cf. Louis Gernet, *Platon, Lois, livre IX, traduction et commentaire* [Paris, 1917], p. 85).

138. The text of the ephebic oath, cited on p. 255 n.† and p. 257 n.*, is that of the stela of Acharnes (cf. Louis Robert, *Etudes épigraphiques et philologiques* [Paris: Champion, 1938], pp. 296–307; and Georges Daux, "Deux steles d'Acharnes," in *Mélanges Orlandos* [Athens, 1964], pp. 79–84). On the democratic character of this oath, see Georges Mathieu, "Remarques sur l'éphébie attique," in *Mélanges Desrousseaux* (Paris: Hachette, 1937), p. 313.

139. Stroud observes ("Theozotides," p. 294) that "Theozotides is dealing with a new situation. The sons [of the dead] are not exactly war orphans, for, if they were, there would have been no need for his decree."

140. Cf. Eiliv Skard, *Zwei religiös-politische Begriffe: Euergetes-Concordia* (Oslo: Jacob Dybwad, 1932), pp. 8–13, on the transformation of the meaning of this term in the fourth century (transformation of the ancient civic duties into gracious gifts, and so on).

141. Jean Pouilloux, "L'Apport des inscriptions comparé à celui des textes littéraires au Vème et au IVème siècle: Deux exemples, Thasos et Salamine de Chypre," in *Akten des VI internationalen Kongresses für Griechische und Lateinische Epigraphik, München 1972*, Vestigia, 17 (Munich: Beck, 1973), pp. 363–65.

142. An uneasy repression, since the epitaphios uses the word that it is trying to avoid, even to the point of referring to the democratic combatants as *huper tēs dēmokratias stasiasantes*; this expression may be compared with the much more neutral formula of Theozotides's decree: *boēthountes tēi dēmokratiai*.

143. De Romilly, *Thucydide et l'impérialisme athénien*, pp. 128–30.

144. Examples seem to be legion. I shall be content to cite Ehrenberg ("When Did the Polis Rise?" p. 158), who, after describing the polis in broad outline, sees Pericles's epitaphios as the best illustration of the ideal of the polis. The shift is perpetual, from the polis to the democratic polis and from the democratic polis to Pericles's Athens.

145. Cf. Finley, *Democracy Ancient and Modern*, pp. 28–29.

146. Schröder, "De laudibus Athenarum," pp. 25–28.

147. Under the name Argos, *The Suppliants* in fact refers to the model of democratic Athens: cf. Podlecki, *Political Background of Aeschylean Tragedy*, ch. 4.

148. Lévêque and Vidal-Naquet, *Clisthène*, p. 48: "The political reversal carried out in Athens under Cleisthenes was accompanied by a symmetrical reversal in the external policy of the Lacedaemonians."

149. Eugène Napoleon Tigerstedt, *The Legend of Sparta in Classical Antiquity* (Lund, 1965), p. 86. Similarly, Finley ("Sparta," p. 157) declares that for Herodotus the Greek world was divided into two kinds of communities, those ruled by tyrants ... and those ruled by themselves. The latter in turn were either fully democratic or they were not," and it is certain that this latter opposition, however important it may be, is not the dominant one.

150. Think of the attitude of the Melians refusing to listen to the Athenians before the assembled people (Thucydides 5.84.3–85).

151. As Goossens observes (*Euripide et Athènes*, pp. 420ff.).

152. Larsen, "Judgment of Antiquity on Democracy," p. 9; Larsen declared: "The Rejection of Democracy by Antiquity may appear to be the proper title of this paper."

153. *Ibid.* Cf. also André Aymard ("Le Protocole royal grec et son évolution," *REA* 50 [1948], repr. in *Etudes d'Histoire ancienne*, pp. 73–99): beginning with the

Diadochi, "never had the word *dēmokratia* enjoyed such success, because it meant in fact, nothing more than *republic*" (pp. 94–95).

154. On the "normal" character of the demokratia/oligarchia opposition, cf. Debrunner, *"Demokratia,"* pp. 15–16 (even at the linguistic level, it is difficult to determine which of the two terms was the older); on the gradual replacement of the isonomia/tyrannis antithesis by the democracy/oligarchy opposition, cf. Debrunner, *ibid.*, p. 22, and Meier, "Drei Bemerkungen," p. 13, and *Entstehung des Begriffs "Demokratie,"* pp. 39–42. I would agree with Gauthier ("La Cité," p. 35) that "in the Pericles period, democracy was defined in relation to government by the *aristoi,* more than in opposition to government by a single man."

155. The community of hopes in danger is democratic, and traditionally opposed to the difficulties encountered by oligarchies in case of war (Plato, *Republic* 8.511d–e, elucidated by Thucydides 3.27 and 6.39.2).

156. At least we should observe that in 464 this antithesis still governs the evocation of democratic principles in *The Suppliants.*

157. Cf. Chapter Three, p. 217 and n.77.

158. Will (*MGO,* p. 142) observes that "the reforms of 462 were to prove the existence of a debate on the development of *politeia,* and that Cimon was hostile to this development."

159. Even if the memory of tyranny did represent a "permanent trauma" in the Athenian collective consciousness (Arnaldo Momigliano, "L'excursus di Tucidide in Vl, 549," in *Studi di storiografia antica in memoria di Leonardo Ferrero* [Turin: Bottega d'Erasmo, 1971], p. 32), Thucydides himself stresses that beginning in 415, fear of tyranny was also a fear of oligarchy (6.60.1).

160. Cf. Lorenzo Braccesi, "L'epitafio di Iperide come fonte storica," *Athenaeum* 58 (1970), p. 287.

161. This is the case with Lysias 19, where, behind the bia/nomos opposition that dominates the passage, one may detect (1) a Spartan or at least a general theme, that of the sovereignty of law, which Sparta tended to appropriate (*nomos despotes:* cf. Herodotus 7.104) — there is no need to attack Sparta openly: the agon also consists in "borrowing" its values; (2) an Athenian theme traditionally opposed to the Spartans' mistrust of the *logos:* the theme of the instructor logos evokes Thucydides 2.40.3.

162. On *spoudaios,* the term that holds an important place in Aristotelian ethics, see Pierre Aubenque, *La Prudence chez Aristote* (Paris: PUF, 1963), pp.

45–51, esp. 45 n.2. The term *spoudaios* refers to an aristocratic ethic, and Aubenque recommends the translation "valorous" ("le valeureux").

163. Robert Clavaud (CUF, p. 21) believes that Demosthenes is explicitly referring here to Thucydides 2.37.2–3. In "Zu den attischen Reden auf die Gefallenen," *Symbolae Osloenses* (1948), p. 63, Mat Pohlenz observes that unlike Thucydides, who associated deos with aischune (2.37.3), the orator here represses deos within the oligarchy, reserving for democracy only aischune (similarly, in Lysias 12 and 25, aischune is opposed to phobos). He compares this text with a passage from *Laws* (3.698b) in which Plato makes aidos the eminently aristocratic guiding principle of Athens during the Persian Wars before defining this term as "fear of dishonor."

164. The aristocratic character of this text appears even more clearly when compared with the eulogy of demokratia in *Against Leptinus* (106), in which Demosthenes tries to define the characteristics of oligarchy as compared with those of democracy, whereas the epitaphios does the opposite.

165. *Oneidos,* however, is what Sparta considered the unforgivable sin; cf. Thucydides 1.84.3; Plutarch, *Lycurgus* 14, 21, 25; and Xenophon, *Constitution of the Lacedaemonians* 9.4.

166. Cf. Detienne, *The Masters of Truth*, pp. 48 and 75.

167. In the Freudian sense of the word.

168. Kakridis, *Der thukydideische Epitaphios*, p. 27, declares that "Pericles succeeded in bringing together in a fruitful combination democratic and aristocratic features, filling with this ideal image the gap between the two parties that, in the real Greece, were to continue their irreconcilable struggle during the Peloponnesian War." (Cf. also Vretska, "Perikles und die Herrschaft des Würdingsten," p. 114.) It is impossible to follow him in this analysis, which ignores far too much the military character of the oration.

169. Cf. Pierre Vidal-Naquet, "La Tradition de l'hoplite athénien," in *Problèmes de la guerre en Grèce ancienne* (The Hague: Mouton, 1968), p. 171–76.

170. The rejection of the sea must be interpreted in political terms: the absence of naval techne is essential (much more than that of a "geographical" eulogy of Attica as a maritime world, on which Arnaldo Momigliano lays great stress, "Sea-Power in Greek Thought," in *Secondo contributo*, pp. 65ff.).

171. Knox, *Oedipus at Thebes,* esp. ch. 2, "Athens," pp. 53–106: Oedipus is a transposition of the *polis-turannos.*

172. Lévêque and Vidal-Naquet, *Clisthène*, p. 120.

173. Cf. Marcel Detienne, "L'Olivier: Un mythe politico-religieux," in M.I. Finley (ed.), *Problèmes de la terre en Grèce ancienne* (Paris: Mouton, 1973), pp. 293–306.

174. Momigliano ("Sea-Power in Greek Thought," p. 61) believes that unlike Euripides, who had no great opinion of sailors, Aristophanes never expressed disapproval of maritime power. This claim, it seems to me, goes a little too far.

175. Cf. A.W. Gomme, "Aristophanes and Politics," in *More Essays,* pp. 86 and 88 (many references).

176. Will (*MGO,* p. 268 n.3) characterizes *The Constitution of the Athenians* as being "exactly the negative of the picture of the idealized Athens painted by the historian Thucydides in the funeral oration of book 2."

177. In *Ludwig Feuerbach and the End of Classical German Philosophy* (Karl Marx and Friedrich Engels, *Selected Works* [London: Lawrence and Wishart, 1968], p. 590), Engels defines the "system" as the perishable part in any philosopher's work "and for the simple reason that it springs from an imperishable desire of the human mind — the desire to overcome all contradictions."

178. Will, *MGO,* p. 461.

179. In "Athenian Demagogues" (p. 8), Finley stresses this aspect of the author, declaring that he is the single, striking exception in the Greek tradition of political thought, which is always moralistic.

180. Cf. Jean-Pierre Vernant, "Tensions et ambiguïtés dans la tragédie grecque," in *MT,* pp. 21–27 and 30: "Tragedy, at the point at which it passes from one plane to another, strongly marks the distances, stresses the contradictions."

181. See Goossens, *Euripide et Athènes,* pp. 177 and 420–21.

182. Goossens recognizes this; he thinks that this clever distribution functions as a foil for the eulogy (*Euripide et Athènes,* p. 428).

183. Adkins rightly stresses the ambiguity of lines 441–42: if he who can shine is the agathos and if the kakos is he who has the right to remain silent, is equality as real as Theseus claims (*Moral Values and Political Behaviour,* p. 142)?

184. In this, the funeral oration differs profoundly from a Sophistic agon, and the question of its relations with Sophistic practice, raised by Bengl ("Staatstheoretische Probleme," pp. 37–40), is probably a false problem.

185. To the names of Austin and Vidal-Naquet, whom I have quoted here (*Economies et sociétés,* pp. 28 and 30), might be added those of Aymard, Adkins, and even Jones, whose works have been constantly used throughout this study.

186. Adkins, *Moral Values and Political Behaviour,* ch. 5, esp. pp. 119–26.

187. Cf. Lévêque and Vidal-Naquet, *Clisthène*, pp. 49–50.

188. Cf. Vidal-Naquet, "Hoplite athénien," pp. 161–62.

189. Cf. Gernet, "Choses visibles et choses invisibles," in *Anthropologie*, pp. 405–14, esp. 409–12.

190. A.G. Woodhead (*"Isegoria* and the Council of the Five Hundred," *Historia* 16[1967], p. 130) reminds us that isegoria was exceptional in Antiquity and opposes Athens to the other Greek poleis of the classical period, where oligarchy remained the most widespread form of constitution.

191. De Romilly (*Thucydide et l'impérialisme athénien*, p. 122): Thucydides evokes democracy "as represented by the constitution of the ancestors and advocated by the reactionaries against contemporary democracy."

192. The passage on politeia is rather undifferentiated and thus difficult to isolate. For example, Büchner sometimes separates the eulogy of politeia from the passage on civilization, making the latter begin at 40, and sometimes suggests that the eulogy of the constitution covers par. 39–42. In fact, the theme of politeia is absorbed from the outset by the passage on civilization, and it is difficult to claim, as Büchner does (p. 50), that pars. 37–41 constitute a summary of Pericles's epitaphios; unlike this oration, which is imbued throughout by politics, the *Panegyricus* prefers the "cultural" domain.

CHAPTER FIVE: THE FUNERAL ORATION AS POLITICAL GENRE

1. The term is borrowed from M. Bizos, notice to the epitaphios, CUF, p. 45.

2. I have borrowed this term from Jacques Derrida, "La Pharmacie de Platon," in *La Dissémination* (Paris: Seuil, 1972), p. 148 (see, more generally, the methodological discussion on pp. 148–49, which is important for any textual analysis).

3. On the need "to work with the absent words," cf. also Clémence Ramnoux, *Héraclite ou l'homme entre les choses et les mots*, 2nd ed. (Paris: Belles Lettres, 1968), p. 54.

4. See esp. Chapter Two, pp. 154–64.

5. Piero Treves ("Apocrifi demostenici," I, *Athenaeum* 14 [1936], pp. 153–74) stresses the concreteness of Hyperides's epitaphios and declares that there was nothing constricting in the norms of the genos, since every orator could evade them if he so wished.

6. George Kennedy, *The Art of Persuasion in Greece* (Princeton, NJ: Princeton University Press, 1963), p. 154.

7. *Ibid.*

8. Here I am applying to the topoi a method to which Adam Parry subjects Thucydides's style in his excellent article "Thucydides' Use of Abstract Language," *Language as Action, Yale French Studies* 45 (1970), pp. 3–20; on p. 12, he declares: "Thucydides depends far too much on these antitheses for us to brush them off as inconvenient mannerisms."

9. On this notion, developed by Lucien Febvre, cf. Jacques Le Goff, "Les Mentalités: Une Histoire ambiguë," in Jacques Le Goff and Pierre Nora (ed.), *Faire de l'histoire*, 3 vols. (Paris: Gallimard, 1974), vol. 3, p. 87.

10. For many examples of this attitude, see Anthelme-Edouard Chaignet, *La Rhétorique et son histoire* (Paris: Bouillon et Vieweg, 1888): cf. p. 361 (definition of the epideictic genre as "the genre of the eulogy, the funeral oration, the one most exposed to monotony, because it moves in the same circle of ideas").

11. See André Boulanger, *Aelius Aristide et la sophistique dans la province d'Asie au IIème siècle de notre ère* (Paris: E. de Boccard, 1923), pp. 317ff., on [Dionysius of Halicarnassus], *Techne rhetorike* 6.2 and Aristotle, *Rhetoric* 2.22.1396a12–15.

12. Chaïm Perelman and Lucie Olbrechts-Tyteca (*Traité de l'argumentation: La Nouvelle Rhétorique* [Brussels: Editions de l'Université de Bruxelles, 1970], pp. 63–64) remind us that after Quintilian, the Roman rhetors abandoned the epideictic genre to the grammarians, teaching their pupils only the other two genres, regarded as belonging to practical eloquence.

13. Cf. *ibid.* p. 64.

14. With the final decline of rhetoric in the Middle Ages, the epideictic genre was classed as literary prose, whereas the legal and the deliberative were annexed by dialectics and philosophy (cf. *ibid.*).

15. This evolution finally came to an end in the Hellenistic period, when the frontier between speech and book disappeared (cf. Henri-Irénée Marrou, *Histoire de l'éducation dans l'Antiquité* [Paris: Seuil, 1948], p. 294). On the transformation of rhetoric, "the theory of the oratorical art, into a general theory of the art of composing and writing," see also Chaignet, *La Rhétorique et son histoire*, p. 241.

16. This is how Vinzenz Buchheit, *Untersuchungen zur Theorie des Genos epideiktikon von Gorgias bis Aristoteles* (Munich: Huber, 1960), comments on Aristotle's text.

17. It is noteworthy that Aristotle's allusions to the funeral oration are confined to the *Rhetoric*; to my knowledge, no epitaphios is mentioned in the *Politics*.

18. Buchheit (*Genos epideiktikon*, p. 143).

19. Stanley Wilcox ("The Scope of Early Rhetorical Instruction," *HSCP* 53 [1942], pp. 121–55) believes that the funeral oration was taught from the fourth century on. He bases this idea on *Menexenus* 236a6; but Plato does not say there, as Wilcox claims, that Antiphon could *learn to praise* his genius; he says simply that a disciple of Antiphon's has no difficulty winning renown by this eulogy. Roland Barthes more prudently believes that the epitaphioi were *learned* ("L'Ancienne Rhétorique," *Communications* 16 [1970], p. 176): "The funeral eulogies … were, if not written (in the modern sense of the word), at least learned, that is to say, fixed in a certain way." Plato's text suggests that the funeral oration contained passages that were learned "by heart" (cf. *Menexenus* 236b8-c1).

20. Pericles's oration, the first in our list, is known to us *in extenso* and in a more or less faithful form only thanks to Thucydides; we know that apart from his decrees, Pericles left no written work (cf. Plutarch, *Pericles* 8.5).

21. K.J. Dover (*Lysias and the Corpus Lysiacum* [Berkeley: University of California Press, 1968], p. 2) finds Lysias's epitaphios a "splendid piece of formal rhetoric."

22. Chaignet, *La Rhétorique et son histoire*, p. 249.

23. Cf. Chapter One, pp. 52–54.

24. For Octave Navarre (*Essai sur la rhétorique grecque avant Aristote* [Paris: Hachette, 1900]) Gorgias, codifier of Greek prose, marks the funeral oration with an indelible imprint and all the epitaphioi known to us are affected by it. This is also the thesis of Ernst Pflugmacher's "Locorum communium specimen" (Ph.D. diss., Greifswald, 1909), which is much less subtle than Navarre's book.

25. This is the hypothesis of Wilhelm Vollgraff (*L'Oraison funèbre de Gorgias* [Leiden: Brill, 1952]).

26. This is the title that Jean-Paul Dumont gives to his French translation of the epitaphios.

27. Eugène Dupréel (*Les Sophistes: Protagoras, Gorgias, Prodicus, Hippias* [Neuchâtel: Griffon, 1948], p. 87) and Mario Untersteiner (*The Sophists* [Oxford: Blackwell, 1954], ch. 7) use the epitaphios to show that in Gorgias ethics and epistemology are closely linked.

28. As Buchheit remarks (*Genos epideiktikon*, p. 36) in criticizing Vollgraff for overestimating the contribution of Gorgias, who is content to rework *idées reçues*.

29. The opposition between doing and saying, to mention only one, is used long before Gorgias.

30. Among other arguments, Vollgraff states that it is "strange to hear Gorgias declaring openly that the men who had given their lives for their country were bellicose by nature.... Had not panegyrists always said: our action is peaceful?" (*L'Oraison funèbre de Gorgias*, p. 61). Recognizing in spite of everything that the author of an epitaphios "could on any occasion praise the innate valor of his heroes," he declares that Gorgias would have had to avoid the word "Ares," which he regards as pejorative. Yet Vollgraff seems not to have understood that the intersection of the phusis/nomos (emphytou/nomimon) antithesis with the Ares/Eros pun allows the terms used to temper and to neutralize each other (cf. Jean-Paul Dumont, *Les Sophistes* [Paris: PUF, p. 81 n.4).

31. "The sense of spirit of competition, directed, however, *not at others, but at oneself*" (Dumont, *ibid.*, p. 81 n.5).

32. The term is borrowed from Dumont (*ibid.*, p. 81 n.6).

33. Cf. Vollgraff and Untersteiner (in his edition of the epitaphios).

34. On the topos of "affected modesty" in exordiums, see Ernst Robert Curtius, *European Literature and the Latin Middle Ages,* trans. Willard R. Trask (Princeton: Princeton University Press, 1953), pp. 83–85.

35. Whereas the epitaphioi oppose logos to erga, Gorgias seems to have no other aim but that of *making a speech* according to the "rules"; there is no reference is made to a "reality." Perhaps we should remember that for the Sophists, the oration had a separate existence (cf. DK, B 3, 86), with all truth now to be found not in the phusis but in the logos. The stress on the will of the orator corresponds to the privileged position that Gorgias assigns the rhetor (cf. Renzo Vitali, *Gorgia: Retorica e filosofia* [Urbino: Argatìa, 1971], p. 106).

36. Untersteiner and Dumont see this as the very definition of an ethics of kairos.

37. Compare Milman Parry's definition of that other traditional genre, Homeric poetry: "It forced the poets to express, as much as possible, any new idea in words resembling those that had already served to express a similar idea" (*L'Epithète traditionnelle dans Homère* [Paris: Société d'Editions les Belles Lettres, 1928], p. 93).

38. *Ibid.*, p. 103. This statement, which is very questionable as far as Homeric poetry is concerned, would apply much better to a genre made up of topoi.

39. Observing that doubts on the authenticity of an epitaphios are usually based on apparent contradictions between this discourse and those of a different type, Dover (*Lysias and the Corpus Lysiacum*, pp. 54–55) compares *Epitaphios* 58

(*hegemonos kakia*) with 19 (*On Aristophanes' Goods*), in which the orator shows sympathy for Conon, and with 14 (*Against Alcibiades*), 38, in which the "loss of ships" is attributed to treason; he reminds us that these divergences are no proof of the inauthenticity of the epitaphios but are explained by the constraints of the genre.

40. In his introduction to Aristotle's *Topica* (CUF, 1967, p. xxxviii), Jacques Brunschwig reminds us that "it is not the least paradox of the *Topica* that it contains no definition of the concept to which it owes its title," and on p. xxxix he quotes the logician Joseph Bochenski to the effect that "no one has so far managed to say briefly and clearly what *topoi* are."

41. Cf. Barthes, "L'Ancienne Rhétorique," p. 266.

42. Cf. Perelman and Olbrechts-Tyteca, *Argumentation*, p. 113: "The particular places that are accorded special importance in various societies enable us to characterize those societies."

43. The expression is borrowed from Le Goff, "Les Mentalités," p. 87. See also Le Goff's assessment of the topoi as the "basso continuo" of the history of a society (*ibid.*, pp. 86–89).

44. Parry ("Thucydides' Use of Abstract Language," p. 3) reminds us that the raw material of language available to every writer is already in itself a bearer of thought; this observation applies especially to the topoi of the exordiums.

45. Thus Chaignet (*La Rhétorique et son histoire*, p. 361), describing the difficulties of the eulogy genre, surveys the topos of jealousy as developed by Pericles or Gorgias.

46. J.D. Denniston (*Greek Prose Style* [Oxford: Clarendons, 1952]) believes that eloquence at Athens had reached a high level of artistic development long before Gorgias arrived there.

47. Parry, "Thucydides' Use of Abstract Language," p. 5, thus defines the mid-fifth century.

48. On this subject, cf. Barthes, "L'Ancienne Rhétorique," pp. 178–79.

49. Denniston (*Greek Prose Style,*) observes that the poetic turn of phrase, a deliberate choice on Gorgias's part, is on the contrary constitutive of the funeral oration from its very origins, to the extent that an author's style is unrecognizable when he is practicing this genre. Thus Hyperides's epitaphios no more resembles the rest of his oeuvre than, for example, Lysias's *Eroticus* is reminiscent of the style of *Against Eratosthenes*.

50. Opposed to personal poetry and to court poetry, maintaining complex

relations with the victory ode, the funeral oration comes into direct competition with the choral lyric in its new function of civic celebration; after Simonides, the bard of the arete of the citizen-soldiers (cf. Marcel Detienne, *The Masters of Truth in Archaic Greece*, trans. Janet Lloyd (New York: Zone Books, 1996), p. 114), the official elegy outlived itself: at Athens, its place was taken by the funeral oration in prose.

51. Cf. Chapter One, pp. 88–91.

52. On the use of these architectural metaphors, cf. Henry R. Immerwahr, "*Ergon:* History as a Monument in Herodotus and Thucydides," *AJPh* 81, no. 3 (1960), pp. 271ff.

53. Cf. Detienne, *The Masters of Truth*, p. 48.

54. I am referring here to the analysis of DK, 22 B 39, by Jean Bollack and Heinz Wismann, *Héraclite ou la séparation* (Paris: Minuit, 1972), pp. 149–50.

55. Although the logos/ergon antithesis is "the real idiosyncrasy" of Thucydides's style (Parry, "Thucydides' Use of Abstract Language," p. 11), it is also the figure of thought proper to the funeral oration; hence the proliferation of antitheses in Pericles's epitaphios, condemned severely by Denniston, *Greek Prose Style*, p. 13.

56. Ramnoux, *Héraclite*, p. 347 (on frags. 177.53 and 53a, 55, 82).

57. *Ibid.*, p. 27.

58. *Ibid.*, p. 118.

59. Felix Heinimann, *Nomos und Physis* (Basel: Reinhardt, 1945), pp. 43–46. Ramnoux (*Héraclite*, p. 296) also sketches the stages of this evolution, at the end of which "to speak has become nothing more than to speak."

60. The performative statement is defined by Emile Benveniste, following J.L. Austin, as a statement that is equivalent to the carrying out of the act (*Problèmes de linguistique générale*, p. 269).

61. Jean-Pierre Vernant, *Les Origines de la pensée grecque* (Paris: PUF, 1962), pp. 40–41. On the exaltation of the logos in Gorgias, see Parry, "Thucydides' Use of Abstract Language," pp. 15–18.

62. On Thucydides's style as "struggle," see Parry, "Thucydides' Use of Abstract Language," p. 20.

63. See Detienne, *The Masters of Truth*, pp. 108 and 118 (on Gorgias); Vitali, *Gorgia: Retorica e filosofia,* pp. 103–52.

64. I have borrowed this expression from the title of Detienne's chapter in *The Masters of Truth*, pp. 89–106.

65. I have borrowed these expressions from Detienne, *The Masters of Truth*, p. 89 and Jean-Pierre Vernant, "Aspects mythiques de la mémoire et du temps," in *MP*, vol. 1, pp. 83–87.

66. According to Detienne (*The Masters of Truth*, p. 75), "the poet's speech nevers solicits agreement from its listeners or the assent from a social group."

67. The risk is less serious, however, than when it is a matter of actually promoting a political line; we may recall Diodotus's bitter remarks on the responsibility of the orators compared with the irresponsibility of the demos, a passive audience but one always ready to turn against its advisers (Thucydides 3.43.4–5).

68. I am referring here to the excellent analysis of *Nemeans* 7 by Ramnoux (*Héraclite*, pp. 116–18).

69. When the inadequacy of words to express deeds ceases to be a threat weighing on the oration and becomes embodied in the political life of the cities, then all reality crumbles. Thucydides describes this experience in 3.82.

70. Henri-Etienne Caffiaux, *De l'oraison funèbre dans la Grèce païenne* (Valenciennes, 1860), p. 54.

71. The whole of Gorgias's text (DK, 82 B 3, 83–84) might throw some light on the opening of Lysias's epitaphios.

72. In his *Etudes épigraphiques et philologiques* (Paris: Champion, 1938), p. 21, Louis Robert distinguishes between the epideixeis (hearing), given on the occasion of a panegyric, and the regular agones, presided over by the agonothetes; the epideixeis of rhetors were frequent in the fifth century, the competitions between rhetors and encomiographers (for example, the one that took place at the Pythia of Delphi) were the creation of the imperial period and did not begin until the first century B.C.

73. Cf. Robert Clavaud, notice to the epitaphios, CUF, pp. 20–21.

74. On the theme of the agon in the *Menexenus,* see Wilhelm Engelmann, *Platons Menexenos* (Leipzig, 1847), on 235d6 (*agōnizetai*), and Adolf Trendelenburg, *Erläuterungen zu Platos Menexenus* (Berlin: Weidmann, 1905), p. 12.

75. Detienne, *The Masters of Truth*, p. 92; on the funerary games, see also pp. 90–99.

76. According to Dumarsais (quoted by Barthes in "L'Ancienne Rhétorique," p. 206), "the commonplaces are the cells where everybody may go and take, so to speak, material for an oration."

77. One might compare the situation of the orators with that of the com-

petitors in the funerary games described in the epics, confronting one another in a "circular and centered space, within which, ideally, each individual stands in a reciprocal and reversible relationship to everyone else" (Detienne, *The Masters of Truth*, p. 97).

78. On the spatiotemporal context of the rotation of offices, see Pierre Lévêque and Pierre Vidal-Naquet, *Clisthène l'Athénien: Essai sur la représentation de l'espace et du temps dans la pensée politique grecque* (Paris: Belles Lettres, 1964), pp. 22–23.

79. Barthes, "L'Ancienne Rhétorique," p. 173 (my italics).

80. On the adaptability of the topos, see Oddone Longo, "Atene fra polis e territorio: In margine a Tucidide I 143, 5," *Studi italiani di filologia classica* 46 (1974). pp. 5–6.

81. This is the definition given of the work of art by the *Dictionnaire Robert*, which cites in support two texts by Baudelaire (vol. 4, p. 717). It is certain that the concept and the thing appeared — or reappeared — clearly in the mid-nineteenth century and that Baudelaire's entire aesthetic thought is devoted to elaborating this notion.

82. Again, according to the *Dictionnaire Robert*, this term was not used until the eighteenth century to designate "written works, insofar as they bear the trace of aesthetic concerns." Roland Barthes considers the word to be recent and dates it from the early nineteenth century; see *Le Degré zéro de l'écriture*, 2nd ed. (Paris: Gonthier, 1964), pp. 10–11, and "Littérature et méta-langage," in *Essais critiques* (Paris: Seuil, 1964), pp. 106–107.

83. Cf. Marrou, *Histoire de l'éducation*, p. 294.

84. Cf. Pierre Lévêque, *Le Monde hellénistique* (Paris: A. Colin, 1969), pp. 112–23.

85. Marrou (*Histoire de l'éducation*, pp. 296–305) gives a few examples of these declamations, in which the rhetor Polemon was a past master.

86. On Agathon's *Anthos*, an original but isolated attempt in the oeuvre of the poet if not in the tragedy of his period, see Pierre Lévêque, *Agathon* (Paris: Société d'Editions les Belles Lettres, 1955), pp. 105–14 and 154. Vernant's commentary ("in Agathon, in his public, in the whole of Greek culture, the tragic spring is broken"; *MT*, p. 17) should not make us forget that tragedy was to survive for a long time in a philosophical, rhetorical form.

87. Jean-Pierre Vernant and Pierre Vidal-Naquet, *MT*, p. 8.

88. *Ibid.*

89. Examples include Pflugmacher, "Locorum communium specimen," and Jan Lodewijk Chaillet, "De orationibus quae Athenis in funebris publicis habebantur" (Ph.D. diss., Leiden, 1891).

90. Logos and ergon are first opposed through a distinction between the ceremony as such and the *oration* (*Thucydides* 2.35.1); then they are reconciled in the unity of the Athenian character (40); the balance is again broken in 41.2–4 in favor of the "truth of facts," which is identified with the power of Athens finally, in 43.2–3 the orator definitively rejects the pairing formed by the institutional eulogy and the official tomb to declare that ergon and logos are reconciled at a higher level: the sepulchre of the Athenians is the whole earth (*pasa gē,* functioning as *ergon*), but also the memory of all mankind (*mnēmē,* which is *logos*).

91. For Parry, the struggle between logos and ergon is the true historical problem and the true subject of Thucydides's history ("Thucydides' Use of Abstract Language," pp. 19–20).

92. This is an example of the correct use of the *apo kainou* technique, in which the sum of the two topoi constitutes a new original whole: cf. Christopher M. Dawson, "*Spoudaiogeloion*: Random Thoughts on Occasional Poems," *YCS* 19 (1966), pp. 39–76, esp. 41.

93. The author of the article "Epitaphios Logos" in *Der Kleine Pauly* (Stuttgart: Druckenmüller, 1964) declares that lack of originality in the orations attributed to Lysias and Demosthenes is no argument against the authenticity of these epitaphioi. This is a very sensible remark that one cannot but agree with.

94. This argument is used by Max Pohlenz against Lysias's epitaphios and by Treves against Demosthenes's.

95. Chaillet, "De orationibus," pp. 62ff.

96. This is the case with Georges Mathieu, *REG* 47 (1934), pp. 263–64. On the lack of evidence for such assertions, see Clavaud, notice, pp. 24–25, whose common sense I fully approve.

97. To base an argument, as Chaillet ("De orationibus," p. 254 n.149) does, on the presence of two fairly similar groups in Demosthenes's epitaphios and in that of the *Menexenus*, without seeing that the context of the first passage also seems to evoke the passage of Lysias (80: the competitions in strength, knowledge, and wealth), is unconvincing.

98. The references are found in Clavaud's notice, pp. 20–21; cf. also Max Pohlenz ("Zu den attischen Reden auf die Gefallenen," *Symbolae Osloenses* [1948], pp. 65–66).

99. The whole issue of *mimesis* in literature is being raised here. Such a practice presupposes an essentially oral culture; cf. Eric A. Havelock, *Preface to Plato* (Cambridge, MA: Belknap Press of Harvard University Press, 1963), pp. 92ff. and 115–33. On the impossibility of assigning an author to the topoi and therefore of determining precisely the limits of imitation, cf. H.L. Hudson-Williams, "Thucydides, Isocrates, and the Rhetorical Method of Composition," *CQ* 42 (1948), pp. 76–81, and Dawson, *"Spoudaiogeloion,"* pp. 41ff.

100. After Johannes Sykutris and Pohlenz, Clavaud (notice, pp. 25–35 and 61 n.2) has shown that there are no such anachronisms in Demosthenes's passages.

101. On the need to "scrutinize the psittacism of mentalities" in order "to identify when the commonplace loses contact with reality," see Le Goff, "Les Mentalités," pp. 88–89.

102. To borrow a phrase from M.I. Finley (*The Ancient Greeks* [London: Chatto and Windus, 1963], p. 86) that is fairly close to Plutarch's *skiamakhounta* (*Sulla* 13.1).

103. Hermann Strasburger, "Thukydides und die politische Selbstdarstellung der Athener," *Hermes* 86 (1958), p. 22.

104. On the atmosphere in Athens after the defeat of 322, cf. Edouard Will, *Histoire politique du monde hellénistique (323–30 av. J.-C.)* (Nancy: Berger-Levrault, 1966), vol. 1, p. 29.

105. As William Scott Ferguson observes (*Hellenistic Athens* [London: Macmillan, 1911], p. 309), from the second century B.C. on, the political system of Athens may or may not have been regarded as an object for praise by other Greeks; in any case, it was no longer an obstacle.

106. On the circumstances and meaning of the honors paid to Demetrius and Antigonus, cf. Will, *Histoire politique*, p. 307.

107. In the fifth century, Herodotus counted, apart from the Athenians (7.161), few autochthones among the Greeks (8.73: Arcadians and Cynurians and, with some reservations, Achaeans). In the second century A.D., as Claude Bérard observes (*Anodoi: Essai sur l'imagerie des passages chthoniens* [Neuchâtel: Attinger, 1974], p. 35), there was not a single Greek people that did not claim to be autochthonous.

108. Ferguson (*Hellenistic Athens*, p. 308) saw clearly that the eulogy of Athens as a land of culture did not really become dominant until the fourth century, after the loss of the empire.

109. On this episode, related by Arrian (*Anabasis* 16.7), see James H. Oliver,

Demokratia, the Gods, and the Free World (Baltimore: Johns Hopkins Press, 1960), pp. 147–48.

110. I owe the expression to Edouard Will, *Histoire politique du monde hellénistique* (Nancy: Berger-Levrault, 1967), vol. 2, p. 402. For an analysis of the behavior of the Diadochi toward Athens, cf. Ferguson, *Hellenistic Athens,* pp. 307–10.

111. Cf. Will, *Histoire politique,* vol. 1, pp. 197–200.

112. *Ibid.,* p. 205.

113. According to Felix Jacoby (*Atthis: The Local Chronicles of Ancient Athens* [Oxford: Clarendon, 1949], p. 109), this abandonment must be attributed to the lucidity of the Athenians, who were under no illusions as to the loss of their final hopes. The process may have been more unconscious, but it seems no less real.

114. The Epitaphia are certainly *commemorations* rather than real funerals (the ephebes offered a sacrifice at Marathon, in honor of all the dead *of the past*). Henri Jeanmaire (*Couroi et Courètes: Essai sur l'éducation spartiate et sur les rites d'adolescence dans l'antiquité hellénique* [Lille: Bibliothèque Universitaire, 1939], p. 339), did not perhaps make this distinction sufficiently clear.

115. It is unlikely, however, for, according to Robert (*Etudes épigraphiques et philologiques,* pp. 21–22), the eulogy, whether in prose or in verse, had no place in the competitions before the first century B.C. and did not really come into its own until the imperial period.

116. Thus Felix Jacoby ("*Patrios Nomos:* State Burial in Athens and the Public Cemetery in the Kerameikos," *JHS* 64 [1944], pp. 65 n.137) takes Menander's statement seriously and believes that the funeral oration was delivered every year by the polemarch in Hadrian's era.

117. On the paradoxical status of rhetorical art, surviving beyond the historical conditions that gave it birth, but only in the decorative and nonpolitical form of epideictic eloquence, see Marrou, *Histoire de la éducation,* pp. 293–94 and 297.

118. Cf. Marrou, *Histoire de l'éducation,* pp. 298–99. On the other hand, it is not irrelevant that all attempts to present a single, fixed plan of the collective funeral oration come up against insurmountable variations from one oration to another (see, for example, Hermann Schneider's efforts in "Untersuchungen über die Staatsbegräbnisse und den Aufbau der öffentlichen Leichenreden bei den Athenern in der klassischen Zeit" [Ph.D. diss., Berne, 1912]).

119. The (individual) funeral enlogies of Aelius Aristides at our disposal are the only examples of this genre to have survived from the period between the

fourth century B.C. and the fourth century A.D.; cf. Boulanger, *Aelius Aristide et la sophistique*, pp. 317ff.

120. James H. Oliver (*The Civilizing Power: A Study of the Panathenaic Discourse of Aelius Aristides Against the Background of Literature and Cultural Conflict, with Text, Translation, and Commentary, TAPS* 58, no. 1 [1968], pp. 17ff.) thinks the the Panathenaic oration may have become a part of the festival only around 118 B.C.; in any case, the fashion for it developed under the Empire (see Marrou, *Histoire de l'éducation*, p. 298).

121. Oliver, *Civilizing Power*, pp. 12–13, makes this observation.

122. *Ibid.* p. 14: "Sections 225–232 should be read as the key-passage of the whole oration."

123. Ferguson (*Hellenistic Athens*, p. 309) observes that the process that made Athens a universal mother culminates in the rhetors of the imperial period.

124. I have borrowed this expression from Pierre Vidal-Naquet, "Temps des dieux et temps des hommes: Essai sur quelques aspects de l'expérience temporelle chez les Grecs," *RHR* 157 [1960], on the orations of Isocrates.

125. Cf. Adolf Kleingünther, "*Protos heuretes*": *Untersuchungen zur Geschichte einer Fragestellung*, Philologus, supp. 26 (Leipzig: Dieterich, 1933), pp. 90ff.

126. Oliver (*Civilizing Power*, pp. 17–18) sees very clearly that the eulogy of Athens had now been taken over by non-Athenians.

127. Eduard Schwartz ("Diodorus," in *RE*, col. 681) thinks that its source is Ephorus. Gomme (*Commentary*, vol. 2, p. 326), on the other hand, is inclined to opt for Timaeus.

128. The image of Athens in the orations corresponds fairly precisely to its real status; see, for example, Lévêque, *Le Monde hellénistique*, pp. 20–21.

129. The status of the Athenians in Diodorus's text is symbolic: Athens is represented by prisoners handed over to the mercy of the Syracusans; this means that, even if she could be the object of pity or gratitude, she no longer occupied a position of strength and, above all, it was no longer Athens that spoke of Athens.

130. Oliver (*Civilizing Power*, pp. 22–24) thinks that these *genē* refer both to the four ancient Ionian tribes in the pre-Cleisthenean period and to the political structure of Athens from Herodius Atticus on; a structure dominated by the *genē* — that is, ultimately, by rich landowners.

131. I have borrowed this expression from Ernest Renan's *Prière sur l'Acropole* (Paris: E. Pelletan, 1899).

132. The *Panathenaicus* of Aelius Aristides, the pagan predecessor of Byzantine culture, links classical Hellenism and the Byzantine renaissance: cf. Oliver, *Civilizing Power*, p. 8.

133. Nietzsche himself lends his voice to the humanistic concert. In "Attempt at a Self-Criticism," the preface to *The Birth of Tragedy*, trans. Walter Kaufmann (New York: Vintage Books, 1967), p. 21, he cites the passage on the great festivals as balm for suffering (2.38.1), as the lesson of "the great funeral oration ... of Pericles (or Thucydides)" (and also as a reflection of his thoughts on the Greeks' relationship to suffering).

134. This is how Barthes ("L'Ancienne Rhétorique," p. 183) defines the new rhetoric of the second century A.D.

135. *Ekphrasis*, or description, is one of the mainsprings of this rhetoric and could function autonomously as a school exercise. Cf. Marrou, *Histoire de l'éducation*, p. 302.

CHAPTER SIX: UNDER THE SPELL OF AN IDEAL

1. Ferdinand de Saussure uses "mannequin" to designate the phonic whole that indicates in a text the presence of the theme word: cf. Jean Starobinski, *Les Mots sous les mots: Les Anagrammes de Ferdinand de Saussure* (Paris: Gallimard, 1971), pp. 50ff. Saussure looked for the words beneath the words; I am trying to show in the funeral oration a sort of "discourse beneath the discourse" of Athens.

2. As Arnaldo Momigliano reminds us ("Some Observations on Causes of War in Ancient Historiography," in *Studies in Historiography* [London: Weidenfeld and Nicolson, 1966]), the technique of analysis used by Thucydides is more thorough when employed in constitutional history than in determining the causes of the war.

3. Cf. Chapter One, pp. 115–17.

4. And yet, as A.W. Gomme has shown ("Concept of Freedom," in *More Essays in Greek History and Literature* [Oxford: Blackwell, 1962], p. 147), they must be placed among the nine or ten writers of the first rank who praised Athens in the fifth and fourth centuries.

5. Between the intention of beginning with the dead (236d2–3) and the real exordium of the oration comes the image of the city, sole phusis of all Athenians (237a–b); although the epitaphios begins formally with the dead, this is merely a way of excluding them from the oration for a long time.

6. I am referring here to Jean-Pierre Vernant's analysis of Platonic anamne-

sis in "Aspects mythiques de la mémoire," in *MP* vol. 1, pp. 80–107, and in "Le Fleuve *Amélès* et la *mélétè Thanatou*," in *ibid.*, pp. 109–23.

7. On the link between Lethe and Thanatos, see Vernant's articles cited above and Marcel Detienne, *The Masters of Truth in Archaic Greece*, trans. Janet Lloyd (New York: Zone Books, 1996), passim.

8. To believe oneself transported during one's lifetime to the Islands of the Blessed is a dangerous error, for which Plato does not pardon even philosophers who are excessively enamored of study (*Republic* 7.519c5–6); the Athenians of the *Menexenus* must recover consciousness and cast a lucid, disenchanted look at Athens, while the philosophers of the *Republic* must rejoin their fellow men so that the constitution can become a reality and not just a dream (520c7–8); in each case, the illusion of immortality is harmful to the reasonable exercise of politics.

9. For a comparison of this passage with Aristophanes, *Wasps* 631–41, see p. 385.

10. A similar movement is observable in Aristophanes: apart from the passage in *Wasps* in which the old men dream of being jurors in the Islands of the Blessed, one might cite *Knights*, 798, in which the Paphlagonian dangles in front of Demos the possibility of becoming a heliast in Arcadia. Arcadia is, in more ways than one, the essence of utopia for the Athenians: (1) as the scholiast remarks, to dominate Arcadia, Athens would have to have carried off a total victory over the Peloponnesians; (2) no doubt there is an allusion to the oracle, handed back to the Lacedaemonians on possession of Arcadia (Herodotus 1.66): "to ask for Arcadia" soon became the proverbial equivalent of "asking for the impossible"; (3) finally, Arcadia, the country of "acorn eaters," was associated by fifth-century Greeks with the most distant past (or the golden age).

11. The passage from *hēmeis* (235a5) to *egoge* (235a6) eliminates the "we" in order to isolate Socrates and, through him, every Athenian in his borrowed fine "ego." One might interpret this phenomenon as one symptom of the *ideological* effect of the funeral oration, if it is true that ideology has a tendency to "summon" individuals, thus transformed into subjects (Louis Althusser, "Idéologie et appareils idéologiques d'Etat: Notes pour une recherche," *La Pensée* 151 [June 1970], pp. 3–38, esp. 31–33).

12. Thus the Méridier translation (CUF), which goes back at least to Marsilio Ficino (*idem ... accidere tam erga me quam reliquam civitatem*); it is adopted by Léon Robin (Pléiade), Robert Gregg Bury (Loeb), and the large majority of translators.

13. For Plato, this opposition was meaningless, as the *Crito* eloquently shows; at least when the philosopher wanted for a time to contrast Socrates with the rest of his fellow citizens, he did so clearly (*Crito* 52b3).

14. Cf. Jacques Derrida, "La Pharmacie de Platon," in *La Dissémination* (Paris: Seuil, 1972), p. 141.

15. Cf. Eduard Schwyzer and Albert Debrunner, *Griechische Grammatik* (Munich: Beck, 1959), vol. 2, pp. 178–79, and above all Raphael Kuhner and Bernhard Gerth, *Ausführliche Grammatik der griechischen Sprache* (Hannover: Hahnsche, 1898–1904), vol. 2, bk. 1, § 405b; in its adverbial sense, *allos* means "moreover," "furthermore," "and above all."

16. It is possible that only the authority of the andres = polis equivalence has diverted the translators from a grammatically correct reading.

17. Cf. Chapter Six, pp. 387–406.

18. For a more complete list of the occurrences of this theme from Alcaeus to Lycurgus, see Yvon Garlan, *Recherches de poliorcétique grecque* (Athens: Ecole Française d'Athènes, 1974), p. 99, and Oddone Longo, "Ad Alceo 112 L.P.: Per la storia di un *topos*," *Bollettino dell'Istituto di Filologia Greca* (Padua), 1 (1974), pp. 211–28.

19. See André Aymard, "Les Cités grecques à l'époque classique: Leurs institutions politiques et judiciaires," in *Etudes d'histoire ancienne* (Paris: PUF, 1967), p. 275; Victor Ehrenberg, *L'Etat grec* (Paris: Maspero, 1976), pp. 85, 149, esp. 151; M.I. Finley, *The Ancient Greeks* (London: Chatto and Windus, 1963), p. 55; Edouard Will, *MGO*, pp. 415–18.

20. *Hē polis*: the city, that is, "our city" but also "the City." To preserve this term's character as the central (and efficacious) syntagma of the official oration, the attempt to translate it has been abandoned, in favor of transcribing the Greek words.

21. Cf. Chapter Two, pp. 152–54 and Chapter Three, pp. 206–17.

22. On the praise of a city as nurse of its men, see Marcel Detienne, "L'Olivier: Un Mythe politico-religieux," in M.I. Finley (ed.), *Problèmes de la terre en Grèce ancienne* (Paris: Mouton, 1973).

23. On the interdependence of phalanx and city, cf. Marcel Detienne, "La Phalange: Problèmes et controverses," in Jean-Pierre Vernant (ed.), *Problèmes de la terre en Grèce ancienne* (Paris: Mouton, 1968). pp. 130–31.

24. It is used in only two other passages, to characterize poetic embellishment (1.21.1) and to designate a religious chant (3.104.5: purification of Delos).

25. Bernard Knox, *Oedipus at Thebes: Sophocles' Tragic Hero and His Time* (Nerw Haven, CT: Yale University Press, 1966), p. 160.

26. It will be remembered that *theasthai* characterizes the astonished gaze (Plato, *Charmides* 154c9) or contemplation (*Phaedo* 84a7–8).

27. This amorous vocabulary is widely used by Aristophanes in a perfectly clear denunciation of the passion of the demagogues for Demos (*Acharnians* 143; *Knights* 732–34 and 1340–44; *Wasps* 699; cf. Plato, *Alcibiades* 132a and *Gorgias* 481d) and in a much more ambiguous way when dealing with the city (*Birds* 136, 143, 1316, 1342).

28. Knox, *Oedipus at Thebes*, p. 161, sees this passage as "the nearest thing to religious feeling."

29. Cf. Victor Ehrenberg, *From Solon to Socrates* (London: Methuen, 1968), p. 263.

30. Taking into account the "secular" character of the funeral oration and for reasons that will be explained later, I much prefer this term (taken in its active sense) to Knox's "divinization."

31. Knox, *Oedipus at Thebes*, pp. 160–61: "The *polis tyrannos,* Athens, assumes this same quasi-divinity." However, the concept polis-tyrannos is absent from the epitaphios.

32. The importance of the family in Demosthenes's epitaphios (cf. 7, 16, 29) accords perfectly with the spirit of *De corona,* in which Demosthenes congratulates himself on being appointed not so much by the demos as by the fathers and the brothers of the dead (288).

33. A. Meillet and J. Vendryes, *Traité de grammaire comparée des langues classiques* (Paris: Champion, 1963), p. 530; see also Jean Humbert, *Syntaxe grecque* (Paris: Klincksieck, 1972), pp. 17–24.

34. Many examples in Kühner and Gerth, *Grammatik*, vol. 2, bk. 1, p. 53: there is the agreement *kata sunesin* with such nouns as *stratos, stratia, homilos, plethos, demos* (especially when this term designates the democratic party: Thucydides 3.80, 5.82, 6.35). For *polis*, one might note, besides the examples cited by L.H. Jeffery and Anna Morpurgo-Davies (*Kadmos* 9[1970], pp. 127–28), the following uses: Aristophanes, *Knights* 813; Thucydides 2.21.3; and Xenophon, *Hellenica* 3.3.4.

35. The use of this construction in the Cretan inscription BM 1969, 4–2.1 (published by Jeffery and Morpurgo-Davies, *Kadmos* 9 [1970], pp. 118–54) gives the impression of a hapax; moreover, it depends on an epigraphic restoration: *espensames polis* (1. 1). However, all the commentators except A.E. Raubitschek

(*ibid.*, pp. 155–56) have accepted this reference (R.F. Willetts, *Kadmos* 11 [1972], p. 97, and Henri van Effenterre, "Le Contrat de travail du scribe Spensithios," *BCH* 97 [1973], pp. 31–46). "We, the city, have promised Spensithios" is a splendid example of the equivalence between the city-state and the community of citizens. As van Effenterre (*ibid.*, p. 34) puts it, the state is not "they" but "we."

36. On this postulate of the unity of the polis, see, from a rather different point of view, Vernant, "Travail et nature dans la Grèce ancienne," in *MP*, vol. 2, pp. 28–29, and Diego Lanza and Mario Vegetti, "L'ideologia della città," *Quaderni di storia* 2 (July-Dec. 1975), pp. 1–37, esp. 20 and 27.

37. M.I. Finley, *Democracy Ancient and Modern* (New Brunswick, NJ: Rutgers University Press, 1973), pp. 64–68.

38. *Ibid.*, pp. 50–54 (absence of an "ideological cover" for imperialism); see the discussion of these statements above, Chapter Two, p. 132.

39. Finley, *Democracy Ancient and Modern*, p. 64 and n.25.

40. Emile Benveniste, "Deux modèles linguistiques de la cité," in *Echanges et communications: Mélanges offerts à Claude Lévi-Strauss* (The Hague: Mouton, 1970), pp. 589–96, repr. in *Problèmes de linguistique générale* (Paris: Gallimard, 1974), vol. 2, pp. 272–80 (quotation p. 278).

41. Perhaps we minimize the abstract character of the word *polis* only because we always refer to the modern model of the state: it is not difficult in these circumstances to declare, as does Hermann Strasburger, that the Greek language had at its disposal only "partial concepts" (*Teilbegriffe*) to express the idea of the state ("Der Einzelne und die Gemeinschaft im Denken der Griechen," *Historiche Zeitschrift* 177 [1954], pp. 227–48, esp. 241).

42. These analyses compel us to regard with reservations Ehrenberg's statement (*L'Etat grec*, p. 151): "It was neither the territory nor some more or less abstract concept (*res publica*) that gave the Greeks their overall representation of the state, but free men who embodied the state."

43. Cf. Benveniste, "Deux modèles linguistiques de la cité," p. 272.

44. Meiggs-Lewis, no. 37, pp. 82–83.

45. On the monument to the Eponyms, see Homer A. Thompson and R.E. Wycherley, *The Athenian Agora*, vol. 14, *The Agora of Athens: The History, Shape, and Uses of an Ancient City Center* (Princeton, NJ: American School of Classical Studies at Athens, 1972), pp. 38–41; and R.E. Wycherley, *The Athenian Agora*, vol. 3, *Literary and Epigraphical Testimonia* (Princeton, NJ: Amercian School of Classical Studies at Athens, 1957). On the civic importance of this monument,

see Pierre Lévêque and Pierre Vidal-Naquet, *Clisthène l'Athénien: Essai sur la représentation de l'espace et du temps dans la pensée politique grecque* (Paris: Belles Lettres, 1964), p. 72; and Giovanna Daverio Rocchi, "Politica di famiglia e politica di tribu nella *polis* ateniese (V. secolo)," *Acme* 24 (1971), pp. 39–42.

46. On the "national" meaning of Cleisthenes's choice of eponyms, see Lévêque and Vidal-Naquet, *Clisthène*, pp. 50–51.

47. Cf. Chapter One, pp. 104–106.

48. See Francis Vian, "La Fonction guerrière dans la mythologie grecque," in *Problèmes de la guerre*, pp. 59–63.

49. On the *neoi* in the funeral oration, cf. Nicole Loraux, "Hebè et andreia: Deux versions de la mort du combattant athénien," *Ancient Society* 6 (1975), pp. 1–31.

50. Cf. Johannes Th. Kakridis, *Der thukydideische Epitaphios* (Munich: Beck, 1961), p. 63; Lanza and Vegetti reduce the ideology of the city rather too summarily to this homology of polis and the individual ("L'ideologia della città," pp. 25–26).

51. On the Panathenaea as a festival of all Athenians in the constituted social body, see Francis Vian, *La Guerre des géants* (Paris: Klincksieck, 1952), p. 256, and Lilly Kahil, "L'Acropole," in *Athènes au temps de Périclès* (Paris: Hachette, 1965), pp. 131–32.

52. This assumption underlies Ludwig Deubner's description of the Panathenaea in *Attische Feste* (Berlin: Akademie, 1956), pp. 22–35.

53. This feature is not peculiar to the Parthenon but is seen throughout Greek art of the classical period. The hoplites are not completely absent as Albert Martin (*Les Cavaliers athéniens* [Paris: Thorin, 1886], p. 130) and Kahil ("L'Acropole," p. 133) claim; but the few that have been found (tablets 22 and 24 — north side, 30 — south side, British Museum) do not form a body; in their isolated occurrences, they remain secondary characters, lost in the midst of cavalry. The importance accorded cavalry may be explained by both aesthetic and political reasons and raises the question of the role and value of youth in the democratic city (cf. Loraux, "Hebè et andreia," p. 17).

54. See Kahil, "L'Acropole," pp. 134–35.

55. Cf. Adam Parry, "Thucydides' Use of Abstract Language," *Language as Action, Yale French Studies* 45 (1970), pp. 12–15.

56. See Chapter Two, pp. 185–86, and, on the oration cut off from its object, Chapter Five, pp. 292–97.

57. As Hermann Kleinknecht observes ("Die Epiphanie des Demos in Aristophanes *Rittern*," *Hermes* 77 [1939], pp. 58–65, repr. in Hans Joachim Newiger [ed.], *Aristophanes und die alte Komödie* [Darmstadt: Wissenschaftliche Buchgesellschaft, 1975], pp. 144–54), ancient Athens, home of the "god," is "deified" by that very fact and therefore has a right to an epiphany (pp. 150–51).

58. In 1334, *polis* may refer to the Acropolis, as in many decrees; on this use of *polis*, cf. Will, *MGO*, p. 418 n.1.

59. Many references in Charles Picard, *Manuel d'archéologie grecque: La Sculpture* (Paris: Picard, 1939): for the fifth century, vol. 2, p. 838; for the fourth century, vol. 3, p. 104, and vol. 4, pp. 1258–59 (see fig. 492). One might also mention Athena crowning Ares on the stela of Acharnes (*ibid.*, fig. 493).

60. See below, n.64.

61. For example, on the heading of the treaty of 375–74 between Athens and Corcyra (cf. Picard, *Manuel d'archéologie grecque: La Sculpture*, vol. 3, p. 104): three characters — Demos (or Erechtheus), a female figure (Corcyra personified?), Athena.

62. Published by Benjamin Dean Meritt, *Hesperia* 21 (1952), p. 355: "This is *probably* Demos crowned by Demokratia." This identification was accepted by James H. Oliver (*Demokratia, the Gods, and the Free World* [Baltimore: Johns Hopkins Press, 1960], pp. 107–108, 164–66, and pl. 2) and by A.E. Raubitschek ("Demokratia," *Hesperia* 31 [1962], pp. 238–43). Cf. also Picard, *Manuel d'archéologie grecque: La Sculpture*, vol. 4, p. 1263 and fig. 495, and Thompson and Wycherley (*Agora*, vol. 14, p. 102), who see it as a "pale reflection" of Euphranor's painting.

63. See the references in Raubitschek, "Demokratia," p. 239.

64. There is evidence for the cult in the 330s and in the Hellenistic period: cf. *IG*, II², 1011, ll. 62–63 (statue of Democracy), and Raubitschek, "Demokratia," pp. 239–40, on the round altar to Athena Demokratia (89–88 B.C.); for the cult of Demos and of the Charites, founded in 229 B.C., cf. Oliver, *Demokratia*, pp. 106–17, and Raubitschek, "Demokratia," pp. 240–41; inferring from *IG*, II², 1496 (sacrifice to Demokratia on the anniversary of the return of the men from Phyle) the existence of a cult founded in 403, Oliver and Raubitschek are somewhat hasty.

65. I have borrowed the term from Pierre Chantraine, "Réflexions sur les noms des dieux helléniques," *AC* 22 (1953), pp. 65–78.

66. Nor that of Athenai, abundantly used by Aristophanes in the final scene of *Knights*.

---

67. The question of the sex of the city is not otiose: both classical and Hellenistic iconography presents the cities as women, goddesses in the classical period and personified abstractions in the Hellenistic (on Megalopolis personified in the fourth century, cf. W. Deonna, "Histoire d'un emblème: La Couronne murale des cités," *Genava* 18 [1940], pp. 128–29). Deonna tries to give a psychoanalytic interpretation of this phenomenon (pp. 159–65); although his remarks are rather cursory, it is certain that the choice of a female figure to represent the city is no accident: so, conversely, we must regard the sexual nondifferentiation of the city in the funeral oration as significant.

68. Confining ourselves here to a few brief suggestions, we may recall that in the "tragedies with suppliants" by Euripides and Sophocles, the balance between andres and polis is broken, as it often is in the funeral oration, to the advantage of the polis. The balance was better preserved in Aeschylus's *Suppliants* (compare Aeschylus, *The Suppliants* 621 and 625–26, and Euripides, *The Suppliant Women* 779).

69. On these honorary titles, see the "Bulletin épigraphique" by Jeanne Robert and Louis Robert, *REG* (see the bulletin for 1951, no. 219a, for *prōtē endoxos*, and those for 1951, no. 219a, and 1960, nos. 358 and 274, for *lampra* [*lamprotatē*] *polis*).

70. Parry ("Thucydides' Use of Abstract Language," p. 14) dates this type of abstraction from the second half of the fifth century and contrasts it with Aristotelian "dogmatic abstraction," which makes abstract words the true reality.

71. Useful remarks on the relativity of this hierarchy are found in Robert Mandrou, *Introduction à la France moderne, 1500–1640* (Paris: Michel, 1974), pp. 75–82 (the primacy of hearing and touch and the secondary role of sight in the sixteenth century).

72. Before the Stoics, Greek thought developed no systematic theory of the five senses. The cultural age that saw the birth of the funeral oration and imprinted its mark on discourse was concerned with only *two* senses: hearing and sight, between which an agon was constantly in progress. In the late fourth century, Aristotle sometimes settled the question in favor of hearing (*Problems* 919b26), and in fifth-century Athens sight was certainly not the privileged mode of perceiving the city: see John E. Stambaugh, "The Idea of the City: Three Views of Athens," *Classical Journal* 69 (1974), pp. 309–21, esp. 309–12.

73. Gustave Glotz, *La Cité grecque* (Paris: Michel, 1968), p. 38. Are "the boundaries of the fatherland, the wheat, the barley, the vines, the olive trees, the

fig trees," called on to bear witness in the oath, enough to make the city "something concrete"? In fact, as Louis Robert shows (*Etudes épigraphiques et philologiques* [Paris: Champion, 1938], pp. 306–307), the archaic nature of the formula made it obscure to the Athenians themselves from the fifth century on.

74. As an auditory model, the city is in dangerous competition with the daimon.

75. See Jacqueline de Romilly, "L'Utilité de l'histoire selon Thucydide," in *Entretiens de la fondation Hardt*, vol. 4 (Vandoeuvres-Geneva, 1956), pp. 41–81.

76. Hermann Strasburger, "Thukydides und die politische Selbstdarstellung der Athener," *Hermes* 86 (1958), p. 20 and passim.

77. See Bruno Gentili, "Le teorie del racconto storico nel pensiero storiografico dei Greci," in Bruno Gentili and Giovanni Cerri, *La teorie del discorso storico nel pensiero greco e la storiografia romana arcaica* (Rome: Ateneo, 1975), pp. 19–26, and Vernant, "Raisons du mythe," in *MT*, pp. 199–201.

78. Gomme, *Commentary*, vol. 1, p. 139 (see also p. 148), and F.D. Harvey, "Literacy in the Athenian Democracy," *REG* 79 (1966), p. 588.

79. Bernard Knox, "Silent Reading in Antiquity," *GRBS* 9 (Winter 1968), pp. 421–35, reminds us of this while questioning whether Antiquity was totally ignorant of silent reading.

80. Francis Macdonald Cornford, *Thucydides Mythistoricus*, 2nd ed. (London: Routledge and K. Paul, 1965), esp. ch. 8, pp. 129–52.

81. Henry R. Immerwahr, "*Ergon*: History as a Monument in Herodotus and Thucydides," *AJPh* 81, no. 3 (1960), p. 281; A.W. Gomme, "Thucydides," in *The Greek Attitude to Poetry and History* (Berkeley: University of California Press, 1954), p. 149.

82. Immerwahr ("Ergon," p. 285) observes that the epitaphios is the only one of Pericles's speeches that is not necessary to the unfolding of the historical narrative. Similarly, Jacqueline de Romilly writes, in her introduction to the edition of book 2 (CUF, p. xxv): "The first oddity about the funeral oration contained in book 2 lies in its very presence. *A priori* such a speech had no reason to feature in a history of the war."

83. See, for example, Immerwahr ("Ergon," p. 284: the epitaphios is in many respects analogous with the entire work) and Klaus Oppenheimer, *Zwei attische Epitaphien* (Berlin: Ebering, 1933), p. 22.

84. Cf. Immerwahr, "Ergon," pp. 281–84.

85. Eugène Napoleon Tigerstedt (*The Legend of Sparta in Classical Antiquity*

[Lund, 1965], p. 140) observes that in book 1, Sparta is considered from the Athenian point of view.

86. In "Selbstdarstellung," Strasburger systematically compares the two types of narratives and lists the differences that separate or oppose them.

87. On this "historical bloc" (to which he adds democracy), see Garlan, *Recherches de poliorcétique grecque*, p. 97. On the general sociological theory of progress in Thucydides, see M.I. Finley, "Myth, Memory, and History," *H&T* 4 (1955), pp. 281–302.

88. The description of the plague in book 2, following the epitaphios with no transition, has the function of registering the first contradiction of the oration by the facts. Not only are the Athenians *conquered* by the disease (2.47.4 and 51.5) and the evil proves stronger than logos (50, 1), but the very notion of a soma autarkes (2.41.1) is superseded (51.5). Moreover, a new practice of death is established — one without ethics, egalitarian in the bad sense of the word (53.4), since the Athenians die in a herd (51.4): in a world in which arete and aischune are no longer of any use (51.5), in which the patrioi nomoi of the funeral are swept aside (52.4), any ideal becomes an illusion (53.3).

89. See, for example, Garlan, *Recherches de poliorcétique grecque*, p. 29.

90. Konrad Gaiser (*Das Staatsmodell des Thukydides: Zum Rede des Perikles für die Gefallenen* [Heidelberg: Kerle, 1975], pp. 53–54) wants to see it as the absolute center of Thucydides's work in both its complete and its incomplete forms. Without attempting such generalizations, I am content to see it as a turning point.

91. Immerwahr ("*Ergon*," p. 282) remarks that the absence of any reference to renown in the Melian debate, and especially in 5.91.1, is significant.

92. The opposition between the uninterrupted speech and dialogue is a major theme in the *Gorgias*: see, for example, 473e–74b.

93. Cf. Chapter Two, pp. 141–44.

94. The Athenians of Samos behave as if they were a city, and scholars have rightly seen this episode as an illustration of the identity between citizen and soldier (Claude Mossé, "Le Rôle politique des armées dans le monde grec à l'époque classique," in *Problèmes de la guerre,* pp. 222–23), but Thucydides's account stresses the distinction between "the city" (the name given to the oligarchic government of Athens) and the army, with each force trying to impose on the other the political system that it advocates (8.76.1). This amounts to saying that the city as a unity no longer existed, at least for a time. Similarly, in 76.6

the soldiers draw a troubling distinction between army and polis, whose power over the army resides solely in the fact that it sends decisions and money to the soldiers.

95. Immerwahr, "*Ergon*," pp. 279–90.

96. These analyses owe much to Pierre Vidal-Naquet's "Athènes et l'Atlantide," *REG* 77 (1964) pp. 420–44.

97. Conversely, when, in the *Laws*, it is necessary to found a city that no longer has any connection with Athens, the Athenian, transported outside the place of his city, is no longer Socrates, *held to living in Athens*, as Derrida reminds us ("La Pharmacie de Platon," p. 141), but becomes *the foreigner*; but by a very Platonic reversal, Athens *as she is* is then declared to be good: cf. 1.624c–d.

98. In the first pages of *Le Paradigme dans la dialectique platonicienne* (Paris: PUF, 1947), Victor Goldschmidt sets out to distinguish these two uses of the term "paradigm."

99. On the Cureotis, see Henri Jeanmaire, *Couroi et Courètes: Essai sur l'éducation spartiate et sur les rites d'adolescence dans l'antiquité hellénique* (Lille: Bibliothèque Universitaire, 1939), pp. 375ff., esp. 381. It is possible that in connecting the Cureotis with the myth of the ancient Athenian victory over Atlantis, Plato intentionally contrasts it with the etiological myth of the Apaturia, that of the fight between Xanthus and Melanthius (cf. Pierre Vidal-Naquet, "Le Chasseur noir et l'origine de l'éphébie athénienne," *Annales ESC* [Sept.–Oct. 1968], pp. 949–53): the philosopher seems to be contrasting a myth that bases the establishment of civic order on a victory through cunning with a myth in which arete triumphs over otherness.

100. Following Proclus, Francis Macdonald Cornford (*Plato's Cosmology* [London: Routledge and K. Paul, 1937], pp. 4–5) tries to compare this speech with a *logos panathenaikos*. Plato, however, concerns himself explicitly with the funeral oration (and not with the "Panathenaic speech," which in any case had no institutional existence in the fourth century).

101. The speech delivered *eis to meson* has an undeniably political character (cf. Detienne, *The Masters of Truth*, pp. 95–96). But whereas the speech of the funeral oration is addressed to the entire polis, with center and periphery reunited for the occasion, and is delivered in the middle of and for the community, here it is a circle of friends in the Pythagorean manner that collects the logos resuscitated from memory. This is a very great difference.

102. This idea is particularly clear in book 3 of the *Laws* (unlike Argos and

Messenia, Sparta, thanks to its divine legislator, was able to resist evil: 690d and 69ld–92c).

103. Cf. Luc Brisson, "De la philosophie politique à l'épopée: Le *Critias* de Platon," *RMM* (1970), pp. 402–38, esp. 436.

104. Why does Plato lay such stress on *writing* in a context in which logos is supreme? This is quite obviously a very large question and one outside our present concern. However, it is worth noting that since the history of ancient Athens has been wiped out (20c6), only one alternative is left: at Sais and in writing. The narrative has taken refuge *elsewhere*, in a double of ancient Athens and in the writing that ensures permanence and identity (cf. *Timaeus*, 22e4, 23a4–5, 23a6–7, 23a8–b1, 23c2–3, 24a2, 24d6–8, 25e2), all the more easily in that it is sacred writing, handled by priests (and not, as in Greece, disqualified by its profane uses). But by this very fact, this writing symbolizes the unbridgeable gap between the Athens of the present and the Athens of the past. The history of Athens is saved completely only when, inscribed no longer on tablets abroad but in the soul of an Athenian, it becomes logos.

105. Brisson, "De la philosophie politique à l'épopée," pp. 421–22.

106. Although in conquering Atlantis it is, beyond oppositions of land and sea, Greek and barbarian, *herself* that she conquers (see Vidal-Naquet, "Athènes et l'Atlantide," pp. 429ff.).

107. For example, Brisson ("De la philosophie politique à l'épopée," p. 416) places the primitive Athens of the *Critias* and that of the *Menexenus* on the same level.

108. On this subject, cf. Vidal-Naquet, "Athènes et l'Atlantide," pp. 432–33.

109. In Plato, humanity is not always originally political. There are even two different interpretations of the myth of the golden age: in the *Politics*, "the golden age is separated radically from the city"; in the *Laws*, "the age of Cronos comprises *poleis*" (see Pierre Vidal-Naquet, "Le Mythe platonicien du *Politique*: Les Ambiguïtés de l'âge d'or et de l'histoire," in *Langue, discourse société: Pour Emile Benveniste* [Paris: Seuil, 1975], pp. 374–90; quotations pp. 386 and 388).

110. Brisson ("De la philosophie politique à l'épopée," p. 418) sees the *Critias* as "the history of an Athens remarkably resistant to history."

111. See Chapter Three, n.77.

112. In the *Critias* (110d5–8), the territory of ancient Athens includes part of Boeotia: a dream that no epitaphios, however animated by exultant patriotism, formulates.

113. For Freud, there is something *liberating* about humor (*Jokes and Their Relation to the Unconscious*, trans. James Strachey [London: Routledge and Kegan Paul, 1960]).

114. See François Châtelet, *La Naissance de l'histoire* 2 (Paris: Union Générale d'Editions, 1973), vol. 2, p. 71.

115. A.W Gomme ("Aristophanes and Politics," in *More Essays*, p. 86) rightly notes the strange absence of hoplites from the most patriotic passages of *Knights*.

116. See Taillardat, *Les Images d'Aristophane*, p. 59.

117. Roger Goossens, *Euripide et Athènes* (Brussels: Palais des Académies, 1962), pp. 219–22.

118. On *aspis* referring to the belly of Dicaeopolis (*Acharnians* 1122), cf. Taillardat, *Les Images d'Aristophane*, p. 69.

119. *Ampelia, sukidia,* and *phuta,* personified by their smile and their gesture of hospitality (Taillardat, *ibid.*, p. 41) and entrusted with welcoming peace, are essential elements in the peasant life evoked in 572ff.; but they also evoke *puroi/krithai, ampeloi, elaai,* and *sukai,* which the ephebes call upon as witnesses when swearing to protect them.

120. Gomme (*Commentary*, vol. 2, pp. 136–37) and Taillardat (*Les Images d'Aristophane*, pp. 401ff.) compare Thucydides's 2.43.1 and the theme of the demagogue, lover of Demos (*Knights* 732, 1163, 1341; Plato, *Gorgias* 481d5–6 and 513c9–10). For the uses of *eran*, see Taillardat, *Les Images d'Aristophane*, p. 161, and K.J. Dover, *Aristophanic Comedy* (London: Batsford, 1972), p. 91.

121. See the references in Taillardat, *Les Images d'Aristophane*, pp. 437–38.

122. As Goossens remarks (*Euripide et Athènes*, p. 424). On the role played by the criticism of democracy in Eupolis, see frags. 104, 116, 117, 118 (*Demoi*), and 205 (*Poleis*) of the Kock edition.

123. On parody and paratragedy, see Peter Rau, *Paratragodia: Untersuchung einer komischen Form des Aristophanes,* Zetemata, 45 (Munich: Beck, 1967), pp. 1–18, and Taillardat, *Les Images d'Aristophane*, p. 503. For the relationship between parody and epic, see also F.J. Lelièvre, "The Basis of Ancient Parody," *G&R* 1 (1954), pp. 66–81.

124. On the people as "reality," both the source and the object of comedy, see Victor Ehrenberg, *The People of Aristophanes* (New York: Schocken, 1962), pp. 9 and 26–32.

125. Ehrenberg (*ibid.*, p. 8) thinks that if the mere fact of being a comic

author leads one to be against the government, this does not mean that Aristophanes wrote his comedies in opposition to democracy. Gomme ("Aristophanes and Politics") and Dover (*Aristophanic Comedy*, pp. 33–35) take the same position, but their attempts to prove that Aristophanes was not a reactionary are not always convincing (for example, Dover, *ibid.*, p. 97). The opposite view is propounded by G.E.M. De Ste.-Croix, *The Origins of the Peloponnesian War* (London: Duckworth, 1972), pp. 355–76 (app. 29: "The Political Outlook of Aristophanes").

126. Cf. Taillardat, *Les Images d'Aristophane,* pp. 329–30.

127. Cf. Chapter Two, p. 130–31.

128. See Taillardat, *Les Images d'Aristophane,* p. 418. Such an analysis presupposes that Pericles actually used the term *karpousthai,* but Taillardat, who quotes the epitaphios, believes that the expression was in any case one dear to the political orators.

129. On the parabasis in its broad sense, see Dover, *Aristophanic Comedy* (pp. 49–51: structure: 51–57: critical and moralistic function).

130. Cf. Dover, *Aristophanic Comedy,* p. 71 (on the lyrical passages).

131. Perhaps this is not the only text in which Aristophanes alludes to the demosion sema; when, in *Knights* 772, the sausage seller jokingly wishes to be dragged by the testicles to the Kerameikos if he does not love Demos, the comic poet is of course thinking of the Inner Kerameikos, the prostitutes' quarter (see the note to the Coulon van Daele edition, CUF, p. 114). But is he thinking *only* of the Inner Kerameikos? More likely the poet, enjoying the ambiguity to the full, is exploiting the existence of *two* Kerameikoi.

132. The name Cuckoo-Land explicitly evokes the Athenians, said to be as stupid as cuckoos (*Acharnians* 598; see the note of the van Daele edition, CUF, p. 63).

133. See Taillardat, *Les Images d'Aristophane,* pp. 151, 335, 395, 400, 415, 436, 441.

134. To my knowledge, scholars have not compared these two texts as a whole. No commentary on the *Menexenus* refers to the passage in *Wasps*; the Blaydes edition of *Wasps* mentions the *Menexenus* on the subject of the Islands of the Blessed, but in the middle of a group of texts that have no relationship to this passage and without making any particular reference to Plato's dialogue.

135. On Socrates as the reasoned "creation" of the fourth-century writers, see Eugène Dupréel, *La Légende socratique et les sources de Platon* (Brussels: Sand, 1922), esp. pp. 334, 340, 400.

136. This debate was particularly lively in the nineteenth century. More recently, an article written in his youth ("Il *Menesseno*," *RFIC* 58 [1930], pp. 40–53), Arnaldo Momigliano tried, with rather unconvincing arguments, to attack the *Menexenus*'s authenticity, now universally accepted.

137. Momigliano ("Il *Menesseno*") sees the dialogue as a polemical work devoted to the theme of improvisation. On Alcidamas, cf. Marjorie Josephine Milne, "A Study in Alcidamas and His Relation to Contemporary Sophistic" (Ph.D. diss., Bryn Mawr, 1924).

138. Theodor Berndt ("De ironia Menexeni platonici" [Ph.D. diss., Münster, 1881]) has pointed out that there is a parody of *Gorgias* 503d in the *Menexenus*.

139. Plato does not seem to be making the same distinction between these two terms as Aristotle in *Rhetoric* (1.1367b28–35).

140. It is significant that this style achieves the most complete definition at the precise moment when, in the *Symposium*, Socrates embarks on a true eulogy.

141. See Chapter One, pp. 87–88. Thrasybulus, exhorting his troops before the battle of Munichia, is supposed to have cried, "Happy, if there are any, are those who will fall! Nobody, however rich he may be, will have so fine a monument" (Xenophon, *Hellenica* 2.4.17).

142. This interchangeable character is suggested in the alternative offered to the boule: Archinus or Dion (234b10). Archinus of Koile, a moderate dear to Aristotle for his role in the democratic restoration (*Constitution of Athens* 40), is well known. Dion is less so, but for Plato proper names are rarely neutral, and the name Dion inevitably suggests Plato's Syracusan friend, the paradigm of the good politician. The boule proposes to appoint one of these two orators indiscriminately; Plato thus stresses the absence of any normative criterion in Athenian politics.

143. The major theme of the *Gorgias*, the opposition between political speech and philosophical dialogue, may be summed up in this way. If the *Gorgias* provides so clear a grid for reading the *Menexenus*, it may be because, in E.R. Dodds's words, this dialogue is "an after-piece to the *Gorgias*" (E.R. Dodds, *Plato's Gorgias* [Oxford: Clarendon, 1959], p. 24, quoted by Gregory Vlastos, "*Isonomia politikè*," in Jürgen Mau and Ernst Günther Schmidt [eds.], *Isonomia: Studien zur Gleichheitsvorstellung im griechischen Denken* [Berlin: Akademie, 1964], p. 28).

144. Von Loewenclau and Nikolaus Scholl bring out many resemblances

but, without inquiring further into the reasons for them, rush into declaring the absolute difference of the Socratic logos: Socrates must have nothing in common with a discourse that he is criticizing.

145. Plato does not disdain a sudden illumination provided it springs from long, mature thought (Letter 7.344b4–8).

146. Max Pohlenz (*Aus Platos Werdezeit* [Berlin: Weidmann, 1913], p. 259) makes this comparison, without further commentary. On the opposition between long time and short time, see Marcel Detienne, *Les Jardins d'Adonis* (Paris: Gallimard, 1972), pp. 196–97.

147. On the theme of Herakles's choice, cf. Bruno Snell, *Die Entdeckung des Geistes* (Hamburg: Claassen, 1955), pp. 324ff.

148. This passage may be seen as an answer to the accusation of desertion that Callicles makes against the philosopher in the *Gorgias* (485d5).

149. One takes this term in a literal sense — is not Socrates possessed by the devil? — as well as in a figurative one: his oddness dissolves the immediate civic certainties, and the accusation most often brought against him by his perplexed listeners is that of being *atopos* (cf., for example, *Gorgias* 494el and *Symposium*, 221d2).

150. For Plato, homonymy is symbolic of a distant kinship (see the crucial text of the *Politics* 257d–58a and, on the Platonic problem of naming, Gérard Genette, "L'Eponymie du nom," in *Mimologiques* (Paris: Seuil, 1976), pp. 11–37.

151. The resemblance to Callicles, more frequently suggested (cf., for example, Berndt, "De ironia Menexeni platonici," and Ilse von Loewenclau, *Der platonische Menexenos* [Stuttgart: Kohlhammer, 1961]), is indubitable but less directly significant; however, it is true that Callicles, designated the lover of the Athenian Demos, opposes Socrates violently when the latter criticizes Pericles (*Gorgias* 502c and esp. 515e6).

152. Thucydides is probably the target through the intermediary of Antiphon (236a4–5), "Thucydides's master" in the eyes of Antiquity; cf. Charles H. Kahn, "Plato's Funeral Oration: The Motive of the *Menexenus*," *CPhil.* 58 (1963), pp. 220–34.

153. This comparison is universally accepted; a whole series of German studies dealt with this subject in the nineteenth century; an exhaustive list for the years 1782–1881 is in Berndt, "De ironia Menexeni platonici." Pericles is a model for von Loewenclau, *Der platonische Menexenos*, a foil for Kahn, "Plato's Funeral Oration."

154. Karl R. Popper, *The Open Society and Its Enemies* (London: G. Routledge and Sons, 1945), vol. 1, p. 174.

155. As a hoplite at Potidaea or at Delium, Socrates is not an ordinary soldier, and yet he deserves *aristeion* (cf. *Symposium* 219e–21c). But there can be no doubt that all this behavior seems out of place and provocative to the ordinary man, and Dupréel may be right to see this passage as a direct response to Aristophanes's *Clouds* (*La Légende socratique*, pp. 313ff.).

156. As Snell (*Die Entdeckung des Geistes*, p. 253) emphasizes, though perhaps in too obvious a way.

157. See the chapter on the funeral of the euthynoi in Olivier Reverdin, *La Religion de la cité platonicienne* (Paris: E. de Boccard, 1945).

158. It remains ambiguous, however; for those who refuse to accept that a fundamental difference separates the virtuous warriors of the *Republic* from the citizen-soldiers of the classical period, the funerals of the "guards," exceptional funerals that assured them demonization (5.468e–69b), evoke the Athenian ceremony. On the relationship between demonization and heroization, see chs. 2 and 3 of Reverdin, *La Religion de la cité platonicienne*.

159. "Socrates is not a spectacular *exemplum*" (Victor Goldschmidt, "Le Paradigme dans la théorie platonicienne de l'action," in *Questions platoniciennes* [Paris: Vrin, 1970], p. 93).

160. The name Semnai, reserved for the Eumenides, combines within it respect and terror, as is fitting for deities that embody both a quasi-bestial savagery and an ancient, venerable justice.

161. See Vernant on Euripides's *Hippolytus* ("Aspects de la personne dans la religion grecque," in *MP*, vol. 2, pp. 84–85 and n.13).

162. See Taillardat's catalog of the use of *semnos* by the comic poets (*Les Images d'Aristophane*, pp. 173–77).

163. G. de Vries points out that this proportion is inverted in the apocryphal works: the false Plato takes himself more seriously than the real one does ("*Semnos* and Cognate Words in Plato," *Mnemosyne* [1944], pp. 151–56).

164. This is how Vlastos translates *sēmnotéros en tōi parachrēma gignomai* ("*Isonomia politikè*," p. 22).

165. This is another image that Plato has borrowed from Aristophanes: see *Frogs* 537–38 and Taillardat's commentary on this passage (*Les Images d'Aristophane*, p. 117).

166. The arrogant frown, the comic symbol of pride, characterizes the

philosophers in the historian Hegesander (in *Athenaeus* 162a, quoted by Taillardat, *Les Images d'Aristophane*) and would not be out of place in Aristophanes's portrayal of Socrates in *Clouds* (362–63). Euripides's Hippolytus is described as semnos, and this accusation is directed either at the Orphics or, more generally, at the "intellectuals." On the accusations of pride and arrogance brought against Socrates by the comedies, cf. Dupréel, *La Légende socratique,* p. 318.

167. Plato praises Socrates for those features that the theater exploits for comic ends: cf. Dupréel, *La Légende socratique.*

168. This does not mean, as Momigliano would have it, that the *Menexenus* is concerned solely with the problem of improvisation.

169. The pejorative connotation of *sunkollan* is beyond question: see Aristophanes, *Wasps* 1041 and *Clouds* 446. It is probably no accident that Plato borrows this term from comedy.

170. It is on precisely this point that the condemnation of the speech is based: imitation in itself is not necessarily to be condemned; imitation of imitation is. On the simulacrum as copy of a copy, cf. Gilles Deleuze, "Simulacre et philosophie antique," in *Logique du sens* (Paris: Minuit, 1969), pp. 292–300.

171. Like Aspasia (*Menexenus* 249d1: "Aspasia the Milesian"), Diotima is a foreigner (*Symposium* 201e2, 204c7: 211d2: "the foreign woman of Mantinea"); also like Aspasia (*Menexenus* 235e4–5: "She is one of the most distinguished masters in the oratorical art"), Diotima is "a master" (*Symposium* 207a5), who treats Socrates like a child (cf. *Menexenus* 236b7 and c3, *Symposium* 202b7–c2) – but, it is true, for the right reason: the whole difference lies there.

172. On Plato and play, cf. Derrida, "La Pharmacie de Platon," pp. 180–82.

173. When Socrates asks for an answer concerning an essence, his interlocutors reply by boasting of the beauty of the thing. This is a constant theme (for example, *Gorgias* 448e2–7), which lays the foundations for the criticism of the eulogy: the eulogy of the speech opens with *kalon* (*Menexenus* 234c1).

174. Berndt ("De ironia Menexeni") and Oppenheimer (*Zwei attische Epitaphien,* p. 73) observe that for Plato imitation is a form of polemic.

175. Victor Cousin, preface to the *Menexenus* (Paris, 1827). For Cousin, the dialogue is "both a criticism of the ordinary funeral orations and an attempt at a better manner, the accepted genre."

176. For Plutarch (*Pericles* 24.7), only the beginning of the dialogue is written in a lighthearted tone; for Dionysius of Halicarnassus (*Demosthenes* 23, ed.

Hermann Usener and Ludwig Radermacher, p. 180), the *Menexenus* contains the *kratistos pantōn tōn politikōn logōn*.

177. Hymn to the ideal Athens: von Loewenclau; a Socratic model of the genre: Cousin and Scholl; a speech on peace: Piero Treves ("Note sulla guerra corinzia," I, *RFIC* 65 [1937], pp. 136ff.) and Pohlenz (*Aus Platos Werdezeit*, pp. 292–305); a political pamphlet: Kahn; a reflection on immortality: George Kennedy (*The Art of Persuasion in Greece* [Princeton, NJ: Princeton University Press, 1963], pp. 158–64).

178. Because they did not pay enough attention to Adolf Trendelenburg's warnings (*Erläuterungen zu Platos Menexenus* [Berlin: Weidmann, 1905]), for whom the exhortation is just as satirical as the rest of the speech, Treves, Pohlenz, von Loewenclau, Scholl, and many others would like to take seriously at least the prosopopoeia of the dead, in which Pohlenz finds "many terms to which Plato might subscribe." Oppenheimer has tried to base this interpretation on many comparisons and to make this part of the speech "an authentic Platonic protreptic" (*Zwei attische Epitaphien*, p. 56); but in doing so he forgets his own idea of imitation as a polemical mode.

179. Kennedy, *The Art of Persuasion,* pp. 163–64.

180. "Let us be clear that Plato would not have been satisfied if his pastiche had been like a caricature that would have taken nobody in"; Luchaire made this useful comment in his edition of the *Menexenus*, pp. viii–ix.

181. Thus, by accusing the epitaphioi of casting an instant spell, Socrates turns against Pericles's epitaphios the criticisms that this speech made of traditional eloquence (Thucydides 2.41.4 and 42.2).

CONCLUSION: IMAGINARY ATHENS OR THE INVENTION OF THE CITY

1. Cf. Victor Ehrenberg, *L'Etat grec* (Paris: Maspero, 1976), pp. 100 and 137.

2. G.W.F. Hegel, *Lectures on the Philosophy of History,* trans. J. Sibree (New York: Dover, 1956), pp. 255–56.

3. Even if "the political awareness of the citizens, which was the true cement of the city, was based on their identity with the state, that is, on that 'given' that they called *politeia*" (Ehrenberg, *L'Etat grec*, p. 156).

4. On all this, see Chapter Six, pp. 340–57. For Hegel, "Athena, the goddess, is Athens herself, that is to say, the real, concrete spirit of the citizens" (*Philosophy of History*, p. 252); see also Dominique Janicaud, *Hegel et le destin de la Grèce* (Paris: Vrin, 1975), pp. 170–74. Hegelian after his own fashion, Gustave Glotz

saw Pericles's epitaphios as "an admirable commentary, each word of which is like a gold medal bearing the effigy of Athena Poliad" (*La Cité grecque* [Paris: Michel, 1968], pp. 153–54); yet Athena is entirely absent from the epitaphioi.

5. Hegel, *Lectures on the Philosophy of History*, pp. 225ff. See also pp. 252 ("the Greeks occupy the middle ground of *Beauty*"), 261 ("the spectacle of a state whose existence was essentially directed to realizing the Beautiful"), and 269 ("Beauty, as the Greek principle"). On the beautiful as the basis of our loyalty to Greece, see p. 223.

6. To use Thucydides's words (1.10.2). From the third century B.C., it is true, the emphasis begins to shift to sight (and the spectacle of monuments) as a way of access to Athens (cf. John E. Stambaugh, "The Idea of the City: Three Views of Athens," *Classical Journal* 69 (1974), pp. 312ff.); thus "external appearances" soon gained the upper hand.

7. On tragedy, see Jean-Pierre Vernant, "Tensions et ambiguïtiés dans la tragédie grecque," in *MT*, esp. p. 25.

8. Edouard Will, *MGO*, pp. 405–406.

9. Cf. Georges Duby, "Histoire sociale et idéologie des sociétés," in Jacques Le Goff and Pierre Nora (eds.), *Faire de l'histoire,* 3 vols. (Paris: Gallimard, 1974), vol. 3, pp. 147–68.

10. Cf. Karl Marx and Friedrich Engels, *The German Ideology* (London: Lawrence and Wishart, 1970), pp. 35ff.

11. On the institution of bourgeois civil society in the nineteenth century (to give an approximate date), see *ibid.*, pp. 35ff.; in "La Naissance de l'idéologie et l'humanisme: Introduction," *Textures* 6–7 (1973), pp. 27–68, Claude Lefort observes that capitalism is the "primary ideological discourse" (p. 48). On the lack of ideology in ancient Greece see M.I. Finley, *Democracy Ancient and Modern* (New Brunswick, NJ: Rutgers University Press, 1973), pp. 50–54 and 65–66.

12. Finley, *Democracy Ancient and Modern*, p. 15. In Marx's view, the question of ideology in precapitalist society is much more complex: the relationship between production and exploitation is visible and transparent, but a "mystical cloud" or a transcendent order arises and annuls this transparency; see Lefort, "La Naissance de l'idéologie et l'humanisme," p. 46, and Maurice Godelier, "Fétichisme, religion et théorie générale de l'idéologie chez Marx," in *Horizon, trajets marxistes en anthropologie* (Paris: Maspero, 1973), pp. 319–42, esp. 328–29.

13. Diego Lanza and Mario Vegetti have raised this question in an article

that I read after writing this book ("L'ideologia della città," *Quaderni di storia* 2 [July-Dec. 1975], pp. 1–37).

14. In borrowing this expression from Lefort ("La Naissance de l'idéologie et l'humanisme," p. 67), we must not forget the radical distinction between the status of the metic and that of the slave. 15. Cf. Pierre Vidal-Naquet, "Esclavage et gynécocratie dans la tradition, le mythe, l'utopie," in *Recherches sur les structures sociales dans l'Antiquité classique* (Paris: CNRS, 1970), pp. 63–80.

16. Slaves and metics are absent; women are referred to as little as possible: the Amazons earn a passage only because they wanted to act like men; see Chapter Three, pp. 208–209.

17. For example, in Euripides's *Ion* (854–56) the declarations of the servant with the generous soul resemble modern ideologies in that they are based on the universal ground of "humanity" and, by this fact, reflect an attitude that may be aiming to soften slavery but not to attack it as an institution; on the contrary, this type of reflection presupposes the maintenance of the status quo. See H.C. Baldry, *The Unity of Mankind in Greek Thought* (Cambridge, UK: Cambridge University Press, 1965), p. 37.

18. On this general feature of the Greek political logos, see Pierre Vidal-Naquet, "Tradition de la démocratie grecque," introduction to *Démocratic antique et démocratie moderne*, by M.I. Finley (Paris: Payot, 1976), p. 42: "Of slaves there is not a word, and the very possibility of political speech is based on this silence."

19. In his completeness and his autarky, the Athenian man is for Pericles an *aner* (Thucydides 2.41.1); thus in the background of the epitaphios, we can glimpse Thucydides's polemic against Herodotus and his universal (but pessimistic) view of humanity (1.32).

20. See Aelius Aristides, *Panathenaicus* 274 (Oliver); see also Cicero, *Pro Flacco* 26 ("adsunt Athenienses unde humanitas ... [orta]"). According to the lexicon drawn up by Oliver, Aelius Aristides uses *anthropōs* much more frequently than *anēr* (sixty-nine instances versus thirty, not to mention the numerous references to "human nature").

21. In the sense in which Ehrenberg declares that reflection on the best state is a way of putting the polis in the superlative (*L'Etat grec*, p. 169).

22. Plato is alone in claiming that the Athenian soil produced man (*Menexenus* 237e–38a): once again the philosopher tries to subvert the official oration from the inside by cunningly introducing into it a problematic of humanity (see

Baldry's remarks, *Unity of Mankind*, pp. 80–81). It is remarkable that, though closely imitating the *Menexenus,* Demosthenes's epitaphios returns to the orthodox position on this point: the civic land produced the Athenians and not man in general.

23. See Marx and Engels, *German Ideology*, pp. 35ff. On the birth of ideology in Florence, cf. Lefort, "La Naissance de l'idéologie et l'humanisme," pp. 66–67, on *humanitas.*

24. On the role of the imitation of Antiquity during the Renaissance and the French Revolution, see Lefort, "La Naissance de l'idéologie et l'humanisme," pp. 28–29, 49, 62–66, and Vidal-Naquet, "Tradition de la démocratie grecque," pp. 15–20.

25. Finley, *Democracy Ancient and Modern,* p. 66. Reflecting on the ideology of the city, Lanza and Vegetti also challenge this statement.

26. Finley, *Democracy Ancient and Modern*, p. 110.

27. For the Greeks, slavery was not exploitation but the use of an animated tool. Moreover, for Marx, exploitation begins only when the destitute worker is forced to sell his labor power; cf. Jean-Pierre Vernant, "La Lutte des classes," in *Mythe et société en Grèce ancienne* (Paris: Maspero, 1974), pp. 11–29, esp. 22 n.18.

28. The most explicit reference to the Athenian policy of consumption is found in Pericles's epitaphios (2.38.2), and it is remarkably discreet: see Chapter Two, p. 130.

29. M.M. Austin and Pierre Vidal-Naquet, *Economies et sociétés en Grèce ancienne* (Paris: A. Colin, 1972), p. 30 (see also pp. 28–29); cf. Louis Gernet, "Les Nobles dans la Grèce antique," in *Anthropologie,* p. 343 ("there is a quality of human pride in the citizen that makes him comparable with the nobles"), and Will, *MGO*, p. 429.

30. I am not denying that the Greeks were capable of developing thought on slavery (see Pierre Vidal-Naquet, "Réflexions sur l'historiographie grecque de l'esclavage," in *Actes du Colloque sur l'esclavage, Besançon, 1971* [Paris: Belles Lettres, 1973], pp. 25–44); but I want to show that Athenian ideology was not situated at the level of the relationship between citizens and slavery.

31. The definition of ideology as "the domain of illusory representations of reality" (Godelier, "Fétichisme," p. 337) is therefore not entirely satisfactory for our purposes.

32. On Pericles's epitaphios, Nietzsche speaks of "trompe-l'oeil" (*Trugbild*) (*Human, All Too Human*, §474).

33. Cf. Ehrenberg, *L'Etat grec*, p. 155.

34. Cornelius Castoriadis, *L'Institution imaginaire de la société* (Paris: Seuil, 1975), pp. 182–84.

35. This "us" is the name of the community of historians at a particular period. I am using it in the sense in which Hegel says that the works of Antiquity "have become what they are for us now" (*Phenomenology of Spirit*, 2, p. 455).

36. Michel de Certeau, *L'Ecriture de l'histoire* (Paris: Gallimard, 1975), p. 48; see also pp. 46–47.

37. See Jacques Bompaire, "Les Historiens classiques dans les exercices préparatoires de rhétorique (Progymnasmata);" in *Recueil Plassart* (Paris, 1976), pp. 1–7.

38. Thus Aelius Aristides bases his own speech on the practice of the public funeral (*Panathenaicus* 253 [Oliver]), and the rhetors Hermogenes and Aphthonios give a definition of the eulogy that involves the eulogy of Athens (Hermogenes: *Rhetores graeci* [Spengel], 2, 12; Aphthonios: *ibid.*, p. 36).

Index

EARTH, 72, 90, 268, 275, 376, 378, 418. *See also* Autochthony.

Education, see *Paideia*.

Eion, epigram of, 92, 96, 99–100, 111, 196.

Ekklēsia, 40, 132, 230, 231, 237, 255, 339, 414, 415, 479 n.50.

Eleutheria, 33, 61, 109–10, 137, 138, 172–74, 180–81, 183, 211–12, 223, 229, 243–44, 247–48, 257–58, 264, 267, 272, 320–21, 455 n.46.

Elite, 77, 88, 147, 156, 210, 219, 224, 233, 239, 244, 347, 410, 426 n.7.

Eloquence, 30, 36–39, 42, 43, 83, 196, 205, 252, 281, 293, 302, 308, 309, 361–62, 364, 388–90, 396, 493 n.12, 496 n.46, 502 n.117, 522 n.181.

Empire, 33, 38, 48, 56, 65, 95, 101, 124, 127–33, 136, 144, 175, 249, 250, 268, 269, 325–26, 343, 365, 367, 369, 370, 372, 378, 383, 411, 414, 452 n.17, 454 n.37, 498 n.72, 501 n.108, 502 n.115, 503 n.123, 508 n.38. *See also Archē*.

Enemy, 49, 51, 85, 99, 107, 111, 112, 116, 122–26, 135, 141, 162, 182, 183, 193, 196, 198–201, 203, 204, 208, 212, 255, 262, 263, 267, 273, 274, 345, 367, 372, 376, 381, 406, 426 n.7, 456 n.54, 468 n.27, 470 n.43, 487 n.137.

Encomium (*egkōmion*), 78, 84, 88, 164, 185, 282, 322, 323, 330, 362, 390, 391, 481 n.66.

Epainos, 22, 84–86, 168–70, 333, 337, 389–90, 444 n.11. *See also* Celebration; Eulogy; Praise.

Ephebes (*ephēboi*), 53, 57, 67, 205, 210, 213, 255, 257, 359, 380, 433 n.18, 472 n.65, 487 n.138, 502 n.114, 516 n.119.

Ephialtes, 21, 94, 101, 102, 105, 112, 229, 247, 258, 262, 477 n.36.

Ephorus, 41, 100, 200, 202, 327, 438 n.49, 447 n.151, 469 nn.32, 39.

Epitaphia, 70–72, 321–22, 502 n.114.

Epitaphs, epigrams, 79, 87, 92, 93, 165–67, 255, 350, 445 n.131.

Eponyms, 50, 127, 149, 161, 182, 195, 201, 319, 348, 431 n.53, 508 n.45, 509 n.46.

Equality, 32, 40, 42, 51, 97, 141, 222–23, 233, 236, 239, 245, 258, 260, 350, 391, 428 n.23, 482 n.79, 491 n.183. *See also Isēgoria; Isonomia*.

Erechtheidai, 90.

Erechtheus, 82, 104, 211, 256, 349, 371, 418, 448 n.157, 483 n.91, 510 n.61.

Erichthonius, 349, 371, 418

Erga, 77, 113, 191, 196, 202, 232, 294–96, 299–304, 312, 324, 370, 377, 412, 495 n.35. *See also* Exploits.

Ergon, 47, 69, 129, 149, 297, 324, 364, 376, 446 n.143. *See also Logos/ergon*.

Eris, 141–42, 157, 286.

Eudaimonia, 74–75, 170, 442 n.93, 463 nn.128, 129.

Euergesia, 155, 255, 460 n.92.

Eugeneia, 203, 210, 245. *See also* Autochthony; Nobility.

Eulogy, 25–26, 76–94, 97, 134–35, 145–50, 154, 158, 164, 177, 182, 184, 295–96, 299, 329–30, 332–34, 360–79, 381, 387–92, 397, 400–404, 420, 457 n.65, 502 n.115; collective and individual, 97–98, 156–57, 160–64, 256, 280, 283, 292, 502 nn.118. *See also* Athens, eulogy of; Democracy, praise and criticism of; Praise.

Eumolpus, 95, 104, 106, 112, 318.

Eunomia, 248, 258.

Euripides, 38, 82, 104, 105, 106, 107, 125, 127, 143, 156–58, 243,

Zone Books series design by Bruce Mau
Typesetting by Archetype
Printed and bound by Maple-Vail on Sebago acid-free paper